New Perspectives on Computer Concepts
4th Edition

COMPREHENSIVE

Includes an interactive Book-on-CD
that contains the entire contents of the textbook,
plus videos, software tours, Course Labs,
computer-scored practice tests, and more!

June Jamrich Parsons
Dan Oja

COURSE
TECHNOLOGY

Thomson Learning™

ONE MAIN STREET, CAMBRIDGE, MA 02142

Australia • Canada • Denmark • Japan • Mexico • New Zealand • Philippines
Puerto Rico • Singapore • South Africa • Spain • United Kingdom • United States

New Perspectives on Computer Concepts 4th Edition—Comprehensive; June Jamrich Parsons, Dan Oja.

Senior Editor	Donna Gridley	**Cover Designer**	Douglas Goodman
Developmental Editor	Pam Conrad	**Photo and Video Researcher**	Abby Reip
Production Editor	Debbie Masi	**Book-on-CD Development**	MediaTechnics Corp.
Product Manager	Donna Gridley	**Media Specialist**	Fatima Nicholls
Text Design and Composition	MediaTechnics Corp.	**Prepress Production**	GEX, Inc.

For more information, contact Course Technology, One Main Street, Cambridge, MA 02142;
or find us on the World Wide Web at www.course.com.

For permission to use material from this text or product, contact us by
- Web: www.thomsonrights.com
- Phone: 1-800-730-2214
- Fax: 1-800-730-2215

ISBN 0-7600-6499-7

Printed in the United States
2 3 4 5 BM 03 02 01 00

BRIEF CONTENTS

CONTENTS

PREFACE

About New Perspectives on Computer Concepts, 4th Edition

With the 4th edition of *Computer Concepts*, we're building on a legacy of excellence. With each new edition we are able to offer you more. The 4th edition is no exception. We've retained the great features of the previous editions that you've told us you liked and added some new features we know you're going to love. If you want a truly excellent introduction to computers, look no further than *Computer Concepts, 4th Edition*.

Flexibility

Whether you use the book alone, or use it with the Book-on-CD and/or the dedicated Web site, it's your choice. Let your needs dictate how you use this integrated text and technology package. Our goal is to provide you with you with flexible, innovative teaching and learning tools. With our solid pedagogy and proven technology, *New Perspectives on Computer Concepts* is reaching new students everyday.

Classic Features

As with the popular 3rd edition, the 4th edition features a CD-ROM that contains the entire contents of the book. Every page of this **Book-on-CD** looks exactly like the printed book, so you can use either one—or both. The Book-on-CD also contains animated software tours, videos, Course Labs, InfoWeb links, and more. Students, instructors, and beta testers have given high marks to the Book-on-CD because it adds an interactive dimension to the learning experience.

Start
Screentour

For the 4th edition we've added more **animated software tours** that demonstrate popular software packages, such as Microsoft's Internet Explorer Web browser, Coda Software's Finale MIDI music toolkit, Caligari TrueSpace 3-D graphics, and more!

User
Interfaces

We've updated our highly interactive, computerized **Course Labs**. The labs combine illustrations, animation, digital images, and simulations. They make computer skills and concepts fun and easy to understand. The labs provide step-by-step tutorials, present reinforcement questions, and allow independent exploration. For the 4th edition, we've added an exciting new lab on Photo Editing. See page xi for a complete listing of the Course Labs that accompany this book.

QUICKCHECK

We've retained our interactive assessment options such as **QuickCheck questions** at the end of every section. **Practice Tests** at the end of each chapter generate computer-scored tests from a test bank of 150 questions per chapter. You will also find a rich selection of end-of-chapter **Projects**, **Lab Assignments**, and **InfoWeb links** that helped make the 3rd edition such a success.

If you're looking for a solution for local or distance learning courses, **CyberClass** might be for you. It is a Web-based tool designed for on-campus or distance learning. To learn more, go to: *www.cyber-class.com*

New Features in the 4th Edition

A Great New Web Site

Now you can do more on the Web! Explore InfoWeb links to research a topic of interest or participate in a multitude of new interactive end-of-chapter activities that include summary exercises, key terms, quizzes, study tips, and additional projects. Or, simply sit back and watch a video. It's all at your fingertips at the new, NP4 Web site, *www.cciw.com/np4*.

Issue Feature

Students can read about current ethical, social, and cultural computing issues in the new *Issue* section at the end of each chapter, then provide their opinions verbally or electronically. Instructors can collect, summarize, and display a chart of student responses using the Consolidation Module found on the IRK. It's a great way to spark classroom discussion!

Interactive Key Terms, Pop-up Definitions & Glossary

Computer terms that can be difficult to remember won't be a problem anymore. Students can now interact with the Key Terms list at the end of each chapter to review new terms. We've also added pop-up definitions that appear on screen when using the Book-on-CD and a Glossary button provides easy access to all definitions from any page in the book.

WebCT

If you want to take your course online, you can use WebCT to help you. WebCT is a flexible course management tool that allows instructors to host a course Web site on a campus server. Course Technology offers FREE content-specific information for *Concepts, 4th Edition*. To learn more, go to: *webct.course.com*

Supplements

The following supplements accompany *New Perspectives on Computer Concepts, 4th Edition*.

Course Labs: Bring Concepts to Life Computer skills and concepts come to life with the New Perspectives Course Labs—27 highly interactive tutorials that present step-by-step instruction, allow independent exploration, and provide printed feedback.

Course Online: A Site Dedicated to Keeping You Up To Date We offer a dedicated Web site for students and instructors who use *New Perspectives on Computer Concepts*. Instructors may visit the site's password-protected Faculty Online Companion for solutions, frequently asked questions with answers, articles, content updates, and more.

Course Presenter: Ready-Made or Customizable Presentations Course Presenter is a CD-ROM-based presentation tool that provides instructors with a wealth of resources for use in the classroom, replacing traditional overhead transparencies with computer-generated presentations. Presenter includes a structured presentation along with videos, animations, Course Labs, and more for each chapter of the textbook. It also provides flexibility to create customized presentations.

Course Test Manager: Testing and Practice Online or On Paper Course Test Manager is a powerful testing and assessment package that enables instructors to create and print tests from testbanks designed specifically for Course Technology titles. In addition, instructors with access to a networked computer lab can administer, grade, and track tests online. Students can also take online practice tests, which generate customized study guides that help students locate review information in the book.

Electronic Instructor's Manual: Help is Only a Few Keystrokes Away This enhanced Instructor's Manual offers an outline for each chapter; suggestions for instruction on the chapter content, including how to effectively use and integrate the InfoWebs, the CD content, and the labs; answers to the end-of chapter materials (Review, Projects, and Lab Assignments); and numerous teaching tips.

Consolidation Module: Find Out What Your Students Are Thinking The Consolidation Module allows instructors to gather student data from interactive activities (including the Issue sections), consolidate student scores, and print assessment reports.

Acknowledgments

Every edition of New Perspectives requires extraordinary effort by a dedicated and creative team. The content of every page is subjected to the scrutiny of professional educators, such as Chuck Calvin, Ed Mott, Catherine Perlich, and David Primeaux. Student reviewers and testers, such as Heather House help us target our readers. We get additional help from professionals all over the world, such as Andrew Hodges at Oxford and Jeffrey Goldberg at Cranfield who helped us verify some information about Alan Turing; Steve Kapsinow at Webopaedia for clearing up some technical terms; and Jeffrey Harrow for the excellent and up-to-date information he supplies in his online newsletter, *The Rapidly Changing Face of Computing*.

The book would not exist—and certainly would not arrive on schedule—were it not for the efforts of our media, editorial, and production teams: Donna Gridley for tireless work on the entire New Perspectives series. Deborah Masi for managing production. Fatima Nicholls and Donna Schuch for creating videos, screentours, and interactive tests. Marilyn Freedman for designing and maintaining our Web sites. Melissa Dezotell, Stacie Parillo and Karen Bartlett for keeping everyone on schedule. Pam Conrad for her insightful developmental edit. Abby Reip for photo research. Jennifer Hambly and Doug Goodman for design work on the cover. We would like to thank you all!

June Parsons and Dan Oja

COURSE LABS

 Using a Mouse

 Keyboarding & Typing Tutor

 User Interface

 DOS Command-Line Interface

 Photo Editing NEW!

 Word Processing

 Spreadsheets

 Databases

 Computer History Hypermedia

 Multimedia

 Using Files

 Defragmentation and Disk Operations

 Windows Directories, Folders, and Files REVISED!

 DOS Directories and File Management

 Troubleshooting REVISED!

 CPU Simulator

 Buying a Computer UPDATED!

 E-mail

 The Internet: World Wide Web

 Web Pages and HTML

 Data Backup

 Data Representation

 Binary Numbers

 Building a Network

 System Testing

 SQL Queries

 Visual Programming

Before You Begin

BEFORE YOU BEGIN

You're going to enjoy using *New Perspectives on Computer Concepts 4th Edition* and the accompanying Book-on-CD. It's a snap to start the Book-on-CD and use it on your computer. So don't delay—get started right away! The answers to the FAQs (frequently asked questions) in this section will help you begin.

FAQ

Will the Book-on-CD work on my computer? The Book-On-CD works on most computers that run Windows. The easiest way to find out if the Book-on-CD works on your computer is to try it! Just follow the steps below to start the CD. If it works, you're all set. Otherwise, check with your local technical support person. If you are technically inclined, the system requirements are listed inside the front cover of this book.

FAQ

How do I start the Book-on-CD? The *New Perspectives on Computer Concepts 4th Edition* Book-on-CD is easy to use and requires no installation. Follow these simple steps to get started:

1. Make sure your computer is turned on.

2. Press the button on your computer's CD-ROM drive to open the drawer-like "tray" as shown in the photo below.

3. Place the Book-on-CD into the tray with the label facing up.

4. Press the button on the CD-ROM drive to close the tray, then proceed with Step 5 on the next page.

FIGURE 1

To use the Book-on-CD, your computer must have a CD-ROM drive. If you have any questions about its operation, check with your local technical support person.

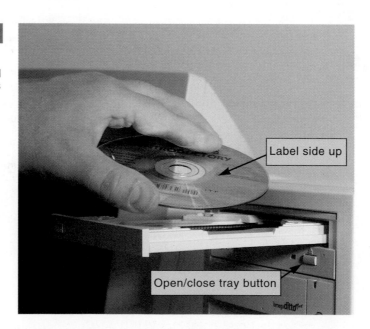

Label side up

Open/close tray button

5. Wait about 15 seconds. During this time, the light on your CD-ROM drive should flicker. Soon you should see the Computer Concepts Welcome screen.

FIGURE 2

The Welcome screen displays the menu of options for the Book-on-CD. Typically, you'll click the **Contents menu**, then select the chapter that you want to read.

Use the **Media menu** to jump to pages containing a video, animation, or software tour.

Use the **Labs menu** to jump to any Lab.

Use the **Tests menu** to jump to a computer-scored Practice Test for any chapter.

Use the **Tools menu** to view your Tracking Disk data, turn sound on or off, and change the default browser.

Use the **File menu** to exit.

FIGURE 3

Manual Start: Follow the instructions in this figure only if the Welcome screen did *not* appear automatically in Step 5.

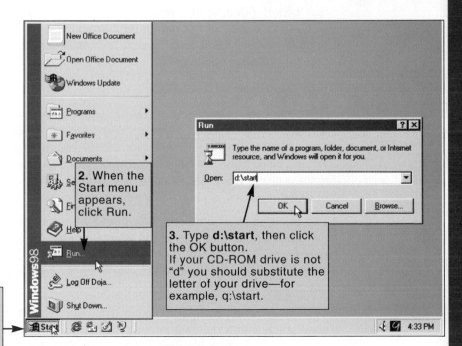

1. Use the mouse to position the arrow-shaped pointer on Start, then click the left button on your mouse.

2. When the Start menu appears, click Run.

3. Type **d:\start**, then click the OK button. If your CD-ROM drive is not "d" you should substitute the letter of your drive—for example, q:\start.

FAQ

How do I end a session? You'll need to leave the Book-on-CD disk in the CD-ROM drive while you're using it. Before you remove the CD from the drive, exit the program by clicking the Exit button at the top of the screen.

Before You Begin

Before You Begin

How do I navigate from page to page? Click the Contents menu to jump to any chapter, section or page number of the book. To move from page to page, you can click the navigation buttons at the top of the screen. To read down to the text at the bottom of a page, drag the scroll box or click the scroll bar at the side of the screen.

FIGURE 4

The **Jump To button** lets you enter any page number.

The **Page ▶ button** takes you to the next page.

The **◀ Page button** takes you to the previous page.

You can use the mouse to drag the **scroll box** or click the **scroll bar** to view the rest of the page.

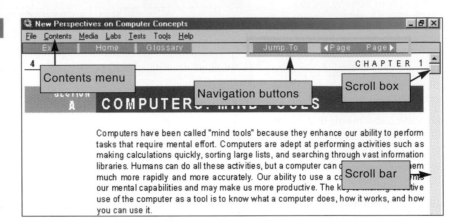

How do I view videos, animations, and screentours? Many of the figures contain a Start Video, Start Animation, or Start Screentour button, such as the sample one pictured to the left of this paragraph. When using the Book-on-CD, you can click these buttons to see videos clips, watch animated conceptual diagrams, and tour through popular software packages.

Start Video

What's an InfoWeb? The InfoWebs provide up-to-date links to Web sites where you will find additional information about important topics covered in each chapter. When you're using the Book-on-CD, you can click any InfoWeb icon that you see in the margin of the book to be connected to a list of corresponding Web sites. This list is updated regularly, so that you'll be getting the most current information.

The InfoWeb links work only if you have a browser and an Internet connection. If you can send e-mail and access the Web with your computer, you probably have such a connection. If this is the case, when you click an InfoWeb icon, your Book-on-CD will automatically start your Web browser software and dial up your connection.

If you do not have an Internet connection, you will not be able to access the auxiliary material provided by InfoWeb links. You might want to consider setting up an Internet connection with a national Internet service provider (ISP), such as America Online, or with a local ISP that you find in the Yellow Pages of your telephone book (look under "Internet"). The InfoWebs are a helpful supplement to the NP4 textbook, but, an Internet connection is **not** required to use the book or the Book-on-CD.

When you complete your exploration of InfoWeb links, you can return to the Book-on-CD by closing your browser. Click your browser's File menu, then click Close or Exit .

FAQ

What is the NP4 Web site? The NP4 Web site contains the first two pages of every chapter, including the chapter preview video, list of chapter topics, chapter objectives, and opening feature story. In addition, the Web site contains the Issue section and all of the end-of-chapter activities, including the interactive summary, key terms, quizzes, study tips, practice tests, projects, lab assignments, and InfoWebs.

You can interact with the Web-based material just as you would with the Book-on-CD. You can watch videos, complete interactive activities, view your scores, and save your scores on a Tracking Disk. The NP4 Web site is a handy—and portable—companion to the book.

FAQ

How do I access the NP4 Web site? To access the NP4 Web site, you need Microsoft Internet Explorer (included with Windows). You will also need an Internet connection provided by your school or by an Internet service provider (ISP).

Whenever you want to visit the NP4 Web site, start your browser software and connect to the Internet. Enter the address www.cciw.com/np4.

The first time that you access the site, your browser will download a program that allows you to view the NP4 pages, interact with the end-of-chapter activities, and receive computer-scored results. The download takes approximately five minutes, depending on the speed of your Internet connection. When the download is complete, follow the instructions on the screen to make sure that your computer will display everything correctly.

For those of you with some technical background, note that the download is digitally signed to ensure that it is a legitimate program and that it does not carry a virus.

FAQ

How do the interactive summaries, quizzes, and practice tests work? When you use the Book-on-CD or the NP4 Web site, you can use a variety of activities to review the chapter material and make sure that you understand the important points. Simply follow the instructions for these activities to enter your answers. When you've completed an activity, the computer will automatically check your responses and provide you with a score. For Practice Tests, you will also receive a study guide to help you find the answers to questions that you answered incorrectly. You can print this study guide by following the instructions on the screen.

You have the option of saving your results on a Tracking Disk, as explained on the next page.

FAQ

What about the Interactive Key Terms? At the end of each chapter, a list of key terms helps you review new terminology. Follow the directions at the top of the page to interact with the key terms list. Your results are not scored or saved.

Before You Begin

Before You Begin

FAQ

What's a Tracking Disk? A Tracking Disk tracks your progress by saving your responses to the "What do you think?" questions on the Issues pages as well as your scores on the QuickChecks, Interactive Summary, Interactive Quizzes, and Practice Tests.

When you complete an activity, such as a QuickCheck, you'll see a message that asks if you would like to save your score. If you click the OK button, you will be prompted to insert your Tracking Disk, then your score will be saved on it.

The first time you save a score, you will need to follow the directions on the screen to create a Tracking Disk. To do so, click the Create button and insert a blank, formatted floppy disk. You only need to create a Tracking Disk one time. Once you've created the Tracking Disk, just insert it into the floppy disk drive of your computer when you insert the Book-on-CD or when prompted to do so.

You can view or print a summary report of all your scores by using the Tools menu on the Welcome screen. In an academic setting, your instructor might request your Tracking Disk data to monitor your progress. If this is the case, you might want to make a copy of your Tracking Disk (refer to page 420 in the Introductory or Comprehensive editions).

FAQ

What about sound? If your computer is equipped for sound, you should hear audio during the videos. If you don't, check the volume control on your computer by clicking the speaker icon in the lower-right corner of your screen. If you're working any place where sound would be disruptive, consider using earphones. You can also use the Tools menu on the Welcome screen to turn sound off.

FAQ

Can I make the type appear larger on my screen? If the type in the Book-on-CD appears small, your monitor is probably set at a high resolution. The type will appear larger if you reduce the resolution by using the Start menu to access Settings and Control Panel. Double-click the Display icon, then select the Settings tab. Move the Screen Area slider to 640 x 480. This setting is optional. You can view the Book-on-CD at most standard resolutions.

If your Book-on-CD text looks jumbled, your computer might be set to use Windows large fonts, instead of the standard font. The standard fonts setting is located on the Scheme list that you can access by double-clicking the Display icon in Control Panel, then selecting the Appearance tab.

FAQ

What if I have additional questions about how to use the CD or Web site? Additional technical information about the NP4 Book-on-CD and NP4 Web site is provided in the Readme file on your CD. To read this information, use the Programs option on the Start menu to view a list of programs on your computer. Select Windows Explorer from the list. Click the icon that represents your CD-ROM drive. Locate the program Readme or Readme.txt in the list on the right side of the screen and double-click it.

COMPUTER CONCEPTS 4th Edition

CHAPTER 1

USING COMPUTERS: ESSENTIAL CONCEPTS

➡ Start Video

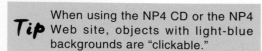

Tip When using the NP4 CD or the NP4 Web site, objects with light-blue backgrounds are "clickable."

PREVIEW

Chapter 1 is a practical introduction to computers that you can immediately apply at home, at school, or at work. In this chapter you will learn which computer components help you to communicate with a computer. You will also learn how to use the controls that you see on the computer screen. This chapter concludes with a demonstration of how to start a computer, start a program, use a Web browser, and search for information on the Internet.

When you have completed this chapter you should be able to:

■ Define the term "computer"
■ Describe the relationship between computer hardware and software
■ Identify the parts of a typical microcomputer system
■ List the peripheral devices that are typically found on microcomputer systems
■ Define the term "user interface"
■ Describe how you use interface elements such as prompts, commands, menus, and graphical objects
■ Describe the resources that help you learn how to use computers and software
■ Use a Web browser and Web search engine

CHAPTER 1 LABS

User
Interfaces

DOS User
Interface

Using a
Mouse

Keyboard &
Typing Tutor

2001: A SPACE ODYSSEY

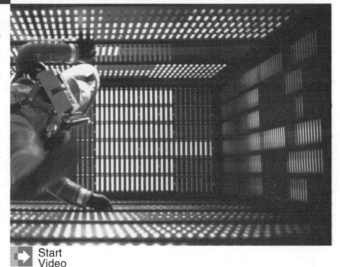

Start
Video

In the classic science-fiction film *2001: A Space Odyssey*, astronauts Dave Bowman and Frank Poole depart on a mission to Jupiter. The mission objective: to discover the source of a mysterious object from space. Midway through the mission, the onboard computer, named HAL, begins to exhibit strange behavior.

HAL warns the crew that an antenna is about to fail, so Frank ventures outside to make repairs. In a suspicious "accident," Frank's lifeline is cut and he begins to drift into deep space. Dave leaves the spacecraft to retrieve Frank's body.

When Dave is ready to reboard, he says to the computer, "Open the pod bay door, HAL. Open the pod bay door!" HAL's reply is chilling, "I'm sorry, Dave, I'm afraid I can't do that." This dialog between a human and a computer raises some intriguing questions. How realistic is it? Can humans and computers communicate this fluently? What went wrong with the communication? Why won't the computer let Dave back into the spaceship?

InfoWeb
1
2001: A
Space
Odyssey

To use a computer effectively, you must communicate tasks to the computer and accurately interpret the information that the computer provides to you. The means by which humans and computers communicate is the central theme of Chapter 1.

The year 2001 is no longer far in the future. Has science fiction become science fact? Could today's technology produce an intelligent computer like HAL? Chapter 1 concludes with a look at the question, "Can computers think?"

> *Tip* InfoWeb icons, such as the one above and to the right, connect you to Web links, film, video, TV, print, and electronic resources. If you're using the New Perspectives CD (NP4 CD) and have Internet access, click an InfoWeb icon to go directly to resources on the Internet. Otherwise, refer to the InfoWeb section at the end of each chapter.

SECTION A COMPUTERS: MIND TOOLS

Computers have been called "mind tools" because they enhance our ability to perform tasks that require mental effort. Computers are adept at performing activities such as making calculations quickly, sorting large lists, and searching through vast information libraries. Humans can do all these activities, but a computer can often accomplish them much more rapidly and more accurately. Our ability to use a computer complements our mental capabilities and may make us more productive. The key to making effective use of the computer as a tool is to know what a computer does, how it works, and how you can use it.

Von Neumann's Definition

InfoWeb 2

John von Neumann

What is a computer? If you look in a dictionary printed before 1940, you might be surprised to find a computer defined as a *person* who performs calculations! Machines also performed calculations back then, but they were referred to as calculators, not computers. The modern definition and use of the term "computer" emerged in the 1940s, when the first electronic computing devices were developed as a response to World War II military needs.

In 1945, a team of engineers began working on a secret military project to construct the Electronic Discrete Variable Automatic Computer, referred to by the acronym EDVAC. At the time, only one other functioning computer had been built in the United States. Plans for the EDVAC were described in a report by the eminent mathematician John von Neumann, pictured in Figure 1-1.

FIGURE 1-1

When this photo was published in 1947, the caption read, "Dr. John von Neumann stands in front of a new Electronic 'Brain,' the fastest computing machine for its degree of precision yet made. The machine which can do 2,000 multiplications in one second and add or subtract 100,000 times in the same period was displayed today for the first time at the Institute for Advanced Study. Its fabulous memory can store 1,024 numbers of 12 decimal places each. Dr. von Neumann was one of the designers of the wonder machine."

Von Neumann's report has been described as "the most influential paper in the history of computer science." It was one of the earliest documents to specifically define the components of a computer and describe their functions. In the report, von Neumann used the term "automatic computing system." Today, popular usage has abandoned this cumbersome terminology in favor of the shorter terms "computer" or "computer system."

CHAPTER 1

Based on the concepts presented in von Neumann's paper, we can define a **computer** as a device that accepts input, processes data, stores data, and produces output. Let's look more closely at the elements of this definition.

A Computer Accepts Input

What kinds of input can a computer use?   Computer **input** is whatever is put into a computer system. The word "input" is also a verb that means to feed information into a computer. Input can be supplied by a person, by the environment, or by another computer. Examples of the kinds of input a computer can process include the words and symbols in a document, numbers for a calculation, pictures, temperatures from a thermostat, audio signals from a microphone, and instructions for completing a process.

An input device gathers and translates input into a form that the computer can process. As a computer user, you will probably use the keyboard as your main input device.

A Computer Processes Data

In what ways can a computer process data?   **Data** refers to the symbols that represent facts and ideas. Computers manipulate data in many ways, and we call this manipulation "processing." Some of the ways that a computer can process data include performing calculations, sorting lists of words or numbers, modifying documents and pictures according to user instructions, and drawing graphs. In the context of computers, then, we can define a **process** as a systematic series of actions that a computer uses to manipulate data. A computer processes data in a device called the **central processing unit** (CPU).

A Computer Stores Data

Why does a computer store data?   A computer must store data so that it will be available for processing. Computers typically have more than one location for storing data, depending on how the data is being used. The computer puts data in one place while it is waiting to be processed and in another place when it is not needed for immediate processing. **Memory** is an area of a computer that holds data that is waiting to be processed. **Storage** is the area where data can be left on a permanent basis while it is not needed for processing.

A Computer Produces Output

What kinds of output does a computer produce?   Computer **output** is the results produced by a computer. The word "output" is also a verb that means the process of producing output. Some examples of computer output include reports, documents, music, graphs, and pictures. An output device displays, prints, or transmits the results of processing.

Although von Neumann defined computers as they existed in the 1940s, his definition still applies to today's computers. Study Figure 1-2 to make sure that you understand fundamental computer functions and see if you recognize the devices that help the computer accomplish each function.

FIGURE 1-2

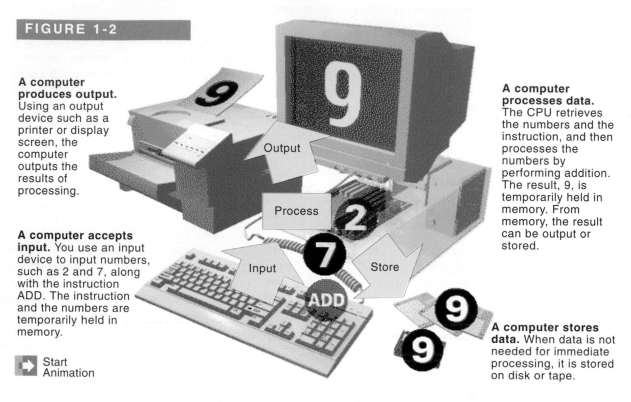

A computer produces output. Using an output device such as a printer or display screen, the computer outputs the results of processing.

A computer accepts input. You use an input device to input numbers, such as 2 and 7, along with the instruction ADD. The instruction and the numbers are temporarily held in memory.

▶ Start Animation

A computer processes data. The CPU retrieves the numbers and the instruction, and then processes the numbers by performing addition. The result, 9, is temporarily held in memory. From memory, the result can be output or stored.

A computer stores data. When data is not needed for immediate processing, it is stored on disk or tape.

QUICKCHECK   A

Tip   At the end of each section in this book, you can fill in "QuickCheck" answers to make sure that you understand what you have read before you continue. The answers to the QuickChecks are at the end of the book. When using the NP4 CD or NP4 Web site, type your answers in the box, then click the Check Answers button.

1 The four functions performed by a computer are input, [＿＿＿＿], storage, and output.

2 [＿＿＿＿＿] refers to the symbols processed by a computer.

3 A computer processes data in a device called the [＿＿＿＿] processing unit.

4 The computer puts data temporarily in [＿＿＿＿＿] while the data is waiting to be processed.

5 When data is not needed for processing, the computer puts it in [＿＿＿＿].

▶ Check Answers

SECTION B
COMPUTER SYSTEM BASICS

A computer system typically includes a computer, peripheral devices, and software. The electronic and mechanical devices that manipulate data are known as **hardware**. The term "hardware" refers to the computer itself and to components called **peripheral devices** that expand the computer's input, output, and storage capabilities. Computer hardware in and of itself does not provide a particularly useful mind tool. To be useful, a computer requires a computer program or **software**, which is a set of instructions that tells a computer how to perform a particular task. Computers can become even more effective when connected to other computers so that that people can share information.

Software

Why does a computer need software? Software sets up a computer to do a particular task, tells the computer how to interact with the user, and specifies how to process the user's data. For example, music composition software sets up a computer to show you a musical staff. It tells the computer to let you input notes from your keyboard or synthesizer. Then the software tells the computer how to process this input into electrical signals that will play your music through a speaker.

A computer without software is like a record player without any records, a tape player without any tapes, or a CD player without any CDs. Without software, a computer is just a useless gadget with a power switch. Fortunately, software is plentiful; indeed, it is available for an astonishing number of tasks. Walk into a large computer store and you will see shelves full of software, including software for producing resumes, software for managing a small business, software to help you study for the Graduate Record Examination, software that teaches you Spanish, software to help you plan your diet, software for composing music, and software that takes you on an adventure through a dangerous labyrinth.

One of the best things about using a computer is browsing through a computer store or a computer software catalog to find just the right software to make your life easier and more interesting.

Categories of Computers

How and why are computers categorized? Traditionally, computers have been classified into four categories that provide some indication of their processing capabilities or "power." The four categories, from least to most powerful, are microcomputers, minicomputers, mainframe computers, and supercomputers. A computer is placed in one of these categories based on its technology, function, physical size, performance, and cost.

The criteria for these categories evolve as technology advances. Therefore, the lines that divide the different computer categories are fuzzy and tend to shift as more powerful computers become available.

By taking a quick look at each of these computer categories, you can compare their processing capabilities and the types of tasks they perform.

InfoWeb
3

Microcomputers

Microcomputers, also known as personal computers, are typically found in homes and small businesses. Prices range from $500 to $5,000, but consumers typically purchase systems in the middle of this range, spending from $1,000 to $2,000. One measure of microcomputer power is the speed of the processor, which on today's models exceeds 500 million operations per second. The microcomputer you use might be a stand-alone unit, or it might be connected to other computers so that you can share data and software with other users. However, even when your computer is connected to others, it will generally carry out processing tasks for only one user. Microcomputers come in many shapes and sizes, as you can see in Figure 1-3.

FIGURE 1-3

A **desktop microcomputer** fits on a desk and runs on power from an electrical wall outlet. The display screen is usually placed on top of the horizontal desktop case.

Some desktop microcomputers feature a vertically oriented tower case, which typically allows more room for expansion than a horizontal case. The tower unit can be placed on the floor to save desk space.

A **notebook computer**, sometimes called a "laptop," is small and light, giving it the advantage of portability that standard desktop computers do not have. A notebook computer can run on power from an electrical outlet or batteries.

A **personal digital assistant** (PDA), or "palm-top" computer achieves even more portability than a notebook computer by shrinking or eliminating some standard components, such as the keyboard. On a keyboardless PDA, a touch-sensitive screen accepts characters drawn with your finger. PDAs easily connect to desktop computers to exchange and update information.

Minicomputers

A **minicomputer** is somewhat more powerful than a microcomputer and can carry out the processing tasks for several people working at terminals that are connected to the minicomputer. A **terminal** is an input and output device that resembles a microcomputer because it has a keyboard and screen. A terminal, however, does not have processing capability, whereas a microcomputer does. When you input a processing request from a terminal, your request is transmitted to the minicomputer. The minicomputer processes data as necessary, then sends the results back to your terminal. The minicomputer system shown in Figure 1-4 is a fairly typical example.

FIGURE 1-4

A typical minicomputer handles processing tasks for multiple users.

Terminals act as each user's main input and output device. The terminal has a keyboard for input and a display screen for output, but it does not process the user's data. Instead, processing requests must be transmitted from the terminal to the minicomputer.

This minicomputer stores data for all users in one centralized location.

Minicomputer systems, which cost between $5,000 and $200,000, typically help small and medium-sized businesses perform specific tasks such as accounting, payroll, and shipping. For example, the main office of Royal Caribbean Cruises uses a minicomputer to track passenger bookings.

FIGURE 1-5

Stop in at any Caribbean port and you'll see ships emblazoned with the distinctive blue-anchor logo of Royal Caribbean Cruises, Ltd. With more than a dozen ships and more than five million passengers a year, the company uses IBM minicomputers to keep track of passenger bookings and corporate accounting.

InfoWeb
5

Mainframe
Computers

Mainframes are large, fast, and fairly expensive computers, generally used by business or government to provide centralized storage, processing, and management for large amounts of data. Like a minicomputer, one mainframe computer carries out processing tasks for multiple users, who input processing requests from terminals. However, a mainframe generally services more users than a minicomputer—some mainframes handle thousands of users. To process large amounts of data, mainframes process billions of instructions per second and often include several central processing units. One processing unit might direct overall operations, while a second unit handles communication with all users requesting data. A third unit could then find the data requested by users.

Mainframes remain the computer of choice in situations where reliability, data security, and centralized control are necessary. The price of a mainframe computer typically starts at several hundred thousand dollars and can easily exceed $1 million. A mainframe computer is housed in a closet-sized cabinet, as shown in Figure 1-6, and its peripheral devices are contained in separate cabinets.

FIGURE 1-6

The closet-sized system unit for an IBM S/390 G5 mainframe computer contains the processing unit, memory, and circuitry to support multiple terminals.

When you use a mainframe, your processing requests are transmitted from your terminal to the computer. At the same time, other users may also transmit requests. The computer processes each request in turn and transmits back the results. Mainframes handle user requests quickly. Even though 500 people might be submitting processing requests, the speed of the computer's response makes it seem as if you are the only user.

FIGURE 1-7

During peak times, an airline reservation mainframe might process more than 4,000 transactions per second.

InfoWeb
6

Supercomputers

Supercomputers, such as the one in Figure 1-8, are the fastest and most expensive type of computer. The cost of a supercomputer ranges from $500,000 to $35 million.

Originally designed for "compute-intensive" tasks such as molecular modeling, code breaking, and weather prediction, supercomputers have expanded into business markets, where the sheer volume of data would cause lengthy processing delays in a traditional mainframe environment. For example, MCI WorldCom uses supercomputer technology to manage its huge pool of customer data. Queries that once took more than two hours now take about a minute of supercomputer time.

A supercomputer can process more than 1 trillion instructions per second, making it possible to perform complex tasks such as modeling the movement of thousands of particles in a tornado or creating realistic animations (Figure 1-9).

FIGURE 1-8

The Cray T3E supercomputer, configurable with as many as 2,048 processors, provides the computing power to tackle the world's most challenging computing problems.

FIGURE 1-9

When creating the animated dinosaur skeleton for a McDonald's commercial, processing each frame might have required one hour of computer time on a very fast microcomputer. At 24 frames per second, it would take 24 hours to complete one second of animation. The animators at Synchromics used the supercomputer at the Maui High Performance Computing Center to reduce this time from 24 hours to 2 hours.

Start
Video

System Components

When I use a computer system, what hardware components will it include?

Microcomputer, minicomputer, mainframe, and supercomputer systems include devices to input, process, store, and output data. This book focuses on microcomputers because you are most likely to use this type of computer. Nevertheless, most of the concepts you will learn apply to the other categories of computers as well. Study Figure 1-10 to learn about the hardware components you are likely to use on a typical microcomputer system.

FIGURE 1-10

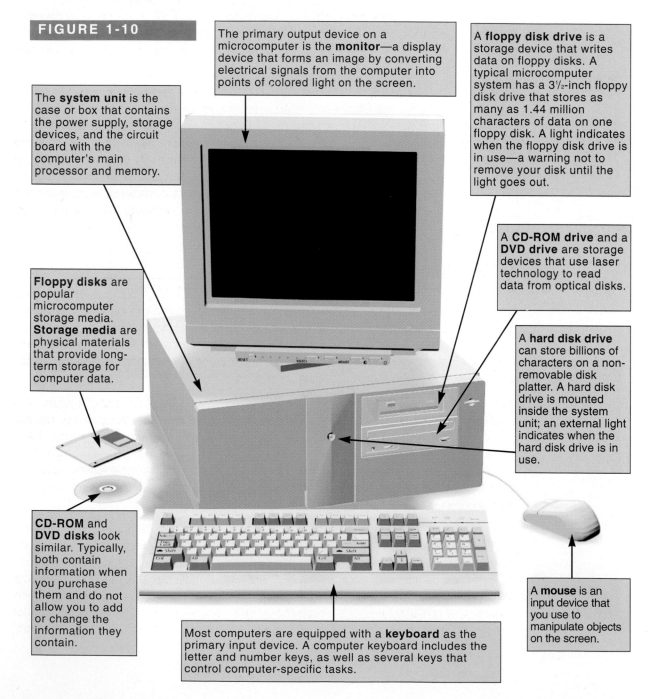

The primary output device on a microcomputer is the **monitor**—a display device that forms an image by converting electrical signals from the computer into points of colored light on the screen.

A **floppy disk drive** is a storage device that writes data on floppy disks. A typical microcomputer system has a 3½-inch floppy disk drive that stores as many as 1.44 million characters of data on one floppy disk. A light indicates when the floppy disk drive is in use—a warning not to remove your disk until the light goes out.

The **system unit** is the case or box that contains the power supply, storage devices, and the circuit board with the computer's main processor and memory.

A **CD-ROM drive** and a **DVD drive** are storage devices that use laser technology to read data from optical disks.

Floppy disks are popular microcomputer storage media. **Storage media** are physical materials that provide long-term storage for computer data.

A **hard disk drive** can store billions of characters on a non-removable disk platter. A hard disk drive is mounted inside the system unit; an external light indicates when the hard disk drive is in use.

CD-ROM and **DVD disks** look similar. Typically, both contain information when you purchase them and do not allow you to add or change the information they contain.

Most computers are equipped with a **keyboard** as the primary input device. A computer keyboard includes the letter and number keys, as well as several keys that control computer-specific tasks.

A **mouse** is an input device that you use to manipulate objects on the screen.

CHAPTER 1

Microcomputer Compatibility

Can all computers use the same software? Today, hundreds of companies manufacture microcomputers. Nevertheless, just about all of the computers that they produce are based on a small number of microcomputer designs or **computer platforms**. Today's two major microcomputer platforms are PCs and Macs.

PCs are based on the architecture of the first IBM microcomputers, which were built with standard off-the-shelf components. Today, PCs are manufactured by many companies, including IBM, Compaq, Dell, and Gateway. The software designed for PCs is usually called **Windows software**, and therefore the PC platform is sometimes referred to as the Windows platform. **Macs** are based on the proprietary Macintosh computer architecture, sometimes referred to as the "Mac platform," which is manufactured almost exclusively by Apple Computer, Inc.

Computers that operate in essentially the same way are said to be **compatible**. Two computer platforms are compatible if they can share the same software and use the same peripheral devices. Not all microcomputers are compatible with each other. PCs and Macs are not regarded as compatible platforms because they cannot use the same hardware devices or use the same programs without hardware or software to translate between them. In the past, sharing data between platforms was often difficult and sometimes impossible. Today, sharing data between these two platforms is inconvenient, but not impossible. Because more than 90% of the microcomputers in use today are PCs, the examples in this book focus on the PC platform.

Peripheral Devices

Is it possible to expand or modify a basic computer system? The term "peripheral device" designates equipment that might be added to a computer system to enhance its functionality. For example, a printer is a popular peripheral device used with microcomputers, minicomputers, and mainframe computers. Keyboards, monitors, disk drives, and mice are sometimes classified as peripheral devices, even though they are included with most basic computer systems.

Peripheral devices allow you to expand and modify a basic computer system. For example, you might purchase a computer that includes a mouse, but you can replace it with a trackball if you prefer. You might want to expand your computer's capabilities by adding a scanner so you can input photographs. If you're an artist, you might want to add a graphics tablet, so that you can sketch pictures using a pencil-like stylus. A peripheral device called a modem connects your computer to the telephone system so that you can access information stored on other computers.

Most microcomputer peripheral devices are designed for installation by users without technical expertise. When you buy a peripheral device, it usually comes with installation instructions and specially designed software. You should carefully follow the instructions to install the device and its software. Also, make sure the computer is turned off before you attempt to connect a peripheral device, so you don't damage your computer system. Figure 1-11 on the next page provides a brief overview of popular microcomputer peripheral devices. Many of these devices are discussed in more detail in later chapters.

FIGURE 1-11

Monitors come in many shapes and sizes, including this flat panel liquid crystal display (LCD).

A color ink-jet printer creates characters and graphics by spraying ink onto paper.

A computer projection device produces a large display of the information shown on the computer screen.

A laser printer uses the same technology as a photocopier to produce professional-quality text and graphics.

A scanner converts a page of text or images into an electronic format that the computer can display, print, and store.

A dot matrix printer creates characters and graphics by printing a fine pattern of dots using a 9-pin or 24-pin print mechanism.

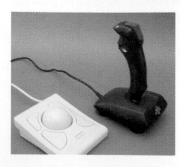
A digital camera records an image, then special digitizing hardware and software convert the image into a signal that a computer can store and transmit.

A multifunction device like this combination printer, scanner, fax, and answering machine provides an alternative to purchasing several separate devices.

A trackball and a joystick are pointing devices that you might use as an alternative to a mouse.

A graphics tablet accepts input from a pressure-sensitive stylus, converting pen strokes into images on the screen.

CHAPTER 1

Computer Networks

What's different about using a network? A **computer network** is a collection of computers and other devices that have been connected in order to share data, hardware, and software. Network users can send messages to other users on the network and retrieve data from a centralized storage device. Using a computer on a network is not much different from using a stand-alone computer, except that you have access to more data and the ability to communicate with others, but you'll have to follow network security procedures.

A network must be secured against unauthorized access to protect the data it stores. Most organizations restrict access to the software and data on a network by requiring users to log in with a unique user ID and password.

A **user ID** is a combination of letters and numbers that serve as your "call sign" or "identification." Your user ID is public—it is usually part of the address someone would need to send you messages over the network. You can let people know your user ID, but you should never reveal your password.

A **password** is a special set of symbols known only to you and to the person who supervises the network. You should not reveal your password to anyone because it would violate your responsibility to help maintain network security. Also, you should understand that if someone logs in to a network using your user ID and sends offensive messages or erases important files, it will look as if you did it. Figure 1-12 shows you what to do when a computer asks you to log in.

FIGURE 1-12

Many computer networks allow
access only if you have a
user ID and password.

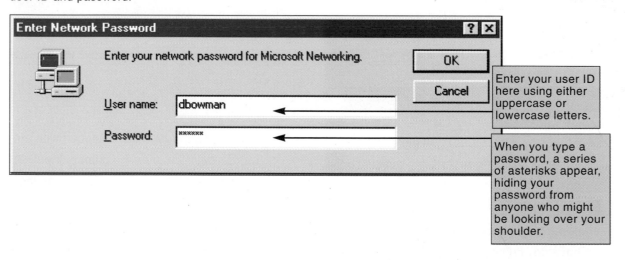

The Internet

What's the Internet? A network can connect microcomputers, minicomputers, and mainframes. Small networks connect a few computers within a building, whereas larger networks can stretch across the country. The world's largest computer network, the **Internet**, provides connections for millions of computers all over the globe. The Internet provides many information services, but the most popular is the World Wide Web, often referred to simply as the **Web**.

The Web is a sort of "flea market" for information. Computer sites all over the world store data of various sorts, such as weather maps, census data, product information, course syllabi, music, and images. When you connect your computer to the Web, you can access this information. The User Focus section of this chapter explains how.

FIGURE 1-13

The Internet provides access to the Web, where you'll find information, discussion groups, library card catalogs, online shopping, and more.

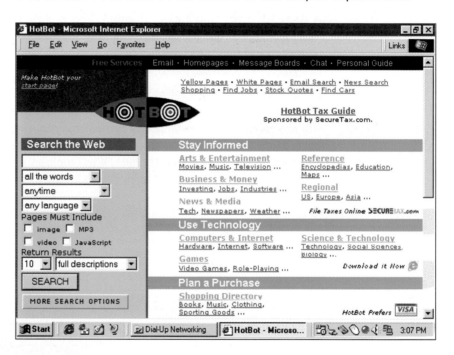

QUICKCHECK B

1 A(n) _____ is generally devoted to carrying out the processing tasks of only one user.

2 A(n) _____ is a device that resembles a microcomputer but does not have any processing capability.

3 If an organization wants to provide processing for more than 200 users and reliability, security, and centralized control are necessary, a(n) _____ computer would best meet its needs.

4 Most microcomputers are equipped with a(n) _____ as the primary input device and a(n) _____ as the primary output device.

5 An IBM computer is _____ with a Compaq computer because it operates in essentially the same way.

6 A computer _____ allows you to access data from a centralized storage device.

→ Check Answers

SECTION C   THE USER INTERFACE

InfoWeb
7
User Interfaces

To effectively use a computer as a mind tool, you must communicate with it; you must tell the computer what tasks to perform and you must accurately interpret the information provided by the computer. The means by which humans and computers communicate is referred to as the **user interface**. Through the user interface, the computer accepts your input and presents you with output.

Ideally, a good user interface makes a computer easy to use, intuitive, and unobtrusive. However, this ideal is not always the reality. Donald Norman, a well-known cognitive scientist, wrote a delightful book called *The Psychology of Everyday Things* in which he says, "Well-designed objects are easy to interpret and understand. They contain visible clues to their operation. Poorly designed objects can be difficult and frustrating to use. They provide no clues—or sometimes false clues. They trap the user and thwart the normal process of interpretation and understanding."

As with many objects in everyday life, some computer user interfaces are not well conceived, and using them may prove frustrating. User interfaces are still evolving in response to the needs of a rapidly growing community of computer users that includes children, teens, adults, and seniors.

FIGURE 1-14

A good user interface is easy to learn and use.

Start
Video

Lab
User Interfaces

Interacting with a Computer

Is a user interface hardware or software? A user interface is a combination of software and hardware. The software that controls a user interface defines its characteristics. For example, it determines whether you accomplish tasks by manipulating graphical objects or typing commands. The hardware controls the way you physically manipulate the computer to establish communication—for example, whether you use a keyboard or your voice to input commands. After you have a general understanding of user interfaces, you will be able to quickly figure out how to make the computer do what you want.

The software interface elements you'll typically encounter include prompts, wizards, commands, menus, dialog boxes, and graphical objects. The hardware interface elements you'll use include pointing devices, keyboards, and monitors.

Prompts

Why is it sometimes hard to figure out what the computer wants me to do?

A **prompt** is a message displayed by the computer that asks for input from the user. In response to a computer prompt, you enter the requested information or follow the instruction. Some prompts, such as "Enter your name:", are helpful and easy to understand, even for beginners. Other prompts, like A:\>, are less helpful to beginners.

A sequence of prompts is sometimes used to develop a user interface called a prompted dialog. In a prompted dialog, a conversation of sorts takes place between the computer and user. In the following example of a prompted dialog, the computer's prompts are shown in uppercase; the user's responses are shown in bold type.

HOW MUCH MONEY IS CURRENTLY IN YOUR ACCOUNT?
1000
HOW MUCH MONEY WILL YOU DEPOSIT EACH MONTH?
100
WHAT IS THE YEARLY INTEREST RATE PERCENT?
6
WHAT IS THE LENGTH OF THE SAVINGS PERIOD IN MONTHS?
36
O.K. AFTER 36 MONTHS YOU WILL HAVE $5149.96 IN YOUR SAVINGS ACCOUNT.

A prompted dialog is rarely found in microcomputer software packages for two reasons. First, the process of interacting with such a dialog is very linear. You must start at the beginning of the dialog and respond sequentially to each prompt. It can be difficult to back up if you make an error.

Second, a prompted dialog may be difficult to use because of the ambiguity of human language. If a prompt is not clear and you respond to it with some unexpected entry, the dialog will not function correctly. In Figure 1-15, you can see an example of this difficulty in a dialog with a computer-based library card catalog system.

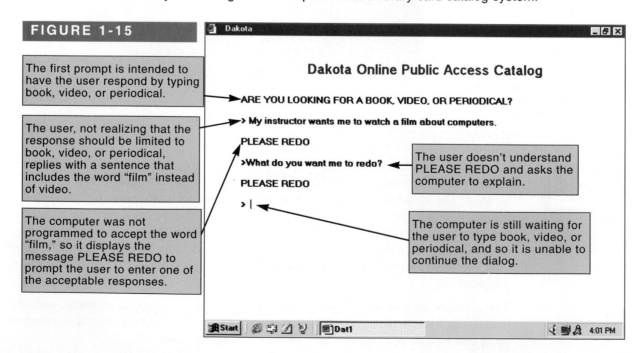

FIGURE 1-15

The first prompt is intended to have the user respond by typing book, video, or periodical.

The user, not realizing that the response should be limited to book, video, or periodical, replies with a sentence that includes the word "film" instead of video.

The computer was not programmed to accept the word "film," so it displays the message PLEASE REDO to prompt the user to enter one of the acceptable responses.

Dakota

Dakota Online Public Access Catalog

ARE YOU LOOKING FOR A BOOK, VIDEO, OR PERIODICAL?

> My instructor wants me to watch a film about computers.

PLEASE REDO

>What do you want me to redo?

PLEASE REDO

> |

The user doesn't understand PLEASE REDO and asks the computer to explain.

The computer is still waiting for the user to type book, video, or periodical, and so it is unable to continue the dialog.

Start   Dat1   4:01 PM

The difficulty encountered with the dialog in Figure 1-15 was not necessarily the fault of the user. The prompts should have provided more specific instructions, and the software should have accepted a wider vocabulary. Unfortunately, if this were the interface on your online library card catalog, you would need to learn how to work within its limitations.

Today's microcomputer software tends to use an updated type of dialog called a "wizard." A **wizard** is a sequence of screens that direct you through multistep software tasks, such as creating a graph, a list of business contacts, or a fax cover sheet. Wizards, like the one shown in Figure 1-16, use graphics to help explain the prompts and allow users to back up and change their responses.

FIGURE 1-16

The Business Card Wizard helps you create business cards that you can print on a laser printer. Click the Screentour button to design and print your own customized business cards.

The wizard prompts you at each step. First, you enter the information you want printed on the card.

Start
Screentour

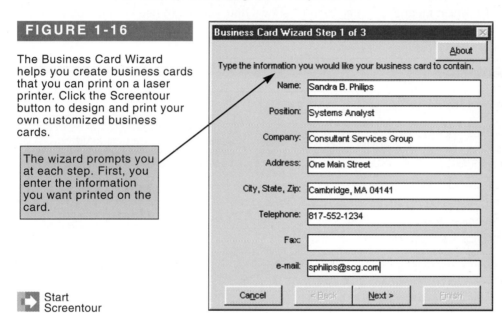

Next, you decide what style you'd like for your business card. The wizard lets you move forward or backward to change your responses until the business card is set up to your satisfaction.

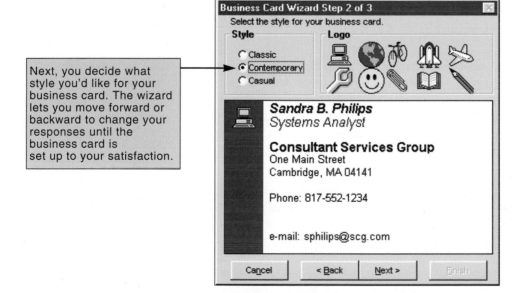

Commands

Do I have to memorize lots of commands to use a computer? A **command** is an instruction you input to tell the computer to carry out a task. When you use older microcomputer interfaces and many mainframe interfaces, you must type commands, then press the Enter key to indicate that the computer should now carry out the command. Each word in a command results in a specific action by the computer. Command words are often English words, such as *print*, *begin*, *save*, and *erase*, but they can also be more cryptic and might even use special symbols. Examples of cryptic command words include the following: *ls*, which means list; *cls*, which means clear the screen; and *!*, which means quit. Figure 1-17 shows how you might use commands to find out what is on your disk.

FIGURE 1-17

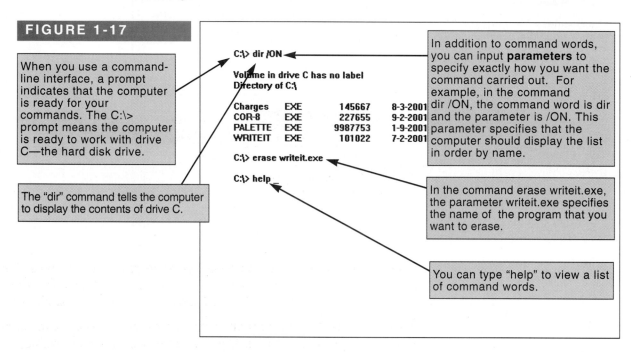

When you use a command-line interface, a prompt indicates that the computer is ready for your commands. The C:\> prompt means the computer is ready to work with drive C—the hard disk drive.

The "dir" command tells the computer to display the contents of drive C.

In addition to command words, you can input **parameters** to specify exactly how you want the command carried out. For example, in the command dir /ON, the command word is dir and the parameter is /ON. This parameter specifies that the computer should display the list in order by name.

In the command erase writeit.exe, the parameter writeit.exe specifies the name of the program that you want to erase.

You can type "help" to view a list of command words.

The commands you input must conform to a specific syntax. **Syntax** specifies the sequence and punctuation for command words and parameters. If you misspell a command word, leave out required punctuation, or type the command words out of order, you have made a **syntax error** and the computer will display an error message. When an error message appears, you must figure out what is wrong with the command and retype it correctly.

DOS User Interface

An interface that requires the user to type commands is referred to as a **command-line interface**. Learning to use a command-line interface is not easy. You must memorize the command words and know what they mean. To make the situation more difficult, there is not a single set of commands that you can use for every computer and every software package. If you forget the correct command word or punctuation, or if you find yourself using an unfamiliar command-line interface, you can usually enter the Help command. If online Help is not available, you'll need to use a reference manual. Command-line interfaces are typical of first-generation microcomputers, sometimes referred to as "DOS machines." You can use the DOS User Interface lab to see what it was like to use one of these "old" computers.

CHAPTER 1

Menus and Dialog Boxes

Are menus easier to use than commands? Menus were developed in response to the difficulties many people experienced when trying to remember the command words and syntax for command-line user interfaces. A **menu** displays a list of commands or options. Each line of the menu is referred to as a menu option or a menu item. Figure 1-18 shows you how to use a menu.

FIGURE 1-18

Menus make it easy to select commands and options.

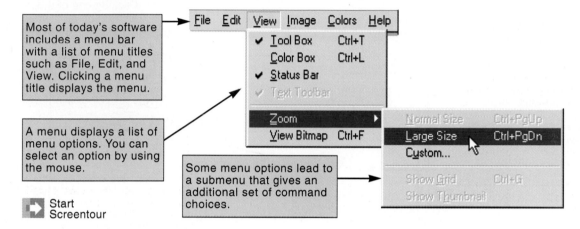

Most of today's software includes a menu bar with a list of menu titles such as File, Edit, and View. Clicking a menu title displays the menu.

A menu displays a list of menu options. You can select an option by using the mouse.

Start Screentour

Some menu options lead to a submenu that gives an additional set of command choices.

Menus are a popular user interface element because they do not require you to remember command words. You just choose the command you want from a list. Also, because all of the options on the list are valid commands, it is not possible to make syntax errors.

You might wonder how a menu can present all of the commands you would ever want to input. Obviously, there are many possibilities for combining command words, so hundreds of menu options might exist. Software designers typically use two methods to present a reasonably sized list of menu options: submenus and dialog boxes.

A **submenu** is an additional set of commands that the computer displays after you make a selection from the main menu. Sometimes a submenu displays another submenu providing even more command choices.

Instead of leading to a submenu, some menu options lead to a dialog box. A **dialog box** displays the options associated with a command. You fill in a dialog box to indicate specifically how you want the command carried out, as shown in Figure 1-19.

FIGURE 1-19

A dialog box displays controls that help you enter command parameters.

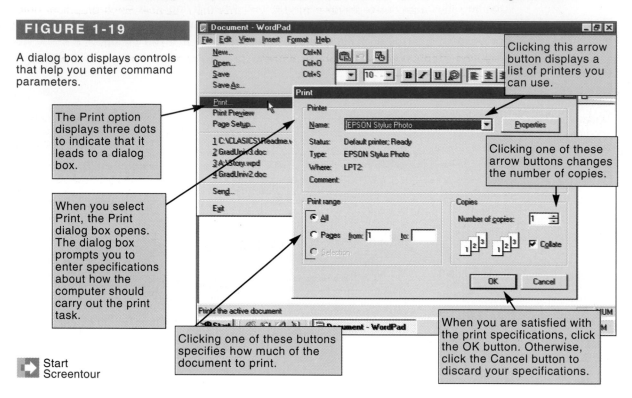

The Print option displays three dots to indicate that it leads to a dialog box.

When you select Print, the Print dialog box opens. The dialog box prompts you to enter specifications about how the computer should carry out the print task.

Clicking this arrow button displays a list of printers you can use.

Clicking one of these arrow buttons changes the number of copies.

Clicking one of these buttons specifies how much of the document to print.

When you are satisfied with the print specifications, click the OK button. Otherwise, click the Cancel button to discard your specifications.

▶ Start
Screentour

Dialog boxes display on-screen "controls," such as buttons and lists, that you can manipulate with the mouse to specify settings and command parameters. Figure 1-20 explains how to use some of the dialog box controls that you are likely to encounter.

FIGURE 1-20

Round **option buttons**, sometimes called "radio buttons," allow you to select one of the options.

Square **check boxes** allow you to select any or all of the options.

Drop-down lists display options when you click the arrow button.

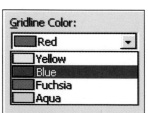

Spin boxes let you increase or decrease a number by clicking the arrow buttons. You can also type a number in the box.

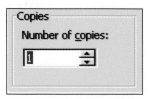

CHAPTER 1

Graphical Objects

Why are GUIs so popular? A **graphical object** is a small picture on the screen that you can manipulate using a mouse or other input device. Each graphical object represents a computer task, command, or a real-world object. You show the computer what you want it to do by manipulating an object instead of entering commands or selecting menu options. Graphical objects include icons, buttons, and windows, as explained in Figure 1-21.

FIGURE 1-21

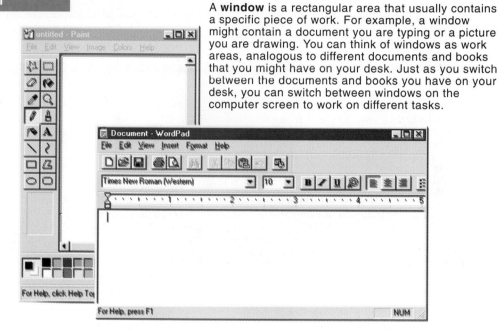

A **window** is a rectangular area that usually contains a specific piece of work. For example, a window might contain a document you are typing or a picture you are drawing. You can think of windows as work areas, analogous to different documents and books that you might have on your desk. Just as you switch between the documents and books you have on your desk, you can switch between windows on the computer screen to work on different tasks.

An **icon** is a small picture that represents an object. When you select an icon, you indicate to the computer that you want to manipulate the object. A selected object is highlighted. The My Computer icon on the right is selected, so it is highlighted with dark blue.

A **button** helps you make a selection. When you select a button, its appearance changes to indicate that it has been activated. The Paintbrush button is selected here, and it appears to be pushed in. Buttons are sometimes referred to as "tools."

As an example of manipulating on-screen objects, consider how you might delete a document. Your computer uses icons that look like sheets of paper to represent the documents you've created. A Recycle Bin icon represents the place where you put the documents that you no longer want. Suppose you used your computer to write a report named "Sport Statistics," but you no longer need it. You can use the mouse to drag the Sport Statistics icon to the Recycle Bin and erase the report from your computer system, as shown in Figure 1-22.

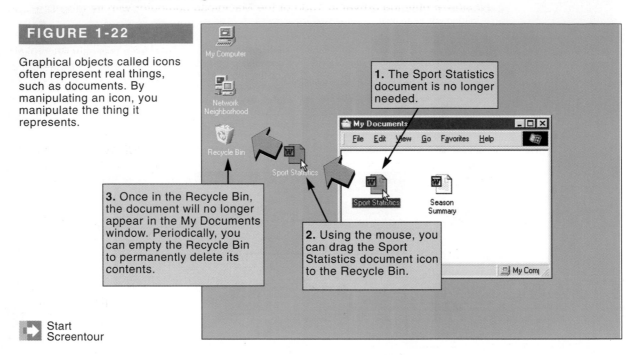

FIGURE 1-22

Graphical objects called icons often represent real things, such as documents. By manipulating an icon, you manipulate the thing it represents.

1. The Sport Statistics document is no longer needed.

3. Once in the Recycle Bin, the document will no longer appear in the My Documents window. Periodically, you can empty the Recycle Bin to permanently delete its contents.

2. Using the mouse, you can drag the Sport Statistics document icon to the Recycle Bin.

Start Screentour

Graphical objects are a key element of the **graphical user interfaces**, or GUIs (pronounced "gooies"), found on most of today's microcomputers. GUIs are based on the philosophy that people can use computers intuitively—that is, with minimal training—if they can manipulate on-screen objects that represent tasks or commands.

GUIs often display menus and prompts in addition to graphical objects, because graphical user interface designers found it difficult to design icons and tools for all possible tasks. Typically, all of the commands for a software program will be listed in the menus. The commands that you tend to use most frequently might also be represented by graphical objects that provide a quick shortcut for carrying out a task.

Most graphical user interfaces are based on a metaphor in which computer controls and components are represented by real-world objects. For example, a user interface with a desktop metaphor might represent documents as pages of paper and storage as a filing cabinet. Metaphors are intended to make the tasks you perform with computers more concrete, easier to explore, and more intuitive.

Lab
Using a Mouse

Pointing Devices

Some mice have three buttons, but others have only one or two—why?

As part of the user interface, a pointing device such as a mouse, trackball, or joystick helps you manipulate objects and select menu options. The most popular pointing device, the mouse, was developed by Douglas Engelbart in the early 1970s to provide an input method that was more efficient than the keyboard. The popularity of the mouse grew slowly, until the arrival in 1983 of the Macintosh computer with its graphical user interface. Now virtually every computer comes equipped with a mouse.

When you move the mouse on your desk, a **pointer**—usually shaped like an arrow—moves on the screen in a way that corresponds to the mouse movement. You select an object on the screen by pressing the left mouse button once. This action is referred to as "clicking." Some operations require you to click the mouse twice in rapid succession, an action referred to as "double-clicking." You can also use the mouse to "drag" objects from one screen location to another by pointing to the object, holding down the mouse button, and moving the mouse to the new location for the object. When the object is positioned in its new location, you release the mouse button. Figure 1-23 shows how to hold a mouse and use it to manipulate graphical objects.

FIGURE 1-23

Using a mouse is an important computing skill.

A pointer on the screen, usually shaped like an arrow, moves as you move the mouse. To select an object, use the mouse to position the pointer on the object, then click the left mouse button.

To hold the mouse, rest the palm of your right hand on the mouse so that your index finger is positioned over the left mouse button. Lightly grasp the mouse using your thumb and ring finger. Move the mouse right, left, forward, and back to move the pointer on the screen.

➡ Start Video

The pointer moves only while the mouse remains in contact with a hard surface like a desk. If you pick up the mouse and move it, the pointer will not move. This fact can come in handy. Suppose you are dragging an object, but your mouse encounters an obstacle on your desk. You can just pick up the mouse, move it to a clear space, and continue dragging.

The mouse you use with a Macintosh computer has only one button. PCs use either a two- or three-button mouse. A two-button mouse allows you to "right-click" an object and provides another way of manipulating it. For example, if clicking the left button selects an object, clicking the right button might bring up a menu of actions you can do with the object. On a three-button mouse, you rarely use the third button. Some three-button mice, however, allow you to click the middle button once instead of double-clicking the left mouse button. This feature is useful for people who have trouble double-clicking. It also helps prevent some muscular stress injuries that result from excessive clicking.

CHAPTER 1

Keyboard

Do I need to be a good typist to use a computer? Virtually every computer user interface requires you to use a keyboard at some point. You don't have to be a great typist, but to use a computer effectively you should be familiar with the computer keyboard because it contains special keys to manipulate the user interface. Study Figure 1-24 on the next page and try the Keyboard & Typing Tutor lab, which includes a typing tutorial so that you can brush up your typing skills.

Lab
Keyboard &
Typing Tutor

You use the typing keys to input commands, respond to prompts, and type the text of documents. A cursor or an insertion point indicates where the characters you type will appear. The **cursor** appears on the screen as a flashing underline. The **insertion point** appears on the screen as a flashing vertical bar. You can change the location of the cursor or insertion point by using the arrow keys or the mouse.

Two keys allow you to delete characters: the Backspace key and the Delete (or Del) key. The Backspace key deletes characters to the left of the insertion point. The Delete key deletes characters from the right of the insertion point. It is also the key to use if you want to delete an object or section of a drawing.

The **numeric keypad** provides a calculator-style input device for numbers and arithmetic symbols. Notice that some keys on the numeric keypad contain two symbols. When the Num Lock key is activated, the keys on the numeric keypad produce numbers. When Num Lock is not activated, these keys move the insertion point in the directions indicated by the arrows on the keys.

The Num Lock key is an example of a toggle key. A **toggle key** switches back and forth between two modes. The Caps Lock key is also a toggle. When you press the Caps Lock key, you switch or "toggle" into uppercase mode. When you press the Caps Lock key again, you toggle back into lowercase mode. The Insert key is a toggle as well. When the Insert key is activated, any text that you type is added at the position of the insertion point. When the Insert key is not activated, any text you type will overwrite your old text. Indicator lights at the top of the keyboard show the status of the toggle keys.

Here's an interesting problem that faced the designers of word processing software that uses a command-line interface. Suppose someone is typing in the text of a document and wants to issue a command to save the document on a disk. If the person types SAVE, it will appear as just another word in the document. How does the computer know that SAVE is supposed to be a command and not just part of a sentence such as "Save your money."? Interface designers solved this problem by introducing function keys, Ctrl keys, and Alt keys.

Function keys, like those numbered F1 through F12, are located at the top of your keyboard and can be used to initiate commands. For example, with many software packages, you press the F1 key to get help. Unfortunately, function keys are not standardized. In one program, you press F7 to save a document, but in another program, you must press F5 to perform the same task.

The Alt and Ctrl keys work in conjunction with the letter keys. If you see <Ctrl X>, Ctrl+X, [Ctrl X], Ctrl-X, or Ctrl X on the screen or in an instruction manual, it means to hold down the Ctrl key while you press X. For example, Ctrl+X is a keyboard shortcut for clicking the Edit menu, then clicking the Cut option. A **keyboard shortcut** allows you to use the keyboard rather than the mouse to select menu commands.

CHAPTER 1

FIGURE 1-24

☐ Editing Keypad   ☐ Typing Keypad

☐ Numeric Keypad   ☐ Function Key Array

The *Esc* or "escape" key cancels an operation.

The function of the *Scroll Lock* key depends on the software you are using. This key is rarely used with today's software.

Indicator lights show you the status of each toggle key: Num Lock, Caps Lock, and Scroll Lock. The Power light indicates whether the computer is on or off.

The *Caps Lock* key capitalizes all the letters you type when it is engaged, but does not produce the top symbol on keys that contain two symbols. This key is a toggle key, which means that each time you press it, you switch between uppercase and lowercase modes.

Function keys execute commands, such as saving a document. The command associated with each function key depends on the software you are using.

Each time you press the *Backspace* key, one character to the left of the insertion point is deleted.

The *Print Screen* key either prints the contents of the screen or stores a copy of your screen in memory that you can manipulate or print with graphics software.

The *Insert* key toggles between insert mode and typeover mode.

The *Num Lock* key is a toggle key that switches between number keys and arrow keys on the numeric keypad.

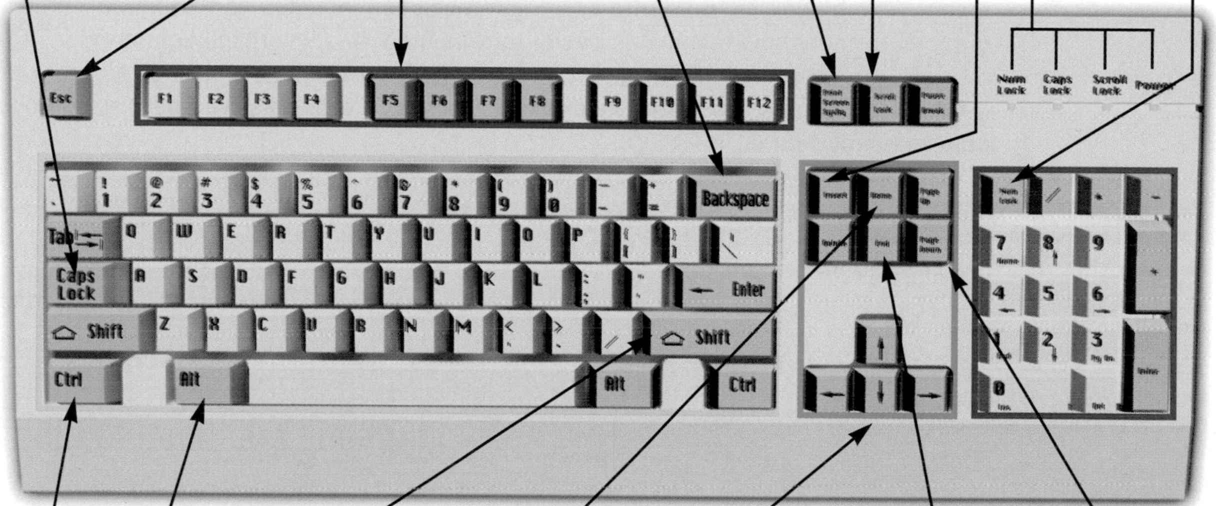

You hold down the *Alt* key while you press another key.

You hold down the *Shift* key while you press another key. The Shift key capitalizes letters and produces the top symbol on keys that contain two symbols.

The *Home* key takes you to the beginning of a line or the beginning of a document, depending on the software you are using.

The *arrow keys* move the insertion point.

The *End* key takes you to the end of the line or the end of a document, depending on the software you are using.

The *Page Up* key displays the previous screen of information. The *Page Down* key displays the next screen of information.

You hold down the *Ctrl* key while you press another key. The result of Ctrl or Alt key combinations depends on the software you are using.

Monitors

How are the monitor and user interface related? A monitor is a required output device for almost every computer user interface. Whereas you manipulate the keyboard and mouse to communicate with the computer, the computer manipulates the monitor to communicate with *you* by displaying results, prompts, menus, and graphical objects. The monitor's display technology determines whether the interface designer can include color and graphical objects.

The first microcomputer monitors and the displays on many mainframe terminals still in use today are character-based. A **character-based display** divides the screen into a grid of rectangles, each of which can display a single character. The set of characters that the screen can display is not modifiable; therefore, it is not possible to display different sizes or styles of characters. The only graphics possible on character-based displays are those composed of underlines, exclamation points, and other symbols that already exist in the character set. One reason that mainframes rarely support graphical user interfaces is because of the legacy of character-based terminals connected to mainframe systems.

A **bitmap display** divides the screen into a matrix of tiny, square "dots" called **pixels**. Any characters or graphics that the computer displays on the screen must be constructed of dot patterns within the screen matrix. The more dots your screen displays in the matrix, the higher its **resolution**. A high-resolution monitor can produce complex graphical images and text that is easier to read than on a low-resolution monitor. Most monitors on microcomputers have bitmap display capabilities, which gives them the flexibility to display characters in different sizes and styles as well as the graphical objects needed for GUIs.

FIGURE 1-25

Most of today's PCs feature a color monitor that displays text and graphics within a matrix of pixels. The more pixels in the matrix, the higher the resolution, and the smoother, more realistic the image.

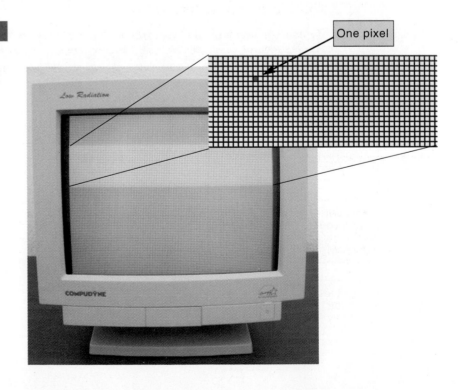

One pixel

CHAPTER 1

Tutorials, Manuals, and Online Help

How do I learn to use the interface on my computer? The Windows software in use on most of today's computers provides a fairly intuitive graphical user interface. Typically, the software that you'll use to produce documents, play games, and access the Internet has a standard set of Windows controls. Once you learn how to use these controls, you'll have a head start on learning any new software that you acquire. The sources of information on Windows software include tutorials, manuals, and online Help.

A tutorial is a guided, step-by-step learning experience; it is especially useful when you're just starting out with a new computer or a new software application. To learn how to use basic Windows controls, look for a tutorial on Microsoft Windows. You can also find tutorials on specific software, such as the graphics program CorelDRAW. Typically, a tutorial teaches generic skills that you can later apply to specific tasks. For example, suppose you purchase CorelDRAW software, and you want to start by drawing your company logo. A tutorial that teaches you how to use CorelDRAW will explain how to do such things as draw straight lines and wavy lines, add color to the drawing, and change the sizes of the pictures you draw. The tutorial does not teach you exactly how to draw your company logo. To get the most out of a tutorial, therefore, you need to think about how you can generalize the skills learned so you can apply them to other tasks. Tutorials come in a variety of forms, such as books, audio cassettes, videos, and on-screen computer-based training (CBT).

The term "online" refers to resources that are immediately available on your computer screen. Most software includes **online Help** that you can access by clicking Help on the menu bar at the top of the screen. Online Help is your best bet when you have a specific question about how to accomplish a task. It is less useful if you want to learn how to use a new software application.

Typically, when you use Help, you'll search through a list of keywords until you find one related to what you're trying to do. Some online Help also provides an online "assistant," like the one in Figure 1-26, that seems to intelligently answer your questions.

FIGURE 1-26

Online Help provides information about the features of a software application.

The Office Assistant responds to questions that you type.

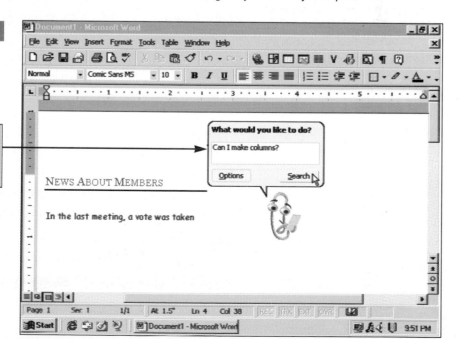

Start
Screentour

Reference manuals usually consist of printed books or online resources that describe each feature of a hardware device or software package. They might also include examples of how to use these features. Think of a reference manual as an encyclopedia, containing descriptions of all features of the software. A reference manual can be quite long, so do not assume that you should read it from cover to cover. Instead, leaf through it to get an overview of features. When you are searching for the answer to a specific question, the index is usually the place to begin.

Computer Terminology

Independent publishers also produce reference manuals for popular hardware and software. You might want to purchase one of these resources if it is easier to understand or better organized than the manual that comes with the hardware or software you purchased. You might also want to consider purchasing a comprehensive computer dictionary to answer your questions about general computer terminology.

Some software and hardware companies provide telephone support for customers who have questions about how to use their products. Sometimes these support line calls are free; sometimes they are not. In addition to paying for the phone call, you might also pay a fee for the time it takes the support person to answer your question.

Learning Styles

Individuals have different learning styles. Whereas some people enjoy discovery learning, others prefer structured lectures. Your learning style is related to the way you'll best learn how to use a computer. If you like reading and easily remember the things you read in books, you will probably like using printed reference manuals and tutorials. If you are a visual learner, you will probably like video tutorials. If you are an adventurous learner, you might enjoy exploring software applications without referring to printed materials or video tutorials. Graphical and menu-driven user interfaces make this sort of exploration possible, as do interfaces that include online Help.

QUICKCHECK C

1 A(n) [_____], such as "Enter your name:", is one way that a computer can tell the user what to do.

2 Instead of prompted dialogs, today's software tends to use [_____] to direct a user through multistep software tasks, such as creating a graph or creating a fax cover sheet.

3 When you use a command-line interface, you press the [_____] key when you have finished typing a command.

4 If you type a command, but leave out a required space, you have made a(n) [_____] error.

5 When you make a menu selection, a(n) [_____] or a dialog box might appear to let you enter more details on how you want the computer to do a task.

6 [_____] are work areas on the screen analogous to different documents and books you might have open on your desk.

7 The flashing underline that marks your place on the screen is called the [_____]; the flashing vertical bar is called the [_____].

8 You can use the [_____] key and the Alt key in conjunction with letter keys instead of using the mouse to control menu commands.

➡ Check Answers

USER FOCUS: BOOT, RUN, BROWSE, AND SEARCH

In today's technological society, many people have used a computer. Some, however, consider themselves beginners. Others are Mac users who are switching to the PC platform. Both types of users can benefit from a review of basic computer procedures, such as turning on equipment and starting programs. The next step, assuming that you have an Internet connection, is to access the Internet and learn how to search for information. Though you'll learn more about accessing the Internet later in the book, this User Focus section will get you started.

Boot Your Computer

What should I turn on first? In most cases, it doesn't matter in what order you turn on your computer, monitor, and printer. Because your monitor might take a few seconds to "warm up," you could turn it on first. Next, you can turn on your printer to make sure that your computer will find an active printer to use for your printouts. Finally, you can fire up the computer, using the switch on the system unit.

When your computer starts, the keyboard lights flash, the disk drives clatter, and a variety of startup messages appear on the screen. All of this activity is part of the "boot" process in which your computer runs a series of self-tests to ensure that everything is in good working order. The boot process is complete when the Windows desktop, shown in Figure 1-27, appears on your screen.

FIGURE 1-27

Your computer is "ready to roll" when the Windows desktop appears. Notice the placement of important icons and controls.

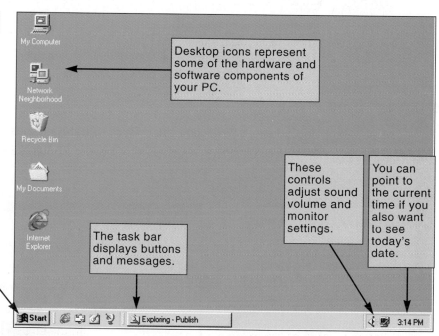

Desktop icons represent some of the hardware and software components of your PC.

The Start button provides access to your software and to hardware settings.

The task bar displays buttons and messages.

These controls adjust sound volume and monitor settings.

You can point to the current time if you also want to see today's date.

Run Programs

How do I start a program? In the jargon of computing, the process of starting and using a software program is referred to as "running" it. You can use one of several methods to start and run a program. Suppose that you want to access the Internet and "surf" for information on the Web using software called a **Web browser**. You'll need to start this software. Figure 1-28 on the next page shows you how.

FIGURE 1-28

To access the Internet and surf the Web, you first need to start a type of software called a Web browser.

1. Position the arrow-shaped pointer on the Start button, then click the left mouse button.

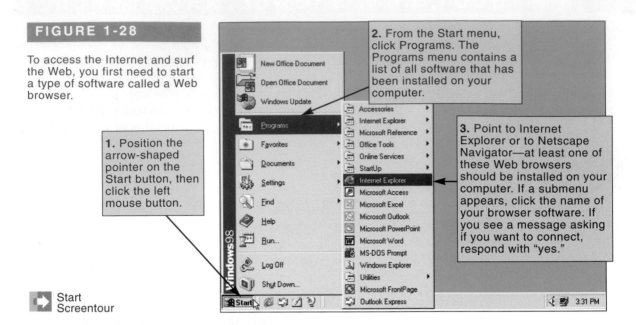

2. From the Start menu, click Programs. The Programs menu contains a list of all software that has been installed on your computer.

3. Point to Internet Explorer or to Netscape Navigator—at least one of these Web browsers should be installed on your computer. If a submenu appears, click the name of your browser software. If you see a message asking if you want to connect, respond with "yes."

Start Screentour

Searching the Web

How do I find information on the Web? After you start your Web browser software, you can find information in one of two ways. If you know the address where the information is stored, such as www.abcnews.com, you can type it in the Address box at the top of the screen. You can also search for information on a specific topic using a **Web search engine**—a sort of online reference librarian that keeps track of the locations of millions of Web-based resources.

To use a search engine, first type its address in your browser. Popular search engines include Yahoo! (www.yahoo.com), Lycos (www.lycos.com), Excite (www.excite.com), and Infoseek (www.go.com). Once you have access to the search engine, you can select topics from a list or enter keywords for the topics that interest you, as shown in Figure 1-29.

FIGURE 1-29

Browser software, such as Microsoft Internet Explorer, helps you navigate the Web.

To access a Web site, enter its address.

Enter keywords for a topic.

Select topics from a list provided by the search engine.

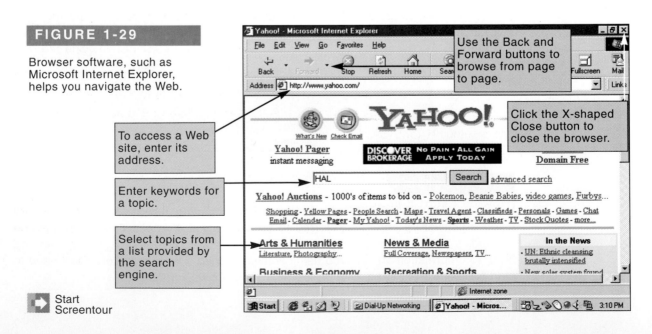

Use the Back and Forward buttons to browse from page to page.

Click the X-shaped Close button to close the browser.

Start Screentour

ISSUE CAN COMPUTERS THINK?

Science fiction usually depicts computers as intelligent devices. In the film *2001*, HAL certainly seemed to think for himself. But are thinking machines just the stuff of science fiction? In 1950, the well-respected British mathematician Alan Turing wrote, "I believe that at the end of the century the use of words and general educated opinion will have altered so much that one will be able to speak of machines thinking without expecting to be contradicted." Can computers think? This subject has inspired a debate that has raged among computer scientists and philosophers for more than half a decade.

Putting aside for a moment the question of whether computers can think, consider how you "know" that other people can think. How can you tell if a person is able to think? You can't "get inside" someone's mind to find out first-hand. Instead, you probably use logic something like: "I am a person and I can think. Therefore, other people must be able to think, too." This logic seems correct, but you can't apply it to entities that are not people. You could not use it, for example, to determine if an extra-terrestrial being can think, or if computers can think. So, do you have an alternative way of assessing whether someone or something can think? You might be able to tell by observing behavior. If, for example, a person or an extra-terrestrial behaves in an intelligent way, you would assume that he or she can think. Is it possible to use behavior as the criteria for determining whether a computer can think? In fact, just this strategy was proposed by Alan Turing.

Turing described a "test" of machine intelligence. The Turing test, as it is now called, is somewhat like a TV game show. It pits a contestant against two backstage opponents—one a computer and one a human. The contestant asks questions to try to identify the computer. Turing suggested that if the computer could not be identified, then it was acting just as intelligently as the human. A computer that can behave as intelligently as a human must, therefore, be intelligent and must be able to think.

Since 1950, designing a computer that can pass the Turing test has become the holy grail for a field of research known as artificial intelligence. **Artificial Intelligence** (AI) refers to the ability of computers to solve problems and perform tasks that were once thought to be uniquely human. AI researchers have produced computers that can move and manipulate robotic limbs, respond to human speech, diagnose diseases, translate documents from one language to another, play chess at the grand master level, and learn new tasks. So far, however, no computer has passed the Turing test.

Even if a computer can eventually pass the Turing test, not everyone would agree that it can think. Philosopher John Searle, for example, attempted to refute the Turing test using the now famous Chinese-Room Thought Experiment. Suppose you are an

English-speaking person who cannot understand written or spoken Chinese. You are locked in a room and given a stack of papers containing Chinese writing. You receive other papers containing a set of simple rules, written in English, that tell you how to manipulate Chinese characters. Next, someone slides a sheet of paper under the door of your room and you see that it contains Chinese writing. Using the simple set of rules, you squiggle something on the sheet of paper and return it to the person on the other side of the door.

It happens that the person outside of the room speaks and reads Chinese. The paper you received under the door actually contained a question in Chinese. By following your set of English rules, the squiggle that you wrote on the paper turned out to be the correct answer to the question. So, your written response makes it look like you can communicate in Chinese, even though you can't understand a word of it.

Searle suggests that a similar process occurs in a computer. Rather than using intelligence, the computer mindlessly manipulates symbols. Searle contends that even if a computer passed the Turing test, it would have no understanding of the conversation it was having with humans—rather, it would simply be processing symbols, while appearing to answer the questions of the game show contestant.

Does Searle's Chinese-Room Thought Experiment effectively refute the possibility that computers can think? Consider this—could the person in the Chinese room manipulate the symbols without using any intelligence? The answer seems to be "No." Therefore, you might conclude that a computer requires intelligence to pass the Turing test or to perform any sort of processing task.

Despite many years of debate, the question "Can computers think?" has yet to be answered, but the debate has spurred fruitful AI research and produced technologies that improve the way we live. AI has not, however, fulfilled the prophesies of science fiction or Turing's expectation that by the year 2000 computers would generally be considered thinking machines.

WHAT DO YOU THINK?

1. Can computers think?   ◯ Yes   ◯ No   ◯ Not sure

2. Is human intelligence different from machine
intelligence?   ◯ Yes   ◯ No   ◯ Not sure

3. Would a computer that could beat chess
champion Gary Kasparov also pass the
Turing test?   ◯ Yes   ◯ No   ◯ Not sure

➡ Save Responses

CHAPTER 1 REVIEW ACTIVITIES

INTERACTIVE SUMMARY

The Interactive Summary helps you select important concepts and facts from this chapter. Fill in the blanks to best complete each sentence. When using the NP4 CD or NP4 Web site, you can click the Check Answers buttons to automatically score your answers. Place your Tracking Disk in the floppy disk drive if you want to save your scores.

A computer is a device that accepts input, processes data, stores data, and produces output. _____ devices, such as a keyboard, feed data into a computer. When data is not needed for immediate processing, it is _____ on disk or tape. Before the computer processes data, it is temporarily held in _____. This data is then processed in the _____ (CPU). The results of processing are called _____.

The electronic and mechanical components of a computer system that process data are referred to as _____. Computers also require a set of instructions called _____, which tells the computer how to interact with the user and how to process the user's data.

Traditionally, computers are classified into four categories: microcomputers, minicomputers, mainframe computers, and supercomputers. Of these four categories, _____ are typically found in homes and small businesses. Although hundreds of companies manufacture these computers, only two major _____ exist: PCs and Macs. PCs are generally not regarded as being _____ with Macs because they cannot use the same hardware devices or use the same programs without hardware or software translation.

Check Answers

A computer _____ is a collection of computers and other devices connected to share data, hardware, and software. The _____ is the world's largest computer network and supplies services such as the World Wide _____. Access to the Web requires _____ software, such as Microsoft Internet Explorer.

The combination of hardware and software that enables humans and computers to communicate is called the user _____. When using today's popular _____ user interfaces (GUIs), you use a mouse to select commands from a(n) _____ and manipulate small pictures called _____ that represent objects. Rectangular _____ contain a specific piece of work, such as a document.

The continual stream of new computer technology means that experts, as well as novices, frequently have to learn how to use new hardware and software. Most software includes a printed reference _____ and online _____ that explain how to use its features.

 Check Answers

INTERACTIVE KEY TERMS

Make sure that you understand all of the boldfaced key terms presented in this chapter. If you're using the NP4 CD or NP4 Web site, you can use this list of terms as an interactive study activity. First, try to define a term in your own words, then click the term to compare your definition with the definition that is presented in the chapter.

Artificial intelligence (AI), 33
Bitmap display, 28
Button, 23
CD-ROM disk, 12
CD-ROM drive, 12
Central processing unit (CPU), 5
Character-based display, 28
Check box, 22
Command, 20
Command-line interface, 20
Compatible platforms, 13
Computer, 5
Computer network, 15
Computer platform, 13
Cursor, 26
Data, 5
Desktop microcomputer, 8
Dialog box, 22
Drop-down list, 22
DVD disk, 12
DVD drive, 12
Floppy disk, 12
Floppy disk drive, 12
Function key, 26
Graphical object, 23
Graphical user interface (GUI), 24
Hard disk drive, 12
Hardware, 7
Icon, 23
Input, 5
Insertion point, 26
Internet, 16
Keyboard, 12
Keyboard shortcut, 26
Macintosh computer (Mac), 13
Mainframe, 10
Memory, 5
Menu, 21
Microcomputer, 8
Minicomputer, 9
Monitor, 12
Mouse, 12
Notebook computer, 8
Numeric keypad, 26

Online Help, 29
Option button, 22
Output, 5
Parameter, 20
Password, 15
PC, 13
Peripheral device, 7
Personal digital assistant (PDA), 8
Pixel, 28
Pointer, 25
Process, 5
Prompt, 18
Resolution, 28
Software, 7
Spin box, 22
Storage, 5
Storage media, 12
Submenu, 21
Supercomputer, 11
Syntax, 20
Syntax error, 20
System unit, 12
Terminal, 9
Toggle key, 26
User ID, 15
User interface, 17
Web, 16
Web browser, 31
Web search engine, 32
Window, 23
Windows software, 13
Wizard, 19

INTERACTIVE QUIZZES

Quiz yourself on important concepts from this chapter by filling in the blanks. When using the NP4 CD or NP4 Web site, you can type your answers, then use the Check Answers buttons to automatically score your responses. Place your Tracking Disk in the floppy disk drive if you want to save your scores.

1 A computer accepts [_____] such as numbers and processing instructions.

2 The processor retrieves data from temporary [_____], then processes it.

3 A computer without [_____] is like a CD player without any CDs.

4 A small business is likely to run its accounting system on a(n) [_____] that employees access using terminals.

5 Computers that specialize in running a single program and can achieve processing speeds in excess of 1 trillion instructions per second are called [_____].

6 An airline might typically use a(n) [_____] computer for its reservation system.

7 PCs and Macs are two microcomputer [_____].

8 The [_____] is a sort of information "flea market" that's accessible using the Internet.

9 A user interface is a combination of [_____] and software.

10 [_____] refers to the field of research that produces computers, devices, and programs that exhibit human-like intelligence and behavior.

➡ Check Answers

Enter the correct letter from the photo into each box.

1 Monitor [_____]

2 Mouse [_____]

3 Floppy disk drive [_____]

4 CD-ROM drive [_____]

5 Function keys [_____]

6 Numeric keypad [_____]

7 Arrow keys [_____]

8 Hard disk drive [_____]

9 CD-ROM disk [_____]

➡ Check Answers

INTERACTIVE PRACTICE TESTS

When you use the NP4 CD or NP4 Web site, you can take practice tests that consist of 10 multiple-choice, true/false, and fill-in-the-blank questions. The 10 questions are selected at random from a large test bank, so each time you take a test, you'll receive a different set of questions. Your tests are scored immediately and you can print study guides that help you find the correct answers for any questions that you missed. If you are using a Tracking Disk, insert it in the floppy disk drive to save your test scores.

 Start Practice
Test

STUDY TIPS

Study Tips help you organize and consolidate the information in a chapter by making lists, outlines, charts, and sketches. You can use paper and pencil or word processing software to complete most of the Study Tips activities.

1 Using your own words, write out the answers to the questions found below each heading in this chapter.

2 At the top of a sheet of paper, write "Definition of the term computer," then make a list of important words, names, and phrases that are related to your list.

3 Use lines to divide a sheet of paper into four equal sections. In the upper-left corner, write "microcomputer." Write "minicomputer" in the upper-right corner, "mainframe" in the lower-left corner, and "supercomputer" in the lower-right corner. Place words, phrases, and definitions in each section that describe and differentiate each type of computer.

4 Draw a sketch of a microcomputer system, without referring to this book. Then label as many components as you can. When you have finished, look at Figure 1-10 to see if you omitted anything.

5 List as many peripheral devices as you can, without referring to this book. Indicate whether each is an input device, an output device, or both. Refer to Figure 1-11 and review any devices you omitted.

6 Make a list of the user interface elements covered in this chapter. Write at least three terms or phrases associated with each. For example, user interface element: prompt. Associated terms and phrases: (a) prompted dialog, (b) wizards, (c) can be ambiguous or confusing.

7 Make a list of information resources that might help you install hardware and learn to use software. Write a one-sentence description of each resource.

8 Write a paragraph that explains the difference between the pointer, the cursor, and the insertion point.

PROJECTS

A project is an open-ended activity that will help you apply the concepts you have learned. Many projects require resources in addition to your textbook, such as current magazines, library materials, or Web access. When you tackle a project, be prepared to use your critical thinking skills, logical analysis, and your creativity.

1 **Your Library Card Catalog Interface** Find out if your library has a computerized card catalog. If it does, use it to answer the following questions:

    a. What is the name of the software that your library uses for its computerized card catalog?

    b. What type of user interface does it have?

    c. Explain the steps you would take to find the call number for the book War and Peace.

    d. Is the computerized card catalog easy to learn and to use?

    e. What kind of online Help is available?

    f. Is the computerized card catalog efficient to use? Explain why or why not.

    g. How much had you used the computerized card catalog before this assignment?

2 **Research Tool: The Internet** Do this project only if you have access to the Internet. The Internet is a worldwide computer network that provides access to a wealth of information, including a World Wide Web site designed to accompany this textbook. Although the Internet is the main topic of Chapter 8, using the Internet can come in handy even as you begin using this book. Several of the end-of-chapter projects refer you to information resources on the Internet. If you would like to use the Internet for these projects, now is a good time to get started.

Several software tools are available to help you use the Internet, such as Netscape Navigator and Microsoft Internet Explorer. It is not possible to cover these software tools here. Therefore, you can accomplish this exploratory project with the help of your instructor or with a tutorial prepared by your school or Internet service provider. Find out how to use the Internet and then answer the following questions:

    a. What is the name of the software tool that you used to access the Internet?

    b. How do you access the "home page" for your school?

    c. Use your Internet software to access the World Wide Web site *http://www.cciw.com/np4*. How can the information at this site help you with the end-of-chapter projects in this textbook?

    d. List at least five other locations or "sites" that are available from your home page. How do you reach these other sites?

    e. How can you keep track of where you have been on the Internet? (In other words, is there a way to backtrack to sites?)

    f. When you have finished browsing on the Internet, how do you quit?

3 **Reference Manuals** Locate a software reference manual in your computer lab, home, or library; then answer the following questions:

    a. What is the title of the reference manual?

    b. How many pages does it have?

    c. What are the titles of each section of the manual? For example, there might be a "Getting Started" section, or an "Installation" section, and so on.

    d. Does the reference manual include an index? If so, does it look complete? You should be suspicious of a large reference manual with a short index—it might be difficult to find the information you need.

    e. Does the reference manual contain a list of features? If so, is this list arranged alphabetically? If not, how is it arranged? (continued on next page)

(continued on next page)

CHAPTER 1

f. Read a few pages of the reference manual. Write one or two sentences describing what you read. Does the reference manual seem to be well written and easy to follow? Why or why not?

4 **Identify Your Learning Style** In this chapter, you learned that you can take many approaches to learning how to use hardware and software. For this project, think about your own learning style and how it might influence which resources you select for learning about computers and software. Use the resources in InfoWeb 9 to assess your learning style. Write a one-page paper and include the following information:

a. Describe the way you like to learn things in general—do you like to read about them, take a class, listen to a cassette, watch a video, think about them, do library research, or follow a different approach?

b. If you have access to the Internet, provide the results of your learning style assessments. Do these results seem to accurately reflect your learning style?

c. If you had to learn how to use a new software application, which approach would you like best: working through a tutorial, using a reference manual, exploring on your own, taking a class, or asking an expert? Why?

d. How does your answer in (c) relate to the way you like to learn other things?

5 **Why Not Just Talk to It?** Computer scientists have discovered that it is quite difficult to develop a "conversational" user interface that you could use to simply "talk" to a computer. One major stumbling block is the ambiguity of human speech. For example, if someone tells you "My friend was looking at a bicycle in the store window, and she wanted it," you assume that "it" refers to the bicycle, not the store window. But English grammar does not make the meaning of "it" explicit, so a computer would have a hard time understanding what you mean. Hubert Dreyfus discusses this problem in the video *The Machine That Changed the World* and in the book entitled *What Computers Still Can't Do*. To pursue this topic, do one or more of the following activities:

a. With a small group of students, try to think of other examples of ambiguity in human conversation that a computer would probably have difficulty understanding. You can share your list with the rest of the class or turn it in to your instructor.

b. Use the resources from InfoWeb 10 to research this topic so that you more fully understand the problem. Write a term paper summarizing your research.

ADDITIONAL PROJECTS

Click the underlined text to link to the NP4 Web site (www.cciw.com/np4) where you can view and print additional projects for this chapter.

<u>**Getting Started on Your Network**</u>

<u>**Evaluate a User Interface**</u>

<u>**Microcomputers, Minicomputers, Mainframes, and Supercomputers**</u>

CHAPTER 1

LAB ASSIGNMENTS

Software for these labs is provided on the NP4 CD and may also be available in your school's computer lab. To start a lab, click the lab icon.

Each lab has two parts: Steps and Explore. Use the Steps first to learn and review concepts. Read the information on each page and complete the numbered steps. As you work through the lab, you will be asked to answer QuickCheck questions about what you have learned. At the end of the lab, you will see a report that scores your answers to the QuickChecks. If your instructor wants you to turn in this report, click the Print button on the QuickCheck Report screen.

When you have completed the Steps, you can click the Explore button to complete the Lab Assignments. You can also use Explore to practice the skills you learned and to explore concepts on your own.

User
Interfaces

You have learned that the hardware and software for a user interface determine how you interact and communicate with the computer. In the User Interfaces lab, you will try five user interfaces to accomplish the same task—creating a graph.

1 Click the Steps button to find out how each interface works. As you work through the Steps, answer all of the QuickCheck questions. When you complete the Steps, you will see a report that summarizes your performance on the QuickChecks. Follow the directions on the screen to print the QuickCheck Report.

2 In Explore, use each interface to make a 3-D pie graph using data set 1. Title your graphs "Cycle City Sales." Use the percent style to show the percentage accounted for by each slice of the pie. Print each of the five graphs (one for each interface).

3 In Explore, select one of the user interfaces. Write a step-by-step set of instructions for how to produce a line graph using data set 2. This line graph should show lines and symbols, and have the title "Widget Production."

4 Using the user interface terminology you learned in this lab and in this chapter, write a description of each of the interfaces you used in the lab. Then, suppose you work for a software publisher and you are going to create a software package for producing line, bar, column, and pie graphs. Which user interface would you use for the software? Why?

DOS User
Interface

The DOS command-line user interface provides a typical example of the advantages and disadvantages of command-line user interfaces. DOS was included with the original IBM PC computers to provide users with a way to accomplish system tasks such as listing, moving, and deleting files on disk. Although today's typical computer user prefers to use a graphical user interface such as Windows, DOS commands still function on most IBM-compatible computers.

1 Click the Steps button to learn how to use the DOS command-line interface. As you work through the Steps, answer all of the QuickCheck questions. When you complete the Steps, you will see a report that summarizes your performance on the QuickChecks. Follow the directions on the screen to print the QuickCheck Report. Remember to use the EXIT command to close the DOS window when you're ready to quit.

2 In Explore, write out your answers to (a) through (d).
   a. Explain the different results you get when you use the commands DIR, DIR /p, and DIR /w.
   b. What happens if you make a typing error and enter the command DIT instead of DIR? What procedure must you follow to correct this error? (continued on next page)

    c. Enter the command DIR /? and explain what happens. Enter the command VER /? and explain what happens. What generalization can you make about the /? command parameter?

    d. Enter the command VER /w. Why do you think /w does not work with the VER command word, but works with DIR?

3 Write a one-page paper summarizing what you know about command-line user interfaces and answering the following questions:

    a. Which DOS commands do you now know how to use?

    b. How do you know which commands to use to accomplish a task?

    c. How do you know what parameters work with each command?

    d. What kinds of mistakes can you make that will produce an error message?

    e. Can you enter valid commands that don't produce the results you want?

Lab
Using a Mouse

A mouse is a standard input device on most of today's computers. You need to know how to use a mouse to manipulate graphical user interfaces and to use the rest of the labs.

1 The Steps for the Using a Mouse lab show you how to click, double-click, and drag objects using the mouse. Click the Steps button and begin the Steps. As you work through the Steps, answer all of the QuickCheck questions that appear. When you complete the Steps, you will see a report that summarizes your performance on the QuickChecks. Follow the directions on the screen to print the QuickCheck Report.

2 In Explore, demonstrate your ability to use a mouse and to control a Windows program by creating a poster. To create a poster for an upcoming sports event, select a graphic, type the poster caption, then select a font, font styles, and a border. Print your completed poster.

Lab
Keyboard & Typing Tutor

To become an effective computer user, you must be familiar with your primary input device—the keyboard.

1 The Steps for the Using a Keyboard lab provide you with a structured introduction to the keyboard layout and the functions of special computer keys. Click the Steps button and begin the Steps. As you work through the Steps, answer all of the QuickCheck questions that appear. When you complete the Steps, you will see a report that summarizes your performance on the QuickChecks. Follow the directions on the screen to print the QuickCheck Report.

2 In Explore, start the typing tutor, which helps you develop your typing skills. Take the typing test and print out your results.

3 In Explore, try to improve your typing speed by 10 words per minute. For example, if you currently type 20 words per minute, your goal would be 30 words per minute. Practice each typing lesson until you see a message that indicates you can proceed to the next lesson. Create a Practice Record as shown here to keep track of how much you practice. When you have reached your goal, print out the results of a typing test to verify your results.

Practice Record for (Name) :_____

Start Date: _____ Start Typing Speed: _____ wpm

End Date: _____ End Typing Speed: _____ wpm

Lesson #: _____ Date Practiced/Time Practiced: _____

INFOWEB

InfoWeb Site
Chapter 1

The InfoWeb is your guide to print, film, television, and electronic resources. Use it to obtain updates on quickly changing technical information and to locate information for research papers. If you're using the NP4 CD, click the InfoWeb Site icon on the left side of this paragraph to access the online InfoWeb links. Otherwise, use your Web browser and type in the address of the NP4 Web site: www.cciw.com/np4. At the Web site you'll find up-to-date links to the topics covered in this chapter.

1 2001: A Space Odyssey

One of the themes in the 1968 science-fiction classic, *2001: A Space Odyssey*, is the relationship between humans and computers. Written by scientist and novelist Arthur C. Clarke, the book *2001: A Space Odyssey* (New York: New American Library, 1968) was the basis for a movie directed by Stanley Kubrick. The film, produced by MGM in 1968, is thought-provoking, and its special effects are still considered impressive, even after 30 years. Perhaps Clarke's vision of the future was so powerful because of his strong background in science and research. Clarke is well known for his  theoretical contribution to the invention of the communications satellite. Visit the NP4 Web site for links to soundtracks and images from the film, critical commentary, and essays by Arthur C. Clarke.

2 John von Neumann

Perhaps the greatest mathematician of his time, John von Neumann (1903–1957) had a photographic memory and a superhuman ability to perform mental calculations. Von Neumann's security clearance allowed him access to ENIAC and EDVAC, the first large-scale digital computers developed in the United States. Find out more about von Neumann by following links from the NP4 Web site. Von Neumann's 1945 paper, "First Draft of a Report on the EDVAC," is reprinted in Nancy Stern's book *From ENIAC to UNIVAC: An Appraisal of the Eckert Mauchly Computers* (Digital Press, 1981).

For information about the exciting early days of computing, visit the Computer Museum's Web site at *www.tcm.org* and look at the years 1945–1952. If you'd like more information, check your library for the video, *The Machine That Changed the World*, Episode 1: Giant Brains (WGBH Television in cooperation with the British Broadcasting Corp., 1991).

3 Microcomputers

In 1977, Digital Equipment Corporation CEO Ken Olsen proclaimed, "There is no reason for any individual to have a computer in their home." It was a statement he would later regret. Microcomputer technology and the vision of pioneers like Apple Computer's Steve Jobs made personal computers a reality. Check the NP4 Web site for links to a detailed history of Apple Computers. For more information about the heady days of the microcomputer industry, read the fast-paced book *Accidental Empires: How the Boys of Silicon Valley Make Their Millions, Battle Foreign Competition, and Still Can't Get a Date* by Robert X. Cringely (published by HarperCollins, 1996).

4 Minicomputers

In 1957, Kenneth Olsen and Harland Anderson formed a company called Digital Equipment Corporation (DEC). Their original objective was to grab a slice of IBM's business market and sell million-dollar mainframes. Financial realities prevailed, however, and a new plan emerged—build a slightly scaled-down computer and sell it for $125,000 to scientific and engineering markets. DEC computers proved successful even in other markets and by 1969—during the era of miniskirts and miniseries—these computers were universally referred to as "minicomputers."

The book *Computer: A History of the Information Machine* by Campbell-Kelly and Aspray (Basic Books, 1996) contains a good history of minicomputers. Links from the NP4 Web site will point you to information about minicomputer history.

Digital Equipment Corporation merged with Compaq in 1998. Today's minicomputer vendors include IBM, Digital/Compaq, and Hewlett Packard. IBM's AS/400 has probably been the most popular microcomputer of all time. Check it out at *www.as400.ibm.com*. For an update on minicomputer technology, look for links at the NP4 Web site.

5 Mainframe Computers

IBM is synonymous with mainframe computers. The company traces its lineage back to the Tabulating Machine Company built around an 1890s card-punch device invented by Herman Hollerith. IBM did not dominate the computer market until 1964, when it introduced the IBM System/360 mainframes that were to be the staple of business computing for a quarter of a century. The history of IBM is expertly chronicled in *Building IBM: Shaping an Industry and Its Technology* by Emerson W. Pugh (MIT Press, 1995), and the video *The Computer Revolution: Birth of the Computer* (available from Films for the Humanities and Sciences).

IBM is not the only mainframe vendor, but its Web site at *www.ibm.com* is a good place to find information on the latest mainframe technology.

6 Supercomputers

It takes a supercomputer to beat the world's best chess player. In 1997, Gary Kasparov admitted defeat to IBM's Deep Blue supercomputer. IBM has an excellent Web site devoted to the match, at *www.chess.ibm.com*.

In the past three years, supercomputer technology and applications have changed remarkably. Today, supercomputer technology is largely based on "super" versions of the same processors that you find in microcomputers. Although supercomputers have not abandoned their specialized markets, they frequently perform the same tasks as mainframes. Seymour Cray was the well-known pioneer of supercomputer technology. You can read a 1994 interview with Cray from the Smithsonian archives at *www.si.edu/resource/tours/comphist/cray.htm* or an excellent book, *The Supermen: The Story of Seymour Cray and the Technical Wizards Behind the Supercomputer* by Charles J. Murray (John Wiley & Sons, 1997). Cray's company, Cray Research, was purchased by Silicon Graphics in 1996.

The NP4 Web site provides you with links to readable articles about supercomputer technology and supercomputer manufacturer's sites.

7 User Interfaces

In the film *2001: A Space Odyssey*, HAL refused to carry out Dave's voice command to open the pod bay door. Like Dave, users every day run into examples of computers that stubbornly refuse to open a particular file, locate a Web site, or carry out a requested command. Why does this problem arise? Although hardware and software bugs account for some user frustrations, many problems are due to miscommunication—a breakdown in the human–computer interface. Donald Norman's *Things That Make Us Smart: Defending Human Attributes in the Age of the Machine* (Perseus Press, 1994) is a book about how technology could enhance human intelligence, but only if it is user-friendly.

Today's graphical user interfaces have come a long way toward making computers usable. Many people believe that GUIs were "invented" for Apple computers, because Apple's Macintosh was the first commercially successful computer with a GUI. In fact, GUIs evolved from Alan Kay's 1970 vision of the "Dynabook"—a portable, personal computer much like today's notebook computers and PDAs. The links on the NP4 Web site point you to lots of resources about user interfaces.

8 Computer Terminology

Whether you're learning about computers for the first time or you're a computer pro, an up-to-date computer dictionary is always a handy companion to help you read computer magazines or look at computer ads. *The Computer Desktop Encyclopedia* by Alan Freedman (American Management Association, 1999) is one of the best references available today. You'll find the Web version at *www.techweb.com/encyclopedia*. Another excellent Web-based compendium of computer terms is the *Webopedia* at *www.webopedia.com*. Visit the NP4 Web site for links to additional online dictionaries and encyclopedias.

Check your library for a more in-depth reference, *Encyclopedia of Computer Science* by Anthony Ralston (Van Nostrand Reinhold, 4th ed., 1999). Microsoft's multimedia encyclopedia called *Encarta* also provides a good assortment of computer definitions.

9 Learning Styles

What's the best way for you to learn? Do you absorb more information from a lecture than a book? Would you rather watch a demonstration or do it yourself? Educators agree that people learn in different ways, including auditory (hear it), kinesthetic (do it), and visual (see it). Several "tests" have been designed to evaluate a person's learning style, such as the Group Embedded Figures Test (GEFT), Felder's Index of Learning Styles, and Kolb's Learning Style Inventory. You can take a quick inventory of your learning style by connecting to *www.howtolearn.com/personal.html*.

10 Artificial Intelligence

In the film *2001: A Space Odyssey*, the computer HAL became operational on January 12, 1997. At the film's 1968 release, computer scientists were not altogether uncomfortable with the prediction that a computer like HAL might be achievable in 30 or so years. The science of artificial intelligence (AI) was in its infancy, but technology and software were developing at a dizzying pace. However, 2001 is here and HAL-like intelligence still seems a long way in the future.

The question "Can computers think?" is still under debate. Alan Turing and Marvin Minsky would argue "Yes!" Alan Turing's paper, "Computing Machinery and Intelligence" (*Mind 59*, 1950) got the discussion rolling and describes the famous Turing test of machine intelligence. For an expanded perspective on the argument, read Minsky's paper, "Why People Think Computers Can't" at *www.ai.mit.edu/people/minsky/papers/ComputersCantThink.txt*.

On the computers-can't-think side of the argument are John Searle and Hubert Dreyfus. A "must read" is *What Computers Still Can't Do: A Critique of Artificial Reason* by Hubert L. Dreyfus (MIT Press, 1992). Another classic in this continuing argument is "Minds, Brains, and Programs" by John Searle (*Behavioral and Brain Sciences* 3, 1980). The fourth episode of *The Machine that Changed the World: The Thinking Machine* sums up the arguments for and against machine intelligence and describes the challenges still in the forefront of artificial intelligence research. The NP4 Web site also contains links to interesting resources on the topic of AI.

CHAPTER 2

SOFTWARE AND MULTIMEDIA

▶ Start Video

CONTENTS

PREVIEW

Chapter 2 provides an overview of computer software—the way it is categorized and the laws that attempt to protect it from unauthorized use. This chapter includes some practical information on using a scanner, taking digital photos, and editing desktop video. The User Focus section explains how to install new software.

When you have completed this chapter you should be able to:

■ Determine the legal restrictions placed on your use of software by copyright laws and license agreements

■ Describe the purpose of a computer operating system

■ Recognize popular operating systems, such as Windows, DOS, Mac OS, UNIX, and Linux

■ Classify software as either system or application software

■ Determine the best type of software to use for a specific task

■ Describe the computer equipment that you need to play and create multimedia

■ Determine if a software package is compatible with your computer system

Multimedia   Photo Editing

MULTIMEDIA MACHINES

The quest for multipurpose machines has always enchanted inventors. Soon after horseless carriages appeared, inventors dreamed about creating a multipurpose vehicle that could be driven on water or land. Car-boats never really caught on, but today we have a multipurpose machine that is far more useful—the computer.

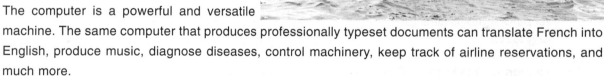

The computer is a powerful and versatile machine. The same computer that produces professionally typeset documents can translate French into English, produce music, diagnose diseases, control machinery, keep track of airline reservations, and much more.

A computer's versatility is particularly evident in the realm of multimedia. "Silent" movies were early attempts at multimedia productions. While Rudolph Valentino made goo-goo eyes at Theda Bara, an organist played live mood music. The "talkies" finally combined film and sound, but budget multimedia persisted. In the 1960s and 1970s, teachers set up old-fashioned multimedia presentations. A film strip projector showed a series of slides stored on one continuous length of film. The sound track was provided by a reel-to-reel tape recorder or—and this technology is really ancient—a record player and 78 rpm records. The narration was punctuated periodically by a clicking sound that meant it was time for the teacher to advance the film strip to the next frame.

Old-fashioned multimedia required a different machine for every type of medium—the projector that displayed film strips was not the same as the projectors for 8 mm films, video tapes, slides, or overhead transparencies. Most projectors had no sound capabilities, so a separate device was required for the sound track. Today, the term "multimedia" has taken on a new meaning. Oddly enough, it now means "one medium" and that medium is digital. Videos, photos, slides, animation, music, and narration no longer require separate machines. They can be combined and played on a single machine—a computer.

A computer's versatility is possible because of software. But how does software give a computer such versatility? What kinds of software can you buy? How do you know what kind of software works with your computer? What equipment do you need to create multimedia projects? You'll find the answers to these questions and more in Chapter 2.

SECTION A

COMPUTER SOFTWARE BASICS

Computer software determines what a computer can do. In a sense, software transforms a computer from one kind of machine to another—from a drafting station to a typesetting machine, from a flight simulator to a calculator, from a filing system to a music studio.

Computer Programs

Do I need to write programs for my computer? A **computer program** is a set of detailed, step-by-step instructions that tells a computer how to solve a problem or carry out a task. Some computer programs handle simple tasks, such as converting feet and inches to centimeters. Longer and more complex computer programs handle very complicated tasks, such as maintaining the accounting records for a business.

The steps in a computer program are written in a language that the computer can interpret and process. As you read through the simple computer program in Figure 2-1, notice the number of steps required to perform a relatively simple calculation.

FIGURE 2-1

This computer program converts feet and inches to centimeters.

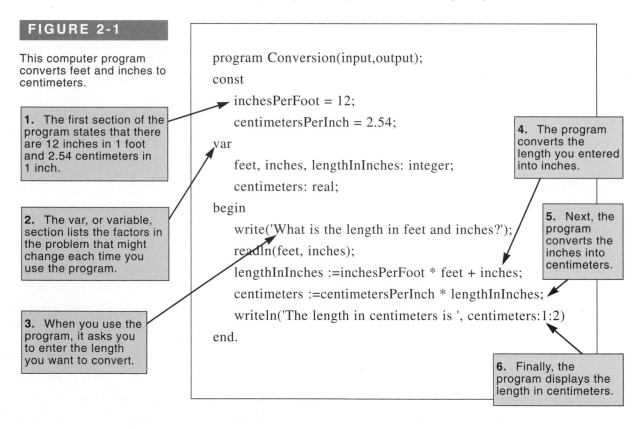

1. The first section of the program states that there are 12 inches in 1 foot and 2.54 centimeters in 1 inch.

2. The var, or variable, section lists the factors in the problem that might change each time you use the program.

3. When you use the program, it asks you to enter the length you want to convert.

4. The program converts the length you entered into inches.

5. Next, the program converts the inches into centimeters.

6. Finally, the program displays the length in centimeters.

```
program Conversion(input,output);
const
    inchesPerFoot = 12;
    centimetersPerInch = 2.54;
var
    feet, inches, lengthInInches: integer;
    centimeters: real;
begin
    write('What is the length in feet and inches?');
    readln(feet, inches);
    lengthInInches :=inchesPerFoot * feet + inches;
    centimeters :=centimetersPerInch * lengthInInches;
    writeln('The length in centimeters is ', centimeters:1:2)
end.
```

At one time, organizations and individuals had to write most of the computer programs they wanted to use. Today, however, most organizations purchase commercially written programs to avoid the time and expense of writing their own. Individuals rarely write computer programs for their personal computers, preferring to select from thousands of commercially written programs, sold as software. Although most computer users do not write their own programs, working as a computer programmer for a government agency, business, or software publisher is a challenging career.

CHAPTER 2

Computer Software

Are computer programs, data, and software the same thing? Software is a basic part of a computer system, but the term "software" has more than one definition. In the early days of the computer industry, it became popular to use the term "software" for all non-hardware components of a computer. In this context, software referred to computer programs and to the data used by the programs.

The U.S. Copyright Act of 1980 defines software as "a set of statements or instructions to be used directly or indirectly in a computer in order to bring about a certain result." This definition implies that computer software is essentially the same as a computer program. It also implies that a collection of data, such as a list of dictionary words, is not software.

In practice, the term "software" is typically used to describe a commercial product, which might include more than a single program and might also include data, as shown in Figure 2-2.

FIGURE 2-2

A commercial software package typically contains a reference manual and floppy disks, a CD-ROM, or a DVD.

The Microsoft Office 2000 software pictured to the right includes programs that help you to draw graphics, write documents, and make calculations. The software also includes some data, such as a thesaurus of words and their synonyms.

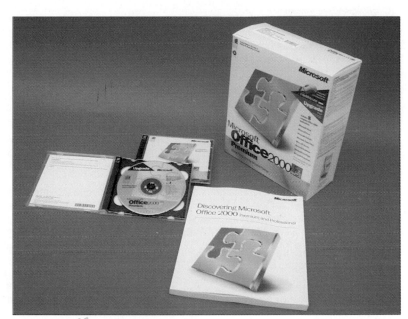

In this textbook, we define **software** as the instructions and associated data, stored in electronic format, that direct the computer to accomplish a task. Under this definition, computer software may include more than one computer program, if those programs work together to carry out a task. Software also can include data, but data alone is not software. For example, word processing software might include the data for a dictionary, but the data *you create* using a word processor is not called software. Suppose you write a report using a software package, then store the report on a disk. Your report consists of data rather than instructions for the computer to carry out. Because your report does not contain instructions, it is not software.

"Software" is a plural noun, so there is no such thing as "softwares" or "one software." How would you talk about software in the singular? You can use the term "software package" to talk about a particular example of software, as in "I bought only one software package, even though the store was having a huge sale."

Copyrighted Software

Is it illegal to copy software? Just because you can copy software doesn't make it legal to do so. Like books and movies, most computer software is protected by a copyright. A **copyright** is a form of legal protection that grants the copyright owner exclusive rights to copy the software, to distribute or sell it, and to modify it.

InfoWeb 1

Copyright

When you purchase copyrighted software, you do not become the owner of the copyright. Instead, you have purchased only the right to use the software. Your purchase allows you to use the software on your computer, but you cannot make copies to give away or sell. People who illegally copy, distribute, or modify software are sometimes called **software pirates**, and their illegal copies are referred to as **pirated software**.

Most software displays a copyright notice, such as "© 2001 eCourseWare" on one of its screens. This notice is not required by law, however, so programs without a copyright notice are still protected by copyright law. Most countries have copyright laws that allow you to copy or modify software only under certain circumstances. If you read the sections of the U.S. Copyright Act shown in Figure 2-3, you will discover under what circumstances you can and cannot legally copy copyrighted software.

FIGURE 2-3

Sections 106 and 117 of the 1980 U.S. Copyright Act.

Only the copyright owner can reproduce, sell, or distribute the copyrighted software.

It is legal to copy the software from the distribution disks to the hard disk of your computer.

It is legal to make an extra copy of the software in case the copy you are using becomes damaged.

If you give away or sell the software, you cannot legally keep a copy.

You cannot legally sell or give away modified copies of the software without permission.

Section 106. Exclusive Rights in Copyrighted Works
Subject to sections 107 through 118, the owner of copyright under this title has the exclusive rights to do and to authorize any of the following:

(1) to reproduce the copyrighted work in copies or phonorecords;
(2) to prepare derivative works based upon the copyrighted work;
(3) to distribute copies or phonorecords of the copyrighted work to the public by sale or other transfer of ownership, or by rental, lease, or lending...

Section 117. Right to Copy or Adapt Computer Programs in Limited Circumstances
Notwithstanding the provisions of section 106, it is not an infringement for the owner of a copy of a computer program to make or authorize the making of another copy or adaptation of the computer program provided:

1. that such a new copy or adaptation is created as an essential step in the utilization of the computer program in conjunction with a machine that is used in no other manner; or

2. that such new copy or adaptation is for archival purposes only and that all archival copies are destroyed in the event that continued possession of the computer program should cease to be rightful. Any exact copies prepared in accordance with the provisions of this section may be leased, sold, or otherwise transferred, along with the copy from which such copies were prepared, only as part of the lease, sale, or other transfer of all rights in the program. Adaptations so prepared may be transferred only with the authorization of the copyright owner.

Licensed Software

Do I need to read the small print before I purchase software? In addition to copyright protection, computer software is often protected by the terms of a software license. A **software license** is a legal contract that defines the ways in which you may use a computer program. For microcomputer software, you will find the license on the outside of the package, on a separate card inside the package, or on the CD packaging. Mainframe software licenses are usually a separate legal document, negotiated between the software publisher and a corporate buyer.

A software license may extend the rights given to you by copyright laws. For example, although copyright law makes it illegal to copy software for use on more than one computer, the license for Claris Works software allows you to buy one copy of the software and install it on both your home computer and your office computer as long as you are the primary user of both computers.

Software licenses are often lengthy and written in "legalese," but your legal right to use the software continues only as long as you abide by the terms of the software license. Therefore, you should understand the software license for any software you use. To become familiar with a typical license agreement, you can read through the one in Figure 2-4.

FIGURE 2-4

When you read a software license agreement, look for answers to the following questions:

Am I buying the software or licensing it?

When does the license go into effect?

How many copies can I make?

Can I rent the software?

Can I sell the software?

What if the software includes a CD-ROM and a set of disks?

Does the software publisher provide a warranty?

Software License Agreement

Important - READ CAREFULLY: This License Agreement ("Agreement") is a legal agreement between you and eCourseWare Corporation for the software product, eCourse GraphWare ("The SOFTWARE"). By installing, copying, or otherwise using the SOFTWARE, you agree to be bound by the terms of this Agreement. The SOFTWARE is protected by copyright laws and international copyright treaties. The SOFTWARE is licensed, not sold.

GRANT OF LICENSE. This Agreement gives you the right to install and use one copy of the SOFTWARE on a single computer. The primary user of the computer on which the SOFTWARE is installed may make a second copy for his or her exclusive use on a portable computer.

OTHER RIGHTS AND LIMITATIONS.

You may not reverse engineer, decompile, or disassemble the SOFTWARE except and only to the extent that such activity is expressly permitted by applicable law.

The SOFTWARE is licensed as a single product; its components may not be separated for use on more than one computer.

You may not rent, lease, or lend the SOFTWARE.

You may permanently transfer all of your rights under this Agreement, provided you retain no copies, you transfer all of the SOFTWARE, and the recipient agrees to the terms of this Agreement. If the software product is an upgrade, any transfer must include all prior versions of the SOFTWARE.

You may receive the SOFTWARE in more than one medium. Regardless of the type of medium you receive, you may use only one medium that is appropriate for your single computer. You may not use or install the other medium on another computer.

WARRANTY. eCourseWare warrants that the SOFTWARE will perform substantially in accordance with the accompanying written documentation for a period of ninety (90) days from the date of receipt. TO THE MAXIMUM EXTENT PERMITTED BY APPLICABLE LAW, eCourseWare AND ITS SUPPLIERS DISCLAIM ALL OTHER WARRANTIES AND CONDITIONS EITHER EXPRESS OR IMPLIED, INCLUDING, BUT NOT LIMITED TO, IMPLIED WARRANTIES OF MERCHANTABILITY, FITNESS FOR A PARTICULAR PURPOSE, TITLE, AND NON-INFRINGEMENT, WITH REGARD TO THE SOFTWARE PRODUCT.

Shrink-Wrap Licenses

Do I have to sign a software license for it to be valid? Formally signing and submitting a license agreement every time you purchase software would be inconvenient, so the computer industry makes extensive use of **shrink-wrap licenses**. When you purchase computer software, the floppy disks, CD-ROM, and/or DVD in the package are usually sealed in an envelope or plastic shrink wrapping. A notification, such as the one in Figure 2-5, states that opening the wrapping signifies your agreement to the terms of the software license.

FIGURE 2-5

When software has a shrink-wrap license, you agree to the terms of the license agreement by opening the package. If you do not agree with the terms, you should return the software unopened.

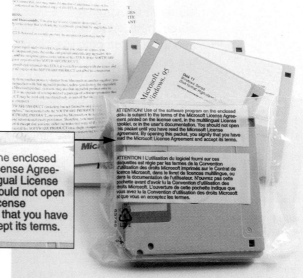

ATTENTION! Use of the software program on the enclosed disks is subject to the terms of the Microsoft License Agreement printed on the license card, in the multilingual License booklet, or in the user's documentation. You should not open this packet until you have read the Microsoft License Agreement. By opening this packet, you signify that you have read the Microsoft License Agreement and accept its terms.

With a shrink-wrap license, a software publisher avoids the cumbersome process of negotiating the terms of the license and obtaining your signature. It is essentially a "take it or leave it" approach to licensing. Court rulings in 1996 and 1997 have upheld the validity of shrink-wrap licensing, one of the most frequently used methods for providing legal protection for computer software.

Licenses for More Than One User

If my company has a computer network, does it still have to pay for a license for each user? Most software publishers offer a variety of license options; some are designed for a single user, others are geared toward more than one user. A **single-user license** limits the use of the software to only one user at a time. Most **commercial software** is distributed with a single-user license.

A **multiple-user license** allows more than one person to use a particular software package. This type of license is beneficial in cases where users each require their own personalized version of the software. An electronic mail program would typically have a multiple-user license because multiple users each require their own mailbox. Multiple-user licenses are generally priced per user, but the price for each user is typically less than the price of a single-user license.

A **concurrent-use license** allows a certain number of copies of the software to be used at the same time. For example, suppose that an organization with a computer network has a concurrent-use license for five copies of a word processor. At any one time, as many as five employees may use the software. Concurrent-use licenses are usually priced in increments. For example, a company might be able to purchase a concurrent-use license for up to 50 users for $2,500 or up to 250 users for $10,000.

A **site license** generally allows the software to be used on any and all computers at a specific location, such as within a corporate office building or on a university campus. A site license is priced at a flat rate—for example, $5,000 per site.

Shareware

My friend gave me a copy of some "shareware." Was that illegal?

InfoWeb
2
Shareware

Shareware is copyrighted software marketed under a "try before you buy" policy. It usually includes a license that allows you to use the software for a trial period. If you want to use it beyond the trial period, you must send in a registration fee. A shareware license typically allows you to make copies of the software and distribute them to others. These shared copies provide a low-cost marketing and distribution channel. Unfortunately, registration fee payment relies on the honor system, so many shareware authors collect only a fraction of the money they deserve for their programming efforts. Take a look at the shareware license in Figure 2-6 and notice the rights it includes.

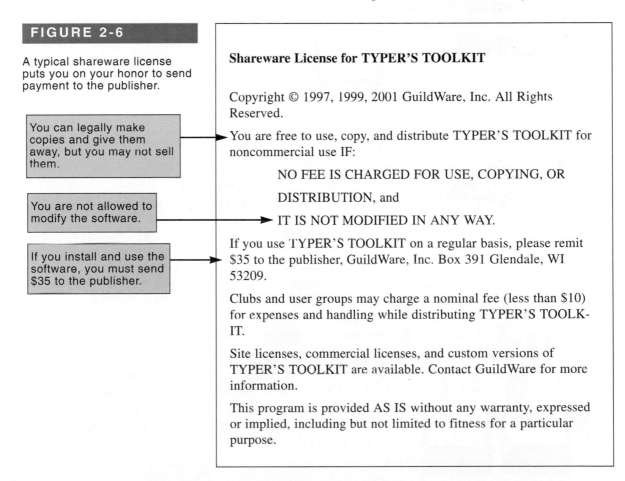

FIGURE 2-6

A typical shareware license puts you on your honor to send payment to the publisher.

You can legally make copies and give them away, but you may not sell them.

You are not allowed to modify the software.

If you install and use the software, you must send $35 to the publisher.

Shareware License for TYPER'S TOOLKIT

Copyright © 1997, 1999, 2001 GuildWare, Inc. All Rights Reserved.

You are free to use, copy, and distribute TYPER'S TOOLKIT for noncommercial use IF:

    NO FEE IS CHARGED FOR USE, COPYING, OR

    DISTRIBUTION, and

IT IS NOT MODIFIED IN ANY WAY.

If you use TYPER'S TOOLKIT on a regular basis, please remit $35 to the publisher, GuildWare, Inc. Box 391 Glendale, WI 53209.

Clubs and user groups may charge a nominal fee (less than $10) for expenses and handling while distributing TYPER'S TOOLKIT.

Site licenses, commercial licenses, and custom versions of TYPER'S TOOLKIT are available. Contact GuildWare for more information.

This program is provided AS IS without any warranty, expressed or implied, including but not limited to fitness for a particular purpose.

Public Domain Software

Isn't some software free? Sometimes an author abandons all rights to a particular software title and places it in the public domain, making the program available without restriction. Such software, referred to as **public domain software**, is owned by the public rather than by the author. Public domain software may be freely copied, distributed, and even resold. The primary restriction on public domain software is that you are not allowed to apply for a copyright on it.

Public domain software is sometimes called "freeware," but the term freeware is also sometimes applied to shareware. This ambiguous use of terminology makes it even more important for consumers to check license agreements to determine how they are allowed to use, copy, and distribute a particular software program.

Software Categories

What's the difference between system software and application software?

Because there are so many software titles, categorizing software as either system software or application software is useful. **System software** helps the computer carry out its basic operating tasks. **Application software** helps the human user carry out a task. System software and application software are further classified into subcategories. As you continue to read this chapter, use Figure 2-7 to help you visualize the hierarchy of software categories.

FIGURE 2-7

Software can be classified into categories.

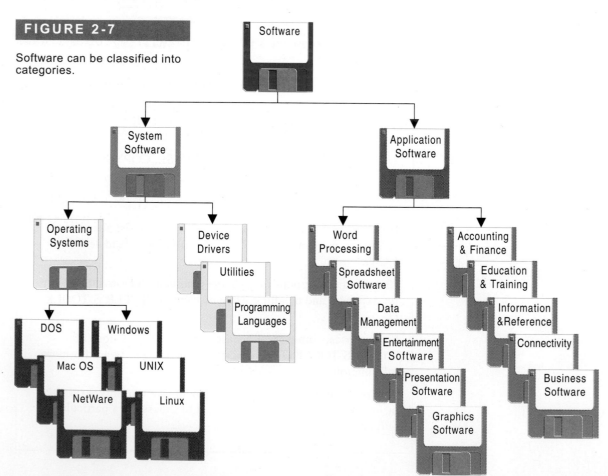

To many computer users, the difference between system software and application software seems somewhat arbitrary. To clarify the difference, you can generally classify software as *system software* if the only reason you need that software is because you have a computer. For example, if you didn't have a computer, you would not need an operating system, device drivers, or computer programming languages.

You would classify software as *application software* if it computerizes something you might do even without a computer. For example, you could write letters and reports even if you didn't have a computer, so the software that you use to create documents would be classified as application software.

Admittedly, some software remains difficult to classify. For example, you use a type of application software to connect your computer to the Internet. You would not connect to the Internet if you did not have a computer, but the software that you use to establish a connection provides additional capabilities, such as voice calls, voice mail, and faxing that you might do without a computer. As you read the next section of this chapter on system software, you'll develop a better idea of how it differs from application software.

concurrent user lic so 40cpplusers

QUICKCHECK A

1 If you use a computer to write a report, the report is considered _____ software. True or false?

2 To use a computer effectively, you need to be a computer programmer. True or false?

3 Illegal copies of software are sometimes called `Pirated` software.

4 The instructions that tell a computer how to convert inches to centimeters are a computer `Program.`.

5 A(n) `multiple-user` license would be useful in a situation where each network user needs a personalized version of the software.

6 A(n) `site` license generally allows the software to be used on any and all computers at a specific location.

7 The "try before you buy" policy refers to `Shareware` licenses.

8 `System soft` software helps the computer carry out its basic operating tasks, whereas `Application.` software helps a computer user carry out tasks.

 Check Answers

SYSTEM SOFTWARE

System software performs tasks essential to the efficient functioning of computer hardware. It directs the fundamental operations of a computer, such as displaying information on the screen, storing data on disks, sending data to the printer, interpreting commands typed by users, and communicating with peripheral devices. This section covers the four subcategories of system software: operating systems, utilities, device drivers, and computer programming languages.

Operating Systems

What is an operating system? An **operating system** (OS) is essentially the master controller for all of the activities that take place within a computer. More importantly, from the user's perspective, a computer's operating system sets the standard for all of the application software that a computer runs. You might be familiar with the names of several operating systems, such as Microsoft Windows, Mac OS, Linux, UNIX, and DOS. These operating systems have different user interfaces and allow your computer to run only compatible software. When your computer uses the Windows operating system, for example, it allows you to run Windows software. A computer that uses the UNIX operating system can typically run only UNIX software.

InfoWeb
3
Operating
Systems

An operating system works like an air traffic controller to coordinate the activities within a computer. Just as an airport cannot function without air traffic controllers, a computer cannot function without an operating system. Therefore an operating system is an essential software component of microcomputers, minicomputers, mainframes, and supercomputers.

If you envision computer hardware as being the core of a computer system, then the operating system provides the next layer of functionality by assisting the computer with basic hardware operations. The operating system also interacts with the next functional layer—application software—to carry out application tasks such as printing and saving data. Figure 2-8 helps you envision how the operating system interacts with computer hardware and application software.

FIGURE 2-8

The operating system interacts with application software and computer hardware.

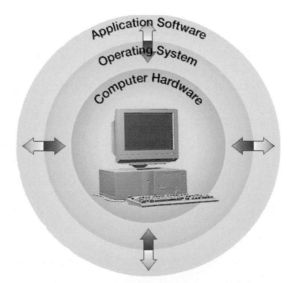

As a specific example of how the operating system works as a liaison between your computer hardware and application software, suppose that you use word processing software to write a letter, which you then want to print. The operating system makes it possible for the application software to communicate with the printer, as shown in Figure 2-9.

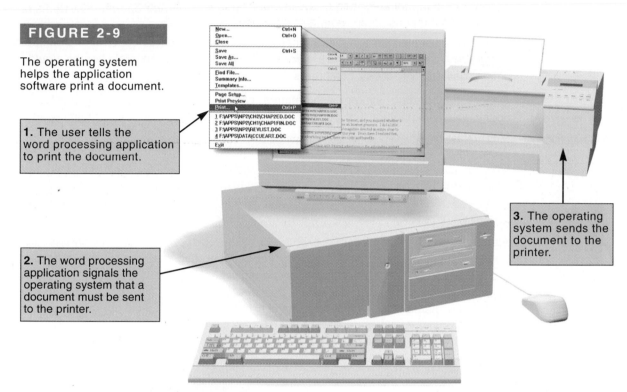

FIGURE 2-9

The operating system helps the application software print a document.

1. The user tells the word processing application to print the document.

2. The word processing application signals the operating system that a document must be sent to the printer.

3. The operating system sends the document to the printer.

An operating system performs many different tasks, often referred to as "services." These services can be classified as either "external" or "internal."

An operating system provides **external services** that help users start programs, manage stored data, and maintain security. You, as the computer user, control these external functions. An operating system provides you with a way to select the programs you would like to use. It also helps you find, rename, and delete documents and other data stored on disk or tape. On some computer systems, the operating system helps maintain security by checking for a valid user ID and password before allowing the user to access programs and data.

In addition, an operating system provides **internal services** "behind the scenes" to ensure that the computer system functions efficiently. These internal services are not generally under your control, but instead are controlled by the operating system itself. The operating system controls input and output, allocates system resources, manages the storage space for programs and data, and detects equipment failure without any direction from you. A **system resource** is any part of a computer system, such as disk drive space, memory capacity, or processor time, that might be used by a computer program. An operating system allocates system resources so that programs can run efficiently.

Desktop and Server Operating Systems

| Which operating systems am I likely to encounter? | Today, roughly a dozen
different operating systems are in common use. Although that number might sound like
a lot, you are likely to use only a few of them.

Operating systems can be classified into two categories: server operating systems and
desktop operating systems. Picture a computer at a Web site providing information to
hundreds of people sitting in their homes and working on their computers. The computer
at the Web site would be called a "server." The computers in people's homes would be
called "desktop" or "client" computers.

A server operating system—sometimes called a network operating system—is
designed for computers that provide centralized storage facilities and communications
capabilities for networks and Web sites. A desktop operating system—also referred to
as a client operating system—is designed for a single-user microcomputer. You will
typically interact directly only with desktop operating systems. But what about when
you use a network or access a Web site? Because you aren't actually sitting at the network or Web site server computer, you won't have to use its operating system.
Therefore, you will still interact only with your desktop operating system.

Although you will likely interact exclusively with desktop operating systems, you are
bound to hear chit chat about popular server operating systems, too. A little background on today's popular operating systems will help you sort through the hype. For
example, you might hear that Linux is the greatest thing since sliced bread, but when
you've completed this section and have a basic background on operating systems,
you'll know why you might not want to buy it for your home PC.

FIGURE 2-10

Millions of computer users
interact with desktop operating
systems, whereas only a few
network and Web site
managers need to deal with
server operating systems.

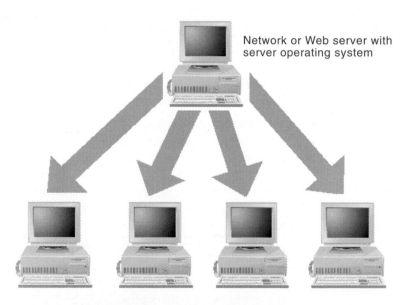

Network or Web server with
server operating system

Network workstations and stand-alone
computers with desktop operating systems

Windows 3.1, 95, 98

Which operating system is the most popular? **Microsoft Windows** is the most popular operating system for today's microcomputers because it supports a vast array of application software and peripheral devices. If you purchase a new PC, it is a virtual certainty that the latest version of Windows has been preinstalled on its hard disk.

The first versions of the Windows operating system, Windows 1.0, 2.0, and 3.0, did not generate much interest among computer users. Windows 3.1, introduced in 1992, really established Windows as the microcomputer operating system of choice. In 1995, Microsoft introduced Windows 95 and three years later launched Windows 98.

Like other graphical user interfaces, Windows provides icons, buttons, and other on-screen controls that can be manipulated by a mouse or similar pointing device. Windows gets its name from the rectangular work areas visible on the screen. Each window can display a different document or program, allowing you to work on more than one project at a time—a service called **multitasking**. *—important for exam*

Windows 95 and 98 provide some basic networking capabilities, making them a suitable operating system for small networks in homes and businesses. However, they are classified as desktop operating systems and would not be found on a minicomputer, mainframe, or supercomputer.

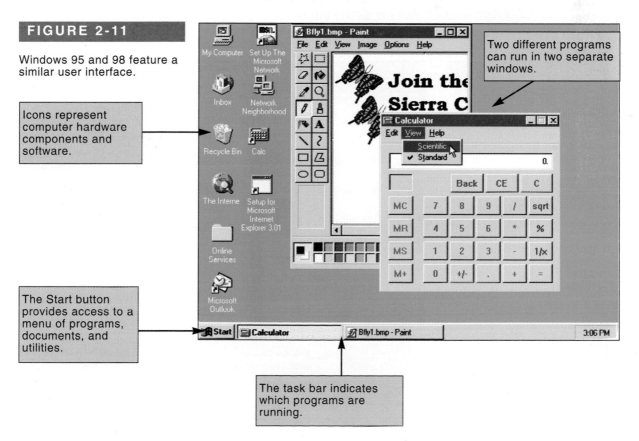

FIGURE 2-11

Windows 95 and 98 feature a similar user interface.

Icons represent computer hardware components and software.

Two different programs can run in two separate windows.

The Start button provides access to a menu of programs, documents, and utilities.

The task bar indicates which programs are running.

Windows NT/2000 Workstation

What about Windows 2000? Microsoft offers workstation versions of the Windows operating system, such as Windows NT Workstation and Windows 2000 Professional. The word "workstation" has several meanings in the computer industry. In this context, it refers to a high-performance, single-user microcomputer that would typically be used for advanced or "high-end" computing tasks, such as professional video editing, scientific visualization, and computer-aided design.

Like Windows 95 and 98, Windows 2000 Professional is designed for the desktop, although it will support small networks. The differentiating features of Windows 2000 Professional include increased security, greater reliability, and the ability to support some specialized software applications designed for high-performance workstations. You might, for example, find professional video editing software that is designed to run on a computer that uses Windows 2000 Professional as its operating system, but will not run on a computer that uses Windows 98.

Interestingly, the Windows 2000 Professional user interface looks almost identical to the Windows 98 interface. They are, however, totally different programs, which accounts for the unfortunate fact that Windows 2000 Professional cannot run some software or support all of the peripheral devices designed for Windows 98. Microsoft plans to eventually consolidate its desktop and workstation operating systems into a single product that will satisfy the needs of people who use either high-end workstations or standard desktop PCs.

FIGURE 2-12

Microsoft Windows 2000 Professional features essentially the same interface as Windows 98.

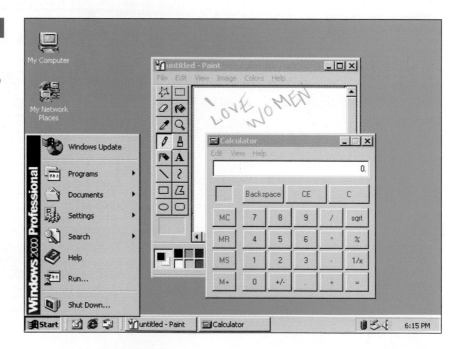

Mac OS

What about Macintosh computers? In 1984, Apple Computer introduced the revolutionary Apple Lisa computer. Its key features included a graphical user interface featuring menus and on-screen icons that could be manipulated by using a mouse. The Lisa computer was not a commercial success, but Apple's next product, the Macintosh computer, sold like hot cakes. Its graphical user interface, **Mac OS**, was a major factor contributing to its success. Apple's snazzy iMac computer, introduced in 1998, also features Mac OS. Like Windows, Mac OS has evolved through many versions in which features have been modified and added, including multitasking capabilities and support for small networks.

FIGURE 2-13

The iMac computer features an elegant design and the easy-to-use Mac OS.

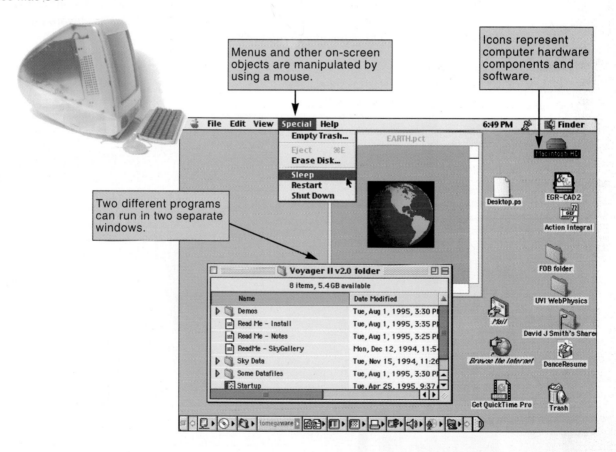

Menus and other on-screen objects are manipulated by using a mouse.

Icons represent computer hardware components and software.

Two different programs can run in two separate windows.

The software that is compatible with Mac OS is referred to as Macintosh software, or "Mac software" for short. Although Macintosh and iMac users can select from a large pool of Macintosh software, fewer software titles are available for Mac OS than for Windows. Special emulation hardware and software add-ons make it possible to run some Windows software on a Macintosh computer, but performance is not optimal and so most Mac OS users stick to Macintosh software.

DOS

Why do I keep hearing about DOS? Old-timers in the computer industry can't help but talk about DOS. It was the first operating system they used, and its difficult-to-use command-line user interface left an indelible impression. **DOS** (which rhymes with "toss") stands for Disk Operating System. It was developed by Microsoft—the same company that later produced Windows—and introduced on the original IBM PC under the name PC-DOS. Microsoft marketed the same operating system to other computer manufacturers under the trade name MS-DOS.

Contrary to popular opinion, DOS is not yet dead; in fact, it has been incorporated into Windows. DOS operates behind the scenes, however, so Windows users do not have to memorize and type complex commands.

During the peak of its popularity, thousands of software programs were produced for computers running DOS. Many of these programs are still available on the Internet. Windows users can sometimes run these programs using the MS-DOS prompt located on the Programs menu. Nevertheless, most DOS software looks pretty unsophisticated by today's standards; so, for most computer users, DOS and DOS software are nothing more than historical highlights of the computer industry.

FIGURE 2-14

The first version of DOS was the operating system for the original IBM PC, shipped in 1982. The DOS user interface seems exceedingly stark compared to today's graphical user interfaces.

The C:\> DOS prompt is a distinguishing feature of MS-DOS and PC-DOS.

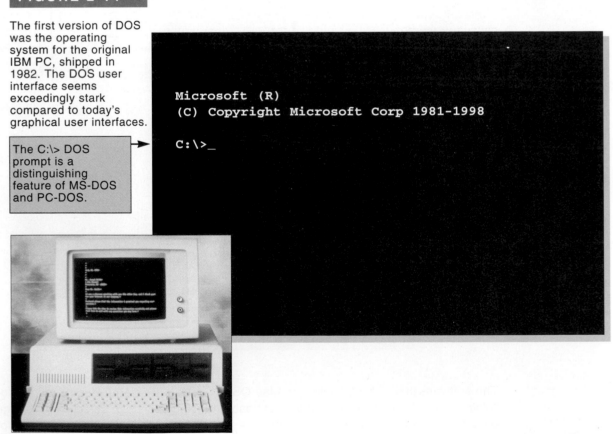

```
Microsoft (R)
(C) Copyright Microsoft Corp 1981-1998

C:\>_
```

Windows Server, NetWare, UNIX, and Linux
Which operating systems are used on servers?

The computers that provide centralized storage and communications services for local area networks and Internet sites typically use a server operating system, rather than a desktop operating system. Today's popular server operating systems include Microsoft Windows NT Server and Windows 2000 Server. As you might expect, these operating systems are similar in appearance to the workstation versions of Windows NT and 2000, but they provide additional features for managing the flow of data on large networks and Web sites.

Novell NetWare is a server operating system designed specifically for microcomputer networks. It is considered ideal in a situation where many users must access document or other data files from a centrally located computer. As a server operating system, NetWare is typically used by network managers, not by the average game-playing, Web-browsing, word-processing computer user.

UNIX was originally developed at AT&T's Bell Laboratories in 1969 as a minicomputer operating system, but has since become popular for network and Web servers of all sizes. A variation of UNIX, called **Linux**, has recently gained prominence as a server operating system for microcomputers and minicomputers. The fact that Linux is available as freeware contributes to its popularity, but network and Web managers have discovered that it also provides a secure and stable operating environment.

Early versions of UNIX and Linux featured a command-line interface that was somewhat difficult to master. Happily, add-ons for these operating systems now make it possible to essentially "paste" on a graphical user interface and ignore the old-fashioned and cumbersome command-line interface.

UNIX and Linux are similar to Windows 2000 because they provide an operating system appropriate for servers and high-performance workstations, but they are not typically found on the PC desktop.

FIGURE 2-15

The Linux operating system, popular with network and Web site managers, typically sports a graphical user interface.

Two or more programs can run in separate windows.

The task bar and menus look much like the Windows interface.

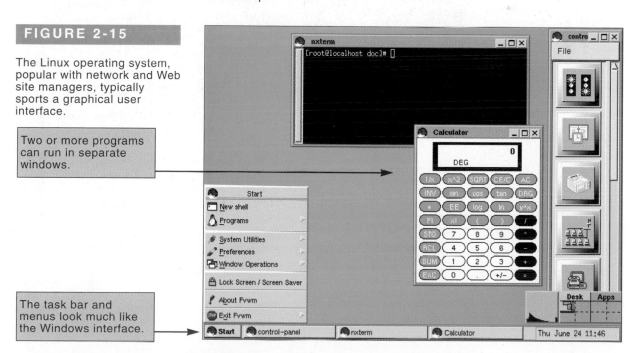

Utilities

Does the operating system include all of the system software I need?

Utilities are a subcategory of system software designed to augment the operating system by providing a way for a computer user to control the allocation and use of hardware resources. Some utilities are included with the operating system; they perform tasks such as preparing disks to hold data, providing information about the files on a disk, and copying data from one disk to another. Additional utilities can be purchased separately from software publishers and vendors. For example, Norton Utilities, published by Symantec, is a very popular collection of utility software. It retrieves data from damaged disks, makes your data more secure by encrypting it, and helps you troubleshoot problems with your computer's disk drives. You can also purchase utility software to protect your computer from viruses that could damage or erase your data.

One important task performed by an operating system utility is disk **formatting**. Each disk must be formatted before you can store data on it. You can think of the formatting process as creating the electronic equivalent of storage shelves. Before you can place items on the shelves, you must assemble the shelves. In a similar way, before you can store data on a disk, you must make sure that the disk is formatted.

Although you can buy preformatted disks, you still might need a disk format utility if you use a disk that has not been preformatted or one that was formatted previously for a different type of computer. Figure 2-16 shows how to use the format utility that's included with the Windows operating system.

FIGURE 2-16

Formatting a disk with the Windows format utility.

1. Insert the disk you want to format and click the My Computer icon to select it, then press Enter.

2. Click the floppy disk drive icon in the My Computer window.

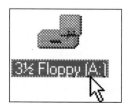

3. Click File on the menu bar, then click Format to open the Format window.

Start Screentour

4. Make sure the Capacity box matches the size of the disk you want to format, then click the Start button.

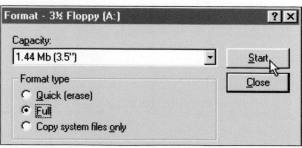

CHAPTER 2

Device Drivers

| How do I use a device driver? | When you purchase a peripheral device, such as a CD-ROM drive, mouse, or scanner, you often need to install software that tells your computer how to use the new device. The system software that helps the computer control a peripheral device is called a **device driver**.

When you purchase a new peripheral device, its installation instructions usually tell you how to install both the device and the necessary device drivers. You "use" a device driver by installing it according to the instructions. Once the device driver is installed correctly, the computer uses it "behind the scenes" to communicate with the device.

Computer Programming Languages

| Is a programming language included with a basic computer system? | As you know, a computer program is a series of instructions that the computer follows to perform a task. A **computer programming language** allows a programmer to write a program using English-like instructions, such as those you saw in Figure 2-1. The programmer's instructions must be translated into electrical signals that the computer can manipulate and process. A programming language also takes care of this translation process.

As mentioned earlier in this chapter, most computer users do not need to write programs. Therefore, computers do not typically come equipped with a computer programming language. If you want to write programs, you must purchase programming language software. Some of the most popular programming languages are BASIC, Visual Basic, C, C++, COBOL, and Java.

QUICKCHECK   B

1 UNIX and Linux are server operating systems, whereas Windows 98 is a(n) _desk Top._ operating system.

2 DOS, Windows, and Mac OS are typically used on _Micro._ computer systems.

3 To run more than one program at a time, you must use an operating system with _Multitasking_ capabilities. (or Exam")

4 A freeware operating system called _Linux_ is gaining popularity for network and Web site servers.

5 _Utility_ software helps the computer accomplish such tasks as preparing a disk for data, providing information about the files on a disk, and copying data from one disk to another.

6 You install a(n) _device driver_ to tell the computer how to use a new peripheral device.

7 A(n) _Prog. language_ allows you to write computer programs using English-like instructions.

Check Answers

SECTION C APPLICATION SOFTWARE

Although system software handles internal computer functions and helps the computer use peripheral devices, it does not transform the computer into the various kinds of machines that you need to write reports, "crunch" numbers, learn how to type, or draw pictures. Instead, it is application software that enables a computer to become a multipurpose machine and to perform many different tasks.

As you'll recall, application software helps you accomplish a specific task using the computer. For example, it can help you produce documents, perform calculations, create graphics, manage financial resources, compose music, play games, maintain files of information, and so on. Application software packages are often referred to simply as "applications." This section of the chapter provides an overview of the most popular application software categories.

Software Jargon

What's all this talk about groupware, suites, and productivity software?

InfoWeb
4
Application
Software

When you shop for computer software in catalogs or stores, you might encounter terms such as "productivity software," "suites," and "groupware." These terms describe broad categories of application software.

As you might expect from its name, **productivity software** is designed to help you work more effectively. Used by individuals, businesses, or organizations, the most popular types of productivity software include word processing, spreadsheet, and data management. The term **office suite** refers to a number of applications that are packaged together and sold as a unit. A typical office suite includes software you would use to write documents, work with numbers, create graphics, and keep track of data. **Groupware** provides a way for more than one person to collaborate on a project. It facilitates group document production, scheduling, and communication. Often it maintains a pool of data that can be shared by members of a workgroup.

Software is also categorized by how it is used. Document production software, for example, helps you create, edit, and publish documents. Software in the connectivity category connects your computer to the Internet, to other computers, and to networks. The names of these functional categories are not used consistently. For example, when

FIGURE 2-17

Computer superstores provide a good software source, but many people also order software from catalogs and download software from the Internet.

browsing through software catalogs or perusing the shelves of computer stores, you might notice that connectivity software is sometimes referred to as communications software. As with much of the terminology that is in daily use by nontechnical people, software categories might seem somewhat imprecise, but you often can figure them out by using common sense.

How much you use a computer, how much time its use saves, and how much it improves the quality of your work depends on the software you select and use. The array of available software applications is extensive, as you can see from Figure 2-17 and as you read on.

Document Production Software

What software should I use to produce documents? Whether you are writing a 10-page term paper, writing software documentation, designing a brochure for your new startup company, or laying out the school newspaper, you will probably use some form of document production software. Document production software assists you with composing, editing, designing, printing, and electronically publishing documents. The three most popular types of document production software are word processing, desktop publishing, and Web authoring.

Word processing software has replaced typewriters for producing documents such as reports, letters, papers, and manuscripts. Individuals use word processing software for correspondence, students use it to write reports and papers, writers use it for novels, reporters use it to compose news stories, scientists use it to write research reports, and business people use it to write memos, reports, letters, and marketing materials. When documents exist in an electronic format, it is easy to reuse them, share them, and even collaborate on them. Word processing software gives you the ability to create, spell-check, edit, and format a document on the screen before you commit it to paper. When you are satisfied with the content of your document, you can use the page layout and formatting features of your word processing software to create a professional-looking printout. Today's best-selling word processing software includes Microsoft Word, Corel WordPerfect, and Lotus Word Pro.

InfoWeb
5
Desktop
Publishing

Desktop publishing software takes word processing software one step further by helping you use graphic design techniques to enhance the format and appearance of a document. Although today's word processing software offers many page layout and design features, desktop publishing software provides more sophisticated features to help you produce professional-quality output for newspapers, newsletters, brochures, magazines, and books. Figure 2-18 illustrates the professional results you can achieve with desktop publishing software such as QuarkXPress, Adobe PageMaker, Corel Ventura, and Microsoft Publisher.

FIGURE 2-18

For documents with many graphics that will be produced by a professional printer, you should consider using desktop publishing software instead of word processing software. Desktop publishing software is typically the tool of choice for newspapers, magazines, and books, such as the one you are reading.

Web authoring software helps you design and develop customized Web pages that you can publish electronically on the Internet. Only a few years ago, creating Web pages was a fairly technical task that required authors to insert special formatting "tags" such as <A HREF = "contents.htm">. Now, Web authoring software helps nontechnical Web authors by providing easy-to-use tools for composing the text for a Web page, assembling graphical elements, and automatically generating formatting tags. Best-selling software in this category includes Claris Home Page, SoftQuad HoTMetaL, MacroMedia DreamWeaver, and Microsoft FrontPage.

Graphics Software

What's the best graphics software? | **Graphics software** helps you create, edit, and manipulate images. These images could be photographs that you're planning to insert in a real estate brochure, a freehand portrait, a detailed engineering drawing of a Harley-Davidson motorcycle, or a cartoon animation. Best-selling graphics packages include Adobe Illustrator, CorelDRAW, and Micrografx Picture Publisher. Many graphics software packages specialize in manipulating one type of image, such as photos, bitmap images, vector graphics, or 3-D objects.

If you have artistic talent and you want to use a computer to create paintings, sketches, and other images, you can use **paint software** (sometimes called "image editing software") to create and edit bitmap images. A **bitmap image** (or "bitmap graphic") is stored as a series of colored dots. Photos are typically bitmap images and they can be manipulated with paint software or photo editing software. **Photo editing software**, includes features specially designed to fix poor-quality photos by modifying contrast and brightness, cropping out unwanted objects, and removing "red eye."

Images composed of lines and filled shapes are called **vector graphics**. Vector graphics require a relatively small amount of storage space and are ideal for diagrams, corporate logos, and schematics.

InfoWeb 6

3-D Graphics

3-D graphics software helps you to create a **wireframe** that represents a three-dimensional object. The wireframe acts much like the framework for a pop-up tent. Just as you would construct the framework for the tent, then cover it with a nylon tent cover, 3-D graphics software can cover a wireframe object with surface texture and color to create a graphic of a 3-D object. The process of covering a wireframe with surface color and texture is called **rendering**.

FIGURE 2-19

You can create a wireframe drawing of a car, then rotate it to view it from the back, side, or front. A process called rendering creates a 3-D solid image by covering the wireframe and applying computer-generated highlights and shadows.

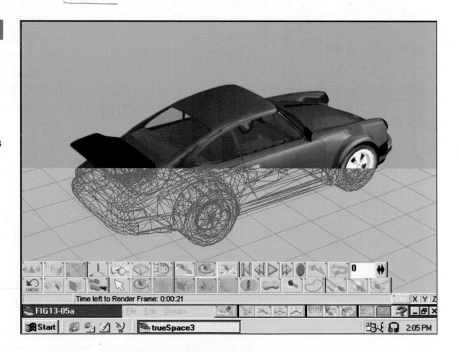

Start Screentour

CHAPTER 2

Presentation Software

How do I use the computer to create snazzy speeches and presentations?

School, business, and even community activities require public speaking from time to time. **Presentation software** provides all of the tools you need for combining text, graphics, graphs, animations, and sound into a series of electronic slides like the one shown in Figure 2-20.

FIGURE 2-20

A slide typically contains a title, a bulleted list, and a graphic.

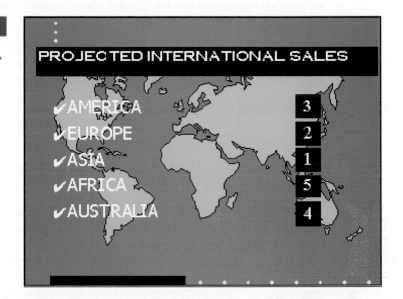

PROJECTED INTERNATIONAL SALES

✔AMERICA   3
✔EUROPE   2
✔ASIA   1
✔AFRICA   5
✔AUSTRALIA 4

InfoWeb
7

Presentations

Two of the most popular presentation software packages are Microsoft PowerPoint and Lotus Freelance Graphics, which also include collections of graphics and sounds to enhance your presentations. After creating your slides, you can use the presentation software to organize them into a compelling visual story for your audience. You can then display the slides on a color monitor for a one-on-one presentation or display the slide show to a group by using a computer projection device as shown in Figure 2-21. You can also output the presentation as overhead transparencies, paper copies, or 35 mm slides.

FIGURE 2-21

A projection device connected to a computer displays the presentation on a large wall screen.

Spreadsheet and Statistical Software

What software can I use for number crunching? **Spreadsheet software** performs calculations based on numbers and formulas that you enter. It is frequently used by financial analysts to examine investment opportunities, by managers to create budgets, by educators to keep track of student grades, and by individuals to track household budgets, analyze retirement investments, and balance checkbooks. Top-selling packages include Microsoft Excel and Lotus 1-2-3. Chapter 3 provides more details on spreadsheet software.

Spreadsheet software also helps you transform complex data into meaningful graphs that allow you to visualize and explore trends. When numerical data appears in the form of a graph, you can see patterns and relationships that might not otherwise be obvious.

Statistical software helps you analyze large sets of data to discover relationships and patterns. It is a helpful tool for summarizing survey results, test scores, experiment results, or population data. Most statistical software includes graphing capability so that you can display and explore your data visually. Software, such as SPSS, JMP, and Data Desk, provides a full line of sophisticated statistical analysis tools.

Mathematical modeling software, such as Mathcad and Mathematica, provides tools for solving a wide range of math, science, and engineering problems. Students, teachers, mathematicians, and engineers, in particular, appreciate how this software helps them recognize patterns that can be difficult to identify in columns of numbers.

FIGURE 2-22

With mathematical modeling software, you can visualize numbers, formulas, and transformations. For example, you can plot the *x, y, z* coordinates of a Mobius band, then manipulate its 3-D display.

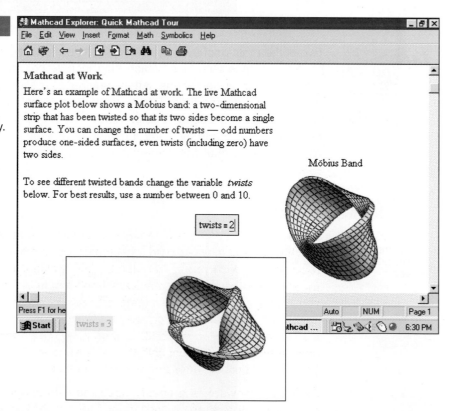

CHAPTER 2

Data Management Software

How can I keep track of information? We live in a society that values and collects information—tons of it. Data management software helps us store, find, organize, update, and report information.

In computer jargon, a **flat file** stores information in records similar to 3 x 5 index cards or Rolodex cards. After you've entered the information for your electronic file cards, software can help you organize these records, find records that match specific criteria, and print lists based on the information. File management software is ideal for working with simple lists of information such as holiday card addresses, doctor visits, and household valuables. It might seem odd, but spreadsheet software is the best tool for managing simple flat files. It includes special data-handling features that allow you to enter data, sort data, search for data that meets specific criteria, and print reports. As a rule of thumb, spreadsheet software can handle any data that you could put on a set of index cards.

FIGURE 2-23

Spreadsheet software provides basic data-handling features. It allows you to display data in rows and columns or as file "cards."

Data can be displayed in row and column format.

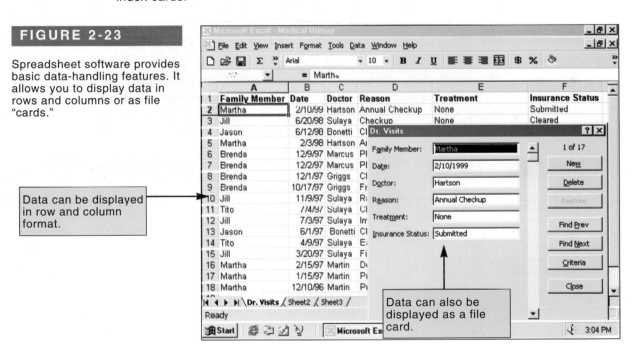

Data can also be displayed as a file card.

Unlike a single flat file, a **database** is a collection of related files. **Database software** provides a flexible way to join and summarize the information in more than one file. For example, suppose you are the curator for an extensive collection of classic rock videos for MTV. You have one computer file containing all the video information and another containing the performer information. While looking at the information on Michael Jackson's *Thriller* video, you wonder how old he was when the video was recorded. Instead of closing the video file and opening the performer file, you can use your database software to, in effect, join the two files together to see all of the information about *Thriller* and Michael Jackson at the same time.

Database software is probably used more frequently in business, government, and education rather than by individuals. Microsoft Access, Lotus Approach, and Claris FileMaker Pro are popular examples of database software for microcomputers. If you're using a database on a mainframe computer, it is likely to be Oracle or IBM's DB2.

Information and Reference Software

How do I locate data, facts, figures, and other information? Information and reference software provides you with a collection of information and a way to access that information. This type of software includes massive amounts of data—unlike data management software, which is shipped without any data. The information and reference software category spans a wide range of applications, from encyclopedias to medical references, from map software to trip planners, and from cookbooks to telephone books. The options are as broad as the full range of human interests.

Information and reference software is generally shipped on a CD-ROM because of the quantity of information it includes. Many of these products provide links to a Web site that contains updates for the information on the CD-ROM. Other software publishers have eliminated the CD-ROM entirely and placed all of their reference materials on the Web. Access to that information often requires a fee or a subscription.

FIGURE 2-24

A multimedia encyclopedia provides a rich selection of text, graphics, sound, animation, and video.

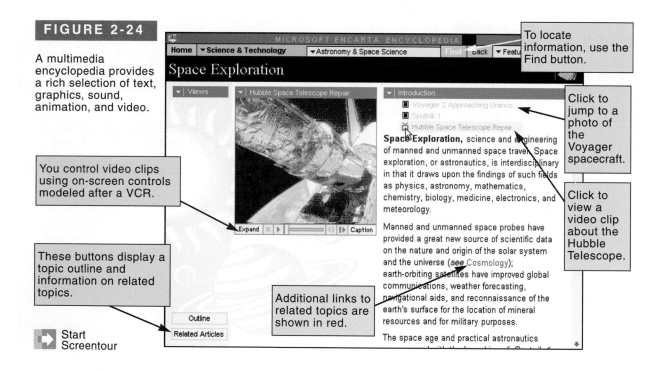

You control video clips using on-screen controls modeled after a VCR.

These buttons display a topic outline and information on related topics.

Start Screentour

To locate information, use the Find button.

Click to jump to a photo of the Voyager spacecraft.

Click to view a video clip about the Hubble Telescope.

Additional links to related topics are shown in red.

The most popular software packages in this category—encyclopedias—contain text, graphics, audio, and video on a full range of topics from apples to zenophobia. Best sellers include Microsoft's Encarta, Grolier's encyclopedia, Compton's encyclopedia, IBM's World Book encyclopedia, and Britannica's CD. All of these titles contain the standard information you would expect from an encyclopedia, such as articles written by experts on various topics, maps, photographs, and timelines. An encyclopedia on CD-ROM has several advantages over its printed counterpart. Finding information is easier, for example. Also, a CD-ROM takes up less space, and includes interesting video and audio clips. Lower production costs translate to more affordable products and allow an average person to own a comprehensive encyclopedia.

Connectivity Software

Do I need software to connect to other computers and the Internet? By now, most people know that networks and the Internet are the hot technology ticket to an amazing world of information and interaction. **Connectivity software** connects your computer to a local computer network or the Internet and provides tools that you can use to take advantage of the information and communications they offer. Connectivity software includes communications software, remote control software, e-mail software, and Web browsers.

InfoWeb
8

Web
Browsers

To access information on the Web, you need **communications software** to dial your connection; you also need Web browser software to view Web pages and navigate links from one document to the next. Basic communications software is now built into most microcomputer operating systems and is sometimes classified as system utility software. The two leading Web browsers are Netscape Navigator and Microsoft Internet Explorer.

CHAPTER 2

FIGURE 2-25

Communications software, such as Windows Dial-up Networking, connects your computer to a phone line or other communications channel.

1. Use the Dial-Up Networking box to select the connection that you want to use.

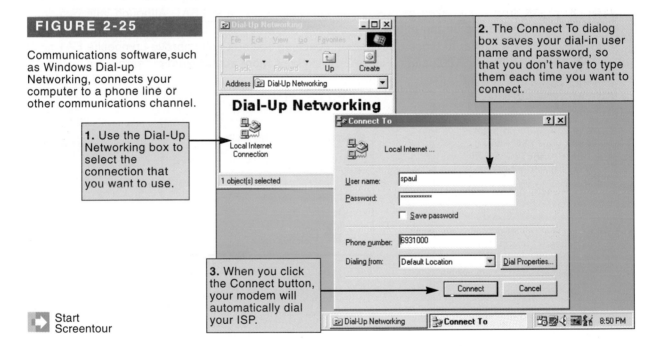

2. The Connect To dialog box saves your dial-in user name and password, so that you don't have to type them each time you want to connect.

3. When you click the Connect button, your modem will automatically dial your ISP.

Start
Screentour

Suppose that you have a computer in your office and a notebook computer at home. You are working at home one evening and need some information that is stored on your office computer. If both computers have modems and the computer in your office is on, you can use **remote control software** to establish a connection between the two machines. Using the keyboard of your notebook computer, you can control your office computer to locate and view the information you need. Popular remote control software includes Symantec's pcANYWHERE and Traveling Software's LapLink.

E-mail is perhaps the heart of Internet activity. It helps you stay in touch with friends, relatives, and business associates. **E-mail software** manages your computer mailbox. Qualcomm's Eudora provides good e-mail shareware. Microsoft bundles its Outlook Express mail program with the Windows operating system. Lotus Notes is a popular alternative for corporations.

Education and Training Software

Can I use software to improve my grades? Do your keyboarding skills need a bit of polish? Do you want to help your children learn and have fun at the same time? Are you the head of human resources and find that your company's managers don't understand all the fuss about diversity? Where can you turn for help? You might very well find your answers in education and training software.

Education and training software helps you learn and practice new skills. For the youngest users, educational software, such as The Learning Company's Reader Rabbit and Math Rabbit, teach basic reading and counting skills. Instruction is presented as games that children can play, and the levels of play are adapted to the child's age and ability.

For older students and adults, software is available to help learn languages, learn how to play the piano, prepare for standardized tests, improve keyboarding skills, and even learn managerial skills for a diverse workplace. Exam preparation software is available for standardized tests such as the SAT, GMAT, and LSAT. Although little research is available on the effectiveness of this software, experts believe that the results should be similar to those of in-person coaching courses that improve composite SAT scores by about 100 points. Figure 2-26 explains more about exam preparation software.

FIGURE 2-26

Exam preparation software assesses your skill level, coaches you on your weak skills, and provides test-taking tips.

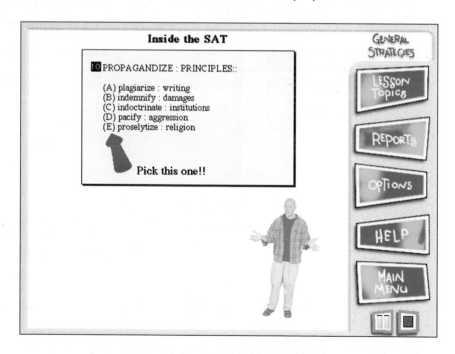

Some education and training software is called "edutainment software" because it blurs the line between learning and game playing. By far, the most active segment of the edutainment industry is children's software. Entertainment and education software titles account for more than 60 percent of all software sold. The average price of an edutainment program is about $40.

Entertainment Software

Are computers changing the way we spend our spare time? Worldwide computer and video game software sales annually exceed $10 billion. Publishers invest as much as $2 million to create and produce a successful entertainment software title. The entertainment software industry employs about 90,000 workers and is increasing its work force by 26 percent per year—a more rapid growth rate than most *Fortune* 500 companies. Clearly, entertainment software is big business as well as fun business. What is entertainment software? It includes games of all sorts, simulations, software toys, and software designed to help you enjoy hobbies and leisure activities.

InfoWeb
9

Games
Galore

Generally, game software is classified into subcategories such as action, adventure, role playing, puzzles, simulations, and strategy/war games. Many of the most popular games are available in multiple formats. You can play them alone on your own PC, in multiplayer environments via the Internet, or on a stand-alone game console such as Sega or Nintendo.

Adventure and role-playing software features realistic 3-D graphics, allows players to interact with the environment, and has weapons and monsters galore. Some of the most popular adventure and role-playing titles are Duke Nukem, Doom, Diablo, Quake, and Tomb Raider. Games vary in their level of violence, and many new games come with password options that allow parents to reduce the amount of R-rated material. Action games like the one shown in Figure 2-27 are similar to arcade games.

FIGURE 2-27

Entertainment software frequently features a snappy soundtrack and splashy graphics.

▶ Start
Video

Simulation software covers a broad range of interests. With SimCity, for example, you develop a city. The computer populates it with "Simmies" that clog your streets, trash your parks, and threaten to remove you from office if you don't supply better city services. With another simulation called Nascar Racing, you can get in the driver's seat of a stock car and test your driving skills on 16 authentic Nascar tracks. With other simulation titles, you can shoot a round of golf with Tiger Woods, fly fighter planes, command a nuclear submarine, or even strap into the pilot's seat of an X-wing fighter.

With the industry growing at a rapid pace and new technology creating ever more sophisticated multimedia capabilities, the future of entertainment software appears to be limited only by how much money consumers are willing to spend.

Accounting and Finance Software

Can software help me manage my money? If you've been tuning into the news, then you are probably aware of the predictions that the Social Security system is likely to run out of money within the next 50 years. It is never too early to start saving and investing money. If retirement seems a distant prospect, you probably have some short-term financial goals, such as earning enough money for next year's tuition, buying a new computer, or saving $5,000 for a trip to Australia. Without a financial plan, you might never reach these goals. Software can help you keep track of your money and your progress toward financial goals.

InfoWeb
10

Money
Management

Accounting and finance software helps you keep a record of monetary transactions and investments. In this software category, **personal finance software** is geared toward individual finances; it helps you keep track of bank accounts, investments, credit card balances, and bills. Some packages also support **online banking**—a way to use your computer and modem to download transactions directly from your bank, transfer funds among accounts, and pay bills. The best-selling personal finance software programs are Microsoft Money and Intuit Quicken.

FIGURE 2-28

Personal finance software can help you track your money and investments.

Quicken Trial 99 - QDATA - [FirstNational: Bank]

File Edit Lists Features Online Reports Window Help

FirstNational: Bank

Delete Find Transfer Reconcile Edit Account   Report ▾ Options ▾ How Do I ▾   Register

Date	Num	Payee/Category/Memo	Payment	Clr	Deposit	Balance
6/15/99		Opening Balance		R	440 50	440 50
		[FirstNational]				
6/15/99	1056	Knollwood Apts	365 00			75 50
		Rent				
6/21/99					200 00	275 50
		Gift Received				
6/21/99	1057	Big Dollar Foods	28 50			247 00
		Groceries				
6/26/99	1058	The Gap		Payment	Deposit	
		Category	Memo		Enter	Edit ▾	Split

Can I afford to pay for my child's ec   Current Balance: 75.50   Ending Balance: 247.00

FirstNational

Banking | Planning | Investing | Home & Car | Taxes

Start | Quicken Trial 99 - Q... | 12:11 PM

Some accounting and finance software is geared toward business. If you're an entrepreneur—even if you have a part-time business while you're in college—small business accounting software can be a real asset. These easy-to-use programs don't require more than a basic understanding of accounting and finance principles. Best sellers include Peachtree Complete Accounting, Intuit QuickBooks, and Best!Ware M.Y.O.B. This type of software helps you invoice customers and keep track of what they owe. It stores additional customer data, such as contact information and purchasing history. Inventory functions keep track of the products you carry. Payroll capabilities automatically calculate wages and deduct federal, state, and local taxes.

CHAPTER 2

Business Software

| What other kinds of software are available for businesses? | Business software helps organizations efficiently accomplish routine tasks. Often, business software is classified into two categories: horizontal market software and vertical market software.

Horizontal market software is any generic software package that can be used by many different kinds of businesses. Much of this software comes from other software categories, such as accounting and finance. Payroll software provides a good example of horizontal market software. Almost every business has employees and needs to maintain payroll records. Payroll software keeps track of employee hours and produces the reports required by the government for income tax reporting.

Vertical market software is designed to automate specialized tasks in a specific market or business, such as construction, health insurance, or used car sales. For example, tasks in the construction industry include estimating the cost of labor and materials for a new building and providing the customer with a price quote for the finished building. Estimating software for the construction industry would automate the task of gathering labor and materials costs and perform the calculations needed to arrive at an estimate. Other examples of vertical market software include software that handles billing and insurance for medical practices and software that tracks the amount of time attorneys spend on each case. Advertisements for vertical market software can be found in trade journals and on the Web.

QUICKCHECK   C

1 If you purchase a software _suite_, you will get several applications in one package.

2 _Desktop Publishing_ software provides sophisticated features for producing professional-quality newspapers, magazines, and books.

3 3-D graphics software helps you create a(n) _Wireframe_ that represents a three-dimensional object.

4 The major characteristic of data management software is that it contains data. True or <u>false</u>? _FALSE_

5 _Communication_ software is instrumental for dialing and connecting to the Internet.

6 _Verticle_ market software is designed for specialized tasks in a specific market or business.

▸ Check Answers

SECTION D MULTIMEDIA

InfoWeb
11
Multimedia

The term "multimedia" isn't new—it refers to the integrated use of multiple media, such as slides, videotapes, audiotapes, records, CD-ROMs, and photos. Now, however, the computer is replacing the slide projectors, tape recorders, and record players previously used for multimedia presentations. Advances in computer technology have made it possible to combine text, photo images, speech, music, animated sequences, and video into a single interactive computer application. A new definition of multimedia has emerged from this blend of technology. Today, **multimedia** is defined as an integrated collection of computer-based media including text, graphics, sound, animation, photo images, and video.

Although multimedia was once considered a special software category, digital media are now found in many different types of application software. For example, reference software such as encyclopedias typically contain multimedia elements such as sound and film clips. Some word processors are equipped with sound and will "read" your documents aloud. A popular office suite features an animated assistant to give you help. Computer games include fast-action animation and sound effects. With the widespread integration of multimedia into software of all types, having a special category for "multimedia software" is no longer necessary.

Today, multimedia provides a rich and interesting computing environment. Additionally, computers with multimedia capabilities provide an awesome set of tools that you can use to pursue your artistic and creative interests.

Multimedia Equipment

Lab
Multimedia

Does my computer need special equipment for multimedia? Multimedia requires sound and graphics capability. A speedy processor chip plus a CD-ROM drive or DVD drive are also desirable. Ten years ago, multimedia components were costly "extras." Today, they are standard equipment even on many inexpensive computers. A $500 computer, however, probably will not provide the same sound and image quality as a $2,000 computer. The multimedia equipment in more expensive computers tends to be faster and have "bells and whistles" that produce better quality output.

A **sound card** gives a computer the capability to record and play sound files as well as video sound tracks. Housed within the system unit, a sound card contains connectors that project from the back of the computer so that you can attach speakers, headphones, and a microphone. Expensive sound cards include circuitry for special audio effects, such as 3-D sound. The quality of your computer's speakers and headphones can also affect the quality of the sound that you hear. The sound quality produced by $200 speakers is far superior to that produced by $10 speakers, and $60 headphones provide much better sound than the $5 headphones you use with your portable CD player.

A CD-ROM drive allows your computer to access audio and software CD-ROMs. Multimedia elements—especially videos—require lots of storage space. Rather than store huge amounts of multimedia data on a computer's hard disk, the data can be stored on a CD-ROM, which you insert only when you want to access the multimedia elements. A DVD drive can access multimedia data from CD-ROMs as well. A DVD drive also allows you to watch feature-length movies on your computer, using the same DVDs that you might rent at your local video store.

Your computer's **graphics card** takes signals from the processor and uses them to "paint" an image on the screen. A graphics card is installed inside the computer's system unit and provides a connection for the monitor's data cable. Your computer's graphics card has to do a lot of work and must do it quickly. To display videos, for example, it repaints every pixel on the screen 15 times per second. More expensive "accelerated" graphics cards are equipped with circuitry that optimizes such tasks.

A fast processor can quickly handle the huge amount of digital data that is required to store and produce multimedia. The faster the processor, the more data it can process each second. A computer with a fast processor outputs smooth video sequences with a sound track that is perfectly coordinated with the action. The popularity of multimedia has caused chipmakers to equip processor chips with special multimedia capabilities that speed up multimedia features such as sound and video. Processor chips with Intel's MMX or AMD's 3DNow! can enhance a computer's multimedia performance.

FIGURE 2-29

Even many inexpensive computers now come equipped for multimedia, but the quality of a computer's sound and display systems can affect the audio and video quality.

You can use the inexpensive headphones from your portable CD player, but remember that better-quality headphones produce clearer sound.

DVD drives work with CD-ROMs as well as DVDs. Many computer manufacturers are now equipping computers with DVD drives to provide access to both CD-ROM and DVD formats.

A sound card provides a connection for speakers, headphones, and a microphone. High-performance sound cards support special audio effects such as 3-D sound.

A faster processor provides better multimedia quality, but the newest, fastest processors are always the most expensive.

A basic computer microphone is suitable for voice recording and dictation. For recording instrumental music and vocals, higher-quality results can be achieved with a professional microphone.

Inexpensive speakers provide basic radio-quality sound. A top-quality speaker system with subwoofer boosts the bass sound and screens out background noise.

Sound Recording

Can I make my own multimedia? You can incorporate graphics, voice, music, animation, and video into the work you create with your computer. Sound recordings, for example, are easy to digitize using a basic microphone and software that's included with the Windows operating system. Figure 2-30 explains how to use software called Sound Recorder to digitally record a narration, vocal segment, or music clip, then store it on disk.

FIGURE 2-30

Using the Sound Recorder software, click the Record button, then speak into the microphone. Click the Stop button when you're finished recording. Use the Save option on the File menu to store the recording on disk.

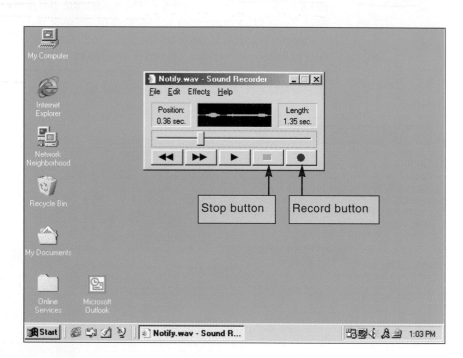

Stop button   Record button

Start
Screentour

Digital Scanning

How do I get images into the computer? Photos and other stationary images are often referred to as "still images" to distinguish them from videos and animation. To convert still images from paper format to digital format, you can use a scanner. A scanner converts a printed image into a bitmap graphic by essentially dividing it into a fine grid-work of cells and assigning a digital value for the color in each cell. These values are then stored by your computer and can be manipulated with graphics software, added to documents, and incorporated in multimedia projects. Scanners, such as the one pictured in Figure 2-31, are inexpensive and easy to use.

FIGURE 2-31

To use a scanner, place a document or photo face down on the glass surface, then close the cover. Activate your scanning software, check the scan settings, then initiate the scan.

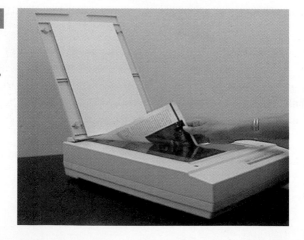

Lab
Photo
Editing

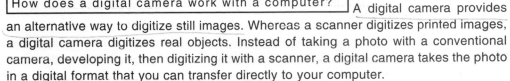

Digital Photography

How does a digital camera work with a computer? A digital camera provides an alternative way to digitize still images. Whereas a scanner digitizes printed images, a digital camera digitizes real objects. Instead of taking a photo with a conventional camera, developing it, then digitizing it with a scanner, a digital camera takes the photo in a digital format that you can transfer directly to your computer.

When you take a photo with a digital camera, the image that enters the camera lens is divided into a fine gridwork of cells. Higher-quality, more expensive digital cameras use a finer gridwork that produces a smoother, sharper image. As with a scanner, the digital color values for each cell in an image are saved on a storage device within the camera. Different cameras use different types of storage, including standard computer floppy disks and small flash memory cards, such as the one pictured in Figure 2-32.

CHAPTER 2

FIGURE 2-32

This digital camera saves as many as 32 images on the small flash memory card pictured in front of the camera.

Start
Video

The way that you transfer digital image data from the camera to your computer depends on the camera's storage mechanism. With cameras that use floppy disk storage, you simply remove the floppy disk from the camera and place it in the disk drive of your computer. You can then transfer the image to your hard disk before manipulating it with a photo editing program, incorporating it into a project, or attaching it to an e-mail message.

With cameras that use flash memory modules, you typically transfer the image data over a cable that runs between the camera and computer. The cable is necessary only for the transfer process and need not be connected while you are taking photos. Typically, the image data is transferred from the camera directly to your computer's hard disk. You can then view the photo, manipulate it with photo editing software, paste it into multimedia projects, and so on.

Digital Animation and Video

What kind of quality can I expect from digital video and animation? Digital animation and video encompass a number of technologies, including those that produce theater-quality special effects, DVD movies, and desktop videos. To differentiate between video and animation, consider their source. A **digital animation** is typically created "from scratch" by an artist with the help of a computer. A **digital video** is based on footage of real objects. The quality of each technology depends on the equipment that is used to create it and to play it.

Hollywood is the driving force behind advances in animation technology. In the 1983 "Star Trek" movie *The Wrath of Kahn*, the Genesis Effect transformed a dead planet into a lush earth-like habitat. The spectacular transformation was the first computer-generated graphics sequence to appear in a feature film. Within 10 years, work was in progress for *Toy Story*, the first feature film created entirely with digital animation.

Computer-generated special effects are created one frame at a time using powerful microcomputers, workstations, mainframes, and even supercomputers. The process is similar to rendering an image from a 3-D wireframe. An animator creates 3-D wireframes for the objects in each scene, specifies their color, texture, and opacity, then determines the position of light sources. Using these specifications, the computer creates a frame. The frames—30 per second—are then transferred sequentially to film.

FIGURE 2-33

Since their debut, computer graphics have provided memorable visual effects including the liquid-metal cyborg in *Terminator II*, dinosaurs in *Jurassic Park*, the doomed ship in *Titanic*, and assorted creatures in *Star Wars: Episode I*. The quality of computer-generated special effects has become so outstanding, that it is difficult to identify them on screen. If you watch the movie *Titanic* again, try to pick out some of the more than 450 computer-generated special effects.

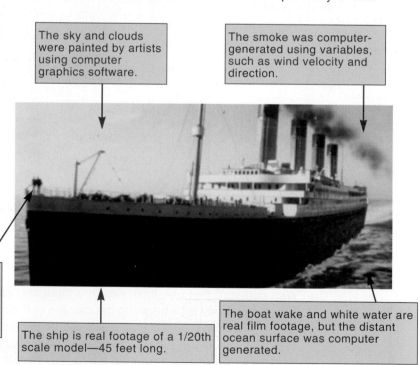

The sky and clouds were painted by artists using computer graphics software.

The smoke was computer-generated using variables, such as wind velocity and direction.

The passengers are digital renderings of real actors wearing special motion suits that digitize the movement of body parts.

The ship is real footage of a 1/20th scale model—45 feet long.

The boat wake and white water are real film footage, but the distant ocean surface was computer generated.

Today, DVDs seem to be replacing video tapes, as the number of movies available in DVD format continues to grow. This technology allows your computer to display full-screen, full-motion video that looks better than a television display, but not as good as a movie screen. Special technology enables a DVD disk to hold the huge amount of data produced by digitizing all of the frames of a motion picture. Creating feature-length MPEG videos on DVD currently requires some rather expensive equipment. For this reason, most multimedia authors prefer to work with desktop video.

Desktop video refers to videos that are constructed using a microcomputer. Typically, the footage for a desktop video has been captured by a digital video camera or has been converted into digital format from a video tape. Unfortunately, today's microcomputers have storage and processing speed limitations that prevent the quality of desktop videos from reaching the standard of DVD movies. Instead of 30 frames per second, desktop videos typically display only 15. Instead of a full-screen display, desktop videos usually appear in a small window on the screen. On older computers with a relatively slow processor, video images might be somewhat blurry, the sound track might not fully coordinate with the action, and skipped frames might produce gaps in the motion.

Despite its current drawbacks, desktop video is a popular addition to many multimedia projects such as encyclopedias, computer-based training lessons, and Web sites. The Windows operating system includes software called Media Player that allows you to play the most popular types of desktop videos. To create your own desktop video, you can purchase video editing software, such as Adobe Premiere. Figure 2-34 shows you how to use this software to assemble a video.

FIGURE 2-34

After you capture video footage from a camera or video tape, you can use video editing software to assemble the video and add a sound track.

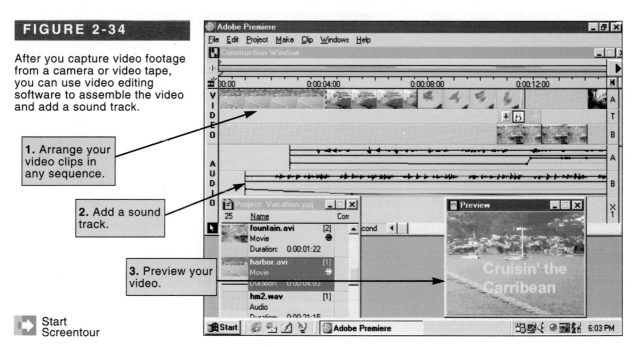

1. Arrange your video clips in any sequence.

2. Add a sound track.

3. Preview your video.

Start Screentour

QUICKCHECK D

1 Multimedia is a blend of technologies, such as text, photo images, speech, music, animated sequences, and video. True or false?

True

2 Computers equipped for multimedia include a(n) Soundcard to which you connect speakers, headphones, and a microphone.

3 A DVD drive works with CD-ROMs as well as DVDs. True or false? True

4 Because of personal computer storage and processing speed limitations, DeskTop video usually appears in a small window instead of filling the screen.

 Check Answers

USER FOCUS | INSTALLING SOFTWARE

Many microcomputers are sold with pre-installed system and application software, but eventually most computer users want to install additional software.

Software Compatibility

How do I know which software will work on my computer? Before you install software, you must make sure that it is compatible with your computer system. To be compatible, the software must be written for the type of computer you use and for the operating system installed on your computer. You should also make sure that your computer meets or exceeds the system requirements specified by the software. **System requirements** specify the operating system type and minimum hardware capacity needed for a software product to work correctly. The system requirements are usually listed on the outside of a software package, as shown in Figure 2-35. They might also be explained in more detail in the software reference manual.

FIGURE 2-35

The system requirements on a software package describe the equipment and operating system necessary to run the software.

Determining Compatibility

Does the version of my computer's operating system affect compatibility?

Suppose you want to purchase software for your PC. First, you need to make sure that the software is written for PCs, rather than for the Apple Macintosh. Sometimes the same software title is available for more than one type of computer. For example, Microsoft Word is available for both PCs and Macs, but these two software packages are two distinct versions. You cannot use the Macintosh version of Microsoft Word on your PC.

Once you know that the software is compatible with your computer hardware, you must make sure that the software will work with your operating system. If your PC uses the DOS operating system, you must select DOS software. If it uses the Microsoft Windows operating system, you will typically use Windows software. Windows runs some DOS software, too.

Operating systems go through numerous revisions. A higher version number indicates a more recent revision; for example, DOS 6.22 is a more recent version than DOS 6.0. Windows 95 and Windows 98 are more recent versions than Windows 3.1. Operating systems are usually **downwardly compatible**, which means that you can use application software designed for earlier versions of the operating system, but not those designed for later versions. For example, if Windows 98 is installed on your computer, you can generally use software designed for earlier versions of Windows, such as Windows 3.1. On the other hand, your software might not work correctly if it requires Windows 98 but you have Windows 3.1 on your computer. If you would like to use software that requires a newer version of your operating system, you must first purchase and install an operating system upgrade. Figure 2-36 summarizes the concept of downward compatibility.

CHAPTER 2

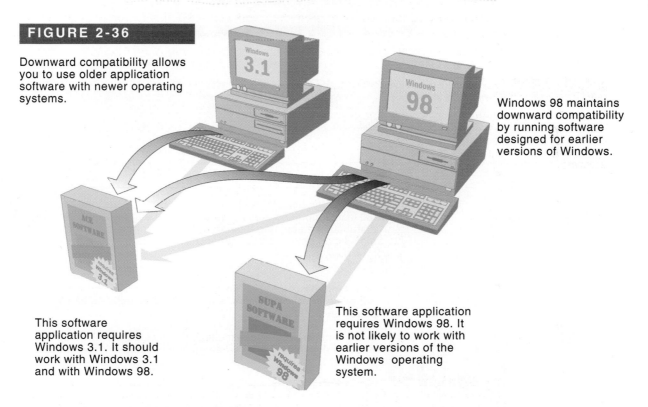

FIGURE 2-36

Downward compatibility allows you to use older application software with newer operating systems.

Windows 98 maintains downward compatibility by running software designed for earlier versions of Windows.

This software application requires Windows 3.1. It should work with Windows 3.1 and with Windows 98.

This software application requires Windows 98. It is not likely to work with earlier versions of the Windows operating system.

Software Setup

When I purchase software, what do I do with the disks? Computer software is usually shipped on floppy disks, CD-ROMs, or DVDs. Before you can use the software, you usually must install it on your computer. During the **installation process**, programs and data for the software are copied to the hard disk of your computer system.

When you install software using a command-line operating system, such as DOS, you should carefully follow the installation instructions provided in the reference manual. No consistent installation procedure exists for DOS software, so each software application might require a unique set of steps.

On the other hand, the installation process is more consistent and usually much easier for Windows software. The new software you purchase will typically include a **setup program** that ushers you through the installation process. Figure 2-37 shows you how to install application software.

FIGURE 2-37

A setup program guides you through the steps required to install Windows application software.

Start Video

1. Insert the setup disk, CD-ROM, or DVD and start the setup program.

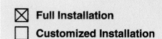

☒ **Full Installation**
☐ **Customized Installation**

2. Select the installation option that best meets your needs. During a full installation, the setup program copies all files and data from the distribution medium to the hard disk of your computer system. A full installation provides you with access to all features of the software.

During a customized installation, the setup program displays a list of software features for your selection. After you select the features you want, the setup program copies only the selected program and data files to your hard disk. A customized installation can save space on your hard disk.

3. If the software includes multiple disks or CD-ROMs, insert each one in the specified drive when the setup program tells you to do so.

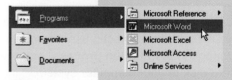

4. When the setup program has finished, start the program you have just installed to make sure that it works.

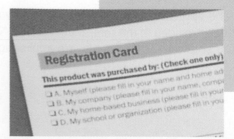

5. Fill out the registration card and send it in. When you send in the card, you become a registered user. The perks of being a registered user vary with each software publisher, but they might include receiving free technical support, product information, or discounts on new versions of the software.

When you install non-multimedia applications such as word processing or accounting software, the computer copies all program modules from the distribution medium to the hard disk of your computer. You do not need to insert the disk or CD-ROM every time you want to use the program because everything you need is on your hard disk. For multimedia applications, the procedure might be different. You generally copy only a small startup program to your hard disk, leaving most of the multimedia images, videos, and sounds on the CD-ROM.

Why wouldn't you copy all of the multimedia components to your hard disk? The answer is to save hard disk space. Multimedia applications require lots of storage space. For example, Microsoft's Encarta encyclopedia takes up about twice as much space as Microsoft Office 2000, which includes word processing, spreadsheet, presentation, and database software applications. You are likely to have many multimedia applications, but use them infrequently. Rather than devoting a large portion of your hard disk space to a multimedia application, you can insert its CD-ROM into the CD-ROM drive only when you need access to its images, animations, videos, and sound.

ISSUE   ARE COPYRIGHTS FAIR?

Software is easy to steal. You don't have to walk out of a CompUSA store with a Microsoft Office 2000 box under your shirt. You can simply borrow your friend's CD-ROM and install a copy of the program on your computer's hard disk. It seems so simple that it couldn't be illegal. But it is.

In many countries, including the United States, software pirates are subject to criminal prosecution. And yet, piracy continues to grow. According to the Software and Information Industry Association (SIIA), a leading anti-piracy watchdog, revenue losses from business software piracy typically exceed $12 billion per year. This figure reveals only a part of the piracy problem—it does not include losses from rampant game and educational software piracy.

A small, but vocal minority of software users believe that data and software should be freely distributed. Richard Stallman writes in the GNU (which stands for "Gnu's Not UNIX") Manifesto, "I consider that the golden rule requires that if I like a program I must share it with other people who like it. Software sellers want to divide users and conquer them, making each user agree not to share with others. I refuse to break solidarity with other users in this way. I cannot in good conscience sign a nondisclosure agreement or a software license agreement."

Is software piracy really damaging? Who cares if you use Microsoft Office without paying for it? Software piracy is damaging because it has a negative effect on the economy. Software production is the third-largest industry in the United States, employing more than 2 million people and growing at a phenomenal rate of 5.8 percent per year. This industry, however, is losing an estimated $32 million every day, which translates to 130,000 lost jobs and $1 billion in lost tax revenues.

Decreases in software revenues can have a direct effect on consumers, too. When software publishers have to cut corners, they tend to reduce customer service and technical support. As a result, you, as the consumer get put on hold when you call for technical support, you find fewer free technical support sites, and you encounter customer support personnel who are only moderately knowledgeable about their products. The bottom line—software piracy negatively affects customer service.

As an alternative to cutting support costs, some software publishers might build the cost of software piracy into the price of the software. The unfortunate result is that those who legitimately license and purchase software pay an inflated price.

Software piracy is a global problem. Although the United States accounts for the highest dollar amount of software piracy, approximately two-thirds of the piracy occurs outside the United States. The countries with the highest piracy rates include China, Japan, Korea, Germany, France, Brazil, Italy, Canada, and the United Kingdom. But piracy is a problem in other countries, also. By some estimates, more than 90 percent of all business software used in Bulgaria, Indonesia, Russia, and Vietnam is pirated.

InfoWeb
12
Anti-piracy

As a justification of high piracy rates, some observers point out that people in many countries simply might not be able to afford software that is priced for the U.S. market. This argument would make sense in China, where the average annual income is equivalent to about $3,500, and in Korea, where the average income is only $900. A Korean who legitimately purchases Microsoft Office for $250 would be spending more than one-quarter of his or her annual income. Most of the countries with a high incidence of software piracy, however, have strong economies and respectable per capita incomes. To further discredit the theory that piracy stems from poverty, India—which has a fairly large computer-user community, but a per capita income of only $1,600—is not among the top ten countries with high rates of software piracy.

If economic factors do not account for the pervasiveness of software piracy, what does? Some analysts suggest that people need more education about software copyrights and the economic implications of piracy. Other analysts believe that copyright enforcement needs to be increased by supporting and implementing more vigorous efforts to identify and prosecute pirates.

WHAT DO YOU THINK?

1. Do you believe that software piracy is a serious issue?   ⭘ Yes   ⭘ No   ⭘ Not sure

2. Do you know of any instances of software piracy?   ⭘ Yes   ⭘ No   ⭘ Not sure

3. Do you think that most software pirates understand that they are doing something illegal?   ⭘ Yes   ⭘ No   ⭘ Not sure

4. Should software publishers try to adjust software pricing for local markets?   ⭘ Yes   ⭘ No   ⭘ Not sure

➡ Save Responses

CHAPTER 2

CHAPTER 2   REVIEW ACTIVITIES

INTERACTIVE SUMMARY

The Interactive Summary helps you select important concepts and facts from this chapter. Fill in the blanks to best complete each sentence. When using the NP4 CD or NP4 Web site, you can click the Check Answers buttons to automatically score your answers. Place your Tracking Disk in the floppy disk drive if you want to save your scores.

A computer _____ is a set of detailed, step-by-step instructions that tells a computer how to solve a problem or carry out a task. In many countries—including the United States and Canada—software is protected by a(n) _____ that grants certain exclusive rights to its author. Most commercial _____ is protected by a license agreement that extends or modifies the basic rights provided by copyright. Another type of software called _____ is marketed under a "try before you buy" policy. When a copyright holder explicitly relinquishes all rights to a software program, it is called public _____ software.

Software can be broadly categorized as system software and application software. System software includes operating systems, utilities, device drivers, and programming _____. An operating system serves as the master control center for all of the activities that take place within a computer. Some operating systems, such as UNIX and Windows NT were designed as _____ or network operating systems. Other operating systems, such as DOS, Windows 98, and Mac OS, were designed primarily for use as _____ operating systems. The _____ software that has been installed on a computer helps a computer user carry out tasks and includes productivity, document production, business, and game software.   ➡ Check Answers

_____ is defined as an integrated collection of computer-based media including text, graphics, sound, animation, photo images, and video. Most computers today are equipped with the _____ and graphics capabilities necessary to use multimedia software applications and Web sites. Peripheral devices such as a digital camera or a(n) _____ help you to capture still images that you can incorporate into your own multimedia projects. A digital video camera helps you to capture video images.

Many microcomputers are sold with preinstalled system and application software, but eventually most computer users want to install additional software. Most Windows software includes a _____ program that escorts you through the steps in the installation process. Software that is illegally installed, copied, and used is called _____ software. When you install software, make sure that you understand the terms of the license agreement.   ➡ Check Answers

CHAPTER 2   **91**

I N T E R A C T I V E   K E Y   T E R M S

Make sure that you understand all of the boldfaced key terms presented in this chapter. If you're using the NP4 CD or NP4 Web site, you can use this list of terms as an interactive study activity. First, try to define a term in your own words, then click the term to compare your definition with the definition that is presented in the chapter.

3-D graphics software, 68
Application software, 54
Bitmap image, 68
Commercial software, 52
Communications software, 73
Computer program, 48
Computer programming language, 65
Concurrent-use license, 53
Connectivity software, 73
Copyright, 50
Database, 71
Database software, 71
Desktop publishing software, 67
Desktop video, 83
Device driver, 65
Digital animation, 82
Digital video, 82
DOS, 62
Downwardly compatible, 85
E-mail software, 73
External services, 57
Flat file, 71
Formatting, 64
Graphics card, 79
Graphics software, 68
Groupware, 66
Horizontal market software, 77
Installation process, 85
Internal services, 57
Linux, 63
Mac OS, 61
Mathematical modeling software, 70
Microsoft Windows, 59
Multimedia, 78
Multiple-user license, 52
Multitasking, 59
Novell NetWare, 63
Office suite, 66
Online banking, 76
Operating system (OS), 56
Paint software, 68
Personal finance software, 76
Photo editing software, 68
Pirated software, 50

Presentation software, 69
Productivity software, 66
Public domain software, 54
Remote control software, 73
Rendering, 68
Setup program, 86
Shareware, 53
Shrink-wrap license, 52
Single-user license, 52
Site license, 53
Software, 49
Software license, 51
Software pirates, 50
Sound card, 78
Spreadsheet software, 70
Statistical software, 70
System requirements, 84
System resource, 57
System software, 54
UNIX, 63
Utilities, 64
Vector graphics, 68
Vertical market software, 77
Web authoring software, 67
Wireframe, 68
Word processing software, 67

CHAPTER 2

INTERACTIVE QUIZZES

Quiz yourself on important concepts from this chapter by filling in the blanks. When using the NP4 CD or NP4 Web site, you can type your answers, then use the Check Answers buttons to automatically score your responses. Place your Tracking Disk in the floppy disk drive if you want to save your scores.

1 If an organization with a computer network has a concurrent-use license for five copies of a word processor, at any one time as many as five employees may use the software. True or false? ☐.

2 An operating system provides ☐ services "behind the scenes" to ensure that the computer system functions efficiently.

3 A(n) ☐ operating system, sometimes referred to as a client operating system, is designed for a single-user microcomputer.

4 The Windows operating system includes a feature called ☐ that allows you to work with more than one software program at a time.

5 The term ☐ suite would refer to a software package containing word

processing, spreadsheet, database, and presentation applications.

6 A process called ☐ prepares a disk to hold data.

7 If you purchase a new scanner, it will probably include device ☐ software that, once installed, will help your computer control the scanner's operation.

8 The limitations of today's computer hardware mean that ☐ video typically appears in a small window on the screen and may not equal the quality of DVD video.

9 If Windows 98 is installed on your computer, you cannot use software designed for earlier versions of Windows, such as Windows 3.1. True or false? ☐

➡ Check Answers

Enter T if the statement is true, F if the statement is false.

1 In a multimedia system, item A could be a CD-ROM drive or DVD drive. ☐

2 Item B is a good backup if item A fails. ☐

3 Items C, D, and E are connected to the sound card. ☐

4 If item F contains multimedia software, the installation process will transfer everything to the computer's hard disk. ☐

➡ Check Answers

INTERACTIVE PRACTICE TESTS

When you use the NP4 CD or NP4 Web site, you can take practice tests that consist of 10 multiple-choice, true/false, and fill-in-the-blank questions. The 10 questions are selected at random from a large test bank, so each time you take a test, you'll receive a different set of questions. Your tests are scored immediately and you can print study guides that help you find the correct answers for any questions that you missed. If you are using a Tracking Disk, insert it in the floppy disk drive to save your test scores.

 Start Practice Test

STUDY TIPS

Study Tips help you organize and consolidate the information in a chapter by making lists, outlines, charts, and sketches. You can use paper and pencil or word processing software to complete most of the Study Tips activities.

1 Using your own words, write out the answers to the questions below each heading in this chapter.

2 Under U.S. copyright law, what are the two major rights granted to the copyright holder? What are the three rights granted to the user of copyrighted materials?

3 Explain the difference between internal and external operating system services.

4 Complete the following "legal" matrix to clarify the difference between copyrighted software, licensed software, shareware, and public domain software.

	Copyrighted Software	Licensed Software	Shareware	Public Domain Software
Legal to make a backup copy?				
Legal to sell a copy?				
Legal to give a copy to a friend?				
Protected by copyright?				

5 Make a two-column list of multimedia equipment. In the first column, list the computer components that enable a computer to play multimedia. In the second column, list the devices that enable you to create multimedia.

6 In your own words, explain the concept of downward compatibility and give an example using specific operating system versions and application software.

7 Make a list of the application software categories covered in this chapter. *Hint:* Begin your list with word processing software and desktop publishing software.

CHAPTER 2

PROJECTS

A project is an open-ended activity that will help you apply the concepts you have learned. Many projects require resources in addition to your textbook, such as current magazines, library materials, or Web access. When you tackle a project, be prepared to use your critical thinking skills, logical analysis, and your creativity.

1 Format a Disk In this chapter, you learned how utility software helps you direct the operating system to accomplish tasks such as formatting a disk. Now is a good time to try out this utility. If your lab computers have the Windows operating system, you can do this project on your own by referring to Figure 2-16. Otherwise, your instructor should provide instructions.

2 The Operating System in Your School's Lab In this project, you will explore the operating system in your school computer lab. If you have more than one lab or your computer uses more than one operating system, your instructor should tell you which one to use for this project.

Find out which operating system is used in your school computer lab, including the type and version. You can go into the lab and obtain this information from one of the computers. If you see a command-line user interface, try typing "ver" and then pressing the Enter key. If you see a graphical user interface, click the Apple menu or click the Help menu, then select About. Once you know the operating system used in your school lab, use the operating system reference manual, online Help, and library resources to answer the following questions:

a. Which operating system and version are used in your school lab?

b. Which company publishes the operating system software?

c. When was the first version of this operating system introduced?

d. Does this operating system have a command-line user interface or a graphical user interface?

e. Does this operating system support multitasking?

f. Do you need a password to use the computers in your school lab? Even if you do not need to use a password, does the operating system provide any security features?

g. What is the anticipated arrival date for the next version of this operating system?

h. How much does the publisher of this operating system usually charge for upgrades if you are a registered user?

3 Multimedia Tools To digitize still images, you would typically need to add a digital camera or a scanner to your computer system. Is one better than the other, or do you need both? For this project, use your library and Web resources to locate information on digital cameras and scanners. Computer magazines often include product comparisons that not only evaluate the strengths and weaknesses of a group of products, but also provide some solid background material and practical tips. You can look for product comparisons by thumbing through computer magazines in your library or by connecting to a Web site, such as *www.zdnet.com*, and entering "digital camera" or "scanner" in the Search box.

Gather information about the current prices for digital cameras and scanners. Which products seem to offer the best slate of features at a reasonable price? Also, look for information on the quality of the images that they produce. Is it better, for example, to scan a photo that you've taken with a conventional camera, or do you get better quality if you take the photo directly with a digital camera?

When you have completed your research, write a one-page analysis of your findings that includes your recommendation on the best tools for digital still images.

4 **The Legal Beagle: Analyzing a License Agreement** When you use a software package, it is important to understand the legal restrictions on its use. In this project, you have an opportunity to read a real software license agreement and make decisions based on how you interpret what it says. You can do this project on your own or discuss it in a small group, as specified by your instructor. Read the license agreement provided below, then answer these questions:

a. Is this a shrink-wrap license? Why or why not?

b. After you pay your computer dealer for the program covered by this license, who owns the program?

c. Can you legally have one copy of the program on your computer at work and another copy of the program on your computer at home if you use the software only in one place at a time?

d. Can you legally sell the software? Why or why not?

e. Under what conditions can you legally transfer possession of the program to someone else?

f. If you were the owner of a software store, could you legally rent the program to customers if you were sure they did not keep a copy after the rental period was over?

g. Can you legally install this software on one computer, but give more than one user access to it?

h. If you use this program for an important business decision and you later find out that a mistake in the program caused you to lose $500,000, what legal recourse is provided by the license agreement?

IMPORTANT - READ CAREFULLY BEFORE USING THIS PRODUCT

License Agreement and Limited Warranty

By using the software included with this Agreement ("Program") you accept the terms of this license. If you do not agree to the terms of this Agreement, and you are also the original purchaser of this program license "Original Purchaser"), promptly return the software together with all accompanying items to your dealer for a full refund.

LIMITED USE LICENSE. The publisher grants you the right to use one copy of the Program for your personal use only. All rights not expressly granted are reserved by the Publisher. You must treat the Program and associated materials and any elements thereof like any other copyrighted material (e.g., a book or musical recording).

YOU MAY NOT:
- Use the Program, or permit use of the Program, on more than one computer, terminal, or workstation at the same time.
- Except as permitted by the Program, copy the Program onto a hard drive or other device and you must run the Program from the CD-ROM.
- Use the Program, or permit use of the Program, in a network or other multi-use arrangement or on an electronic bulletin board system or other remote access arrangement.
- Reverse engineer, decompile, disassemble, or create derivative works of, the Program.
- Publicly perform or display this Program.

- Rent, lease, license or otherwise transfer this Program without the express written consent of the Publisher, except that you may transfer the complete Program copy and accompanying materials on a permanent basis, provided that no copies are retained and the recipient agrees to the terms of this Agreement.

LIMITED WARRANTY. The Publisher warrants to the Original Purchaser only, that the Program shall perform substantially in accordance with the accompanying written materials for ninety (90) days from the date of purchase.

EXCLUSIVE REMEDY. The Original Purchaser's exclusive remedy for the breach of this license shall be, at Publisher's option, either (a) the repair or replacement of the Program that does not meet Publisher's Limited Warranty and which is returned to Publisher with a copy of your receipt; or (b) a refund of the price, if any, which you paid for the Program and associated materials. This Limited Warranty is void if the failure of the Program has resulted from accident, abuse, misapplication, or use of the Program with incompatible hardware.

NO OTHER WARRANTIES. The Publisher disclaims all warranties with respect to the program and accompanying materials, either express or implied, including but not limited to implied warranties of merchantability, non-infringement of third party rights, and fitness for a particular purpose. In no event shall the Publisher be liable for any consequential or incidental damages whatsoever arising out of the use of or inability to use this program or program package. The Publisher's liability shall not exceed the actual price paid for the license to use the Program.

5 **What Software Tool Would You Recommend?** Folk wisdom tells us to use the appropriate tool for a job. This idea holds true for software tools, too. In this project, you decide what software tool is most appropriate for a task. You can do this project on your own or discuss it in a small group.

For each of the scenarios that follow, decide which software tool (e.g., word processing) would accomplish the task most effectively.

a. You want to keep track of your monthly expenses and try to figure out ways to save some money.

b. As the leader of an international team of researchers studying migration patterns of Canada geese, you want all team members to communicate their findings to each other quickly.

c. You are the office manager for a department of a *Fortune* 500 company and one of your responsibilities is to arrange meetings and schedule facilities for the employees in your department.

d. As a partner in a law firm, you need to draft and modify legal briefs.

e. You are in charge of a fund-raising campaign and you need to track the names, addresses, phone numbers, and donations made by contributors.

f. You are going to design and produce the printed program for a community theater play listing the actors, director, lighting specialists, and so on.

g. A sales manager for a cosmetics company wants to motivate the sales force by graphically showing the increases in consumer spending in each of the past five years.

h. The marketing specialist for a new software company wants to send out announcements to 150 computer magazines.

i. The owners of five golf courses in Jackson County want to design a promotional brochure that can be distributed to tourists in restaurants and hotels.

j. The owner of a small business wants to keep track of ongoing income and expenses and print out monthly profit and loss statements.

k. The superintendent of a local school system wants to prepare a press release explaining why student test scores were 5 percent below the national average.

l. A contractor wants to calculate his cost for materials needed to build a new community center.

m. A college student wants to send out customized letters addressed to 20 prospective employers.

n. The parents of three children want to decide whether they should invest money for their children's education in the stock market or whether they should buy into their state's prepaid tuition plan.

o. The director of fund raising for a large nonprofit organization wants to keep a list of prospective donors.

ADDITIONAL PROJECTS

Click the underlined text to link to the NP4 Web site (www.cciw.com/np4) where you can view and print additional projects for this chapter.

Software Applications: What's Available

Multimedia Top Ten

Productivity Suites and Groupware

Where's the Shareware?

LAB ASSIGNMENTS

Software for these labs is provided on the NP4 CD and may also be available in your school's computer lab. To start a lab, click the lab icon.

Each lab has two parts: Steps and Explore. Use the Steps first to learn and review concepts. Read the information on each page and complete the numbered steps. As you work through the lab, you will be asked to answer QuickCheck questions about what you have learned. At the end of the lab, you will see a report that scores your answers to the QuickChecks. If your instructor wants you to turn in this report, click the Print button on the QuickCheck Report screen.

When you have completed the Steps, you can click the Explore button to complete the Lab Assignments. You can also use Explore to practice the skills you learned and to explore concepts on your own.

Lab
Multimedia

Multimedia brings together text, graphics, sound, animation, video, and photo images. If you are using the CD version of this book, you have already seen multimedia in action. In this lab, you will learn how to apply multimedia and then have the chance to see what it might be like to design some aspects of multimedia projects.

1 Click the Steps button to learn about multimedia development. As you proceed through the Steps, answer the QuickCheck questions. When you complete the Steps, you will see a report that summarizes your performance on the QuickChecks. Follow the directions on the screen to print the QuickCheck Report.

2 In Explore, browse through the STS-79 Multimedia Mission Log. How many videos are included in the Multimedia Mission Log? The image on the Mission Profile page is a vector drawing. What happens when you enlarge it?

3 Listen to the sound track on Day 3. Is it a WAV file or a MIDI file? Why do you think so? Is it a synthesized sound or a digitized sound? Listen to the sound track on page 8. Can you tell if it is a WAV file or a MIDI file?

4 Suppose you were hired as a designer for a multimedia series targeting fourth- and fifth-grade students. Describe the changes you would make to the multimedia Mission Log so that it would be suitable for these students. Also, include a sketch showing a screen from your revised design.

5 When you view the multimedia Mission Log on your computer, do you see palette flash? Why or why not? If you see palette flash, list the images that flash.

6 Multimedia can be effectively applied to projects such as encyclopedias, atlases, and animated storybooks; to computer-based training for foreign languages, first aid, or software applications; for games and sports simulations; for business presentations; for personal albums, scrapbooks, and baby books; for product catalogs and Web pages.

Suppose you were hired to create one of these projects. Write a one-paragraph description of the project you would develop. Describe some of the multimedia elements you would include. For each element, indicate its source and whether you would need to obtain permission for its use. Finally, sketch a screen or two showing your completed project.

A digital camera or scanner produces digital still photos that you can include in multimedia projects and e-mail. But digital photos—like their film and paper counterparts—are not necessarily "perfect." They are sometimes out of focus, too bright, too dark, or poorly framed. The good news is that fixing a digital photo is relatively simple. To alter a digital image, you can use generalized bitmap graphics software or specialized photo editing software. In this lab, you will have the opportunity to use both types of software to compare features and ease of use.

1 Click the Steps button to learn about photo editing software. As you proceed through the Steps, answer the QuickCheck questions. After you complete the Steps, you will see a QuickCheck Report. Follow the instructions on the screen to print this report.

2 When you click the Explore button, Microsoft Paint opens and displays a photo called Dog.bmp. You can continue the Explore activities using Paint, or you can save Dog.bmp on a disk, close Paint, and proceed using the photo editing software of your choice.

3 Using Microsoft Paint or the photo editing software of your choice, try to complete the list of editing tasks below. The number of tasks that you can complete will depend on the software that you have elected to use.

Crop the photo so that you see only the dog and the toys.

Remove the "green" eye.

Change the bear's nose from red to black.

Remove the small scar from the dog's forehead.

Smooth or despeckle the photo.

Decrease the brightness until you can see the details of the white bear's fur.

4 Save your revised photo and print it out. Use a color printer if one is available otherwise, use a back-and-white printer.

5 On the back of your printout, indicate which software you used and list the photo editing tasks that you were able to complete.

INFOWEB

*The InfoWeb is your guide to print, film, television, and electronic resources. Use it to obtain updates on quickly changing technical information and to locate information for research papers. If you're using the NP4 CD-ROM, click the InfoWeb Site icon on the left side of this paragraph to access the online InfoWeb links. Otherwise, use your Web browser and type in the address of the NP4 Web site: **www.cciw.com/np4**. At the Web site you'll find up-to-date links to the topics covered in this chapter.*

1 Copyright and Software Law

Software copyright law is the focus of an ongoing discussion among legal experts, law makers, software publishers, and consumers' rights advocacy groups. There seems to be general agreement that current laws should be updated. Cornell University provides a hypertext version of the U.S. Copyright Act that is currently in effect at *www.law.cornell.edu/uscode/17*. If you have questions about what's legal and what's not, you'll find copyright FAQs at the Electronic Frontier Foundation site at *eff.org/pub/Intellectual_property*. For "plain speak" information on the difference between copyrighted, licensed, shareware, and public domain software, you can connect to The Copyright Web site at *www.benedict.com*.

2 Shareware: Try Before You Buy

The Internet provides an ideal distribution channel for shareware. You can connect to a shareware site, select the program that you want to try and "download it" by transferring it to your computer. At sites such as *www.shareware.com*, you can search for, browse, and download freeware, shareware, demos, fixes, patches, and upgrades from various software archives and computer vendor sites on the Internet. Before you download shareware, be sure that you understand the copyright and license. Also, make sure that your shareware source is reputable and guarantees that its software is virus-free.

3 Operating Systems

To learn more about operating systems, head for the Web sites of the companies that produce them. DOS and Windows operating systems are at *www.microsoft.com*, the Mac OS is at *www.apple.com*, UNIX is at *www.sco.com*, and Linux is at distributor sites such as Red Hat (*www.redhat.com*) and Caldera Systems (*www.calderasystems.com*). On bookstore shelves, you'll find many good desktop references for the Windows operating system, such as *Windows Secrets* by Brian Livingston and Davis Straub (IDG Books Worldwide). Most college-level computer curricula include an operating systems course in which

students learn about operating system services and the specific ways that an operating system controls computer hardware. One standard text for this course is *Operating Systems: Design and Implementation* by Andrew S. Tanenbaum and Albert S. Woodhull (Prentice Hall, 1997).

4 Shopping for Application Software

These days you can buy software without leaving your house—as long as you have Internet access and a credit card. Egghead Computer operates a chain of computer superstores. Connect to its Web site (*www.egghead.com*), where you'll find descriptions and system requirements for software packages as well as articles and reviews detailing their strengths and weaknesses. Micro Warehouse. offers catalog sales of hardware and software and also has a Web site at *www.warehouse.com*. At the CNET Shopper.com Web site, *www.shopper.com*, you can choose a software package and compare prices from stores and catalogs across the country. Students can often get discounts on software at sites such as *www.studentdiscount.net* or *www.micromaster.com*.

Computer magazines are good sources of information about software—look for them in your library, on newsstands, or on the Web. Two of the biggest computer magazine publishers are Ziff-Davis and CMP. Ziff-Davis publications include *PC Week, PC Computing, Mac Week,* and *Computer Shopper.* CMP publishes *Computer Reseller News, Home PC, InformationWeek, NetGuide,* and *Windows Magazine.* You can find their magazines online at the ZDNet Web site, *www.zdnet.com,* and the TechWeb site, *techweb.cmp.com,* respectively. *Computerworld* at *www.computerworld.com* has great product comparisons, as does *InfoWorld* at *www.infoworld.com.*

5 Desktop Publishing

The popularity of desktop publishing increases every year. Why? Find out how an assortment of companies save money and publicize their messages at *www.adobe.com/studio/casestudies/main.html,* the Web site maintained by the publisher of the popular PageMaker DTP software. You can download your own trial version of desktop publishing software at *www.quark.com.* The Quark site, home of the highly-rated QuarkXpress software, also contains a detailed list of software features—useful option if you want to know what desktop software really does. Look for desktop publishing articles and design tips on the Web at sites like *www.publish.com* and *www.dtpjournal.com.*

6 3-D Graphics

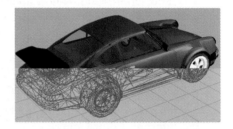

One of the most exciting developments in graphics is 3-D rendering. Premier packages include AutoCad and Caligari trueSpace. To find out more about 3-D software, click the Gallery link on the Caligari site at *www.caligari.com.* This site also features a great collection of samples and a free trial version of the software. Persistence of Vision also hosts a site, *www.povray.org/java-index.html,* that contains stunning 3-D samples. While at the site, you can download a well-regarded free ray-tracing program. To find out what kind of graphics you can generate with a supercomputer, connect to *www.ncsa.uiuc.edu/SDG/DigitalGallery/DG_science_theater.html.* You'll find additional cool 3-D graphics links at the NP4 Web site.

7 Presentations

Using Microsoft PowerPoint software to create presentations? Your local bookstore might have just the desk reference you need to master all of its features. The 400-page book and CD-ROM for *Creating Cool PowerPoint 97 Presentations* by Glenn E. Weadock and Emily Sherrill Weadock (IDG Books Worldwide, 1997) are chock full of great hints. Using presentation software won't guarantee a successful presentation, however. For tips on how to plan, prepare, and deliver a presentation, check your library for books such as *Business Presentations and Public Speaking* by Peter H. Engel (Harvard Business School Press, 1996) and *How to Give a Terrific Presentation* by Karen Kalish (Amacom, 1996). Online you can connect to *Presentations* magazine at *www.presentations.com* for tips on making presentations, selecting presentation hardware, and making effective use of presentation software.

8 Web Browsers

To access the Web, you need Web browser software. At the Microsoft site, check out *www.microsoft.com/ie* for a description of the Internet Explorer browser and plug-in Internet tools. Information about Netscape Navigator can be found at *www.netscape.com.*

9 Games Galore

Most software publishers give away free playable demos of their game software. A fun site with downloads, including children's games, is *www.happypuppy.com.* "Serious" and more violent game demos are supplied by *www.avault.com.* If you want to know which games are today's best sellers, connect to *www.gamespot.com.*

10 Money Management

Money problems? Personal financial management can't promise to solve them, but can supply the software tools you need to get your finances in order. Visit the Intuit Web site at *www.intuit.com* where you can read about the popular Quicken and QuickBooks software, then download a free trial version. A related site, the Quicken Financial Network at *www.qfn.com*, has articles about retirement planning, managing a stock portfolio, and online banking. The site also features QuickAnswers that help you make actual calculations to predict your financial future.

11 Multimedia

Digital imaging technology changes rapidly. To keep up with the latest developments in digital cameras, video cameras, and scanners, check out any of the Web-based digital camera review sites, such as *www.plugin.com/digitalcameraguide/index.html* or *www.inconference.com/digicam/ index.htm*l. For specifications on current camera models, connect to manufacturer Web sites—for example, Agfa (*www.agfa.com*), Canon (*www.canon.com*), Kodak (*www.kodak.com*), Olympus (*www.olympusamerica.com*), Nikon (*www.nikonusa.com*), and Epson (*www.epson.com*).

Once you have the images, you'll want to add them to multimedia projects. For information about Adobe Premiere video editing software, connect to the Adobe site *www.adobe.com*. Visit the Macromedia Web site for information about other multimedia software packages, such as Macromedia Director and Shockwave. Multimedia development training is offered on a number of college campuses, such as California Institute of the Arts, Minneapolis College of Art and Design, and Savannah College of Art and Design. You might check your college's catalog for courses on digital photography, 3-D animation, and special effects. If you would like to try your hand at digital photo editing, you can check out sites such as *www.microsoft.com* (the publisher's site for PhotoDraw 2000) and *www.adobe.com* (the publisher's site for Adobe Photoshop), where you can download trial versions of photo editing software.

12 Anti-piracy

For updates on global software piracy, check the Web sites of the Business Software Alliance (*www.bsa.com*) and The Software and Information Industry Association (formerly the Software Publishers Association) at *www.siia.net*. Because these organizations represent the software industry, their sites also contain plenty of facts and figures that point out the economic and social pitfalls of piracy. For analysis of all sides of the piracy issue, you must look elsewhere. You can enter the search keyword "software piracy" in a Web search engine, then follow the resulting links. You can also check the NP4 Web site for links to other up-to-date articles. What should you do if you discover a software pirate? You can report suspected violations of copyright law to the Business Software Alliance by dialing (888) NOPIRACY or to the SIIA anti-piracy hotline at (800) 388-7478.

CHAPTER 3

DOCUMENTS, WORKSHEETS, AND DATABASES

→ Start Video

PREVIEW

Chapter 3 is filled with tips about working with computerized documents, worksheets, and databases. These tips can help you use software to improve the quality of your work, to get better grades, and to enhance your career. The *User Focus* section explains how to integrate word processing, spreadsheet, database, Web, and presentation software tools to create great reports and presentations.

After you have completed this chapter you should be able to:

■ Discuss and demonstrate how document production software can help you improve the quality of your writing

■ Describe how spreadsheets work and explain how you create, format, and audit a worksheet

■ Discuss your responsibilities for creating accurate worksheets and graphs

■ Differentiate between a structured database and a freeform database

■ Describe the techniques you can use to search for data in databases

■ Describe how to integrate word processing, spreadsheet, and database software

CHAPTER 3 LABS

Computer History   Word Processing   Spreadsheets   Databases

GOOD NEWS, BAD NEWS

The news in 1979 and 1980: The Shah of Iran flees into exile. A partial meltdown at the Three Mile Island nuclear power plant horrifies environmentalists. In Teheran, members of the U.S. embassy are taken hostage and will remain in captivity for over a year. The Mount St. Helens volcano erupts, leveling 120 square miles of Washington State forest. John Lennon is murdered.

For microcomputer owners, however, the news in 1979 and 1980 is more positive. Three super software packages arrive on the market. They quickly become best sellers and form the bedrock of microcomputer software. Computer users gladly tackle the complex interface of the WordStar word processing software so they can create professional-looking documents. VisiCalc, a totally new invention in a category dubbed "spreadsheet software," seems to make it relatively painless for novices to set up complex numerical calculations. A third product, dBase, helps computer users organize their information by creating and maintaining databases.

Lab
Computer History

Word processing, spreadsheet, and database software have been referred to as "the Big Three" and as "productivity software." How do these software packages affect the way you work? Can word processing software improve the quality of your writing? Will spreadsheet software help you enjoy working with numbers? Do you need database software to access information on the Web? Chapter 3 looks at the features and foibles of word processing, spreadsheet, and database software, then wraps up with some tips on how to use these tools together to create dynamic documents and presentations.

DOCUMENTS

Lab
Word
Processing

InfoWeb
1

Literacy

Documents are an integral part of our society and culture. Historical documents, such as the Declaration of Independence and the U.S. Constitution, promote political and social philosophies. Literary documents, such as *To Kill a Mockingbird* and *War and Peace,* record the issues and dilemmas facing societies and cultures. Fiction books entertain. Weekly magazines and daily newspapers provide information on current events. Contracts keep a record of agreements for corporations and individuals.

Despite the popularity of radio, television, and film, documents remain an important component of our everyday lives. Literacy rates reflect the growing importance of reading and writing and seem to correspond to social and economic progress.

As literacy increased throughout the world, the tools of document production changed. Hand-copied manuscripts were produced too slowly to satisfy the demands of a literate populace. The printing press, and later the photocopier, made it easy to produce multiple copies of books, magazines, newspapers, pamphlets, and newsletters. The quill pen was inconvenient because it required the writer to pause every few words to dip the pen into an inkwell. Fountain pens, and later ball-point and felt-tip pens, provided writers with more free-flowing writing tools. The pencil and erasable ink were notable innovations for providing writers with editing capabilities. The typewriter became what might now be called a "personal printing device" and enabled individuals to produce professional-looking documents without using an expensive printing press.

FIGURE 3-1

Throughout history, technology has had a significant impact on document production tools. At one time, pen and ink were considered state-of-the-art document production technologies.

Start
Video

For most of today's document production tasks, computers with document production software have replaced pencils with chewed-up erasers, smudgy ball-point pens, and clacking typewriters. **Document production software** includes word processing software and desktop publishing software. You might also include the software that helps you create e-mail and hypertext documents for the Internet's World Wide Web.

Today, it seems that everyone uses computers to produce documents. Using computers, college students write research papers, elementary school students write short essays, secretaries write memos, grandmothers write thank-you notes, executives write corporate reports, job hunters produce resumes, novelists write books, reporters write news stories, and so on. Should you use a computer for your writing? Check out some good and bad reasons in Figure 3-2 on the next page.

FIGURE 3-2

Good and bad reasons to use a computer for your writing.

Good reasons to use a computer for your writing

- You want to improve the technical aspects of your writing, such as spelling, grammar, and writing style.
- When you proofread your work, you see sections that you know you can improve.
- You have good ideas, but bad handwriting.
- You're a perfectionist.
- You're not a good typist and can't can't afford to hire one.
- You want to post your documents on the Web or e-mail them to friends or colleagues.

Bad reasons to use a computer for your writing

- You never get started until the last minute.
- You're too lazy to proofread your document.
- You want to "borrow" your roommate's report from last semester.
- You hope that your readers will be so impressed with your graphics and layout that they don't read what you have written.

Typing and Keyboarding

Do I really have to know how to type? Typing was once a specialized skill practiced mainly by women in secretarial positions. Today, however, a sizable percentage of the population in highly literate nations has basic typing or "keyboarding" skills. The pervasiveness of keyboarding ability stems from the popularity of computerized document production.

Typing

To use a computer to produce documents, typing on a keyboard is generally required. Surprisingly, typing class enrollments have not increased. Although there are advantages to being a good keyboarder, you don't need to be an expert typist to create documents. Document production software has a variety of features that can help you create error-free documents. Typing tutor software can help you quickly increase your typing speed and accuracy without taking a course. Indeed, you might find that your typing skills quickly improve beyond hunt-and-peck just by using computers on a daily basis.

The Writing Process

Does using a computer change the writing process? Individual writers use different methods for composing documents with a computer, but typically you can begin by using word processing software to type a rough draft of your document. Next, you edit the document until you are satisfied with its content and writing style. Then, you might use your word processing software to format and print the document. Alternatively, you might transfer your document to desktop publishing software to complete the layout and printing.

As you type your document, don't become distracted by how your final product will look. Instead, concentrate on expressing your ideas. Later, when you're satisfied with the content of your document, you can shift your focus to the details of how your document will look on paper.

Word processing software makes it easy to change the wording in a document, but don't fall into the "tweaking trap." Some writers dither around while writing their first draft, trying to perfect each sentence before continuing. Writing instructors suggest that you can produce better documents more quickly if you just let your words flow. When you reach a tricky spot, mark the place with a few question marks or asterisks, then continue. You can return to these spots later and insert the exact words you want to use.

Word processing makes it easy to let your ideas flow because the software automatically handles many tasks. For example, you don't need to worry about fitting words within the margins. With document production software, a feature called **word wrap** determines how your text will flow from line to line by automatically moving words down to the next line as you reach the right margin. Imagine that the sentences in your document are ribbons of text; word wrap bends the ribbons. Changing the margin size just means bending the ribbon in different places. Even after you've typed an entire document, adjusting the size of your right, left, top, and bottom margins is simple.

FIGURE 3-3

The late Isaac Asimov was one of this century's most prolific writers. When describing the writing process, he said, "My routine was (and still is) to write a story in its first draft as fast as I can. Then I go over it, and correct errors in spelling, grammar, and word order."

Improving the Quality of Your Writing

Does document production software improve writing quality? Computers have been accused of dumping a mountain of poor-quality documents into circulation. To anyone who reads electronic mail, it soon becomes painfully clear that many literate people still have trouble with spelling and grammar. Some observers characterize the material exchanged in online discussions and newsgroups as crude, silly, uninformed, and self-serving. This criticism implies that instead of helping writers, computers have somehow lowered literary standards.

Perhaps much of this criticism is misplaced. After all, pulp fiction lined bookstore shelves long before computers graced the drawing boards of IBM and Apple. In any case, people—not computers—create documents. Those spelling errors, grammatical blunders, incoherent arguments, and unverified assertions are probably attributable to human fallibility, rather than to some computer-sponsored plot to subvert literature.

InfoWeb 3

Improve Your Writing

When used skillfully, computerized document production tools can help you improve the quality of your writing. With such tools, it is easy to create the first draft of a document, refine its overall organization, then zero in to make detailed improvements to sentence structure and word usage. You can easily insert text, cut sections of text, and move entire paragraphs or pages to improve the structure and logical flow of a document. In document production terminology, sections of your document are sometimes referred to as **text blocks**.

Although document production software simplifies block operations, such as moving and deleting paragraphs, you first need to decide how to arrange, and perhaps rearrange, your document to present an effective progression of ideas. Some writers find that the limited amount of text displayed on the screen prevents them from getting a good look at the overall flow of ideas throughout the document. One solution is to use the outline feature of your software.

An **outline feature** helps you develop a document as a hierarchy of headings and sub-headings. This textbook, for example, is structured into a series of chapters, sections, and subsections. When you create a hierarchical document, you "tag" each heading to identify whether it starts a chapter, section, or subsection. To get an overall view of the document, use your software to show only the chapter headings. To view the structure in more detail, use the outline feature to display the chapter headings and the section headings. When you move a heading in outline view, the outline feature automatically moves all of its subheadings and paragraphs.

As an alternative to using the outline feature, you might try a time-tested, but low-tech technique that works for creative writing as well as hierarchically structured documents. Print out your first draft, then cut it into pieces, paragraph by paragraph. Spread these paragraphs out on the floor and rearrange them until you're satisfied that you have the most logical, effective, and compelling organization. Finally, you can use the cut and paste commands of your software to move text blocks and duplicate your new organization.

Once you have taken care of the overall structure of your document, you can turn to the details of word usage, spelling, and grammar. For example, you might use your software's **thesaurus** to find more descriptive words to clarify and enliven your writing.

Some writers know that they tend to overuse certain words or use them incorrectly. For instance, you might tend to overuse the word "however." You could use your software's **search feature** to hunt for all occurrences of this problem word. For each occurrence, you can decide to leave it or revise it. A variation of this feature, called **search and replace**, is handy if you want to substitute one word or phrase for another. For example, after you finish the first draft of a short story, you might change a character's name by using search and replace to change every occurrence of "Tim" to "Jeff."

Now, what about spelling? A document with spelling errors reflects poorly on the writer. Most document production tools, including newer e-mail editors, have some type of spelling checker. As you type, an **in-line spelling checker** marks errors with a colored background or wavy underline. You can backspace and correct the error manually, or you can click the misspelled word and then select from a list of correctly spelled options.

If you do not want to hassle with spelling while you concentrate on composition, an alternative spelling checker looks through your entire document any time you activate it. You would generally use this type of spelling checker (shown in Figure 3-4) when you have completed your first draft, then again just before you print.

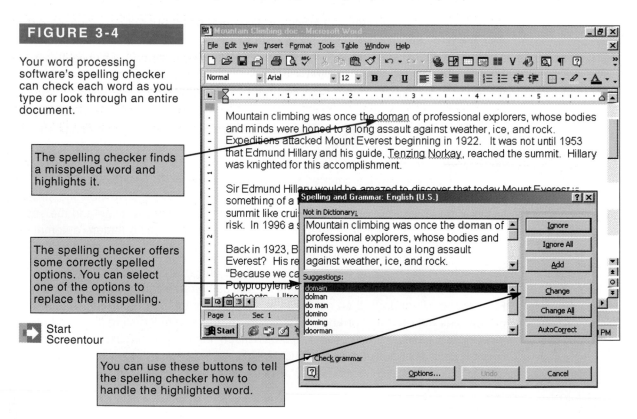

FIGURE 3-4

Your word processing software's spelling checker can check each word as you type or look through an entire document.

The spelling checker finds a misspelled word and highlights it.

The spelling checker offers some correctly spelled options. You can select one of the options to replace the misspelling.

Start Screentour

You can use these buttons to tell the spelling checker how to handle the highlighted word.

Although your software's spelling checker helps you correct misspellings, it cannot guarantee an error-free document. A spelling checker works by looking for each word from your document in an online list called a "spelling dictionary." If the word from your document is in the dictionary, the spelling checker considers the word correctly spelled. If the word is not in the dictionary, the word is counted as misspelled. Sounds OK, right? But, suppose your document contains a reference to the city of "Negaunee." This word is not in the dictionary, so the spelling checker considers it misspelled, even though it is spelled correctly. The spelling checker might even suggest that you change the word to "negate"—a word that does appear in the dictionary. Proper nouns and scientific, medical, and technical words are likely to be flagged as misspelled, even if you have spelled them correctly because they do not appear in the spelling checker's dictionary. If you plan to use such words often, you can add them to the dictionary.

Now suppose that your document contains the phrase "a pear of shoes." Although you meant to use "pair" rather than "pear," the spelling checker will not catch your mistake because "pear" is a valid word in the dictionary. Your spelling checker won't help if you have trouble deciding whether to use "there" or "their," "its" or "it's," or "too" or "to." Remember, then, that a spelling check cannot substitute for a thorough proofread.

InfoWeb
4
Grammar

All languages are complex. English, for example, is characterized by many linguists as having an exception to every rule. You can clear up many grammatical questions by using a **grammar checker**, a feature of most word processing software that coaches you on correct sentence structure and word usage. Think of a grammar checker as an assistant that will help you proofread a document by pointing out potential trouble spots and suggesting alternatives.

A grammar checker will not change your document for you. Instead, it highlights possible problems, suggests alternate words or phrases, and gives you the option of making changes. For example, if a document contains the sentence "The design team was never hesitant to accept these sort of assignments," then a grammar checker might point out that you should consider using "sorts" instead of "sort." Refer to Figure 3-5.

FIGURE 3-5

A grammar checker points out possible grammar errors, and might suggest alternatives.

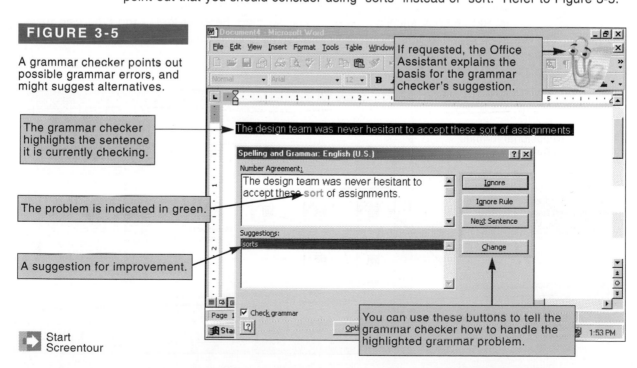

The grammar checker highlights the sentence it is currently checking.

The problem is indicated in green.

A suggestion for improvement.

If requested, the Office Assistant explains the basis for the grammar checker's suggestion.

You can use these buttons to tell the grammar checker how to handle the highlighted grammar problem.

Start
Screentour

CHAPTER 3

Formatting a Document

How does document production software help create documents that look great? Before the printing press, documents were hand-copied. In the Middle Ages, artists and monks huddled in cavernous rooms called "scriptoria" to painstakingly hand-copy religious documents. Many of these hand-copied documents, called "illuminated manuscripts," were works of art in addition to a means of communicating information. These manuscripts often contained illustrations, elaborately detailed initial letters on each page, and decorative borders. Most of these manuscripts were commissioned by wealthy aristocrats. Figure 3-6 shows a page from an illuminated manuscript.

FIGURE 3-6

Illuminated manuscripts, such as this one from the Vatican library, were hand-crafted works of art.

Today, beautifully crafted documents are no longer a special perk of wealth. Modern printing techniques make it cost-effective to mass-produce documents that are available to everyone in libraries, bookstores, and newsstands. In addition, today's document production software provides individuals with the tools necessary to produce professionally formatted and illustrated documents. When you create documents, you'll want to take advantage of formatting tools such as document templates, wizards, fonts, styles, borders, and clip art.

A **document template** is a preformatted document into which you type your text. Most document production software encourages you to select a template before you type the text for your first draft. If you don't select a template, the software will select one for you—usually a plain template suitable for letters and reports. In a document template, format settings such as margins, line spacing, heading fonts, and type size have all been set up for you. Figure 3-7 shows some of the document templates typically available with today's word processing software.

FIGURE 3-7

Document templates provide preset professional formats for your documents.

Template categories include letters and faxes, memos, reports, and Web pages.

Within each category, you can choose from several templates.

A preview window displays an example of a document created using the selected template.

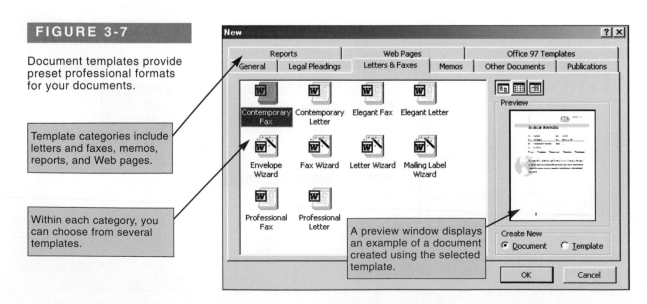

You might wonder if selecting a template before you begin to type contradicts the conventional advice to ignore formatting issues for your first draft. In practice, you'll want to select a template before you type and perhaps format your headings as you type. You can postpone the rest of your formatting activities until you're satisfied with the content.

Some software goes a step beyond templates by furnishing **document wizards** that not only provide you with a document format, but also provide step-by-step guidance on the process of entering the text for a wide variety of documents. You might want to check out the templates and wizards provided by your software before you struggle with creating your own formats. For example, to create an entry-level resume, you might find it easy to use a resume wizard like the one shown in Figure 3-8.

CHAPTER 3

FIGURE 3-8

Document wizards can help you with the content and format for a variety of documents, such as an entry-level resume.

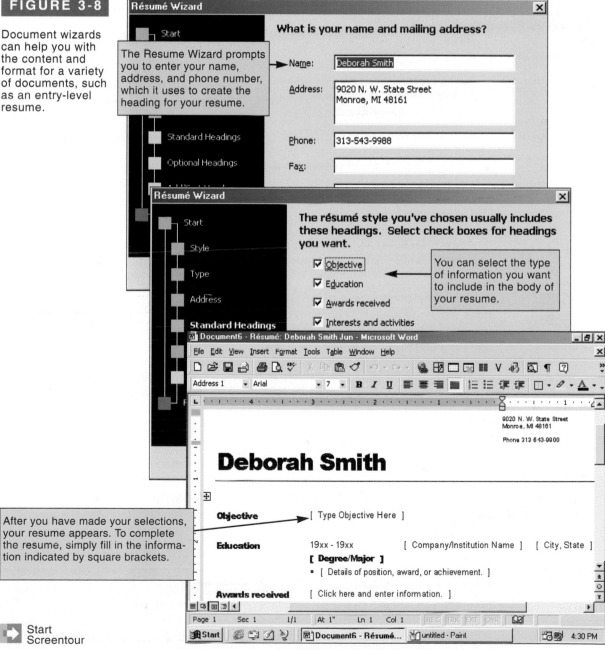

The Resume Wizard prompts you to enter your name, address, and phone number, which it uses to create the heading for your resume.

You can select the type of information you want to include in the body of your resume.

After you have made your selections, your resume appears. To complete the resume, simply fill in the information indicated by square brackets.

Start
Screentour

InfoWeb
5

Fonts

The font you select has a major effect on the look of your document. A **font** is a specific type design, such as Arial, Times New Roman, Gothic, Courier, or Commercial Script. Your document production software generally supplies many fonts. If you want even more variety, you can purchase and install additional font collections. Typeset fonts such as Times New Roman and Arial make your document look formal and professionally produced. Research studies show that serif fonts are easier to read on the printed page, whereas sans serif fonts are easier to read on a computer screen. In addition, a kerned font is easier to read than a monospaced font. Figure 3-9 explains the difference between a serif and a sans serif font, and the difference between a kerned font and a monospaced font.

FIGURE 3-9	Font serifs and kerning can affect the look and readability of your documents.	
Font Treatment	**Description**	**Example**
Serif	A serif font has embellishments called "serifs" on the ends of the lines that form the characters.	Look at this!
Sans Serif	A sans-serif font lacks serifs.	Look at this!
Kerned	A kerned font provides a wider space for wide letters, such as the "w," but reduces the amount of space allotted to narrow letters, such as "t."	wwwww ttttt
Monospaced	Each character in a monospaced font takes up the same amount of space.	wwwww t t t t t

To give your document a more personal appeal, you can use simulated handwriting fonts . You can also mix handwriting fonts with more conventional, typeset fonts. Some companies will convert a sample of your handwriting into your own handwritten font for use on a computer.

In addition to selecting fonts, you can manipulate the look of your document by adjusting the line spacing, margins, indents, tabs, borders, and frames. Additional space makes a document easier to read. Larger margins and double-spacing generate white space, make your document appear less dense, and make reading seem easier. The margins for most papers and reports should be set at 1 inch or 1.5 inches.

Justification defines how the letters and words are spaced across each line. Typeset documents are often fully justified so that the text is aligned evenly on both the right and left margins, like the text on this page. Your document will look more formal if it is fully justified, rather than if it has an uneven or "ragged" right margin.

Columns enhance readability and tables organize data. In document production terminology, columns generally mean a newspaper-style layout of paragraphs of text. Tables arrange data in a grid of rows and columns. Tables are more appropriate than columns for numeric data and for lists of information. For example, to create a "two-column" resume, you should use the table function in your word processing software. Don't waste your time trying to arrange columns or tables using the Tab key and spacebar. Instead, use your software's automatic column format feature or table feature.

When you summarize or list information, or even when you type your answers to homework questions, your points will stand out if you use hanging indents, bulleted lists, or numbered lists, as shown in Figure 3-10.

FIGURE 3-10

A hanging indent makes numbered points stand out.

The number is positioned at the left margin.

The hanging indent text is aligned under the tab stop, not at the left margin.

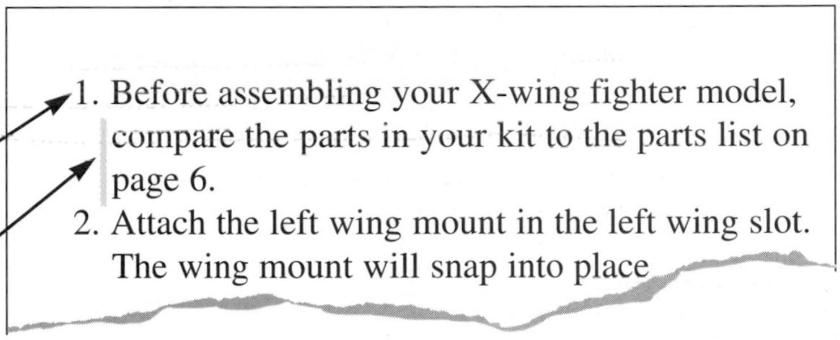

1. Before assembling your X-wing fighter model, compare the parts in your kit to the parts list on page 6.
2. Attach the left wing mount in the left wing slot. The wing mount will snap into place

To add visual interest to documents, you can incorporate borders, rules, and graphics. A border is a box around text or graphics—usually around a title, heading, or table. A rule is a line, which is usually positioned under text. Rules can be horizontal, vertical, or diagonal. The thinnest rule is one pixel thick or less and is called a "hairline rule."

Graphics are pictures and illustrations. **Clip art** collections provide hundreds of graphics that you can insert into documents. You can find clip art on CD-ROMs and the Internet. With the right equipment, you can also scan pictures from books and magazines, then add them to your documents. Just be sure to check for permission before you use clip art or other people's graphics in your documents.

Most document production software uses frames as containers for graphics. A **frame** is an invisible box that you can position anywhere on a page. Generally, you can flow text around the frame and layer frames one on top of another to achieve complex layout effects, like those shown in Figure 3-11.

FIGURE 3-11

Frames act as containers for text and graphics.

A frame can contain graphics or text.

A frame can be positioned anywhere on the page—even in the top margin.

Frames allow you to produce eye-catching layouts—for example, by wrapping text around a frame.

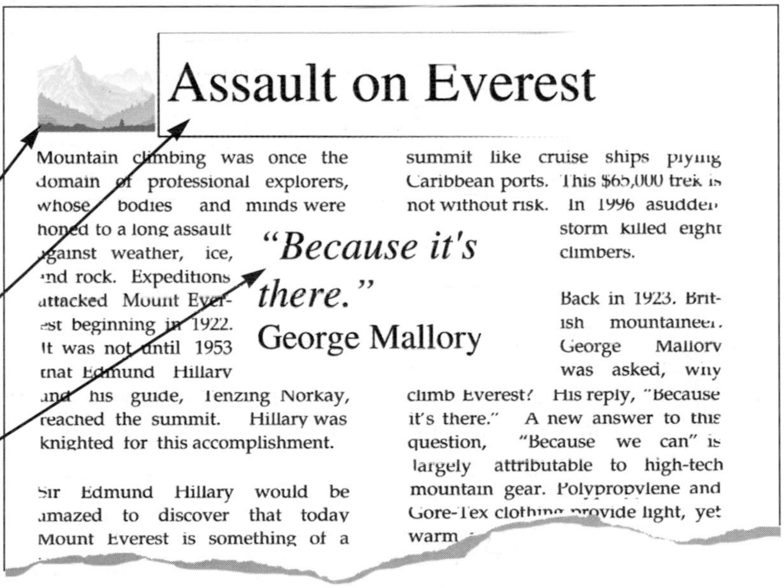

Assault on Everest

Mountain climbing was once the domain of professional explorers, whose bodies and minds were honed to a long assault against weather, ice, and rock. Expeditions attacked Mount Everest beginning in 1922. It was not until 1953 that Edmund Hillary and his guide, Tenzing Norkay, reached the summit. Hillary was knighted for this accomplishment.

Sir Edmund Hillary would be amazed to discover that today Mount Everest is something of a

"Because it's there."
George Mallory

summit like cruise ships plying Caribbean ports. This $65,000 trek is not without risk. In 1996 a sudden storm killed eight climbers.

Back in 1923, British mountaineer George Mallory was asked, why climb Everest? His reply, "Because it's there." A new answer to this question, "Because we can" is largely attributable to high-tech mountain gear. Polypropylene and Gore-Tex clothing provide light, yet warm

Paper and Electronic Publishing

What are the options for printing and publishing documents? Printing with movable type existed in Asia as early as 1000 A.D. However, until Johann Gutenberg demonstrated his printing press in 1448, this technology did not exist in Europe. The printing press had a massive effect on Western culture by making information available to all who could read. Publications spread ideas and have been instrumental in the development of many social, political, and religious movements.

FIGURE 3-12

Thomas Paine harnessed the power of the printed word in 1776 when he sold 500,000 copies of a 50-page pamphlet, *Common Sense*. This document asserted that it was just common sense for the American colonies to become independent from Great Britain. Six months later, the Declaration of Independence was signed.

American revolutionary Thomas Paine and his compatriot, Thomas Jefferson, envisioned a free press as the cornerstone of a free society. They believed that publishing would spread ideas, foster dialog between diverse interest groups, and help to establish a common social agenda. Putting their beliefs to the test, Paine and Jefferson published documents such as *Common Sense* to spread ideas about democracy and freedom.

Early expectations were that computerized document production would make it easy for individuals, not just publishing companies, to produce professional-quality books and pamphlets. Technology has made it possible for individuals to create many more documents, such as newsletters and manuscripts. Nevertheless, computerized document production technology has had only a moderate effect on traditional paper-based publishing. If you assumed that this technology would produce a huge glut of new books, think again. Although computers help produce documents faster, the cost of paper and the economics of distribution still limit the number of books published each year.

InfoWeb
6

Publishing

One of the most significant effects of computerized document production came as a somewhat unexpected surprise. The Internet has opened up amazing new opportunities for **electronic publishing**. Today, it is old-fashioned to think of a computer as just a place to store information before it is committed to paper. Once a document is in electronic format, why not keep it there? Electronic documents are easy to send, store, and manipulate. They might even bring us closer to the global democracy that Thomas Paine envisioned. Today, virtually anyone can post a document on the World Wide Web, send an e-mail message, or participate in online discussion groups. The power of the printed word seems to be evolving into the power of the electronically published word.

The Internet provides a powerful communications channel for disseminating many kinds of information. A single e-mail letter can be sent to hundreds of recipients and forwarded from those recipients to hundreds more. Political pamphlets and position papers can be linked to popular search sites such as Yahoo! For individuals, organizations, and special-interest groups that cannot afford to produce paper publications, the Internet provides a low-cost means of distributing ideas and other information.

FIGURE 3-13

Many activists believed that certain provisions of the U.S. Telecommunications Act of 1996 would limit freedom of speech on the Internet. Activists organized massive protests on electronic forums and supported a well-engineered lawsuit. The Supreme Court eventually declared that many parts of the Act were unconstitutional.

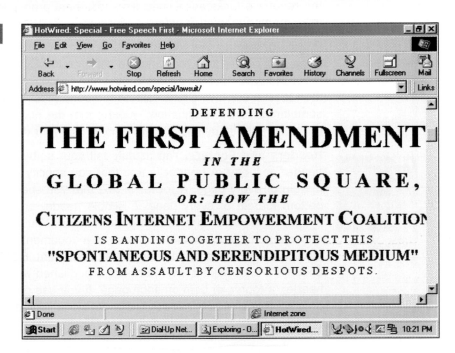

Suppose that you want to publish a document on the Web for all the world to see. Before you can post a document on the Web, it must be converted into a Web-compatible format, such as HTML. **HTML** (hypertext markup language) is a set of codes or "tags" that you can insert into a document. These HTML tags provide a standardized way of handling text and graphics so that the pages of your document can be viewed using a Web browser such as Microsoft Internet Explorer or Netscape Navigator.

Most word processing and desktop publishing software provides a feature that converts documents into HTML format. You would usually find this feature as a menu option, perhaps labeled "Save as HTML." You would write your document as usual and save it just as for any normal project. When the document is complete, you would use the Save as HTML option to save an HTML version of your document. Saving a document in HTML format does not, however, typically place it on the Web for public access. To actually post a document on the Web, you must transfer your HTML file to a Web site. This process differs from one Web site to the next. For specific details on how to post a document, you would check with the Webmaster at your school, office, or local Internet service provider (ISP).

Automating Document Production

How can I harness the power of a computer to automate document production tasks? Computers are quite talented when it comes to repetitive tasks such as counting, numbering, searching, and duplicating. Document production software makes clever use of the computer's talents in these areas to automate many of the repetitive tasks associated with document production. Automating such tasks can save time and increase your productivity.

Page Numbering. As you edit a document and change its format, you might remove large sections of text, reducing the page count. Or, your professor or publisher might insist that you double-space the document, doubling the page count. It makes sense then to let the software take care of numbering your pages. Automatic page numbering, sometimes called "pagination," means that the computer automatically numbers and renumbers the pages as you edit and format your document.

InfoWeb 7

Who Wrote It?

Headers and Footers. You usually tell your software to include page numbers in a header or footer. A **header** is text that you specify to automatically appear in the top margin of every page. A **footer** is text that you specify to automatically appear in the bottom margin of every page. A simple header or footer might consist of the word "Page," followed by the current page number. You might also put your name and the document title in the header or footer of a document so that its printed pages won't get mixed up with those of another printed document. Headers and footers help identify a document and make it look more like a published work. Published books often have a header, a footer, or both on each page. If you use document production software, your documents can easily have these professional elements.

FIGURE 3-14

Using concordance techniques, Joe Klein, was identified as the mystery author of *Primary Colors*.

Word Count. Does your English professor want a 1,000-word essay? Your document production software can easily count the words in a document so that you can check the length of an essay or any other document. Another use for a computer's ability to count words is for literary analysis. A **concordance** is an alphabetized list of words in a document and the frequency with which each word appears. Concordance has been used to determine the authorship of historical and contemporary documents by comparing the frequencies of words used in a document by an unknown author with the frequencies of words used in a document of known authorship. The anonymously authored novel, *Primary Colors*, was widely speculated to be based on behind-the-scenes wheeling and dealing during Bill Clinton's first presidential campaign. Vassar professor Donald Foster used concordance techniques to compare the text of *Primary Colors* to a series of columns written by journalist Joe Klein. Mr. Klein later admitted his authorship of the book.

Readability Formulas. Most grammar checkers use readability formulas to identify the reading level required to understand a document. You can use this readability information to target your writing to your audience. The longer your sentences and words, the higher the reading level required to understand your writing. Most writers aim for a seventh- or eighth-grade reading level on documents intended for the general public.

Index and Table of Contents. Longer documents benefit from having an index and table of contents. Because of document production technology, many people expect that all long documents—not just those created by professional publishers—will include these elements. Most document production software can automatically generate an index and table of contents, then automatically update them as you edit your document.

Mail Merge. The process of creating a series of personalized letters by combining the information in a mailing list with a blank form letter is called **mail merge**. Most word processing software provides mail merge capabilities. A mail merge requires two documents: one containing your mailing list, and another containing a form letter. Your mailing list is simply a list of names and addresses typed as a single column. Your form letter is a document that includes specially marked containers for a name, address, or other information from the mailing list. The way you create these containers varies from one word processor to another, so you should refer to your software documentation for specific instructions. Once you have created the documents that contain your mailing list and form letter, you can initiate the merge routine, which enters one name and address on each letter, then prints it. Figure 3-15 further explains this process.

CHAPTER 3

FIGURE 3-15

To set up a mail merge, you create a document containing specially marked containers. You also create a file of information that goes in the containers each time the document is printed. Your document production software will merge the document and the information.

➡ Start Animation

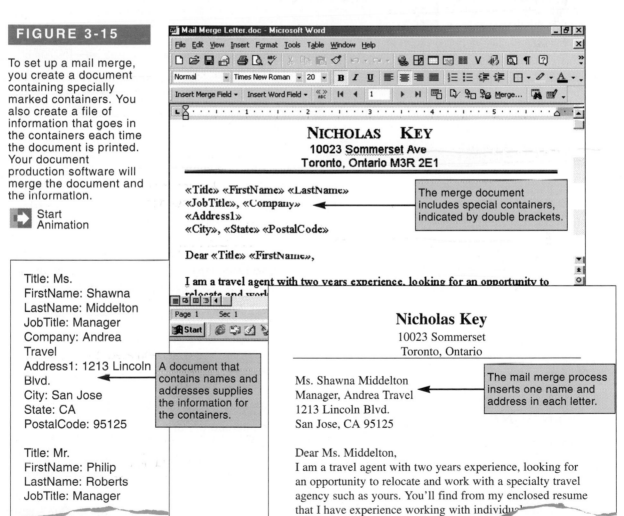

The merge document includes special containers, indicated by double brackets.

A document that contains names and addresses supplies the information for the containers.

The mail merge process inserts one name and address in each letter.

Title: Ms.
FirstName: Shawna
LastName: Middelton
JobTitle: Manager
Company: Andrea Travel
Address1: 1213 Lincoln Blvd.
City: San Jose
State: CA
PostalCode: 95125

Title: Mr.
FirstName: Philip
LastName: Roberts
JobTitle: Manager

Footnotes. Scholarly documents often require numbered footnotes that contain citations for works mentioned in the text. As you revise a document, the footnotes need to stay associated with their source in the text and must be numbered sequentially. Most document production software includes footnoting facilities that correctly position and number the footnotes even if you move blocks of text. But what if you need endnotes instead of footnotes? Your software can gather your citations at the end of your document and print them in order of their appearance in the document or in alphabetical order. Some word processors even have wizards that help you enter your citations in the correct format, depending on whether the citations are books or magazine articles.

FIGURE 3-16

Your word processing software can help you number footnotes and adjust the layout of text in your document so that the footnote appears on the the same page as its reference number.

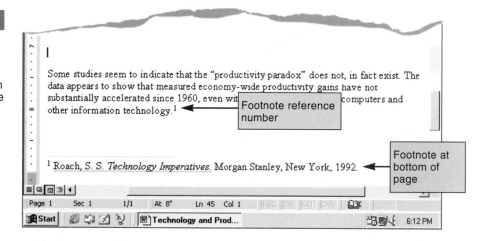

QUICKCHECK   A

1 The spread of literacy went hand-in-hand with technology developments, culminating in today's use of computers and document [Production] software.

2 When you type a document, it is best not to get distracted by how the final product will look. Instead, you should concentrate on expressing your ideas. True or false? [   ]

3 A feature of word processing software called [word wrap] takes care of where to break lines of text.

4 The spelling checker feature of word processing software would alert you if you accidentally used the word "see" instead of "sea" when referring to a large body of water. True or false? [   ]

5 A(n) [template] *(document)* provides preset formats for a document, whereas a(n) [wizard] is a feature that coaches you step-by-step through the process of entering text into a document.

6 One of the most significant effects of computerized document production has been to encourage [electronic] publishing.

7 [Concordance] has been used to establish the authorship of historical and contemporary documents.

8 Documents that are posted on the World Wide Web must be in [HTML] format.

 Check Answers

SECTION B — SPREADSHEETS AND WORKSHEETS

Mathephobia /maθ(ə) 'fəʊbɪə/ mathe after Fr *mathematiques* the abstract deductive science of number and quantity + phobia L f. Gk, f. *phobos* denoting fear, dislike, antipathy as in hope to never take another math class.

Lab
Spreadsheets

The United States is one of the most technological societies on earth. Therefore, the population's resistance to math, as evidenced by standardized test scores, is somewhat surprising. People with mathephobia hate to balance their checkbooks, calculate their tax returns, work out expense budgets, or decide what to do about financing their retirement.

Sensing financial opportunity, entrepreneurs have devised a number of tools to ease the burden of making calculations. To date, the most ambitious of these tools is the computerized spreadsheet. A **spreadsheet** is a numerical model or representation of a real situation. For example, your checkbook register is a sort of spreadsheet because it is a numerical representation of the cash flowing in and out of your bank account.

FIGURE 3-17

Your checkbook register is an example of a manual spreadsheet—it is essentially a numeric model of your checking account activity.

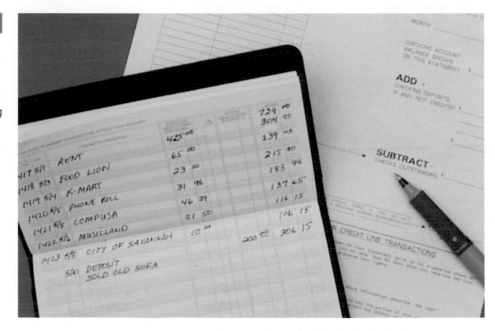

Today, the term "spreadsheet" usually refers to the data for numerical models that are created and stored on a computer by a person using spreadsheet software. One expert describes spreadsheets as "intuitive, natural, usable tools for financial analysis, business and mathematical modeling, decision making, simulation, and problem solving."

Imagine a "smart" piece of paper that automatically adds up the columns of numbers that you write on it. Your smart paper can make other calculations, too, based on simple equations that you write. Computerized spreadsheets can do all this and more.

The Spreadsheet Advantage

Is spreadsheet software better than a hand-held calculator? Using spreadsheet software is fairly straightforward. You enter the numbers you want to calculate and then indicate how the computer should manipulate those numbers. For example, you can follow the instructions on the back of your bank statement to reconcile your checkbook balance with the balance on your bank statement, as shown in Figure 3-18.

FIGURE 3-18

Spreadsheet software displays all of the numbers on screen so that you can keep track of what you've entered, as well as the results of your calculations.

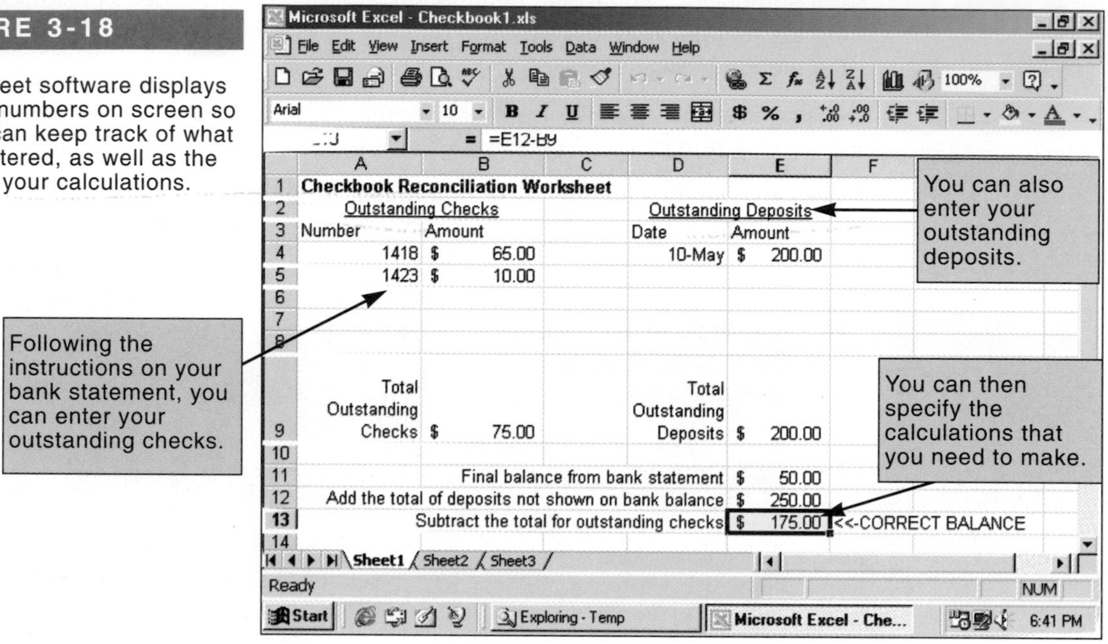

Following the instructions on your bank statement, you can enter your outstanding checks.

You can also enter your outstanding deposits.

You can then specify the calculations that you need to make.

A hand-held calculator might be useful for simple calculations, but it becomes less convenient as you deal with more numbers and as your calculations get more complex. For example, when balancing your checkbook with a hand-held calculator, you'll probably have to make the calculation in stages. You'll first total your cleared checks and jot down the amount on paper. Next, you'll total your deposits and jot down that amount. Finally, you'll re-enter these amounts to compute the actual balance for the account.

The biggest disadvantage of most calculators is that the numbers you entered are stored, but you can't see them. You can't verify their accuracy. Also, it is difficult to change the numbers that you have entered without redoing the entire calculation. By contrast, if you use spreadsheet software, all of your numbers are visible on the screen, and they are easy to change. You can print your results as a nicely formatted report, convert your numbers into a graph, and save your work and revise it later. You can easily incorporate your calculations and results into other electronic documents, post them as Web pages, and e-mail them to your colleagues.

Spreadsheet Basics

What does a computerized spreadsheet look like? A company that publishes spreadsheet software estimates that today more than 20 million people in the world are busily using spreadsheets. Certainly, this software has had a major effect on the way people work with numbers. What's the big attraction? To answer this question, it's important to understand how spreadsheets work.

You use spreadsheet software to create a type of on-screen spreadsheet called a **worksheet**. A worksheet is based on a grid of columns and rows. Each column is lettered and each row is numbered. The intersection of a column and row is called a **cell**. Each cell has a unique **cell reference** or "address" derived from its column and row location. For example, A1 is the cell reference for the upper-left cell in a worksheet because it is in column A and row 1.

A cell can contain a number, text, or formula. A **number** is a value that you want to use in a calculation. **Text** is used for the worksheet title and for the labels that identify the numbers. For example, suppose that your worksheet contains the number $2,559.81. You could use text to identify this number as "Income." A **formula** tells the computer how to use the contents of cells in calculations. You can use formulas to add, subtract, multiply, and divide numbers. Figure 3-19 illustrates a simple spreadsheet that performs subtraction to calculate savings.

FIGURE 3-19

A typical worksheet displays numbers and text in a grid of rows and columns. Cell B6 contains the result of a calculation performed by the spreadsheet software.

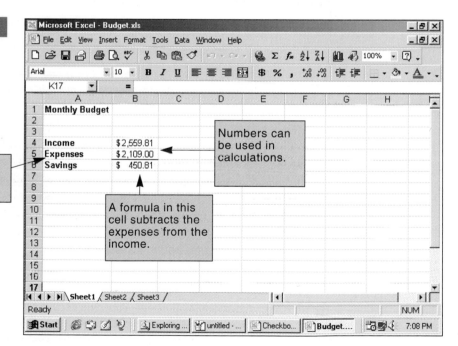

Text labels describe your data.

Numbers can be used in calculations.

A formula in this cell subtracts the expenses from the income.

 Start
Screentour

Calculations

How does spreadsheet software work? The value of spreadsheet software lies in the way it handles the numbers and formulas in a worksheet. Think of the worksheet as having two layers—the layer you see and a hidden layer underneath. The hidden layer can hold formulas, but the result of these formulas appears on the visible layer. Figure 3-20 shows how this process works.

FIGURE 3-20

The formula =B4-B5 works behind the scenes to tell the computer to subtract the number in cell B5 from the number in cell B4. The formula is located in cell B6, but what appears in cell B6 is not the formula but rather its results.

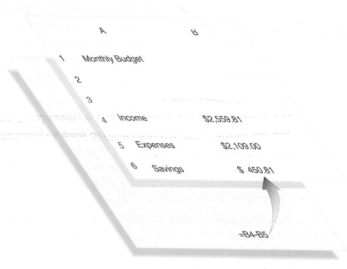

Whenever you add or change something in a cell, the spreadsheet recalculates all of the formulas. Consequently, the results displayed on a worksheet always reflect the current figures contained in the cells.

Formulas typically begin with an equal sign and include references to other cells. These references allow you to easily change your data and recalculate results. For example, if you have a formula that says "subtract the contents of cell B5 from the contents of B4," it doesn't matter what those cells contain. The result will be accurate even if you later change the contents of these cells. Using cell references such as B5 and B4, you can create generic formulas such as =B4-B5 that work no matter how many times you change the data in cells B4 and B5. This aspect of computerized spreadsheets means that you can reuse worksheets, instead of recreating them. For example, you can use the same checkbook worksheet month after month by simply entering the amounts for new checks and deposits.

When you construct a worksheet, you can enter your own formulas to specify how to carry out calculations. As another option, you can select a predefined formula called a **function**. Suppose that you've got a research assignment and you need to find the standard deviation of test scores for a school district. You can't find your old statistics textbook. No problem. Your spreadsheet software has a built-in function to calculate standard deviations. You simply enter the test scores in a series of cells and tell the computer to use the standard deviation function for the calculation. Most spreadsheet software includes hundreds of functions for mathematical, financial, date, and statistical calculations.

Creating a Simple Worksheet

How do I create a simple worksheet? Building a worksheet from scratch requires thought and planning so that you end up with an accurate and well-organized worksheet. When you create your own worksheets, use these steps as guidelines:

InfoWeb 8

Spreadsheet Tips

1. **Visualize your worksheet.** Make sure that you have a clear idea of the worksheet's purpose, then make a list of the calculations that you'll need. For example, checkbook reconciliation calculations include adding the total amount of outstanding deposits to the bank balance and subtracting the total amount of outstanding checks. Also, try to picture how your data will fit in columns and rows. Think about which labels you'll use across the top of the worksheet and which labels you'll use down the left side.

2. **Enter numbers and labels in the cells, then enter the formulas.** When you enter the numbers, make sure you put a descriptive label in an adjoining cell, usually to the left of the data. It's also a good idea to include a title at the top of the worksheet.

3. **Format the worksheet.** To improve readability, you might want to increase the font size of titles and boldface key labels. You can use color to emphasize numbers and results, create graphs from your data, and add graphics.

4. **Test the worksheet.** Later in this chapter, you'll learn about various ways to test a worksheet, but the first question to ask yourself is, "Do these results make sense?" If the results shown on the worksheet don't seem to be "in the ballpark" of what you expected, perhaps you've made a typo when entering a formula. Check your numbers and formulas and make revisions until the worksheet produces correct results.

5. **Save and print the worksheet.** Figure 3-21 provides some tips to help you create a professional-looking worksheet.

CHAPTER 3

FIGURE 3-21

As a rule of thumb, most worksheets should have a title, documentation, and a layout that makes it easy to understand the calculations.

Every worksheet should have a title.

Documentation helps you keep track of revisions and explains how the sheet was created, in case someone else needs to revise it.

Data is usually organized in vertical columns.

Lines called "cell borders" help divide the worksheet into sections.

You can use bold, italics, and colors to highlight important data.

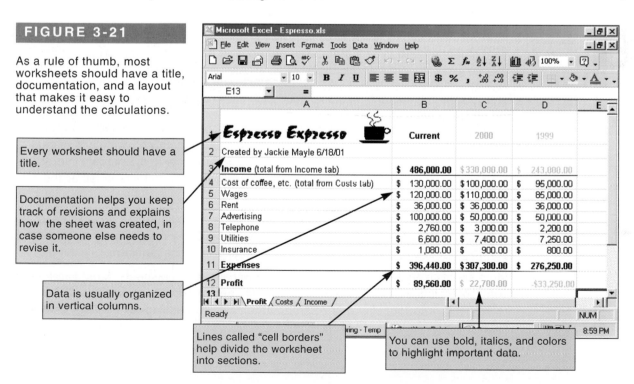

Worksheet Templates

What if I'm not sure how to set up a worksheet? If you have trouble creating a worksheet from scratch, you might find a predefined template that meets your needs. A **worksheet template** is a worksheet form created by spreadsheet professionals who have already developed the formats and formulas for you. To use a template, simply select the one you want and then fill in your numbers. Popular spreadsheet programs typically offer templates for the following tasks:

- Tracking a household budget
- Deciding on the best car lease option
- Creating a business plan
- Invoicing customers
- Providing customers with sales quotes

- Creating purchase orders
- Calculating monthly loan payments
- Recording business expenses while you travel
- Tracking the time you work on various projects

Who's Responsible?

How do I know if my spreadsheet is producing correct results? The United States has more lawyers per capita than any other country in the world. In a society where lawsuits seem as common as weddings, it might be prudent to consider who is responsible for the accuracy of a spreadsheet. For example, whose fault is it when a project runs over budget because the formula to total up the costs was not accurate?

Spreadsheet
Errors

In a well-publicized case, a company discovered that an incomplete worksheet formula resulted in a loss of several hundreds of thousands of dollars. The company sued the spreadsheet publisher, claiming that the software was faulty. The lawsuit was dropped. Responsibility for the accuracy of a worksheet lies with the person who creates it.

In a business situation, an error in a worksheet formula can cost a company a great deal of money. But even if the stakes are not that high for the worksheets you create, you should still verify the accuracy of your data and formulas. The prime directive of worksheet design is "Don't rely on your worksheet until you test it." Testing, called **auditing** in spreadsheet jargon, is important.

To test a worksheet, enter some test data for which you already know the result. For example, if you are designing a worksheet to calculate monthly payments for a car loan, use a loan table to find the actual payment for a $12,000 car at 8.5 percent interest on a three-year loan. Then enter this data into your worksheet and see whether the result matches the actual payment.

Another test strategy is to enter simple data that you can figure out "in your head." For example, if you were creating the Espresso worksheet shown previously in Figure 3-21, you might test it by entering "1" for all income and expense numbers.

More sophisticated tests are required for more complex worksheets. Most spreadsheet software includes auditing features to help you find references to empty cells, cells not referenced, and formulas that reference themselves, causing an endless calculating loop.

Modifying Worksheets

Can I modify my spreadsheets? Modifying the text, numbers, and formulas on a worksheet is as easy as using a word processor's insert and delete features. As soon as you enter new numbers in a worksheet, the computer recalculates all formulas, keeping the results up-to-date.

You can modify the structure of a worksheet by inserting rows and columns, deleting rows and columns, or moving the contents of cells to other cells. Many inexperienced spreadsheet users might hesitate to make such structural changes. Why? Suppose you've created a spreadsheet and tested all of its formulas. You decide to delete row 3, which is currently blank. All labels, numbers, and formulas move up one row. But what's happened to the formula that previously referenced cells B4 and B5? Now those numbers have moved up to cells B3 and B4. Do you have to revise all of the formulas on your worksheet? Happily, the answer is no.

When you insert, delete, or move cells, the spreadsheet software attempts to adjust your formulas so that the cell references they contain are still accurate. Unless you specify otherwise, a cell reference is a **relative reference**—that is, a reference that can change from B4 to B3, for example, if the data in column B moves up one row.

What if you don't want a cell reference to change? You can define any reference in a formula as an absolute reference. An **absolute reference** never changes when you insert rows or copy or move formulas. Understanding when to use absolute references is one of the key aspects to developing spreadsheet design expertise. Figure 3-22 and its associated Screentour provide some additional information about relative and absolute references.

FIGURE 3-22

Spreadsheet software adjusts formulas when you insert, move, or delete cells.

	A	B
1	**Monthly Budget**	
2		
3		
4	**Income**	$2,559.81
5	**Expenses**	$2,109.00
6	**Savings**	$ 450.81
7		

= B4-B5

A formula in cell B6 calculates savings based on numbers in cells B4 and B5.

	A	B
1	**Monthly Budget**	
2		
3	**Income**	$2,559.81
4	**Expenses**	$2,109.00
5	**Savings**	$ 450.81
6		
7		

= B3-B4

The spreadsheet software automatically changes the formula to reflect the new location of the Income and Expenses numbers.

Start
Screentour

Spreadsheet "Intelligence"

In what sense is spreadsheet software intelligent? When mainframe computers first made the headlines in the 1950s, they had an unsettling effect on the American public. And no wonder. Headlines dubbed these computers "Giant Brains," and journalists speculated about how long it might be until computers "took over." The public was pacified when word spread that computers could only follow the instructions of their human programmers. Fifty years have passed since the "Giant Brain" headlines appeared. Computer technology has improved to the point where it sometimes seems that computers do have some sort of intelligence—or at least they seem to anticipate what you want them to do. You'll run into some examples of this computer "intelligence" when you use spreadsheet software.

An example that you'll recognize as soon as you begin to use spreadsheet software is its ability to distinguish between the data you're using for text and the data you're using for numbers. At first, this task might seem easy—text is letters and numbers are, well, numbers. But suppose that you want to enter a Social Security number in a cell. When you enter 375-80-9876, should the spreadsheet regard it as the subtraction formula 375 minus 80 minus 9876? Should the spreadsheet regard it as a single number, 375809876, that can be used for mathematical operations? Or should the spreadsheet regard it as text that cannot be mathematically manipulated? The answer is that your spreadsheet software will regard 375-80-9876 as text. If you think about it, you'll see that the computer is correct. Although they are called Social Security numbers, we don't add, subtract, multiply, or divide them. We treat them as text.

Shortcuts are another example of spreadsheet "intelligence." Spreadsheet software contains many handy shortcuts to help simplify the process of creating, editing, and formatting a worksheet. For example, Fill operations continue a series you have started. Type "January" in one cell and "February" in the next, then use a Fill operation and the spreadsheet will automatically enter the rest of the months in the next 10 cells. Fill operations also complete numerical sequences such as "1, 2, 3, 4, ..." or "1990, 1995, 2000, ...". Figure 3-23 shows how a Fill operation works.

FIGURE 3-23

Most spreadsheet software contains handy shortcuts, such as the Fill operation that automatically completes a series of numbers.

1. Type the first few numbers in a series.

2. The spreadsheet software will fill in the rest of the series.

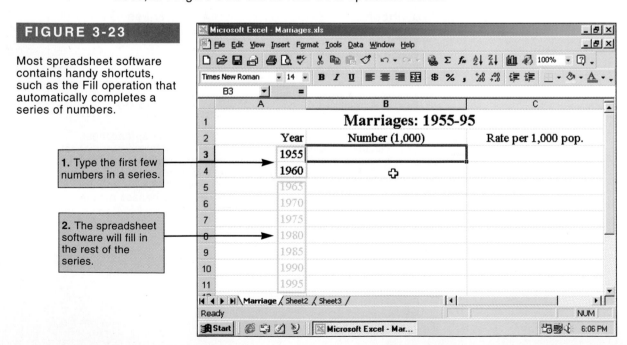

Formatting Worksheets

Does spreadsheet software provide formatting options similar to those provided by word processing software? Spreadsheet software provides many formatting options to improve the appearance of your worksheet. The formatting you use for a spreadsheet depends on your output plan. Worksheets that you intend to print might be formatted differently from worksheets that you intend to view only on the screen. Worksheets that you want to project for presentations often require a format different from printed worksheets.

Worksheets for routine calculations are much handier to use if you can see all of the information without scrolling, so try to place all labels, numbers, and formulas on one screen. If necessary, you can make the columns narrow so that more of them fit on the screen. If you're creating a worksheet for your own use, there's probably no need to spend time making it look attractive.

If you plan to print your spreadsheet, you might want to spend some time creating an attractive format. Use a larger font for the title, and consider italicizing or boldfacing important numbers and their labels. Your worksheet will look more polished if you omit the grid lines between rows and columns. Maintain a liberal amount of white space on the page just as you would when you format documents with a word processor. Don't skip every other row to give the appearance of double spacing, however. If you do so, you'll have trouble graphing the data because half of your data points will be zero. Figure 3-24 provides some worksheet formatting tips.

CHAPTER 3

FIGURE 3-24

When formatting a worksheet for printing, your goal is to make it look like a typeset document.

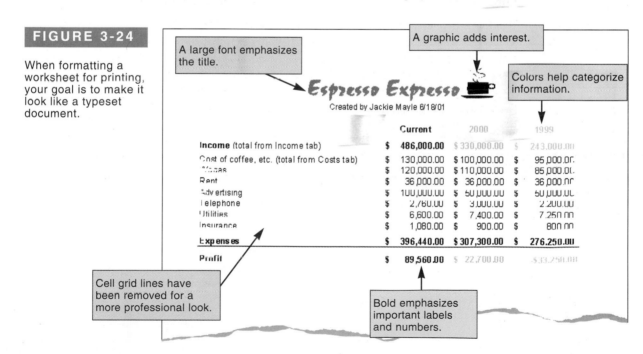

A large font emphasizes the title.

A graphic adds interest.

Colors help categorize information.

Cell grid lines have been removed for a more professional look.

Bold emphasizes important labels and numbers.

Espresso Expresso
Created by Jackie Mayle 6/18/01

	Current	2000	1999
Income (total from Income tab)	$ 486,000.00	$ 330,000.00	$ 243,000.00
Cost of coffee, etc. (total from Costs tab)	$ 130,000.00	$ 100,000.00	$ 95,000.00
Wages	$ 120,000.00	$ 110,000.00	$ 85,000.00
Rent	$ 36,000.00	$ 36,000.00	$ 36,000.00
Advertising	$ 100,000.00	$ 50,000.00	$ 50,000.00
Telephone	$ 2,760.00	$ 3,000.00	$ 2,200.00
Utilities	$ 6,600.00	$ 7,400.00	$ 7,250.00
Insurance	$ 1,080.00	$ 900.00	$ 800.00
Expenses	$ 396,440.00	$ 307,300.00	$ 276,250.00
Profit	$ 89,560.00	$ 22,700.00	-$33,250.00

Spreadsheets for presentations must be legible when displayed by a projection device. You might consider a larger type size—one that can be easily viewed from the back of the room in which your worksheet will be projected. Scrolling is usually not desirable in a presentation situation, so try to fit the worksheet on one screen. You can create a **workbook** containing several worksheets if you need to present multiple charts and graphs.

The use of color will make your presentation more interesting and help to highlight important data on the worksheet. If you are also planning to print your worksheet in black and white, select your colors carefully. Colors appear in shades of gray on a black-and-white printout. Some colors produce a dark shade of gray that obscures labels and numbers. Figure 3-25 provides some examples of worksheets formatted for presentations.

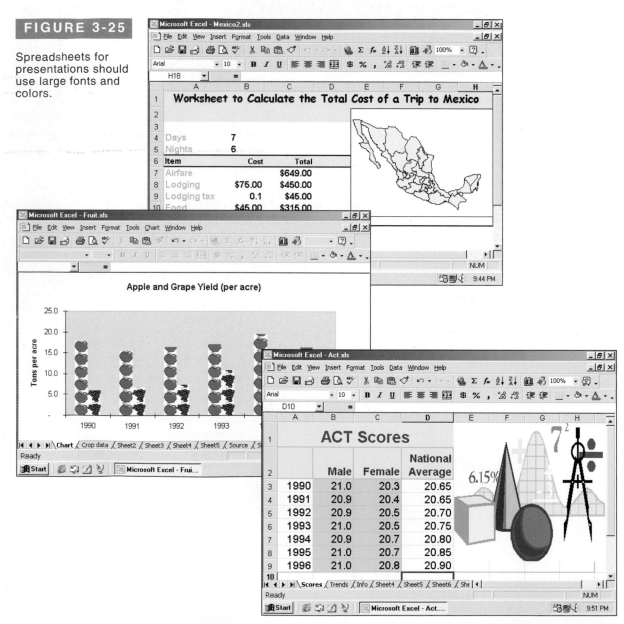

FIGURE 3-25

Spreadsheets for presentations should use large fonts and colors.

Charting Your Proposal

What about graphs and charts? Many television viewers are familiar with the whimsical Kinko's commercial in which a young man proposes to his sweetheart in a posh restaurant by hauling out a series of large and colorful charts describing his future earning potential. If this commercial is any indication, charts and graphs would seem to be spilling over from the business world into popular culture.

FIGURE 3-26

Charts and graphs are popping up everywhere.

Spreadsheet software provides you with an easy way to create polished graphs and charts. Remember the unsatisfactory results you got by using graph paper and colored pencils? With spreadsheet software, it is simple to create an attractive pie graph that illustrates opinion poll data, a line graph that drives home the alarming increase in the national debt, or a bar graph that compares market share for U.S. and foreign automobile manufacturers.

InfoWeb
10

Lie

Graphs, as you know, provide a quick summary or overview of a set of data. Trends that might be difficult to detect in columns of figures come into focus when skillfully graphed. Graphs are an effective presentation tool because they are visually interesting and easy to understand. However, when creating graphs, you have a responsibility to your audience to create a visual representation of the truth. Although you might not intentionally design a graph to "lie," it is all too easy to design a graph that implies something other than the truth. For example, which of the two graphs from Figure 3-27 do you think a sales manager would prefer to show?

The sales figures represented by the graph on the right certainly look better than those on the left. Look closely. The data for both graphs is the same, but changing the shape of the graph causes the trend in sales to look either pretty tame or very dramatic. When you design a graph, try to consider how the average person would interpret it, then make sure that the interpretation coincides with reality.

FIGURE 3-27

Graphs can "stretch the truth."

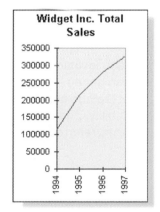

Claw Your Way to the Top with Spreadsheet Software

In what situations can I use spreadsheet software? Spreadsheet software was invented in 1978 by a Harvard Business School student, Dan Bricklin. Many computer historians believe that his software, called VisiCalc, not only launched a new genre of computer software, but also launched the Digital Age by putting a rocket under the fledgling microcomputer industry. Before VisiCalc became available, consumers couldn't think of much use for a personal computer. VisiCalc provided business people with a handy tool for making calculations without visiting a statistician or accountant. It contained all of the basic elements of today's electronic spreadsheets—a screen-based grid of rows and columns, predefined functions, automatic calculations, formatting options, and rudimentary "intelligence" for copying and replicating formulas.

A spreadsheet works well for recording and graphing data, for making calculations, and for constructing numerical models of the real world. The main advantage of spreadsheet software is the time it saves—once you create a worksheet, you can change your data without redoing your calculations. In addition, worksheet data is stored in electronic format, so it can be merged with word processing documents, posted on the Internet, or transmitted as part of an e-mail message.

FIGURE 3-28

Humorist Dave Barry explains spreadsheets in his book, *Claw Your Way to the Top.*

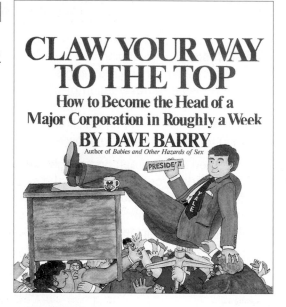

In his tongue-in-cheek book, *Claw Your Way to the Top*, Dave Barry defines a spreadsheet as "a kind of program that lets you sit at your desk and ask all kinds of neat 'what if?' questions and generate thousands of numbers instead of actually working." These what-if questions are part of a process called **spreadsheet modeling**, which consists of setting up numbers in a worksheet to describe a real-world situation. For example, spreadsheets are often used for business modeling. The worksheet data represents or describes financial activities in a business, such as products sold, expenses for employees, rent, inventory, and so forth. By looking at the numbers in such a business model, you can get an idea of its current profitability. You can also experiment with changing some of the numbers in the model to see how changes in business activities might affect profitability. The process of setting up a model and experimenting with different numbers is often referred to as **what-if analysis**.

What-if analysis is certainly a useful tool. Imagine having answers to questions such as "What if I get an A on my next two economics exams? But what if I get Bs?"; "What if I invest $100 per month in my retirement plan? But what if I invest $200 per month?"; "What if our sales reps increase sales by 10 percent? But what if sales decline by 5 percent?"; "What if I take out a 30-year mortgage at 8.5 percent? But what if I take out a 15-year mortgage at 7.75 percent?". Spreadsheets make these questions easy to answer.

Spreadsheet software is applicable in just about every profession. Educators use spreadsheets for gradebooks and analysis of test scores. Farmers use spreadsheets to keep track of crop yield, to calculate the amount of seed to purchase, and to estimate expenses and profits for the coming year. At home, spreadsheets help you balance your checkbook, monitor your savings and investments, track your household expenses, and calculate your taxes.

Entrepreneurs use spreadsheets to define business plans. Corporate executives use spreadsheets to keep tabs on finances. Scientists use spreadsheets to analyze data from experiments. Contractors use spreadsheets to bid on construction projects. Athletes use spreadsheets to track training programs and sports statistics. The list goes on and on, as more people recognize the advantages of spreadsheet software. You'll want to consider how spreadsheets can help you in your career field.

CHAPTER 3 (side tab)

QUICKCHECK B

1 In a spreadsheet grid, each
~~Column~~ is lettered; each
~~Row~~ is numbered.

2 B3 and B4 are called cell ~~references'~~.

3 Most spreadsheet software includes hundreds of predefined formulas called ~~functions'~~ for mathematical, financial, and statistical calculations.

4 The spreadsheet software publisher is responsible for the validity of the figures and formulas in your worksheets. True or false?

5 Relative references change if the data they reference changes location on the worksheet. In contrast, an absolute reference will not change. True or false?

6 A worksheet that will be viewed on the screen would generally be formatted differently than a worksheet that will be printed in black and white. True or false?

7 The process of setting up a model and experimenting with different numbers is often referred to as ~~what-if~~ analysis.

Check Answers

SECTION c DATABASES

Databases

Sometime in the middle of this century, our industrial society began to evolve into an information society. The way we live has changed in many ways. We interact with information more frequently, we enter careers connected to information management, we increasingly attach a cash value to information, we tend to depend on information, and we are becoming aware of the potential problems that can occur when information is misused. We have moved from the Industrial Age to the Information Age.

The Information Age is fueled by an explosion of data that is generated by individuals, corporations, and government agencies. Some experts estimate that the amount of information doubles every year. This information is stored in an uncountable number of databases, most of them computerized. In the course of an ordinary day, whether you realize it or not, you will likely interact with more than one of these databases.

FIGURE 3-29

The rock group Police sings "Too much information running through my brain. Too much information, driving me insane."

The term "database" is a slippery thing. Although a technical definition exists for the term, it is largely ignored in popular usage. This section focuses on the popular rendition of databases, using a broad, nontechnical definition of a **database** as a collection of information stored on one or more computers.

This section also focuses on software that's designed to search for information in databases, rather than on database management software that's designed to create and manipulate databases. You might like this focus because it's so practical. After all, 95 out of 100 times that you encounter a database, you'll be looking for information, not creating or adding information.

Structured and Freeform Databases

What kind of databases am I likely to use? During a typical day, you're likely to encounter many types of databases, such as a library card catalog, a banking database that contains your checking account balances, CD-ROM encyclopedias, your computer's directory of files, and your e-mail address book. You might also interact with collections of information accessed via the Internet, such as Web sites devoted to hip-hop music, the stock market, the job market, or travel.

Databases come in two "flavors": structured databases and freeform databases. A **structured database** (also called a "structured data file") is a file of information organized in a uniform format of records and fields. Figure 3-30 shows an example of a record from a structured database for a library card catalog.

FIGURE 3-30

A structured database stores data in a series of records. Each record contains the same field names, such as "Title" and "Author." The data in each field, such as "Roots" and "Haley, Alex," depends on the entity that the record describes.

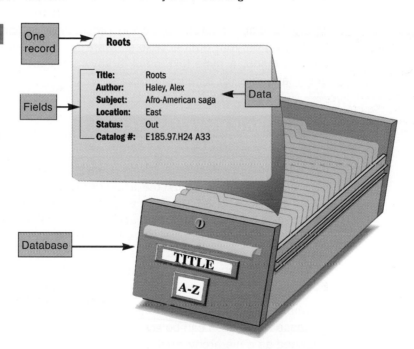

Structured databases typically store data that describes a collection of similar entities. For example, a medical database stores data for a collection of patients. An inventory database stores data for a collection of items stocked on store and warehouse shelves.

A **freeform database** is a loosely structured collection of information, usually stored as documents rather than as records. For example, you might consider the collection of word processed documents stored on your computer to be a freeform database of your own writing. A CD-ROM containing documents and videos of the Civil War would be another example. The World Wide Web, with its millions of documents stored worldwide, is another example of a freeform database. Whether stored on your hard disk, a CD-ROM, or the Internet, freeform databases have the potential to contain varied and useful information for you as a student or as a career professional.

Searching for Information

How do I find information in a database? When searching for information in a database, as opposed to creating and maintaining a database, you typically don't need to know whether you're accessing a structured database or a freeform database because your data access software hides the details of the database structure. **Data access software** is the interface you use to search for information in a database. You tell the data access software what you're seeking, and it will attempt to find it. The data access software understands the structure of the database, so you don't need to worry about the technical details.

The source that supplies the database, also usually provides the data access software, because different databases inevitably use different data access software. Becoming an effective information gatherer in the Information Age requires you to be flexible and willing to learn different searching procedures for different data access software. Depending on your data access software, you might enter your search specifications using a menu, a hypertext index, a keyword search engine, a query by example, a query language, or a natural language.

Menus and Hypertext Indexes

What's the easiest way to access database information? The Information Age has had a major effect on our lives. Consider how it has changed the way we do our banking. Information is now the basic product of the banking industry. As one expert points out, "Money is today only a special case of information." You've probably used your bank's phone-in automated account information system that asks you to "press 1 for account information, press 2 for help with your PIN number" and so on. Such a system provides your interface to the bank's database of checking and savings account information. Because so many people use this type of database, access must be simple. Consequently, most data access software for bank customers is based on menus.

Database menus are similar to those used in most other software. Menus that access database information can be screen-based or consist of audio cues. Menus are typically arranged as a hierarchy, so that after you make a choice at the first level of the menu, a second series of choices appears.

The trick to using telephone menus is to place your finger over the best choice as you hear it. Leave your finger there until you hear a better choice. Then, when the voice finishes explaining the menu options, you don't have to recall the number of the one you want.

Screen-based menus are typically easier to use than telephone menus because you always have all options in view. For this reason, they can also be more complex, displaying many options on multiple levels. If you frequently use the same menu-based data access software, you'll become more proficient at gathering information if you try to envision the hierarchy of menus.

Screen-based menus have become a popular format for providing access to information via the Internet. AltaVista, Yahoo!, and other popular indexes to the World Wide Web feature a **hypertext index** that links you to information in categories such as education, entertainment, and business. To use a hypertext index, you select a general category such as Society & Politics. That selection links you to a list of subtopics. You might select Politics from this list and then see another list from which to choose. Eventually, after you have navigated enough lists, you'll reach a document containing the information you were seeking. Figure 3-31 shows AltaVista's hypertext index.

FIGURE 3-31

AltaVista's hypertext index helps you find information on the Web by selecting topics and subtopics.

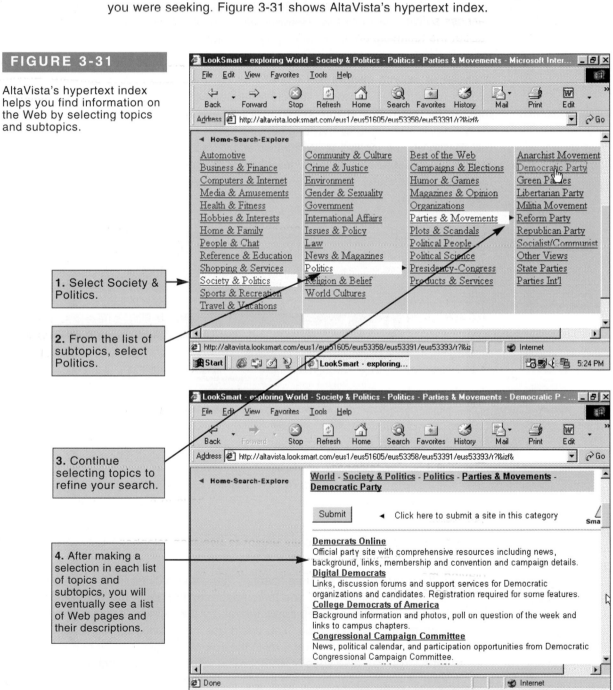

1. Select Society & Politics.

2. From the list of subtopics, select Politics.

3. Continue selecting topics to refine your search.

4. After making a selection in each list of topics and subtopics, you will eventually see a list of Web pages and their descriptions.

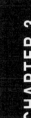

Keyword Searches

What if I don't want to wander through all levels of a menu or index to find information?

InfoWeb 11
Information Careers

Libraries have influenced the way that we organize information. Traditionally, we have found it handy to place information into categories—for example, by following John Dewey's classifications or those of the Library of Congress. It therefore seems natural to use similar classifications to organize electronic information, such as World Wide Web documents. Yahoo!'s menu structure, for example, reflects just such a classification scheme. Unfortunately, not everything can be neatly classified. Nevertheless, using the power and speed of computers, you can search for information by keyword, instead of by topic.

A **keyword search engine** lets you access data without slogging through a menu of subject categories. Keyword search engines are especially popular for searching through the many documents stored in a freeform database such as the World Wide Web. To use a keyword search engine, you simply type in a word such as "parties" and the search engine locates related information. Usually, it displays short summaries of the documents that contain the word you typed. You can then select those documents that seem most useful. The user interface for a keyword search engine is usually very simple, as shown in Figure 3-32.

FIGURE 3-32

A keyword search engine lets you search for data by entering words and phrases that describe a topic.

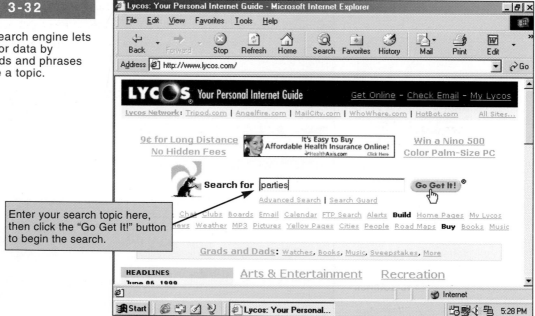

Enter your search topic here, then click the "Go Get It!" button to begin the search.

InfoWeb 12
Search Engines

A search for a broad topic such as "parties" generally provides too much information. Therefore, search engines allow you to compose "expert" searches using more specific search criteria. For example, you could search for the *phrase* "political parties" to limit your search to the political arena. You could use *operators* such as "and" and "or" to look for more than one specific item, as in the search for "democratic party *and* political conventions." You can also specify whether you want an exact match or an "in the ballpark" match. If you ask for an exact match to "political parties," you won't get articles on party politics.

Query by Example (QBE)

What about finding data in structured databases? You might remember the scene at the end of the classic old adventure film *Raiders of the Lost Ark*, in which Indiana Jones' valuable archeological discovery is unloaded from a forklift in a cavernous government warehouse full of crates and boxes. How long would it take to find it again?

Today, we expect to have information instantly. We want to know our bank balance right away. We want our Social Security checks on time. We want our tax refunds sooner, rather than later. We don't want to wait for a clerk to run back to the dairy aisle to check the price of a carton of yogurt.

When the information in a database needs to be accessed quickly, it is usually stored as a structured database. Because of its structure, a computer can generally locate data in a structured database more rapidly than it can locate information in a freeform database. In a structured database, the description of an item is stored in a particular field. Suppose that you tell the computer to find the records for any item described as "Lost Ark." The computer simply looks at the data in the description field of each record until it finds a record containing the words "Lost Ark."

Although computers can more easily find information in structured databases, the structure can cause a problem for humans. The problem is that users might not know the format for the records in a database. For example, how would you know whether an online library card catalog stores book titles in a field called Title, BookTitle, or T? Is the title the first field? Or does the first field contain the name of the author? One way to help users search structured databases is by providing a **query by example** (QBE for short) user interface like the one shown in Figure 3-33.

FIGURE 3-33

When you use a QBE interface, you see a blank record on the screen. Into this record, you enter examples of what you want the computer to find. In this case, the user is looking for a book published in 1993 or later that includes "Economics" in the title.

As you might guess from this example, using QBE requires you to learn a few "tricks," such as the use of the asterisk and dash. Different QBE software might use different symbols. Your best bet when using a new QBE is to read the Help instructions carefully before you set up your query.

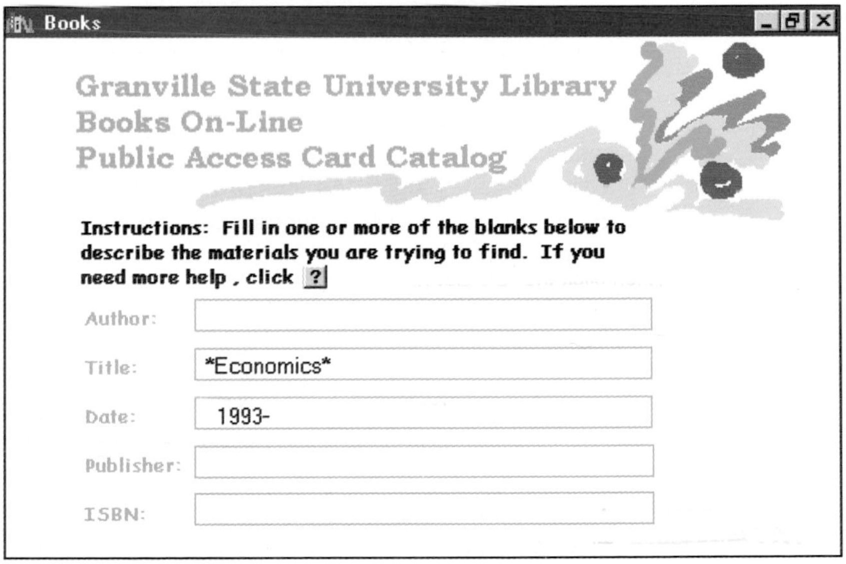

Books   [_] [□] [X]

**Granville State University Library
Books On-Line
Public Access Card Catalog**

Instructions: Fill in one or more of the blanks below to describe the materials you are trying to find. If you need more help , click [?]

Author:	
Title:	*Economics*
Date:	1993-
Publisher:	
ISBN:	

Query Languages and Natural Language

Can I just type in a question to find information? Many science-fiction writers and film makers have speculated about how intelligent computers and robots might affect society and culture. Of course, one aspect of such intelligence would be the ability to understand human speech. It would be handy if we could access databases in the same way that we describe to a reference librarian the type of data we wanted to find. The first step in this direction involves the use of query languages.

FIGURE 3-34

Robots with intelligence are a common theme in science fiction and films. When will computers respond to our database queries with the insight of a skilled reference librarian?

A **query language** is a set of command words that you can use to direct the computer to create databases, locate information, sort records, and change the data in those records. In situations where a fairly sophisticated user wants to access a structured database, a query language provides good flexibility for pinpointing information.

To use a query language, you need to know the command words and the grammar or syntax that will let you construct valid query "sentences." For example, the SQL (Structured Query Language) command word to find records is "select." When you type the command "select *", the computer will look for all records. To locate all of the Byzantine statues in an art museum database, you would enter an SQL query something like this:

*Select * from Artworks where Style = 'Byzantine' and Media = 'statue'*

Before you can compose such a query, you must have a fairly extensive knowledge of the database and its structure. You must know that the name of the database is "Artworks." You must also know that the artistic style of each work is stored in a field called "Style" and that works are categorized as painting, statue, pottery, and so on, in a field called "Media." As you can see, this interface is not suitable for casual users. Imagine if you had to compose SQL queries to use your library card catalog! Many people would find it easier to just wander around the stacks.

Advances in artificial intelligence have led to some progress in the ability of computers to understand queries formulated in a **natural language** such as English, French, or Japanese. To make such natural language queries, you don't need to learn an esoteric query language. Instead, you just enter questions such as the following:

What Byzantine statues are in our museum collection?

Computers still have some interpretation difficulties arising from ambiguities in human languages, so the use of natural language query software is not yet widespread.

Using Search Results

What can I do with the information I find? The power of information comes not only from finding it, but also from using it. In an information-rich society, finding information that is astonishing, amusing, and informative is not difficult. Finding information that is bizarre, offensive, destructive, and confidential is not difficult either. Keep in mind that the information you seek, collect, and disperse reflects your values and ethics. Laws and regulations on the publication and use of information in electronic form have not really kept up with the technology. Therefore, it is up to you to "use it, but don't abuse it." Once you have found information in a database, you can use it in a number of ways.

Print It. When you find information in a structured database, you can generally print out a single record or a list of selected records. You might want to print a particular record, for example, if you're looking through a real estate database and find your dream house. In another scenario, suppose you were looking in the ERIC database to find some academic articles for a paper you're writing about male role models in elementary schools. You could print out a list of article titles and the journals in which they appeared. If call numbers for the journals are available, including that information on the printout would make it much easier to locate the articles in your library. Likewise, you can print information that you find in a freeform database.

Copy and Paste. Most of today's graphical user interfaces provide a way to highlight database information you see on the screen and copy it to a worksheet or document. This technique is especially useful with the information you find in freeform databases, because often you want just the information from one section of one document. For example, suppose you've been cruising the Internet for information on the formation of the Cascade Mountains for your geology seminar. You locate a Web document that contains relevant information. Figure 3-35 shows you how to copy this information from the Web to one of your own word processing documents.

FIGURE 3-35

You can copy text and graphics from Web pages to your own word processing documents. Make sure that you include appropriate references in your paper for any material you copy.

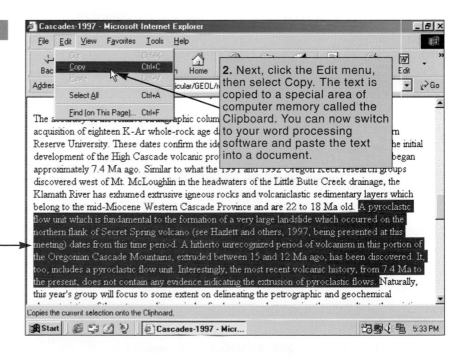

1. Highlight the text you want to copy.

2. Next, click the Edit menu, then select Copy. The text is copied to a special area of computer memory called the Clipboard. You can now switch to your word processing software and paste the text into a document.

Start
Screentour

Export It. You might find some data that you want to analyze or graph using spreadsheet software. Many databases automatically **export data** by transforming it into a format that's acceptable to your spreadsheet software. If your database does not have this capability, your spreadsheet software might be able to **import data** by reading the database data and translating it into a worksheet. As another option, your spreadsheet software might include a wizard to help you transport data between databases and worksheets.

Save It. When you find a group of records in a structured database that you want to manipulate later, your database software might provide you with an option to save the records as a file on a hard or floppy disk. If you opt for this route, you should be aware that you are likely to need the same database software that was originally used to enter and create the records in order to work with the records later. This requirement is not always practical, so you might have to use export or copy options instead. If you find data on the Web, the software you're using to access the information usually provides you with a way to save it on your own computer. This ability is particularly useful if you find a long document that you want to read at your leisure.

Transmit It. Today, you're plugged into a "global village" where e-mail arrives just minutes after it was sent and where you can "chat" online with people from all over the world. You can electronically distribute the information you collect; an easy way is to insert information into e-mail messages. A more ambitious project would be to develop your own World Wide Web site from which people could view Web pages and download databases.

Whether you print, import, copy, save, or transmit the data you find in databases, it is your responsibility to use it appropriately. Respect copyrights by giving credit to the original author in a footnote or endnote. The information in corporate and government databases is often confidential. When you have access to such data, respect the privacy of the individuals who are the subject of the data. Don't divulge the information you find or introduce inaccuracies into the database.

QUICKCHECK   C

1 A(n) ⌊*Structured*⌋ database is a file of information organized in a uniform format of records and fields, whereas a(n) ⌊*free form*⌋ database is a loosely structured collection of information.

2 To use a keyword search engine, you simply type in a word such as "music" and the search engine locates all related information in the database. True or false? ⌊ ⌋

3 When using a(n) ⌊*query by example*⌋ user interface to search a database, you use a blank record to enter examples of the data you want the computer to find.

4 A(n) ⌊*query language*⌋ such as SQL consists of a set of command words that you can use to direct the computer to locate information in a structured database.

5 Once you locate information in a database, you can print it, export it to other software packages, copy and paste it into other software, save it for future reference, or transmit it. True or false? ⌊ ⌋

Check Answers

USER FOCUS PUTTING IT ALL TOGETHER

You shouldn't finish this chapter with the impression that you use only one software tool per project. It is true that word processing, spreadsheet, and database software tools each have their own strengths. But you often can be more productive if you use the tools together. Suppose you are writing a report. How can you use the tools you've learned about to gather information, organize it, analyze it, and report your results? This section illustrates one possible scenario of how you might use a variety of computer and print resources to put together a research project.

Researching a Topic

Where do I start?   Suppose that you have to write a paper, but find yourself staring at a blank sheet of paper or a blank computer screen. Just take one step at a time. Use your technology tools. You'll be surprised at how fast your paper materializes.

InfoWeb
13

Online Card
Catalogs

First, choose your topic. As you research it, you will use a variety of databases. Next, browse around your library and the Internet to find sources of information. Whereas most research once took place in library buildings, the trend today is to use a computer to search online. From your home or office, you can look through millions of Web documents and search through the card catalogs of many libraries, including the Library of Congress.

You might want to make photocopies of interesting articles, check out relevant books, and save any information you find on the Web. If you seem to be finding bits and pieces of information on the Web, copy and paste them into a document you create with word processing software. Don't worry about the organization of the document for now. Just think of it as notes that you can use later.

Make sure that you keep track of where you obtain your information. Make a note of the magazine name and issue date on any photocopies you make. For information you gather from the Internet, make note of its source. Every document on the World Wide Web has a unique address called a URL. Most Web browser software has a setting to include the URL on any Web pages you send to your printer. If you note the URL for every bit of information you gather, you will be able to give credit to the authors in your final report. Figure 3-36 illustrates a Web page URL.

FIGURE 3-36

To make note of a URL, you can drag your mouse pointer over a URL, then use the Copy and Paste options on the File menu.

As you gather information, make sure that you have a way to distinguish between information you have copied verbatim and information you have paraphrased using your own words. You might simply put quotes around the material that you have copied verbatim. This approach will help keep you honest about which parts of the report are your own work.

Organizing and Analyzing Information

How do I add my own viewpoint and analysis to the report? After you collect information, you need to read through it and think about what it means. What are the trends? What are the controversies? What stands out as interesting? With this background, you can determine what you want to say.

Begin a new document using your word processing software and type in your main point. You should be able to write this main idea as a single, clear sentence. Use the editing features of your software to work on this sentence until it is perfect.

The next step is to create an outline of items that will support your main point. Use the outlining feature of your word processor to type in the headings and subheadings for your report. Refer back to the information you have gathered when necessary. You can have two or more documents open at the same time when using word processing software, so it's easy to flip back and forth between the document that contains your outline and the one that contains your research notes.

With your outline in place, you can begin to move your research notes into the appropriate places in your outline. Use the copy and paste feature while both documents are open to make this process a breeze.

FIGURE 3-37

Remember to proofread your work. You cannot depend on your spelling and grammar checkers to find all of your errors.

Of course, you don't want your paper to simply be a collage of other people's work. As a rule of thumb, in your final paper at least 8 of every 10 paragraphs should be your own words. Now is your chance to add your viewpoint and skillfully weave together the facts. Don't be misled into thinking that paraphrasing just means rearranging a few words in each of the sentences you copied from someone else's work. If you're tempted to copy, read your research note, then delete it and rewrite it using your own words.

Work on your document until you're satisfied, then run a spelling check and a grammar check if one is available. Don't forget to proofread your paper!

Before you finalize the content of your paper, you might consider whether some sections would be clearer if you included a graph or other illustration. You can use spreadsheet software to create graphs for data you have gathered. You can use the copy and paste functions to insert the graphs into your document.

When you're happy with the content of your document, save it on disk. Make an extra copy of your work on a different disk, just to be safe. You might also want to print your document even though you have not formatted it yet. If you lose your electronic copies, you can still reconstruct your document from the printout.

Following a Style Guide

How do I know how to format my paper? If you have not been provided with style guidelines from your instructor or boss, you should follow a standard style manual such as the *Publication Manual of the American Psychological Association*, *The Chicago Manual of Style*, or Turabian's *Student's Guide for Writing College Papers*. These manuals stipulate how large to make your margins, what to include in headers and footers, how to label graphs and illustrations, how to format your footnotes or endnotes correctly, and so forth. You'll use the formatting features of your word processing software to follow the style guidelines.

InfoWeb 14

Internet Citations

A style guide devotes many pages to the correct format for the book and magazine citations you include at the end of a paper or in footnotes. But what is the correct citation format for materials you use from Web pages or other Internet sources? Most style guides now include this information. If your style guide does not, you can access one of several Web sites that provide formats for electronic citations.

Presentations

What if I have to give a speech? If you plan to present your report, you need some speaking notes and some visual aids. Create your speaking notes using your word processing software. Use a large boldface font and double or triple spacing. After you print these notes, use different color highlighters to mark the first word in each paragraph. This device will help you keep your place as you speak.

Visual aids could mean handouts or computer-generated "slides." Consider whether an outline, graph, list of important points, or graphic image would be most useful for your audience. Your word processing software can help you produce printed handouts. Your spreadsheet software might help you put together a few graphs to support your main point. You could also consider using presentation software to assemble a computer-generated slide presentation (Figure 3-38). Don't forget to practice before you're "on stage"!

As you continue to work with electronic documents, you'll discover even more "tricks" for harnessing their features to increase your productivity and the quality of your work. Watch for tips in magazines and newspapers, on computer TV shows, and on the Web.

FIGURE 3-38

Use presentation software to create effective visual aids. Remember, however, that your slides should highlight your main points, rather than display the entire text of your speech.

ISSUE   DO COMPUTERS INCREASE PRODUCTIVITY?

Word processing, spreadsheet, and database software have been called "productivity software" because they are supposed to increase the amount of work that a person can produce. It seems to be a sensible supposition. Computers increase productivity, right? Without computers, life would certainly be different. For example, we take it for granted that we can make as many telephone calls as we want. However, futurist Paul Saffo points out that if telephone companies still used human operators instead of computer switching, they would have to employ over one-third of the U.S. population to handle the volume of telephone calls for a typical day. Without computers, phone usage would be severely restricted.

Computers are everywhere and common sense seems to indicate that they should increase productivity. They help us sift through mountains of data on the Internet much more easily than we could search through the stacks of a large research library. They help us communicate via e-mail much faster than old-fashioned ground mail. They let us plan and budget far more effectively with spreadsheet software than with a calculator.

InfoWeb
15

Productivity
Paradox

Unfortunately, as Nobel Prize-winning economist Robert Solow has said, we see computers everywhere except in the productivity statistics. According to the U.S. Bureau of Labor Statistics, during the 1950s and 1960s, the U.S. economy posted a 3 percent annual increase in productivity. To measure productivity, you count how many units a person, group, or machine can make in a given period of time. In the past 30 years, however, productivity growth has slowed to about 1 percent per year. These statistics are curious because the slow down in productivity coincides with the introduction of microcomputers and their massive deployment in homes and businesses. Despite the personal computer "revolution" and the billions of dollars that have been invested in computer technology, productivity actually appears to have decreased. Economists have coined the phrase **productivity paradox** to describe this discrepancy between increasing technology deployment and decreasing productivity.

What could possibly account for the productivity paradox? Some experts suggest that we need to look no further than our own desktops to discover how computers might actually reduce productivity. The "dither factor," for example, encourages us to tinker with every sentence that we type, revising it over and over in a quest for literary perfection. A document that might take us only 30 minutes to scribble out by hand, could end up taking three hours on the computer.

The "futz factor" kicks in when we run into a software bug or a hardware problem. In the past, only technicians had to worry about mechanical and electronic problems. Now those problems face every person who works with a PC. A few years ago, a survey by SBT Accounting Systems of San Rafael, California, showed that the typical computer user in a business setting wastes 5.1 hours per week on PCs.

The "game factor" can also have a negative effect on productivity. How many times have you been sidetracked by an interesting Web site, a chat room, or a computer game? A study by Forrester Research showed that 20 percent of employees' time on the Internet at work didn't involve their jobs. Employers, who quickly translated this statistic into overpaid wages and lost income, became alarmed. And yet, intuition told these employers that removing computers from the workplace would be even more counter-productive. Is there another perspective to the productivity paradox?

Some experts have suggested that, although productivity might be a valid measure of success in an industrialized society, it might not be as important in an information or service society such as the United States, the European Union, Australia, and Canada. As mentioned earlier, productivity measures how many units a person, group, or machine can make in a given period of time. Increasing productivity means increasing the number of units. But does this increase translate into better customer service, better product quality, or faster availability? Perhaps measuring units leads the statisticians to miss more important measures of success and effectiveness.

The growth of the U.S. economy seems to indicate that some positive factor is at work. Whether it is technology or some other yet-to-be-identified factor is a question that challenges economists. Businesses and individuals are also interested in the economics of prosperity. If productivity is a measure of economic success, prosperity and employment opportunities might be expected to increase as productivity increases. If computers can't provide a productivity boost, what other aspect of the economy can?

CHAPTER 3

WHAT DO YOU THINK?

1. Have computers increased the quantity of work that you produce?   ○Yes   ○ No   ○ Not sure

2. Have computers increased the quality of work that you produce?   ○Yes   ○ No   ○ Not sure

3. Can you recall an example of when a computer actually made you less productive?   ○Yes   ○ No   ○ Not sure

4. Do you believe that computers have had a beneficial effect on your country's economy?   ○Yes   ○ No   ○ Not sure

 Save Responses

CHAPTER 3 REVIEW ACTIVITIES

INTERACTIVE SUMMARY

The Interactive Summary helps you select important concepts and facts from this chapter. Fill in the blanks to best complete each sentence. When using the NP4 CD or NP4 Web site, you can click the Check Answers buttons to automatically score your answers. Place your Tracking Disk in the floppy disk drive if you want to save your scores.

Document production software includes word _____ software, desktop publishing software, e-mail editors, and the software that helps you create Web pages. Document production software makes it easy to compose, edit, and revise the content of your documents, using software features such as block move, outlining, search and replace, the spelling checker, the thesaurus, and the grammar checker. Your software takes care of many behind-the-scenes tasks, such as using the _____ feature to fit the words within margins . You should not, however, depend on your software to find all of the errors in your document—you should carefully _____ your documents before you print, submit, or publish them.

Spreadsheet software helps you create numeric models in a(n) _____ that's based on a grid of rows and columns. Each cell in this grid has a cell _____, such as A1, and can hold a number, text, or formula. Your spreadsheet software automatically calculates formulas whenever you enter or change data in the cells. This feature makes it easy to create _____ analyses to experiment with different numbers and different scenarios. Spreadsheet software also provides an easy way to create line, bar, and pie _____ based on the data in a worksheet. You can format worksheets for on-screen viewing, presentations, or printouts.

▶ Check Answers

A(n) _____ database stores data in a format that is similar to a card file—that is, it contains a series of records and each record contains a series of _____ containing data. A(n) _____ database, such as a collection of Web pages, is a loosely structured collection of information. Data _____ software, such as a search engine, provides a way to search for information in a database. Typically, when you search a structured database, you use query by example or a query _____. When searching through a freeform database, you are likely to use a keyword search or a hypertext _____.

In today's Information Age, you'll typically use a combination of document production, spreadsheet, and database tools to create documents, graphs, Web pages, and presentations. Always make sure that you exercise honesty when you incorporate material that you find in the library, on your bookshelf, or at Web sites.

▶ Check Answers

INTERACTIVE KEY TERMS

Make sure that you understand all of the boldfaced key terms presented in this chapter. If you're using the NP4 CD or NP4 Web site, you can use this list of terms as an interactive study activity. First, try to define a term in your own words. Then click the term to compare your definition with the definition that is presented in this chapter.

Absolute reference, 125
Auditing, 124
Cell, 121
Cell reference, 121
Clip art, 113
Concordance, 116
Data access software, 134
Database, 132
Document production software, 104
Document template, 110
Document wizards, 111
Electronic publishing, 114
Export data, 140
Font, 112
Footer, 116
Formula, 121
Frame, 113
Freeform database, 133
Function, 122
Grammar checker, 109
Header, 116
HTML (Hypertext Markup Language), 115
Hypertext index, 135
Import data, 140
In-line spelling checker, 108
Justification, 112
Keyword search engine, 136
Mail merge, 117
Natural language, 138
Number, 121
Outline feature, 107
Productivity paradox, 144
Query by example (QBE), 137
Query language, 138
Relative reference, 125
Search and replace, 108
Search feature, 108
Spelling checker, 108
Spreadsheet, 119
Spreadsheet modeling, 130
Structured database, 133

Text, 121
Text block, 107
Thesaurus, 108
What-if analysis, 130
Word wrap, 106
Workbook, 128
Worksheet, 121
Worksheet template, 124

CHAPTER 3

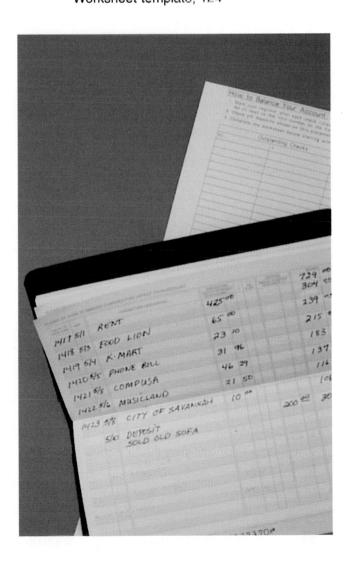

INTERACTIVE QUIZZES

Quiz yourself on important concepts from this chapter by filling in the blanks. When using the NP4 CD or NP4 Web site, you can type your answers, then use the Check Answers buttons to automatically score your responses. Place your Tracking Disk in the floppy disk drive if you want to save your scores.

1 Document production software helps you improve the _____ of your writing in addition to improving the way it looks.

2 Document production software was expected to create a surge in print publishing, but surprised many people by creating amazing opportunities in _____ publishing instead.

3 A(n) _____ is an electronic version of a(n) _____, used to create numeric models of real situations.

4 When you change the value in a worksheet cell, your spreadsheet software recalculates all of the _____.

5 When you copy, move, or delete cells in a worksheet, your spreadsheet software adjusts _____ cell references as necessary.

6 When you are searching for information in a database, the necessary data _____ software is usually supplied by the the same source that provides the database.

7 When you collect information from a Web site, make sure that you keep track of the site's _____.

Check Answers

Refer to the Checkbook Balance worksheet at the right and enter T in the box if the statement is true; enter F if the statement is false.

1 The worksheet is most probably formatted for printing. _____

2 To produce the correct results, the formula in cell B7 should be =B4+B5+B6. _____

3 The formula in cell B7 should contain absolute cell references or it will not produce the correct results. _____

4 If you change the number in cell B4 to $500.00, the worksheet will automatically change the contents of cell B7 to $300.00. _____

5 If you delete row 3, the current balance will automatically change to $0.00. _____

	A	B
1	**Checkbook Balance**	
2		
3		
4	**Last month's balance**	**$400.00**
5	**Total for all checks**	**$300.00**
6	**Total for all deposits**	**$100.00**
7	**Current balance**	**$200.00**
8		

Check Answers

INTERACTIVE PRACTICE TESTS

When you use the NP4 CD or NP4 Web site, you can take practice tests that consist of 10 multiple-choice, true/false, and fill-in-the-blank questions. The 10 questions are selected at random from a large test bank, so each time you take a test, you'll receive a different set of questions. Your tests are scored immediately, and you can print study guides that help you find the correct answers for any questions that you missed. If you are using a Tracking Disk, insert it in the floppy disk drive to save your test scores.

 Start Practice
Test

STUDY TIPS

Study Tips help you organize and consolidate the information in a chapter by making lists, outlines, charts, and sketches. You can use paper and pencil or word processing software to complete most of the Study Tips activities.

1 In your own words, answer the questions below each heading in this chapter.

2 Make a list of the document production features discussed in this chapter.

3 Explain the differences between a document template, a font, a style, and a document wizard.

4 Describe the steps in the writing process recommended in this chapter.

5 Write one or two paragraphs describing how a spreadsheet works to someone who has never seen or used one.

6 Briefly describe how a mail merge works.

7 Explain each of the following spreadsheet items: a number, a formula, a function, and a cell reference.

8 Explain what happens to the cell references in a formula when you copy that formula to a different column. How does this process relate to absolute and relative references?

9 Describe three techniques for auditing a worksheet.

10 Make a list of tips for formatting worksheets. Divide your tips into three categories: on-screen, printed, and projected.

11 Provide your own example of a what-if analysis.

12 Explain the difference between a structured database and a freeform database.

13 List and describe at least six search procedures that you might use to locate information in a database.

14 Outline the steps from the *User Focus* section of this chapter for using computer tools to create a research report.

15 Describe the productivity paradox.

PROJECTS

A project is an open-ended activity that will help you apply the concepts you have learned. Many projects require resources in addition to your textbook, such as current magazines, library materials, or Web access. When you tackle a project, be prepared to use your critical thinking skills, logical analysis, and your creativity.

1 **Who's pear of shoes our over their?** Most word processing software includes a grammar checker that helps you locate potential problems with sentence structure, punctuation, and word usage. When you use a grammar checker, it is important to remember that you must evaluate its suggestions and decide whether to implement them. In this project, you'll use a grammar checker to revise some of your own writing.

Begin with a first draft of at least one page of your writing. You can use something you have previously composed, or you can write something new. You'll need to type your document using word processing software with grammar checking capabilities. Print out your first draft.

After you've printed your first draft, activate the grammar checker. Consider each of its suggestions and implement those that you think will improve your writing. Proofread your document after you've completed the changes to ensure that it still flows well. Print out your revised document, then use a highlighter to indicate the changes you made. Turn in both drafts of your document.

2 **See Dick Run. See Jane. See Spot Play.** Although close to 80 percent of the population for most industrialized countries has completed high school, journalists supposedly write for an audience with only an eighth-grade reading level. Is this true? To find out, you can use your word processing software to discover the reading level of typical articles in popular magazines and newspapers.

To complete this project, locate two articles that you think are typical of the writing style for the magazines or newspapers you read. Using your word processor, enter at least 10 sentences from the first article. Use your word processor's reading-level feature to find the reading level for the passage you typed. Print out the passage and on it note the reading-level statistics you obtained from your word processor. Do the same with the second article. Turn in both of your printouts. Be sure to include full bibliographical data on both articles.

3 **True Lies.** Arnold Schwarzenegger and Jamie Lee Curtis starred in an action-thriller spoof about a secret agent who pretended to be a nerdy computer technician. Another character in the film was actually a used car salesman, but pretended to be a secret agent. The theme of *True Lies*—that things are not always what they seem—applies to spreadsheet graphs as well. What graphs appear to show is not always what the data actually means.

For this project, look through magazines, books, and newspapers to find an example of a misleading graph. You might find that the dimensions of the graph distort the true picture. Perhaps a line graph was used when a pie graph would have been more meaningful. Maybe some of the data was omitted.

Photocopy the graph, then write a paragraph describing how the graph is misleading and what you would suggest to make it better depict the real data.

4 **Searching for Godot.** Knowing how to use a search engine is becoming a pivotal skill for the Information Age. Most keyword search engines include instructions or short tutorials on their use. For this project, you'll connect to one of the Web search engines and learn how to use it.

To complete this project, you must have access to the Internet and you must have a Web browser such as Netscape Navigator or Microsoft Internet Explorer. Start your browser and connect to one of the following sites:

www.lycos.com   *www.altavista.com*

www.excite.com   *www.hotbot.com*   (continued on next page)

Read through the instructions carefully, paying close attention (and maybe taking notes) on the options available for advanced searches, exact matches, and Boolean operators (AND, OR, NOT). Next, try a few searches to make sure you've got the hang of it.

Write a mini-manual about how to use your keyword search engine, providing examples of different types of searches.

5 **Brave New World.** Because computerized databases have become such an integral part of our society, we don't often consider what life would be like without them. In fact, without computerized databases, banking, shopping, communications, entertainment, education, and health care would probably be far different from what they are today. For this project, you should first make a list of assumptions about how your life would be different if no computerized databases existed. For example, one of your assumptions might be, "Without computerized databases, we would have to pay for everything in cash because banks couldn't process enough checks by hand and credit card companies couldn't verify charges."

After you have a list of assumptions, write a short story about one day in the life of a person who lives in a society without computerized databases. In your story, try to depict how this person's life would differ from what we think of as "normal."

Turn in your list of assumptions and your short story.

6 **Edit Yourself.** After reading the *User Focus* section of this chapter, you might have some ideas about how you can use software tools to collect facts, improve your writing, analyze numeric data, and give presentations. Select a report, paper, or presentation that you recently created. Think about specific ways in which you could improve it.

Make a list of possible improvements, indicating the tools you would use. Be specific. For example, you might say, "Gather additional facts about per capita coffee consumption using a Web search engine" or "Check the reading level using a word processor and make adjustments to bring it to the eighth- to tenth-grade level." Turn in a photocopy of your original project as well as your list of improvements.

ADDITIONAL PROJECTS

Click the underlined text to link to the NP4 Web site (www.cciw.com/np4), where you can view and print additional projects for this chapter.

The March of Progress: Create a Timeline of Important Events in the History of Document Production

Information Science Careers

Exploring Software Menus

Font Master: Analyzing How Fonts Affect the Look of a Document

LAB ASSIGNMENTS

Software for these labs is provided on the NP4 CD and may also be available in your school's computer lab. To start a lab, click the lab icon.

Each lab has two parts: Steps and Explore. Use the Steps first to learn and review concepts. Read the information on each page and do the numbered steps. As you work through the lab, you will be asked to answer QuickCheck questions about what you have learned. At the end of the lab, you will see a report that scores your answers to the QuickChecks. If your instructor wants you to turn in this report, click the Print button on the QuickCheck Report screen.

When you have completed the Steps, you can click the Explore button to complete the Lab Assignments. You can also use Explore to practice the skills you learned and to explore concepts on your own.

The Computer History Lab is an example of a multimedia hypertext, or hypermedia that contains text, pictures, and recordings that trace the origins of computers.

1 Click the Steps button to learn how to use the Computer History Lab. As you proceed through the Steps, answer all QuickCheck questions that appear. After you complete the Steps, you will see a QuickCheck Report. Follow the instructions on the screen to print this report.

2 Click the Explore button. Find the name and date for each of the following:

a. First automatic adding machine

b. First electronic computer

c. First electronic stored-program computer

d. First widely used, high-level programming language

e. First microprocessor

f. First microcomputer

g. First word processing program

h. First spreadsheet program

3 Select one of the following computer pioneers and write a one-page paper about that person's contribution to the computer industry: Grace Hopper, Charles Babbage, Augusta Ada, Jack Kilby, Thomas Watson, or J. Presper Eckert.

4 Use this lab to research the history of the computer. Based on your research, write a paper explaining how you would respond to the question, "Who invented the computer?"

Word processing software is the most popular computerized productivity tool. In this lab you will learn how word processing works. When you have completed this lab, you should be able to apply the general concepts you learned to any word processing package you use at home, at work, or in your school lab.

1 Click the Steps button to learn how word processing software works. As you proceed through the Steps, answer all of the QuickCheck questions that appear. After you complete the Steps, you will see a QuickCheck Report. Follow the instructions on the screen to print this report.

2 Click the Explore button to begin. Click File, then click Open to display the Open dialog box. Click the file *Timber.tex*, then press the Enter key to open the letter to Northern Timber Company. Make the following modifications to the letter, check the spelling, then print it out. You do not need to save the letter.

a. In the first and last lines of the letter, change "Jason Kidder" to your name.

b. Change the date to today's date.

c. The second paragraph begins "Your proposal did not include..." Move this paragraph so it is the last paragraph in the text of the letter.

d. Change the cost of a permanent bridge to $20,000. (continued on next page)

3 In Explore, open the file *Stars.tex*. Make the following modifications to the document, then print it out. You do not need to save the document.

   a. Center and boldface the title.

   b. Change the title font to size 16 Arial.

   c. Boldface the words DATE, SHOWER, and LOCATION.

   d. Move the January 2-3 line to the top of the list.

   e. Double-space the entire document.

4 In Explore, compose a one-page, double-spaced letter to your parents or to a friend. Make sure you date the letter and check your spelling. Print the letter and sign it. You do not need to save your letter.

Lab
Spreadsheets

Spreadsheet software is used extensively in business, education, science, and humanities to simplify tasks that involve calculations. In this lab, you will learn how spreadsheet software works. You will use spreadsheet software to examine and modify worksheets as well as to create your own worksheets.

1 Click the Steps button to learn how spreadsheet software works. As you proceed through the Steps, answer all of the QuickCheck questions that appear. After you complete the Steps, you will see a QuickCheck Report. Follow the instructions on the screen to print this report.

2 Click the Explore button to begin this assignment. Click OK to display a new worksheet. Click File, then click Open to display the Open dialog box. Click the file *Income.xls*, then press the Enter key to open the Income and Expense Summary worksheet. Notice that the worksheet contains labels and values for income from consulting and training. It also contains labels and values for expenses such as rent and salaries. The worksheet does not, however, contain formulas to calculate Total Income, Total Expenses, or Profit. Do the following:

   a. Calculate the Total Income by entering the formula =sum(C4:C5) in cell C6.

   b. Calculate the Total Expenses by entering the formula =sum(C9:C12) in cell C13.

   c. Calculate the Profit by entering the formula =C6-C13 in cell C15.

   d. Manually check the results to make sure you entered the formulas correctly.

   e. Print your completed worksheet showing your results.

3 You can use a spreadsheet to keep track of your grade in a class. In Explore, click File, then click Open to display the Open dialog box. Click the file *Grades.xls* to open the Grades worksheet. This worksheet contains all of the labels and formulas necessary to calculate your grade based on four test scores.

Suppose you receive a score of 88 out of 100 on the first test. On the second test, you score 42 out of 48. On the third test, you score 92 out of 100. You have not taken the fourth test yet. Enter the appropriate data in the Grades worksheet to determine your grade after taking three tests. Print out your worksheet.

4 Worksheets are handy for answering "what if" questions. Suppose you decide to open a lemonade stand. You're interested in how much profit you can make. What if you sell 20 cups of lemonade? What if you sell 100? What if the cost of lemons increases?

In Explore, open the file *Lemons.xls* and use the worksheet to answer questions (a) through (d), then print the worksheet for question (e):

   a. What is your profit if you sell 20 cups per day?

   b. What is your profit if you sell 100 cups per day? (continued on next page)

c. What is your profit if the price of lemons increases to $0.07 and you sell 100 cups?

d. What is your profit if you raise the price of a cup of lemonade to $0.30? (Lemons still cost $0.07 and assume you sell 100 cups.)

e. Suppose your competitor boasts that she sold 50 cups of lemonade in one day and made exactly $12.00. On your worksheet, adjust the cost of cups, water, lemons, and sugar and the price per cup to show a profit of exactly $12.00 for 50 cups sold. Print this worksheet.

5 It is important to make sure that the formulas in your worksheet are accurate. An easy way to test accuracy is to enter 1's for all values on your worksheet, then check the calculations manually. In Explore, open the *Receipt.xls*, which calculates sales receipts. Enter 1 as the value for Item 1, Item 2, Item 3, and Sales Tax %. Manually calculate what you would pay for three items that cost $1.00 each in a state where sales tax is 1% (.01). Do your manual calculations match those of the worksheet? If not, correct the formulas in the worksheet and print out a formula report of your revised worksheet.

6 In Explore, create your own worksheet showing your household budget for one month. You may use real or fictional data. Make sure you put a title on the worksheet. Use formulas to calculate your total income and your total expenses for the month. Add another formula to calculate how much money you were able to save. Print a formula report of your worksheet. Also, print your worksheet showing realistic values for one month.

Databases

The Database Lab demonstrates the essential concepts of file and database management systems. You will use the lab to search, sort, and report the data contained in a file of classic books.

1 Click the Steps button to review basic database terminology and to learn how to manipulate the classic books database. As you proceed through the Steps, answer the QuickCheck questions that appear. After you complete the Steps, you will see a QuickCheck Report. Follow the instructions on the screen to print this report.

2 Click the Explore button. Make sure that you can apply basic database terminology to describe the classic books database by answering the following questions:

a. How many records does the file contain?

b. How many fields does each record contain?

c. What are the contents of the Catalog # field for the book written by Margaret Mitchell?

d. What are the contents of the Title field for the record with Thoreau in the Author field?

e. Which field has been used to sort the records?

3 In Explore, manipulate the database as necessary to answer the following questions:

a. When the books are sorted by title, what is the first record in the file?

b. Use the Search button to search for all books in the West location. How many do you find?

c. Use the Search button to search for all books in the Main location that are checked in. What do you find?

4 In Explore, use the Report button to print out a report that groups the books by status and sorts them by title. On your report, circle the four field names. Put a box around the summary statistics showing which books are currently checked in and which books are currently checked out.

INFOWEB

The InfoWeb is your guide to print, film, television, and electronic resources. Use it to obtain updates on quickly changing technical information and to locate information for research papers. If you're using the NP4 CD, click the InfoWeb Site icon on the left side of this paragraph to access the online InfoWeb links. Otherwise, use your Web browser and type in the address of the NP4 Web site: www.cciw.com/np4. At the Web site, you'll find up-to-date links to the topics covered in this chapter.

1 Literacy

According to the United Nations, almost 97 percent of adult populations in Western developed countries are literate. But the media in the United States often claim that 20 to 30 percent of Americans are functionally illiterate—they cannot read well enough to understand a newspaper, understand a paycheck stub, or complete a simple form. What is the cause of this discrepancy? To find out, you can read the article, "Measuring the Nation's Literacy: Important Considerations" by Terrence Wiley at *www.ed.gov/databases/ERIC_Digests/ed334870.html.* Literacy is important because how well you read and write influences your ability to participate in economic, social, and political life. Although more than 10 years old, the classic book *Illiterate America* by Jonathan Kozol (New American Library Trade, 1988) will give you a good start in understanding what problems are associated with illiteracy, why literacy is critical to success in life, and what you can do about illiteracy. Check the NP4 Web site for more links.

2 Typing

Gregory Arakelian holds the record as the world's fastest typist at 158 words per minute. A "good" typist's speed is around 60 words per minute. If you are still hunting and pecking, you might want to try working with typing software, such as *Typing Tutor* or *Mavis Beacon Teaches Typing.* You might want to visit *www.zdnet.com/familypc/content/960819/columns/parental/960819.html* and read the article "Time to Start Typing?" Some researchers claim that the arrangement of keys on the QWERTY keyboard limits typing speed. Read the article "Typing Errors" at the Reason Online site, *www.reasonmag.com/9606/Fe.QWERTY.html,* for a different discussion of the facts. At the Mavis Beacon Teaches Typing Web site, *www.mavisbeacon.com,* you can find information about the history of typing, links to information on repetitive stress injuries, and more.

3 Improve Your Writing

The World Wide Web has many, many resources for writers of all experience and talents. A number of universities have online writing labs that offer writing tips, style guidelines, advice about conducting research, and tips for writing term papers. Writing labs, such as The Writing Place at Northwestern University, *www.writing.nwu.edu/wwriters/heller.html* offer plenty of good advice. Look for other writing links at the NP4 Web site. If you need inspiration, connect to *www.clark.net/pub/edseiler/WWW/asimov_home_page.html,* the Isaac Asimov Home Page, where you'll find advice from one of the world's most prolific and broad-based writers.

4 Grammar

How's your grammar? You can take a grammar quiz (more interesting than it sounds) by connecting to *www.greyowltutor.com/quiz3.html.* For an entertaining viewpoint on grammar, read the Grammar Lady's column at *www.grammarlady.com.* At this site, you can also submit questions to the grammar hotline. A good desk reference available at your library is *Webster's New World Guide to Current American Usage* by Bernice Randall (Prentice Hall, 1988).

5 Fonts

Fonts or typefaces are the clothes that your words wear. The book *Typographic Design: Form and Communication* by Rob Carter, Ben Day, and Philip Meggs (John Wiley & Sons, 1985) provides a comprehensive introduction to typeforms, their organization, and their relationship to content. At the Web site for Graphion's Online Type Museum, *www.slip.net/~graphion/museum.html*, you can learn about the history and practice of typesetting. Then venture over to the typoGRAPHIC Web site, *www.typographic.rsub.com/typo*, where you can learn about the evolution and development of letterforms, view a timeline of the recent history of typography, find a glossary of typographic terms, and browse a gallery of typographic imagery. Microsoft Typography at *www.microsoft.com/truetype* contains free TrueType fonts and a discussion of typography on the Web. At the Shareware and Freeware Fonts Web page, *desktoppublishing.com/fonts-free.html*, you can find links to many Web sites that provide electronic fonts either for free or for a small fee.

6 Publishing: Electronic New Frontiers

Some inventions and discoveries have not only changed the trajectory of human endeavor, but have also changed the way that we see the world around us. The printing press and, as many suspect, electronic publishing are two such inventions. At the Media History Project Web site, located at *www.mediahistory.com/histhome.html*, you can contemplate these types of questions. You can also find at that site a timeline of media from 5,000 BCE to the present, reviews of books, archives of the Dead Media Project, and links to Internet resources on various media, from oral history to the printing press to digital media. You can find a discussion of Thomas Paine as the moral father of the Internet at "The Age of Paine," by Jon Katz at *www.wired.com/wired/archive/3.05/paine.html*. To learn what the experts predict about the future of books and electronic publishing, read "The Future of the Book" by Nicholas Negroponte at *www.wired.com/wired/4.02/negroponte.html*.

7 Who Wrote It?

Concordance was the tool used to unmask the anonymous author of *Primary Colors*. The Concordances and Corpora site discusses how computerized concordances work and presents information on several concordance programs (*www.georgetown.edu/cball/corpora/tutorial3.html*).You can learn more about concordances, by connecting to the Web Concordances and Workbook Web site at *www.dundee.ac.uk/english/wics/wics.htm*, a site in Dundee, Scotland, that includes concordances of selected poems of Shelley, Coleridge, Keats, Blake, and other poets. You might want to read *End of the Game* by L. Reilbstein (*Newsweek*, July 29, 1996), which describes the controversy over the authorship of *Primary Colors*.

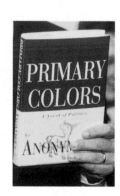

8 Spreadsheet Tips

The Spreadsheet Page at *www.j-walk.com/ss* contains information, files, and FAQs about Excel, Lotus 1-2-3, and Quattro Pro. At the Unofficial Microsoft Excel Page, *www.vex.net/~negandhi/excel*, you can find tips, reports on bugs, and files to download. You can link to tutorials, tips, free software and templates at the Microsoft Excel site, *www.microsoft.com/excel/*. For some tips and guidance on how to create a well-designed spreadsheet, connect to Spreadsheet Etiquette at *www.melbpc.org.au/pcupdate/9409/409sset.htm*.

9 Spreadsheet Errors

Research on spreadsheet errors has been carried out by Raymond R. Panko at the University of Hawaii. You can find out more about the alarming rate of spreadsheet errors at *www.panko.cba.hawaii.edu.* Also, check the NP4 Web site for additional links.

10 Lie: Don't Do it with Statistics or Graphs

You should avoid the temptation to tell tall tales with statistics. Find out how with the video *How Numbers Lie: Self-Defense Against Misleading Statistics* (1996). If you need to brush up on statistics, head for *nilesonline.com/stats,* where you'll find an entertaining tutorial. The updated 1954 classic, *How to Lie with Statistics*, by Darrell Huff (W W Norton & Co., 1993) is still a "must read." For more information on creating effective and truthful graphs, read *The Visual Display of Quantitative Information* by Edward R. Tufte (Graphics Press, 1992).

11 Information Careers

A career in information science is not new in the 1990s, but this career has new challenges In the Information Age. What is information science? Is it the career for you? To learn more about information science, read "Careers in Research Libraries and Information Science: The Dynamic Role of the Research Librarian" at *arl.cni.org/careers/CareersPaper.html.* At the Education and Careers for the 21st Century Web site, *www-slis.lib.indiana.edu/21stCentury/,* you can learn more about careers for information professionals in areas such as social informatics or content management. The American Society for Information Science (ASIS) was founded in 1937 and brings together information professionals from fields as diverse as computer science, linguistics, librarianship, engineering, and medicine. To learn more about ASIS, visit its Web site at *www.asis.org/.*

12 Search Engines

Search engines such as Yahoo! and Excite can help you locate information. There are many search engines available. But how do you use them most effectively? For a basic introduction to searching for information, connect to *www1.zdnet.com/complife/fea/9708/findny10.html* and read "Find Anything Online" by Reva Basch. "The Spider's Apprentice: How to Use Web Search Engines" at *www.monash.com/spidap4.html* provides helpful guidance about some of the Internet's main search engines. If you've ever asked yourself how these search engines work, read Steve Steinberg's online article, "Seek and Ye Shall Find (Maybe)," at *www.wired.com/wired/archive/4.05/ /indexweb.html.* The Search Engine Watch Web site at *searchenginewatch.com/* includes reviews and tutorials. For a more in-depth discussion of searching the Web, connect to "Beyond Surfing: Tools and Techniques for Searching the Web" by Kathleen Webster and Kathryn Paul at *magi.com/~mmclick/it96jan.htm.*

13 Online Card Catalogs

From your computer, you can search through the 4-million book card catalog of the Library of Congress. Just connect to *lcweb2.loc.gov/catalog.* Another great card catalog is located at the U.S. National Archives and Records Administration at *www.nara.gov,* where you'll find, among other things, the Kennedy Assassination Records Collection. The British Library also has an online card catalog that you can access at *opac97.bl.uk.*

14 Internet Citations

As you become an expert at locating information on the Web and Internet, you will want to start using that information in your term papers and reports. The *MLA Handbook for Writers of Research Papers* and the *APA Manual*, two books you can find in your library's reference department, present discussions and examples of how to cite source material from the Internet. Visit *www.colleges.org/ecite.html* for links to citation styles for Internet resources.

15 The Productivity Paradox

Before you formulate an opinion on the productivity paradox that was discussed in the *Issue* section of this chapter, you might want to check the Web for additional information. Use a search engine and enter "productivity paradox" as the keyword or check the NP4 Web site for some links to get you started.

CHAPTER 4
COMPUTER FILES AND DATA STORAGE

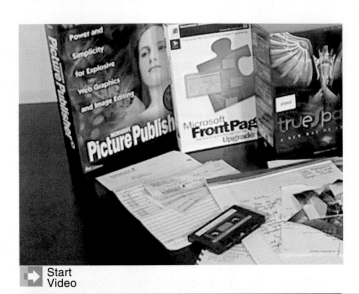

Start Video

CONTENTS

PREVIEW

This chapter provides a practical foundation for using a computer to manage your data. You will find out which storage device to use when you save data and how to create a valid filename that the computer will accept. You will learn how to use file manager utility software to organize the files on your disks so that they are easy to locate. You will also learn what happens in the computer when you store a file.

When you have completed this chapter you should be able to:

■ Correctly use the terms "data" and "information"

■ Create valid filenames under DOS and Windows

■ Explain how wildcards and file extensions simplify file access

■ Determine if a file is an executable file or a data file

■ Describe the difference between logical and physical file storage

■ Discuss how the directory and the FAT help you access files

■ Select a storage device based on characteristics such as its capacity and access speed

■ Describe the process of saving, retrieving, revising, deleting, and copying files

CHAPTER 4 LABS

Directories, Folders, Files

DOS File Management

Defragmentation

Using Files

TINY WRITING

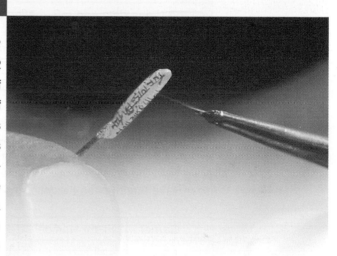

How much data can you pack into a small area? In 1968, Frederick Watts hand-printed 9,452 characters on a piece of paper the size of a postage stamp. In 1983, Tsutomu Ishii of Tokyo, Japan wrote the Japanese characters for *Tokyo, Japan*, on a human hair. A few years later, Surendra Apharya of Jaipur, India, managed to squeeze 241 characters on a single grain of rice. That seems like a lot of data packed into a small area, but a computer can store hundreds of times as much data in the same area. For example, an entire encyclopedia can fit on a single 4.75-inch CD-ROM disk.

How can computers store so much data in such a small area? Obviously, computers do not store data by somehow writing very small documents on a disk or CD-ROM. Instead, computers digitize data so that it can be stored using electronic, magnetic, or optical technologies. When you understand how these storage technologies differ, you can make better decisions about which storage devices you'll want to use.

With the potential to store thousands of pages or pictures on a disk, you might wonder how you can search through all that data to find what you want. This chapter explains how to use popular software utilities to locate and organize your data and answers other commonly asked questions about computer storage—for example, Can you change data once it is stored? What happens if you run out of disk space? What's the life span of the data that's stored on floppy and hard disks?

InfoWeb 1

World Records

SECTION A   DATA, INFORMATION, AND FILES

Computer professionals have special definitions for the terms *data*, *information*, and *file*. Although we might refer to them as technical definitions, they are not difficult to understand. Knowing these technical definitions will help you to communicate with computer professionals and understand phrases such as "data in, information out."

Data and Information: Technically Speaking

Aren't data and information the same thing? In everyday conversation, people use the terms *data* and *information* interchangeably. However, some computer professionals make a distinction between the two terms. **Data** is the words, numbers, and graphics that describe people, events, things, and ideas. Data becomes information when you use it as the basis for initiating some action or for making a decision. **Information**, then, is defined as the words, numbers, and graphics used as the basis for human actions and decisions.

To understand the distinction between data and information, consider the following: AA 4199 ORD 9:59 CID 11:09. These letters, numbers, and symbols describe an event— a flight schedule—and are typical of the *data* stored in a computer system. Now, suppose that you decide to take a trip from Chicago (ORD) to Cedar Rapids, Iowa (CID). Your travel agent sees the following on the computer screen:

Carrier	Flight Number	From	Departs	To	Arrives
AA	4199	ORD	9:59	CID	11:09

Within the context of making a flight reservation, these letters, numbers, and symbols would be considered *information* because your travel agent is using them to help you make a decision about your travel itinerary.

The distinction between data and information might seem somewhat elusive, because "AA 4199 ORD 9:59 CID 11:09" can be both data and information. When should you use the term "data," and when should you use the term "information"? As a rule of thumb, remember that technically speaking data is used by computers; information is used by humans. Usually, the letters, numbers, and symbols stored in a computer are referred to as data. When letters, numbers, and symbols are being used by a person to complete an action or make a decision, they are referred to as information.

Incidentally, in Latin, the word *data* is the plural for *datum*. According to this usage, it would be correct to say "The January and February rainfall *data* are stored on the disk," and "The March *datum* is not yet available." Most English dictionaries, however, accept the use of *data* as either singular or plural. In this text, *data* is used with the singular verb, as in "The *data is* stored on the disk."

Computer Files

What kinds of files are stored on a computer? A computer file, usually referred to simply as a **file**, is a named collection of data that exists on a storage medium such as a hard disk, a floppy disk, or a CD. A file could contain a computer program or data, such as a document, a graphic, a digital video, or digitized sound. For example, if you use a computer to write a memo to your employer, the words contained in the memo are stored on a disk as a file. You provide the file with a name to distinguish it from other files on the disk and to help you locate your memo in the future.

Project Due
MARCH 28th.

File Naming Conventions

May I use any name I want when I create my own files? A **filename** is a unique set of letters and numbers that identifies a file and usually describes the file contents. For example, *Pbrush* is the name of the file that contains the Microsoft Paint software.

A filename might be followed by a **filename extension** that further describes the file contents. Filename extensions are also referred to as "file extensions" or simply "extensions." In *Pbrush.exe*, *Pbrush* is the filename and *.exe* is the extension. As you can see, the extension is separated from the filename with a period, called a *dot*. To tell someone the name of this file, you would say "Pbrush dot e-x-e". You will learn more about using file extensions later in this chapter.

When you create a file, you must provide it with a valid filename that adheres to specific rules, referred to as **file naming conventions**. Each operating system has a unique set of file naming conventions. You can use Figure 4-1 to determine whether filenames such as *Aux, My File.doc,* and *Bud93/94.txt* are valid under the operating system that you use.

FIGURE 4-1	File Naming Conventions			
	DOS and Windows 3.1	**Windows 95/98/NT/2000**	**MacOS**	**UNIX/Linux**
Maximum length of filename	8-character filename plus an extension of 3 characters or less	255-character filename including an extension of 3 characters or less	31 characters (no extensions)	14-256 characters (depending on UNIX/Linux version) including an extension of any length
Spaces allowed	No	Yes	Yes	No
Numbers allowed	Yes	Yes	Yes	Yes
Characters not allowed	/ [ ] ; = " \ : , l * ?	\ ? : " < > l * /	None	! @ # $ % ^ & * () {} [] " \ ' ; < >
Filenames not allowed	Aux, Com1, Com2, Com3, Com4, Con, Lpt1, Lpt2, Lpt3, Prn, Nul	Aux, Com1, Com2, Com3, Com4, Con, Lpt1, Lpt2, Lpt3, Prn, Nul	None	Depends on the version of UNIX or Linux
Case sensitive	No	No	Yes	Yes (use lowercase)

Using DOS or Windows file naming conventions, *Aux* is in the list of filenames that are not allowed. *My File.doc* is not valid under DOS, Windows 3.1, or UNIX because it contains a space between *My* and *File*. The filename *Bud93/94.txt* would be valid only under MacOS because it contains a slash. Filenames such as *Session, Report.doc, Budget1.wks,* and *Form.1* are valid under all of the operating systems listed in Figure 4-1.

CHAPTER 4

Wildcards

Is *.* a filename? Files have unique names, but sometimes you might want to refer to more than one file. For example, suppose that you want to list all of the files on your disk with an .exe extension. You can specify **.exe* (pronounced "star dot e-x-e") to request such a list. The asterisk is a **wildcard character** used to represent a group of characters in the filename or extension. **.exe* means all of the files with an .exe extension. You can use the wildcard character to locate or delete groups of files on a disk.

Wildcards come in very handy when a disk, CD, or DVD contains hundreds of files and you don't want to manually scan through them. But, to understand how wildcards work, consider a sample disk that contains only the following nine files:

Word.exe	*Word.cfg*	*Sam.bmp*
Spell.exe	*Recruits.doc*	*Silver.exe*
Report.doc	*Mail.dat*	*Middle.bat*

Using the wildcard in *Word.** means that the filename must be *Word* but the extension can be anything. On the sample disk, two files fit this description: *Word.exe* and *Word.cfg*.

Some additional examples will help you recognize the many ways that you can use wildcards. **.doc* means any files with .doc extensions. On the sample disk, two files fit this description: *Recruits.doc* and *Report.doc*. *S** means any filename that begins with the letter "S." On the sample disk, *Spell.exe*, *Sam.bmp*, and *Silver.exe* match this description.

. (pronounced "star dot star") means all files. When you use DOS, the command *DEL *.** will delete all files in a directory. Be careful if you use this command. You wouldn't want to inadvertently wipe out all of your files!

Most operating systems allow you to use wildcards to make it easier to manipulate a collection of files. You will encounter wildcards even with a graphical user interface, as shown in Figure 4-2.

Wildcards help you locate filenames—for example, if you want to find a document that begins with the letter "R" when using Microsoft Word.

By typing R* in the File name box, you would be using the * wildcard to request a list of all files that begin with the letter "R".

*.doc uses a wildcard to specify all files that have a .doc extension.

The list includes only those files that begin with the letter "R" and have a .doc extension.

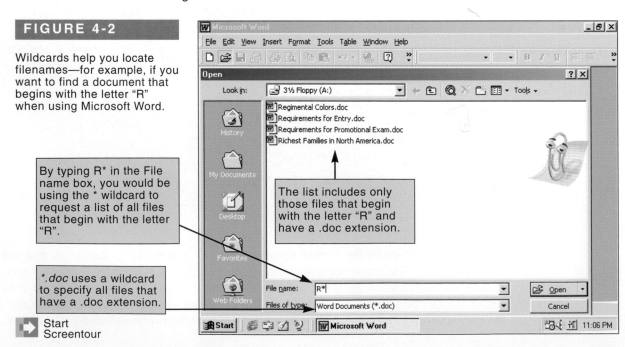

Start
Screentour

File Extensions and File Types

Why do I need to know about file extensions? Typically, a file extension indicates the category to which the file belongs. A computer file is categorized based on the data it contains, the software that was used to create it, and the way you should use it. You'll find it useful to understand the characteristics of file categories, so that you can access files efficiently. As you read on, you will learn about the most typical file categories: executable files, data files, configuration files, drivers, and modules.

Executable Files

How do I use executable files? An **executable file** contains the program instructions that tell a computer how to perform a specific task. For example, the word processing program that tells your computer how to display and print text is stored as an executable file. The executable files on your computer system include the operating system, utilities, and other application software programs. You can identify executable files by their filename extensions. Most executable files have an .exe extension, and a few have a .com extension.

Most have .exe or .com extensions.

To use an executable file, such as an application program, you "run" it or "start" it. In Chapter 1, you learned how to run a program by clicking the Start button, then selecting the program name from the Programs menu. You can also start a program by double-clicking its icon, as shown in Figure 4-3.

FIGURE 4-3

When using the Windows operating system, you can identify executable files by their unique program icons and by the .exe file extension.

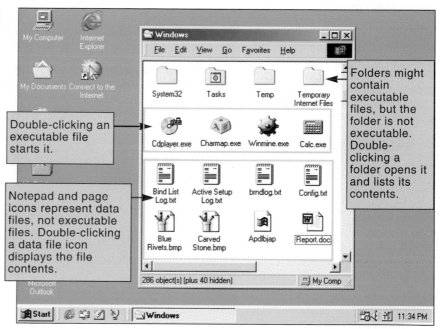

Double-clicking an executable file starts it.

Notepad and page icons represent data files, not executable files. Double-clicking a data file icon displays the file contents.

Folders might contain executable files, but the folder is not executable. Double-clicking a folder opens it and lists its contents.

CHAPTER 4

Data Files

How do I use data files? A **data file** contains words, numbers, and pictures that you can view, edit, save, send, and print. You can think of data files as passive—the data does not instruct or direct the computer to do anything. Executable files, on the other hand, are active—the instructions stored in the file cause the computer to carry out some action.

Typically, you create data files when you use application software. For example, you create a data file when you store a document that you've written using word processing software or when you save a picture that you've drawn using graphics software. You also create a data file when you store a spreadsheet, a graph, a sound clip, or a video.

You probably won't create all of the data files you use. Sometimes, you might receive data files as part of a software package that you purchase. For example, you could purchase a CD-ROM that contains a collection of clip art files.

Whether you create or purchase a data file, you typically use it in conjunction with application software that helps you manipulate the data in the file. You usually view, revise, and print a data file using the same software that was used to create it. For example, if you create a data file using word processing software such as Microsoft Word, you would usually use Microsoft Word to edit the file.

To view or edit a data file, you "open" it. The method that you use to open a data file depends on your computer's operating system. Windows, for example, provides several methods for opening data files. Two of these methods are explained in Figure 4-4.

FIGURE 4-4

When using Windows, you can select a data file from the documents list, or you can double-click its icon.

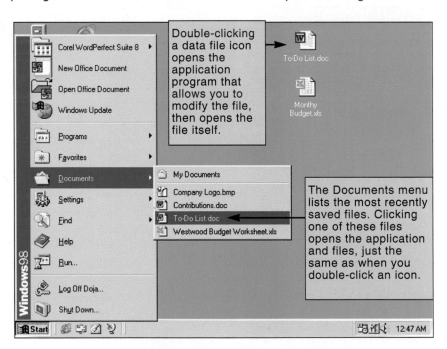

Double-clicking a data file icon opens the application program that allows you to modify the file, then opens the file itself.

The Documents menu lists the most recently saved files. Clicking one of these files opens the application and files, just the same as when you double-click an icon.

[handwritten margin notes: Root dir = C:\ ; A drive A A:\ ; what do text editor do? ex1 .txt ; example in DOS & windows. ; Give the DOS, unix, equivalence to ... web address on the Quiz ; What is the URL or web address of this course.]

The standard method for opening a data file requires that you start an application program, then use the open command provided by the application. This method works with just about any operating system and is preferred by many computer users. In Figure 4-5, for example, an artist has started the Paint application program and used Paint's Open command to view a digital rendition of a Van Gogh painting.

FIGURE 4-5

Most people prefer to open data files by first starting an application program, then using the Open command on the application's File menu.

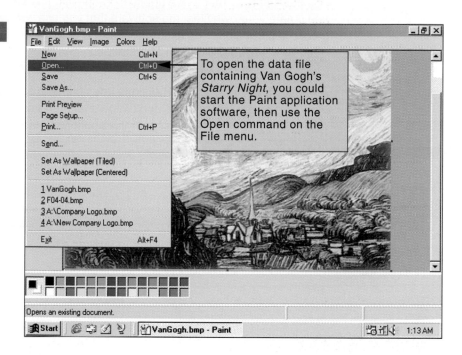

To open the data file containing Van Gogh's *Starry Night*, you could start the Paint application software, then use the Open command on the File menu.

Start
Screentour

You can't open a data file with just any old application software. Typically, you should open documents with word processing software, open worksheets with spreadsheet software, open graphics with paint or draw software, and so on. By looking at a file-name extension, you can get a clue as to the file's contents and the software that you should use to open it.

Filename
Extensions

Filename extensions for data files fall into two categories: generic extensions and application-specific extensions. A **generic filename extension** indicates the general type of data contained in a file, and usually means that you can open the file using one of several software packages. For example, a .bmp extension tells you that the file contains graphical data and that you could open it using almost any any graphics software, such as Microsoft Paint or MicroGrafx Picture Publisher. Figure 4-6 lists some generic filename extensions.

FIGURE 4-6	Generic Filename Extensions
Type of file	**Filename Extension**
Text	.txt .dat .rtf
Sound	.wav .mid
Graphics	.bmp .pcx .tif .wmf .jpg .gif
Animation/video	.flc .fli .avi .mpg .mov
Web documents	.html .htm

[vertical tab, right margin] CHAPTER 4

An **application-specific filename extension** is associated with a particular application and indicates which application software was used to create a file. For example, a file created with Microsoft Word for Windows typically has a .doc extension. You will get the best results if you open that .doc file using Microsoft Word software.

Is it necessary to memorize application-specific filename extensions? Not really. When you create your own files, the software that you use will automatically append the correct filename extension. For example, if you create a document with Microsoft Word, you need to enter only the main filename, such as "Report". The Word software will automatically append a .doc extension, making the full filename *Report.doc*.

A knowledge of filename extensions does come in handy when you receive a file on a disk or over the Internet but don't know much about its contents. By looking at the file extension, you can often discover the application that you should use to open the file. Figure 4-7 lists some application-specific filename extensions that you are likely to encounter.

FIGURE 4-7	Application-specific Filename Extensions
Application Software	**Filename Extension**
WordPerfect (Word processing)	.wpd
Microsoft Word and WordPad (Word processing)	.doc
Lotus Word Pro (Word processing)	.sam
Microsoft Works (Word processing)	.wps
Microsoft Works (Spreadsheet)	.wks
Lotus 1-2-3 (Spreadsheet)	.wk4
Microsoft Excel (Spreadsheet)	.xls
Microsoft Access (Database)	.mdb
Microsoft PowerPoint (Presentation)	.ppt
Adobe Acrobat Reader (Portable file viewer)	.pdf
WinZip (Compression)	.zip

Configuration Files, Program Modules, and Other Files

What other kinds of files will I find on my computer? In addition to executable files and data files, a computer typically contains other kinds of files that are essential for hardware or software operations. These files have extensions such as .bat, .sys, .cfg, .dll, .ocx, .vbx, .ini, .mif, .hlp, and .tmp. Because these files—even the so-called "temporary" files—are crucial for the correct operation of your computer system, it is important not to delete them. Figure 4-8 provides additional information on each of these file categories.

FIGURE 4-8	Filename Extensions for Configuration Files and Program Modules	
Type of File	**Description**	**Filename Extension**
Batch file	A sequence of operating system commands that are executed automatically when the computer boots.	.bat
Configuration file	Information about programs that the computer uses to allocate the resources necessary to run them.	.cfg, .sys, .mif, .ini
Help	The information that is displayed by online Help.	.hlp
Temporary file	A sort of "scratch pad" that contains data while a program is running, but that is discarded when you exit the program.	.tmp
Program support modules	Program instructions that are executed in conjunction with the main .exe file for a program.	.ocx, .vbx, .dll

CHAPTER 4

QUICKCHECK   A

1 As a rule of thumb, _data_ is used by computers; _information_ is used by humans.

2 The asterisk is a(n) _wildcard_ character that is used to represent a group of characters in a filename or extension.

3 Most executable files have a(n) _.exe_ extension.

4 In computer jargon, you _open_ a data file, and you "run" a program.

5 Files extensions, such as .bmp and .txt are _generic_ file extensions, which means that they can be opened using more than one software package.

6 You can delete files with .bat, .sys., and .cfg extensions because they are temporary, unnecessary files. True or false?

 Check Answers

FILE MANAGER UTILITY SOFTWARE

Your computer system might contain hundreds or even thousands of files stored on disks and other storage devices. To keep track of these files, computer operating systems provide **file manager utility software** that helps you locate, rename, move, copy, and delete files. File managers vary from one operating system to another, but all are based on similar concepts. Using the basic concepts about device letters and folders presented in this section, you will be able to navigate most computer systems to locate files so that you can open, rename, delete, move, or copy them.

Device Letters

Why do storage devices have letters? Suppose that you're looking for an old friend from high school. If you know the city in which he lives, you can easily look for his name in the telephone directory for that city. Looking for computer files is similar because knowing which storage device holds the file makes locating it much easier.

Most computers have more than one storage device, such as a floppy disk drive, a hard disk drive, and a CD-ROM or DVD drive. A storage device is typically identified by a letter called a **device letter**, which simply provides a shorthand way to refer to a particular storage device when saving or opening files.

Your computer's floppy disk drive is usually assigned device letter A and is referred to as drive A. The main hard disk drive is usually referred to as drive C. Additional storage devices can be assigned letters from D through Z. A device letter is sometimes followed by a colon, so C: would refer to a computer's hard disk drive. Figure 4-9 shows the device letter assignments for a computer that is "fully loaded" with storage devices.

floppy drive = A
main hard disk =

FIGURE 4-9

On microcomputers, it is conventional for the floppy disk drive to be drive A and the hard disk drive to be drive C. The device letters for other storage devices vary. On one computer the CD-ROM drive might be E, whereas on another computer it might be drive R.

A tape drive typically has no device letter.

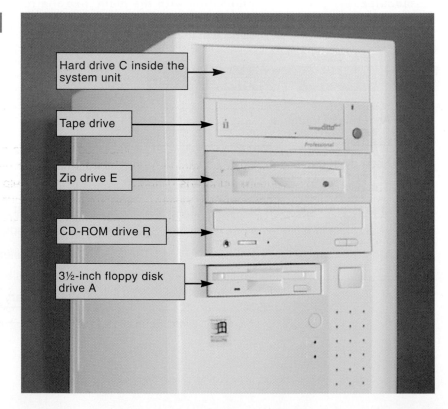

Hard drive C inside the system unit

Tape drive

Zip drive E

CD-ROM drive R

3½-inch floppy disk drive A

Directories and Folders

How can I get a list of files that are stored on a disk? An operating system maintains a list of files called a **directory** for each disk, CD-ROM, or DVD. One way to find a file is to look through the directory listings. A directory contains information about every file on a storage device, including the filename, the filename extension, the date and time the file was created, and the file size. You can use the operating system's file manager utility software to view the directories for a computer's storage devices.

FIGURE 4-10

The operating system's file manager utility displays lots of information about the files stored on a computer.

The highlight indicates which directory you are viewing—in this case, the root directory for drive A.

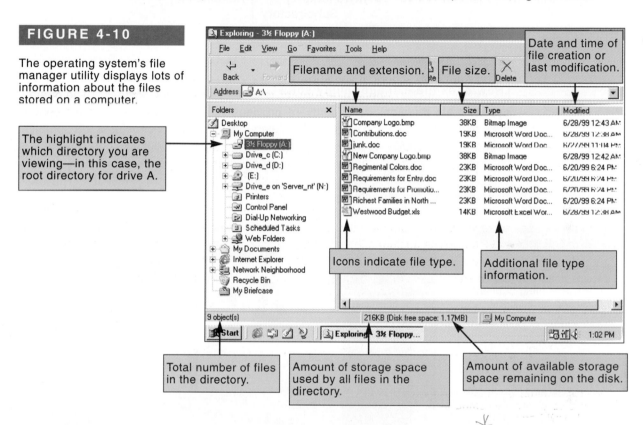

A folder name is separated from a drive letter and a filename by a special symbol. In DOS and Microsoft Windows, this symbol is the backslash \. For example, the root directory of drive C might have a folder called *Graphics*, written as *C:\Graphics*.

Lab

Directories, Folders, Files

The main directory of a disk, sometimes referred to as the **root directory**, provides a useful list of files. Finding a particular file could be difficult, however, if the root directory contains hundreds or thousands of files. To help you organize a large number of files, most operating systems allow you to divide your directory into smaller lists called **folders** or "subdirectories." For example, you can create one folder to hold all of your files that contain documents and another folder to hold all of your files that contain graphical images. Folders can be further divided into other folders, sometimes called "subfolders."

A folder name is separated from a drive letter and a filename by a special symbol. In DOS and Microsoft Windows, this symbol is the backslash \. For example, the root directory of drive C might have a folder called *Graphics*, written as *C:\Graphics*.

instant order

* A **file specification** (sometimes called a "path") is the drive letter, folder, filename, and extension that identifies a file. Suppose that you create a folder on drive A named *Word* for your word processing documents. Now suppose that you want to create a document called *Gumbo* for your favorite soup recipe and store it on drive A in the Word folder. The file specification is

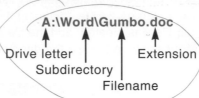

A:\Word\Gumbo.doc

Drive letter   Extension
    Subdirectory
             Filename

Storage Models

> How does file manager utility software depict files and folders?

The operating system's file manager utility software provides you with a symbolic or metaphorical view of the files stored on a computer. Metaphors for directory structures are sometimes called *logical models* because they represent the way you logically conceive of them. Several file storage metaphors are commonly used by file manager utilities, including the "filing cabinet" and "tree structure" metaphors. Figure 4-11 illustrates the filing cabinet metaphor for computer storage systems.

FIGURE 4-11

A file cabinet metaphor depicts a storage device as a drawer of a filing cabinet containing folders and documents.

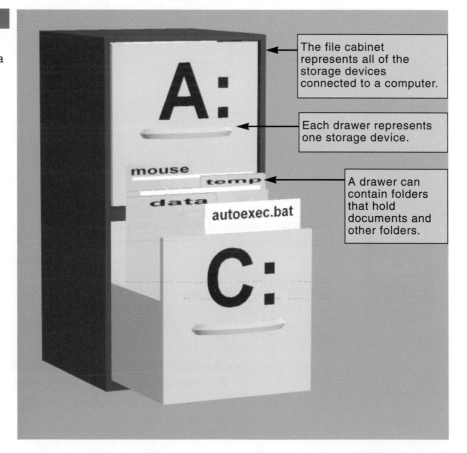

The file cabinet represents all of the storage devices connected to a computer.

Each drawer represents one storage device.

A drawer can contain folders that hold documents and other folders.

Another conceptual model of computer storage is based on a hierarchical diagram that some people refer to as a "tree structure." In this metaphor, illustrated in Figure 4-12, a tree represents a storage device. The trunk of the tree is the root directory. The branches of the tree represent folders. These branches can split into smaller branches or subfolders. The leaves at the end of a branch represent individual files.

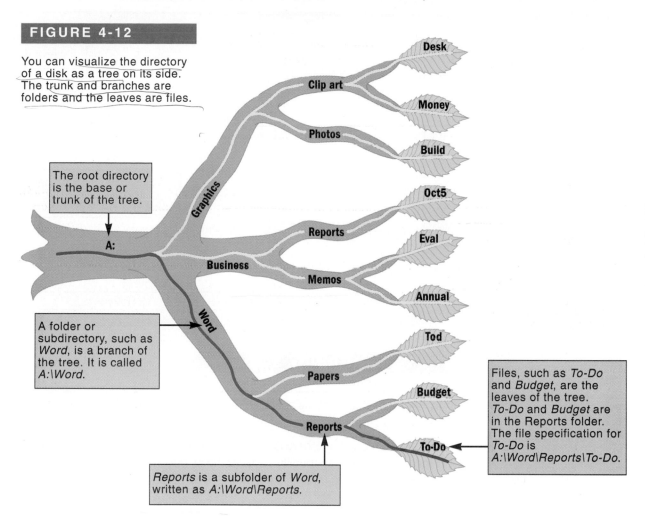

FIGURE 4-12

You can visualize the directory of a disk as a tree on its side. The trunk and branches are folders and the leaves are files.

The root directory is the base or trunk of the tree.

A folder or subdirectory, such as *Word*, is a branch of the tree. It is called *A:\Word*.

Reports is a subfolder of *Word*, written as *A:\Word\Reports*.

Files, such as *To-Do* and *Budget*, are the leaves of the tree. *To-Do* and *Budget* are in the Reports folder. The file specification for *To-Do* is *A:\Word\Reports\To-Do*.

The tree structure metaphor provides a useful mental image of the way in which folders and files are organized. It is not, however, particularly practical as a user interface. Imagine the tree diagram expanded to show a more realistic set of folders that contain hundreds of files. Depicting such a collection of files on little green leaf graphics would be cumbersome.

CHAPTER 4

Graphical user interface designers devised several ways to translate these metaphors into a more practical screen display. Figure 4-13 shows how Microsoft programmers used both the file cabinet and tree structure metaphors to create a file manager utility called Windows Explorer.

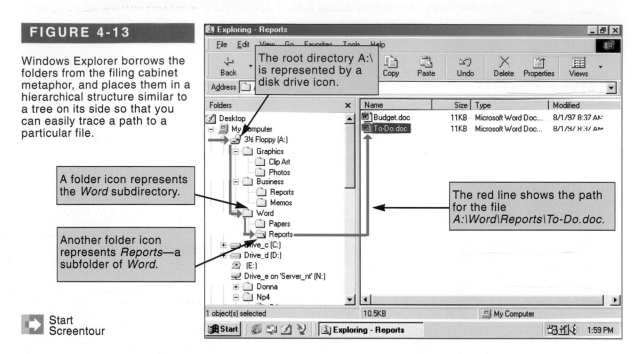

FIGURE 4-13

Windows Explorer borrows the folders from the filing cabinet metaphor, and places them in a hierarchical structure similar to a tree on its side so that you can easily trace a path to a particular file.

A folder icon represents the *Word* subdirectory.

Another folder icon represents *Reports*—a subfolder of *Word*.

The root directory A:\ is represented by a disk drive icon.

The red line shows the path for the file A:\Word\Reports\To-Do.doc.

Start Screentour

Using File Manager Utility Software

How do I use file manager utility software? The purpose of file manager utility software is to help you find, rename, copy, move, and delete files or folders. The list that follows describes when you might want to perform these file operations.

■ **Find.** Before you can open or otherwise manipulate a file or folder, you need to know where it is located. File manager utility software helps you view the directory structure of a storage device to locate folders, then look through the folders to find a particular file.

■ **Rename.** You might want to change the name of a file or folder to better describe its contents. When renaming a file, you typically should be careful to keep the same file-name extension so that you can open it with the correct application software.

■ **Copy.** You can copy a file or folder to a floppy disk—for example, if you would like to send it to a friend or colleague. You might also want to make a copy of a document so that you can revise the copy and leave the original intact. Remember to adhere to copyright and license restrictions when you copy files.

■ **Move.** You can move a file from one folder to another or from one storage device to another. When you move a file, it is erased from its original location, so make sure that you remember the new location of the file. You can also move folders from one storage device to another or move them to a different folder.

■ **Delete.** You can delete a file when you no longer need it. You can also delete a folder. Be careful when you delete a folder because most file manager utilities also delete all the files that a folder contains.

Lab
DOS File
Management

Because different file managers use different metaphors, the exact procedures for these file operations will vary. However, many of today's computers use the Windows operating system, so you are most likely to use Windows Explorer file manager utility software. Figure 4-14 briefly explains how you can use Windows Explorer to locate, rename, copy, move, and delete files. If you would like to compare the same operations under DOS, you can explore the DOS File Management Lab.

FIGURE 4-14

File manager utilities allow you to rename, copy, move, and delete files.

By opening a storage device icon, you can see the first level of folders.

By opening a folder, you can see any subfolders that it contains. If the folder contains files, they are displayed on the right side of the screen.

Start
Screentour

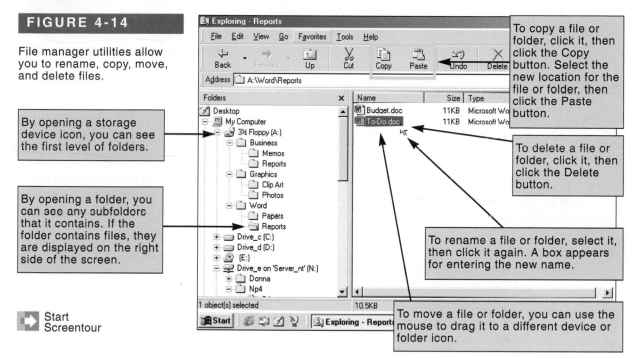

To copy a file or folder, click it, then click the Copy button. Select the new location for the file or folder, then click the Paste button.

To delete a file or folder, click it, then click the Delete button.

To rename a file or folder, select it, then click it again. A box appears for entering the new name.

To move a file or folder, you can use the mouse to drag it to a different device or folder icon.

CHAPTER 4

QUICKCHECK B

1 A computer's floppy disk drive is usually referred to as drive A, and the hard disk drive is drive B. True or false? ☐ *C*

2 The main directory for a disk is called the ☐ *Root* directory.

3 Folders are also called ☐ *Sub directories*.

4 What is the filename extension in the path: A:\Research\Primates\Jan5.dat. ☐ *.DAT* *Root → folder or sub*

5 The file manager utility software that is included with the Windows operating system is called Windows Explorer. True or false? ☐

6 Metaphors of directory structures are sometimes called ☐ *logical* models *know for test*

7 File manager utility software prevents you from illegally copying files. True or false? ☐

 Check Answers

HOW COMPUTERS STORE FILE DATA

The conceptual model of folders and files that you see when using a file manager utility has little relationship to what actually happens when a computer stores data on a disk. Your computer does not mark off a section of a disk for each folder, nor does it necessarily store a file as a unit. Surprisingly, the data for a single file can be scattered all over the surface of a disk.

The way that a computer actually stores data on a disk is referred to as "physical storage." In contrast, a conceptual model of files and folders would be referred to as "logical storage." Although it is not absolutely necessary to understand all of the details that pertain to physical storage, the general background presented in this section will help you understand important differences between storage technologies, such as floppy disks, hard disks, CD-ROMs, and DVDs.

Storage Terminology

What are the basic components of a data storage system? A data storage system has two main components: a storage medium and a storage device. A **storage medium** (storage media is the plural) is the disk, tape, CD, DVD, paper, or other substance that contains data. A **storage device** is the mechanical apparatus that records and retrieves data from a storage medium. Storage devices include floppy disk drives, hard disk drives, CD drives, DVD drives, and tape drives. The term **storage technology** refers to a storage device and the media it uses.

The process of storing data is often referred to as "writing data" or "saving a file" because the storage device *writes* the data on the storage medium to *save* it for later use. The process of retrieving data is often referred to as "reading data," "loading data," or "opening a file." The terms "reading" and "writing" make sense if you imagine that you are the computer. As the computer, you *write* a note and save it for later. You retrieve the note and *read* it when you need the information it contains. The terms *reading data* and *writing data* are often associated with mainframe applications. The terms *save* and *open* are standard Windows terminology.

Bits and Bytes

If I enter a letter or number how is it actually stored? Microcomputers store digital data. Therefore, your computer must translate the information that you enter from documents, graphics, videos, or sound recordings, into a digital series of 1s and 0s. As an example, suppose that you create a document that begins with the word "At". A computer would convert the "A" into 01000001 and the "t" into 01110100. Computers use a variety of methods or "codes" to convert information into digital data. You will learn more about the digital codes that represent data in the next chapter. For now, just envision your documents, graphics, etc., as a continuous series of 1s and 0s.

Each 1 or 0 that represents data is referred to as a **bit** and is the smallest unit for digitizing data. Eight bits are referred to as a **byte** (rhymes with "light"). Four bits are called a "nibble" (really!). In a document, each byte usually represents one character—a letter, punctuation mark, space, or numeral. The phrase "profit margin" requires 13 bytes of storage space because the phrase contains 12 characters and the space between the two words requires an additional byte of storage space.

Magnetic and Optical Technologies

How does a computer get the 1s and 0s onto the storage medium?

You can envision a document stored in your computer's memory as a long series of 1s and 0s. These bits are sent to a storage device, which writes the data on a storage medium. Obviously, the data is not literally written as "1" or "0". Instead, the 1s and 0s have to be transformed into changes in the surface of a storage medium. Exactly how this transformation happens depends on the storage technology. For example, floppy disks store data in a different way than CD-ROMs. Today's microcomputer storage devices typically use either magnetic or optical storage technologies.

Hard disk, floppy disk, and tape storage technologies can be classified as **magnetic storage**, which stores data by magnetizing microscopic particles on the disk or tape surface. The particles retain their magnetic orientation until that orientation is changed, thereby making disks and tape fairly permanent but modifiable storage media. A **read-write head** mechanism in the disk drive reads and writes the magnetized particles that represent data. Figure 4-15 shows how a computer stores data on magnetic media.

FIGURE 4-15

Storing data on magnetic media.

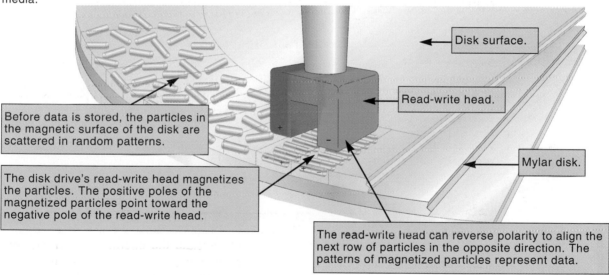

Disk surface.

Read-write head.

Before data is stored, the particles in the magnetic surface of the disk are scattered in random patterns.

The disk drive's read-write head magnetizes the particles. The positive poles of the magnetized particles point toward the negative pole of the read-write head.

Mylar disk.

The read-write head can reverse polarity to align the next row of particles in the opposite direction. The patterns of magnetized particles represent data.

Data that has been stored magnetically can be easily changed or deleted, simply by changing the magnetic orientation of the appropriate particles on the disk surface. This feature of magnetic storage provides lots of flexibility for editing data and reusing areas of a storage medium that contains unneeded data.

Data stored on magnetic media such as floppy disks can be altered by magnetic fields, dust, mold, smoke particles, heat, and mechanical problems with a storage device. Placing a magnet on a floppy disk, for example, is a sure way of losing data.

Magnetic media gradually lose their magnetic charge, resulting in lost data. Some experts estimate that the reliable life span of data stored on magnetic media is about three years. They recommend that you refresh your data every two years by recopying it.

CHAPTER 4

less susceptible to environmental damage?

FIGURE 4-16

The pits on an optical storage disk as seen through an electron microscope. Each pit is 1 micron in diameter—1,500 pits lined up side by side would be about as wide as the head of a pin.

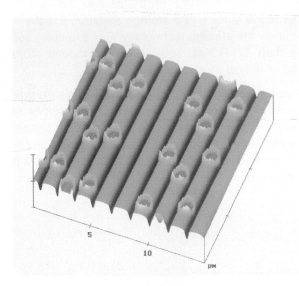

CD and DVD storage technologies can be classified as **optical storage**, which stores data as microscopic light and dark spots on the disk surface. The dark spots, which are shown in Figure 4-16, are called pits. The lighter, non-pitted surface areas of the disk are called lands.

Optical storage gets its name because it is possible to see the data using a high-powered microscope. The transition between pits and lands is interpreted as the 1s and 0s that represent data. An optical storage device uses a low-power laser light to read the data that has been stored on an optical disk, as shown in Figure 4-17.

The data that has been recorded on optical media is generally considered to be less susceptible to environmental damage than data that has been recorded on magnetic media.

FIGURE 4-17

Optical storage devices read data using reflected laser light.

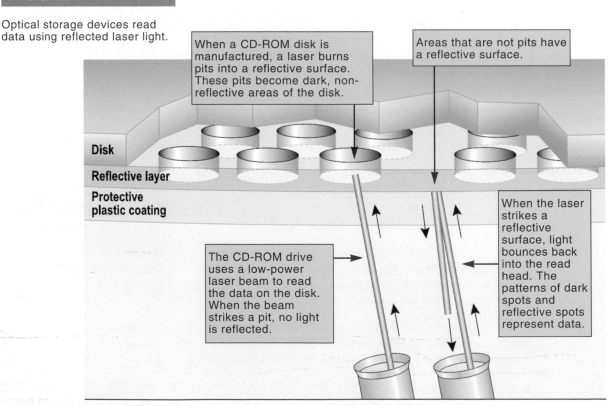

When a CD-ROM disk is manufactured, a laser burns pits into a reflective surface. These pits become dark, non-reflective areas of the disk.

Areas that are not pits have a reflective surface.

Disk

Reflective layer

Protective plastic coating

The CD-ROM drive uses a low-power laser beam to read the data on the disk. When the beam strikes a pit, no light is reflected.

When the laser strikes a reflective surface, light bounces back into the read head. The patterns of dark spots and reflective spots represent data.

Tracks, Sectors, and Clusters

Is data stored in specific places on a disk, tape, or CD? Before a computer stores data on a storage medium, it creates the equivalent of electronic storage bins called **tracks**. Optical technologies store data in tracks that spiral out from the center of the disk. On computer tapes, the tracks run parallel to the edge of the tape. On magnetic disks, the tracks are arranged as concentric circles, which are further divided into wedge-shaped **sectors**, as shown in Figure 4-18.

Know this diagram

FIGURE 4-18

Data is stored in tracks and sectors.

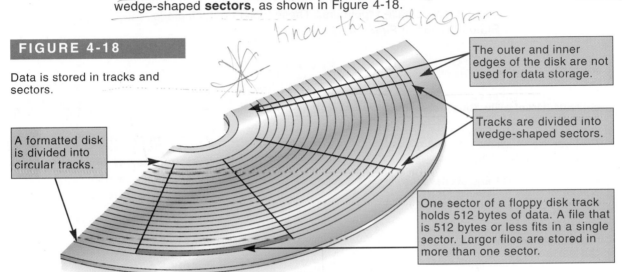

A formatted disk is divided into circular tracks.

The outer and inner edges of the disk are not used for data storage.

Tracks are divided into wedge-shaped sectors.

One sector of a floppy disk track holds 512 bytes of data. A file that is 512 bytes or less fits in a single sector. Larger files are stored in more than one sector.

Tracks and sectors are numbered to provide addresses for the data storage "bins." The numbering scheme depends on the storage device and the operating system. For example, the floppy disks that you use if your computer has the Windows operating system have 80 tracks and 18 sectors on each side.

Tracks and sectors can be handled individually or as a group. To speed up the process of reading and writing data, a disk drive usually handles a group of sectors, called a **cluster**. The number of sectors that form a cluster vary, depending on the capacity of the disk and the technical specifications of the disk drive.

File Allocation Tables

How does a computer keep track of the location for every file? A computer's operating system keeps track of stored files by creating a file similar to a table of contents on every storage medium that contains files. The exact structure of the table of contents varies, based on the type of media. CD-ROMs require a slightly different table of contents than a floppy or hard disk, for example. To illustrate how a computer keeps track of files, consider what happens when you store and retrieve files from a floppy or hard disk.

InfoWeb
3
FAT

When you store a file on a disk, the operating system records the cluster number that contains the beginning of the file in a **file allocation table** (FAT). The FAT is an operating system file that maintains a list of files and their physical location on the disk. It is such a crucial file that if it is damaged by a head crash or other disaster, you generally lose access to all of the data stored on your disk. The possibility of losing data because of a damaged FAT, is one important reason to back up the data on your hard disk.

When your computer stores a file, the operating system looks at the FAT to see which clusters are empty. The operating system then puts the data for the file in empty clusters. The cluster numbers are recorded in the FAT. The name of the new file and the number of the first cluster that contains the file data are recorded in the directory.

A file that does not fit into a single cluster will spill over into the next contiguous (meaning "adjacent") cluster unless that cluster already contains data. If the next cluster is full, the operating system stores the file in a noncontiguous ("nonadjacent") cluster and sets up instructions called "pointers." These "point" to each piece of the file, as shown in the Status column of Figure 4-19.

FIGURE 4-19

Each colored cluster on the disk contains part of a file. Clusters 3 and 4 (blue) contain the *Bio.txt* file. Cluster 9 (aqua) contains the *Pick.wps* file. Clusters 7, 8, and 10 contain the *Jordan.wks* file.

A computer locates and displays the *Jordan.wks* file, by looking for its name in the file allocation table. By following the pointers listed in the Status column, the computer can then see that the file is continued in clusters 8 and 10.

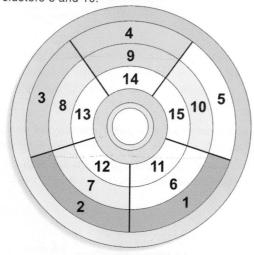

File Allocation Table		
Cluster	**Status**	**Comment**
1	1	Reserved for operating system
2	1	Reserved for operating system
3	4	First cluster of *Bio.txt*. *Points* to cluster 4, which holds more data for *Bio.txt*
4	999	Last cluster of *Bio.txt*
5	0	Empty
6	0	Empty
7	8	First cluster for *Jordan.wks*. Points to cluster 8, which holds more data for the *Jordan.wks* file
8	10	Second cluster for *Jordan.wks*. Points to cluster 10, which holds more data for the *Jordan.wks* file
9	999	First and last cluster containing *Pick.wps*
10	999	Last cluster of *Jordan.wks*

When you want to retrieve a file, the operating system looks through the directory for the filename and the number of the first cluster that contains the file data. The FAT tells the computer which clusters contain the remaining data for the file. The operating system moves the read-write head to the cluster that contains the beginning of the file and reads it. If the file is stored in more than one cluster, the read-write head must move to the next cluster to read more of the file. It takes longer to access a file stored in noncontiguous clusters than one stored in contiguous clusters because the disk or head must move farther to find the next section of the file.

When you erase a file, the operating system changes the status of the appropriate clusters in the FAT. For example, if a file is stored in clusters 5, 7, 9, and 11 and you erase it, the operating system changes the status for those four clusters to "empty." The data is not physically removed or erased from those clusters. Instead, the old data remains in the clusters until a new file is stored there. This rather interesting situation means that if you inadvertently erase a file, you might be able to get it back using the operating system's **undelete utility**. In Windows, such a utility is available as the Recycle Bin's Restore feature. Of course, you can undelete a file only if you haven't recorded something new over it, so undelete works only if you discover and correct mistakes immediately.

As you use random-access storage, files tend to become **fragmented**—that is, each file is stored in many noncontiguous clusters. Drive performance generally declines as the drive works harder to locate the clusters that contain the parts of a file. To regain peak performance, you can use a **defragmentation utility** to rearrange the files on a disk so that they are stored in contiguous clusters. Study Figure 4-20, which explains more about fragmentation and defragmentation.

FIGURE 4-20

Defragmenting a disk helps your computer operate more efficiently.

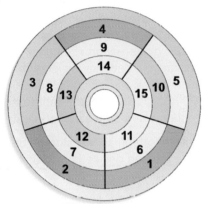

Fragmented disk

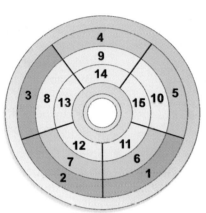

Defragmented disk

On this fragmented disk, the purple, yellow, and blue files are stored in non-contiguous clusters. Accessing the clusters for these files is not efficient because of the time required to move the read-write head over the data.

When the disk is defragmented, the clusters of data for each file are moved to contiguous clusters. Data access becomes more efficient because drive head and disk movement are minimized.

QUICKCHECK C

1 The phrase "Now on Sale" would require 11 bits of storage space. True or false?

2 A computer stores data on a floppy disk by _magnatising_ microscopic particles on the disk surface.

3 _optical_ storage devices store data as microscopic light and dark spots on the surface of a CD or DVD disk.

4 On hard disks and floppy disks, data is stored in concentric _tracks_, which are further divided into sectors.

5 A special file called the _file allocat-_ keeps track of the physical location of data on a floppy or hard disk.

6 Disk drive performance declines as the files stored on a disk become _fragmented_.

 Check Answers

SECTION D — DISKS, TAPES, CDs, AND DVDs

Today's computers sport multiple types of storage devices, each with unique advantages and disadvantages. Computer buyers, faced with the daunting task of selecting from a wide array of storage technologies, find it helpful to understand the characteristics of these devices. To compare storage devices, it is useful to apply four criteria: versatility, durability, capacity, and speed.

■ **Versatility.** Some storage devices can access data from only one type of medium. More versatile devices can access data from several different media.

■ **Durability.** Most storage technologies are susceptible to damage from mishandling or other environmental factors, such as heat and moisture. Some technologies are less susceptible than others. More durable technologies are less susceptible to damage that could cause data loss.

■ **Capacity.** In today's computing environment, higher capacity is almost always preferred. **Storage capacity** is the maximum amount of data that can be stored on a storage medium and is usually measured in kilobytes, megabytes, gigabytes, or terabytes. A **kilobyte** (KB) is 1,024 bytes, but this number is often rounded to 1 thousand bytes. A **megabyte** (MB) is 1,048,576 bytes—approximately 1 million bytes. A **gigabyte** (GB) is 1,073,741,824 bytes—approximately 1 billion bytes. A **terabyte** (TB) is about 1 trillion bytes. When you read that the storage capacity of a computer is 20.4 gigabytes, it means the hard disk on that computer can store as much as 20.4 billion bytes of information. This capacity is equivalent to approximately 5,400,000 single-spaced pages of text—that would be a stack of paper 1,800 feet high!

■ **Speed.** Quick access to data is important, so fast storage devices are preferred over slower devices. The speed of a storage device is measured by its access time and its data transfer rate.

Access time is the average time it takes a computer to locate data on the storage medium and read it. Access time for a microcomputer storage device, such as a disk drive, is measured in milliseconds. One **millisecond** (ms) is one-thousandth of a second. Lower numbers indicate faster access times. For example, a drive with a 6 ms access time is faster than a drive with an access time of 11 ms. Access time is best for random access devices. **Random access** (also called "direct access") is the ability of a device to "jump" directly to the track or sector that holds the requested data. Floppy disk, hard disk, CD, and DVD drives are random access devices. A tape drive, on the other hand, must use slower **sequential access** by reading through the data from the beginning of the tape.

Data transfer rate is the amount of data that a storage device can move from the storage medium to the computer per second. Higher numbers indicate faster transfer rates. For example, a CD-ROM drive with a 600 KBps data transfer rate is faster than one with a 300 KBps transfer rate.

This section provides an overview of microcomputer storage technologies in five major categories: floppy disk, hard disk, tape, CD, and DVD. The CD and DVD categories are divided into subsections because several variations of these technologies are in widespread use.

Floppy Disk Storage

InfoWeb 4

Floppies & Zips

Why is it called a floppy disk?   A **floppy disk** is a round piece of flexible mylar plastic covered with a thin layer of magnetic oxide. The disk is sealed inside a protective casing. Floppy disks are also called "floppies" or "diskettes." Those brightly colored computer disks that fit conveniently in your pocket or backpack are sometimes mistakenly called "hard disks" because of their rigid plastic casing; they are "floppies," however, not hard disks. If you break open the disk casing (something you should never do unless you want to ruin the disk), you would see that the mylar disk inside is thin and, well, floppy. A special high-capacity floppy disk manufactured by Iomega Corporation is called a **Zip disk**.

Floppy disks come in several sizes: 3½ inch, 5¼ inch, and 8 inch. The disk size most commonly used on today's microcomputers is 3½ inch. When a 3½-inch disk is inserted in a disk drive, the spring-loaded access cover slides to the side to expose the disk surface for reading and writing data. Figure 4-21 shows the construction of a 3½-inch floppy disk.

FIGURE 4-21

3½-inch floppy disk construction.

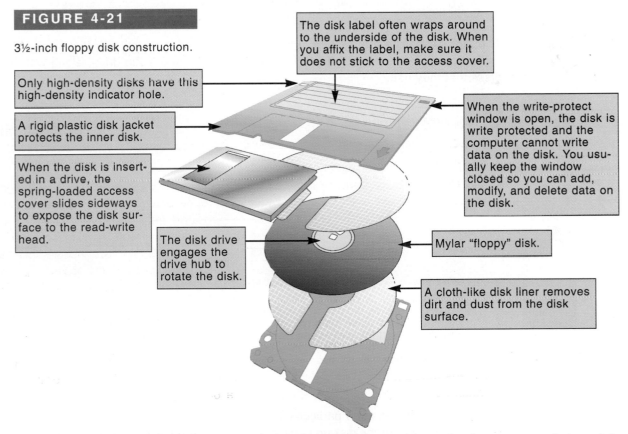

The disk label often wraps around to the underside of the disk. When you affix the label, make sure it does not stick to the access cover.

Only high-density disks have this high-density indicator hole.

A rigid plastic disk jacket protects the inner disk.

When the disk is inserted in a drive, the spring-loaded access cover slides sideways to expose the disk surface to the read-write head.

When the write-protect window is open, the disk is write protected and the computer cannot write data on the disk. You usually keep the window closed so you can add, modify, and delete data on the disk.

The disk drive engages the drive hub to rotate the disk.

Mylar "floppy" disk.

A cloth-like disk liner removes dirt and dust from the disk surface.

In the past, floppy disks stored data only on one side; today, however, most store data on both sides. As you might guess, a **double-sided disk** (sometimes abbreviated as DSD or DS) stores twice as much data as a single-sided disk. The amount of data that a disk stores depends on its density. **Disk density** refers to the closeness and size of the magnetic particles on the disk surface. The higher the disk density, the smaller the magnetic particles it stores, and the more data it can store. Think of it this way: Just as you can put more lemons than grapefruit in a basket, you can store more data on a disk coated with smaller particles than with larger particles. A **high-density disk** (HD or

HDD) can store more data than a **double-density disk** (DDD or DD). Most of today's computers use high-density 3½-inch disks formatted with 18 sectors and 80 tracks per side. Figure 4-22 summarizes floppy disk capacities by size and density.

FIGURE 4-22	Floppy and Zip Disk Capacities		
Size	5¼"	3½"	3½"	3½" Zip
Density	High	Double	High	N/A
Capacity	1.2 MB	720 KB	1.44 MB	100 MB
Sectors per side	15	9	18	32
Tracks per side	80	80	80	3,065

The storage device that records and retrieves data on a floppy disk is a floppy disk drive. Figure 4-23 shows a 3½-inch floppy disk drive and a Zip drive, along with the disks that they use.

FIGURE 4-23

Floppies and Zip disks are typically used for transporting or shipping data files. They do not have the capacity to store most of today's software, however, so they would not be the main storage device for a computer system.

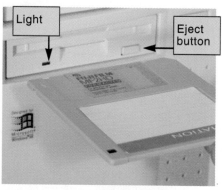

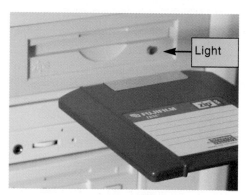

A 3½-inch disk drive has an eject button to release the disk and a drive light to indicate when the drive is in use. You insert the disk so the label goes in last. Virtually every computer has a 3½-inch disk drive.

A Zip drive uses special Zip disks that are slightly larger than a 3½-inch floppy disk. The green light indicates that the drive is ready. A yellow light indicates that the drive is in use. Insert the Zip disk so the label enters last. Zip disks are increasing in popularity.

A floppy disk drive is not a particularly speedy device. It takes about 0.5 second for a 3½-inch drive to spin the disk up to maximum speed and then find a specific sector that contains data. A Zip drive is about 20 times faster.

Newer technologies are decreasing the use of floppy disks. In the past, software was distributed on floppy disks. Today, most software vendors use CD-ROM or DVD-ROM disks instead. Local computer networks and the Internet have made it easy to share data files, so floppy disks are shipped less frequently. Floppies are still used in many college computer labs so that students can transport their data to different lab machines or to their home computers.

Hard Disk Storage

How can a hard disk be the same size as a floppy, but store so much more data? Hard disk storage is the preferred type of main storage for most computer systems because it provides faster access to files than floppy or Zip disk drives. A **hard disk platter** is a flat, rigid disk made of aluminum or glass and coated with a magnetic oxide. A **hard disk** is one or more platters and their associated read-write heads. You will frequently see the terms "hard disk" and "hard disk drive" used interchangeably. You might also hear the term "fixed disk" used to refer to hard disks.

Hard Drive
Update

Microcomputer hard disk platters are typically 3½ inches in diameter—the same size as the circular mylar disk in a floppy. However, the density of the surface particles and the data storage capacity of a hard disk far exceed those of a floppy disk. Also, the access time for a hard disk is significantly faster than that for a floppy disk. Hard disk storage capacities of 20.4 GB and access times of 6 to 11 ms are not uncommon.

You might guess that a hard disk drive would fill one platter before storing data on a second platter. However, it is more efficient to store data at the same track and sector locations on both platters before moving the read-write heads to the next sector. A vertical stack of tracks is called a **cylinder**—the basic storage bin for a hard disk drive. Figure 4-24 provides more information on how a hard disk drive works.

FIGURE 4-24

The hard disk platters are stored inside the drive case or cartridge to prevent dust and other contaminants from interfering with the read-write heads.

The drive spindle supports one or more hard disk platters. Both sides of the platter are used for data storage. More platters mean more data storage capacity. Hard disk platters rotate as a unit on the drive spindle to position a specific sector under the read-write heads. The platters spin continuously, making thousands of revolutions per minute.

The platter surfaces are formatted into cylinders and sectors. A cylinder is a vertical stack of tracks. To find a file, the computer must know the platter, cylinder, and sector, in which the file is stored.

▶ Start
Video

Each data storage surface has its own read-write head, which moves in and out from the center of the disk to locate a specific track. The head hovers only a few micro inches above the disk surface, so the magnetic field is much more compact than on a floppy disk. As a result, more data is packed into a smaller area on a hard disk platter.

CHAPTER 4

Like floppy disks, hard disks provide random access to files. Unlike floppy disks, which begin to rotate only when you request data, hard disks are continually in motion, so there is no delay as the disk spins up to maximum speed. As a result, hard disk access is faster than floppy disk access.

It is important to keep track of how much space is available on your computer's hard disk, so you don't inadvertently fill it up. You can ask your computer operating system to display the capacity of your hard disk and the amount of that capacity currently used for data. Figure 4-25 explains how to find your computer's disk capacity and utilization under DOS and Windows.

FIGURE 4-25

Hard disk capacity information displayed in DOS (top) and Windows (bottom).

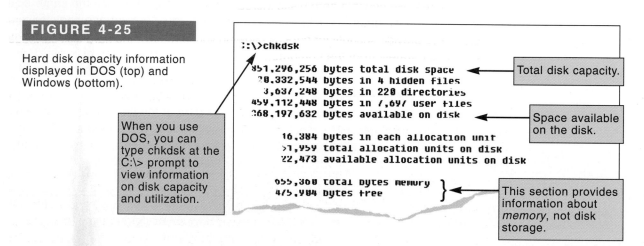

When you use DOS, you can type chkdsk at the C:\> prompt to view information on disk capacity and utilization.

Total disk capacity.

Space available on the disk.

This section provides information about *memory*, not disk storage.

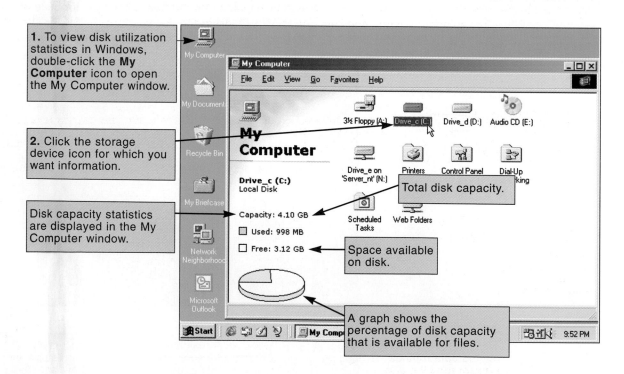

1. To view disk utilization statistics in Windows, double-click the **My Computer** icon to open the My Computer window.

2. Click the storage device icon for which you want information.

Disk capacity statistics are displayed in the My Computer window.

Total disk capacity.

Space available on disk.

A graph shows the percentage of disk capacity that is available for files.

The read-write heads in a hard disk hover a microscopic distance above the disk surface. If a read-write head runs into a dust particle or some other contaminant on the disk, it might cause what is called a **head crash**. A head crash damages some of the data on the disk. To help eliminate contaminants from contacting the platters and causing head crashes, a hard disk is sealed in its case. A head crash can also be triggered by jarring the hard disk while it is in use. Although hard disks have become considerably more rugged in recent years, you should still handle and transport them with care.

Some hard disks are removable. **Removable hard disks** or hard disk cartridges contain platters and read-write heads that can be inserted and removed from the drive much like a floppy disk. Removable hard disks increase the potential storage capacity of your computer system, although the data is available on only one disk at a time. Removable hard disks also provide security for data by allowing you to remove the hard disk cartridge and store it separately from the computer.

RAID, another type of hard disk storage, is found in an increasing number of mainframe and microcomputer installations. A **RAID** (redundant array of independent disks) storage device contains many disk platters, provides redundancy, and achieves faster data access than conventional hard disks. The redundancy feature of RAID technology protects data from media failures by recording the same data on more than one disk platter.

To further increase the speed of data access, your computer might use a disk cache. A **disk cache** (pronounced "cash") is a special area of computer memory into which the computer transfers the data you are likely to need from disk storage. How does a disk cache help speed things up? Suppose your computer retrieves data from a particular sector of your disk. There is a high probability that the next data you need will be from an adjacent sector—the remainder of a program file, for example, or the next section of a data file. The computer reads the data from nearby sectors and stores it in the cache. If the data you'll use next is already in the cache, the computer doesn't need to wait while the mechanical parts of the drive locate and read the data from the disk. Figure 4-26 shows how a disk cache works.

CHAPTER 4

FIGURE 4-26

How disk caching works.

1. The computer asks for data that is stored on disk. The disk-cache manager retrieves the requested data (red arrows) and sends it to the main memory so the computer can use it.

2. The disk-cache manager also reads related data (orange arrows) from the disk and keeps it in the cache.

3. When the computer asks for more data, the disk-cache manager first checks the cache to see if the data is there. If the requested data is in the cache, it is immediately sent for processing. If the requested data is not in the cache, the disk-cache manager must take the time to locate the data on the disk, retrieve the data, then send it to the main memory.

 Start Animation

InfoWeb
6

<u>Tape</u>

Tape Storage

Do they still use those big tape drives on computers that you see in old movies? In the 1960s, magnetic tape was the most popular form of mainframe computer storage. When IBM introduced its first microcomputer in 1981, the legacy of tape storage continued in the form of a cassette tape drive, similar to those used for audio recording and playback.

Using tape as a primary storage device instead of a hard disk would be inconvenient and slow because tape requires sequential, rather than random, access. With sequential access, data is stored and read as a sequence of bytes along the length of the tape. Study the diagram in Figure 4-27 to learn how computers store data on tape.

FIGURE 4-27

The files on magnetic tape are arranged for sequential access.

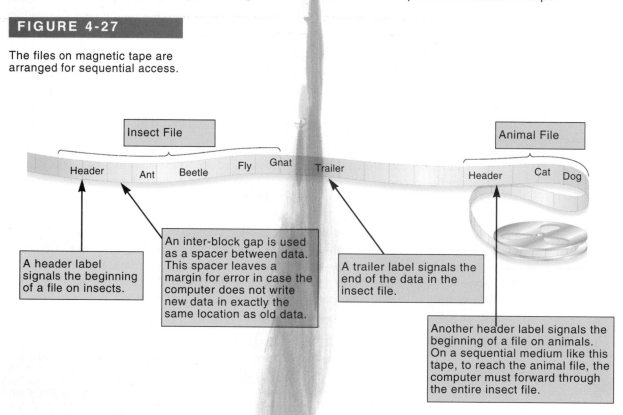

A header label signals the beginning of a file on insects.

An inter-block gap is used as a spacer between data. This spacer leaves a margin for error in case the computer does not write new data in exactly the same location as old data.

A trailer label signals the end of the data in the insect file.

Another header label signals the beginning of a file on animals. On a sequential medium like this tape, to reach the animal file, the computer must forward through the entire insect file.

Microcomputer users quickly abandoned tape storage for the convenience and speed of random access disk drives. Recently, however, tape storage for microcomputers has experienced a revival—not as a principal storage device, but for backing up data stored on hard disks. As you have learned in this chapter, the data on disks can be easily destroyed, erased, or otherwise lost. Protecting the data on the hard disk is of particular concern to users because it contains so much data—data that would be difficult and time-consuming to reconstruct. A **tape backup** is a copy of the data on a hard disk that is stored on magnetic tape, and used to restore lost data. A tape backup is relatively inexpensive and can rescue you from the overwhelming task of trying to reconstruct lost data. If you lose the data on your hard disk, you can copy the data from the tape backup to the hard disk. Typically, you do not use the data directly from the tape backup because sequential access is too slow to be practical.

The large reels of computer tapes you might have seen in old movies are called **open reel tapes** and resemble spools of 16 mm film. Access speeds for open reel tapes are measured in seconds, not milliseconds. Open reel tapes are still used as a distribution medium for some mainframe and minicomputer systems. Newer tape storage devices for these computers typically use half-inch tape cartridges. A **tape cartridge** is a removable magnetic tape module similar to a cassette tape.

The most popular types of tape drives for microcomputers also use tape cartridges, but there are several tape specifications and cartridge sizes, including QIC (quarter-inch cartridge), DAT (digital audio tape), DLT (digital linear tape), Travan, and ADR (advanced digital recording). Check the tape drive manual to make sure that you purchase the correct type of tape for your tape drive.

For a backup device, access time is less important than the time it takes to copy data from your hard disk to tape. Drive manufacturers do not always supply such performance specifications, but most users can expect a tape drive to back up 100 MB in 15–20 minutes. Figure 4-28 shows a typical microcomputer tape backup device.

FIGURE 4-28

Tape drives are typically incorporated in microcomputer systems to back up the contents of the hard drive. An external tape drive such as this one is a stand-alone unit that can be easily moved from one computer to another. Internal tape drives are installed in the system unit, similar to a floppy or CD-ROM drive.

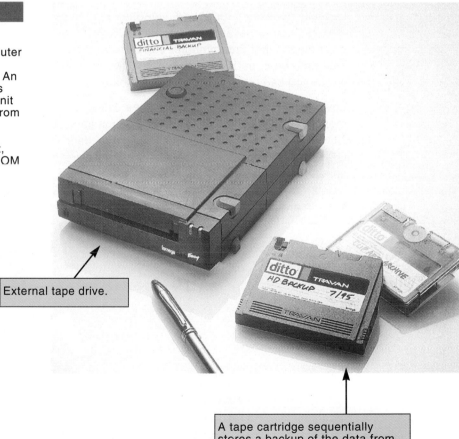

External tape drive.

A tape cartridge sequentially stores a backup of the data from the computer's hard disk drive.

CHAPTER 4

CD-ROM Technology

If CD-ROMs are read-only, doesn't that limit their use? CD-ROMs are based on the same technology as the music CDs that you buy at a music store. **CD-ROM** (pronounced "cee dee rom") stands for Compact Disc Read-Only Memory. A computer CD-ROM disk, like its audio-counterpart, contains data that has been stamped on the disk surface when it was manufactured.

CD-ROM
Update

CD-ROM technology provides storage capacity that far exceeds that of a floppy or Zip disk. A single CD-ROM disk holds up to 680 MB, equivalent to more than 300,000 pages of text. The surface of the disk is coated with a clear plastic, making the disk quite durable. Unlike magnetic media, it is not susceptible to humidity, fingerprints, dust, or magnets. If you spill coffee on a CD-ROM disk, you can just rinse it off and it will be as good as new. The useful life of a CD-ROM disk is estimated to exceed 500 years.

A CD-ROM disk is relatively inexpensive to manufacture, making it an ideal way for software publishers to distribute large programs and data files. CD-ROM is the medium of choice for delivery of multimedia applications because it provides the large storage capacity necessary for sound, video, and graphics files. CD-ROMs supplement, rather than replace, a hard disk because a CD-ROM is a read-only storage medium. **Read-only** means that the computer can retrieve data from a CD-ROM but cannot save any new data on it. In this respect, CD-ROM technology differs from hard disk storage, on which you can read, write, and erase data.

Low-cost CD-ROM drives, sometimes called CD-ROM players, are standard issue on most of today's computer systems, but just about any computer optical drive, including CD-ROM and DVD drives, can read the data on a CD-ROM disk. The speed of CD-ROM drives has increased since they were first introduced. The original single-speed (1X) drives could transfer 150 KB of data per second to computer memory. The next 2X models doubled the transfer rate to 300 KB per second. Today, drives with 40X speeds are common. Figure 4-29 shows how to load a CD into the CD-ROM drive.

FIGURE 4-29

Data is stored on the bottom of a CD-ROM disk in one continuous track that spirals out from the center of the disk. The track is divided into equal-length sectors.

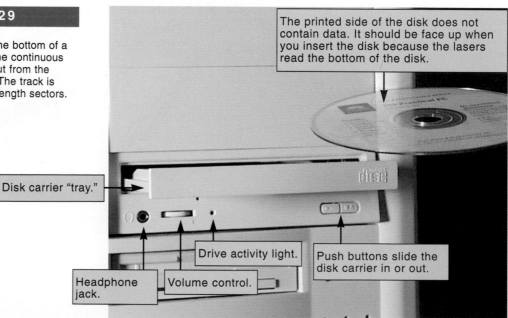

The printed side of the disk does not contain data. It should be face up when you insert the disk because the lasers read the bottom of the disk.

Disk carrier "tray."

Drive activity light.

Push buttons slide the disk carrier in or out.

Headphone jack.

Volume control.

CD-R Technology

Can I make my own CD-ROMs? **CD-R** (compact disc-recordable) technology allows you to essentially create your own CDs by recording data on a CD-R disk using a special CD-R drive. Unlike a CD-ROM drive, which can only read data, a CD-R drive uses a laser to change the reflectivity of a dye layer on a blank CD-R disk. As a result, the data on a CD-R disk is not actually stored as pits in the disk surface. Dark spots in the dye layer, however, appear to be pits. Therefore, disks that have been produced on a CD-R device can be used on most optical drives, such as a CD-ROM or DVD drive.

As with regular CD-ROM disks, the data on a CD-R disk cannot be erased or modified once you have recorded it. However, most CD-R drives allow you to record your data in multiple sessions. For example, you might fill two tracks on a CD-R disk today, then add the data for a few more tracks to the disk tomorrow. The disks that you create in multiple sessions can be read only on drives that have **multisession support**. Most of today's optical drives provide multisession support, but you might not find it on CD-ROM drives manufactured before 1998.

CD-R is a useful technology for archiving data. **Archiving** refers to the process of moving data off a primary storage device when that data is not accessed frequently. For example, a business might archive its accounting data for previous years or a hospital might archive billing records once the accounts are paid. What's the difference between an archive and a backup? Archived data does not generally change, but the data you back up might change frequently.

CD-R technology is not an acceptable replacement for a hard disk. Although multisession support allows you to add data to a CD-R disk, you cannot delete or change data once it has been recorded. Furthermore, the process of storing data on a CD-R is very slow. It can take from 20 to 60 minutes to record a full CD-R.

CD-RW Technology

Is there any way to change the data on a CD? **CD-RW** (compact disc-rewritable) technology allows you to write data on a CD, then change that data. The process requires special CD-RW disks and a CD-RW drive, which uses **phase change technology** to alter the crystal structure on the disk surface. The crystal structure's ability to reflect light depends on its state, so altering the crystal structure creates patterns of light and dark spots similar to the pits and lands on a CD-ROM disk. The crystal structure can be changed from light to dark and back again many times, making it possible to record and modify data much like on a hard disk.

When CD-RW technology was first introduced, other types of optical drives could not read CD-RW disks. Most of today's optical drives now read CD-RW disks.

CD-RW technology is useful for archiving and backing up data. It is not yet an acceptable substitute for a hard disk, however, because the process of accessing, saving, and modifying data on a CD-RW disk is relatively slow.

CHAPTER 4

DVD Technology

How is DVD different from CD technology? **DVD**, which stands for "digital video disc" or "digital versatile disc," is a variation of CD technology that was designed to provide enough storage capacity for a full-length movie. Most people are now familiar with DVD movies that can be played on a DVD player connected to a television set. Most experts predict that DVDs will replace video tape within a few years.

InfoWeb 8

DVD Technology

The computer industry was quick to appropriate DVD technology for data storage. Like a CD-ROM disk, a **DVD-ROM** disk is stamped with data at the time of manufacture and does not allow you to add or change the data on the disk. A single-sided DVD disk can store much more data than a CD-ROM—4.7 GB (4,700 MB) on a DVD compared with 680 MB on a CD-ROM. In addition to holding movies, DVD-ROM disks are ideally suited for distributing large multimedia applications, such as games, encyclopedias, maps, and telephone number databases.

DVD-ROM disks require a DVD drive—they cannot be read by a CD-ROM, CD-R, or CD-RW drive. Remember, however, that a DVD drive can read data from CD-ROM, CD-R, and CD-RW disks, which is why so many computer manufacturers now equip their computers with DVD drives, rather than CD drives. Given the choice, most computer buyers prefer the more versatile DVD-ROM drive to a CD-ROM drive.

DVD+RW and DVD-RAM Technology

Is there a DVD equivalent to CD-RW? In 1999, DVD manufacturers introduced several competing technologies that make it possible to write data on DVD disks. **DVD+RW** uses phase change technology very similar to CD-RWs. A second writable technology called **DVD-RAM** uses a blend of technologies to record data. DVD-RAM and DVD+RW technologies are not compatible. Disks created by a DVD-RAM drive cannot be used in a DVD+RW drive, and vice versa. Disks created with either format cannot be read by many of today's DVD-ROM drives. Most experts predict that eventually the multiple CD and DVD devices of today will be replaced by a single DVD device that reads CD-ROMS, reads DVD-ROMS, and writes DVDs.

QUICKCHECK D

1 Storage capacity is measured in _____, and access time is measured in _____.

2 The computer can move directly to any file on a(n) _____ access device, but must start at the beginning and read through all the data on a(n) _____ access device.

3 A data transfer rate of 150 KBps is better than a rate of 100 KBps. True or false? _____

4 A double-density disk has a higher disk density than a high-density floppy disk. True or false? _____

5 CD-R technology allows you to write data on a disk, then change that data. True or false? _____

6 _____ technology allows you to store 4.7 GB, but does not let you change the data once it has been stored.

 Check Answers

USER FOCUS

Lab
Using Files

Now that you have learned about logical and physical file storage, let's apply what you've learned to how you would typically use files when you work with application soft-

FIGURE 4-30

File operations for a typical word processing session.

Word.cxc is loaded into memory from the hard disk.

Your data is stored in memory while you type.

1 | **Running an Application**

Suppose you want to create a document about the summer vacation packages your company offers. You decide to create the document using the word processing software, Microsoft Word. Your first step is to start the software. When you run Microsoft Word, the program file is copied from the hard drive to the memory of the computer.

2 | **Creating a File**

You begin to type the text of the document. As you type, your data is stored in the memory of the computer. Your data will not be stored on disk until you initiate the Save command.

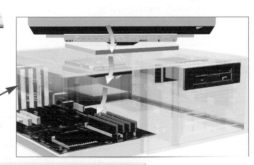

3 | **Saving a Data File**

When you create a file and save it on disk for the first time, you must name the file so that you can later retrieve it by name. Earlier in this chapter, you learned that the name you give to a file must follow the file naming conventions for the operating system. You name the file *A:Vacation.doc*. By typing *A:* you direct the computer to save the file on the floppy disk in drive A. The computer looks for empty clusters on the disk where it can store the file. It then adds the filename to the directory, along with the number of the cluster that contains the beginning of the file. Once you have saved your file, you can continue to work on the document, exit the Word program, or work on another document.

A:Vacation.doc is copied from memory to the floppy disk.

CHAPTER 4

Word.exe is loaded into memory.

A:Vacation.doc is copied from disk into memory.

4 **Retrieving a Data File**

Suppose that a few days later, you decide that you want to re-read *Vacation.doc*. You need to start Microsoft Word. Once the Word program is running, you can retrieve the *Vacation.doc* file from the disk on which it is stored.

When you want to use a data file that already exists on disk storage, you must tell the application to open the file. In Microsoft Word, you either type the name of the file, *A:Vacation.doc*, or select the filename from a list of files stored on the disk. The application communicates the filename to the operating system.

The operating system looks at the directory and FAT to find which clusters contain the file, then moves the read-write head to the appropriate disk location to read the file. The electronics on the disk drive transfer the file data into the main memory of the computer where your application software can manipulate it. Once the operating system has retrieved the file, the word processing software displays it on the screen.

5 **Revising a Data File**

When you see the *Vacation.doc* file on the screen, you can modify it. Each character that you type and each change that you make are stored temporarily in the main memory of the computer, but not on the disk.

The *Vacation.doc* file is already on the disk, so when you are done with the modifications you have two options. Option one is to store the revised version in place of the old version. Option two is to create a new file for your revision and give it a different name, such as *Holiday.doc*.

If you decide to go with option one—store the revised version in place of the old version—the operating system copies your revised data from the computer memory to the same clusters that contained the old file. You do not have to take a separate step to delete the old file—the operating system automatically records the new file over it.

If you decide to go with option two—create a new file for the revision—the application prompts you for a filename. Your revisions will be stored under the new filename. The original file, *Vacation.doc*, will still remain on the disk in its unrevised form.

The changes you make to the document are stored in memory. When you save your revisions, they overwrite the previous version of *Vacation.doc*.

ISSUE IS DATA GETTING LOST?

Before quitting his boring Madison Avenue job and moving to Hollywood, "Mark," a hot-shot advertising designer, copied a collection of his digital graphic and video ideas from his computer at work onto a 12 GB tape. His plan was to purchase a new computer with a 12 GB tape drive, then pull the data off the tape and onto his new hard drive. It was a great plan, except that when he arrived in California, he discovered that the tape drive manufacturer no longer produced the 12 GB model. He was unable to purchase any tape drive that would read the tape that contained his data! Without begging his former boss for access to his old computer, Mark would never be able to retrieve his data.

Mark's data access problem might be indicative of a big problem looming in the future. Today, computers store most of the data generated by banks, credit bureaus, government agencies, and other organizations. In addition, a large amount of historical data is being digitized and stored in computer-readable format. Some experts are concerned that much of this digital data might ultimately be lost as a result of media failures and changes in technology that make some types of media obsolete.

InfoWeb
9
Past &
Future

Storage technology has advanced dramatically over the last 40 years. In 1956, IBM researchers introduced the world's first computer disk storage system. It stored 5 MB of data on fifty 24-inch disks. Today, the capacity of a hard disk exceeds 20 GB—that's 4,000 times the capacity of a 1950s storage device. CD and DVD technologies offer optical storage as an alternative to magnetic storage technology, and we can expect new high-capacity storage technologies in the not-too-distant future.

Research is under way on holographic and molecular storage technologies. Holographic storage is essentially a three-dimensional snapshot of data stored in a crystal medium. In the laboratory, researchers have achieved storage densities of 48 MB per cubic centimeter, but expected storage density is 10 GB per cubic centimeter. To put it in perspective, a couple of holographic storage cubes about the size of a pair of dice could hold the contents of a half-mile-high stack of books. Even higher capacity might be possible with molecular storage, which manipulates individual molecules to represent data bits. Researchers have produced a "nano-abacus" with this technology, though a molecular storage device for your PC is still some years away.

Although these new technologies offer the promise of faster, more dependable data storage, the issue of compatibility still exists. In the future, your holographic storage device is not likely to read the CD-R disks that you use today to archive your data. Five years from now, how will you access today's data? To illustrate the problem, consider a related issue: Could you access data that was stored 20 years ago?

Twenty years ago, 8-inch floppy disks were a popular and state-of-the-art storage medium for microcomputers. Suppose that you needed to read the information stored many years ago on a set of 8-inch floppy disks. Obviously, you would need an 8-inch disk drive—hardly standard equipment on today's PCs. The companies that manufacture storage devices tend to drop support for old technologies soon after introducing new models.

You might have difficulty purchasing a new 8-inch floppy disk drive, but perhaps you might locate a used drive. You would still need the correct type of cable and circuit board to connect the drive to the computer. The circuit board would have to be compatible with a modern PC. You would also need driver software that would enable your computer to control that ancient 8-inch disk drive. Drivers are typically designed for a particular operating system. Drivers designed for the operating systems that were popular 20 years ago are not likely to work under Windows. Ultimately, you would wish that the person who saved those 8-inch disks had also saved the entire computer system, including the 8-inch disk drive.

The data storage problem might be getting worse because of competing standards. For example, the current battle between the incompatible DVD+RW and DVD-RAM formats means that data stored using one technology cannot be read using the other technology. Suppose that consumers decide that they prefer CD+RW technology and DVD-RAM technology becomes obsolete. Five years from now, if you have a DVD containing data, it could be difficult to read it. This situation has led some experts to call for more industry cooperation in setting standards for storage devices and media. For now, however, computer users should be aware that today's data disks, CDs, or DVDs might not be usable on tomorrow's storage devices.

WHAT DO YOU THINK?

1. Can you currently access all of the data that you've stored on computers in the past?   ⦿Yes ◯ No ◯ Not sure

2. Could future data access problems be prevented if the computer industry had a better set of storage standards?   ⦿Yes ◯ No ◯ Not sure

3. Had you heard about this storage compatibility issue before reading this chapter?   ⦿Yes ◯ No ◯ Not sure

 Save Responses

CHAPTER 4   REVIEW ACTIVITIES

INTERACTIVE SUMMARY

The Interactive Summary helps you select important concepts and facts from this chapter. Fill in the blanks to best complete each sentence. When using the NP4 CD or NP4 Web site, you can click the Check Answers buttons to automatically score your answers. Place your Tracking Disk in the floppy disk drive if you want to save your scores.

A named collection of data that exists on a storage medium is usually referred to simply as a file. Computers store many types of files. A(n) _____ file contains the instructions that tell a computer how to perform a specific task. A(n) _____ file contains words, pictures, and numbers that you can view, edit, save, send, and print. A computer system also contains configuration files and program modules that are essential to the operation of hardware and software.

To help you keep track of the files on a computer, the operating system provides file _____ utility software, such as Windows Explorer. This software displays a(n) _____, which lists filenames, filename extensions, file sizes, and creation/modification dates. A directory can be divided into subdirectories, sometimes called _____.

Check
Answers

Computers store digital data, so the information that you enter is changed into 1s and 0s called _____. A series of eight bits is referred to as a(n) _____. Magnetic storage devices such as floppy and hard disk drives magnetize microscopic particles to represent 1s and 0s. Optical storage technologies use a series of dark _____ and reflective lands to represent 1s and 0s. On both magnetic and optical storage media, data is recorded in concentric or spiral _____, which are sometimes divided into sectors. Sectors are sometimes grouped as _____ or stacked into cylinders to expedite data storage and retrieval. A special file, such as the file _____ table, keeps track of the exact physical location for each file.

The capacity of a storage device is measured in bytes. A(n) _____ is about 1,000 bytes; a(n) _____ is about 1 million bytes; a(n) _____ is about 1 billion bytes; and a(n) _____ is about 1 trillion bytes. The speed of a storage device is measured by its _____—the average time that it takes to locate data and read it. Another measure of storage device speed is the data _____ rate—the amount of data that can be moved from storage to the computer memory per second. Today, most computer systems include a hard disk drive, a floppy disk drive, and a CD-ROM or DVD-ROM drive. A _____ drive provides the highest storage capacity and fastest data access of any storage device available for microcomputers. CD-ROM and DVD-ROM drives provide inexpensive access to multimedia games and encyclopedias, but do not allow you to _____ your own data.

Check
Answers

CHAPTER 4

I N T E R A C T I V E   K E Y   T E R M S

Make sure that you understand all of the boldfaced key terms in this chapter. If you're using the NP4 CD or NP4 Web site, you can use this list of terms as an interactive study activity. First, try to define a term in your own words, then click the term to compare your definition with the definition that is presented in this chapter.

Access time, 180
Application-specific filename extension, 166
Archiving, 189
Bit, 174
Byte, 174
CD-R, 189
CD-ROM, 188
CD-RW, 189
Cluster, 177
Cylinder, 183
Data, 160
Data file, 164
Data transfer rate, 180
Defragmentation utility, 179
Device letter, 168
Directory, 169
Disk cache, 185
Disk density, 181
Double-density (DD) disk, 182
Double-sided (DS) disk, 181
DVD, 190
DVD+RW, 190
DVD-RAM, 190
DVD-ROM, 190
Executable file, 163
File, 160
File allocation table (FAT), 177
File manager utility software, 168
File specification, 170
Filename, 161
Filename extension, 161
File naming conventions, 161
Floppy disk, 181
Folders, 169
Fragmented, 179
Generic filename extension, 165
Gigabyte (GB), 180
Hard disk, 183
Hard disk platter, 183
Head crash, 185
High-density (HD) disk, 181
Information, 160
Kilobyte (KB), 180

Magnetic storage, 175
Megabyte (MB), 180
Millisecond (ms), 180
Multisession support, 189
Open reel tapes, 187
Optical storage, 176
Phase change technology, 189
RAID, 185
Random access, 180
Read-only, 188
Read-write head, 175
Removable hard disks, 185
Root directory, 169
Sectors, 177
Sequential access, 180
Storage capacity, 180
Storage device, 174
Storage medium, 174
Storage technology, 174
Tape backup, 186
Tape cartridge, 187
Terabyte, 180
Tracks, 177
Undelete utility, 179
Wildcard character, 162
Zip disk, 181

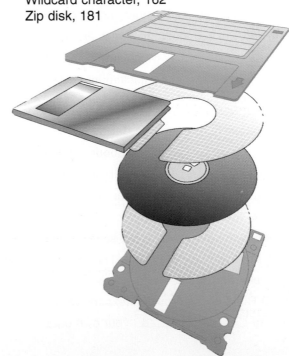

INTERACTIVE QUIZZES

Quiz yourself on important concepts from this chapter by filling in the blanks. When using the NP4 CD or NP4 Web site, you can type your answers, then use the Check Answers buttons to automatically score your responses. Place your Tracking Disk in the floppy disk drive if you want to save your scores.

1 The rules for creating valid filenames are referred to as file naming _____.

2 When you save a data file, your application software adds a(n) _____, such as .doc or .xls.

3 You could probably open the file *Art.bmp* using just about any graphics software. True or false? _____

4 The main directory for a disk is referred to as the _____ directory.

5 When you open a file, the computer is writing data. True or false? _____

6 A bit is larger than a byte. True or false? _____

7 A disk is divided into sectors, but several sectors can be grouped into _____ to expedite data storage.

8 When you delete a file, it is physically removed from the disk. True or false? _____

9 A(n) _____ disk contains files that are stored in noncontiguous clusters.

10 A(n) _____ drive can read most CD-ROM, DVD-ROM, and DVD-RAM disks.

 Check Answers

CHAPTER 4

Refer to the directory listing and then type the correct answer into the boxes.

1 *Lyrics.doc* requires _____ bytes of storage space.

2 The Music directory contains _____ program file(s).

3 The Music directory contains _____ data file(s).

4 The largest file has a(n) _____ extension.

5 The Music directory contains _____ graphics files.

6 How many files match the specification M*.*? _____

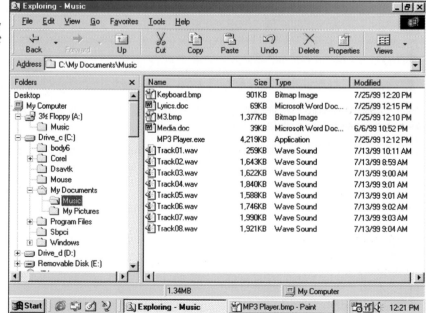

7 The device letter for the drive that contains the Music directory is _____.

 Check Answers

INTERACTIVE PRACTICE TESTS

When you use the NP4 CD or NP4 Web site, you can take practice tests that consist of 10 multiple-choice, true/false, and fill-in-the-blank questions. The 10 questions are selected at random from a large test bank, so each time you take a test, you'll receive a different set of questions. Your tests are scored immediately and you can print study guides that help you find the correct answers for any questions that you missed. If you are using a Tracking Disk, insert it in the floppy disk drive to save your test scores.

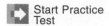 Start Practice Test

STUDY TIPS

Study Tips help you organize and consolidate the information in a chapter by making lists, outlines, charts, and sketches. You can use paper and pencil or word processing software to complete most of the Study Tips activities.

1 Indicate which filenames in the following list are not valid under the operating system used in your school's computer lab. Which file naming convention does each nonvalid filename violate?

Wp.exe	*Ppr*	*Win.exe*
Autoexec.bat	*Results*.wks*	*Monthly.wk1*
Report#1.txt	*Smith&Smith.doc*	*Sep/94.wri*
Asia map.doc	*Ocean.tif*	*Mn43-44.dbf*

2 Explain the difference between the terms in the following pairs: data and information, logical storage and physical storage, executable files and data files, generic filename extensions and application-specific filename extensions, reading data and writing data, magnetic storage and optical storage, bit and byte, random access and sequential access, CD-ROM and CD-RW.

3 Make a list of the file operations that you can perform with file manager utility software.

4 Write a short description of how a file allocation table helps the operating system locate files.

5 Explain how a disk becomes fragmented and why it is a good idea to periodically defragment your computer's hard disk.

6 Suppose that a friend is buying a new computer and can't decide whether to get a CD-ROM drive, a CD-RW drive, a DVD-ROM drive, a DVD-RAM drive, or a DVD+RW drive. Explain the advantages and disadvantages of each.

7 You could specify all the files with a .doc extension by *.doc. How would you specify the following files?

a. All the files with .txt extensions

b. All the files that contain "minutes"

c. All the files that begin with "Ship"

d. All the files on the disk

e. All the files that begin with the letter "R"

8 Suppose you need to retrieve a file from Sarah's computer. She tells you that the file is stored as *D:\Data\Payables.xls*.

a. What is the filename?

b. What is the filename extension?

c. On which drive is the file stored?

d. Will you need a specific software program to retrieve the file?

e. What type of file is it likely to be?

f. In which directory is the file stored?

PROJECTS

A project is an open-ended activity that will help you apply the concepts you have learned. Many projects require resources in addition to your textbook, such as current magazines, library materials, or Web access. When you tackle a project, be prepared to use your critical thinking skills, logical analysis, and your creativity.

1 File Extensions Many software applications use a specific filename extension for data files created with that application. Determine the extensions used by five applications on your own computer or a lab computer. Run each software application and attempt to retrieve a file. If the software application uses a specific filename extension, you will usually see it indicated in a box on the screen. For example, you might see *.doc if you are using Microsoft Word for Windows.

For each of the five programs you select:

a. Specify the program name.

b. Sketch a picture of the program icon (if you are using Windows) or indicate the executable file-name (if you are using DOS).

c. Indicate the filename extension used by the program. If the program does not use a specific file-name extension, indicate that this is the case.

2 Storage Devices You Use You should be aware of the storage devices on your computer so that you use the best device for each task. You will need to take a hands-on look at your computer at home or a computer in your school lab to answer the following questions:

a. Where is this computer located?

b. What is the hard disk capacity? (*Hint:* Refer to Figure 4-25.)

c. Is there a tape storage device?

d. Is there an optical drive? If so, what type?

e. What drive letters are assigned to each storage device?

f. Which storage device do you typically use for the data files you create?

g. Which storage device holds most of the application software that you use?

h. Which storage device would you use for backups?

3 Organizing Files and File Folders How are you going to organize the information you plan to store on your hard drive? As you'll recall from reading the section on logical file storage, your hard disk storage is like a filing cabinet. You can create file folders in which to store your files. There is no one right way to organize your files, but it is important that your filing system work for you. Take time to think about the filing system you plan to create.

Read the following possibilities, and then comment on the advantages and disadvantages of each. Finally, write a description and draw a picture to show how you plan to organize your folders.

a. Create a folder for each file that you make.

b. Create a folder for each application you plan to use and store only documents you generate with that application in that folder.

c. Create folders for broad topics such as Memos, Letters, BudgetItems, and Personal, and store documents that match those headings in the appropriate folder regardless of the application used to create the documents.

d. Create folders around specific topics such as Applications, Personal, Taxes, and so on. Then store all files related to that specific topic in the appropriate folder, regardless of the application used to create the documents.

e. Basically the same as (d), but create additional subfolders to group similar files.

4 CD-Mania As you learned from reading the chapter, there are several CD and DVD formats, including CD-ROM, CD-R, CD-RW, DVD-ROM, DVD-RAM, and so on. In fact, there are additional formats, such as CD-I, CD-DA, and DVD-video. For this project, use your library and Internet resources to write a paper describing five CD formats and three DVD formats. The length of your paper will depend on the scope of the project: a three-page paper is suitable for a short project, a term paper might require 10–15 pages. Be sure to include a bibliography.

Your paper can deal with CDs and DVDs from a technical perspective or from an applied perspective. If you take a technical perspective, you should look for answers to questions such as, but not limited to these:

a. What are the capacity and storage formats for each type of CD or DVD?

b. Why did these specifications originate?

c. What are the advantages and disadvantages of each?

If you take an applied perspective, you should try to find the answers to questions such as, but not limited to these:

a. What are the primary uses for each type of CD or DVD?

b. What are the advantages and disadvantages of each?

c. How do the costs of each format compare?

5 Data Storage in Organizations Organizations take different approaches to data storage, depending on the volume of their data, the value of their data, and the need for data security. The purpose of this project is to interview the person responsible for maintaining the data for an organization and discover the answers to the following questions:

a. What is the job title of the person responsible for this organization's data storage?

b. What preparation did this individual have to qualify for this position?

c. What are this individual's job responsibilities?

d. How does this individual keep up with trends that affect data storage?

e. What type of data does the organization store?

f. What percentage of this data is stored on a computer system?

g. What types of storage devices are used in this organization?

h. What is the capacity of each storage device?

i. What happens when the storage devices are full?

j. What problems are associated with maintaining the data for this organization?

This project works well if the class is divided into teams and each team interviews a person from a different organization. Each team can then present a 15-minute report to the rest of the class, along with a two- to three-page written report of its findings.

ADDITIONAL PROJECTS

Click the underlined text link to the NP4 Web site (www.cciw.com/np4) where you can view and print additional projects for this chapter.

Calculating Storage Requirements

Calculating Hard Disk Capacity

What's in That File?

Troubleshooting a Storage Problem

Sizing Up Future Storage Technologies

LAB ASSIGNMENTS

Software for these labs is provided on the NP4 CD and may also be available in your school's computer lab. To start a lab, click the lab icon.

Each lab has two parts: Steps and Explore. Use the Steps first to learn and review concepts. Read the information on each page and complete the numbered steps. As you work through the lab, you will be asked to answer QuickCheck questions about what you have learned. At the end of the lab, you will see a report that scores your answers to the QuickChecks. If your instructor wants you to turn in this report, click the Print button on the QuickCheck Report screen.

When you have completed the Steps, you can click the Explore button to complete the Lab Assignments. You can also use Explore to practice the skills you learned and to explore concepts on your own.

Lab
Directories,
Folders, Files

Graphical user interfaces such as MacOS and Windows use a filing system metaphor for file management. In this lab, you will learn the basic concepts of these file system metaphors. With this background, you will find it easy to understand how to manage files with graphical user interfaces.

1 Click the Steps button to learn how to manipulate directories, folders, and files. As you proceed through the Steps, answer all of the QuickCheck questions that appear. After you complete the Steps, you will see a QuickCheck Report. Follow the instructions on the screen to print this report.

2 Make sure you are in Explore. Change to drive C as the default drive. Double-click the c:\ folder to display its contents, then answer the following questions:

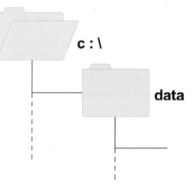

a. How many data files are in the root directory of drive C?

b. How many program files are in the root directory of drive C?

c. Does the root directory of drive C contain any subdirectories? How can you tell?

d. How many files are in the Programs folder?

e. Complete the diagram to show the arrangement of folders on drive C. Do not include files.

3 Click the Explore button. Make sure drive A is the default drive. Double-click the a:\ folder to display the folder contents, then answer the following questions:

a. How many files are in the root directory of drive A?

b. Are the files on drive A data files or program files? How can you tell?

c. Does the root directory of drive A contain any subdirectories? How can you tell?

4 Open and close folders, and change drives as necessary to locate the following files. After you find the file, write out its file specification:

a. *config.sys*   d. *meeting.doc*

b. *explorer.exe*   e. *newlogo3.bmp*

c. *toolkit.wks*   f. *todo.doc*

CHAPTER 4

Lab

DOS File Management

DOS is an operating system used on millions of computers. Even if your computer has a graphical user interface, such as Microsoft Windows, understanding DOS commands helps you grasp the basic concepts of computer file management. In this lab, you learn how to use basic DOS commands.

1. Click the Steps button to learn basic DOS commands. As you proceed through the Steps, answer all of the QuickCheck questions that appear. After you complete the Steps, you will see a QuickCheck Report. Follow the instructions on the screen to print this report.

2. Go through the Steps for this lab once again. This time, create a mini DOS manual by listing each DOS command and its function. For each command, you should also provide a sample of a valid command. For example:

   DIR   Provides a listing of all files on a disk

         Example: DIR A:

3. Click the Explore button and make a new disk. (You can copy over the disk you used for the Steps.) Do each of the following tasks and record the command you used:
   a. Display the directory for drive A.
   b. Display only those files on drive A that begin with the letter "T."
   c. Erase all files that have names beginning with "New".
   d. Create a directory called PAPERS.
   e. Move all files with .DOC extensions into the PAPERS directory.
   f. Rename OPUS27.MID to SONG.MID.
   g. Delete all files with names that start with "BUDGET".

4. In Explore, make a new disk. (You can copy over the disk you used for earlier lab activities.) Do each of the following tasks, then give your disk to your instructor. Don't forget to put your name on the disk label.
   a. Make two subdirectories on your disk: PICS and BUDGETS.
   b. Move all files with .BMP extensions into the PICS directory.
   c. Move all files with .WKS extensions into the BUDGETS directory.
   d. Delete all files except README.TXT from the root directory. (Do not delete the files from PICS or BUDGETS.)
   e. Rename the file README.TXT to READ.ME.

5. Use the TYPE command to view the contents of the START.BAT file. Describe the file contents. Use the TYPE command to view the contents of OPUS27.MID. Describe what you see. Explain the different results you obtained when you used the TYPE command with START.BAT and OPUS27.MID.

Lab

Defragmentation

In this lab, you will format a simulated disk, save files, delete files, and undelete files to see how the computer updates the FAT. You will also find out how the files on your disk become fragmented and what a defragmentation utility does to reorganize the clusters on your disk.

1. Click the Steps button to learn how the computer updates the FAT when you format a disk and save, delete, and undelete files. As you proceed through the Steps, answer all of the QuickCheck questions that appear. After you complete the Steps, you will see a QuickCheck Report. Follow the instructions on the screen to print this report. (continued on the following page)

2   Click the Explore button. Click the Format button to format the simulated disk. Try to save files 1, 2, 3, 4, and 6. Do they all fit on the disk?

3   In Explore, format the simulated disk. Try to save all of the files on the disk. What happens?

4   In Explore, format the simulated disk. Save FILE-3, FILE-4, and FILE-6. Next, delete FILE-6. Now, save FILE-5. Try to undelete FILE-6. What happens and why?

5   In Explore, format the simulated disk. Save and erase files until the files become fragmented. Draw a picture of the disk to show the fragmented files. Indicate which files are in each cluster by using color, crosshatching, or labels. List which files in your drawing are fragmented. Finally, defragment the disk and draw a new picture showing the unfragmented files.

Lab
Using Files

In this lab, you manipulate a simulated computer to view what happens in memory and on disk when you create, save, open, revise, and delete files. Understanding what goes on "inside the box" will help you quickly grasp how to perform basic file operations with most application software.

1   Click the Steps button to learn how to use the simulated computer to view the contents of memory and disk when you perform basic file operations. As you proceed through the Steps, answer all of the QuickCheck questions that appear. After you complete the Steps, you will see a QuickCheck Report. Follow the instructions on the screen to print this report.

2   Click the Explore button and use the simulated computer to perform the following tasks:

a. Create a document containing your name and the city in which you were born. Save this document as NAME.

b. Create another document containing two of your favorite foods. Save this document as FOODS.

c. Create another file containing your two favorite classes. Call this file CLASSES.

d. Open the FOOD file and add another one of your favorite foods. Save this file without changing its name.

e. Open the NAME file. Change this document so it contains your name and the name of your school. Save this as a new document called SCHOOL.

f. Write down how many files are on the simulated disk and the exact contents of each file.

g. Delete all of the files.

3   In Explore, use the simulated computer to perform the following tasks:

a. Create a file called MUSIC that contains the name of your favorite CD.

b. Create another document that contains eight numbers and call this file LOTTERY.

c. You didn't win the lottery this week. Revise the contents of the LOTTERY file, but save the revision as LOTTERY2.

d. Revise the MUSIC file so it also contains the name of your favorite musician or composer, and save this file as MUSIC2.

e. Delete the MUSIC file.

f. Write down how many files are on the simulated disk and the exact contents of each file.

INFOWEB

 The InfoWeb is your guide to print, film, television, and electronic resources. Use it to obtain updates on quickly changing technical information and to locate information for research papers. If you're using the NP4 CD, click the InfoWeb Site icon on the left side of this paragraph to access the online InfoWeb links. Otherwise, use your Web browser and type in the address of the New Perspectives Web site: www.cciw.com/np4. At the Web site, you'll find up-to-date links to the topics covered in this chapter.

1 World Records

In 1951, a hunting party in Ireland shot at, but missed, some golden plovers. The hunters discussed at length whether the golden plover was Europe's fastest game bird. The managing director of Guinness breweries, Sir Hugh Beaver, was a member of the hunting party. With sudden inspiration he realized that what the world needed was a book of records to settle such debates, and the *Guinness Book of World Records* was born. Now published annually, you can find it in your library or bookstore. There's even a *Guinness Disk of Records* published on CD-ROM by Grolier Electronic Publishing. World Record Madness (*www.irsoft.demon.co.uk/Inquirer/records.html*) highlights recent world record attempts in activities such as showering, stamp licking, and crawling. The article discusses the increase in serious accidents during world record attempts and points out that several countries around the world have banned such activities. For world record sites on the Web, connect to *www.imn.htwk-leipzig.de/~saxonia/links.html*, the International Club for Record Breakers.

2 Filename Extensions

You learned that much of today's software adds an application-specific filename extension to the files you save. Suppose you receive a file that has an unfamiliar extension. What software should you use to view the file? On the Web, you'll find a list of filename extensions in alphabetical order at *www2.crosswinds.net/san-marino/~jom/filex/extensio.htm*. You can also connect to a great Web reference called *The PC Guide* at *www.pcguide.com/ref/hdd/file/fat-c.html* that includes plenty of information on filenames and extensions.

3 FAT

You can learn more about file allocation tables by searching for "FAT" and following the links at PCWebopaedia's site, *www.webopaedia.com*. You'll find additional information about the FAT, microcomputer storage, and a wide variety of other computer topics in the best-selling book, *Peter Norton's Inside the PC* (Sams, 1999).

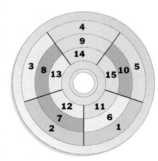

4 Floppies & Zips

How many types of floppy disks are there? Which ones are obsolete? What are the specifications of different floppy disk formats? You can find the answers to these questions and more in PC Guide's discussion of floppy disk formats and logical structures (Floppy Disk Formats and Logical Structures at *www.pcguide.com/ref/fdd/format-c.html*).What if your floppy disk stops working? Get some hints on fixing it at *www.louisville.edu/~ajsmit01/floppy.html*. You can learn more about Zip drives and the new 250 MB capacity disks at Iomega's site, *www.iomega.com*.

5 Hard Drive Update

To find the latest information on disk drive storage capacities and access speeds, check out these manufacturer sites: Seagate at *www.seagate.com* and Western Digital Corporation at *www.wdc.com/tape*. For RAID and mainframe storage solutions, try *www.storage.ibm.com* and *www.storage.digital.com*.

6 Tape

What's new with tape drive capacity and tape technology? Check these manufacturers' sites: Hewlett-Packard at *www.hp.com/tape/colorado/index.html*, Exabyte at *www.exabyte.com*, and Seagate at *www.seagate.com/tape/tapetop.shtml*. For information on the popular Ditto tape drive, connect to its manufacturer's Web site, *www.tecmar.com*.

7 CD-ROM Update

For the latest on CD-ROM access times and transfer rates, connect to manufacturer sites such as Mitsumi at *www.mitsumi.com* or NEC at *www.nec.com*. IBM provides an easy-to-read guide to CD-ROM technology at *www.pc.ibm.com/us/infobrf/cdtech.html*. If you want to get a quick grasp of concepts such as access time and data transfer speeds, this Web page is the place. For general information about CD-ROM drives, check out the CD Information Center at *www.cd-info.com/index.shtml*, sponsored by the CD-Info Company. Thinking of buying a CD-R drive and making your own CDs? There are pitfalls when you burn your own pits! See the advice from *PC Magazine* columnist Jim Seymour at *www8.zdnet.com/pcmag/issues/1507/pcmg0043.htm*. Hewlett-Packard manufactures one of the most popular CD-R drives. Connect to *www.hp.com* and search for CD-R. At HP's site, search for the page "CD Technology Introduction," which includes information on CD standards, data access, data formats, access speed, and more.

8 DVD Technology

You'll find an excellent introduction to DVD at *www.c-cube.com/technology/dvd.html*. If you are most interested in multimedia, then you'll want to keep pace with the latest developments in DVD. E-town's DVD Central (*www.e-town.com,* then click *DVD Central*) provides news stories and information on new DVD products, background stories, and has a special section of links to articles that take a more critical view of the technology. The Computer Shopper has a great site with information on DVD technology and buying DVD drives. Connect to *computershopper.zdnet.com*, then select the DVD-ROM category. Another great site, DVD-Today (*dvdtoday.com*) includes a DVD Technology Overview with links to other sites that provide a comparison of CD and DVD technologies, as well as DVD FAQs. At the Creative Labs Web site, *www.creativelabs.com*, you can follow the multimedia links to find the latest on DVD products.

9 Past & Future of Storage Technology

At IBM's Web site (*www.ibm.com/history*) you can find a computer history timeline with some interesting facts about computer storage devices, such as RAMAC and Winchester disks. What does the future have in store? At *www.almaden.ibm.com/sst,* IBM maintains an illustrated and information-packed Web site about new developments in computer storage. For additional information, connect to *www.disktrend.com*. At this Web site, you can find summaries of recent reports, disk drive industry news, selected storage topics, and links to other storage Web sites.

CHAPTER
5
COMPUTER ARCHITECTURE

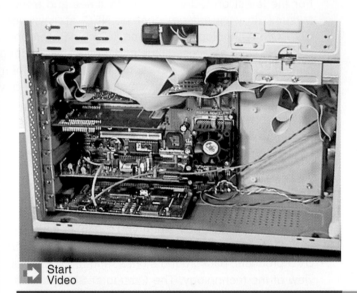

➡ Start Video

PREVIEW

Chapter 5 provides you with a peek "under the hood" of a computer system and explains how a computer works. You can use this information to troubleshoot computer problems at work, home, or school. In addition, you'll learn terminology that will help you understand much of the jargon you read in computer ads and hear in conversations with computer professionals.

When you have completed this chapter you should be able to:

■ Identify the components that are on the main circuit board—the motherboard—of a microcomputer

■ Explain how RAM, virtual memory, ROM, and CMOS differ

■ Explain how the CPU performs the instructions contained in a computer program

■ List the factors that affect CPU performance

■ Describe how the data bus and expansion bus work

■ List the components necessary to connect a peripheral device to a computer and describe each component's role

■ Troubleshoot the boot process of your computer system

CHAPTER 5 LABS

CPU
Simulator

Trouble-
shooting

APRAPHULIAN COMPUTER

An article in the April 1988 issue of *Scientific American* announced that "archaeologists have discovered the rotting remnants of an ingenious arrangement of ropes and pulleys thought to be the first working digital computer ever constructed." The article described in detail how the people of an ancient culture, known as the Apraphulians, built complex devices of ropes and pulleys, housed these devices in huge black wooden boxes, and used them to perform complex mathematical computations. Some of the devices were so colossal that elephants were needed to pull the huge ropes through the pulley system.

A computer constructed of ropes and pulleys? That would indeed be a very unusual architecture for a computer! As you might have guessed, this article was an April Fools' joke. The article went on to explain, however, that it would be possible to construct a very basic digital computer using ropes and pulleys.

Today's computers use electrical power instead of elephants, and computer "chips," rather than ropes and pulleys, perform all of the processing tasks. Nevertheless, the idea that you could build a computer out of ropes and pulleys reinforces the notion that a computer is, in many respects, a very simple device—an important point to keep in mind as you delve into the technical side of computers that is presented in this chapter.

InfoWeb
1
April Fools

How does a computer work? This chapter takes you on a tour inside the case of a modern computer system. You'll become familiar with the devices that store, process, and transport data. You'll also discover how the microscopic circuits in computer chips actually process data. The basic concepts you learn in this chapter apply to microcomputers, minicomputers, computers, and even supercomputers.

SECTION A   DIGITAL ELECTRONICS

Computer architecture refers to the design and construction of a computer system. The architecture of any computer can be broadly classified based on two characteristics: what the computer uses for power and how the computer physically represents, processes, stores, and moves data. Most modern computers are electronic devices; that is, they are powered by electricity. Also, modern computers use electrical signals and circuits to represent, process, and move data.

InfoWeb
2

Inside the
Case

Inside the System Unit

What does the inside of a computer look like? Try to visualize what's inside a computer's system unit. Many people picture a maze of wires and other electronic gizmos. You might be surprised, however, to find that the inside of a computer looks pretty simple. We removed the cover from a microcomputer in Figure 5-1 to show you what's inside.

FIGURE 5-1

A computer's system unit typically contains circuit boards, a power supply, and storage devices. A few wires and cables connect storage devices to the power supply and circuit boards.

The components inside a notebook computer would be more tightly packed together than the components in the tower unit shown in the photo.

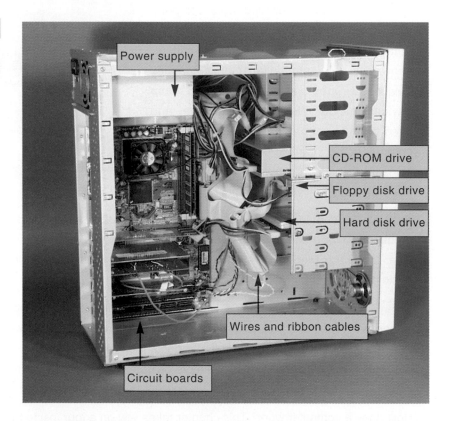

In this chapter, you'll learn about the architecture of microcomputers and you'll find out what makes them "tick." As you read the chapter, keep in mind that the main components of a microcomputer are similar to the components that you would find in a minicomputer, mainframe, or supercomputer. Therefore, most of the microcomputer architecture concepts presented in this chapter also apply to other computer categories.

InfoWeb
3

Integrated
Circuits

Integrated Circuits

Why isn't the system unit filled with a lot of wires?   Most of the electronic components inside a computer are integrated circuits. An **integrated circuit** (IC), like the one pictured in Figure 5-2, is a thin slice of silicon crystal packed with microscopic circuit elements such as wires, transistors, capacitors, and resistors.

FIGURE 5-2

A single integrated circuit less than a quarter-inch square could contain more than 1 million microscopic circuit elements.

Integrated circuits are commonly called "chips" or "microchips."

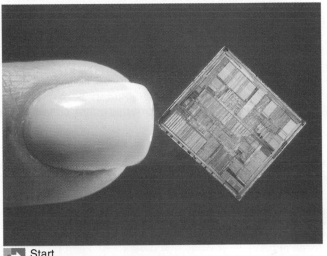

▶ Start
Video

An integrated circuit is packaged in a ceramic carrier that provides connectors to other computer components. Inside of a computer you are likely to find several kinds of **chip packages**, including DIP, DIMM, PGA, and SEC, as shown in Figure 5-3.

FIGURE 5-3

Integrated circuits are housed within a ceramic carrier. These carriers exist in several configurations or chip packages, such as DIPs, DIMMs, PGAs, and SECs.

CHAPTER 5

A DIP (dual in-line pin) has two rows of connecting pins. Once used for memory, DIPs now contain specialized support circuitry.

A DIMM (dual in-line memory module) is a small circuit board containing several chips typically used for memory.

A PGA (pin-grid array) is a square chip package with pins arranged in concentric squares, typically used for the main processing circuitry.

An SEC (single edge contact) cartridge is a popular chip package for many of today's most powerful processors.

The Motherboard

How do the chips fit together to make a computer? Inside the system unit, chips are housed on a circuit board called the **motherboard** or "main board." If you look carefully at a computer circuit board, you'll see that some chips are soldered to the board, but other chips are plugged into the board and can be removed. Soldered chips are permanent and not designed to be removed. In contrast, removable chips allow you to upgrade your computer components.

In a microcomputer, the motherboard contains the processor chip, the chips for computer memory, and chips that handle basic input and output. Circuits etched into the motherboard act like wires, providing a path so the computer can transport data from one chip to another as needed for processing. In addition, the motherboard contains expansion slots that allow you to connect peripheral devices to the computer. Figure 5-4 illustrates how a microcomputer motherboard connects the chips that carry out basic computer functions.

InfoWeb 4

Motherboards

FIGURE 5-4

A computer motherboard provides sockets for chips, slots for small circuit boards, and the circuitry that connects all of these components.

The rest of this chapter provides additional details about each of these components.

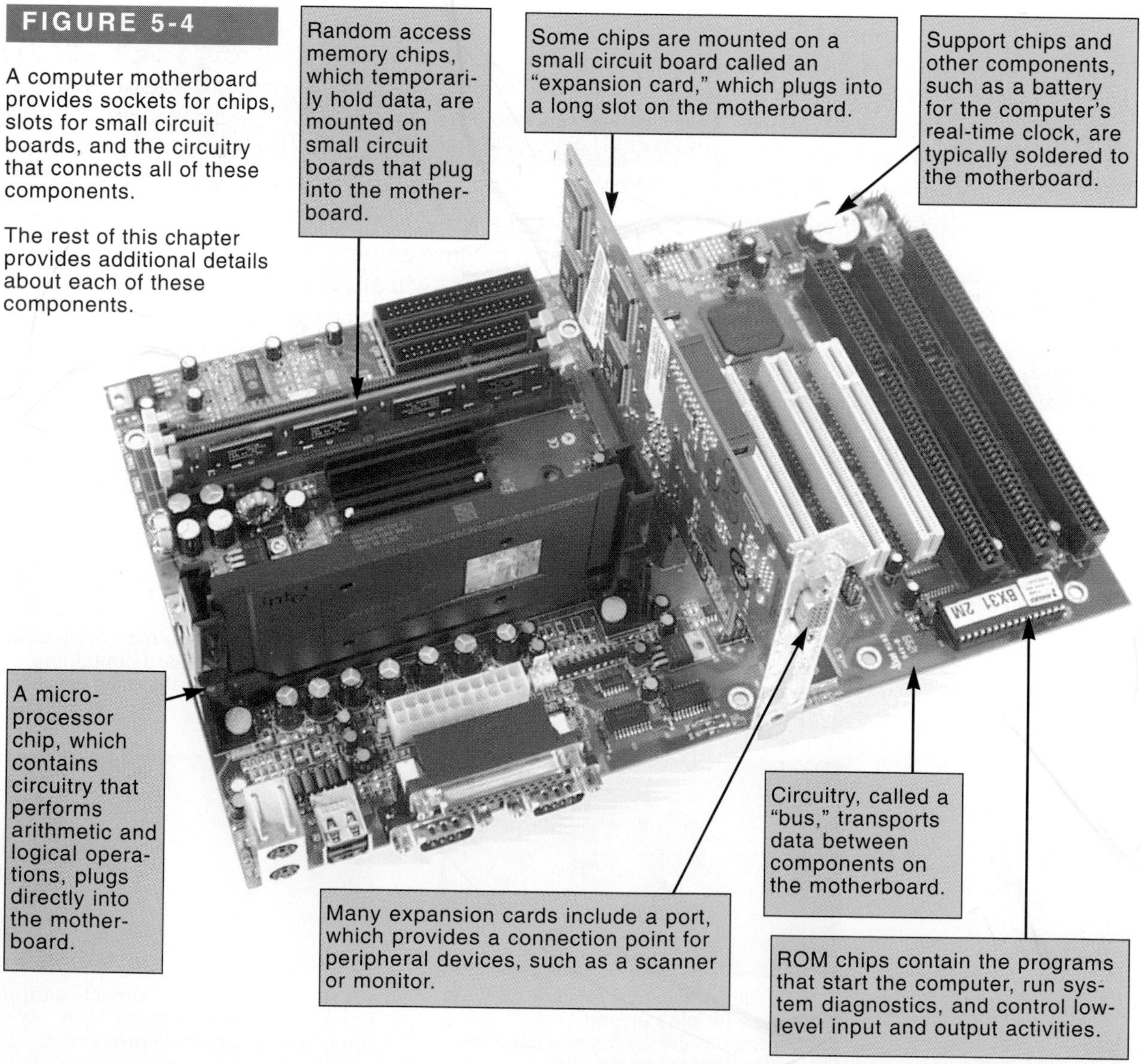

Random access memory chips, which temporarily hold data, are mounted on small circuit boards that plug into the motherboard.

Some chips are mounted on a small circuit board called an "expansion card," which plugs into a long slot on the motherboard.

Support chips and other components, such as a battery for the computer's real-time clock, are typically soldered to the motherboard.

A microprocessor chip, which contains circuitry that performs arithmetic and logical operations, plugs directly into the motherboard.

Many expansion cards include a port, which provides a connection point for peripheral devices, such as a scanner or monitor.

Circuitry, called a "bus," transports data between components on the motherboard.

ROM chips contain the programs that start the computer, run system diagnostics, and control low-level input and output activities.

Digital Data Representation

If a computer is just a bunch of electrical circuits, how can it manipulate numbers and letters? In Chapter 4, you learned that computers work with data that has been coded as a series of bits—1s and 0s—that can be converted into dark and light spots on a CD or DVD, or into magnetically charged particles on a floppy disk, hard disk, or tape. When data is being transported along computer circuitry or processed within an integrated circuit, however, the 1s and 0s have to be converted into some sort of electrical signal.

The type of signal that a computer uses to represent data depends on whether the computer is a digital or analog device. A **digital device** works with discrete—that is, distinct or separate—numbers or digits, such as 1 and 0. An **analog device** operates on continuously varying data. As an analogy, a traditional light switch has two discrete states: on and off, so it is a digital device. A dimmer switch, on the other hand, has a rotating dial that increases or decreases brightness smoothly over a range from bright to dark. A dimmer switch is an analog device.

Today, most computers are digital and their circuits have only two possible states. For convenience, let's say that one of those states is "on" and the other state is "off." If you equate the on state with 1 and the off state with 0, you can grasp the basic principle of how a digital computer works. In a digital computer, each number or letter is represented by a series of 1s and 0s that can be converted into electrical "on" and "off" signals. Figure 5-5 will help you visualize how computers might use electrical pulses to move data along a circuit.

FIGURE 5-5

A pulse of electricity moving down a circuit could represent 1 bit.

Start
Video

CHAPTER 5

Data Representation Codes

Do all digital computers use the same code to represent data? Think about the way Morse code uses dashes and dots to represent letters. In a similar way, digital computers represent numbers, letters, and symbols with codes that use a series of 1s and 0s. Computers do not use Morse code, but instead represent data using the binary number system and several other codes designed especially for computer data. The coding scheme used depends on whether the data is numeric data or character data.

Numeric data consists of numbers that represent quantities and that might be used in arithmetic operations. For example, your annual income is numeric data. You use it in arithmetic operations every April when you calculate your income taxes.

Digital computers represent numeric data using the **binary number system**, also called "base 2." The binary number system has only two digits: 0 and 1. The numeral 2 cannot be used in the binary number system, so instead of writing "2," you would write "10." In the binary number system, the numbers 1 through 8 are 1, 10, 11, 100, 101, 110, 111, and 1000.

The binary number system can represent any number using only 1s and 0s, which can then be converted to electrical "ons" and "offs" inside a computer. Figure 5-6 provides examples of numbers that have been converted into binary format.

FIGURE 5-6	The binary number system can represent any number as a series of 1s and 0s.
Decimal Number	**Binary Representation**
1	1
2	10
3	11
4	100
5	101
6	110
7	111
8	1000
9	1001
10	1010
1,000	1111101000
1,026	10000000010
4,879	1001100001111

Character data is composed of letters, symbols, and numerals that will not be used in arithmetic operations. Examples of character data include your name, address, and hair color.

Digital computers typically represent character data using codes, such as ASCII and EBCDIC. ASCII is the data representation code used on most microcomputers, many minicomputers, and some mainframe computers. **ASCII** stands for American Standard Code for Information Interchange and is pronounced "ASK ee." The ASCII code for an uppercase "A" is 01000001.

IBM-brand mainframe computers often use the EBCDIC code. **EBCDIC** stands for Extended Binary-Coded Decimal Interchange Code (pronounced "EB seh dick"). The EBCDIC code for the letter "A" is 11000001.

When you look at the ASCII and EBCDIC table in Figure 5-7, you might wonder why it contains codes for 1, 2, 3, 4, and so on. Shouldn't these numbers be represented by the binary number system? The ASCII code for "5" is 00110101. Why is it different from the binary representation of "5," which is 101?

Some data that you might think of as "numbers" is really character data. Consider your Social Security number. Because you are not going to use your Social Security number in arithmetic operations, it is considered character data, made up of *numerals*, not numbers. A computer would use ASCII or EBCDIC to represent the *numerals* in your Social Security number, whereas it would use the binary number system to represent a *number*, such as your age.

FIGURE 5-7   Each letter, number, and most symbols have an ASCII and EBCDIC code.

	ASCII	EBCDIC		ASCII	EBCDIC		ASCII	EBCDIC
(space)	00100000	01000000	?	00111111	01101111	^	01011110	
!	00100001	01011010	@	01000000	01111100	_	01011111	
"	00100010	01111111	A	01000001	11000001	`	01100000	
#	00100011	01111011	B	01000010	11000010	a	01100001	10000001
$	00100100	01011011	C	01000011	11000011	b	01100010	10000010
%	00100101	01101100	D	01000100	11000100	c	01100011	10000011
&	00100110	01010000	E	01000101	11000101	d	01100100	10000100
'	00100111	01111101	F	01000110	11000110	e	01100101	10000101
(	00101000	01001101	G	01000111	11000111	f	01100110	10000110
)	00101001	01011101	H	01001000	11001000	g	01100111	10000111
*	00101010	01011100	I	01001001	11001001	h	01101000	10001000
+	00101011	01001110	J	01001010	11010001	i	01101001	10001001
,	00101100	01101011	K	01001011	11010010	j	01101010	10010001
-	00101101	01100000	L	01001100	11010011	k	01101011	10010010
.	00101110	01001011	M	01001101	11010100	l	01101100	10010011
/	00101111	01100001	N	01001110	11010101	m	01101101	10010100
0	00110000	11110000	O	01001111	11010110	n	01101110	10010101
1	00110001	11110001	P	01010000	11010111	o	01101111	10010110
2	00110010	11110010	Q	01010001	11011000	p	01110000	10010111
3	00110011	11110011	R	01010010	11011001	q	01110001	10011000
4	00110100	11110100	S	01010011	11100010	r	01110010	10011001
5	00110101	11110101	T	01010100	11100011	s	01110011	10100010
6	00110110	11110110	U	01010101	11100100	t	01110100	10100011
7	00110111	11110111	V	01010110	11100101	u	01110101	10100100
8	00111000	11111000	W	01010111	11100110	v	01110110	10100101
9	00111001	11111001	X	01011000	11100111	w	01110111	10100110
:	00111010	01111010	Y	01011001	11101000	x	01111000	10100111
;	00111011	01011110	Z	01011010	11101001	y	01111001	10101000
<	00111100	01001100	[	01011011	01001010	z	01111010	10101001
=	00111101	01111110	\	01011100		{	01111011	
>	00111110	01101110	]	01011101	01011010	}	01111101	

Data Transport

What happens to the data in a computer? Typically, data travels from one location to another within the computer on an electronic pathway or circuit called a **data bus**. The data bus is a series of circuits that connect the various electrical components on the motherboard. The bus contains data lines and address lines. **Data lines** carry the signals that represent data. **Address lines** carry the signals that specify where the computer can find the data that it is supposed to process. See Figure 5-8.

FIGURE 5-8

A computer data bus "picks up" a load of bits from one of the components on the motherboard, then transfers these bits to another motherboard component. After dropping off one load of bits, the bus collects another load.

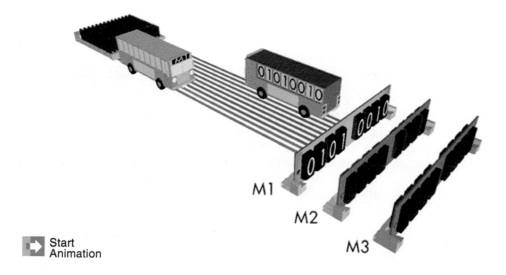

▶ Start
Animation

QUICKCHECK   A

1 A(n) _____ is a collection of microscopic circuit elements such as wires, transistors, capacitors, and resistors packed onto a very small square of silicon.

2 A(n) _____ device works with discrete numbers, whereas a(n) _____ device operates on continuously varying data.

3 Most microcomputers use the _____ code to represent character data.

4 The _____ number system represents numeric data as a series of 0s and 1s.

5 A(n) _____ is an electronic pathway that links the chips on the motherboard of a computer.   ▶ Check Answers

CHAPTER 5

SECTION B MEMORY

So far in this chapter, you have learned that digital computers represent data using electronic signals. You know that the data bus transports these electronic signals from one place to another inside the computer. Now you will find out where the computer puts data when it is not in transit.

InfoWeb 5

Memory Technology

As you learned in Chapter 1, memory holds data and program instructions. Memory is sometimes called *primary storage*, but this term is easily confused with disk storage. It is therefore preferable to use the term *memory* to refer to the circuitry that has a direct link to the processor and to use the term *storage* to refer to media, such as disks, that are not directly linked to the processor.

There are four major types of memory: random access memory, virtual memory, CMOS memory, and read-only memory. Each type of memory is characterized by the kind of data it contains and the technology it uses to hold the data.

Random Access Memory

How does RAM work? **RAM** (random access memory) is an area in the computer system unit that temporarily holds data before and after it is processed. For example, when you enter a document, the characters you type usually are not processed immediately. Instead, they are held in RAM until you tell your software to carry out a process such as printing.

FIGURE 5-9

Each RAM location has an address and holds one byte of data by using eight capacitors to represent the eight bits in a byte.

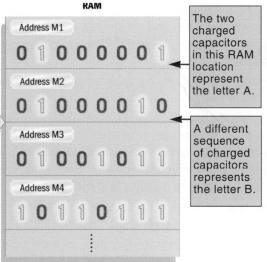

RAM is connected to the data bus so that the computer can transport data to and from the central processing unit.

The two charged capacitors in this RAM location represent the letter A.

A different sequence of charged capacitors represents the letter B.

In RAM, microscopic electronic parts called **capacitors** hold the electronic signals for the ASCII, EBCDIC, or binary code that represents data. You can visualize the capacitors as microscopic lights that can be turned on or off. A charged capacitor represents an "on" bit. A discharged capacitor represents an "off" bit.

Each bank of capacitors holds eight bits, or one byte of data. A **RAM address** on each bank helps the computer locate the data contained in that bank, as shown in Figure 5-9.

In some respects, RAM is similar to a chalkboard. You can use a chalkboard to write mathematical formulas, erase them, and then write an outline for a report. In a similar way, RAM can hold numbers and formulas when you use a spreadsheet, then hold the text of your English essay when you use a word processor. The contents of RAM can be changed just by changing the charge of the capacitors. Because its contents can be changed, RAM is a reusable computing resource.

Unlike hard disk or floppy disk storage, most RAM is *volatile*, which means that it requires power to hold data. If the computer is turned off or the power goes out, all data stored in RAM instantly and permanently disappears. When someone unhappily says, "I have lost all my data!", it often means that the person was entering data for a document or worksheet, and the power went out before the data was saved on disk.

RAM Functions

Why is RAM so important? RAM is the "waiting room" for the computer's processor. RAM holds raw data that is waiting to be processed, as well as the instructions that will process the raw data. In addition, RAM holds processed data before it is stored more permanently on disk or tape. For example, when you use personal finance software to balance your checkbook, you enter raw data for the check amounts, which is held in RAM. The personal finance software sends the instructions for processing this data to RAM. The processor uses these instructions to process the data, then sends the results back to RAM. From RAM, the results can be stored on disk, displayed, or printed.

In addition to data and software instructions, RAM holds operating system instructions that control the basic functions of the computer system. These instructions are loaded into RAM every time you start your computer, and they remain there until you turn off the computer.

RAM Capacity, Speed, and Configuration

How much RAM does my computer need? The storage capacity of RAM is measured in megabytes. Today's microcomputers typically have between 64 and 256 megabytes of RAM, which means they can hold between 64 million and 256 million characters of data or instructions.

The amount of RAM your computer needs depends on the software you use. RAM requirements are usually specified on the outside of the software box. What if the software you want to use requires more RAM than your computer has? You can purchase additional RAM to expand the memory capacity of your computer up to the limit set by the computer manufacturer.

InfoWeb 6

Grace Hopper

The speed of RAM is also important. The processor works at a certain speed, but would be forced to slow down if it had to wait for data from RAM. Today's RAM can have access speeds as fast as 8 nanoseconds. Slower, older memory has access speeds that range from 60 to 80 nanoseconds. How long is a nanosecond? Grace Hopper, a pioneer in the computer industry, used a 12-inch piece of wire to illustrate the distance electricity could travel in a nanosecond—one billionth of a second. By contrast, a microsecond would be a coil of wire nearly 1,000 feet long.

In today's microcomputers, RAM is typically configured as a series of DIPS soldered onto a small circuit board called a **DIMM** (dual in-line memory module). Metallic "teeth" on one edge of a DIMM plug into special RAM slots on the motherboard, which makes it easy to replace defective RAM or add RAM capacity.

FIGURE 5-10

Today, most RAM is configured as small circuit boards called DIMMs, which plug into special slots in the motherboard.

Virtual Memory

What if I run out of RAM? Suppose that you have an older computer with only 32 MB of RAM. You're working on a complex project using a word processing program to edit a document containing several large graphics. The operating system requires 12 MB of RAM, your word processing program requires an additional 4 MB, and your document—with all of the graphics—requires about 15 MB. You're using about 31 MB of your computer's 32 MB RAM capacity. Now, what if you want to also open your spreadsheet software that requires 4 MB of RAM?

With today's operating systems, you shouldn't run out of RAM because a computer can use space on its hard disk as an extension of RAM. A computer's ability to use disk storage to simulate RAM is called **virtual memory**. Figure 5-11 explains how virtual memory works.

FIGURE 5-11

Virtual memory simulates RAM.

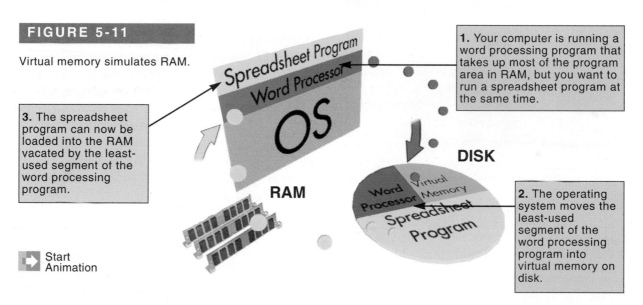

1. Your computer is running a word processing program that takes up most of the program area in RAM, but you want to run a spreadsheet program at the same time.

2. The operating system moves the least-used segment of the word processing program into virtual memory on disk.

3. The spreadsheet program can now be loaded into the RAM vacated by the least-used segment of the word processing program.

Start Animation

RAM

DISK

Virtual memory allows computers without sufficient amounts of real memory to run large programs, manipulate large data files, and run multiple programs simultaneously. Unfortunately, virtual memory is not as fast as RAM. Your computer takes longer to retrieve data from virtual memory because the disk is a mechanical device. A disk access time of 10 milliseconds is quite a bit slower than RAM access speeds of 60 nanoseconds.

Like data held in RAM, data in virtual memory becomes inaccessible if the power fails. You might wonder why—normally disks do not lose data when the power goes off. Data in virtual memory is not erased from the disk if the power fails, but the instructions that direct the computer to the location of virtual memory are stored in RAM and are lost when power fails. Consequently, the computer cannot access virtual memory data even after power is restored.

Read-Only Memory

If a computer has RAM, why does it need ROM? **ROM** (read-only memory) is one or more chips containing instructions that help a computer prepare for processing tasks. The instructions in ROM are permanent, and the only way to change them is to remove the ROM chips from the motherboard and replace them with another set. You might wonder why a computer includes chips with programs permanently stored in them. Why not use the more adaptable RAM?

FIGURE 5-12

The ROM BIOS is housed in one or more ROM chips on the motherboard.

The answer to this question is that when you turn on your computer, the central processing unit receives electrical power and is ready to begin executing instructions. But because the computer was just turned on, RAM is empty—it doesn't contain any instructions for the central processing unit to execute. Now ROM plays its part. ROM contains a small set of instructions called the **ROM BIOS** (basic input/output system). The instructions in the BIOS tell the computer how to access the disk drives and other peripheral devices. When you turn on your computer, the central processing unit performs instructions specified by the ROM BIOS that search the disk drive for the main operating system files. The computer can then load these files into RAM so that they can be used during the remainder of the computing session.

CMOS Memory

If the boot instructions are permanent, does that mean I can't change any hardware on my computer system? A computer is not ready to process data until it has copied certain operating system files from the hard disk into RAM. However, the computer can find data on the hard disk only if it has some information about how the hard disk is formatted. Where does the computer find the information it needs to access the hard disk?

RAM is empty when the computer first boots, so the information cannot be found there. ROM would not be a good place to store this information, either. If information about the hard disk was permanently stored in ROM, you would never be able to replace your hard disk drive with a larger one, because your computer could not access the new hard disk by using information about the old disk. Therefore, a computer must have some semipermanent way of keeping boot data, such as the number of hard disk sectors and cylinders. For this purpose, a computer needs a type of memory more permanent than RAM, but less permanent than ROM.

CMOS memory (complementary metal oxide semiconductor, pronounced "SEE moss") holds data, but requires very little power to retain its contents. Because of its low power requirements, a CMOS chip can be powered by a battery that's integrated into the motherboard. The battery trickles power to the CMOS chip so that it can retain vital data about your computer system configuration, even when your computer is turned off. In many of today's microcomputers, the CMOS chip is housed within the same chip carrier as the ROM BIOS.

When your system configuration changes, the data in the CMOS memory must be updated. Some operating systems have special utilities that help you update the CMOS settings. For example, most of today's computers have a **plug and play** feature that helps you update CMOS if you install a new hard drive. You can manually change the CMOS data by running the CMOS setup program, as shown in Figure 5-13.

FIGURE 5-13

CMOS holds computer configuration settings, such as the date and time, hard disk capacity, number of floppy disks, and RAM capacity.

```
                      ROM PCI/ISA BIOS (2A37IB0B)
                          STANDARD CMOS SETUP

   Date (mm:dd:yy)    :  Sat, Sep 13 1998
   Time (hh:mm:ss)    :  14 : 26 : 56

   HARD DISKS           TYPE  SIZE  CYLS  HEAD  PRECOMP  LANDZ  SECTOR  MODE

   Primary Master    :  Auto   0     0     0       0       0      0     AUTO
   Primary Slave     :  None   0     0     0       0       0      0     ------
   Secondary Master  :  None   0     0     0       0       0      0     ------
   Secondary Slave   :  None   0     0     0       0       0      0     ------

   Drive A           :  1.44M, 3.5in.
   Drive B           :  None

   Video             :  EGA/VGA                    Base Memory :    640K
   Power Management  :  Disabled               Extended Memory : 31744K
                                                  Other Memory :    384K

                                                  Total Memory : 32768K

   ESC : Quit                ↓↑→← : Select Item         PU/PD/+/- :  Modify
   F1  : Help                [Shift] F2 : Change Color
```

Start
Screentour

QUICKCHECK **B**

1 _____ is electronic circuitry that holds data and programs.

2 Having a steady power source is important for a computer because RAM is _____.

3 RAM capacity is measured in _____.

4 In RAM, microscopic electronic parts called _____ hold the electrical signals that represent data.

5 RAM speed is measured in _____.

6 If your computer does not have enough RAM to run several programs at once, your computer operating system might simulate RAM with disk-based _____ memory.

7 The series of instructions that a computer performs when it is first turned on are permanently stored in _____.

8 System configuration information, such as the number of the hard disk cylinders and sectors, is stored in battery-backed _____ memory.

 Check Answers

CHAPTER 5

SECTION C CENTRAL PROCESSING UNIT

So far in this chapter, you have learned that digital computers represent data by using a series of electrical signals. You know that data can be transported over the data bus or held in memory. A computer does more than transport and store data, however. It is supposed to process data—perform arithmetic, sort lists, format documents, and so on.

The central processing unit (CPU) is the circuitry in a computer that executes instructions to process data. It retrieves instructions and data from RAM, processes those instructions, then places the results back into RAM so they can be displayed or stored. Figure 5-14 will help you visualize the flow of data and instructions through the processor.

FIGURE 5-14

The data bus transports data and instructions between RAM and the CPU.

The data bus transports data and instructions from RAM to the CPU for processing.

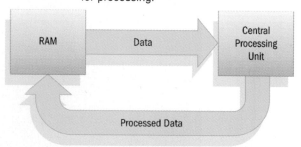

RAM contains data and instructions about how to process the data.

The CPU processes data.

The data bus transports the processed data to RAM so it can be displayed, output, or stored on disk.

InfoWeb 7

CPUs

Central Processing Unit Architecture

What does the CPU look like? At one time, computer CPUs were huge, unreliable expensive devices that guzzled a tremendous amount of electrical power. In 1945, the size of a CPU was measured in feet (Figure 5-15), whereas today it is measured in **mils** (0.001 inch).

FIGURE 5-15

The ENIAC, built in 1944, had 20 processing units, each about two feet wide and eight feet high. Today, this circuitry fits on an integrated circuit less than 560 mils (0.56 inch) square.

The central processing unit of a mainframe computer usually contains several integrated circuits and circuit boards. In a microcomputer, the central processing unit is a single integrated circuit called a **microprocessor**. Figure 5-16 illustrates a microprocessor similar to the one that is probably in the computer you use.

FIGURE 5-16

The microprocessors in today's microcomputers might be housed in a large SEC (as pictured) or in a smaller, square PGA.

Start
Video

The central processing unit has two main parts: the arithmetic logic unit and the control unit. Each unit performs specific tasks to process data.

The **ALU** (arithmetic logic unit) performs arithmetic operations such as addition and subtraction. It also performs logical operations such as comparing two numbers to see if they are the same. The ALU uses **registers** to hold data that is being processed. In the ALU, the result of an arithmetic or logical operation is placed the **accumulator**. From the accumulator, data can be sent to RAM or used for further processing. Figure 5-17 diagrams how the ALU processes data.

FIGURE 5-17

How the ALU works.

1. The data to be processed arrives from RAM and is held in registers.

2. A signal from the control unit indicates which arithmetic or logical operation to perform.

4. The results are usually sent to RAM so they can be output or stored on disk.

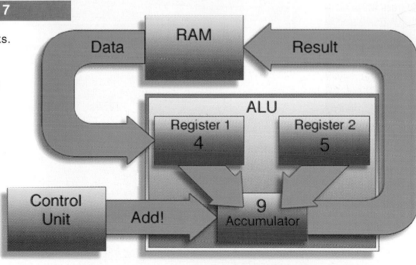

Start
Animation

3. The ALU performs the operation and places the result in the accumulator.

CHAPTER 5

How does the ALU get data, and how does it know which arithmetic or logical operation it must perform? The CPU's **control unit** directs and coordinates processing.

The control unit uses an **instruction pointer** to keep track of the sequence of instructions that is supposed to be processed. Using this pointer as a guide, the control unit retrieves each instruction in sequence from RAM and places it in a special **instruction register**. The control unit then interprets the instruction to find out what needs to be done. According to its interpretation, the control unit sends signals to the data bus to fetch data from RAM, and to the ALU to perform a process.

The control unit makes a significant contribution to processing efficiency. It is analogous to the director on a movie set, because it executes a series of instructions just as a director follows a script. The control unit directs the movement of data, just as a director positions actors and props on the set. A movie director schedules a production to ensure that the camera operators, actors, sound technicians, and lighting crew are ready to film each scene. The control unit schedules processing by making sure that the data and instructions arrive in the ALU when they are needed for processing. Figure 5-18 diagrams the role of the control unit.

FIGURE 5-18

How the control unit works.

1. The control unit retrieves an instruction from RAM and puts it in the instruction register.

2. The RAM address of the instruction is kept in the instruction pointer. When the instruction has been executed, the address in the instruction pointer changes to indicate the RAM address of the next instruction to be executed.

3. The control unit interprets the instruction in its instruction register.

4. Depending on the instruction, the control unit will get data from RAM, tell the ALU to perform an operation, or change the memory address in the instruction pointer.

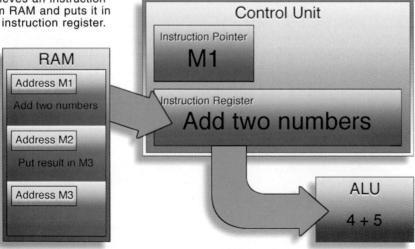

 Start Animation

Instructions

What specifies the steps that the CPU must perform to accomplish a task?

Lab
CPU
Simulator

A computer accomplishes a complex task by performing a series of very simple steps, referred to as instructions. An **instruction** tells the computer to perform a specific arithmetic, logical, or control operation.

An instruction has two parts: the op code and the operands. An **op code**, which is short for "operation code," is a command word for an operation such as add, compare, or jump. The **operands** for an instruction specify the data or the address of the data for the operation. Let's look at an example of an instruction:

op code ⟶ **JMP M1** ⟵ operand

InfoWeb
8

Instruction
Sets

In the instruction JMP M1, the op code is JMP and the operand is M1. The op code JMP means jump or go to a different instruction. The operand M1 is the RAM address of the instruction to which the computer is supposed to go. The instruction JMP M1 has only one operand, but some other instructions have more than one operand. For example, the instruction ADD REG1 REG2 has two operands: REG1 and REG2.

The list of instructions that a CPU is able to execute is known as its **instruction set**. Every task a computer performs is determined by the list of instructions in its instruction set. As you look at the instruction set in Figure 5-19, consider that the computer must use instructions such as these for all of the tasks it helps you perform—from database management to word processing.

CHAPTER 5

FIGURE 5-19	A simple microprocessor instruction set	
Op Code	**Operation**	**Example**
INP	Input the given value into the specified memory address	INP 7 M1
CLA	Clear the accumulator to 0	CLA
MAM	Move the value from the accumulator to the specified memory location	MAM M1
MMR	Move the value from the specified memory location to the specified register	MMR M1 REG1
MRA	Move the value from the specified register to the accumulator	MRA REG1
MAR	Move the value from the accumulator to the specified register	MAR REG1
ADD	Add the values in two registers, place the result in the accumulator	ADD REG1 REG2
SUB	Subtract the value in the second register from the value in the first register, place the result in the accumulator	SUB REG1 REG2
MUL	Multiply values in two registers, place the result in the accumulator	MUL REG1 REG2
DIV	Divide the value in the first register by the value in the second register, place the result in the accumulator	DIV REG 1 REG2
INC	Increment (increase) the value in the register by 1	INC REG1
DEC	Decrement (decrease) the value in the register by 1	DEC REG1
CMP	Compare the values in two registers; if values are equal, put 1 in the accumulator, otherwise put 0 in the accumulator	CMP REG1 REG2
JMP	Jump to the instruction at the specified memory address	JMP P2
JPZ	Jump to the specified address if the accumulator holds 0	JPZ P3
JPN	Jump to the specified address if the accumulator does not hold 0	JPN P2
HLT	Halt program execution	HLT

FIGURE 5-20

The instruction cycle.

1. Fetch instruction

2 Interpret instruction

3 Execute instruction

4 Increment instruction pointer

Instruction Cycle

How does a computer process instructions? The term **instruction cycle** refers to the process in which a computer executes a single instruction. The instruction cycle is repeated each time the computer executes an instruction. The steps in this cycle are summarized in Figure 5-20.

You now have all the pieces that you need to understand the details of the instruction cycle. You know how the ALU performs arithmetic and logical operations and how the control unit retrieves data from RAM and tells the ALU which operation to perform. Figure 5-21 explains how the ALU, control unit, and RAM work together to process instructions.

FIGURE 5-21

Processing instructions.

1. The instruction pointer indicates the memory location that holds the first instruction (M1).

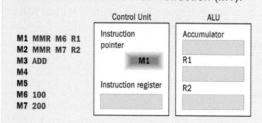

2. The computer fetches the instruction and puts it into the instruction register.

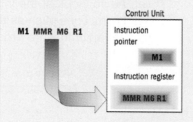

3. The computer executes the instruction that is in the instruction register; it moves the contents of M6 into register 1 of the ALU.

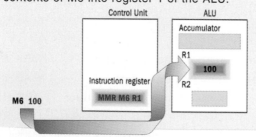

4. The instruction pointer changes to point to the memory location that holds the next instruction.

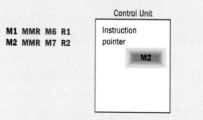

5. The computer fetches the instruction and puts it in the instruction register.

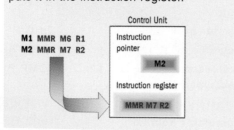

6. The computer executes the instruction; it moves the contents of M7 into register 2 of the ALU.

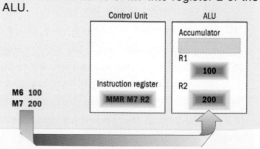

(Figure continued on next page)

Exit | Home | Glossary | Jump Back | Jump To | ◀Page | Page▶

CHAPTER 5   **225**

FIGURE 5-21**FIGURE 5-21**

Processing instructions
(continued).

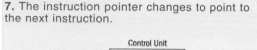

7. The instruction pointer changes to point to the next instruction.

8. The computer fetches the instruction and puts it in the instruction register.

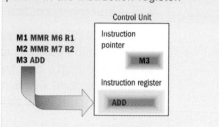

9. The computer executes the instruction. The result is put in the accumulator.

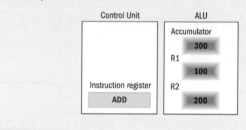

CPU Performance Factors

How does the architecture of a computer contribute to its performance?

Integrated circuit technology is the basic building block of CPUs in today's microcomputers, minicomputers, mainframes, and supercomputers. Remarkable advances in this technology have produced exponential increases in computer speed and power. In 1965, Gordon Moore, co-founder of chip-production giant, Intel Corporation, predicted that the number of transistors on a chip would double every 18 to 24 months. Much to the surprise of engineers and Moore himself, "Moore's law" accurately predicted 30 years of chip development. In 1958, the first integrated circuit contained two transistors. The Pentium III Xeon processor, introduced in 1999, has 9.5 million transistors.

More transistors mean more processing power, today's CPU chips are generally faster than those of the past. However, all CPUs are not created equal; some process data faster than others. CPU speed is influenced by several factors, including clock rate, word size, cache, and instruction set size. Specifications for these factors allow you to compare different CPUs.

Before you learn more about the factors that affect CPU performance, you should understand that a computer system with a high-performance CPU might not necessarily provide great overall performance. You know the old saying, "a chain is only as strong as its weakest link." A computer system might also have weak links. Even with a high-performance processor, a computer system with a slow hard disk, no disk cache, and a small amount of RAM is likely to be slow at tasks such as starting programs, loading data files, printing, and scrolling through long documents.

Clock Rate

What does the date and time have to do with CPU performance? A computer contains a **system clock** that emits pulses to establish the timing for all system operations. The system clock is not the same as a "real-time clock" that keeps track of the time of day. Instead, the system clock sets the speed or "frequency" for data transport and instruction execution.

To understand how the system clock works, visualize a team of oarsmen on a Viking ship. The ship's coxswain beats on a drum to coordinate the rowers. A computer's system clock and a ship's coxswain accomplish essentially the same task—they set the pace of activity. Boom! A stream of bits takes off from RAM and heads to the CPU. Boom! The control unit reads an instruction. Boom! The ALU adds two numbers.

The clock rate set by the system clock determines the speed at which the computer can execute an instruction and, therefore, limits the number of instructions that a computer can complete within a specific amount of time. The time to complete an instruction cycle is measured in **megahertz** (MHz), or millions of cycles per second.

The microprocessor in the original IBM PC performed at 4.77 MHz. Today's processors perform at speeds exceeding 600 MHz. If all other specifications are identical, higher megahertz ratings mean faster processing.

Word Size

Which is faster, an 8-bit processor or a 64-bit processor? **Word size** refers to the number of bits that the central processing unit can manipulate at one time. Word size is based on the size of the registers in the CPU and the number of data lines in the bus. For example, a CPU with an 8-bit word size is referred to as an 8-bit processor; it has 8-bit registers and manipulates 8 bits at a time.

A computer with a large word size can process more data in each instruction cycle than a computer with a small word size. Processing more data in each cycle contributes to increased performance. For example, the first microcomputers contained 8-bit microprocessors, but today's faster computers contain 32-bit or 64-bit microprocessors.

Cache

Disk cache speeds up access to data on disk; is there a similar process that speeds access to data from RAM? Another factor that affects CPU performance is cache. **Cache**, sometimes called "RAM cache" or "cache memory," is special high-speed memory that gives the CPU more rapid access to data. A very fast CPU can execute an instruction so quickly that it often must wait for data to be delivered from RAM, which slows processing. The cache ensures that data is immediately available whenever the CPU requests it.

As you begin a task, the computer anticipates what data the CPU is likely to need and loads this data into the cache area. When an instruction calls for data, the CPU first checks to see if the required data is in the cache. If so, it takes the data from the cache instead of fetching it from RAM, which takes longer. All other factors being equal, more cache means faster processing.

InfoWeb
9

RISC

Instruction Set Complexity

What's the difference between CISC and RISC? As programmers developed various instruction sets for computers, they tended to add increasingly more complex instructions that took up many bytes in memory and required several clock cycles for execution. A computer based on a central processing unit with a complex instruction set came to be known as a **CISC** (complex instruction set computer) machine.

In 1975, John Cocke, an IBM research scientist, discovered that most of the work done by a microprocessor requires only a small subset of the available instruction set. Further research showed that only 20 percent of the instructions of a CISC machine do about 80 percent of the work. Cocke's research resulted in the development of microprocessors with streamlined instruction sets, called RISC machines.

The microprocessor of a **RISC** (reduced instruction set computer) machine has a limited set of instructions that it can perform very quickly. In theory, therefore, a RISC machine should be faster than a CISC machine for most processing tasks. Some computer scientists believe, however, that a balance or hybrid of CISC and RISC technologies produces the most efficient and flexible computers.

InfoWeb
10

Parallel and
Pipelining

Pipelining and Parallel Processing

Can a CPU increase its performance by executing more than one instruction at a time? Computers with a single processor execute instructions "serially"—that is, one instruction at a time. Usually, the processor must complete all four steps in the instruction cycle before it begins to execute the next instruction. However, using a technology called **pipelining**, the processor can begin executing an instruction before it completes the previous instruction. Pipelining speeds up processing, as shown in Figure 5-22.

CHAPTER 5

FIGURE 5-22

Pipelining allows a computer to process more than one instruction at a time.

Instructions

1 MAM M30

2 MOV M10 R1

3 MOV M11 R2

RAM

Control Unit

Registers

MOV M10 R1

Accumulator

MAM M30

The control unit decodes **instruction 3** while...

the data for **instruction 2** moves into a register, while...

instruction 1 is completed.

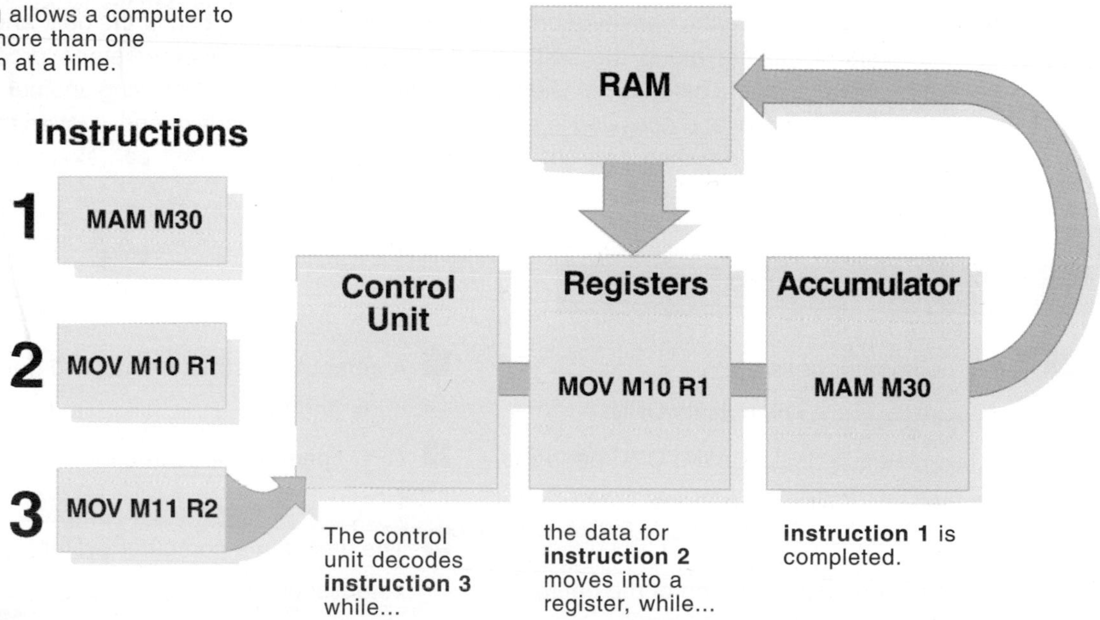

A computer that has more than one processor can execute multiple instructions at the same time. **Parallel processing** increases the amount of processing that a computer can accomplish in a specific amount of time. A computer that is capable of parallel processing is called a **parallel computer** or "non-von Neumann machine." Figure 5-23 explains the concept of parallel processing.

FIGURE 5-23

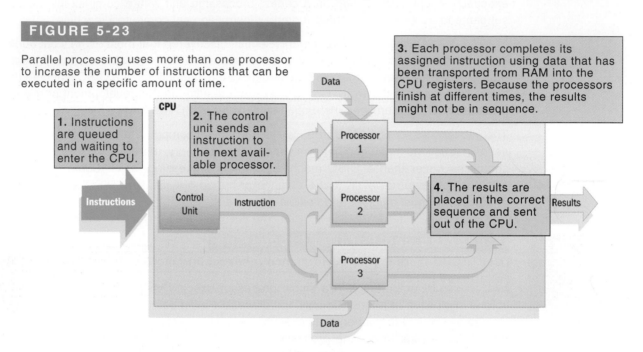

Parallel processing uses more than one processor to increase the number of instructions that can be executed in a specific amount of time.

3. Each processor completes its assigned instruction using data that has been transported from RAM into the CPU registers. Because the processors finish at different times, the results might not be in sequence.

1. Instructions are queued and waiting to enter the CPU.

2. The control unit sends an instruction to the next available processor.

4. The results are placed in the correct sequence and sent out of the CPU.

CPU

Instructions

Control Unit   Instruction

Processor 1

Processor 2

Processor 3

Data

Data

Results

To get a clearer picture of serial, pipelining, and parallel processing techniques, consider an analogy in which computer instructions are pizzas. Serial processing executes only one instruction at a time, just like a pizzeria with only one oven that can bake only one pizza (instruction) at a time. Pipelining is similar to a pizza conveyor belt. A pizza starts moving along the conveyor belt, but, before it reaches the end of the belt, another pizza starts moving along the belt. Likewise, a pipelining computer starts processing an instruction; but before it completes the instruction, it begins processing another instruction. Finally, parallel processing is similar to a pizzeria with many ovens. Just as these ovens can bake more than one pizza at a time, a parallel computer can execute more than one instruction at a time.

QUICKCHECK   C

1 A microcomputer uses a(n) _____ chip as its CPU.

2 The _____ in the CPU performs arithmetic and logical operations.

3 The _____ in the CPU directs and coordinates the operation of the entire computer system.

4 A computer instruction has two parts: the op code and the _____.

5 CPU speed is measured in _____.

6 The timing in a computer system is established by the _____.

➡ Check Answers

SECTION D | INPUT/OUTPUT

When you purchase a computer, you can be fairly certain that before its useful life is over, you will want to add equipment to expand its capabilities. When you understand computer input/output, you will see how it is possible to expand a computer system. **I/O**, pronounced "eye-oh," is computer jargon for input/output. I/O refers to collecting data for the microprocessor to manipulate, and transporting results to display, print, and storage devices.

You have already learned that a data bus transports data between RAM and the CPU. The data bus also extends to other parts of the computer. The segment of the data bus that transports data between RAM and peripheral devices is called the **expansion bus**. I/O often involves a long path that moves data over the expansion bus, slots, cards, ports, and cables. Figure 5-24 provides an overview of the I/O architecture described in the rest of this section.

FIGURE 5-24

I/O architecture transports data to motherboard components and to peripheral devices.

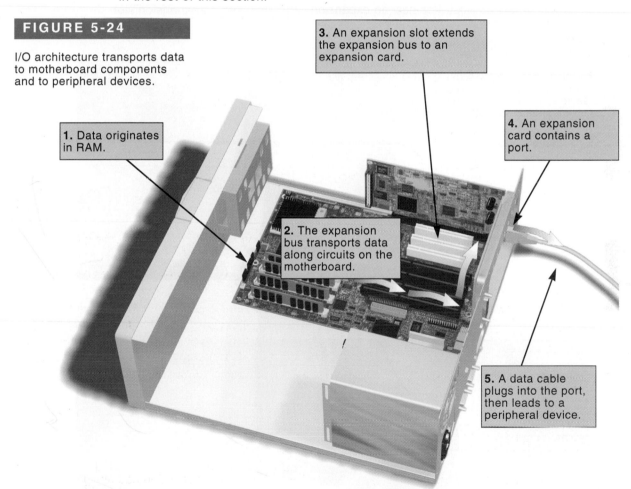

3. An expansion slot extends the expansion bus to an expansion card.

1. Data originates in RAM.

4. An expansion card contains a port.

2. The expansion bus transports data along circuits on the motherboard.

5. A data cable plugs into the port, then leads to a peripheral device.

CHAPTER 5

Expansion Slots and Cards

How do I use expansion slots? On the main board, the expansion bus terminates at an expansion slot. An **expansion slot** is a long, narrow socket on the motherboard into which you can plug an expansion card. An **expansion card** is a small circuit board that provides a computer with the ability to control a storage, input, or output device. Expansion cards are also called "expansion boards" or "controller cards."

Most microcomputers have four to eight expansion slots, but some of these slots usually contain expansion cards when you purchase the computer. Today's microcomputers typically contain a **graphics card** for connecting the monitor, a **modem** for transmitting data over phone or cable lines, and a **sound card** for connecting speakers, headphones, and a microphone. You would usually have to add expansion cards if you want to connect a scanner, digitize videos, or connect your computer to a network. Figure 5-25 illustrates how an expansion card plugs into an expansion slot.

FIGURE 5-25

Expansion cards simply slide into an expansion slot, then can be secured to the system unit case with a small screw.

Start
Video

An expansion card has a "card edge" connector with metal contacts that connect the circuitry on the card to the circuitry on the motherboard.

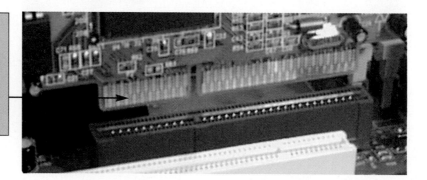

The number and type of empty expansion slots in your computer dictates its expand-ability. A microcomputer motherboard typically has three types of expansions slots:

- **ISA** (industry standard architecture). ISA slots are an older technology, used today for some modems and other relatively slow devices. Many new computers have few or no ISA slots.

- **PCI** (peripheral component interconnect). PCI slots offer fast transfer speeds and a 64-bit data bus. These slots typically house a graphics card, sound card, video capture card, modem, or network interface card.

- **AGP** (accelerated graphics port). Primarily used for graphics cards, and faster than a PCI slot, an AGP slot provides a high-speed data pathway that is particularly handy for 3-D graphics.

Expansion cards are built for only one type of slot. If you plan to add or upgrade a card in your computer, you must therefore make sure that you have a slot that matches the type of card you want to install. For example, suppose that you plan to replace your computer's modem with a faster one. Before making your purchase, take a peek inside your computer's system unit to see which type of slot holds the current modem. As you shop, you can read the connection information on the modem boxes to make sure that you select a new modem that fits in the same type of slot as your old modem. Figure 5-26 shows you how to identify AGP, PCI, and ISA slots.

FIGURE 5-26

AGP, PCI, and ISA slots are different lengths, so you can easily identify them by opening your computer's system unit and looking at the motherboard.

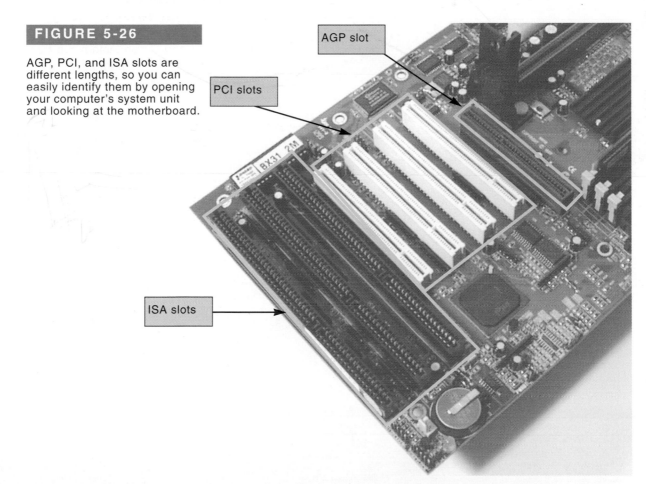

AGP slot

PCI slots

ISA slots

CHAPTER 5

Expansion Ports and Cables

How do I connect a peripheral device to an expansion card? To connect a peripheral device to an expansion card, you plug a cable from the peripheral device into an expansion port. An **expansion port** is any connector that passes data in and out of a computer or peripheral device. Ports are sometimes called "jacks" or "connectors"—the terminology is inconsistent.

FIGURE 5-27

To many computer users, the back of a computer is a confusing array of unlabeled ports, connectors, and cables. This figure will help you become familiar with the shapes of the most frequently used expansion ports.

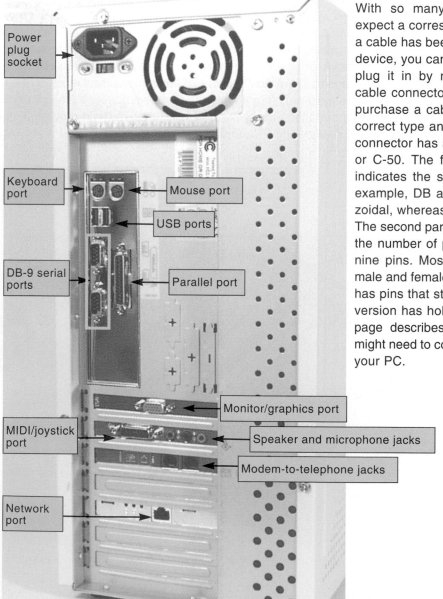

An expansion port is often housed on an expansion card so that it is accessible through a hole in the back of the computer system unit. A port might also be connected directly to the main board, instead of to an expansion card.

With so many types of ports, you can expect a corresponding variety of cables. If a cable has been supplied with a peripheral device, you can usually figure out where to plug it in by matching the shape of the cable connector to the port. If you have to purchase a cable, you'll need to know the correct type and designation. Each type of connector has a designation such as DB-9 or C-50. The first part of the designation indicates the shape of the connector. For example, DB and C connectors are trapezoidal, whereas DIN connectors are round. The second part of the designation indicates the number of pins. A DB-9 connector has nine pins. Most types of connectors have male and female versions. The male version has pins that stick out, whereas the female version has holes. Figure 5-28 on the next page describes the cable connectors you might need to connect a peripheral device to your PC.

InfoWeb 11

Connectors

FIGURE 5-28	Microcomputer cables and connectors		
	Connector	**Description**	**Devices**
	Serial DB-9	Connects to serial port, which sends data over a single data line one bit at a time at speeds of 56 Kbps.	Mouse or modem
	Parallel DB-25M	Connects to parallel port, which sends data simultaneously over eight data lines at speeds of 12,000 Kbps.	Printer, external CD-ROM drive, Zip drive, external hard disk drive, tape backup device
	USB	Connects to universal serial bus (USB), Which sends data over a single data line at speeds of 12,000 Kbps; supports up to 127 devices.	Modem, keyboards, joystick, scanner, mouse
	SCSI C-50F	Connects to SCSI ("scuzzy") port, which Sends data simultaneously over 8 or 16 Data lines at speeds between 5 MBps And 80 MBps; supports up to 16 devices.	Hard disk drive, scanner, CD-ROM drive, tape backup device
	IEEE 1394	Connects to the "FireWire" port, which sends data at 400,000 Kbps.	Video camera, DVD drive
	VGA DB-15	Connects to the video port	Monitor

CHAPTER 5

QUICKCHECK D

1 A(n) _____ is an electronic path that transports data between RAM and expansion slots.

2 A(n) _____ is a small circuit board that plugs into an expansion slot.

3 An expansion _____ is located inside the system, whereas an expansion _____ is located on the exterior of the system unit.

4 A(n) _____ port allows you to connect up to 127 peripheral devices to a single port. *Hint:* Refer to Figure 5-28.

Check Answers

TROUBLESHOOTING THE BOOT PROCESS

Lab
Trouble-
shooting

Now that you have an understanding of how I/O, RAM, ROM, CMOS, and the CPU operate, you're ready to learn how they all work together to prepare a computer for accepting commands each time you turn it on.

The sequence of events that occurs between the time you turn on a computer and the time it is ready for you to issue commands is referred to as the **boot process**. Microcomputers, minicomputers, mainframes and supercomputers all require a boot process. In this section of the chapter, you'll learn about the microcomputer boot process because you are most likely to use this type of computer.

You'll find out what happens during each step of the boot process for a typical PC and what you should do when the boot process doesn't proceed smoothly. Of course, even when you know how to troubleshoot computer problems, you should always follow the guidelines provided by your school or employer when you encounter equipment problems.

An Overview

InfoWeb 12
Trouble-
shooting

If the computer memory is blank when I turn it on, how does it know how to start up? As you learned earlier, one of the most important components of a computer—RAM—is volatile, so it cannot hold any data when the power is off. It also cannot hold the operating system instructions when the power is off. Therefore, the computer cannot use RAM to "remember" any basic functions, such as how to deal with input and communicate output to the external world. A computer needs some way to get operating system files into RAM. That's one of the main objectives of the boot process. In general, the boot process follows these six steps:

1. **Power up.** When you turn on the power switch, the power light is illuminated, and power is distributed to the motherboard.

2. **Start boot program.** The microprocessor begins to execute the instructions stored in ROM.

3. **Power-on self-test.** The computer performs diagnostic tests of several crucial system components.

4. **Load operating system.** The operating system is copied from a disk to RAM.

5. **Check configuration and customization.** The microprocessor reads configuration data and executes any customized startup routines specified by the user.

6. **Ready for commands and data.** The computer is ready for you to enter commands and data.

Power Up

| What if I turn the computer on, but nothing happens? | The first stage in the

boot process is the power-up stage. The fan in the power supply begins to spin, and the power light on the case of the computer comes on, as shown in Figure 5-29.

FIGURE 5-29

When you turn on a computer, you should see the power light and hear the fan.

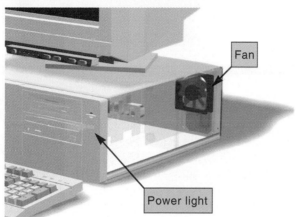

If you turn on the computer and the power light does not come on, the system is not getting power. You should check the power cord at the back of the computer to make sure it is firmly plugged into the wall and into the system unit. Also, make sure that the wall outlet is supplying power. If the power light still does not come on, then the computer's power supply might have failed. If you encounter this problem, you should contact a technical support person for assistance.

Start Boot Program

| What happens if the ROM is malfunctioning? | As soon as power reaches the

motherboard, the microprocessor begins to execute the boot program stored in ROM, as shown in Figure 5-30.

If the ROM chips, RAM modules, or microprocessor are malfunctioning, the microprocessor is unable to run the boot program and the computer stops or "hangs." You know you have a problem at this stage of the boot process if the power light is on and you can hear the fan, but there is no message on the screen and nothing else happens. This problem requires the assistance of a technical support person.

FIGURE 5-30

Most computers beep once when the ROM-based boot program begins.

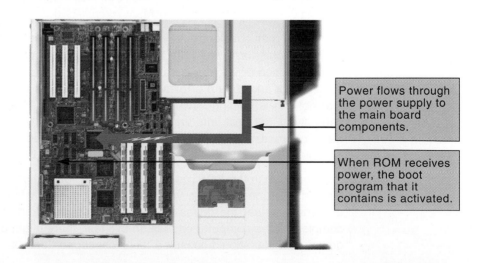

Power flows through the power supply to the main board components.

When ROM receives power, the boot program that it contains is activated.

Power-On Self-Test

Can the computer check to determine if all its components are functioning correctly? The next step in the boot process is the **power-on self-test** (POST), which diagnoses problems in the computer, as shown in Figure 5-31.

FIGURE 5-31

The power-on self-test checks system components.

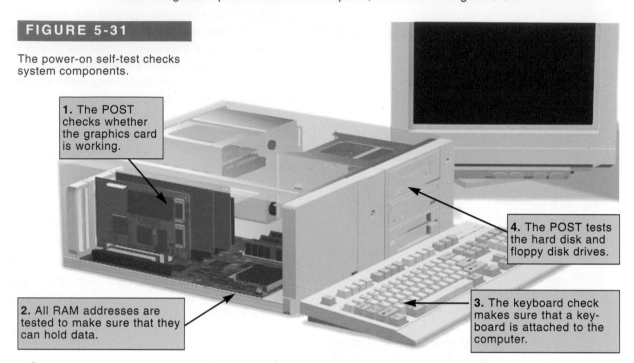

1. The POST checks whether the graphics card is working.

2. All RAM addresses are tested to make sure that they can hold data.

3. The keyboard check makes sure that a keyboard is attached to the computer.

4. The POST tests the hard disk and floppy disk drives.

The POST first checks the graphics card that connects your monitor to the computer. If the graphics card is working, you'll see a message such as "Video BIOS ver 2.1 2000." If your computer beeps and does not display the video BIOS message, the graphics card is probably malfunctioning. You should contact a technical support person to have the graphics card checked.

Next, the computer tests RAM by placing data in each memory location, then retrieving that data to see if it is correct. The computer displays the amount of memory tested. If any errors are encountered during the RAM test, the POST stops and displays a message that indicates a problem with RAM.

The POST then checks the keyboard. On most computers, you can see the keyboard indicator lights flash when the keyboard test is in progress. If the keyboard is not correctly attached or if a key is stuck, the computer beeps and displays a keyboard error message. If a keyboard error occurs, you should turn the computer off and make sure that nothing is holding down a key on the keyboard. Next, unplug the keyboard and carefully plug it back into the computer. Finally, turn on the computer again to repeat the boot process. If the problem recurs, you might need to have your keyboard repaired or replaced.

The final step in the POST is the drive test. If you watch the hard disk drive and floppy disk drives during this test, you will see the drive activity lights flash on for a moment, and you will hear the drives spin. The drive test should take only a second or two to complete. If the computer pauses on this test, there might be a problem with one of the drives, and you should consult a technical support person.

Load Operating System

How does the computer load the operating system into RAM? After successfully completing the POST, the computer continues to follow the instructions in ROM to load the operating system, as shown in Figure 5-32.

FIGURE 5-32

Loading the operating system.

1. If the computer finds a disk in drive A, that drive becomes the default drive.

2. If the computer cannot find a disk in drive A, it uses drive C as the default drive.

3. The computer loads the operating system from the default drive into RAM.

The computer first checks drive A to see if it contains a disk. If it does, drive A becomes the **default drive**. The computer uses the default drive for the rest of the computing session unless you specify a different one.

If there is no disk in drive A but the computer has a drive C, the computer uses drive C as the default drive. If your computer has a hard disk, you generally want drive C to be the default drive, so it is best not to put a disk in any of the floppy disk drives until the boot process is complete; otherwise, the computer will recognize the floppy disk drive as the default drive.

Next, the computer tries to locate and load operating system files from the default drive. The computer looks for two operating system files: *Io.sys* and *Msdos.sys*. If these files do not exist on the disk, the boot process stops and displays a message such as "Non-system disk or disk error" or "Cannot load a file." If you see one of these messages, there is probably a disk in drive A that should not be there. Remove the disk from drive A so that your computer looks on the hard drive for the operating system files.

The microprocessor next attempts to load an operating system file called *Command.com*. Two problems can occur at this stage of the boot process, and both problems have the same error message—"Bad or missing command interpreter." First problem: the file *Command.com* might be missing because someone inadvertently erased it. Second problem: your disk might contain the wrong version of *Command.com* because someone inadvertently copied a different version onto the computer.

If you encounter either problem, you should turn the computer off, then find a bootable floppy disk. A **bootable floppy disk** contains a minimal set of operating system files. Put this floppy disk in drive A and turn on the computer again. Even if you are successful using a floppy disk to boot your system, you need to correct the *Command.com* problem on your hard disk. A technical support person or experienced user can help you fix the *Command.com* problem.

Check Configuration and Customization

Does the computer get all of its configuration data from CMOS? Early in the boot process, the computer checks CMOS to determine the amount of installed RAM and the types of available disk drives. Often, however, more configuration data is needed for the computer to properly access all available devices and set up your screen-based desktop. In the next stage of the boot process, the computer searches the root directory of the boot disk for configuration and customization settings.

Configuration information can be stored in a variety of files, including *Config.sys* and the Windows Registry. The **Windows Registry** contains the settings that a computer needs to correctly use its hardware devices and software. The Registry also includes information about the colors and fonts that you've selected for the Windows desktop, passwords for authorized users, and a list of the programs that have been installed on your computer system. Registry information is stored in two files: *System.dat* and *User.dat*.

FIGURE 5-33

Configuration data is stored in the *System.dat* and *User.dat* files that make up the Windows Registry.

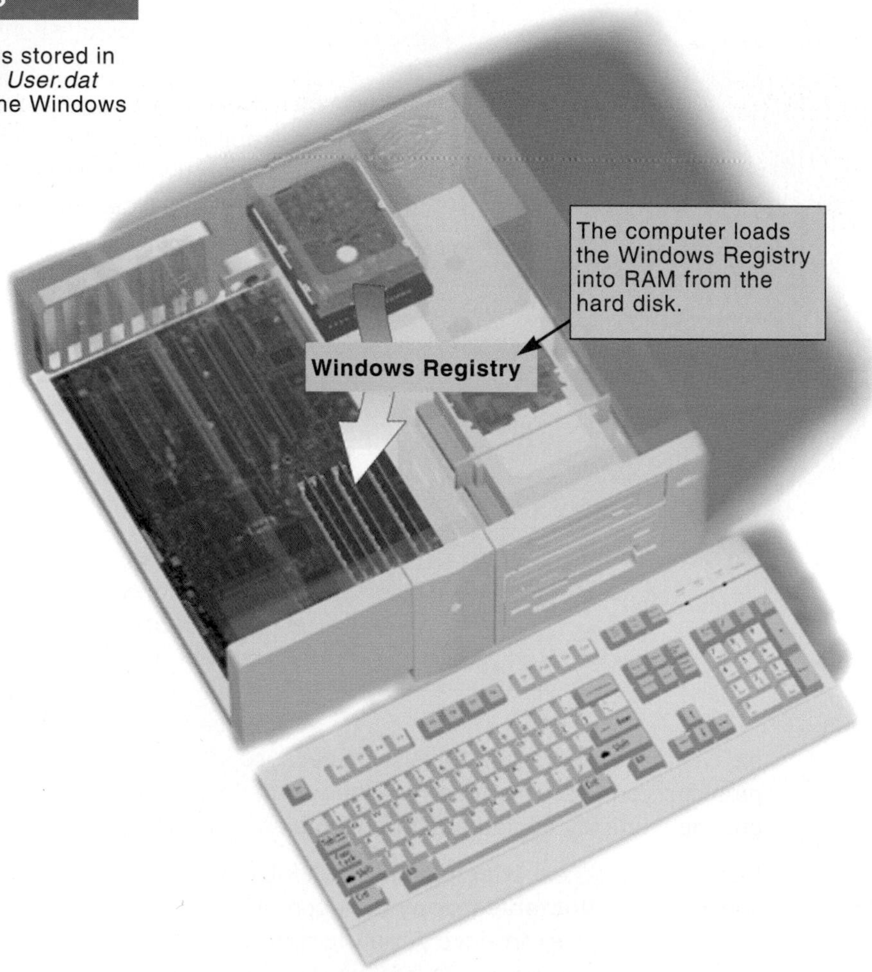

The computer loads the Windows Registry into RAM from the hard disk.

Windows Registry

Ready for Commands and Data

How do I know when the computer has finished booting? The boot process is complete when the computer is ready to accept your commands. Usually, the computer displays the operating system main screen or prompt at the end of the boot process. If you are using DOS, you will see the operating system prompt; if you are using Windows, you'll see the Windows desktop (Figure 5-34)

If Windows cannot complete the boot process, you are likely to see a menu that contains an option for Safe Mode. **Safe Mode** is a limited version of Windows that allows you to use your mouse, monitor, and keyboard, but no other peripheral devices. This mode is designed for troubleshooting, not for real computing tasks. After your computer enters Safe Mode, you should use the Shut Down option on the Start menu to properly shut down and turn off your computer. You can then turn on your computer again, and it should complete the boot process in regular Windows mode. If your computer enters Safe Mode again, consult a technician.

FIGURE 5-34

You can enter commands and launch programs when the computer displays the Windows desktop or the DOS operating system prompt C:\>.

FIGURE 5-35

If Windows cannot compete the boot process, you can select Safe Mode, shut down your computer, and then restart it.

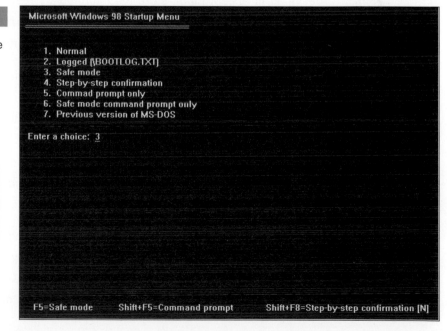

Microsoft Windows 98 Startup Menu

1. Normal
2. Logged (\BOOTLOG.TXT)
3. Safe mode
4. Step-by-step confirmation
5. Commad prompt only
6. Safe mode command prompt only
7. Previous version of MS-DOS

Enter a choice: 3

F5=Safe mode   Shift+F5=Command prompt   Shift+F8=Step-by-step confirmation [N]

Start
Screentour

WHO INVENTED THE COMPUTER?

Just think how wealthy you would be if you had invented the computer, held a patent for its technology, and could collect even $1 in royalties for every computer ever sold. In 1973, a company called Sperry-Rand claimed to hold a patent on the technology for electronic digital computers. If the courts had upheld this claim, then no company would have been able to manufacture computers without obtaining a license from and paying royalties to Sperry-Rand. As you might expect, other computer companies, such as IBM, took issue with Sperry-Rand's claim. During the ensuing court battle, opposition lawyers suggested a surprising number of candidates as the "inventor" of the computer. You can read the brief sketches of these candidates and their machines, and then do some supplementary research on the Web before deciding who you think invented the computer.

During the period 1821-1832, Charles Babbage drew up plans for a machine that he called the Analytical Engine. Like modern computers, this device was designed to be programmable. It would accept input from a set of punched cards that contained the instructions for performing calculations. The plans for the Analytical Engine called for it to store the results of intermediary calculations in a sort of memory. Results would be printed on paper. Babbage intended to power his device using a steam engine, which was the cutting-edge technology of his day. Unfortunately, Babbage worked on this machine for 11 years, but never completed it.

In 1939, John Atanasoff began to construct a machine that came to be known as the Atanasoff-Berry Computer (ABC). Like today's computers, the ABC was powered by electricity, but it used vacuum tubes instead of integrated circuits. This machine was designed to accept input, store the intermediary results of calculations, and produce output. Unlike today's computers, the ABC was not a multipurpose machine. Instead, it was designed for a single purpose—finding solutions to systems of linear equations.

Atanasoff never completed the ABC, but he shared his ideas and technology with John Mauchly and J. Presper Eckert, who were working on plans for the ENIAC (Electronic Numerical Integrator and Computer). Like the ABC, the ENIAC was powered by electricity and used vacuum tubes for its computational circuitry. The machine could be "programmed" by rewiring its circuitry and it produced printed output. ENIAC went online in 1946. Eckert and Mauchly filed for a patent on their technology and formed a company that became Sperry-Rand.

The ENIAC was not originally designed to store a program in memory, along with data. The stored program concept—a key feature of today's computers—was proposed by John von Neumann, who visited the ENIAC project and then collaborated with Eckert and Mauchly on the EDVAC computer, which was completed in 1949. As you know from Chapter 1, the EDVAC was an electronic, digital computer that could accept input, process data, store data and programs, and produce output. Like the ENIAC, the EDVAC used vacuum tubes for its computational circuitry. Whereas the ENIAC worked with decimal numbers, however, the EDVAC worked with binary numbers much like today's computers.

In 1938, German scientist Conrad Zuse developed a binary, digital computer called the Z-1. Zuse had designed his machine as a programmable, general-purpose device with input, storage, processing, and output capabilities. Unlike the ABC and ENIAC, the Z-1 was not a fully electronic device. Instead of using electrical signals to represent data, it used mechanical relays.

Zuse's work was cloaked in secrecy during World War II, and scientists in Allied countries had little or no knowledge of his technology. It is somewhat surprising, therefore, that a similar machine was constructed in the United States by Howard Aiken, who was working with funding from IBM. The Harvard Mark I, completed in 1944, was powered by electricity, but used mechanical relays for its computational circuitry.

No list of computer inventors would be complete without Alan Turing, who worked with a group of British scientists, mathematicians, and engineers to create a completely electronic computing device in 1943. Called the Colossus, Turing's machine was essentially a huge version of Atanasoff's ABC—a special-purpose device (designed to break Nazi codes) powered by electricity, with vacuum tubes for its computing circuitry.

The roster of possible computer "inventors" includes Babbage, Atanasoff, Eckert and Mauchly, von Neumann, Zuse, Aiken, and Turing. Patents were filed only by IBM for Aiken's Mark I and by Eckert and Mauchly for the ENIAC. Should any of these inventors be collecting royalties on computer technology?

WHAT DO YOU THINK?

1. The Sperry-Rand lawsuit ended with a ruling that the Eckert and Mauchly patent was not valid because the ENIAC inventors derived their ideas from Atanasoff. Do you think that this decision was correct?   ○ Yes   ○ No   ○ Not sure

2. To be credited with the invention of the computer, do you think that the inventor would be required to have completed a working model?   ○ Yes   ○ No   ○ Not sure

 Save Responses

CHAPTER 5 — REVIEW ACTIVITIES

INTERACTIVE SUMMARY

The Interactive Summary helps you select important concepts and facts from this chapter. Fill in the blanks to best complete each sentence. When using the NP4 CD or NP4 Web site, you can click the Check Answers buttons to automatically score your answers. Place your Tracking Disk in the floppy disk drive if you want to save your scores.

Computer _____ refers to the design and construction of a computer system. Virtually all of today's computers are digital devices because they work with data that has been converted into 1s and 0s. Once converted, the data can travel along computer circuitry as pulses of electricity. Computers use several codes for data, such as the _____ number system for numeric data and the ASCII or _____ codes for character data.

Most of the electronic components inside a computer are _____ circuits, commonly referred to as "chips." These chips plug into a main circuit board called the motherboard, which provides a circuit called a(n) _____ that transports data from one chip to another. While data is waiting to be processed, it is held in random access memory (RAM) chips. When a computer is on, this memory typically contains program instructions, data, and the _____ system. RAM chips are usually configured on a small circuit board called a(n) _____. These chips hold data only when the computer is receiving power, so they are said to be _____. In contrast, read-only memory (ROM) contains "hard wired" instructions called the ROM _____, which are a critical part of the boot process. A third type of memory called _____ provides a semi-permanent storage area for configuration settings, such as hard disk capacity and the current date and time.

 Check Answers

The central processing unit of a microcomputer is a single chip called a(n) _____. Within this chip, the _____ performs arithmetic and logical operations. The _____ unit directs and coordinates processing based on a set of instructions. Microprocessor performance depends on several factors, including clock rate, word size, cache capacity, and instruction set complexity. Performance is enhanced by processing more than one instruction at a time by pipelining or _____ processing.

A computer's input/output architecture is a segment of the data bus called the _____ bus, which carries data from the computer motherboard to peripheral devices. On the motherboard, an expansion _____ provides a receptacle for an expansion card. This card usually contains a(n) _____ that protrudes through the back of the system unit, allowing you to plug in a cable from a peripheral device. A computer also provides some expansion ports that are connected directly to the motherboard, such as a parallel printer port, a serial mouse port, and a VGA monitor port.

 Check Answers

INTERACTIVE KEY TERMS

Make sure that you understand all of the boldfaced key terms presented in this chapter. If you're using the NP4 CD or NP4 Web site, you can use this list of terms as an interactive study activity. First, try to define a term in your own words, then click the term to compare your definition with the definition that is presented in the chapter.

Accumulator, 221
Address lines, 214
AGP, 231
ALU (arithmetic logic unit), 221
Analog device, 211
ASCII, 212
Binary number system, 212
Bootable floppy disk, 237
Boot process, 234
Cache, 226
Capacitors, 215
Character data, 212
Chip packages, 209
CISC, 227
CMOS memory, 218
Computer architecture, 208
Control unit, 222
Data bus, 214
Data lines, 214
Default drive, 237
Digital device, 211
DIMM, 216
EBCDIC, 213
Expansion bus, 229
Expansion card, 230
Expansion port, 232
Expansion slot, 230
Graphics card, 230
I/O (input/output), 229
Instruction, 223
Instruction cycle, 224
Instruction pointer, 222
Instruction register, 222
Instruction set, 223
Integrated circuit (IC), 209
ISA, 231
Megahertz, 226
Microprocessor, 221
Mils, 220
Modem, 230
Motherboard, 210
Numeric data, 212
Op code, 223
Operands, 223
Parallel computer, 228

Parallel processing, 228
PCI, 231
Pipelining, 227
Plug and play, 219
Power-on self-test (POST), 236
RAM, 215
RAM address, 215
Registers, 221
RISC, 227
ROM, 218
ROM BIOS, 218
Safe Mode, 239
Sound card, 230
System clock, 226
Virtual memory, 217
Windows Registry, 238
Word size, 226

CHAPTER 5

I N T E R A C T I V E   Q U I Z Z E S

Quiz yourself on important concepts from this chapter by filling in the blanks. When using the NP4 CD or NP4 Web site, you can type your answers, then use the Check Answers buttons to automatically score your responses. Place your Tracking Disk in the floppy disk drive if you want to save your scores.

1 A(n) _____ device works with discrete numbers, whereas a(n) _____ device works with continuously varying data.

2 A Social Security number is an example of _____ data that would be represented by the ASCII or EBCDIC codes.

3 On the data bus, _____ lines carry the signals that represent data and _____ lines carry the location of the data that the computer is supposed to use.

4 RAM speed is measured in _____ .

5 Today's computer typically contain at least 32 GB of RAM. True or false? _____ .

6 _____ memory allows a computer to use disk storage to simulate RAM.

7 A CISC machine has a larger instruction set than a RISC machine. True or false? _____

8 The Windows _____ is a data file that contains configuration information.

9 If a Windows computer cannot complete the boot sequence, it displays a menu that lets you boot into _____ Mode.

Check Answers

Enter the correct letter from the photo into each box.

1 Microprocessor _____

2 RAM _____

3 ROM _____

4 Expansion card _____

5 Expansion slot _____

6 Port _____

Check Answers

INTERACTIVE PRACTICE TESTS

When you use the NP4 CD or NP4 Web site, you can take practice tests that consist of 10 multiple-choice, true/false, and fill-in-the-blank questions. The 10 questions are selected at random from a large test bank, so each time you take a test, you'll receive a different set of questions. Your tests are scored immediately and you can print study guides that help you find the correct answers for any questions that you missed. If you are using a Tracking Disk, insert it in the floppy disk drive to save your test scores.

 Start Practice
Test

STUDY TIPS

Study Tips help you organize and consolidate the information in a chapter by making lists, outlines, charts, and sketches. You can use paper and pencil or word processing software to complete most of the Study Tips activities.

1 Below each heading in this chapter, there is a question. Look back through this chapter and answer each of these questions using your own words.

2 Use Figure 5-7 to write out the ASCII code for the following phrase: *Way Cool!*

3 Imagine you are a teacher. Write a one- or two-page script explaining the instruction cycle to your class, and design at least three visual aids you would use as illustrations.

4 Think about the concepts in the first four sections of this chapter: Digital Electronics, Memory, Central Processing Unit, and I/O. Using these concepts, put together your own description of how a computer processes data. You can use a narrative description and/or sketches.

5 For each type of memory (RAM, ROM, CMOS, and virtual), answer the following questions:
   a. What role does it play in the overall process of computing?
   b. What types of data does it hold?
   c. Does it store data permanently or temporarily?

6 Assume that a computer has the following instructions and data in its RAM and CPU. After the processor executes the instructions in RAM, what are the final values in Register 1, Register 2, and the accumulator? (*Hint:* Refer to Figure 5-19.)

RAM	Program	
	P1	MMR M1 REG1
	P2	MMR M2 REG2
	P3	ADD REG1 REG2
	P4	MAM M3
	P5	HLT
	Data	
	M1	5
	M2	3

CPU	Control Unit	
	Instruction Pointer	P1
	Instruction Register	
	ALU	
	Accumulator	
	REG1	

CHAPTER 5

PROJECTS

A project is an open-ended activity that will help you apply the concepts you have learned. Many projects require resources in addition to your textbook, such as current magazines, library materials, or Web access. When you tackle a project, be prepared to use your critical thinking skills, logical analysis, and your creativity.

1 Looking from the Inside Out After disconnecting the power cable, carefully open the case of a computer system unit. Draw a sketch and label each of the components you see inside. Try to locate and label all of the components discussed in this chapter.

2 The History of the IC Computers would not be available to individuals today if not for the invention of the integrated circuit. Just four months apart in 1959, Jack Kilby and Robert Noyce independently created working models of the circuit that was to transform the computer industry. Jack Kilby worked at Texas Instruments, and you can find reproductions of his original research notes on the Web site *www.ti.com/corp/docs/history/firstic.htm.* Robert Noyce developed the integrated circuit while CEO of Fairchild Semiconductor, before he left Fairchild to form Intel.

Use your library and Internet resources to research the effect of the integrated circuit on the computer industry, then do one of the following:

a. Write a two- to three-page paper summarizing how the integrated circuit was used in the first five years after it was invented.

b. Write two one-page biographical sketches: one of Jack Kilby and one of Robert Noyce.

c. Create a diagram of the "family tree" of computer technologies that resulted from the development of the integrated circuit.

d. Based on the facts you have gathered about the development of the computer industry, write a two- to three-page paper describing the computer industry today if the integrated circuit had not been invented.

3 Scanning a Computer Ad for Key Terms Photocopy a full-page computer ad from a current issue of a computer magazine, such as *Computer Shopper.* On the copy of the ad, use a colored pen to circle any of the key terms that were presented in this chapter. Make sure you watch for abbreviations; they are frequently used in computer ads. On a separate sheet of paper or using a word processor, make a list of each term you circled and write a definition of each.

4 Researching and Writing about RAM Suppose you are a computer industry analyst preparing an article on computer memory for a popular computer magazine. Gather as much information as you can about RAM, including current pricing, the amount of RAM that comes installed in a typical computer, tips for adding RAM to computers, and so forth. Use a word processor to write a one- to two-page article that would help your magazine's readers understand all about RAM.

5 Expansion Ports Look in computer magazines or on the Web to find advertisements for three peripheral devices that connect to a computer using different ports or buses. For example, you might find a modem that connects to the serial port. Photocopy each of these three ads. For each device, circle on the photocopy the device's brand name, model name and/or number, and the port or bus it uses. Make sure that you provide the name and publication date of the magazine and the page number on which you found the information.

6 Interview with a Computer User Complete steps (a) through (d) to interview one of your friends who has a computer and write a report that describes how your friend could expand his or her computer system.

a. Find out as many technical details as you can about your friend's computer, including the type of computer, the type and speed of the microprocessor, the amount of memory, the configuration of disk drives, the capacity of the disk drives, the resolution of the monitor, and so on. (continued on next page)

b. Find out how your friend might want to expand his or her computer system either now or in the future. For example, your friend might want to add a printer, a sound card, a DVD drive, memory, or a better-quality monitor.

c. Look through computer magazines to find a solution for at least one of your friend's expansion plans. What would you recommend as a solution? If money was no object, would your recommendation change? Why or why not?

d. Write a two-page report describing your friend's computer and his or her expansion needs. Then describe the solution(s) you found.

7 **Observing the Boot Process** Using the *User Focus* section of this chapter as your guide, make a detailed list of each step in the boot process. Take your list into the computer lab and boot one of the computers. As the computer boots, read your list to make sure it is correct. For which steps in the boot process can you see or hear something actually happening?

8 **Troubleshooting Scenarios—What Would You Do?** Your instructor might want you to do this project individually or in a small group. For each of the following scenarios, indicate what might be wrong:

a. You turn on the computer's power switch and nothing happens—no lights, no beep, nothing. What's the most likely problem?

b. You turn on your computer and the computer completes the POST test. You see the light on drive A and you hear the drive power up, but you get a message on the screen that says "Non-system disk or disk error." Explain what caused this message to appear and explain exactly what you should do to complete the boot process.

c. Your computer begins to boot, but instead of showing the Windows desktop, it displays a menu that includes an option for Safe Mode. What should you do before you begin using any application software?

d. You turn on your computer, see the power light, and hear the fan. Then, the computer begins to beep repeatedly. What would you suspect is the problem?

ADDITIONAL PROJECTS

Click the underlined text to link to the NP4 Web site (www.cciw.com/np4), where you can view and print additional projects for this chapter.

The Apraphulian's Computer

Researching and Writing about RISC

Can a Computer Make Errors?

LAB ASSIGNMENTS

Software for these labs is provided on the NP4 CD and may also be available in your school's computer lab. To start a lab, click the lab icon.

Each lab has two parts: Steps and Explore. Use the Steps first to learn and review concepts. Read the information on each page and do the numbered steps. As you work through the lab, you will be asked to answer QuickCheck questions about what you have learned. At the end of the lab, you will see a report that scores your answers to the QuickChecks. If your instructor wants you to turn in this report, click the Print button on the QuickCheck Report screen.

When you have completed the Steps, you can click the Explore button to complete the Lab Assignments. You can also use Explore to practice the skills you learned and to explore concepts on your own.

In a computer's CPU, the ALU performs instructions orchestrated by the control unit. Processing proceeds at a lightning pace, but each instruction accomplishes only a small step in the entire process. In this lab, you work with an animated CPU simulation to learn how computers execute assembly language programs. In the Explore section of the lab, you have an opportunity to interpret programs, find program errors, and write your own short assembly language programs.

1 Click the Steps button to learn how to work the simulated CPU. As you proceed through the Steps, answer all of the QuickCheck questions that appear. After you complete the Steps, you will see a QuickCheck Report. Follow the instructions on the screen if you want to print this report.

2 Click the Explore button. Use the File menu to open the program called *Add.cpu*. Use the Fetch Instruction and Execute Instruction buttons to step through the program. Then answer the following questions:

   a. How many instructions does this program contain?

   b. Where is the instruction pointer after the program is loaded, but before it executes?

   c. What does the INP 3 M1 instruction accomplish?

   d. What does the MMR M1 REG1 instruction accomplish?

   e. Which memory location holds the instruction that adds the two numbers in REG1 and REG2?

   f. What is in the accumulator when the program execution is complete?

   g. Which memory address holds the sum of the two numbers when program execution is completed?

3 In Explore, use the File menu to open the program called *Count5.cpu*. Use the Fetch Instruction and Execute Instruction buttons to step through the program. Then answer the following questions:

   a. What are the two input values for this program?

   b. What happens to the value in REG1 as the program executes?

   c. What happens when the program executes the JPZ P5 instruction?

   d. What are the final values in the accumulator and registers when program execution is complete?

4 In Explore, click File, then click New to make sure the CPU is empty. Write a program that follows these steps to add 8 and 6:

   a. Input 8 into memory address M3.

   b. Input 6 into memory address M5. (continued on next page)

    c. Move the number in M3 to Register 1.

    d. Move the number in M5 to Register 2.

    e. Add the numbers in the registers.

    f. Move the value in the accumulator to memory address M1.

    g. Tell the program to halt.

Test your program to make sure it produces the answer 14 in address M1. When you are sure that your program works, use the File menu to print your program.

5 In Explore, use the File menu to open the program called *Bad1.cpu*. This program is supposed to multiply two numbers together and put the result in memory location M3. However, the program contains an error.

    a. Which memory location holds the incorrect instruction?

    b. What instruction will make this program produce the correct result?

6 In Explore, use the CPU simulator to write a program to calculate the volume, in cubic feet, of the inside of a refrigerator. The answer should appear in the accumulator at the end of the program. The inside dimensions of the refrigerator are 5 feet by 3 feet by 2 feet. Test your program, then print it.

Lab
Trouble-
shooting

Computers sometimes malfunction, so it is useful to have some skill at diagnosing, if not fixing, some of the hardware problems you might encounter. In this lab, you use a simulated computer that has trouble booting. You learn to make and test hypotheses that help you diagnose the cause of boot problems.

1 Click the Steps button to learn how to make and test hypotheses about hardware malfunctions during the boot process. As you proceed through the Steps, answer all of the QuickCheck questions that appear. After you complete the Steps, you will see a QuickCheck Report. Follow the instructions on the screen if you want to print this report.

2 Click the Explore button. Use the File menu to load *System11.trb*. Click the Boot Computer button and watch what happens on the simulated computer (in this case, what does not happen!). State an hypothesis about why this computer does not boot. Use the Check menu to check the state of various cables and switches. When you think you know the cause of the problem, select it from the Diagnosis list. If you correctly diagnosed the problem, write it down. If your diagnosis was not correct, form another hypothesis and check it, until you correctly diagnose the problem.

3 Sometimes problems that appear very similar result from different causes. In Explore, use the File menu to load *System03.trb*, then diagnose the problem. Do the same for *System06.trb*. Describe the problems with these two systems. Then describe the similarities and differences in their symptoms.

4 In Explore, use the File menu to load *System02* and *System08*. Both systems produce keyboard errors, but these errors have different causes. Describe what caused the problem in *System02*, and what caused the problem in *System08*. Once you have diagnosed these problems, what can you do about them?

5 In Explore, use the File menu to load Systems 04, 05, 07, 09, and 14. These systems produce similar symptoms on boot up, but they have different problems. Diagnose the problem with each system and indicate the key factor (the symptom or what you checked) that led to your diagnosis.

INFOWEB

The InfoWeb is your guide to print, film, television, and electronic resources. Use it to obtain updates on quickly changing technical information and to locate information for research papers. If you're using the NP4 CD, click the InfoWeb Site icon on the left side of this paragraph to access the online InfoWeb links. Otherwise, use your Web browser and type in the address of the NP4 Web site: www.cciw.com/np4. At the Web site, you'll find up-to-date links to the topics covered in this chapter.

1 April Fools

The Apraphulian computer was the subject of A. K. Dewdney's article, "Computer Recreations: An ancient rope-and-pulley computer is unearthed in the jungle of Apraphul" published in *Scientific American*, April 19, 1988. What begins as an April Fools' joke turns out to be an excellent explanation on the basic circuitry in a digital computer. Although this article is not online, you'll find more recent editions of *Scientific American* at *www.sciam.com*. Each issue contains at least one article about computers. Don't miss "Ask the Experts," where you'll find authoritative answers to questions such as "Can computers be made from strands of DNA?" in the Ask the Experts Archive.

2 Inside the Case

If you have a chance to visit the Computer Museum in Boston, make sure you tour the Walk-through Computer 2000 exhibit, where you'll walk inside the system unit of a gigantic PC to get an up-close view of the computer components discussed in this chapter. The Computer Museum Web site at *www.tcm.org* contains a text-based description of the exhibit; select Resources, Building Exhibits, then scroll down the page and click "The Walk-through Computer 2000: Behind the Scenes."

3 Integrated Circuits

Without the invention of the integrated circuit, computers would still be room-sized devices affordable to only the largest and most powerful governments and organizations. You can see a picture of the first IC and read the inventor's original notes at the Texas Instruments site at *www.ti.com/corp/docs/history/firstic.htm*. For information on Marcian (Ted) Hoff and other inventors, visit the Invention Dimension site at *web.mit.edu/invent* and go to the Inventor of the Week archives. To get an idea of how many ICs have been manufactured and to see what kinds of products they're in, check out the QuestLink Technology site at *www.questlink.com*.

4 Motherboards

For an update on what's new in motherboard technology, connect to the Mainboard Guide Web site at *sysdoc.pair.com/mainboard.html*, where you'll find FAQs and recommendations for selecting a motherboard. A more technical site with links to motherboard manufacturers and other motherboard sites is the Motherboard Homeworld at *www.motherboards.org*. Intel produces motherboards for its line of microprocessors. You'll find its information at *developer.intel.com/design/motherbd*.

5 Memory Technology

For a great online guide to PC memory—ROM, RAM, SRAM, DRAM—read PCGuide's "Memory Technology Types" at *www.pcguide.com/ ref/ram/types.htm*. Another Web site worth browsing is the Memory Manual at *pdpsys.com/mem_man.htm*. Here you can search an acronym dictionary to discover the meaning of terms such as EDO and FPM. In addition, you will find up-to-date information on memory speed and capacity.

6 Grace Hopper

Never one to follow gender stereotypes, Grace Hopper graduated with a Ph.D. in mathematics, joined the United States Naval Reserves, and in 1944 became one of the first computer programmers. Until her death in 1992, Dr. Hopper presented fascinating lectures peppered with her particular brand of wit and wisdom. You can read about her life and contribution to computer science at *www.cs.yale.edu/HTML/YALE/CS/HyPlans/tap/Files/hopper-wit.html*. In 1997, the U.S. Navy commissioned a destroyer in her honor, the *U.S.S. Hopper*. It is the first time a destroyer has been named after a woman. You'll find additional information at *web.mit.edu/invent/www/inventorsA-H/hopper.html*.

7 CPUs

A microprocessor is a fascinating microworld of nearly invisible circuitry. To get a glimpse into this world, visit *micro.magnet.fsu.edu/chipshot.html*, where you'll find links to excellent pictures of microprocessors taken through an electron microscope. You'll find more pictures if you connect to *infopad.eecs.berkeley.edu/CIC/die_photos*. Don't leave without looking at some of the photos with overlays—they show you the location of the microscopic ALU, registers, and control unit. For updates on current microprocessor technology, follow the site links for microprocessor manufacturers, such as *www.intel.com, www.amd.com, www.cyrix.com, www.motorola.com,* and *www.ibm.com*.

8 Instruction Sets

For a more in-depth look at what happens in a microprocessor, ask your local librarian for a copy of the book *How Microprocessors Work* by Wyant and Hammerstrom (Ziff-Davis Press, 1994). This book has many excellent illustrations that help you visualize what happens within the microprocessor circuitry. Microprocessor instruction sets are a pretty esoteric subject. The instruction set you saw in Figure 5-19 is very small, compared to those of most CISC processors. To get a taste of a real instruction set, look at the instruction set cards at at *www.comlab.ox.ac.uk/archive/cards.html*.

9 RISC

You can read a fascinating interview with the founder of RISC technology, John Cocke, by connecting to *www.rs6000.ibm.com/resource/interviews*. A good discussion of CISC versus RISC architectures is available at *www.zdnet.com/pcmag/issues/1418/pcm00082.htm*. In this *PC Magazine* article, Jeff Prosise discusses the following questions: Is a reduced instruction set chip better than a complex instruction set chip? What is the difference between RISC and CISC? What does a reduced instruction set mean, and are RISC chips really less complex than CISC chips?

10 Parallel and Pipelining

Parallel processing technology is a key to today's supercomputer architecture. In a test run, an Intel computer using 9,200 Pentium Pro microprocessors running in parallel clocked a new record by performing 1.34 trillion operations per second. You can read more about this engineering feat by connecting to *www.intel.com/pressroom/archive/releases/CN0611B.HTM*. Spend a few minutes with Tony Wesley at *www.acs.oakland.edu/~awesley/pipetop.htm* for an easy-to-understand tutorial on pipelining. To get an idea of how parallel architecture is applied in the real world, visit the Lawrence Livermore National Laboratory Web site on parallel computing at *www.llnl.gov/liv_comp/parcomp*.

11 Connectors

You'll find everything you wanted to know about ports, cables, and connectors in the Hardware Book at *www.dataplus.se/hwb*. Also, check out the pictures of PC cables and connectors at ConnectPro's online catalog at *www.connectpro.com/catalog.htm*. For a tour of USB technology, link to Intel's USB page at *www.intel.com/design/usb/index.htm*.

12 Troubleshooting

The PC Mechanic site at *pcmech.pair.com* is where to go if you want to learn more about the parts of a PC. You'll find all sorts of handy information, such as the meaning of those beeps you hear when your computer doesn't boot up. If you really get into computer hardware, you might want to build your own computer. Before you get started, visit the Build Your Own PC site at *www.verinet.com/pc*. You'll love the graphics here and the casual, easy-to-understand style. If you're having trouble with a computer, try A:1 Computer's site at *a1computers.net*, where you can click the links to Preventive Maintenance Tips or Troubleshooting Tips (scroll down the page to find these links). The Troubleshooting Flowchart is particularly useful. Successful troubleshooting begins with an organized approach to problem solving. You can read tips from an expert at the Troubleshooters.Com site, *www.troubleshooters.com*. Another source of good troubleshooting information might be a users group near you. Search for "users groups" on Yahoo! for a group you might visit or join.

CHAPTER 6

THE COMPUTER MARKETPLACE

CONTENTS

→ Start Video

PREVIEW

Chapter 6 provides you with the background you need to become a smart consumer in the computer marketplace. This chapter includes an in-depth guide to interpreting a computer ad, shopping tips, and insights into the computer industry that sets the prices for the products you purchase. In addition, you'll learn a bit about employment opportunities in the computer industry. The *Issue* section wraps up the chapter with a look at the options for recycling your old computers and electronics equipment.

When you have completed this chapter, you should be able to:

■ Read a computer ad and understand how the technical specifications affect price and performance

■ Explain why there are so many models of computers at so many different prices

■ Find reliable information about computer products

■ Determine which products are of good quality and value

■ Take a systematic approach to shopping for a computer

■ Use technology resources to research career options and create an effective resume

CHAPTER 6 LAB

Buying a
Computer

SHOP 'TIL YOU DROP

It is one of those dreary afternoons when the rain fogs up the windows. Your friend Matt is sprawled on the floor amidst a small mountain of computer magazines. Now and then he tags a page with a Post-it note or jots down the price of a computer system. You munch on grapes while browsing employment sites on the Web.

"Hey, what's up?" you ask.

"See all these magazines! See all these ads! How's a person supposed to know what to buy? The more I look, the more confused I get!" He opens the latest issue of *Computer Shopper*—all 400 pages of it—and you see that he has marked at least 30 ads with Post-it notes!

"Look," he says, "here's a computer with a Pentium III processor...$1,395. Here's another one from a different company...$1,445."

"There's got to be some difference between them," you exclaim, trying to help.

Matt frowns. "Yeah. That's the trouble. One has more RAM, but the other one has a better monitor. I could spend $1,695 and get Surround Sound plus a larger hard drive, but that would wreck my budget. What am I going to do?"

Whether you're shopping for a computer or considering a career, the computer industry offers a huge variety of choices. For a consumer, understanding the computer industry is just as important as understanding world events. In fact, much of the news about the computer industry has global significance for today's Information Age. As a result, there is increasing coverage of computers and the computer industry on the evening news, in magazines, on the Internet, and on TV.

The purpose of this chapter is to help you learn about the computer industry. You'll discover what you need to know to be a smart computer shopper. You'll discover who does what in the computer industry, and maybe you'll even identify a computer career that appeals to you.

SECTION A — CONSUMER'S GUIDE TO COMPUTERS

Sometime in the not-too-distant future, you might participate in a computer purchase—if not for your own computer, then one for a friend, your parents' small business, your employer, or your children. Buying the right computer and keeping within your budget are challenges.

Suppose that you decide to buy a computer. You'll probably look at computer ads to get an idea of features and prices. Most computer ads list technical specifications describing the computer's components, capabilities, and special features. Do you need to understand the technical specifications to make an intelligent purchase decision? The answer is definitely "yes!" Suppose that you see a computer ad, such as the one in Figure 6-1. This computer system costs $1,499. Would it be a good "deal"?

FIGURE 6-1

A typical computer ad.

MicroPlus Home PC XL550

MicroPlus award-winning computers offer strong performance at a reasonable price. Simply the fastest Windows machines you can buy. MicroPlus computers feature superior engineering, starting with a genuine Intel processor and a motherboard designed specifically to take advantage of the latest technological advancements. Of course, you are covered by the MicroPlus one-year, on-site parts and labor warranty.*

- Intel Pentium 550 MHz with 512K cache
- 128 MB SDRAM expandable to 384 MB
- 3.5" 1.44 MB floppy drive
- 13 GB Ultra ATA hard drive
- 40X variable CD-ROM drive
- Turtle Beach Montego Sound Blaster-compatible PCI sound card
- Stereo speakers
- 16 MB Diamond Viper AGP graphics card
- 56 K V.90 PCI data/fax modem
- 15" (13.8 vis) .26 dp monitor 1024 x 768 max. res
- 7-bay mid-tower case
- 2 USB, 1 parallel port
- Multifunction keyboard and mouse
- Windows 98
- Microsoft Office 2000
- MicroPlus Edutainment Pak

$1,499

MicroPlus!
www.micropluscomputers.com

*On-site service available for hardware only and only in the continental U.S. Shipping and handling costs are not covered by warranty. All returns must be in original box and packaging. Shipping and handling costs are nonrefundable. Call for an RMA number. Prices and availability subject to change without notice.

You can't tell if the MicroPlus computer is a good deal unless you compare its specifications to those of computers from other vendors. Let's take a closer look at what the specifications mean in terms of price and performance.

Selecting a Microprocessor

Does the microprocessor affect the price of a computer? A microprocessor (sometimes referred to simply as a "processor") is the core component in a computer and is featured prominently in product descriptions. Processor specifications have a significant effect on the price of a computer, so it is useful to be able to decipher the processor information provided in a computer ad. Typically, computer ads indicate the processor manufacturer, model, speed, and cache capacity.

InfoWeb
1
Which Chip?

Manufacturer. Intel and AMD are currently the two major PC microprocessor manufacturers. Intel created the processor for the first IBM PC and is considered the industry leader in microprocessor research and development. Computers that contain Intel processors command higher prices than computers that contain other manufacturers' processors. The "Intel Inside" logo, shown in Figure 6-2, helps you quickly identify computers with Intel processors.

FIGURE 6-2

"Intel Inside" is the trademark for Intel microprocessors.

Intel's rival, AMD, produces "work-alike" processors for PC-compatible computers. AMD processors offer manufacturers and customers an alternative to those produced by Intel. Both Intel and AMD are reputable chipmakers and consumers are generally quite satisfied with the performance of their processors. Other reputable chipmakers, such as Cyrix and Texas Instruments, have produced processors in the past and may again in the future. If you have questions about unfamiliar processors or manufacturers, look for product reviews or other consumer information in magazines or on Web sites.

Processor models. Ever since Henry Ford christened his Model A, car makers have used model names to identify different car styles and designs. Chipmakers have followed suit by assigning model names or model numbers to processors. A chip model indicates its architecture. For example, the original IBM PC contained an Intel model 8086 processor, which had a 16-bit word size and a 16-bit bus. In 1982, Intel produced the 80286 model, with the same word size and bus architecture as the 8086, but with the ability to access more memory. Intel's 80386 model featured a 32-bit word size and bus. The 80486 model featured enhanced number-crunching capability. In 1993, Intel introduced the 64-bit Pentium model, which was followed by the Pentium Pro, Pentium MMX, Pentium II, Pentium II Xeon, Pentium III, and Pentium III Xeon. Each Pentium model featured enhancements that increased processing speed and efficiency.

Intel also produces a "budget" processor called the Celeron, which has a slightly less sophisticated architecture than the Pentium models. Most people can discern no difference in the operation of a computer with a Pentium processor and one with a Celeron processor. Both processors use the same instruction set and therefore use the same software. Computers with a Celeron processor are typically less expensive than computers with Pentium processors. If you are shopping on a budget, a Celeron processor might mean a savings of $100 to $300.

AMD produces K6 and Athlon processors that compete directly with Intel's Pentiums and Celerons. From the user's perspective, it is virtually impossible to find any operational differences between computers that use AMD processors and those with Intel processors. You can run the same software and add the same peripheral devices. Computers with AMD processors typically retail for less than computers with Intel processors—a good deal for shoppers on a limited budget.

CHAPTER 6

Speed. Virtually every computer ad indicates processor speed. How does this information factor into your purchase decision? Processor speed is a measure of its clock rate, which indicates the number of instructions that can be processed per second. A computer with a 550 MHz processor would be faster than a computer with a 500 MHz processor if all other specifications for the two computers are equal. As you learned in Chapter 5, however, a computer's ability to process data can be limited by factors other than processor speed.

The clock speed for the latest-model processor tends to be faster than the speed of previous models, and manufacturers charge a premium price for speed. For certain applications, such as 3-D games and desktop publishing, the fastest processor can be very desirable, but applications like word processing and e-mail don't seem to benefit much from cranking up the clock speed. Before you are tempted to spend an extra $200 to $300 for a computer with the fastest processor on the market, visit a computer store for a speed comparison. If you can't discern any speed difference with the software that you typically use, you might be able to save money by purchasing a computer with a slightly slower processor.

Cache capacity. You should recall from Chapter 5 that RAM cache is special high-speed circuitry that holds data just before the processor needs it. In theory, a large cache area increases processing speed. With the architecture of today's computers, the cache capacity is tied to the processor model. For example, a Celeron processor typically has a 128 KB cache. A Pentium III processor typically has a 512 KB cache.

Some computer ads specify the cache architecture in addition to cache capacity. The circuitry for a **Level 1 cache** (L1 cache) is built into the processor chip. Circuity for a **Level 2 cache** (L2 cache) is housed outside the processor, on a separate chip. The cache chip connects to the main processor via a dedicated high-speed bus and is often housed in the same chip carrier as the processor. Level 2 cache is much faster than RAM and almost as fast as cache built into the processor chip. Although many computer ads include cache specifications, it is not of particular significance to consumers because it is not configurable—for example, a consumer can't request more cache for a computer with a Celeron processor.

InfoWeb
2

Benchmarks

If you are really concerned with processor performance, you have two avenues of research. As mentioned earlier, you can compare the performance of two computers that use different processors to see if you can discern any difference on the tasks you typically perform. Another option would be to look for data from benchmark tests. A **benchmark test** is a set of standard processing tasks that measure the performance of computer hardware or software. Some benchmark tests provide ratings for basic processing operations, such as adding whole numbers, whereas other benchmark tests provide task-oriented ratings, such as how fast a computer can load a software package or copy a large graphic. The task-oriented benchmark tests provide better data for answering the question: "Will I be happy about the speed of this computer when I use it with my software, documents, and multimedia?"

RAM: Requirements and Cost

How much RAM is enough? The amount of RAM a computer needs depends on the operating system and application software that you plan to use. To run Windows software effectively, your computer should have at least 32 MB of RAM. Most computers today include at least 128 MB of RAM. RAM costs have dropped in recent years from $10 per megabyte to about $2.50 per megabyte, so it is now less costly to load up your computer with plenty of RAM.

You might notice the term "SDRAM" in some computer ads. **SDRAM** (synchronous dynamic RAM) is a type of volatile memory circuitry that runs in synchronization with the bus that transports data to and from the processor. This type of RAM is faster than other types of RAM, such as EDO and FPM, so it works well even with processor speeds that exceed 500 MHz.

You can also add RAM after purchasing a computer system. For example, the MicroPlus computer described in Figure 6-1 includes 128 MB of RAM, but additional SDRAM DIMMs—up to a maximum of 384 MB—can be added. Most consumer advocates recommend that you get as much RAM as you can afford with your initial computer purchase.

FIGURE 6-3

The amount of RAM that you'll need depends on the software that you plan to use and might vary by operating system. For example, the Microsoft Office 2000 package lists these RAM requirements.

■ For Windows 95 or Windows 98:

16 MB of RAM for the operating system, plus an additional 4 MB of RAM for each application running simultaneously (8 MB for Outlook, Access, or FrontPage; 16 MB for PhotoDraw)

■ For Windows NT Workstation:

32 MB of RAM for the operating system, plus an additional 4 MB of RAM for each application running simultaneously (8 MB for Outlook, Access, or FrontPage; 16 MB for PhotoDraw)

Floppy Disk Drives: How Many?

Do I need more than one floppy disk drive? Most microcomputers today are configured with a single 3½-inch floppy disk drive that reads and writes 1.44 MB disks. A popular misconception is that a computer needs two disk drives to copy the contents of one disk to another, but this is not the case. Both Windows and DOS allow you to make a copy of an entire disk by reading data from the original disk into memory, then inserting the destination disk and copying the data from memory to the destination disk. One 3½-inch floppy disk drive should be sufficient for your computing needs.

Many computers also include a Zip drive as standard equipment or as a low-cost add-on. For about $100, a Zip drive provides good flexibility for backing up and transporting large files. Zip drives are available with 100 MB or 250 MB capacity. The 250 MB drives can read and write to both 100 MB or 250 MB Zip disks. The 100 MB drive works only with 100 MB disks.

CHAPTER 6

Hard Drive Specifications

What's Ultra ATA? A hard disk drive (often referred to as a "hard drive" in computer ads) is standard equipment on virtually every PC. You will use it as the main storage area for programs and data files, so a high-capacity hard drive is desirable.

Computer ads typically specify a hard drive's storage capacity, speed, and controller type. Capacity is measured in gigabytes (GB)—that's billions of bytes. Although this capacity might seem excessive, many application programs are quite large. For example, Microsoft Office requires more than 500 MB of hard disk space. Most computers today are shipped with at least 10 GB of hard disk capacity.

Hard drive speed can be specified in terms of access time or the speed at which the disk platters rotate. Access times between 6 ms and 11 ms are typical for today's micro-computer hard drives. Faster access times mean that programs start more quickly and data files open more quickly. Realistically, however, the difference between a "slow" 11 ms drive and a "fast" 6 ms drive would be virtually unnoticeable in day-to-day use.

Another measure of hard drive speed is revolutions per minute (rpm). The faster a drive spins, the more rapidly it can position a specified sector under the read-write head and the more quickly it can access data. For example, a 7,200 rpm drive would be able to access data faster than a 5,400 rpm drive.

A hard drive mechanism includes a circuit board called a **controller** that positions the disk and read-write heads to locate data. Disk drives are classified according to the type of controller they have. Popular drive controllers include Ultra ATA, EIDE, and SCSI. **Ultra ATA** (AT attachment) and **EIDE** (enhanced integrated drive electronics) use essentially the same basic drive technology. Both feature high storage capacity and fast data transfer. Ultra ATA drives, which are commonly found in today's PCs, are twice as fast as their EIDE counterparts. **SCSI** (small computer system interface) drives provide a slight performance advantage over EIDE drives and are typically found in high-performance workstations and servers.

Some computer ads specify DMA hard drives. **DMA** (direct memory access) allows a computer to transfer data directly from a drive into RAM, without intervention from the processor. This architecture relieves the processor of data-transfer duties and frees up processing cycles for other tasks. DMA and Ultra ATA are companion technologies. The fastest drive access will occur when a computer has an Ultra ATA drive that implements DMA data transfer.

After processing speed, hard drive capacity is probably the most popular yardstick for comparing computer systems. All other factors (price, processor, and so on) being equal, a computer with a higher-capacity hard drive is probably your best buy.

CD and DVD Drives

Should I get a CD drive or a DVD drive? Virtually every computer on the market today comes equipped with a CD-ROM or DVD-ROM drive. CD-ROM drives typically accompany less expensive computer systems, whereas DVD-ROM drives are more likely to be included with more expensive systems. Most experts recommend a DVD-ROM drive because it can read CD-ROM, CD-R, CD-RW, DVD-ROM, and DVD movie formats. A CD-ROM drive cannot read DVD-ROM or DVD movie formats.

Some computer manufacturers offer the option of substituting a DVD-ROM drive for a CD-ROM drive. The cost of this upgrade is less than $100 and is probably a good investment. Whether you purchase a CD-ROM drive or a DVD-ROM drive with your computer, get the fastest one available.

Judging the speed of a CD-ROM or DVD-ROM drive can be a bit tricky. For example, a 1X DVD-ROM drive is just about the same speed as an 8X CD-ROM drive. The table in Figure 6-4 will help you compare CD-ROM and DVD-ROM drive speeds.

FIGURE 6-4	Comparative data transfer rates for CD-ROM and DVD-ROM drives.	
Speed	**CD-ROM Drive**	**DVD-ROM Drive**
1X	150 KBps	1,250 KBps
2X	300 KBps	2,500 KBps
4X	600 KBps	5,000 KBps
6X	900 KBps	7,500 KBps
8X	1,200 KBps	10,000 KBps
16X	2,400 KBps	
20X	3,000 KBps	
40X	6,000 KBps	
48X	7,200 KBps	

The computer ad in Figure 6-1 described the CD-ROM drive as "40X variable," which indicates that the data transfer rate of the CD-ROM drive varies between a minimum transfer rate of 2,500 KBps (17X) and a maximum speed of 6,000 KBps (40X). Alternative terminology for 40X variable includes "17–40X" and "40X max."

CD-ROM and DVD-ROM drives are not the only optical storage options available. Drives that support writable formats, such as CD-R, CD-RW, DVD-ROM, and DVD+RW, are becoming popular for archiving data. Another popular use for writable optical drives is storing tracks from Web sites and music CDs. Many musicians have Web sites featuring files that contain sample tracks of their music. A hard disk cannot store many of these large music files, but a CD makes a perfect storage medium. And, yes, the CDs can be played on a DiscMan or car CD player.

As this textbook goes to press, the two most popular options for adding writable optical storage are (1) replacing a CD-ROM drive with a CD-RW drive and (2) adding a CD-RW drive to a system that also contains a DVD-ROM drive. Advances in writable DVD technology are likely to change these options in the future.

CHAPTER 6

Input Devices

> **Should I settle for a standard keyboard and mouse?**

Most desktop computers include a standard 104-key keyboard and a mouse. It is easy and inexpensive to upgrade these input devices after you have used your computer for a while (refer to Figure 6-5). You can read about upgrade options in your favorite computer magazine. Avid fans of computer games will probably want to add a joystick as soon as possible.

FIGURE 6-5

Cases of carpal tunnel syndrome, a stress-related wrist injury, are on the rise. Intensive keyboard and mouse use are the suspected culprits. Ergonomically designed keyboards, such as Microsoft's Natural Keyboard, may prevent computer-related injuries.

Although a mouse is the standard pointing device used with desktop computers, it can be inconvenient to carry and use while traveling with a notebook computer. Most notebook computers include an alternative pointing device. The three most popular options—track point, trackball, and touchpad—are explained in Figure 6-6.

FIGURE 6-6

Notebook pointing devices provide a portable alternative to a conventional mouse.

Track point

A **track point** is a small, eraser-like device embedded among the typing keys. To control the on-screen pointer, you push the track point up, left, right, or down. Buttons for clicking and double-clicking are located in front of the spacebar.

Trackball

A **trackball** is like an upside-down mouse. By rolling the ball with your fingers, you control the on-screen pointer. Buttons for clicking are often located above or to the side of the trackball.

Touchpad

A **touchpad** is a touch-sensitive device. By dragging your finger over the surface, you control the on-screen pointer. Two buttons equivalent to mouse buttons are located in front of the touchpad.

Sound Systems

What's wavetable synthesis, and do I need it? With the proliferation of multimedia applications, a sound system has become an essential piece of computing equipment. A basic computer sound system includes a sound card and speakers. The sound card circuitry for a notebook computer is often built into the motherboard and the speakers are built into the case. In a desktop computer, a sound card usually resides in an expansion slot, as shown in Figure 6-7, and the stand-alone speakers plug into it. In a computer ad, specifications for the sound card typically appear on a separate line from the specifications for the speakers.

InfoWeb
3

Sound
Systems

FIGURE 6-7

In a desktop computer, a sound card plugs into an expansion slot.

A sound card converts the digital data in a sound file into analog signals for instrumental, vocal, and spoken sounds. In addition, a sound card lets you make your own recordings by converting analog sounds into digitized sound files that you can store on disk. Computer ads typically specify the sound card manufacturer, model, and expansion slot type. For example, the computer advertised in Figure 6-1 comes equipped with a Turtle Beach (manufacturer) Montego (model) Sound Blaster-compatible PCI (slot type) sound card.

Sound cards are typically manufactured by companies other than those that manufacture computers. Popular sound card manufacturers include Turtle Beach, Diamond, and Creative Labs. New sound card models arrive regularly. If you are curious about the features of a sound card that you see in a computer ad, you can usually find reviews and product descriptions on the sound card manufacturer's Web site or in computer magazines. Most sound cards feature Sound Blaster compatibility and wavetable synthesis.

The Sound Blaster was one of the first sound cards designed for PCs. Because many games and business software packages were programmed to use Sound Blaster sound cards, it became a de facto standard. "Sound Blaster-compatible" simply means that a sound card adheres to this standard.

Wavetable synthesis creates music by playing digitized sound samples of actual instruments. These sound samples are stored in the card or are loaded into main RAM each time your computer boots. The size of the wavetable affects sound quality—the larger the wavetable, the more realistic the sound. Numbers such as 64, 128, and 512 in the sound card specification usually indicate the size of the wavetable.

In a desktop computer, the sound card typically plugs into a PCI slot or into an ISA slot. The newest sound cards tend to use the PCI slot.

A sound card outputs sound to speakers or headphones. As with any audio system, higher-quality speakers provide richer sound and enhanced volume. Speaker manufacturers, such as Altec Lansing, Koss, and Yamaha, are familiar names in the audio business. A good shopping tip is to use the speakers that are standard with a computer system before deciding to upgrade to a more expensive set.

CHAPTER 6

Computer Displays

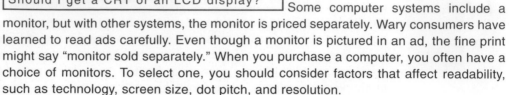

Should I get a CRT or an LCD display? Some computer systems include a monitor, but with other systems, the monitor is priced separately. Wary consumers have learned to read ads carefully. Even though a monitor is pictured in an ad, the fine print might say "monitor sold separately." When you purchase a computer, you often have a choice of monitors. To select one, you should consider factors that affect readability, such as technology, screen size, dot pitch, and resolution.

InfoWeb
4
Display
System

For many years, CRT monitors were the only game in town for desktop computer displays. **CRT** (cathode ray tube) technology uses a gun-like mechanism to spray the screen with dots of color. Because the technology is similar to a television set, CRT monitors offer an inexpensive and dependable computer display. As an alternative to CRT monitors, an **LCD** (liquid crystal display) produces an image by manipulating light within a layer of liquid crystal cells. Modern LCD technology is compact in size, lightweight, and provides an easy-to-read display. LCDs are standard equipment on notebook computers. Recently, stand-alone LCDs, referred to as "LCD monitors" or "flat panel displays," have also become available for desktop computers (Figure 6-8).

FIGURE 6-8

A flat panel LCD monitor provides good image quality and requires only a small amount of desk space.

The advantages of an LCD monitor include display clarity, low radiation emission, portability, and compactness. Unfortunately, an LCD monitor can be triple the price of an equivalent CRT monitor, so most people consider one to be a luxury item. In addition to their high cost, LCD monitors have a limited viewing angle. The brightness and color tones that you see depend on the angle of the screen, because of the way that light reflects off the LCDs. For this reason, graphical artists prefer CRT technology, which displays uniform color from any viewing angle.

FIGURE 6-9

As with a TV, a monitor's viewable image size is less than the screen size.

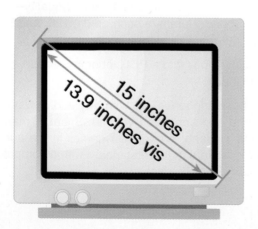

Screen size is the measurement in inches from one corner of the screen diagonally across to the opposite corner. Typical monitor screen sizes include 13", 15", 17", 19", and 21". The 13" and 15" monitors are considered to be "small," whereas the 17", 19", and 21" monitors are considered to be "large." Prices, as you might expect, increase with the size of the monitor.

On most monitors, the viewable image does not stretch to the edge of the screen. Instead, a black border makes the image smaller than the size specified. Many computer vendors now include a measurement for the **viewable image size (vis)**. A 15" monitor has approximately a 13.9" vis, as shown in Figure 6-9.

Dot pitch is a measure of image clarity; a smaller dot pitch means a crisper image. Technically, dot pitch is the distance in millimeters between like-colored pixels. A .28 or .26 dot pitch is typical for today's monitors.

The specifications for a monitor include its **maximum resolution**—the maximum number of pixels it can display. Standard resolutions include 640 x 480, 800 x 600, 1024 x 768, 1280 x 1024, and 1600 x 1200. Today's monitors typically have a maximum resolution of 1280 x 1024; many people continue to use 640 x 480 resolution, however, because it provides large, easy-to-read text. At higher resolutions the text appears smaller, but you can display a larger work area—for example, an entire page of a document. The two screen shots in Figure 6-10 help you compare a display at 640 x 480 resolution with a display at 1024 x 768 resolution.

FIGURE 6-10

The upper screen shows a simulation of a computer display set at 1024 x 768 resolution. Notice the size of characters and other screen objects.

The lower screen shows a 640 x 480 resolution. Characters and icons appear larger, but the screen-based desktop appears to be a smaller work area than it appeared with the higher resolution.

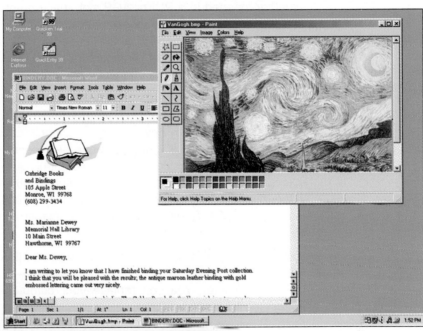

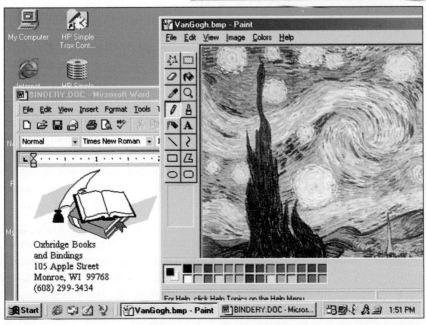

CHAPTER 6

Graphics Cards

Is a graphics card an "extra," too? Virtually all new computers include a graphics card, even if a monitor is not included. Computer ads provide graphics card specifications that include the manufacturer, model, slot type, accelerator technology, and video memory capacity.

Graphics cards are manufactured by many of the same companies that produce sound cards, including Diamond, ATI, and Creative Labs. These companies produce models with colorful names, such as Rage, XPert, Stealth, and Viper. Today's fastest graphics cards fit in the AGP expansion slot. Cards that fit in the PCI slot typically take a bit longer to update the screen.

Whether inserted in a PCI or AGP slot, many graphics cards contain special graphics accelerator technology to boost performance. An **accelerated graphics card** can greatly increase the speed at which images are displayed. 3-D accelerator features are especially beneficial for 3-D architectural drawing and for playing computer games.

Graphics cards carry their own memory circuitry, called **video memory**, which stores graphics images as they are processed and before they are displayed. The amount of memory on the card determines the maximum screen resolution and color depth that can be sent to a display device, such as a monitor. **Color depth** (also called "bit depth") refers to the number of colors that can be present on the screen at any one time. A 24-bit color depth, considered to be photographic quality, can display more than 16 million colors. To display a 24-bit, full-screen graphic at 640 x 480 resolution requires 1 MB of video memory. To display the same graphic at 1024 x 768 resolution requires slightly more than 2 MB. To display two of these images in rapid succession, your video card needs more than 4 MB of video memory.

Today's video cards typically contain between 8 MB and 32 MB of video memory. Cards with more memory capacity are more expensive—a cost that can raise the price of a computer system. You can replace your computer's graphics card with the latest, hottest model for about $250.

Notebook Displays

The ads for notebook computers seem to use different display terminology. What do these terms mean? Although notebook computers use the same LCD technology as stand-alone flat panel monitors, most ads use a different set of terminology to describe notebook displays.

Many older notebooks have passive matrix screens, sometimes referred to as "dual-scan." A **passive matrix screen** relies on timing to make sure the liquid crystal cells are illuminated. As a result, the process of updating the screen image does not always keep up with moving images, and the display can appear blurred. Newer notebooks feature an **active matrix screen**, sometimes referred to as "TFT" (thin film transistor), which updates rapidly and is essential for a crisp display of animations and video.

Notebook computer ads usually specify screen resolution as SVGA or XGA. **SVGA** (super video graphics array) is 800 x 600 resolution. **XGA** (extended graphics array) is 1024 x 768 resolution. The specified resolution might be the *only* resolution available, meaning that you would not be able to switch from, say, 800 x 600 to 640 x 480. Ads do not typically provide much information on switching resolutions, but you can usually ask a salesperson or e-mail a query to the manufacturer's customer service department.

Planning for Expansion

How can I make sure that I can expand my computer system? No matter how many bells and whistles your new computer system includes, you'll want to add to it in the future. Before you purchase a computer, make sure that it provides plenty of expansion options.

A desktop computer's system unit case provides openings, called "bays," for mounting storage devices. An **external bay** provides an opening for installing a device that you need to access from the outside of the case, such as a floppy disk drive, Zip drive, removable hard disk drive, or tape drive. When an external bay does not contain a device, it is covered with a rectangular plate. An **internal bay** provides a mounting bracket for devices that do not need to be accessible from outside the system unit case. A hard disk drive typically uses an internal bay because it doesn't require you to insert and remove disks.

A system unit with many bays provides greater expansion capability. The computer ad in Figure 6-1 on page 254 specified a tower case with seven bays. The picture in the ad shows five external bays, so two of the bays must be internal. The hard disk drive occupies one internal bay, and the floppy disk drive and CD-ROM drive each occupy one external bay. That leaves three external bays and one internal bay for expansion— probably enough for most home and business uses.

To add peripheral devices such as a printer, scanner, or graphics tablet, your computer needs an open port or expansion slot. In Chapter 5, you learned that you can plug an expansion card for a peripheral device into an AGP, PCI, or ISA expansion slot on the motherboard. When you purchase a new computer, some slots will already be connected to peripheral devices. Be sure to ask how many slots are free for later expansion.

Notebook computers typically do not have space inside the case for expansion cards. A **PCMCIA slot** (Personal Computer Memory Card International Association) is a special type of expansion slot developed for notebook computers. A **PCMCIA card**, also called a "PC card," is a credit-card-sized circuit board that contains circuitry and devices, such as a modem, memory expansion card, network interface card, or hard disk drive. You can plug in and remove a PCMCIA card without turning the computer off. In this way you can switch from one PCMCIA device to another without disrupting your work.

FIGURE 6-11

To add a modem, network interface card, or hard disk to a notebook computer, plug in a PCMCIA card.

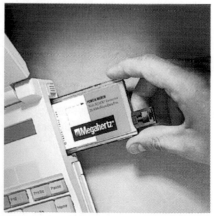

PCMCIA

PCMCIA slots are classified according to their size. Type I slots accept only the thinnest PCMCIA cards, such as memory expansion cards. Type II slots accept most of the popular PCMCIA cards—those that contain modems, sound cards, and network cards. Type III slots accept the thickest PCMCIA cards, which contain devices such as hard disk drives. Many notebooks provide a multipurpose PCMCIA slot that will accept two Type I cards, two Type II cards, or one Type III card.

Both notebook and desktop computers feature a variety of built-in ports for connecting peripheral devices. A desktop computer typically includes

- 1 keyboard port

- 1 mouse port

- 2 USB ports for devices such as scanners

- 1 parallel port for a printer, scanner, or external hard disk drive

- 2 serial ports, one of which might be used for an external modem

As described earlier in the chapter, a graphics port for connecting a monitor is supplied on the graphics card. The sound card supplies ports for speakers and a microphone, plus a MIDI/joystick port that can be used to connect a MIDI keyboard or a joystick.

A notebook computer often features more built-in ports than a desktop computer, because user-installable expansion options are limited. A notebook computer typically includes

- 1 keyboard port for connecting an external keyboard

- 1 mouse port for connecting an external pointing device, such as a mouse

- 1 graphics port for connecting an external monitor

- 1 parallel port for a printer or other parallel device (scanner, external hard drive)

- 1 USB port for a scanner or other USB device

- 1 serial port, typically not used

- 1 infrared port for printers or PDAs that support wireless data transfer

- 1 audio-out port for external speakers or headphones

- 1 audio-in port for an external microphone

Many notebook computers also provide a port for a device called a **port replicator**, which allows you to conveniently connect multiple external devices. For example, you could plug an external monitor, mouse, and printer into the ports of a port replicator, then plug the port replicator into your notebook computer. When you want to transport your notebook without the external devices, you simply disconnect the one connector for the port replicator. Without the port replicator, you would have to disconnect each of the devices individually.

Notebook Power Sources

How long will a notebook computer run on batteries? Most notebook computers operate on power from either rechargeable batteries or a wall outlet. The length of time that a notebook computer can work on battery power depends on many factors. Fast processors, active matrix LCDs, and additional peripheral devices demand significant power from notebook computer batteries. Notebook manufacturers have attempted to reduce power consumption by building power-saving features into their computers. These features automatically switch off the hard disk drive, LCD display, or even the processor if you do not interact with the computer within a short period of time. These devices are reactivated when you press a key or move the mouse.

Most of today's notebook computers use lithium ion batteries, which typically provide two to four hours of operating time. Consumers need to be aware that many ads indicate maximum operating times. An ad that proclaims "Runs up to four hours!" might mean that the battery can supply four hours of operating time with no additional devices attached and with minimal use of the hard disk drive. Under typical working conditions, this computer with fully charged batteries may run for significantly less than four hours.

The easiest way to extend the operating time of your notebook computer is to purchase extra batteries. When the first battery wears down, you can swap it with a second battery and get back to work. Some notebook computers allow you to swap batteries while the computer is on, a process called a **hot swap**.

Most notebook computers require an external AC adapter to plug into a wall outlet. Such an adapter—about the size and weight of a small brick—can add significantly to the traveling weight of the notebook. Some notebook computers have eliminated the external adapter and require only a power cable to plug into a wall outlet. It is a good idea to use AC power whenever possible, such as when you use your notebook at home. Using AC power saves your batteries so that you have battery power when AC power is not available.

CHAPTER 6

QUICKCHECK A

1 A(n) [＿＿＿＿＿] test can provide a consumer with information on processor or computer performance.

2 If you want to copy a file from one floppy disk to another, you need a computer with two floppy disk drives. True or false? [＿＿＿＿]

3 Ultra ATA refers to a type of "souped-up" memory that is required for computers with 500 MHz processors. True or false? [＿＿＿＿]

4 A 6X CD-ROM drive is the same speed as a 6X DVD-ROM drive. True or false? [＿＿＿]

5 Most sound cards feature [＿＿＿＿＿] compatibility.

6 Computer ads use terms such as TFT and SVGA to describe the display device on [＿＿＿＿＿] computers.

7 A(n) [＿＿＿＿＿] slot is important for adding peripheral devices to a notebook computer.

 Check Answers

CONSUMER'S GUIDE TO PRINTERS

Occasionally, a computer vendor offers a hardware bundle that includes a computer, printer, and software. More often, however, printers are sold separately so that consumers have a choice of quality, features, and price. Printer options include ink jet printers, laser printers, dot matrix printers, and multifunction printers. When you purchase a printer, consider the following factors:

■ **Resolution.** The quality or sharpness of printed images and text depends on the printer's resolution—the density of the gridwork of dots that create an image. Printer resolution is measured by the number of dots it can print per linear inch, abbreviated as **dpi**. At normal reading distance, a resolution of about 900 dots per inch appears solid to the human eye, but a close examination of color sections will reveal a dot pattern. Although 900 dpi might be considered sufficient for magazines, expensive coffee-table books are typically produced on printers with 2,400 dpi or higher. Microcomputer printer resolutions vary from 60 dpi to 1,500 dpi.

■ **Color capability.** Some printers are capable of printing in color, whereas other printers are limited to black, white, and shades of gray. If you have a printer that does not print color, the colorful graphics and Web pages that you see on your computer screen will be printed as shades of gray. Surprisingly, some of the least expensive microcomputer printers have color capability. Most computer users like their Web pages and photos printed in color, so they overwhelmingly choose color printers.

■ **Print speed.** Printer speeds are measured either by pages per minute (ppm) or characters per second (cps). Color printouts typically take longer than black-and-white printouts. Documents that contain mostly text tend to print more rapidly than graphics. Ten pages per minute is a typical speed for a microcomputer printer.

■ **Printer cost.** Microcomputer printers range in price from $100 to $5,000. Typically, more expensive printers provide higher resolution, faster printing speeds, and a high-capacity duty cycle. A **duty cycle** is an indication of the number of pages a printer can be expected to print per month without undue wear and tear. Low-cost printers are typically designed for personal use and have a duty cycle of about 3,000 pages per month—about 100 pages a day. More expensive printers, designed for business and commercial use, have a duty cycle that exceeds 10,000 pages per month.

■ **Per-copy cost.** Printing requires ongoing costs for printer supplies, such as ribbons, ink cartridges, and toner. These costs vary with different types, brands, and models of printers. In comparative reviews, these costs are often expressed as "per-copy costs"—the cost of printing a page with an average amount of text, graphics, and color. As a consumer, you can easily check the price of printer supplies before you make a final printer selection.

■ **Warranty.** Printers tend to be fairly reliable devices, but problems with circuit boards, paper-handling mechanisms, and print heads occasionally crop up. Printer warranties typically cover mechanical and electronic problems, but require that you send the printer to a service center for repair. Many people regard a low-cost printer as a consumable item, because the cost of sending it in for repair and the nuisance of being without a printer is more costly than simply buying a new one.

Ink Jet Printers

What's the most popular type of printer? An **ink jet printer** has a nozzle-like print head that sprays ink onto paper to form characters and graphics. Today's most popular printer technology, ink jet printers produce low-cost color or black-and-white printouts. The print head in a color ink jet printer consists of a series of nozzles, each with its own ink cartridge. Most ink jet printers use CMYK color, which requires only cyan (blue), magenta (pink), yellow, and black inks to create a printout that appears to have thousands of colors. Alternatively, some printers use six ink colors to print midtone shades that create slightly more realistic photographic images.

InfoWeb 7

Printers

Operating costs for an ink jet printer are reasonable. You'll need to periodically replace the black ink cartridge and a second cartridge that carries the colored inks. Each replacement ink cartridge costs between $25 and $35. Under realistic use, the cost for color printing will be between 5 and 15 cents per page. A potential hidden cost of operating an ink jet printer is special paper. Although you can satisfactorily print documents with small graphics and line art on the same type of inexpensive paper that you might use in a photocopier, high-quality photo printouts require special paper that can cost between $0.08 and $1.50 per sheet. Typically, this special paper has a super-smooth finish that prevents the ink from bleeding and creating dull colors.

Today's ink jet printers have excellent resolution; depending on the model, it can range from 600 dpi to 1,440 dpi. If you want better quality when printing photographic images, you need a printer with a high resolution. Some ink jet printers can produce ultra-high resolution by making multiple passes over the paper. Although it might seem logical that this technique would slow down the printing process, multiple-pass ink jet printers produce a respectable five pages per minute. You can purchase a good-quality ink jet printer for about $300. You can expect to pay more for a printer with a higher resolution. Manufacturers include Hewlett-Packard, Epson, Lexmark, Okidata, Canon, and NEC.

CHAPTER 6

FIGURE 6-12

An ink jet printer produces characters and graphics by spraying ink onto paper. The print head is a matrix of fine spray nozzles. Patterns are formed by activating selected nozzles. An ink jet printer typically forms a character in a 20 x 20 matrix, producing a high-quality printout.

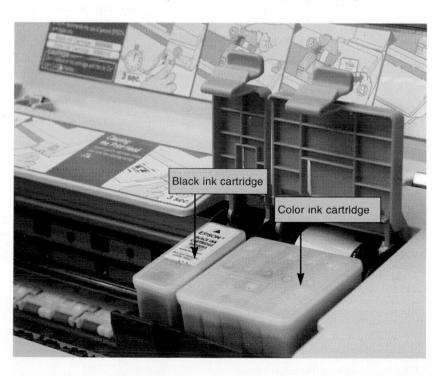

Black ink cartridge

Color ink cartridge

Laser Printers

Is a laser printer better than an ink jet? A **laser printer** uses the same technology as a photocopier to paint dots of light on a light-sensitive drum. Electrostatically charged ink is applied to the drum, then transferred to paper. An expensive laser printer can produce better quality than an ink jet printer, but it cannot match an ink jet's ability to print in color for less than $500.

You can buy laser printers at two price points. Inexpensive desktop or personal models, priced for less than $400, are quite suitable for black-and-white printing of a limited number of copies. More expensive professional laser printers with color or extended-run capacity begin at $1,000 and quickly exceed the $3,000 mark.

As with other printer technologies, print speed and resolution will be key factors in your purchase decision. Personal laser printers produce six to eight pages per minute at a resolution of 600 dpi. Professional models pump out 15 to 25 pages per minute at 1,200 dpi. A personal laser printer has a duty cycle of about 3,000 ppm—that means roughly 100 pages per day. You wouldn't want to use it to produce 5,000 campaign brochures for next Monday, but you would find it quite suitable for printing 10 copies of a five-page outline for a meeting tomorrow.

Some people are surprised to discover that laser printers are less expensive to operate than ink jet printers. On average, you can expect to pay about 2 cents per page for black-and-white laser printing. This per-page cost includes periodically replacing the toner cartridge and drum. A toner cartridge and a drum unit each cost about $70, though prices vary by manufacturer and model.

Laser printers accept print commands from a PC, but use their own printer language to construct a page before printing it. **Printer Control Language** (PCL) is the most widely used printer language, but some printers also use the **PostScript** language, which is preferred by many publishing professionals. Printer languages require memory, and most laser printers have between 2 MB and 8 MB. A large memory capacity is required to print color images and graphics-intensive documents. A laser printer comes equipped with enough memory for typical print jobs. If you find that you need more memory, check the printer documentation for information.

FIGURE 6-13

Laser printers use the same technology as duplicating machines. A laser charges a pattern of particles on a drum, which picks up a powdery black substance called toner. The toner is transferred onto paper that rolls past the drum. In the past, the high price of laser printers limited their use to businesses and large organizations. Laser printer prices have decreased, however, making these devices affordable for individuals.

Color laser printers work by reprinting each page for each primary color. For each reprint, the paper must be precisely positioned so that each color is printed in exactly the right spot. This requirement dramatically increases the complexity of the print mechanism and the amount of time required to print each page.

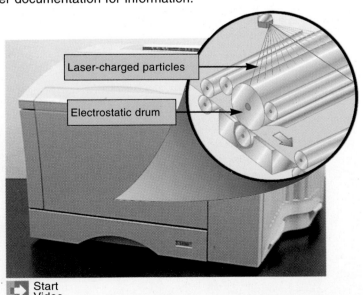

Laser-charged particles

Electrostatic drum

▶ Start
Video

Dot Matrix Printers

Why would anyone want a dot matrix printer? When PCs first began to appear in the late 1970s, dot matrix printers were the technology of choice and they are still available today. A **dot matrix printer**, which is sometimes referred to as an "impact printer," produces characters and graphics by using a grid of fine wires. As the print head noisily clatters across the paper, the wires strike the ribbon and paper in a pattern prescribed by your PC. Dot matrix printers can print text and graphics—some even print in color using a multicolored ribbon.

With a resolution of 140 dpi, a dot matrix printer produces low-quality output with clearly discernible dots forming letters and graphics. Dot matrix speed is typically measured in characters per second (cps). A fast dot matrix device can print at speeds up to 455 cps—about five pages per minute.

Who would want a slow, noisy printer that produces low-quality output? Today, dot matrix printers, like the one in Figure 6-14, are used primarily for "back-office" applications that demand low operating cost and dependability, but not high print quality. Unlike laser and ink jet technologies, a dot matrix printer actually strikes the paper and, therefore, can print multipart carbon forms. A $4 ribbon can print more than 3 million characters before it needs to be replaced.

FIGURE 6-14

The print head in a dot matrix printer contains a row of fine wires that strike the ribbon and paper to produce a matrix of dots that form characters or graphical images.

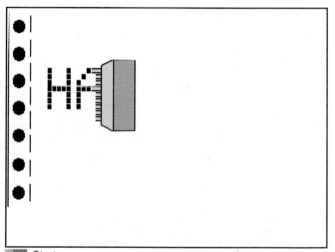

➡ Start Animation

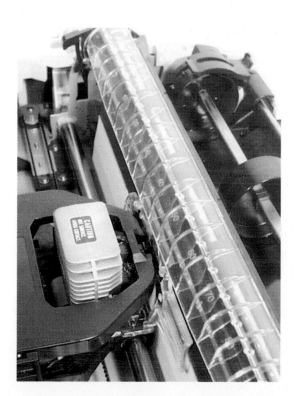

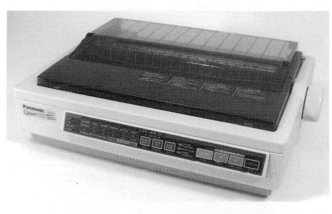

CHAPTER 6

Multifunction Printers

Can I use a computer printer as a copier? A home office can get cluttered with equipment, such as a fax machine, telephone, answering machine, copier, computer, printer, and scanner. Why not combine these devices into one? That is precisely the solution offered by manufacturers, such as Brother, Hewlett-Packard, and Okidata. A **multifunction printer** uses either laser or ink jet technology to take the place of a variety of printing and communication devices, such as the following:

Computer printer. A multifunction printer connects to your PC just like a standard printer to print documents and graphics. Multifunction ink jet printers typically have color capability, whereas multifunction laser printers do not.

Fax machine. A multifunction printer can connect to your phone line to send and accept faxes. To send a fax, you feed a document into an input slot. A multifunction printer can also receive and print faxes on plain paper.

FIGURE 6-15

At about $500, a multifunction printer is relatively inexpensive, considering the variety of functions it can offer. Before you purchase one, however, consider whether limitations such as single-sheet copying and black-and-white scanning fit your needs.

Answering machine. When a multifunction printer is attached to a phone line, it might just as well act as an answering machine. Many, but not all, multifunction printers have answering machine capabilities.

Telephone. Many multifunction printers include a handset and a dialing keypad to take the place of a standard telephone.

Copier. You can use a multifunction printer to copy a single sheet by feeding it through the input slot. On most multifunction printers, you will be limited to copying single sheets because the input slot is not designed for books and other thick materials. Your printer might be able to create only black-and-white copies, even if it can print from your computer in color.

Scanner. Most multifunction printers can scan pictures and documents that you feed through the input slot. If your multifunction printer produces only black-and-white copies, it will probably produce only black-and-white scans because it uses the same mechanism for both scanning and copying.

QUICKCHECK B

1 The most popular type of microcomputer printer uses [   ] technology.

2 The [   ] cycle of a business or commercial printer is more than that for a personal printer.

3 For inexpensive color printing, a(n) [   ] printer is the best choice.

4 For printing multipart carbon forms, a(n) [   ] printer is the best choice.

5 A(n) [   ] is designed to take the place of several devices such as a copier, computer printer, fax machine, and scanner.

 Check Answers

SECTION C — THE COMPUTER INDUSTRY

The **computer industry** consists of corporations and individuals that supply goods and services to people and organizations that use computers. It is in a continual state of change as new products appear and old products are discontinued; as corporations form, merge, and die; as corporate leadership shifts; as consumers' buying habits evolve; and as prices steadily continue to decrease. Before you venture out to buy computers, peripheral devices, or software, you should arm yourself with some basic knowledge about the computer industry, such as the effect of product life cycles on prices, the tiered structure of computer vendors, the four market channels from which you can purchase hardware and software, and the types of publications offered by the computer press.

Hardware Product Life Cycle

Does the computer industry introduce new models annually? Automobile manufacturers introduce new models every year, which incorporate new features and give customers an incentive to buy. Likewise, computer manufacturers introduce new models—for the same reasons as their counterparts in the automotive industry. The computer industry is not on an annual cycle, however, so the computer marketplace seems rather chaotic because new product announcements, ship dates, and availability dates all occur at irregular intervals. In the computer industry, the life cycle of a new computer model typically includes five phases: product development, product announcement, introduction, maintenance, and retirement.

Product development often takes place "under wraps." Developers use fanciful code names, such as Merced and Camelot, to refer to their products. Inevitably, news of these products "leaks" out and causes much speculation among industry analysts.

Sometime during the development process, a company makes a product announcement to declare its intention to introduce a new product. Products are often announced at trade shows and press conferences. As a consumer, you should be wary of making decisions based on product announcements. A product announcement can precede the actual launch of the product by several years. Some products, referred to as **vaporware**, are announced but never produced.

When a hardware product is first introduced, initial supplies of the product generally remain low while manufacturing capacity increases to meet demand. Consumers who want a scarce product must pay a relatively high price. As supply and demand for the product reach an equilibrium, the price of the product decreases slightly. Usually the price decrease is due to discounting by dealers rather than a change to the manufacturer's list price. In Figure 6-16, you can follow the price of a Compaq Presario 1650 from July 20, 1998, through August 16, 1999.

FIGURE 6-16

The price of a Compaq Presario 1650 dropped significantly between July, 1998 and August, 1999. The red line indicates the high price, the blue line the average price, and the green line the low price. Graph courtesy of PriceSCAN.

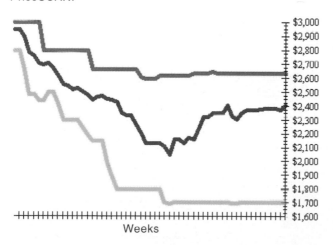

$3,000	
$2,900	
$2,800	
$2,700	
$2,600	
$2,500	
$2,400	
$2,300	
$2,200	
$2,100	
$2,000	
$1,900	
$1,800	
$1,700	
$1,600	

Weeks

When a new product becomes available, it is usually added to the vendor's product line. The prices of products with older technology, such as Pentium II processors, are reduced to keep them attractive to buyers. Gradually, the oldest products are discontinued as demand for them declines. As you can see from the ad in Figure 6-17, the less expensive products tend to have slower processors, less RAM, and lower-capacity hard disk drives. If your budget is not severely limited, a computer in the middle of a vendor's product line usually gives you the most computing power per dollar.

FIGURE 6-17

A microcomputer product line typically provides a good variety of choices at several price points.

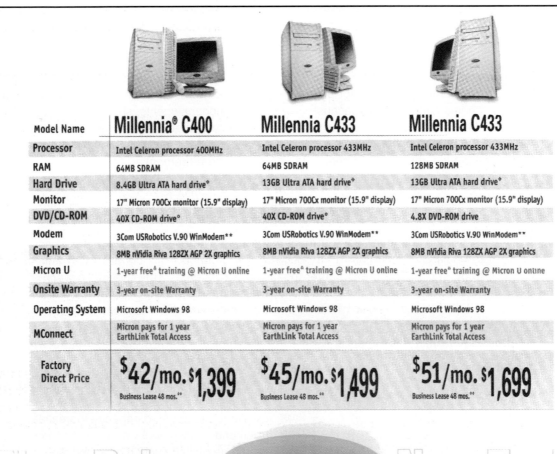

Model Name	Millennia® C400	Millennia C433	Millennia C433
Processor	Intel Celeron processor 400MHz	Intel Celeron processor 433MHz	Intel Celeron processor 433MHz
RAM	64MB SDRAM	64MB SDRAM	128MB SDRAM
Hard Drive	8.4GB Ultra ATA hard drive◊	13GB Ultra ATA hard drive◊	13GB Ultra ATA hard drive◊
Monitor	17" Micron 700Cx monitor (15.9" display)	17" Micron 700Cx monitor (15.9" display)	17" Micron 700Cx monitor (15.9" display)
DVD/CD-ROM	40X CD-ROM drive°	40X CD-ROM drive°	4.8X DVD-ROM drive
Modem	3Com USRobotics V.90 WinModem**	3Com USRobotics V.90 WinModem**	3Com USRobotics V.90 WinModem**
Graphics	8MB nVidia Riva 128ZX AGP 2X graphics	8MB nVidia Riva 128ZX AGP 2X graphics	8MB nVidia Riva 128ZX AGP 2X graphics
Micron U	1-year free△ training @ Micron U online	1-year free△ training @ Micron U online	1-year free° training @ Micron U online
Onsite Warranty	3-year on-site Warranty	3-year on-site Warranty	3-year on-site Warranty
Operating System	Microsoft Windows 98	Microsoft Windows 98	Microsoft Windows 98
MConnect	Micron pays for 1 year EarthLink Total Access	Micron pays for 1 year EarthLink Total Access	Micron pays for 1 year EarthLink Total Access
Factory Direct Price	$42/mo. $1,399 Business Lease 48 mos.**	$45/mo. $1,499 Business Lease 48 mos.**	$51/mo. $1,699 Business Lease 48 mos.**

New Rules. MICRON ELECTRONICS New Tools.

Software Product Life Cycle

What's the difference between a version and a revision? A company that produces computer software is referred to as a **software publisher**. Software, like hardware, begins with an idea that is then shaped by a design team and marketing experts. Most software products undergo extensive testing before they are released. The first phase of testing, called an **alpha test**, is carried out by the software publisher's in-house testing team. Errors and "bugs" found during the alpha test phase are fixed, then the software enters a second testing phase called a **beta test**. Typically, a beta test is conducted by a team of off-site testers, such as a professional testing company. Sometimes a software publisher releases a "beta version" of the software to selected individuals and companies in the general public in order to expose the software to the widest possible variety of computers and operating environments. Although it can be exciting to test a yet-to-be-released software package, beta versions are typically "buggy" and can cause unexpected glitches in your computer. Beta testing requires a high tolerance for frustration.

FIGURE 6-18

Microsoft asked for individuals and companies to participate in beta testing for Office 2000, but beta testers had to pay for the beta software.

OFFICE 2000 PREVIEW PROGRAM
As a Microsoft Preferred Customer, you're always among the first to hear the latest information about Microsoft Office. Now you can be among the first to experience Office 2000 - by taking advantage of this limited-time offer to participate in the Office 2000 Consumer Preview Program.

Sign up today for the Office 2000 Consumer Preview Program for just $19.95US* The Consumer Preview Program delivers everything you need to experience all the new features and improvements of Office 2000. You get:

* Office 2000 Premium beta version - including new versions of Word, Microsoft Excel, Outlook(r) messaging and collaboration client, PowerPoint(r) presentation graphics program, Publisher and Microsoft Access. Plus, two products making their Office debut: PhotoDraw 2000(tm), the all-in-one illustration and photo-editing program for creating professional-looking graphics for your marketing materials, and FrontPage (r)2000, the latest version of Microsoft's popular web site creation and management tool.

CHAPTER 6

A newly published software package can be an entirely new product, a new **version** (also called a "release") with significant enhancements, or a **revision** designed to add minor enhancements and eliminate bugs found in the current version. Before you buy software, you should be familiar with the difference between versions and revisions.

The original *version* of a software product is typically called version 1.0. A major improvement to a software product would be indicated by a new version number, such as 2.0. The numbers in the title of a software product do not always indicate a version. Obviously, Windows 2000 is not the 2000th version of the Windows operating system!

Software publishers release a *revision* to fix bugs or make small changes to product features. The revision number is separated from the version number with a period. The first revision of a product will be 1.1. If you discover a software bug that affects usability, check with the software vendor to see if a revision of the product exists that includes a "bug fix." The publisher will often supply a revision for free or nominal shipping costs. You can usually find the revision and version numbers in a Windows program by clicking Help, then selecting About.

"No one pays list price for software!" say industry analysts. A variety of discounts and special offers make it worthwhile to shop around. You can purchase a $495 software package for less than $100 if you're a smart shopper.

When a new software product first becomes available, the publisher often offers a special introductory price that's designed to entice customers. Several software products that now carry a list price of $495 were introduced at a special price of $99. Even after the introductory price expires, most vendors offer sizable discounts. The average discounted price is referred to as the **street price**. Expect software with a list price of $495 to be offered for a street price of about $299.

If you own an earlier version of a software package, you are probably eligible for the **version upgrade price**. By supplying the vendor with proof that you own the earlier version, you can get the new version at a discount. For example, if your word processing software is version 7 and you want to upgrade to version 8, you might be able to upgrade for $75 instead of paying for an entirely new package.

A **competitive upgrade** is a special price offered to consumers who switch from one company's software product to the new version of a competitor's product. For example, suppose you've been using ClarisDraw, but you decide to switch to GRAFIX 7, published by a different company. The company that produces GRAFIX 7 might offer a competitive upgrade to lure customers away from its competitor, ClarisDraw. You might pay only $149 for this competitive upgrade, instead of paying the $399 street price, as shown in Figure 6-19.

FIGURE 6-19

Competitive software upgrades provide an incentive for switching from a competitor's product.

Unlike computer hardware products, older versions of software do not remain in the vendor's product line. Soon after a new version of a software product is released, the software publisher usually stops selling earlier versions. When a publisher offers a new version of the software that you are using, it is a good idea to upgrade; but you can wait for several months until the initial rush for technical support on the new product decreases. If you don't upgrade, you might find that the software publisher offers minimal technical support for older versions of the program. Also, if you let several versions go by without upgrading, you might lose your eligibility for special upgrade pricing.

Market Tiers

What accounts for price differences for computers with the same specifications from different vendors? Since 1981, hundreds of companies have produced personal computers. Industry analysts often classify these companies into three tiers, or categories. Although the analysts do not necessarily agree on which companies belong in each tier, the concept of tiers helps to explain price differences.

The top tier consists of large companies that have been in the computer business for many years and have an identifiable share of total computer sales—companies such as IBM, Apple, Compaq, Dell, and Hewlett-Packard. The second tier includes newer companies with high sales volume but with somewhat less financial resources than companies in the first tier. Most analysts place companies such as Gateway and Packard Bell in the second tier. The third tier consists of smaller startup companies that sell primarily through mail order.

Computer prices vary by tier. Computers from the top-tier vendors generally are more expensive than computers offered by second-tier or third-tier vendors. For example, a computer with specifications similar to the MicroPlus computer featured in the ad at the beginning of this chapter might cost $1,999 from a first-tier vendor, $1,495 from a second-tier vendor, and $1,295 from a third-tier vendor.

What accounts for such price differences? First-tier companies often have higher overhead costs, management is often paid higher salaries, and substantial financial resources are devoted to research and development. These companies are responsible for many of the innovations that have made computers faster, more powerful, and more convenient. Also, many consumers believe that computers sold by first-tier companies offer better quality and are a safe purchasing decision. They believe there is less risk that computers from first-tier companies will become obsolete quickly or that the vendor will go out of business.

Computers from second-tier companies are generally less expensive than those from first tier firms, although the quality can be just as good. Most PCs are constructed from off-the-shelf circuit boards, cables, cases, and chips. Consequently, the components in the computers sold by second-tier companies are often the same as those in computers sold by first tier firms. Second-tier companies often maintain low prices by minimizing operating costs. These companies have limited research and development budgets. Also, they try to maintain a relatively small work force by contracting with other companies to provide repair and warranty work.

Computers from third-tier companies often appear to be much less expensive than those in other tiers. Sometimes this difference reflects the low overhead costs of a small company, but other times it reflects poor-quality components. A consumer who is knowledgeable about the market and has technical expertise can often get a bargain on a good-quality computer from a third-tier company. But some consumers think it's risky to purchase computers from third-tier companies. Third-tier companies are smaller and perhaps more likely to go out of business, leaving their customers without technical support.

Marketing Channels

Is it safe to buy a computer by mail? Computer hardware and software are sold through marketing outlets, or "channels." These channels include computer retail stores, mail-order/Internet outlets, value-added resellers, and manufacturer direct.

A **computer retail store** purchases computer products from a variety of manufacturers and then sells those products to consumers. Computer retail stores are either small local shops or nationwide chains that specialize in the sale of microcomputer software and hardware. The employees at computer retail stores are often knowledgeable about a variety of computer products and can help you select a hardware or software product to fit your needs. Many computer retail stores also offer classes and training sessions, answer questions, provide technical support, and repair hardware products. A computer retail store is often the best shopping option for buyers who are likely to need assistance after their purchase, such as beginning computer users or those with complex computer systems such as networks. Such stores can be a fairly expensive channel for hardware and software, however. Their prices reflect the cost of purchasing merchandise from a distributor, maintaining a retail storefront, and hiring a technically qualified staff.

FIGURE 6-20

Computer retail stores range from small, locally owned businesses to gigantic superstores, such as CompUSA.

A **mail-order supplier** takes orders by telephone or from an Internet site, then ships the product directly to consumers. Mail-order suppliers generally offer low prices but might provide limited service and support. A mail-order supplier is often the best source of products for buyers who are unlikely to need support or who can troubleshoot problems with the help of a technical support person on the telephone. Experienced computer users who can install components, set up their software, and do their own troubleshooting are often happy with mail-order suppliers. Inexperienced computer users might not be satisfied with the support and assistance they receive from these suppliers.

A **value-added reseller** (VAR) combines commercially available products with specialty hardware or software to create a computer system designed to meet the needs of a specific industry. Although VARs charge for their expertise, they are often the only source for specialized computer systems. For example, if you own a video rental store and want to automate the rental process, the best type of vendor might be a VAR that offers a complete hardware and software package that is tailored to the video rental business. Otherwise, you would have to piece together the computer, scanner, printer, and software components yourself. VARs are often the most expensive channel for hardware and software, but their expertise can be crucial to ensure that the hardware and software work correctly in a specific environment.

Manufacturer direct refers to hardware manufacturers that sell their products directly to consumers using a sales force or mail order. The sales force usually targets large corporate or educational customers where large-volume sales can cover costs and commissions. Manufacturers also use mail order to sell and distribute products directly to individual consumers. Products sold directly by manufacturers are usually less expensive than the same products sold by retailers. In most cases, manufacturers do not offer the same level of support and assistance as a local retailer. In an effort to improve customer support, some manufacturers have established customer support lines and provide repair services at the customer's home or place of business.

Smart shoppers understand the advantages and disadvantages of each computer marketing channel, and apply this knowledge when they shop. Figure 6-21 summarizes the computer industry's marketing channels.

FIGURE 6-21

The computer industry provides a variety of marketing channels.

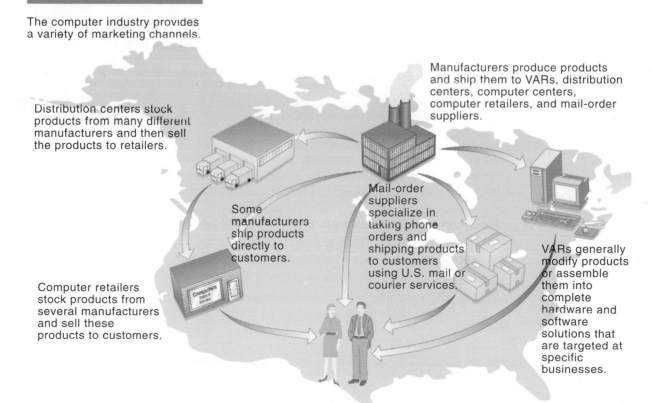

Distribution centers stock products from many different manufacturers and then sell the products to retailers.

Manufacturers produce products and ship them to VARs, distribution centers, computer centers, computer retailers, and mail-order suppliers.

Some manufacturers ship products directly to customers.

Mail-order suppliers specialize in taking phone orders and shipping products to customers using U.S. mail or courier services.

Computer retailers stock products from several manufacturers and sell these products to customers.

VARs generally modify products or assemble them into complete hardware and software solutions that are targeted at specific businesses.

CHAPTER 6

The Computer Press

Where can I get reliable information about computers to help me make informed purchases? Computer publications provide information on computers, computing, and the computer industry. The type of computer publication you need depends on the kind of information you want.

Publications

Computer magazines. These publications contain articles and advertisements for the latest computer products and generally target users of both personal and business computers. Articles focus on product evaluations, product comparisons, and practical tips for installing hardware and using software. These magazines are full of product advertisements, which are useful if you want to keep informed about the latest products available for your computer. You can find computer magazines such as those shown in Figure 6-22 on virtually any newsstand and at the library. Many computer magazine publishers also maintain Web sites containing articles, product reviews, and links to shopping and manufacturers' sites.

FIGURE 6-22

Just about every newsstand includes a section of computer publications.

Computer industry trade journals. These publications have a different focus than computer magazines because they target computer professionals. Computer trade journals, such as *InfoWorld* and *Computer Reseller News*, focus on company profiles, product announcements, and sales techniques. Often, corporate decision makers are provided with free subscriptions to trade journals because advertisers want them to be aware of their products. Trade journals are not always available on newsstands, and subscriptions are not always available to the general public.

Computing journals. These publications offer an academic perspective on computers and computing issues. Such journals focus on research in computing, with articles on such topics as the most efficient sorting technique to use in a database management system, the implications of copyright law for educational institutions, or the prevalence of spreadsheet use by executives in *Fortune* 500 companies. Academic journals rarely advertise hardware and software products because it might appear that advertisers could influence the content of articles.

An article in a computing journal is usually "refereed," which means that it is evaluated by a committee of experts who determine if the article is original and based on sound research techniques. The best place to find computing journals is a university library. Some of the most respected journals in the computing field include *Communications of the ACM* (Association for Computing Machinery), *Communications of the IEEE* (Institute of Electrical and Electronics Engineers), *SIAM* (Society of Industrial and Applied Mathematics), *Journal on Computing*, and *Journal of Information Science*.

Web
Resources

Internet sites. The Internet provides an excellent source of information about the computer industry and computer products. Several computer magazines and trade journals maintain Internet sites with articles from back issues. Current issues are also available from some sites. Many computer companies have Internet sites where consumers can access up-to-date information about products and services. Here you can usually find product specifications, product announcements, sales literature, technical support forums, and pricing information.

Computer
TV

Television shows. A new crop of television shows about computers provide hardware and software reviews, tips, and computer industry news for new and experienced users. The CMPTV network produces shows such as *Net Cafe*, *Computer Chronicles* (Figure 6-23), *@Home*, and *User Group*. CNET produces *The Web*, *The New Edge*, and *CNET Central*. Jones Cable Network and Mind Extension University offer *Computer Kids*, *Home Computing*, and *New Media News*. CNN Financial Network includes a high-tech overview called *Digital Jam*, also available in video format on the Internet. ZDTV, operated by Ziff-Davis, has teamed up with Microsoft to broadcast technology news on MSNBC. Most of these networks are carried on cable TV. Check your cable listings for airtimes.

CHAPTER 6

FIGURE 6-23

For almost 20 years, viewers have tuned into *Computer Chronicles* on the Public Broadcasting System. Hosted by Steward Chiefet, the show features demonstrations of new hardware and software products.

 Start
Video

Industry analysts. Journalists and columnists monitor computer industry trends, evaluate industry events, and make predictions about what the trends seem to indicate. Computer industry analysts range from professional financial analysts, who report on the computer industry for the *Wall Street Journal* and *Forbes* magazine, to the "rumor-central" analysts (Figure 6-24) who spark up the back pages of computer magazines and trade journals with the latest gossip about new computer products.

FIGURE 6-24

Robert X. Cringely is one of the best-known computer columnists. Look for his column, "Notes From the Field," on the back pages of *InfoWorld* magazine.

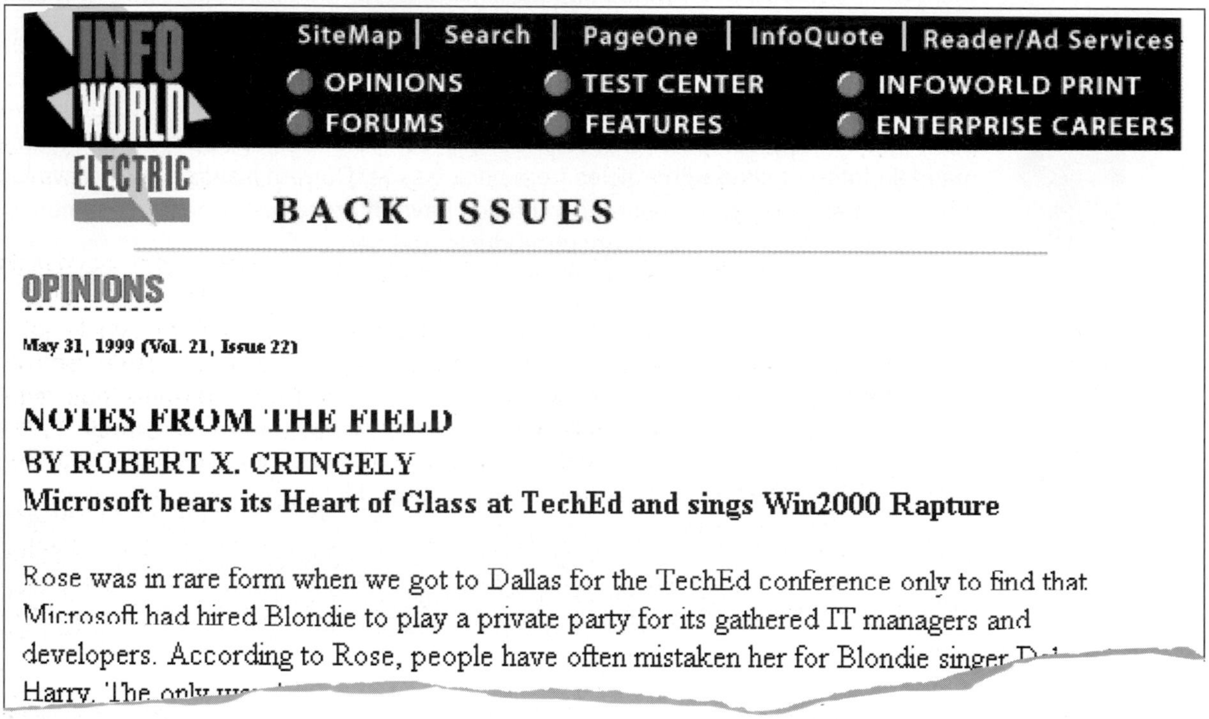

INFO WORLD ELECTRIC

SiteMap | Search | PageOne | InfoQuote | Reader/Ad Services

● OPINIONS   ● TEST CENTER   ● INFOWORLD PRINT
● FORUMS   ● FEATURES   ● ENTERPRISE CAREERS

BACK ISSUES

OPINIONS

May 31, 1999 (Vol. 21, Issue 22)

NOTES FROM THE FIELD
BY ROBERT X. CRINGELY
Microsoft bears its Heart of Glass at TechEd and sings Win2000 Rapture

Rose was in rare form when we got to Dallas for the TechEd conference only to find that Microsoft had hired Blondie to play a private party for its gathered IT managers and developers. According to Rose, people have often mistaken her for Blondie singer Deborah Harry. The only w...

QUICKCHECK   C

1 Products that are announced, but never shipped are called ⬚.

2 If your budget is not severely limited, a computer in the middle of a vendor's product line usually gives you the most computing power per dollar. True or false? ⬚

3 A(n) ⬚ upgrade is a special price offered to consumers who switch from one company's software product to a new version of a competitor's product.

4 Computer vendors are often classified into three ⬚ based on market share and financial resources.

5 A(n) ⬚ sells complete computer solutions for a specific industry, such as video stores or medical offices.

6 Computer books offer the most up-to-date information about computer products. True or false? ⬚

➡ Check Answers

SECTION D COMPUTER INDUSTRY CAREERS

InfoWeb 11

BLS

The $290 billion computer industry employs more than 1.5 million people. Over the past 50 years, it has created jobs that never before existed and financial opportunities for individuals with motivation, creative ideas, and technical skills. Since 1970, high-tech business has produced more than 7,000 millionaires and more than a dozen billionaires. According to the U.S. Bureau of Labor Statistics, computer and data processing services are projected to be the third fastest-growing industry; computer engineers, systems analysts, and data processing equipment repairers are expected to be among the 30 fastest-growing occupations between now and the year 2005.

Computer Industry Job Categories

Does the computer industry include every job that involves a computer?

It seems today that just about everyone uses computers at work. In fact, it is difficult to find a job nowadays that does not make use of computers in some capacity. Nevertheless, not everyone who uses a computer is employed in the computer industry. For a clear picture of computer jobs, it is useful to consider three categories. These categories can be somewhat loosely defined as computer-specific jobs, computer-related jobs, and computer-use jobs.

Computer-specific jobs, such as computer programmer, Webmaster, and chip designer would not exist without computers. **Computer-related jobs**, on the other hand, are variations of more generic jobs that you might find in any industry. For example, jobs in computer sales, high-tech recruiting, and graphics design are similar to sales, recruiting, and design jobs in the automobile or medical industries. **Computer-use jobs** require the use of computers to accomplish tasks in fields other than computing. Writers, reporters, accountants, retail clerks, medical technicians, auto mechanics, and many others use computers in the course of their everyday job activities.

The individuals who hold computer-specific jobs are usually referred to as "computer professionals." Of the three computer career categories, computer-specific jobs require the most preparation and will appeal to those who like working with, learning about, and thinking about computers (Figure 6-25).

CHAPTER 6

FIGURE 6-25

Jay Nunamaker, a computer science professor and chairman of a computer consulting firm, explores how computers can facilitate group interaction.

Computer Majors

What are the qualifications for computer jobs? Jobs for people who design and develop computer hardware and software require a high degree of training and skill. Virtually any of these jobs require a college degree and many require a master's degree or doctorate.

InfoWeb 12

College Connection

Most universities, colleges, and vocational schools offer degrees in computer engineering, computer science, and information systems that provide good qualifications for computer-specific jobs. There is some overlap among these fields of study, but the emphasis for each is different.

Computer engineering degrees require a good aptitude for engineering, math, and electronics. Career opportunities for computer engineering graduates focus on the design of computer hardware and peripheral devices, often at the chip level (Figure 6-26).

FIGURE 6-26

Technicians in a chip fabrication plant wear "bunny suits" to maintain a sterile environment.

Start
Video

Computer science degrees require a good aptitude for math and computer programming. The main object of study in a computer science program is the digital computer, and the main objective is to make the computer work effectively and efficiently. Computer science graduates generally find entry-level jobs as programmers with good possibilities for advancement to software engineers, object-oriented/GUI developers, and project leaders in technical applications development.

Information systems degree programs focus on the application of computers in a business or organizational environment. Coursework in business, accounting, computer programming, communications, systems analysis, and human psychology is usually required. For students who want to become computer professionals but lack strong math aptitude, most academic advisors recommend the information systems degree. An information systems degree usually leads to an entry-level programming or PC support job with good possibilities for advancement to systems analyst, project manager, database administrator, network manager, or other management positions.

Preparing for a Computer Career

How do I prepare for a computer industry career? Education and experience are the keys to a challenging computer job with good potential for advancement. In addition to a degree in computer science, computer engineering, or information systems, think about how you can get on-the-job experience through internships, military service, government-sponsored training programs, or work-study programs. Remember, however, these experiences are only supplements to formal education.

FIGURE 6-27

Not all computer science majors wear their computers around campus, but computer science and information systems degrees provide excellent credentials for a career in computing.

The MIT Wearable Computing Web Page

InfoWeb 13
Organizations

Owning your own computer, installing software, and troubleshooting hardware and software problems provide good experience with mass-market computing standards. You can gain additional experience from projects sponsored by clubs and organizations. The three largest computer organizations in North America are the Association for Computing Machinery (ACM), the Association of Information Technology Professionals (AITP), and the Institute of Electrical and Electronics Engineers–Computer Society (IEEE-CS).

InfoWeb 14
Certification

To beef up your credentials, you might also consider certification. The Institute for Certification of Computing Professionals (ICCP) has a regular schedule of exams for computer jobs such as computer programming, systems analysis, and network management. If you are considering a career in computer network management, it might be worthwhile to complete the test for Novell NetWare, Microsoft Certified Systems Engineer, or Microsoft NT certification. MOUS (Microsoft Office User Specialist) certification for application software such as Microsoft Word and Excel is also available.

It is essential to keep track of the job market in your area of specialty and develop a good mix of generalized knowledge and specialized skills. Generalized knowledge and your ability to apply it will help you generate creative and feasible solutions to problems. Specialized skills, such as experience with Visual Basic programming, will give you marketable tools to match specific jobs. The trick is to anticipate which computer skills will be in demand when you next search for a job. By obtaining those skills, you put yourself in a good competitive position against other applicants.

Working Conditions

What are the advantages of working in the computer industry? Graduates with degrees in computer engineering, computer science, and information systems generally work in a comfortable office or laboratory environment. Many technology companies offer employee-friendly working conditions that include child care, flexible hours, and the opportunity to telecommute—that is, conduct business electronically from home or a satellite office. As in any industry, the exact nature of a job depends on the company and the particular projects that are in the works. Some jobs and some projects are more interesting than others.

Many computer professionals like to pick and choose projects, which might account for the recent trend toward contract work and consulting. Contract programmers, consultants, and technical writers are self-employed, seek out short-term projects, and negotiate a per-project compensation rate. They set their own schedule, but often work 60-hour weeks. It takes motivation and discipline to be successful, but the rewards include control over your working environment.

In the computer industry, as in most industries, management positions command the highest salaries and salary levels increase with experience. Salaries vary somewhat by geographic location. In the Northeast and on the West Coast, salaries tend to be higher than in the Southeast, Midwest, Southwest, and Canada. Figure 6-28 provides sample 1999 salaries for computer-related jobs in the Midwest.

FIGURE 6-28		1999 computer industry salaries in the Midwest	
Job Title	**Salary**	**Job Title**	**Salary**
Chief information officer	$144,600	Software engineer	$60,800
IS director	100,900	Senior database analyst	75,100
Manager of analysts and programmers	88,100	Object-oriented/GUI developer	68,600
Network manager	79,100	Web/Internet developer	60,800
Data center manager	67,900	Systems analyst/programmer	57,900
Telecommunications manager	88,300	Telecommunications specialist	55,100
PC workstation manager	60,900	PC applications specialist	46,500
Tech support manager	84,900	Security specialist	75,500
Entry-level programmer	33,000	Help desk specialist	39,000

Using Technology to Find a Job

How do I find a computer industry job? The first step in a job search is to realistically assess your qualifications and needs. Your qualifications include your computer skills, educational background, previous work experience, communications skills, and personality. By comparing your qualifications with the requirements for a job, you can assess your chances of being hired. Your needs include your preferred geographical location, working conditions, corporate lifestyle, and salary. By comparing your needs with the information you discover about a prospective employer, you can assess your chances of enjoying a job once you've been hired. Several excellent books and Web sites provide information to help you assess your qualifications and needs. It is an important step. Your goal is not to "get a job," but to get a job that you like, that provides you with opportunity for advancement, and that rewards you with a good salary.

InfoWeb
15
Career
Resources

Today, researching the job market has become much easier, thanks to the Internet. In 1999, an estimated one of every three employers in North America used the Internet for recruiting. Popular Web-based "want ads" post descriptions of job openings. Usually the employers pay for these postings, so access is free to prospective employees. Web sites, such as the one shown in Figure 6-29, include general information about jobs, employment outlook, and salaries in computer industry jobs.

FIGURE 6-29

One of the most popular career Web sites.

Because the salaries for most jobs are stated vaguely as "commensurate with experience," it is useful to discover what you're worth by studying Web-based salary reports. If you're asked to name a figure during a job interview, you can use information from these reports to provide your prospective employer with your salary requirements, based on occupation, experience, and geographic area. The Web is not the only source of job listings. You can and should consult newspaper want ads, attend job fairs, and consider using the services of a professional recruiter.

You will need to prepare a resume containing your career goal, experience, skills, and education. Some career counselors suggest that high-tech candidates should not follow many of the rules delineated in traditional resume guidebooks. For example, if you have a substantial list of technical skills, you might not be able to limit your resume to a single page. Your resume should demonstrate technical savvy without appearing overly "packaged." For example, dot matrix printing is hard to read and old-fashioned, but would not automatically qualify for the wastebasket in a stack of engineering resumes. By contrast, unless you're applying for a job as a Web site or graphical designer, you don't want your resume to look like a page from *Wired* magazine. Such advice is interesting, but remember that corporate cultures differ. What might get your foot in the door at a shirt-and-tie corporation such as IBM could be different than at a jeans-and-sandals startup, such as Yahoo! Don't despair. You can use your word processor to tailor your resume to the corporate culture of each prospective employer.

CHAPTER 6

Contacting Prospective Employers

How do I get my information out? The standard procedure for mailing letters of application and resumes remains appropriate even in this age of high technology. Nevertheless, alternatives sometimes prove even more effective. Many companies will accept resumes by fax to reduce the time it takes to process applicants. E-mail is another route that speeds up the process. Use it if you can, and make sure you include your e-mail address on your application materials. In addition to speeding communication, using e-mail demonstrates your familiarity with one of the most pervasive technology tools in the world today.

You can post your resume on a placement Web site where it can be viewed by corporate recruiters. Some of these Web sites charge a small fee for posting resumes; others are free. You can also post your resume along with your personal Web page, if you have one. This course of action is particularly effective if you design these pages to show-case technical skills that are applicable to the job you're seeking. College students beware. Some employers have discovered much more than they bargained for by visiting the Web pages created by job applicants. If you are searching for employment, take a moment to look at your Web page through the eyes of a middle-aged, conservative, corporate recruiter. Remember that this page is public. Even if you don't include its Web address in your application materials, it is not difficult to find.

QUICKCHECK   D

1 The U.S. Bureau of Labor Statistics estimates that computer and data processing services will be the fastest-growing industry between now and 2001. True or false?

[_____]

2 A(n) [_____] degree program focuses on the application of computers in a business or organizational environment.

3 High-tech salaries tend to be highest on the West Coast and in the [_____] section of the United States.

4 Education and [_____] are the keys to a challenging computer job with good potential for advancement.

5 The AITP, ACM, and IEEE-CS are professional [_____].

6 In addition to using Web-based job listings, you can consult newspaper want ads, attend [_____], and use the services of a professional recruiter to find a job in the computer industry.

➡ Check Answers

COMPUTER SHOPPING STRATEGIES

If you are like most consumers in pursuit of a good computer value, you will talk to salespeople, read computer magazines, look through computer catalogs, chat with your friends who own computers, and compare prices on the Web. Here are some shopping strategies that should help you purchase a computer that meets your needs, while staying within a budget you can afford.

Lab
Buying a Computer

Determine Your Needs and Budget

Where do I start? Start by setting a budget and stick to it! Computer vendors have very carefully priced the computers in their product line so that you will be tempted to spend "just a few hundred dollars more" to get a model with more features. The trouble is that if you decide to spend that few hundred dollars, you will be tempted to spend even a little more to get even more features.

Once you have established a budget, consider how you plan to use the computer. A computer can be a valuable asset for completing your college degree, it can be a useful educational tool for your children, and it can increase your competitive edge in your career. Consider these factors before you begin shopping for a computer:

Notebook or desktop? If you plan to carry your computer with you, a notebook computer is the optimal choice. A notebook costs more than a similarly configured desktop, however, so you will either pay for portability or give up features.

Compatibility? Most computers sold today are IBM-compatible PCs. However, you should consider a Macintosh computer if most of the computers in your school are Macintoshes, if the computer is intended for your children who are using Macintosh computers in school, or if Macintosh is the major computer used in your career field.

Support? Equipment breaks. Circuits fail. Your computer does "odd" things while you are trying to complete a task. Where can you turn for help? Earlier in this chapter, you learned about the technical support offered by computer vendors in the three market tiers. You should be aware that support can vary even within a tier. A little pre-purchase research on the Web or with past customers can help you determine whether a vendor can offer the level of support you need.

InfoWeb 16
Consumer Information

Warranty. When you purchase a computer, ask about the warranty. Most computers come with a one-year parts and labor warranty. Before you buy, you should find out whether you could expect on-site service in your home or whether you would have to send in your computer for repairs or bring it to a local store. Read the warranty carefully so that you understand what it covers and exactly which repair services it provides. Many merchants offer extended warranties—some lasting as long as five years. Depending on the price and coverage, an extended warranty can be an excellent deal.

Printer? Remember that you must include the cost of a printer in your budget. Unless you need to print multipart forms, you should not buy a dot matrix printer. A color ink jet printer is in the same price range and produces better print quality. Inexpensive laser printers, referred to as "personal laser printers," cost $100 to $300 more than ink jet printers. Make sure that you consider a printer's operational cost. If you are on a very limited budget, it is easier to replace a $15 ink cartridge than a $100 toner cartridge.

Collect the Facts

What information do I need? Before you make a decision, shop around to collect information on pricing, features, and support. You can find computer system specifications and pricing information in magazine ads and on the Web.

As you look at computer ads, pay particular attention to (1) processor manufacturer and model, (2) processor speed, (3) RAM capacity, (4) hard disk capacity, (5) monitor size, and (6) price. After looking at several ads, a pattern will emerge. You'll notice that the specifications in each price range tend to be similar. Once you recognize these specifications, you can be assured of getting a reasonable deal. Be wary of any computer that doesn't meet the specifications for the price range—it is probably overpriced. Also, be careful of a computer that has far better specifications than you would expect for that price range. A super-low-cost computer might be reconditioned, used, or a floor model—not necessarily a bad deal, if the computer works and can be serviced.

In addition to computer ads, you can find comparative pricing at Web-based "price quote" sites. At these sites, you can search for information by processor speed or price range. These sites also allow you to enter the brand and model of the PC that you'd like to purchase. After a brief search, the site will display a list of vendors that sell that computer model, along with the prices that each vendor charges. When you use a price quote site, be aware that some of these sites search only those merchants that have paid to participate. Figure 6-30 provides more information about Web-based price quote sites.

FIGURE 6-30

Price quote sites search the Web for computer prices offered by a variety of vendors.

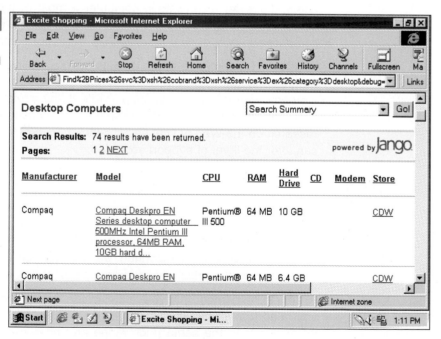

Start
Screentour

Although you might be tempted to buy the computer with the best features and lowest price, don't forget to consider the warranty and the quality of the support offered by the vendor. The list in Figure 6-31 will help you gather facts about pricing, features, and support.

FIGURE 6-31

A feature list can help you keep track of the comparative data that you find in computer magazine ads and price quote Web sites. You can fill in specifications for each computer that you are considering.

Comparative Shopping Feature List

- **Manufacturer:**_____
- **Model:**_____
- **Price:**_____
- Processor model:_____
- Processor speed:_____
- Cache capacity:_____
- RAM capacity:_____
- Hard disk drive capacity:_____
- Hard disk drive type and speed:_____
- CD/DVD drive speed:_____
- Zip drive capacity?:_____
- Modem speed:_____
- Sound card model:_____
- Speaker description:_____
- Graphics card slot type (desktop only):_____
- Graphics card accelerator features:_____
- Graphics card video RAM capacity:_____
- Display type (LCD/CRT):_____
- Display screen size and dot pitch:_____
- Type of pointing device:_____
- Number and type of expansion ports:_____
- Number and type of expansion slots:_____
- Overall weight (notebook only): _____
- Battery operating time (notebook only):_____
- Operating system version:_____
- Bundled software (list):_____
- Warranty coverage:_____
- Technical support quality:_____

CHAPTER 6

Evaluate the Facts

How do I make the decision? After you have collected the facts, your decision might be obvious. In an ideal situation, a local vendor with a reputation for excellent support is selling a computer with features and price comparable to those sold by many reputable mail-order vendors. In the real world, however, your local vendor's price might be higher, and then your decision is not so clear. You might want to make a decision support worksheet like the one shown in Figure 6-32.

FIGURE 6-32

A decision support worksheet can help you select the best deal.

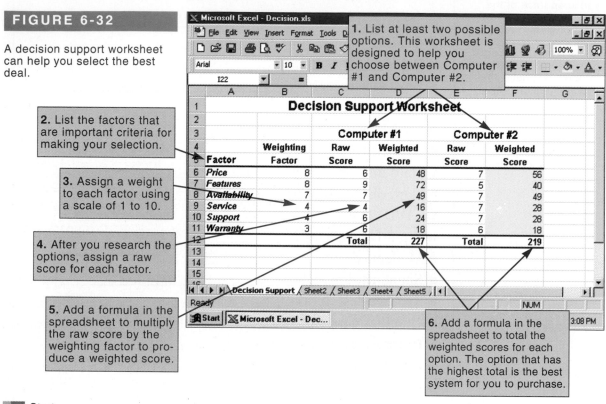

1. List at least two possible options. This worksheet is designed to help you choose between Computer #1 and Computer #2.

2. List the factors that are important criteria for making your selection.

3. Assign a weight to each factor using a scale of 1 to 10.

4. After you research the options, assign a raw score for each factor.

5. Add a formula in the spreadsheet to multiply the raw score by the weighting factor to produce a weighted score.

6. Add a formula in the spreadsheet to total the weighted scores for each option. The option that has the highest total is the best system for you to purchase.

Decision Support Worksheet

	Weighting	Computer #1		Computer #2	
Factor	**Factor**	**Raw Score**	**Weighted Score**	**Raw Score**	**Weighted Score**
Price	8	6	48	7	56
Features	8	9	72	5	40
Availability	7	7	49	7	49
Service	4	4	16	7	28
Support	4	6	24	7	28
Warranty	3	6	18	6	18
		Total	227	Total	219

Start
Screentour

ISSUE   WHAT SHOULD HAPPEN TO OLD COMPUTERS?

Keeping up with technology means replacing your computer every few years, but what should you do with your old, outdated computer? Worldwide, an estimated 150 million computers were discarded by the year 2000. In the United States alone, more than 20 million computers become obsolete each year. According to research conducted by Stanford Resources of San Jose, California, only 11 percent of these obsolete computers will be recycled. It is estimated that U.S. landfills already contain more than 2 million tons of computer and electronic parts, which can contain toxic substances such as lead, phosphorus, and mercury.

An Environmental Protection Agency report sums up the situation: "In this world of rapidly changing technology, disposal of computers and other electronic equipment has created a new and growing waste stream."

InfoWeb 17

Recycle & Reuse

Many computers end up in landfills because their owners were unaware of potential environmental hazards. In addition, PC owners are not typically supplied with information concerning the options for disposing of their old machines. Instead of throwing your old computer away, you might be able to sell it; donate it to a local school, church, or community program; have it hauled away by a professional recycling firm; or send it back to the manufacturer.

With the growing popularity of Internet auctions and dedicated computer reclamation sites, you might be able to get some cash for your old computer. At Web sites such as the Computer Recycle Center (www.recycles.com), you can post an ad for your "old stuff." Off the Web, you can find several businesses, such as Computer Renaissance, that refurbish old computers and sell them in retail stores.

Donating your old computer to a local organization doesn't actually eliminate the disposal problem, but it does delay it. Unfortunately, finding a new home for an old computer is not always easy. Most schools and community organizations have few resources for repairing broken equipment, so if your old computer is not in good working order, it could be more of a burden than a gift. In addition, your computer might be too old to be compatible with the other computers that are used in an organization. It helps if you can donate software along with your old computer. To provide a legal transfer, include the software distribution disks, manuals, and license agreement. And remember, once you donate the software, you cannot legally use it on your new computer unless it is freeware or shareware.

If you cannot find an organization to accept your computer donation, look in your local Yellow Pages or on the Internet for an electronics-recycling firm, which will haul away your computer and recycle any usable materials.

CHAPTER 6

Despite the private sector options for selling, donating, or recycling old computers, many governments are worried that these "voluntary" efforts will not be enough to prevent massive dumping of an ever-growing population of computers. Many lawmakers in the United States and the European Union believe that legislation is necessary, but they can't agree on an implementation plan. Basic to the issue is the question of "Who pays?" Should it be the taxpayer, the individual consumer, or the computer manufacturer?

Currently, taxpayers pick up the tab for electronic waste disposal through municipal trash pick-up fees or through local taxes. But is this approach fair to individual taxpayers who generate very little electronic waste?

To make consumers responsible for the cost of recycling the products they buy, some lawmakers have suggested adding a special recycling tax to computers and other electronic devices. A proposal in South Carolina, for example, would impose a $5 fee on the sale of each piece of electronic equipment containing a CRT and require the state treasurer to deposit the fees into an electronic equipment recycling fund.

Other lawmakers propose to make manufacturers responsible for recycling costs and logistics. "Extended producer responsibility" refers to the idea of holding manufacturers responsible for the environmental effects of their products through the entire product life cycle, which includes taking them back, recycling them, and disposing of them. Proposed legislation in Europe would require manufacturers to accept returns of their old equipment free of charge, then take appropriate steps to recycle it. The economics of a mandatory take-back program are likely to increase the costs of products because manufacturers would typically pass on recycling costs to consumers. Some companies currently participate in voluntary extended producer responsibility programs. Compaq, 3M, Hewlett-Packard, Nortel, Frigidaire, and Xerox, for example, provide recycling options for some product components, although none of the companies has instituted a comprehensive product take-back program as yet.

WHAT DO YOU THINK?

1. Have you thrown away an old computer or other electronic device? ○ Yes ○ No ○ Not sure

2. Are you aware of any options for recycling electronic equipment in your local area? ○ Yes ○ No ○ Not sure

3. Would it be fair for consumers to pay a recycling tax on any electronic equipment that they purchase? ○ Yes ○ No ○ Not sure

⏩ Save Responses

<table>
<tr><td>CHAPTER
6</td><td>REVIEW ACTIVITIES</td></tr>
</table>

INTERACTIVE SUMMARY

The Interactive Summary helps you select important concepts and facts from this chapter. Fill in the blanks to best complete each sentence. When using the NP4 CD or NP4 Web site, you can click the Check Answers buttons to automatically score your answers. Place your Tracking Disk in the floppy disk drive if you want to save your scores.

Computer ads, whether in magazines or on the Web, provide most consumers with the information they use to purchase computers. Typically, an ad lists a series of _____ that describe the speed and capacity of processing, storage, input, and output components. Today, most computers contain processors manufactured by one of two companies: _____ or Intel. Intel's two most popular processor models are the _____ and Celeron. A typical storage configuration on both note-book and desktop computers includes a 1.44 MB floppy disk drive, a(n) _____ ATA hard disk drive, and a CD-ROM or DVD-ROM drive. Input devices include a keyboard and pointing device. Notebook computers typically include a flat panel screen that uses _____ technology. With a desktop computer, the display device might not be included in the system price, even if it is pictured in the ad. A printer is usually not included in the price of a computer, so it must be purchased separately. The most popular type of printer is a color _____.   ⟩ Check Answers

The computer _____ consists of corporations and individuals that supply goods and services to people and organizations that use computers. The companies that manufacture computers are some-times classified into three categories, or _____, based on their size, sales volume, and financial stability. Prices tend to vary by category, as does service, quality, and support. Computer hard-ware and software products have a product life _____ that begins with product development. For hardware products, the best "power for your dollar" is often found with products in the middle of a vendor's product line. Unlike hardware, however, old versions of software are quickly _____, so you should always purchase the newest version when buying software.

Computer hardware and software are available from a variety of marketing outlets, or _____, such as computer retail stores, mail-order suppliers, value-added resellers, and manufacturer direct sales. The Web is playing a growing role in the computer marketplace by offering online catalog shopping, manufacturer direct sales sites, and price quote sites.

Computer careers typically provide an excellent salary and comfortable working conditions, but require a good education. Computer _____ degrees provide a good background for jobs such as pro-grammers, software engineers, and project leaders in technical applications development. Computer _____ degrees prepare students for jobs designing computer hardware and peripheral devices. Information _____ degrees emphasize computers within a business setting.

 Check Answers

I N T E R A C T I V E   K E Y   T E R M S

Make sure that you understand all of the boldfaced key terms presented in this chapter. If you're using the NP4 CD or NP4 Web site, you can use this list of terms as an interactive study activity. First, try to define a term in your own words, then click the term to compare your definition with the definition that is presented in the chapter.

Accelerated graphics card, 264
Active matrix screen, 264
Alpha test, 275
Benchmark test, 256
Beta test, 275
Color depth, 264
Competitive upgrade, 276
Computer engineering, 284
Computer industry, 273
Computer-related jobs, 283
Computer retail store, 278
Computer science, 284
Computer-specific jobs, 283
Computer-use jobs, 283
Controller, 258
CRT (cathode ray tube), 262
DMA, 258
Dot matrix printer, 271
Dot pitch, 263
Dpi, 268
Duty cycle, 268
EIDE, 258
External bay, 265
Hot swap, 267
Information systems, 284
Ink jet printer, 269
Internal bay, 265
Laser printer, 270
LCD, 262
Level 1 cache (L1 cache), 256
Level 2 cache (L2 cache), 256
Mail-order supplier, 278
Manufacturer direct, 279
Maximum resolution, 263
Multifunction printer, 272
Passive matrix screen, 264

PCMCIA card, 265
PCMCIA slot, 265
Port replicator, 266
PostScript, 270
Printer Control Language (PCL), 270
Revision, 275
SCSI, 258
SDRAM, 257
Software publisher, 275
Street price, 276
Touchpad, 260
Trackball, 260
Track point, 260
SVGA, 264
Ultra ATA, 258
Value-added reseller (VAR), 279
Vaporware, 273
Version, 275
Version upgrade price, 276
Video memory, 264
Viewable image size (vis), 262
Wavetable synthesis, 261
XGA, 264

INTERACTIVE QUIZZES

Quiz yourself on important concepts from the chapter by filling in the blanks. When using the NP4 CD or NP4 Web site, you can type your answers, then use the Check Answers buttons to automatically score your responses. Place your Tracking Disk in the floppy disk drive if you want to save your scores.

1 A computer containing a Pentium processor is typically more expensive than an equivalent computer with a Celeron processor. True or false? [_____]

2 If you are interested in comparing the speed of two computer systems, you might be able to find comparative data from a(n) [_____] test.

3 A(n) [_____] slot typically provides a faster bus for a graphics card than a PCI slot.

4 To display images at high resolution and at a high color depth, your computer's graphics cards needs lots of video [_____].

5 A(n) [_____] printer is the best solution for printing on multipart carbon forms.

6 Suppose that a software product is designated 2.3. The "2" is the [_____] number, whereas the "3" is the [_____] number.

7 Software publishers use competitive [_____] to try to lure customers away from competitors' products.

8 Computer professionals hold what are sometimes called computer-[_____] jobs that require specific computer-related education and training.

Check Answers

Fill in the blanks with the correct specifications from the ad.

1 Processor speed: [_____]

2 Processor model: [_____]

3 DVD-ROM speed: [_____]

4 Sound card manufacturer: [_____]

5 Graphics card slot type: [_____]

6 Video memory: [_____]

7 Monitor resolution: [_____]

8 Actual screen image size: [_____]

9 RAM capacity: [_____]

10 Operating system: [_____]

The Family PC $1229

- Intel Celeron 466 MHz
- 64 MB SDRAM
- 6.4 GB ATA Hard Drive
- 3.5" Floppy Disk Drive
- 6X DVD-ROM Drive
- 4 MB 3-D AGP Graphics Card
- .28 Dot Pitch 800 x 600 15" Monitor (13.9" vis)
- Creative Labs AudioPCI 64V
- Altec Lansing ACS5 Speakers
- 3Com U.S. Robotics V.90 Modem
- Keyboard and Mouse
- Microsoft Windows 98 and Home Essentials
- One-year Parts and Labor Warranty with On-site Service*

*Warranty terms and conditions available on request. On-site service is administered by PCTS and is not available outside the continental U.S. All pricing and specifications subject to change without notice.

Check Answers

CHAPTER 6

INTERACTIVE PRACTICE TESTS

When you use the NP4 CD or NP4 Web site, you can take practice tests that consist of 10 multiple-choice, true/false, and fill-in-the-blank questions. The 10 questions are selected at random from a large test bank, so each time you take a test, you'll receive a different set of questions. Your tests are scored immediately and you can print study guides that help you find the correct answers for any questions that you missed. If you are using a Tracking Disk, insert it in the floppy disk drive to save your test scores.

 Start Practice
Test

STUDY TIPS

Study Tips help you organize and consolidate the information in a chapter by making lists, outlines, charts, and sketches. You can use paper and pencil, or word processing software to complete most of the Study Tips activities.

1 Make a list of the key points you need to remember about buying a desktop computer, then make a list of the additional factors you must consider when buying a notebook computer.

2 Demonstrate your understanding of the terminology and issues involved in purchasing a computer by answering the following questions about the computer ad in Figure 6-1.

   a. The processor in the MicroPlus computer would be classified in which processor family?

   b. The software that you could run with the MicroPlus computer would not generally be compatible with which other types of computers?

   c. Does the MicroPlus computer have enough RAM to run Windows 98?

   d. About how much would it cost to upgrade the MicroPlus computer to 256 MB of memory?

   e. Why does the MicroPlus computer come with only one 3.5" floppy disk drive?

   f. How fast is the CD-ROM drive?

   g. Can you add a second internal hard disk drive to the MicroPlus computer? Why or why not?

   h. Would you be able to display photographic-quality images at 1024 x 768 resolution? Why or why not?

   i. If you purchase the MicroPlus computer and a week after you receive it, the monitor stops working, what is the MicroPlus company policy on repairs?

3 Draw a diagram to illustrate the life cycle of a computer hardware product.

4 Describe the difference between a version upgrade and a competitive upgrade.

5 Describe the characteristics of each of the three market tiers in the computer industry.

6 List the advantages and disadvantages of purchasing a computer from each computer industry marketing channel.

7 In your own words, describe the difference between computer-specific jobs, computer-related jobs, and computer-use jobs.

8 List the ways in which you can use technology to find a job.

P R O J E C T S

A project is an open-ended activity that will help you apply the concepts you have learned. Many projects require resources in addition to your textbook, such as current magazines, library materials, or Web access. When you tackle a project, be prepared to use your critical thinking skills, logical analysis, and your creativity.

1 **The Computer Shopper Experience** The story about Matt at the beginning of this chapter is fairly realistic. Many people purchase mail-order computers, and *Computer Shopper* is the most popular source of information for mail-order prices. Suppose you decide to buy a computer, and you decide your budget is $1,500. You don't need to buy a printer because your friend is giving you a usable, but older printer. Look through the ads in a recent issue of *Computer Shopper* to find the best computer that fits your computing needs and your budget. Write the list of features, the price, and the vendor for the computer, as well as the month and page of the issue. Then explain why you think this computer is the best one for the money.

2 **Today's Microprocessors** Microprocessor technology changes rapidly. New models arrive every couple of years, and the clock speed for a particular model seems to increase every few months. As you learned in this chapter, computers that contain state-of-the-art processors are usually priced at a premium. Because the latest processors are so expensive, the most popular computers—those that are purchased by the most people—tend to contain a previous-model processor. When you are in the market for a computer, it is useful to be able to differentiate between the state-of-the-art processors and previous models.

Browse through several computer magazines to determine which processor is most popular and which processor is currently state-of-the-art. Write a brief description of your findings. Include the following information:

a. The clock speed, processor model name or number, and word size for the most popular micro-processor

b. The clock speed, processor model name or number, and word size for the state-of-the-art micro-processor

c. Explanation of which factors helped you determine that these particular microprocessors are the most popular and the most state-of-the-art

d. A bibliography of your sources

3 **Comparison Shopping** Comparison shopping is a good strategy for finding the best deal in a computer system. Use the hardware checklist in Figure 6-31 to gather comparative information about two computer systems. You can gather the information from a computer magazine, the Internet, or a local computer retail store. Be sure you exercise courtesy, especially if you visit a small retail store. Let the salesperson know that you are working on a class project, and remember that the salesperson's priority is shoppers who intend to actually buy a computer. Your instructor might assign this project to a group.

4 **Your Dollar Buys a Lot More Today** You have probably heard that computer technology changes at an amazing speed. Today, your money buys much more computing power than it did in previous years. How much more? Look through the computer ads in the June issues of computer magazines dating from this year and back to 1990 (or as many years as you can find). Create a chart that shows the changes in the specifications for computers for a price of $2,000. Be sure you compare the processor speed, RAM capacity, and hard disk drive capacity.

5 **Product Comparison Reviews** Many computer magazines feature extensive product comparison reviews in which several hardware or software products are evaluated and compared. Suppose you are working for an organization and your job is to select hardware and software products.

a. Describe the organization for which you work, then specify which type of product (notebook computers, word processing software, printers, and so on) you are seeking and why.

b. Explain the important factors that will influence your decision, such as budget or special features that your organization requires from the product.

c. Find and read an appropriate comparative review in a recent computer magazine.

d. Based on the comparative review, write a memo to your "boss" that summarizes your recommendation and provides justification for the products that you would select.

6 **Career Research** Books, magazines, and the Web supply plenty of resources to help you choose a career. If you're considering a career change, these resources can help you decide if it is the right thing to do. Use the resources in your library and on the Web to gather information about a career in which you are interested. Unless your instructor requires it, you do not need to limit yourself to computing careers. Answer the following questions:

a. In one paragraph, how would you describe the nature of the work you would perform in this career?

b. What types of businesses and organizations typically hire people in your chosen career field?

c. What are the working conditions?

d. What specific qualifications would you need to successfully compete in this career?

e. What is the employment outlook for this career?

f. What is a typical starting salary? What is the salary range?

g. What sources did you use to locate information about this career?

7 **Web Resume** The Web provides a way to publish your resume where it might be seen by prospective employers. But like a stack of resumes on a recruiter's desk, your Web resume may be quickly rejected if it contains spelling and grammar errors, if it is difficult to read, or if your credentials are not presented in a logical format. It takes several drafts to produce a good resume.

Begin by creating your resume using a word processing program. Use a reference book or Web site about resumes to help organize your content. Spell-check this first draft and print it.

Next, show the first draft to at least three friends, colleagues, or instructors. Make revisions based on their comments. When you are satisfied with your resume, generate a Web page. Store the page on a floppy disk and submit it to your instructor.

ADDITIONAL PROJECTS

The Computer Industry

The Latest "Scoop" from Industry Analysts

Your Compatibility Needs

Using a Decision Support Spreadsheet for Buying a Computer

LAB ASSIGNMENTS

Software for this lab is provided on the NP4 CD and may also be available in your school's computer lab. To start the lab, click the lab icon.

The lab has two parts: Steps and Explore. Use the Steps first to learn and review concepts. Read the information on each page and do the numbered steps. As you work through the lab, you will be asked to answer QuickCheck questions about what you have learned. At the end of the lab, you will see a report that scores your answers to the QuickChecks. If your instructor wants you to turn in this report, click the Print button on the Quick Check report screen.

When you have completed the Steps, you can click the Explore button to complete the Lab Assignments. You can also use Explore to practice the skills you learned and to explore concepts on your own.

Lab
Buying a Computer

When buying from a mail-order or Internet computer vendor, consumers don't have an opportunity to take various computer models for a "test drive." They make their computer purchase decisions based solely on a list of specifications. Thus it is essential to understand the specifications in computer ads. In this lab, you will find out how to use a Shopping Glossary to interpret the specifications.

1   Click the Steps button to learn how to use the Shopping Glossary. As you proceed through the Steps, answer all of the QuickCheck questions that appear. After you complete the Steps, you will see a QuickCheck Report. Follow the instructions on the screen to print this report.

2   Click the Explore button and read the ad for the Nevada Tech Systems computer in Ad 1. Use the Shopping Glossary to define the following terms:
a. L2 cache   d. Wavetable
b. SDRAM   e. Zip
c. AGP   f. V.90

3   In Explore, read the ads for the ZeePlus Value Pak and the ZeePlus Multimedia Pro computers. The two systems differ substantially in price. If you purchase the more expensive system, what additional features do you get?

4   In Explore, read the ad for the ZeePlus Multimedia Pro Computer (500 MHz) and the NP2 Super Systems Computer. What is the price difference between these two systems? What factors might account for this price difference?

5   In Explore, read the ads to find a notebook computer that's priced within $100 of the Nevada Tech Systems desktop computer. Make a list of the features that the desktop computer has, but the notebook computer lacks. Which one would you buy? Why?

6   Photocopy a computer ad from a recent issue of a computer magazine. On a separate sheet of paper, write each specification (for example, Intel Pentium III processor). For each specification, define each term (for example, Intel is a microprocessor manufacturer, Pentium is a type of microprocessor in the x86 family). Write out all acronyms (for example, RAM means "random access memory"). If you have difficulty with some of the terms and acronyms, click the Explore button and use the Shopping Glossary.

INFOWEB

The InfoWeb is your guide to print, film, television, and electronic resources. Use it to obtain updates on quickly changing technical information and to locate information for research papers. If you're using the NP4 CD, click the InfoWeb Site icon on the left side of this paragraph to access the online InfoWeb links. Otherwise, use your Web browser and type in the address of the NP4 Web site: www.cciw.com/np4. At the Web site you'll find up-to-date links to the topics covered in this chapter.

1 Which Chip?

Since 1993, Intel has introduced several versions of the Pentium processor. Competing chipmaker AMD has introduced additional work-alike chips. Which chip is best suited to your computing needs? To answer this question, read *A Gamer's Guide to CPUs* (even if you aren't a gamer!) by Ken Feinstein (2/26/99) at *www.gamecenter.com/Hardware/Roundup/Cpu/?st.cn.sr.rl.gc*. You can get the official party line about Intel and AMD chips at the Web sites for Intel at *www.intel.com* and AMD at *www.amd.com*, respectively. Also, check the NP4 Web site for the latest links on this topic.

2 Benchmarks

Want to test your own PC to see how it performs on standard benchmark tests? You can download benchmark tests and test your own PC using *PC Magazine's* Winstone 99 and WinBench 99 benchmark test files at *www8.zdnet.com/pcmag/pclabs/bench/bench.htm*. You'll find links to results of various benchmark tests at Scott Wainner's System Optimization site, *www.sysopt.com/bench.html*, and the Ideas International site, *www.ideasinternational.com/benchmark/bench.html*.

3 Sound Systems

You can purchase $10 speakers for your computer or you can purchase $500 speakers. What's the difference? The quality of sound you hear depends on the quality of your speakers, the capabilities of your sound card, and the quality of the sound file you're playing. To compare the quality of sound cards, download the files at *pubweb.nwu.edu/~jll544/sndsmpl.html* and take the wavetable sound card test drive. Are you interested in which speakers produce the most dynamic sound? Look for a comparative review, such as CNET's roundup of the latest speaker systems at *www.computers.com/reviews/comparative/intro/0,23,0-19-646924,00.html*. For an update on the latest speaker technology, check out Altec Lansing's Web site at *www.altecmm.com* and click the Line link. Then check out the site of other popular speaker vendors: Creative Labs at *www.creativelabs.com*, Labtec at *www.labtec.com*, and Koss at *www.koss.com*.

4 Display System: Two to Tango

It takes two to tango and your display system is only as good as your monitor and graphics card. For advice on choosing a monitor, read page 123 of the October 7, 1996, issue of *Computerworld* magazine and search for "How to Select a PC Display System" at *www.techweb.com/encyclopedia*. Look for comparative reviews by connecting to *www.cnet.com* and searching for "monitor reviews." Computer Shopper's Web site at *www.computershopper.com* contains a good collection of tips and answers to such questions as "How do I choose a monitor?" and "Should I buy a CRT or LCD?" Just connect to the site and follow the links for Monitors. For an update on current monitor models, connect to vendor sites, such as NEC Technologies at *www.nec.com*, Sony Electronics at *www.sony.com*, Samsung Electronics America at *www.samsung.com*, and Philips Electronics at *www.philips.com*. You can check out graphics card manufacturers' Web sites: Diamond Multimedia Systems at *www.diamondmm.com*, ATI Technologies at *www.atitech.com*, Matrox Electronic Systems at *www.matrox.com*, and STB Systems at *www.stb.com*.

5 Notebooks

Thinking of buying a notebook computer? *PC World* magazine has an excellent Web site just for you at *www.pcworld.com/top400/category/0,1377,Portable_PCs,00.html*. You might also want to connect to *www.computershopper.com* and follow links for notebooks. An illustrated tutorial, *Introduction to Liquid Crystal Displays*, at *abalone.phys.cwru.edu/tutorial/enhanced/files/lcd/Intro.htm* provides a solid background in LCD technology. Just for fun, you might want to visit AT&T Bell Labs gallery of exquisite liquid crystal photos at *www.bell-labs.com/new/gallery/thumbnails.html*.

6 PCMCIA

The definitive site about PCMCIA is the PCMCIA home page at *www.pc-card.com*. Here you'll find links to PCMCIA FAQs, products, and press releases. You'll find a good primer on PCMCIA technology and markets at the Accurite Technologies site, *www.accurite.com/PCMCIAprimer.html*.

7 Printers

Most computer users have heard of Epson, the printer manufacturer that set the standard for dot matrix printing. What many people don't know is that Epson's history spans more than 100 years and includes the invention of the world's first quartz watch. In 1964, Epson created printing timers for the Tokyo Olympics. Epson (*www.epson.com*) competes for the lion's share of the computer printer market with Hewlett-Packard (*www.hp.com*). You can visit either Web site for an update on current printer technology. For buyer's guidelines, look in recent editions of computer magazines. On the Web, connect to *www.computershopper.com* and follow the links for Printers, or connect to *www.cnet.com* and search for "printer reviews."

8 Publications: Computer Industry Magazines and Journals

The number of computer publications reflects our interest in computing. On the Web, you can find listings of currently published computer magazines and journals at *www.internetvalley.com/top100mag.html*. For PC users, the most popular hardware and software magazines are probably *Computer Shopper* (*www.cshopper.com*), *InfoWorld* (*www.infoworld.com*), *PC Magazine* (*www.zdnet.com/pcmag*), *PC Computing* (*www.zdnet.com/pccomp*), and *Windows* (*www.winmag.com*). The most readable academic journal is *Communications of the ACM*. For general commentary about the computer industry, check your newsstand or the Web for *Forbes* (*www.forbes.com*), *Upside* (*www.upside.com*), and the *Wall Street Journal* (*www.wsj.com*).

9 Web Resources: News and Views

For the latest breaking news about the computer industry, check out Yahoo! Technology Headlines at *www.yahoo.com/headlines/tech*, Infoseek's computer page at *www.infoseek.com* (then link to Computing), or WebCrawler's computer page at *webcrawler.com/Computers*. You can see live video of the CNN Financial Network Digital Jam show at *cnnfn.com/news/technology*. You can also connect to *www.computernewsdaily.com* for articles from the New York Times Syndicate, a collection of excellent newspapers from North America, Europe, and Asia. Another great source of news on computing is Jeffrey Harrows' The Rapidly Changing Face of Computing at *www.digital.com/info/rcfoc*.

10 Computer TV

You'll have to check your local listings for the broadcast schedule for computer TV shows such as *Computer Chronicles* and *@Home*. To find out the topics on this week's shows, you can use the Web. Check the CNET site at *www.cnet.com* for information about *The Web*, *The New Edge*, and *CNET Central*. The PCTV Web site *www.cmptv.com* provides information on *Net Cafe*, *Computer Chronicles*, and *TechWeb Today*. Jones Cable Network at *www.meu.edu/ktv/index.html* gives you the rundown on several high-tech shows, including *Computer Kids*, *Home Computing*, and *DiskDoctors*. Also, check out schedules and technology links for MSNBC at *www.msnbc.com*.

11 BLS: Bureau of Labor Statistics

The U.S. Bureau of Labor Statistics (BLS) provides projections for computer industry employment at *stats.bls.gov/news.release/ecopro.table6.htm* and *stats.bls.gov/news.release/ecopro.table7.htm*. The BLS's *Occupational Outlook Handbook* describes computer industry jobs, typical working conditions, and salary levels at *stats.bls.gov/ocohome.htm*.

12 College Connection

An excellent site that lets you interactively search for a college by major, location, size, and tuition is CollegeNET at *www.collegenet.com*.

13 Organizations

What's up with computer professional organizations? Check out their Web sites or call for information. Your campus might have a student chapter of one or more of these organizations:

Association for Computing Machinery (*www.acm.org*) 212-626-0500
IEEE Computer Society (*www.computer.org*) 714-821-8380
Association for Women in Computing (*www.awc-hq.org*) 415-905-4663
Association of Information Technology Professionals (*www.aitp.org*) 800-224-9371

14 Certification

The ICCP claims that its certification is "recognized worldwide by employers and peers as validation of its holders' computing knowledge and experience." Find out more about the ICCP certification program for students and professionals at *www.iccp.org*. Information about preparing for and taking the Novell certification exams for computer networking is at *education.novell.com*. Connect to the Microsoft site *www.microsoft.com/train_cert/* to discover the benefits of becoming a Microsoft Certified Professional (MCP). To find out how to get certification for your expertise with Microsoft Office software, check out *www.microsoft.com/office/train_cert/default.htm*.

15 Career Resources

The Web site *www.lib.mtu.edu/jrvp/Instruction/seminars/careerjob/present.htm* is a good place to get some tips on job hunting. When you register for the High-Tech Career Alert at the HiTechCareers site *www.hitechcareer.com*, you will receive weekly e-mail of jobs in your career field. The comprehensive CareerBuilder site at *www.careerbuilder.com* contains tips for creating your resume, job listings, an interactive page that helps you compare the cost of living for different cities, and tips on successful job interviews. Another comprehensive site, *CareerMagazine's www.careermag.com*, includes job listings, a resume bank, employer profiles, and products and services to help you manage your career. One of the largest sources of career resources is the Monster Board at *www.monster.com*. Newer, but very active career sites include *www.headhunter.net* and *www.tcm.com*. If you want inspiration, rent the video *Triumph of the Nerds*. Information and script for this video are available at *www.pbs.org/nerds*.

16 Consumer Information: Buying a Computer

The online *UGeek* magazine at *www.geek.com* includes a buyer's guide that features recommendations for selecting a processor, case, storage devices, sound system, and display system. *BusinessWeek* runs a great site at *www.maven.businessweek.com* where you can enter specifications for a computer system or printer to get information on its features, price, and performance. For additional Web shopping, try the following sites:

cnet.shopper.com	*www.compusa.com*
www.cdw.com	*buycomp.com*
www.microwarehouse.com	*www.pricewatch.com*
www.dell.com	

PC Magazine sponsors an annual survey that evaluates the service and reliability of PC vendors. You can search its site for the most recent survey. Before you purchase anything by mail or online, read "Ten Tips for Direct Success" on page 80 of the July 1997 *Computer Shopper*. Connect to Consumer World at *www.consumerworld.org* for links to consumer information, the Better Business Bureau, and product reviews.

17 Recycle & Reuse

At the Computer Reclaimation Web site (*www.computerreclamation.com*), you can take a tour through a "computer graveyard" guided by William Gibson and Ray Bradbury. Check the NP4 Web site, *www.cciw.com/np4*, for additional links related to the recycling/reuse issue.

ADDITIONAL TIPS

Tip 1: Sound Settings

If your computer is equipped for sound, you should hear audio during the videos and screentours. If you don't, check the volume control on your computer by clicking the speaker icon in the lower-right corner of your screen. You should also check the sound setting for the NP4 Book-on-CD, located on the Options menu. If you're working in a lab or office environment where sound would be disruptive, consider using headphones.

Tip 2: InfoWebs

The information on many Web sites changes frequently. Therefore, some of the Web pages that are referenced in the InfoWebs may not be available. If you type in a Web site address, but do not connect to the specified page, check the NP4 Web site at *www.cciw.com/np4*. At that site, you can link to any chapter and any InfoWeb topic to check for updated Web links.

Tip 3: Practice Tests

Let us help you get the best grade possible! Take a Practice Test anytime you want to prepare for an exam. Every chapter offers a test bank of 100+ questions. The questions are randomly selected every time you take a test, so you can take Practice Tests over and over again. You can even print out your own study guide that will help you prepare for class exams.

Tip 4: Online Glossary

If you're using the Book-on-CD and can't remember the meaning of a word that was defined in a previous chapter, simply click the Glossary button, then enter the word or select it from the list. In the printed text, all key terms are defined in the Glossary pages at the end of the book.

CHAPTER 7

LOCAL AREA NETWORKS AND E-MAIL

CONTENTS

▶ Start Video

PREVIEW

Chapter 7 provides a practical overview of microcomputer networks, such as those in your school labs or in a business where you work. In this chapter, you'll learn how to select a secure password and how to log into a network. You'll also learn how to share files with other users, and you'll pick up some tips for using e-mail.

When you have completed this chapter you should be able to:

■ Describe the resources you would find on a typical local area network

■ Explain how using a computer on a network is different from using a stand-alone computer

■ Explain the difference between sharing files on a network and using groupware

■ Describe how processing differs on networks that use dedicated file servers, peer-to-peer capability, client/server architecture, and time sharing

■ Describe the types of software you can use on a local area network

■ Explain how software licenses for networks differ from those for stand-alone computers

■ Explain how a network uses store-and-forward technology for e-mail

CHAPTER 7 LAB

E-mail

BEYOND THE SNEAKER NET

In the decade between 1976 and 1986, the microcomputer industry boomed. Microcomputer companies made record profits. The editors of *Time* magazine named the microcomputer "Man of the Year." Yet, while mainframe users enjoyed the connectivity provided by e-mail and shared files, microcomputer users were generally isolated on their stand-alone computers. Communication between microcomputers was jokingly referred to as "the sneaker net"—meaning that to transfer a file from one computer to another, you put the file on a floppy disk, then walked with the disk to another computer. White Reeboks were popular corporate footwear at the time.

The idea that microcomputer users could benefit by connecting their computers into a network became feasible about 15 years ago with the introduction of reliable, reasonably priced software and hardware designed for microcomputer networks. The availability of this hardware and software has ushered in a new era of computing, which increasingly provides ways for people to collaborate, communicate, and interact.

The purpose of this chapter is to help you understand the types of local area computer networks you would typically find in a college, university, or business. This chapter emphasizes the user's perspective, beginning with a tour of network resources. It then presents practical information on network hardware and software, including network applications such as groupware and e-mail.

SECTION A   LOCAL AREA NETWORKS

As described in Chapter 1, a computer network is a collection of computers and other devices that communicate to share data, hardware, and software. A network that is located within a relatively limited area such as a building or campus is referred to as a **local area network** (LAN). A network that covers a large geographical area is referred to as a **wide area network** (WAN). In this chapter you will learn about local area networks.

InfoWeb
1

LANs

Local area networks are found in most organizations, businesses, government offices, and educational institutions. They have even found their way into the home computing environment, allowing children and parents to work on different computers but share printers, scanners, and other peripheral devices.

Not all LANs are the same. Different types of networks provide different services, use different technology, and require users to follow different procedures. The information in this section describes how the majority of microcomputer networks work. Because a specific network might require different user procedures, however, don't hesitate to ask questions when you use an unfamiliar network.

Network Resources

What sort of resources does a LAN provide? A computer that is not connected to a network is referred to as a **stand-alone computer**. When you physically connect your computer to a local area network, using a cable or other communications channel, your computer becomes a **workstation** on the network. Note that this use of the term "workstation" differs from its use in Chapter 1, where "workstation" referred to a high-performance microcomputer. Some authors distinguish between the two uses by using the terms "network workstation" and "high-end workstation." If not, you'll have to determine the correct meaning from the context.

Your workstation provides you with your computer's usual resources, referred to as **local resources**, such as its hard drive, software, data, and printer. You also have access to **network resources**, which typically include application software, storage space for data files, and printers other than the one connected to your local workstation.

On a network, application software and storage space for data files are typically provided by a network server. A **network server** is a computer connected to the network that "serves," or distributes, resources to network users. A **network printer** provides output capabilities to network users. Each device on a network, as shown in Figure 7-1, is referred to as a **node**.

FIGURE 7-1

Network nodes include workstations, printers, and servers.

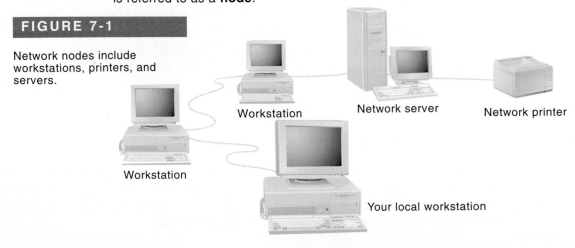

Workstation

Network server

Network printer

Workstation

Your local workstation

The Login Process

Do I have to do anything special to access network resources? Even if your computer is physically connected to a network, you cannot typically use network resources until you log into the network. When you log in, you formally identify yourself to the network by providing your user ID and password. Your user ID and password are the basis for your user account. A **user account** provides access to network resources and accumulates information about your network use by tracking when you log in and log out. A **network administrator**, also called a "network supervisor," is the person who is responsible for setting up user accounts and maintaining a network. The network administrator provides each new user with a user ID and a "starter" password.

On many networks, your user ID is derived from your real name. For example, Nancy Chin's user ID might be "nchin." User IDs typically consist of a set of characters without any spaces, so other options for Nancy's user ID would be "nancychin" or "nancy_chin." In a case-sensitive network, "NancyChin" would not be the same as "nancychin." Therefore, it is is important to carefully duplicate uppercase and lowercase letters when entering your user ID.

Like a user ID, a password is typically a single set of characters without any spaces, and might be case sensitive. On most networks, you can change your starter password to one of your own choosing. If you have this option, you should select a secure password so that other people cannot log in as you and access your files. Your password should be unique, yet something you can easily remember. How do you select a secure password? Refer to Figure 7-2 for some password do's and don'ts.

FIGURE 7-2

Use these tips to select a secure password.

DO:

- Select a password that is at least 5 characters long.
- Try to use both numbers and letters in your password.
- Select a password you can remember.
- Consider making a password by combining two or more words or the first letters of a poem or phrase.
- Change your password periodically.

DON'T:

- Select a password that is a word that can be found in a dictionary.
- Use your name, nickname, Social Security number, birth date, or name of a close relative.
- Write your password where it is easy to find—under the keyboard is the first place a password thief will look.

Entering a valid user ID and password is the beginning of the login process. As the login process continues, your workstation is connected to network drives, allowing you to use programs and data files stored on a server. The login process also connects your workstation to network resources such as a network printer.

Drive Mapping

How does my computer access data files and application software from a network server? Your workstation gains access to the server when the server hard drive is "mapped" to a drive letter. **Drive mapping** is network terminology for assigning a drive letter to a network server disk drive. For example, the login process might automatically map the server hard drive by assigning the letter F to it.

Once a drive letter has been mapped, you can access data files and application software from that drive just as you would from your local hard disk drive. Essentially, you can then use the hard drive on the server just as if it was part of your workstation computer.

Drive mappings vary from one network to another, depending on the requirements of the organization and of its users. One organization might map the server drive as F; another organization might map the server drive as J. In other organizations, multiple drives on more than one server might be mapped as F, I, J, and Z. You'll find it useful to know your network's drive mapping so that you can easily find programs and files.

The Windows operating system provides a utility called Network Neighborhood that helps you discover the network drive mapping and the other network resources that are available to your workstation. The Screentour for Figure 7-3 demonstrates how to use the Network Neighborhood.

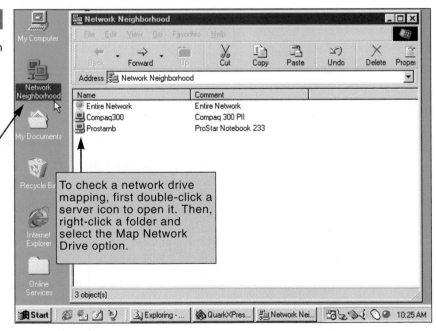

FIGURE 7-3

The Network Neighborhood icon provides information about network drive mapping and printer resources.

Clicking the Network Neighborhood icon opens a dialog box that lists the devices connected to your network.

To check a network drive mapping, first double-click a server icon to open it. Then, right-click a folder and select the Map Network Drive option.

Start
Screentour

Using Programs on a Network

When I start a program supplied by a network server, is it the same as starting a program on a stand-alone computer? As explained in Chapter 5, when you launch a program on a stand-alone computer, it is copied from your hard disk into RAM. Suppose that you want to use a word processing program that is stored on the hard disk of a network server. Will a copy of the program be loaded into the memory of the server or into the memory of your workstation?

On a typical LAN, when you start a program that is stored on a server, the program is copied to your workstation's RAM (Figure 7-4). Once the program is in memory, it runs just as if you had started it from your workstation's hard drive.

FIGURE 7-4

Suppose that you want to use the WordPerfect word processing program that is stored on a network server. Your computer requests the program. The server sends a copy of the program to your workstation's RAM, where it runs just as if it was loaded from your computer's hard disk.

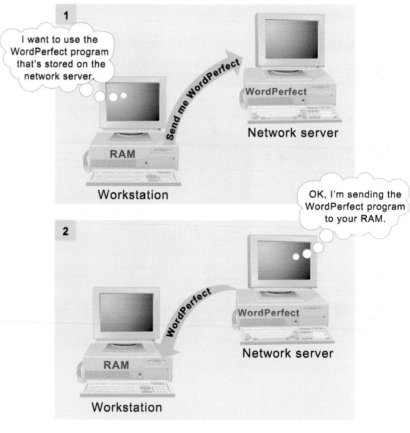

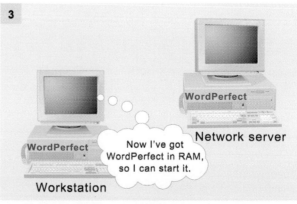

You might wonder if multiple users on the same network can use the same program simultaneously. One advantage of a network is that with proper licensing, many users can access a single program at the same time. This process is called **sharing** a program. For example, while WordPerfect is running on your workstation, other users can start the same program. At each user's request, the network server sends a copy of WordPerfect to the RAM of each user's workstation.

Sharing programs is effective for several reasons. First, less disk storage space is required because the program is stored only once on the server, instead of being stored on the hard disks of multiple stand-alone computers. Second, when a new version of the software is released, it is easier to update one copy of the program on the server than to update many copies stored on stand-alone computers. Third, purchasing a software license for a network can be less expensive than purchasing a single-user license for every workstation on the network (Figure 7-5).

FIGURE 7-5

Sharing programs on a network saves disk space, reduces maintenance, and reduces licensing costs.

Using Data Files on a Network

Is there any advantage to storing data files on the server instead of my local hard disk? You've just read that it is possible to share *programs* on a network. Can you also share *data files?* Suppose that while connected to a network, you create a document using a word processing program. You can store the document either on your local hard disk or on the server hard disk. If you store the file on your local hard disk, you typically can access the file only from your workstation. However, if you store the file on the hard disk of the server, you can access the file from any workstation on the network. Other network users can also access the files that you have stored on the server, as shown in Figure 7-6, although most networks provide you with the option of restricting access.

FIGURE 7-6

Files stored on a server can be accessed from any workstation.

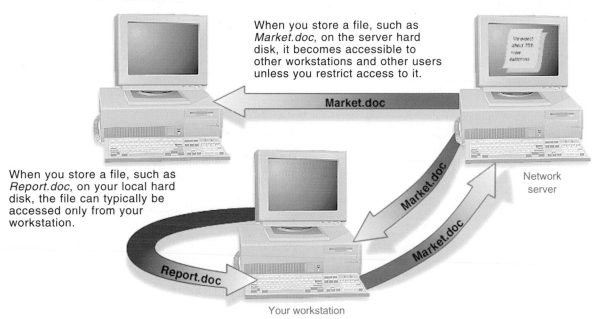

When you store a file, such as *Market.doc*, on the server hard disk, it becomes accessible to other workstations and other users unless you restrict access to it.

Market.doc

When you store a file, such as *Report.doc*, on your local hard disk, the file can typically be accessed only from your workstation.

Network server

Market.doc

Market.doc

Report.doc

Your workstation

 Start Animation

Although a *program file* from the file server can be used on more than one workstation at the same time, most of the *data files* on a network server can be opened by only one user at a time. When one user has a file open, it is locked to other users. **File locking** is a sensible precaution against losing valuable data. If the network allowed two users to open and edit the same data file, both users could make changes to the file. But what if one user's changes contradicted the other user's changes? Whose changes would be incorporated in the final version of the file?

CHAPTER 7

Suppose that two users were allowed to make changes to the same file at the same time. Each user could open a copy of the original file and modify it. The first user to finish making changes would save the file on the server. So far, so good—the first user has replaced the original version of the file with an edited version. Remember, however, that the second user has been making revisions to the *original* file, but she has no idea that the first user's revisions exist. When the second user saves her revised version of the file, the changes made by the first user are overwritten by the second user's version, as shown in Figure 7-7.

FIGURE 7-7

If networks did not lock files, two people could edit the same file at the same time, but one person's revisions would be overwritten by the other person's revisions.

The original document is not well written and the percentage is wrong. Sam and Gracie both decide to fix it.

Sam's workstation

Gracie's workstation

If Sam and Gracie were allowed to open the document at the same time, they could edit the document in two different ways.

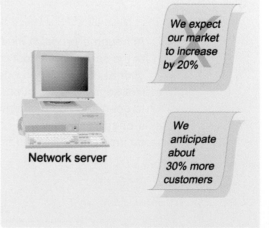

Network server

Start Animation

Sam stores the edited document on the server. Later, when Gracie stores her version of the document on the server, it overwrites Sam's version, erasing all of his work.

Using a Network Printer

How does my software know when it is supposed to send documents to the network printer instead of my local printer?   Suppose that you have a Canon ink jet printer connected to your computer. Your dorm room just got wired to the campus network, and you've been told that you can access the computer lab's Lexmark color laser printer over the network. Before you can access the Lexmark printer, you have to install its driver software. During the installation process, you can indicate that the Lexmark is a network printer. Once Windows has this information, any printouts that you send to the Lexmark printer will be routed over the network. Figure 7-8 provides information on how to add a network printer using the Windows Add Printer Wizard.

FIGURE 7-8

When you use the Add Printer Wizard, you can specify whether a printer is connected to the network or to your local computer.

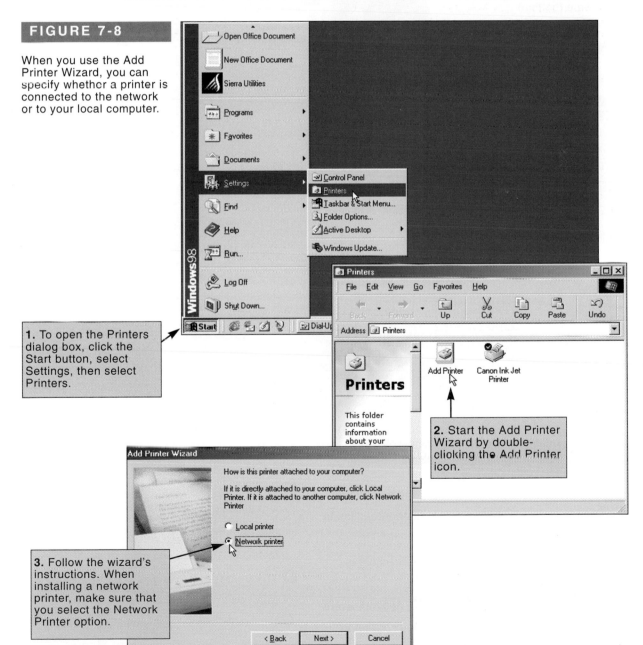

1. To open the Printers dialog box, click the Start button, select Settings, then select Printers.

2. Start the Add Printer Wizard by double-clicking the Add Printer icon.

3. Follow the wizard's instructions. When installing a network printer, make sure that you select the Network Printer option.

CHAPTER 7

When your computer is connected to more than one printer, the printer that you use most frequently is referred to as the **default printer**. If you do not want to use the default printer for a particular document, you can select a different printer using either of the two methods illustrated in Figure 7-9.

FIGURE 7-9

You can select a printer by using the Start button to access the Printers dialog box (top) or you can use the Print dialog box provided by your application software (bottom).

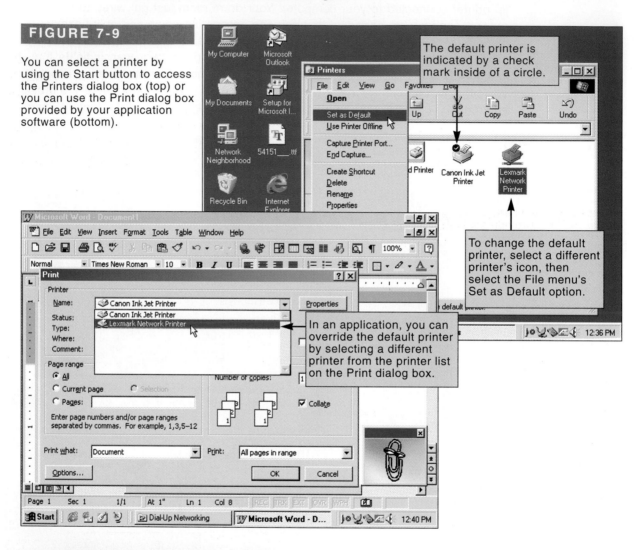

The default printer is indicated by a check mark inside of a circle.

To change the default printer, select a different printer's icon, then select the File menu's Set as Default option.

In an application, you can override the default printer by selecting a different printer from the printer list on the Print dialog box.

QUICKCHECK A

1 A network _____ is a computer connected to a network that distributes files to network users.

2 In many networks, the server hard drive is _____ as drive F.

3 Assuming proper licensing, two network users should be able to use the same program at the same time. True or false? _____

4 While Joan is editing a word processing document called *Budget.doc*, Karl can edit this document at the same time. True or false? _____

5 The printer that you use most frequently is referred to as the _____ printer.

 Check Answers

SECTION B NETWORK HARDWARE

In the previous section, you looked at local area network resources and considered the advantages of computer networks. Now you'll learn about expansion cards, cables, servers, and other hardware components of a network.

Network Interface Cards

What establishes the physical connection for the computers in a network?

A network interface card is the key hardware component for connecting a computer to a local area network. A **NIC** (pronounced "nick;" the acronym for "network interface card") is a small circuit board that sends data from your workstation out to the network and collects incoming data for your workstation. A desktop computer NIC plugs into an expansion slot on the computer motherboard. A notebook computer NIC is usually a PCMCIA card. The photos in Figure 7-10 illustrate desktop and notebook computer NICs.

FIGURE 7-10

Desktop (left) and notebook (right) network interface cards are expansion cards that can be used to connect a computer to a network.

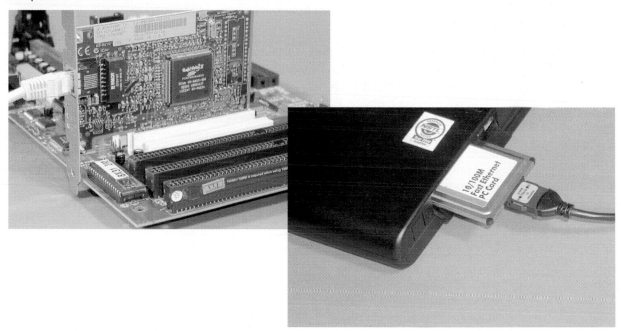

Each server, workstation, printer, or other device on a network must have a NIC. Different types of networks use different types of NICs. If you want to add a computer to a network, you need to know the network type so you can purchase the appropriate NIC. Popular network types include **Ethernet** and **Token Ring**. You can purchase NICs for these networks in either 10 megabit or 100 megabit speeds. The 100 megabit cards provide faster data transfer. The network supervisor can tell you which speed is supported on your network.

InfoWeb
2
Ethernet

CHAPTER 7

Cable and Wireless Networks

Are network nodes always connected by cables? Most networks use cables to connect servers, workstations, and printers. Today's networks typically use **twisted-pair cable**, sometimes called "UTP" (unshielded twisted pair) or "STP" (shielded twisted pair), which looks similar to a telephone cable and has a square, plastic **RJ-45 connector** on either end. Another option is **coaxial cable**, which resembles a cable-TV cable with a round, silver **BNC connector** on either end. Figure 7-11 illustrates both types of cable.

FIGURE 7-11

Twisted-pair cable (left) and coaxial cable (right) can be used to connect a NIC to other network equipment.

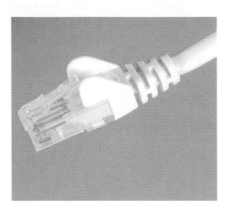 

InfoWeb
3
Wireless Networks

Instead of using cables, **wireless networks** use radio or infrared signals to transmit data from one network device to another. Wireless networks are handy in environments where wiring is difficult to install, such as in historical buildings. In addition, wireless networks provide mobility. For example, a wireless network would make it possible to carry a notebook or hand-held computer throughout a large warehouse to take inventory. A third application for wireless networks is for temporary installations, when drilling holes to install wiring is not practical or economical. The NICs for a wireless network contain the transmitting devices necessary to send data to other devices on the local area network.

Network Hubs

Do workstations connect directly to a server? On most of today's networks, the cable from a workstation NIC connects to a **network hub**, which is a device that joins communications lines together. In a typical network configuration, cables from one or more workstations connect to the hub, then a single cable connects the hub to a server, as illustrated in Figure 7-12.

FIGURE 7-12

A hub serves as a central connection point for workstation and server cables.

Network Servers

> When I am using a network, is my data processed locally or on the network server?

When you use a stand-alone computer, all of your data is processed by your computer's microprocessor. When your computer is connected to a network, on the other hand, the device that processes your data depends on the type of servers included on your network. Server types include dedicated servers, non-dedicated servers, print servers, application servers, and host computers. The rest of this section describes the characteristics of these server types.

A **dedicated file server** is devoted solely to the task of delivering programs and data files to workstations. As you can see in Figure 7-13, a dedicated file server does not process data or run programs for the workstations. Instead, programs run using the memory and processor of the workstation.

FIGURE 7-13

A dedicated file server delivers programs and data to workstations, but does not process data for the workstations.

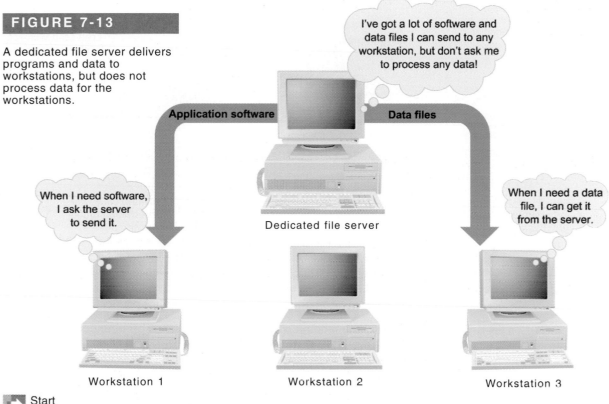

I've got a lot of software and data files I can send to any workstation, but don't ask me to process any data!

Application software

Data files

Dedicated file server

When I need software, I ask the server to send it.

When I need a data file, I can get it from the server.

Workstation 1   Workstation 2   Workstation 3

Start Animation

A typical local area network uses a microcomputer as a file server. A minicomputer or a mainframe computer can also be a file server, however. Many businesses with older minicomputer and mainframe systems have essentially recycled this equipment by adding microcomputer networking capabilities.

CHAPTER 7

In some cases, a computer on a network performs a dual role as both file server and workstation. This setup is referred to as a **non-dedicated file server** or **peer-to-peer** capability. When you use a non-dedicated file server, your computer functions like a normal workstation, but other workstations can access programs and data files from the hard disk of your computer, as shown in Figure 7-14.

FIGURE 7-14

A non-dedicated file server functions like any other workstation. It also can be accessed to provide other workstations with programs and data files.

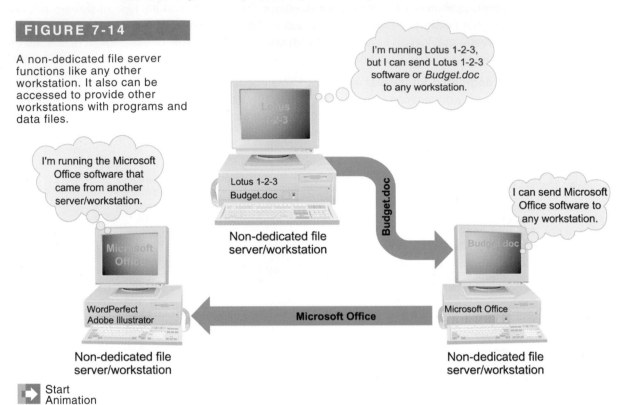

I'm running Lotus 1-2-3, but I can send Lotus 1-2-3 software or *Budget.doc* to any workstation.

I'm running the Microsoft Office software that came from another server/workstation.

I can send Microsoft Office software to any workstation.

Lotus 1-2-3
Budget.doc

Budget.doc

Non-dedicated file server/workstation

WordPerfect
Adobe Illustrator

Microsoft Office

Microsoft Office

Non-dedicated file server/workstation

Non-dedicated file server/workstation

Start Animation

A **print server** receives files from workstations, then forwards these files to a specific network printer. A print server can be the same computer as the file server, or it can be another microcomputer, minicomputer, or mainframe computer connected to the network.

A print server typically manages a **print queue** ("queue" is pronounced like the letter "Q"), which is a special holding area where files are stored until they are printed. A **print job** is a file that has been sent to a print queue. What happens if a print server receives more than one print job? Most networks would not allow two files to travel simultaneously over the network. However, it is possible that before the printer has completed one printout, other files arrive to be printed. When more than one user sends a file to the print queue, the files are added to the print queue and printed in the order in which they are received.

InfoWeb
4

Client/Server

An **application server** is a computer that runs a specific application software package and forwards the results of its processing to workstations as requested. An application server makes it possible to use the processing power of both the server and the workstation. Also referred to as **client/server architecture**, use of an application server splits processing between the workstation *client* and the network *server*. Suppose you want to search for a particular record in a 50,000-record database stored on a network server. Study Figure 7-15 to see how client/server architecture takes advantage of the processing capacity of both the workstation and the server.

FIGURE 7-15

An application server typically runs database software and performs database functions as requested by the workstations. The results received by a workstation can be further processed by that workstation.

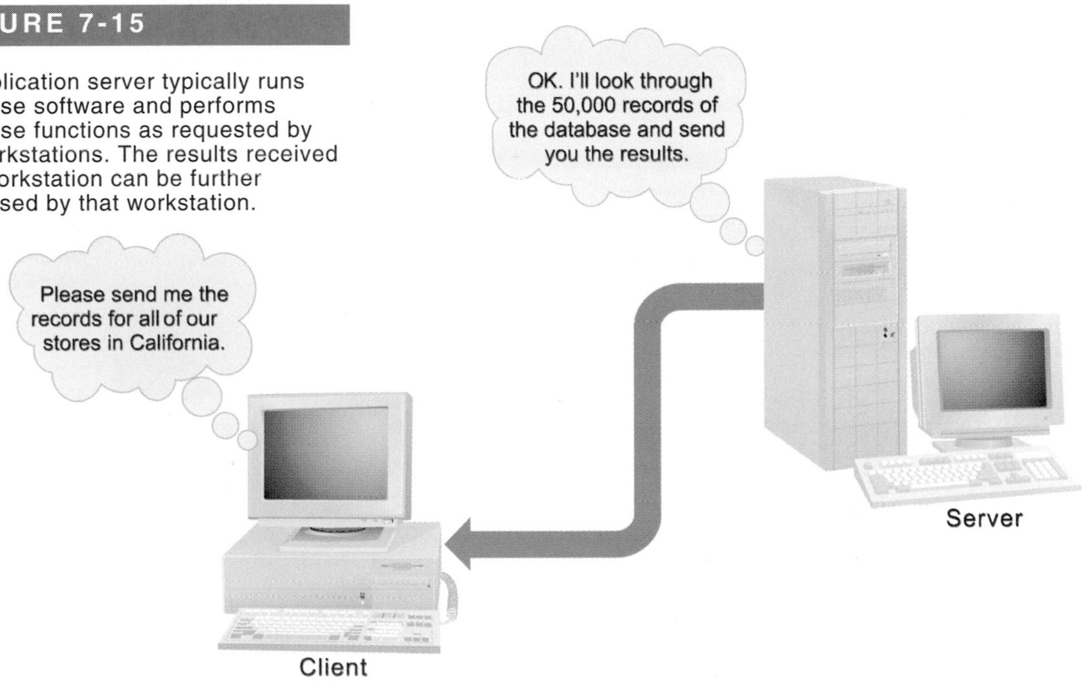

OK. I'll look through the 50,000 records of the database and send you the results.

Please send me the records for all of our stores in California.

Server

Client

▶ Start
Animation

Some networks include a **host computer**, which is typically a minicomputer or a mainframe with attached terminals. When you use a host computer from a terminal, all of the processing takes place on the host. Your terminal has a keyboard and a screen, but it does not have a local storage device, and it does little or no processing on its own. Instead, the host accepts commands from terminals and sends back a display of results. Because the terminals have no processing power of their own, they cannot further process the results they receive. For example, if your terminal receives a list of 50 people sorted by address, you could not sort the list by last name on your terminal. You would have to ask the host to sort the list and send you the new results.

Although a system containing a host computer and terminals fits our general definition of a *network*, it is more customary to call it a **time-sharing system**. Because terminals can perform little or no processing on their own, every terminal must wait for the host to process its request. The terminals essentially *share* the host's processor by being allocated a fraction of a second of processing time. Unlike an application server, a time-sharing system host computer typically runs more than one application because it must provide both the software and the processing power for all of the terminals.

CHAPTER 7

Before powerful microcomputer networks became available, connecting terminals to a host computer provided relatively low-cost computer access. For economic reasons, many organizations have not yet moved important data and programs from mainframe hosts to microcomputer networks.

It is possible to connect a microcomputer to a host using **terminal emulation software**, but your microcomputer will behave just like a terminal and will receive only a display of results, not data that it can process (Figure 7-16). If you want to process data sent by a host, you must use communications software instead of using terminal emulation software to transfer the data to your computer.

FIGURE 7-16

In a typical time-sharing system, a mainframe computer host stores and processes all of the data. Terminals without storage capacity or processing power merely act as input and output devices so that users can input data, specify processing tasks, and read the displayed output.

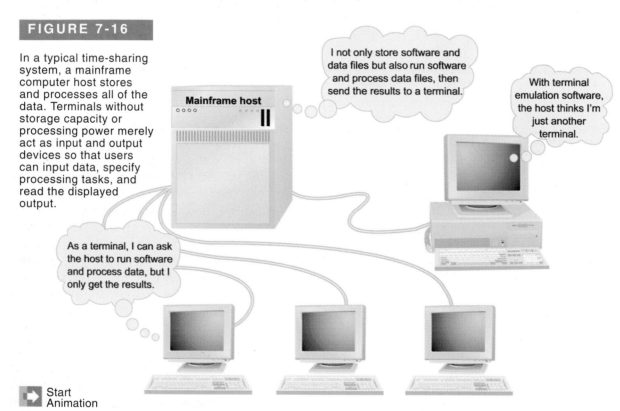

Start Animation

QUICKCHECK   B

1 The circuit board that connects a computer to a local area network is called a(n) _____.

2 A(n) _____ server is devoted to the task of delivering programs and data files to workstations.

3 A computer connected to a network that functions both as a file server and a workstation is referred to as a(n) _____ server.

4 Client/server architecture takes advantage of the processing capabilities of both the workstation and the server. True or false? _____

5 On some networks, a(n) _____ computer processes data, then outputs the results on the screen of a terminal.

Check Answers

SECTION C   SOFTWARE FOR NETWORKS

The software on a local area network typically includes specialized network software as well as many of the same applications that you might use on a stand-alone computer.

Network Operating Systems

InfoWeb 5

NOS

Does a network require any special software? Today's popular desktop operating systems, such as Windows 95, Windows 98, Windows NT Workstation, and Windows 2000 Professional, include the software necessary to establish communication with a network server. When you install a NIC and boot your computer, the operating system will detect the card and guide you through the process of installing its driver software. With that task accomplished, your computer will automatically connect to the network every time it boots. The network software that is built into your computer's operating system handles the communication between your workstation and the network server. For example, if you want to open a file that is stored on the server's hard disk, your workstation's software can relay the request to the server.

FIGURE 7-17

Novell NetWare is a popular network operating system optimized for installations that need an efficient file server.

A **network operating system** (NOS) is the software that manages network resources, controls the flow of data, maintains security, and tracks user accounts. A network operating system has two components: network server software and network client software. **Network server software**, which is installed on a file server, controls file access from the server's hard disk, manages the print queue, and tracks user data such as IDs and passwords. **Network client software**, which is installed on the local hard disk of each workstation, gathers your login information, handles drive mapping, and directs printouts to the network printer.

Contrary to what you might assume, the server and client software components do not necessarily have to match. Suppose that your computer uses the Windows NT Workstation operating system. Can you access only a server that uses Windows NT Server software? No. The network client software that is provided as part of Windows 95, 98, NT Workstation, and 2000 Professional allows you to access servers running a variety of software, including Linux, UNIX, and Novell NetWare (shown in Figure 7-17), as well as Windows NT Server and Windows 2000 Server.

As an additional twist to network operating systems, it is interesting to note that many desktop operating systems have some *server* capabilities. You could, for example, set up a small network by installing Windows 98 on a server and Windows 95, 98, NT Workstation, or 2000 Professional on the workstations. Obviously, multiple options exist for network server software and network workstation software. The important point to remember is that your Windows desktop operating system provides you with client software that is compatible with most of the popular network server software.

CHAPTER 7

Stand-alone Applications on a Network

Do I need to buy a special version of my favorite application software to use it on a network? Most application software designed for stand-alone computers can be installed on a network server, which sends copies to individual workstations as requested. Typically, your favorite word processing, spreadsheet, presentation and graphics software will work on a network just as they do on a stand-alone computer.

Some applications that you use on a stand-alone computer have built-in networking features that appear only when the software is installed on a network. For example, when you use word processing software that has been installed on a network, your software might provide a dialog box that lets you send files to another person on the network.

Installing Windows Software on a Network

How does my Windows menu know what's on the file server? Suppose that the office is buzzing about a great new graphics package that has just been installed on the network server. You check out your Windows menu of programs, but can't find the new software. What's the problem? Before you can access a program on the file server, your local version of Windows needs to know that the software has been installed.

After a new program has been installed on a network server, you or your network manager must also complete a workstation installation of the software. A **workstation installation** copies some—but not all—of the program files to your local hard disk, then updates the Windows Registry and the Windows Start menu to include a listing for the new program. On some networks, the workstation installation can be performed from a remote location such as the network manager's office. Sound complicated? Just remember that if you do not have a listing for a program that resides on a network server, you probably need to complete a workstation installation.

Software Licenses for Networks

Can an organization buy just one copy of a software package and put it on the network for everyone to use? In an organization with 100 users, word processing capability might cost $295 for a single copy. At that price, 100 copies would be $29,000. Because it would be very inexpensive, an organization might be tempted to purchase a single copy of a software package, then place it on the network for everyone to use. However, using a single-user license for multiple users typically violates the software's copyright.

Most single-user software licenses allow only one person to use the software at a time. However, many software publishers also offer a network license that permits use by multiple people on a network. A **network license** is essentially another name for a multiuser license or a site license. It will cost more than a single-user license, but less than purchasing single-user licenses for all of the users. For example, a word processing software package that costs $295 for a single-user license might have a $5,000 network license that allows up to 100 people to use the software. Network licenses can be obtained for most software by contacting the software publisher.

Groupware and Workflow Software

Is there a way for two or more people to work together on the same data file? When local area networks were first introduced, typically only one user could work on a document at any given time. However, this restriction on sharing files did not support many organizational activities that require collaboration and communication among employees. For example, in most organizations, people exchange information using memos, phone conversations, and face-to-face meetings. Employees collect, organize, and share information, which must be stored in a centralized repository. Documents and forms flow through organizations, picking up required signatures and approvals. Employees contribute sections of text that are compiled into a single report.

As the use of networks increased, organizations and businesses began to demand software that would facilitate the flow and sharing of documents. Software publishers responded to this demand by producing groupware and workflow software.

Groupware

Groupware, introduced in Chapter 2, is application software that supports collaborative work by managing schedules, shared documents, and intra-group communications. A key feature of groupware is document version management. When more than one group member revises a document, whose revisions should be accepted for the final version? The solution frequently implemented by groupware is to maintain all revisions within the document so the workgroup can accept or reject each revision, as shown in Figure 7-18.

FIGURE 7-18

In this shared document, one user's revisions are shown in red, and the other user's revisions are shown in blue.

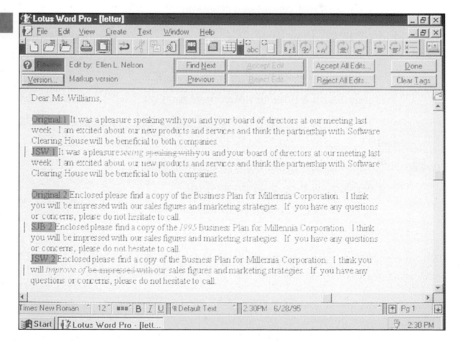

InfoWeb
7

Workflow
Software

Workflow software, also referred to as "document routing software," automates the process of electronically routing documents from one person to another in a specified sequence and time. Workflow software facilitates a process or a series of steps. For example, suppose you apply for a loan. The bank has a specific procedure for processing the loan application. First, a credit officer checks your credit rating and makes a recommendation about whether to accept or reject your application. Next, the bank loan committee must approve the application. Finally, the approved application is processed by your loan officer. To facilitate this process, workflow software would route the loan application to the first bank officer, specify the due date for action, collect the necessary approval, then route the application to the next officer, and so on.

Workflow software is based on a "process-centered model" as opposed to groupware's "information-centered model." With workflow software, the focus is on a series of steps. With groupware, the documents are the focus.

Q U I C K C H E C K   C

1 If your computer uses the Windows 98 operating system and you want to connect to a network that has a Windows NT server, you must switch to the Windows NT server operating system. True or false? [ ]

2 If your computer is connected to a network, you must install a special network version of your favorite application software. True or false? [ ]

3 If an organization is planning to use software on a network, it should purchase a(n) [ ] license so multiple users can legally use the software.

4 If you are a team leader and you want your team members to collaborate on a project using the network, you might try to find a(n) [ ] product.

5 If you were the manager of a loan department in a bank, you might use [ ] software to automatically send loan applications to each member of your department for processing and approval.

➡ Check
Answers

USER FOCUS E-MAIL

Lab
E-mail

E-mail, or "electronic mail," is correspondence conducted between one or more users on a network. E-mail is a more efficient means of communication than ground or air mail. Rather than waiting for a piece of paper to be physically transported by office mail or the Postal Service, you can send an electronic version of a message directly to someone's electronic mail box. E-mail also helps you avoid frustrating "telephone tag."

How E-mail Works

When I send an e-mail message does it go directly to the recipient? What if the recipient's workstation is not turned on? An **e-mail message** is essentially a document sent electronically from one user to another. An **e-mail system** consists of the hardware and software that collect and deliver e-mail messages. Typically, e-mail services are provided by a local area network or by an Internet server. The software on the network or Internet server that controls the flow of e-mail is called **e-mail server software**. The software on a workstation that helps each user read, compose, send, and delete messages is called **e-mail client software**. E-mail systems are sometimes classified as groupware because they facilitate communication among members of a workgroup.

InfoWeb
8

E-mail

E-mail messages are *stored* on a server. When you want to read this mail, the server *forwards* the messages to your workstation. Hence e-mail is a **store-and-forward technology**. Because the server stores the messages, your workstation does not need to be turned on when someone sends e-mail to you. In many ways, an e-mail system works like the traditional postal system. The server that stores your mail is similar to your local post office because it holds your mail until it can be delivered to your house. The mail box located on your computer is similar to the mailbox at your house because it is where your messages wait for you to read them and where you can leave messages that are waiting to be sent.

FIGURE 7-19

E-mail uses store-and-forward technology so that your mail remains stored on a server until you are ready to read it.

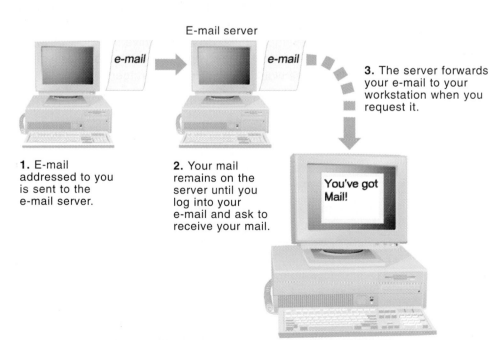

E-mail server

3. The server forwards your e-mail to your workstation when you request it.

1. E-mail addressed to you is sent to the e-mail server.

2. Your mail remains on the server until you log into your e-mail and ask to receive your mail.

You've got Mail!

Your workstation

CHAPTER 7

E-mail Servers

Where is my e-mail server? The computer that stores and forwards your e-mail can be part of a local area network or the Internet. Many businesses and educational institutions operate e-mail servers as part of their LANs. Within a college or university, for example, a LAN-based e-mail server would provide mail services to faculty, staff, and students with network accounts. LAN users can send and receive e-mail any time they are logged into the network.

Mail servers also exist on the Internet. These servers provide e-mail services to the general public for a small monthly fee or for free. For example, an e-mail account is included in the monthly subscription fee for America Online (AOL), AT&T WorldNet, or CompuServe. Free e-mail accounts are provided by advertiser-supported Internet sites, such as Hotmail and MailCity. Typically, if you have an account on an Internet e-mail server, you would collect your mail by establishing an Internet connection using a phone line and your computer's modem. Chapter 8 provides additional information about connecting to the Internet.

FIGURE 7-20

Free e-mail accounts are available on advertiser-supported Internet sites.

E-mail Addresses

How can I find someone's e-mail address? Just like ordinary mail, e-mail must be addressed correctly so that it will arrive at its destination. Typically, an **e-mail address** is a person's network user ID, an @ symbol, and the name of his or her e-mail server. For example, suppose that a university student whose user ID is dee_greene has a mail account on the campus e-mail server called rutgers.edu. This student's e-mail address would be dee_greene@rutgers.edu.

You can discover someone's e-mail address in several ways. First, and perhaps easiest, is to just ask, "Hey, what's your e-mail address?" Alternatively, you might be able to look up an e-mail address in a LAN directory or on the Internet. It is becoming a common practice for businesses and schools to list e-mail addresses along with their telephone numbers. Some e-mail addresses are listed on "people finder" sites on the Internet, such as *peoplefinder.excite.com* or *people.yahoo.com*.

Your e-mail address can change if you "move" to a different network or to a different Internet e-mail server. When your address changes, you should remember to send your friends, colleagues, and clients an e-mail with your new contact information. In recent years, e-mail forwarding has become popular. It works in this way: You subscribe to an e-mail forwarding service, such as *www.bigfoot.com*, which provides you with a permanent e-mail address. The forwarding service does not provide you with post office services or a personal mailbox. Its sole purpose is to forward your mail to whatever LAN-based or Internet-based e-mail server is currently handling your mail. Your address on the e-mail forwarding service remains the same, regardless of where you might "move" your actual e-mailbox.

E-mail Gateways

Can I send e-mail to people on other networks or the Internet? Many LAN-based e-mail systems are connected to other e-mail systems or to the Internet through an electronic link called a **gateway**. These gateways allow you to send e-mail to people who are on other networks. When you send an e-mail message to a user on another computer network, the message is transferred through the gateway and relayed to its destination. For example, subscribers to Internet services such as AOL can communicate with AT&T WorldNet subscribers, as well as with people on university, business, or government networks. In today's connected world, sending e-mail to someone on another continent is essentially the same as sending it to the person in the office next door. With e-mail, you do not need extra postage for overseas mail—the e-mail address is sufficient to route a message to its destination anywhere in the world.

Reading E-mail

How do I use e-mail? Your e-mail messages are transmitted through an e-mail system and stored on a host or network server in an area you can think of as your local post office. When you use your e-mail client software to log into the e-mail system and check your mail, new messages are transferred to your computer's e-mailbox. You can choose to display and read the mail on your computer screen, print it, delete it, reply to it, forward it, or save it on disk. Figure 7-21 shows how a user's mailbox might look when accessed with Microsoft Outlook Express e-mail client software.

FIGURE 7-21

Your e-mailbox lists new messages.

Buttons at the top of the mail window help you reply to, forward, send, and delete messages.

Your Inbox lists all of the messages in your e-mailbox. An icon that looks like an unopened envelope indicates unread mail.

The text of the new message is displayed in the lower section of the window.

Start Screentour

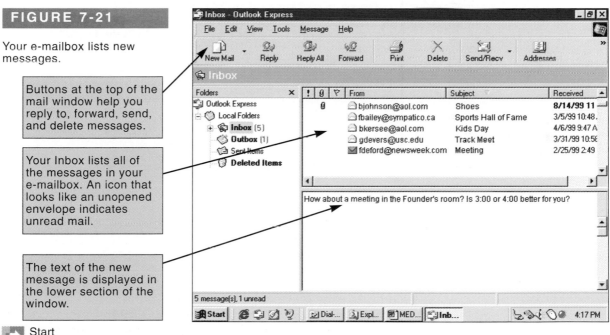

CHAPTER 7

Replying to E-mail

Why are those > symbols in my e-mail? Suppose that you receive e-mail from your supervisor indicating the dates for the next sales meeting. Unfortunately, the meeting conflicts with your vacation. You decide to reply to the supervisor's e-mail to see whether you need to reschedule your vacation. You click the Reply button on your e-mail software. The screen changes so that you now see the supervisor's message, but each line has a > symbol in front of it. What's happened?

As part of your reply, most e-mail client software includes the text of the message to which you are replying. This text is preceded with > symbols. You then type the text of your reply above the text marked with the > symbols. When you send your reply, it will include your message and the message to which you are replying. In that way, your reply contains the text of the original e-mail to help remind the recipient of the context of the discussion.

FIGURE 7-22

Replying to e-mail is easy—simply use the Reply button.

When you reply to an e-mail message, your e-mail client automatically fills in the To, From, and Subject lines.

Typically, you will type the text of your reply above the text of the original message.

The ">" symbol indicates the text of the message to which you are replying.

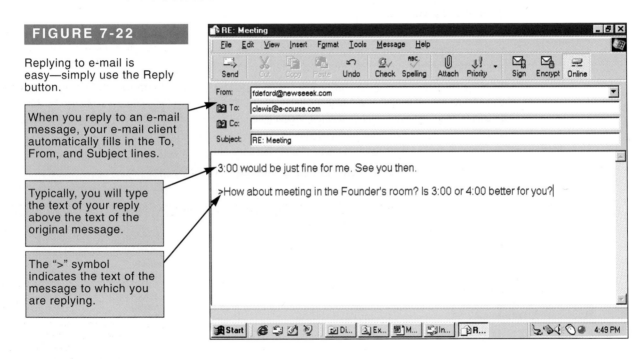

Composing New Messages

How does my e-mail software help me compose and send messages? Your
e-mail software has a button or menu option for New Mail that displays a message
form. The first item for the form is the recipient's mail address. You can type in this
address or select it from an address book that contains a list of e-mail addresses for
the people with whom you correspond frequently. You can even set up groups in your
address book. For example, you could create a "CarPool" group containing the e-mail
addresses of the people in your car pool. You can easily e-mail everyone in the car pool
by sending one e-mail addressed to "Car Pool."

The e-mail form usually contains a cc: option so that you can send a copy of an e-mail
to someone other than the main recipient. The form also includes a subject area in
which you specify the topic of the e-mail.

The e-mail form includes a space in which you can type the text of your message. Like
most word processors, e-mail software takes care of word wrap, but don't expect it to
provide many formatting options. Standard e-mail is plain text—no bold, no underline,
no fancy fonts. If you want to send a formatted document, you'll typically have to use
an attachment.

Most e-mail systems allow you to send an **e-mail attachment**, which is a file such as
a document, worksheet, or graphic that travels through the e-mail system along with an
e-mail message. For example, suppose you've created a poster for a community beach
cleanup day. You stored the file on your disk as *Beach Cleanup.bmp*, and now you want
to send it to the head of the cleanup committee so that she can have it printed. Figure
7-23 shows you how to attach this file to an e-mail message.

FIGURE 7-23

Sending an e-mail attachment.

1. Create a new message and address it to the person to whom you are sending the attachment.

2. Use the menus or the toolbar buttons provided by your e-mail software to attach the file containing the attachment.

3. An icon indicates the name of the file you attached. Send the mail following your usual procedures. The recipient of the message can click the icon to see the attachment.

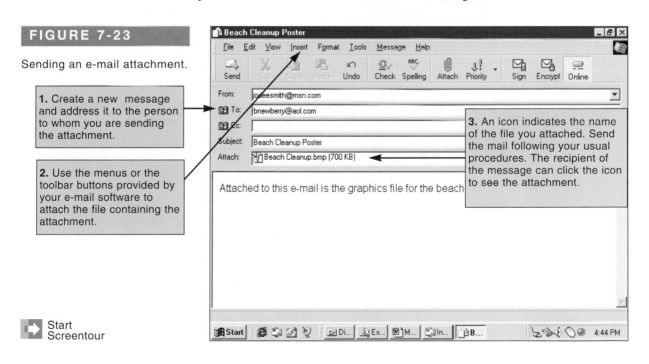

Start
Screentour

Managing Your E-mail

I know how to write letters and memos—is there anything special I need to know about writing e-mail messages? E-mail is not exactly the same as using the post office. With e-mail you can send messages immediately—your letters don't sit around waiting for you to take them to the post office. You can send the same message to multiple people as easily as you can send a message to a single person. It is a simple process to reply automatically to messages you receive as well.

The advantages of e-mail can also create potential problems—for example, you might regret the contents of a message sent off in haste. Also, it's easy to let an overwhelming number of messages accumulate in your mailbox. Here are some tips to help you avoid e-mail problems:

- **Read your mail regularly.** When you use e-mail, your correspondents expect a quick response. You lose much of the advantage of e-mail if you check your mailbox only once every two weeks!

- **Delete messages after you read them.** Your e-mail is stored, along with everyone else's, on a file server where storage space is valuable. Leaving old messages in your mailbox takes up space that could be used more productively.

- **You don't have to reply to every e-mail message.** The purpose of some e-mail messages is to give you information. Don't reply unless you have a reason to respond, such as to answer a question. Sending a message to say "I got your message" just creates unnecessary mail traffic.

- **If you receive mail addressed to a group, it might be better to reply only to one person in the group.** You might receive mail as a member of a mailing list; the same message will be sent to everyone on the list. If you use the automatic reply feature of your e-mail system, your message is likely to be sent to everyone on the list. Use this option only if your reply is important for everyone to see.

- **Think before you send.** It is easy to write a message in haste or in anger and send it off before you have time to think it through. If you're upset, write your message, but wait a day before you send it.

- **Don't write anything you want to remain confidential.** E-mail is easily forwarded to other people. Suppose you write something unflattering about Rob in an e-mail message to Julie. Julie can easily forward your message to Rob.

- **Don't get sloppy.** Your e-mail is a reflection of you, your school, and your employer. Use a spelling checker if one is available; if not, proofread your message before you send it. Use standard grammar, punctuation, and capitalization.

- **Use proper netiquette.** Netiquette is online jargon for "Internet etiquette." It is a series of customs or guidelines for maintaining civilized communication in online discussions and e-mail messages. For example, netiquette guidelines point out that a message in all uppercase means you're shouting. You should avoid this style of message unless you want other people to regard your message as an emotional outburst. You can, however, use "smileys," such as :-) to express emotions and feelings in your e-mail.

ISSUE   HOW PRIVATE IS E-MAIL?

When you drop an envelope in the corner mailbox, you probably expect it to arrive at its destination unopened and with its contents kept safe from prying eyes. When you make a phone call, you might assume that your conversation will proceed unmonitored by wiretaps or other listening devices. Can you also expect an e-mail message to be read only by the person to whom it is addressed?

E-mail Privacy

In a recent poll conducted by *MacWorld* magazine, managers from 25 percent of the companies surveyed said that they read employee e-mail. But this intentional eavesdropping is only one way in which the contents of your e-mail messages might become public. The recipient of your e-mail can forward it to one or more people—people who you never intended for it to reach. Your e-mail messages could pop up on a technician's screen in the course of system maintenance or repairs. Also, keep in mind that e-mail messages—including those that you have deleted from your own PC—might be stored on backups of the e-mail server. You might wonder if such open access to your e-mail is legal. The answer in most cases is yes.

In the United States, the federal Omnibus Crime Control and Safe Streets Act of 1968 and the Electronic Communications Privacy Act of 1986 prohibit public and private employers from engaging in surreptitious surveillance of employee activity through the use of electronic devices. However, two exceptions to these privacy statutes exist. The first exception permits an employer to monitor electronic communications if one party to the communication has consented to the monitoring. An employer must inform employees of this policy before undertaking any monitoring. The second exception permits employers to monitor their employees' electronic communications if there exists a legitimate business need and if the monitoring takes place within the business-owned communications system.

Employees have not been successful in defending their rights to e-mail privacy. For example, in 1996, a Pillsbury employee was fired from his job for making unprofessional comments in an e-mail to his supervisor. The employee sued because he claimed that the company had repeatedly assured its employees that e-mail was private. The court ruled that the employee's right to privacy did not outweigh the interests of the company. Although it would seem that the company violated the requirement to inform employees as required by the first exception to the privacy statutes, the fact that the company owned the e-mail system gave it the right to monitor any correspondence carried out over that system.

Like employees of a business, students who use a school's e-mail system cannot be assured of e-mail privacy. When a CalTech student was accused of sexually harassing a female student by sending lewd e-mail to her and to her boyfriend, investigators retrieved all of the student's e-mail from the archives of the e-mail server. The student was expelled from the university even though he claimed that the e-mail had been "spoofed" to make it look as though he had sent it, when it had actually been sent by someone else.

Why would an employer want to know the contents of employee e-mail? Why would a school be concerned with the correspondence of its students? It is probably true that some organizations simply snoop on the off chance that some important information might be discovered. Other organizations have more legitimate reasons for monitoring e-mail. An organization that owns an e-mail system could be held responsible for the consequences of actions related to the contents of e-mail messages on that system. For example, a school has a responsibility to protect students from harassment. If it fails to do so, it could be sued along with the author of the offending e-mail message. Organizations also recognize a need to protect themselves from false rumors and industrial espionage. For example, a business would want to know if an employee was supplying its competitor with information on product research and development.

Many schools and businesses have established e-mail privacy policies, which explain the conditions under which you can and cannot expect your e-mail to remain private. Court decisions, however, seem to support the notion that because an organization owns and operates its e-mail system, the organization owns the e-mail messages that are generated on its system. The individual who authors an e-mail message does not own it and therefore has no rights related to it. A company can, therefore, legally monitor your e-mail. You should use your e-mail account with the expectation that some of your mail *will* be read from time to time. Think of your e-mail as a postcard, rather than a letter, and save your controversial comments for face-to-face conversations.

WHAT DO YOU THINK?

1. Do you think that most people believe that their e-mail is private?　　　　　　　　◯ Yes　◯ No　◯ Not sure

2. Do you agree with CalTech's decision to expel the student who was accused of sending harassing e-mail to another student?　　　◯ Yes　◯ No　◯ Not sure

3. Should the laws be changed to make it illegal to monitor e-mail without court approval?　　◯ Yes　◯ No　◯ Not sure

4. Would you have different privacy expectations regarding an e-mail account at your place of work and an account that you purchase from an e-mail service provider?　　　　　◯ Yes　◯ No　◯ Not sure

➡ Save Responses

CHAPTER 7 — REVIEW ACTIVITIES

INTERACTIVE SUMMARY

The Interactive Summary helps you select important concepts and facts from this chapter. Fill in the blanks to best complete each sentence. When using the NP4 CD or NP4 Web site, you can click the Check Answers buttons to automatically score your answers. Place your Tracking Disk in the floppy disk drive if you want to save your scores.

A computer _____ is a collection of computers and other devices that communicate to share data, hardware, and software. When a network is located within a relatively limited area, such as a building or campus, it is referred to as a(n) _____. Each device connected to a network is referred to as a(n) _____. A network typically has one or more network _____, which are computers that distribute programs and/or files to the workstations. When you log into a network, the server's hard drive is _____ to a drive letter, making it easy to access the files and programs that it contains.

You and other network users can typically use the same program at the same time, but programs should be shared only if a network, multiuser, or site license has been obtained. Unlike program files, when one user has a data file open, it is _____ so that other users cannot make changes at the same time. The exception to this policy involves data files opened using _____ that supports collaborative work by many users on the same files.

 Check Answers

The key hardware component for connecting a computer to a local area network is a network _____ card, or NIC. A NIC is typically inserted into an expansion slot or PCMCIA slot, then connected by cable to a device called a(n) _____, which is a centralized connection point for all of the network devices. The servers in a network can have different capabilities for processing data. A dedicated _____ server typically does not process data, but is solely devoted to the task of delivering programs and data files to workstations. A non-dedicated file server has the capability to both process data like a workstation and serve out files to other workstations. A print server specializes in managing one or more network printers. A(n) _____ server shares processing tasks with the workstations, typically by handling database functions. A(n) _____ computer performs all of the processing tasks for a series of terminals that serve as its input and output devices.

Today's popular desktop operating systems include network _____ software, which makes it easy to set up a network connection. When your computer is connected to a LAN, you can still access your stand-alone software applications from your workstation's hard disk. These applications can also be installed on a network server and will work just as they do on a stand-alone computer. When new application software is installed on a network server, you must typically also perform a(n) _____ installation, which updates the Windows Registry and adds the program to the Windows Start menu.

Check Answers

CHAPTER 7

INTERACTIVE KEY TERMS

Make sure that you understand all of the boldfaced key terms presented in this chapter. If you're using the NP4 CD or NP4 Web site, you can use this list of terms as an interactive study activity. First, try to define a term in your own words, then click the term to compare your definition with the definition that is presented in the chapter.

Application server, 321
BNC connector, 318
Client/server architecture, 321
Coaxial cable, 318
Dedicated file server, 319
Default printer, 316
Drive mapping, 310
E-mail, 327
E-mail address, 328
E-mail attachment, 331
E-mail client software, 327
E-mail message, 327
E-mail server software, 327
E-mail system, 327
Ethernet, 317
File locking, 313
Gateway, 329
Host computer, 321
Local area network (LAN), 308
Local resources, 308
Network administrator, 309
Network client software, 323
Network hub, 318
Network license, 324
Network operating system (NOS), 323
Network printer, 308
Network resources, 308
Network server, 308
Network server software, 323
NIC (network interface card), 317
Node, 308
Non-dedicated file server, 320
Peer-to-peer, 320
Print job, 320
Print queue, 320
Print server, 320
RJ-45 connector, 318

Sharing, 312
Stand-alone computer, 308
Store-and-forward technology, 327
Terminal emulation software, 322
Time-sharing system, 321
Token Ring, 317
Twisted-pair cable, 318
User account, 309
Wide area network (WAN), 308
Wireless networks, 318
Workflow software, 326
Workstation, 308
Workstation installation, 324

INTERACTIVE QUIZZES

Quiz yourself on important concepts from this chapter by filling in the blanks. When using the NP4 CD or NP4 Web site, you can type your answers, then use the Check Answers buttons to automatically score your responses. Place your Tracking Disk in the floppy disk drive if you want to save your scores.

1 A(n) [_____] area network is located within a limited area, whereas a(n) [_____] covers a large geographical area.

2 The process of drive [_____] assigns a drive letter to the network server disk drive so that it can be accessed from a workstation.

3 When you start a program that is stored on a network server, the program is copied to the [_____] of your workstation.

4 A network typically [_____] data files to prevent two people from accessing the same file at the same time.

5 A network in which the host computer sends data to terminals is called a peer-to-peer network. True or false? [_____]

6 After new software has been installed on a network server, you will not see the software listed on the Start menu until you complete a(n) [_____] installation.

7 If your computer uses the Windows NT Workstation operating system, you can connect only to a Windows NT server. True or false? [_____]

8 An e-mail [_____] is a file that travels through an e-mail system along with an e-mail message.

Check Answers

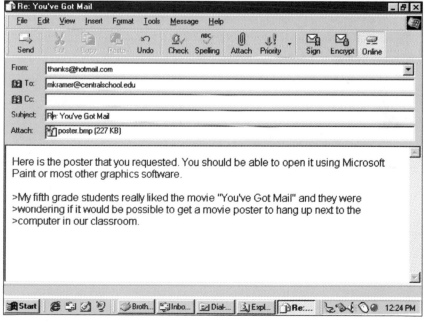

Fill in the blanks according to the information that you see on the screen that is pictured on the right.

1 The *user ID* of the person who is sending the e-mail: [_____]

2 The name of the recipient's *e-mail server*: [_____]

3 The filename of the attachment: [_____]

4 The symbol used to mark the text of the original e-mail message: [_____]

Check Answers

INTERACTIVE PRACTICE TESTS

When you use the NP4 CD or NP4 Web site, you can take practice tests that consist of 10 multiple-choice, true/false, and fill-in-the-blank questions. The 10 questions are selected at random from a large test bank, so each time you take a test, you'll receive a different set of questions. Your tests are scored immediately, and you can print study guides that help you find the correct answers for any questions that you missed. If you are using a Tracking Disk, insert it in the floppy disk drive to save your test scores.

 Start Practice
Test

STUDY TIPS

Study Tips help you organize and consolidate the information in a chapter by making lists, outlines, charts, and sketches. You can use paper and pencil, or word processing software to complete most of the Study Tips activities.

1 List three reasons why sharing programs is effective for an organization.

2 Suppose Latisha Simms needs to select a password for herself. Rank the following, listing the most secure password first: BZ39A (a totally random selection of letters and numbers), LASIMMS (for Latisha Alexandra Simms), SSOSAPFOR (the first letters of "sing a song of sixpence, a pocket full of rye"), SMMIS (Latisha's last name spelled backwards), and Thomas (Latisha's husband's name).

3 Draw a diagram and explain the processing roles for servers and workstations for each of the following types of networks: (1) a network with a dedicated file server, (2) a peer-to-peer network, (3) a client/server network, (4) a time-sharing system.

4 Explain the difference between sharing files on a network and using a groupware product on a network.

5 Draw a conceptual diagram of a network showing the following components: (1) three workstations, (2) one file server, (3) one network printer, (4) a hub, (5) NICs for workstations, printer, and server, (6) cables connecting all of the network nodes.

6 Make a list of important points pertaining to network operating systems.

7 Summarize the software licensing issues that affect local area networks.

8 Explain how store-and-forward technology applies to e-mail systems.

9 Briefly describe the various options for obtaining an e-mail account.

10 Create your own example to explain the purpose of an e-mail attachment.

PROJECTS

A project is an open-ended activity that will help you apply the concepts you have learned. Many projects require resources in addition to your textbook, such as current magazines, library materials, or Web access. When you tackle a project, be prepared to use your critical thinking skills, logical analysis, and your creativity.

1 **Your School Network** Research your school network to answer the following questions:

   a. What is the network operating system?

   b. What drives are mapped to a student workstation?

   c. Is the file server a microcomputer, minicomputer, or mainframe computer?

   d. Is the print server a different device than the file server?

2 **Network Operating System Efficiency** Network operating systems are designed to optimize the process of sending program and data files to workstations. Consequently, the amount of time it takes multiple users to open the same file should not be much longer than it takes a single user to open the file. How efficient is the file server in your lab? To find out, form a team of three to five class members and do the following:

   a. Using a stopwatch or the second hand of your watch, record the number of seconds it takes a word processing software application to start on a workstation in your lab. For example, if your lab has Microsoft Word, click the Word icon to highlight it, then start timing when you press the Enter key to launch the program. Stop timing when the word processor is ready for you to start typing.

   b. Exit the word processing application to get ready for the second part of the test.

   c. Position each member of your team at other workstations on the network. Each team member should click the word processing icon so it is highlighted. One of the team members should give a signal so that all team members press the Enter key at the same time. Each team member should record how long it takes before the word processing application is ready for typing.

   d. Record each team member's results. Prepare a one-page document in which you summarize your experiment and its results. Be sure you explain exactly how you carried out the experiment—how many members were on your team, which lab you used, and which software you used. Also, present your conclusions about the efficiency of your network server.

3 **Client/Server Architecture in Corporations** Client/server architecture is becoming increasingly more popular in corporations. To find out more about client/server computing, use library and Internet resources to look for case studies and articles about corporations using client/server applications. Write a one- or two-page description of an effective use of client/server computing. Be sure to include a list of references.

4 **Networks in Action** Make an appointment to interview the network supervisor in an organization or business related to your career field. To prepare for the interview, make a list of questions that you will ask about how the network works and how it is used. Use the topics in this chapter to help organize your questions about network hardware, network software, application software, and groupware. After the interview, write a two- to three-page summary of your findings. Include the name of the person you interviewed, the business or organization, and the date of the interview. In addition to the report summarizing your findings, attach a list of your questions.

CHAPTER 7

5 **Network Careers** The companies that produce network operating systems encourage computer professionals to obtain professional certification to demonstrate their knowledge of networking. Such certification is often one of the qualifications listed in ads for network supervisor jobs. Novell offers certification as a CNE (Certified NetWare Engineer) or a CNA (Certified NetWare Administrator). Microsoft also offers a certification program for its server operating systems. Write a one- to two-page paper that describes Microsoft's or Novell's certification process. Include answers to the following questions: What is the process for certification? What is the cost? How would you prepare for the certification exam? For what sort of jobs would you qualify once you are certified?

6 **E-mail Smileys** E-mail has spawned a language of "emoticons," or "smileys," that are composed of keyboard characters. For example, the smiley ;-) looks like a person winking. You could use this smiley in an e-mail message to indicate that you are joking. Lists of smileys have been published on the Internet and in books, computer magazines, and newspapers. Find a list of smileys and select five that you would like to use. Describe what each means. Submit your list and indicate the source of your selection.

7 **E-mail Ethics** Assume that you are the network administrator at a small manufacturing company. While doing some maintenance work on the e-mail system, you happen to view the contents of a mail message between two employees. The employees seem to be discussing a plan to steal equipment from the company. What would you do? Write a one-page essay that explains your decision and describes the factors that affected it.

8 **E-mail Practice** Learn how to use the e-mail system available on your school network. Briefly describe how you perform each of the following tasks:

a. Compose and send a message.

b. Reply to a message you received.

c. Delete a message you received.

d. Forward a message you received to someone other than the person who sent the message.

e. Send a carbon copy of the message.

f. Send a message to a mailing list.

A D D I T I O N A L   P R O J E C T S

Click the underlined text to link to the NP4 Web site (www.cciw.com/np4), where you can view and print additional projects for this chapter.

Anonymous E-mail?

N-tier Networks

LAB ASSIGNMENTS

Software for the E-mail Lab is provided on the NP4 CD and may also be available in your school's computer lab. To start the lab, click the lab icon.

The lab has two parts: Steps and Explore. Use the Steps first to learn and review concepts. Read the information on each page and do the numbered steps. As you work through the lab, you will be asked to answer QuickCheck questions about what you have learned. At the end of the lab, you will see a report that scores your answers to the QuickChecks. If your instructor wants you to turn in this report, click the Print button on the QuickCheck Report screen.

When you have completed the Steps, you can click the Explore button to complete the Lab Assignments. You can also use Explore to practice the skills you learned and to explore concepts on your own.

Lab
E-mail

E-mail that originates on a local area network with a mail gateway can travel all over the world. That's why it is so important to learn how to use e-mail. In this lab, you use an e-mail simulator, so even if your school computers don't provide you with e-mail service, you will know the basics of reading, sending, and replying to e-mail messages.

1 Click the Steps button to learn how to work with e-mail. As you proceed through the Steps, answer all of the QuickCheck questions that appear. After you complete the Steps, you will see a QuickCheck Report. Follow the instructions on the screen to print this report.

2 Click the Explore button. Write a message to re@films.org. The subject of the message is "Picks and Pans." In the body of your message, describe a movie you have seen recently. Include the name of the movie, briefly summarize the plot, and give it a thumbs up or a thumbs down. Print the message before you send it.

3 In Explore, look in your Inbox for a message from jb@music.org. Read the message, then compose a reply indicating that you will attend. Send a carbon copy to mciccone@music.org. Print your reply, including the text of JB's original message, before you send it.

4 In Explore, look in your Inbox for a message from leo@sports.org. Reply to the message by adding your rating to the text of the original message as follows:

Equipment:	Your Rating:
Rollerblades	2
Skis	3
Bicycle	1
Scuba gear	4
Snowmobile	5

Print your reply before you send it.

CHAPTER 7

INFOWEB

The InfoWeb is your guide to print, film, television, and electronic resources. Use it to obtain updates on quickly changing technical information and to locate information for research papers. If you're using the NP4 CD, click the InfoWeb Site icon on the left side of this paragraph to access the online InfoWeb links. Otherwise, use your Web browser and type in the address of the NP4 Web site: www.cciw.com/np4. At the Web site you'll find up-to-date links to the topics covered in this chapter.

1 LANs

For more information about LANs, browse through the fine illustrations in *How Networks Work* by Derfler and Freed (Ziff-Davis Press, 1998). For answers to your technical questions about networks, refer to *Novell's Encyclopedia of Networking* by Kevin Shafer (Novell Press, 1997) or Werner Feibel's *The Network Press Encyclopedia of Networking* (Sybex, 1999), which includes a CD-ROM and provides a comprehensive discussion and analysis of networking. Yet another exceptional resource on networking is Tom Sheldon's *Encyclopedia of Networking with CDROM* (McGraw-Hill, 1999). On the Web, connect to *www.internetwk.com* and then link to either Network Infrastructure and Services or Systems and Management for updates on the latest LAN technologies. The British magazine *Network World* at *www2.idg.com.au/nwwdb.NSF/Current* has excellent articles on networking.

2 Ethernet

Today, most networks use the Ethernet standard, which was invented in 1976 by Robert Metcalfe. You can see Metcalfes original sketch of an Ethernet at *wwwhost.ots.utexas.edu/ethernet*. Ethernet tutorials can be found at *www.lantronix.com/technology/tutorials*. The paper "Networking: A Primer," available at *www.baynetworks.com/products/Papers/wp-primer.html*, provides a solid introduction to LANs. It also includes a discussion of Ethernet and clear diagrams. For information on other network standards, connect to *www.webopaedia.com* and look up Token Ring, ARCnet, ATM, and FDDI.

3 Wireless Networks

Wireless networks are popping up everywhere. You'll find an excellent overview about wireless LANs at *www.wlana.com/intro/introduction/index.html*. Lucent Technologies produces a popular wireless system called WaveLAN that you can check out at *www.wavelan.com*. HyperLink Technologies provides information on wireless data collection devices at *www.hyperlinktech.com/products.htm*.

4 Client/Server

"Client/server" is now a somewhat tired buzzword in the computer industry, but it is still mentioned frequently in the press. You'll find a wealth of information on client/server computing if you visit the Client Server Group Web site at *www.isa.co.uk/csg*. For information about 2-tier, 3-tier, and N-tier client/server architecture, connect to *www.ilt.com/AEDIS/Ntier*. You'll find a brief overview of the advantages of N-tier architecture at *www.buzzeo.com/zeologixNTier.html*. The book *Building N-Tier Applications with Com and Visual Basic 6.0* by Ash Rofail and Tony Martin (John Wiley & Sons, 1999) presents the step-by-step process of building an N-tier application.

5 NOS: Network Operating Systems

In the world of PCs, Novell NetWare is the best-selling network operating system for file servers. Visit Novell's Web site at *www.novell.com* for information about local area networks and Novell products. At *www.openvms.digital.com/openvms/whitepapers/nosc/nosc.html*, you'll find a comparison of network operating systems. To read about other network operating systems, visit these vendors: Microsoft, the publisher of the Windows NT Workstation 4.0, at *www.microsoft.com/ntworkstation*; Artisoft, the publisher of the LANTastic network operating system, at *www.artisoft.com/products.htm*; and Banyan, provider of network solutions for over 16 years, at *www.Banyan.com*.

6 Groupware

Lotus Notes has been one of the most popular groupware packages. Connect to the Lotus Notes site at *www2.lotus.com/home.nsf/tabs/lotusnotes* to find out about Notes5. Those just starting to use groupware will probably want to read about Domino.Doc at *www2.lotus.com/home.nsf/tabs/domdoc*. Another popular groupware product is Microsoft's NetMeeting. Look for information and download links at *www.microsoft.com/netmeeting*. Find out about Novell's Groupwise software by visiting *www.novell.com/groupwise*. For an insightful look at groupware from the perspective of management, look for the book *Groupware: Collaborative Strategies for Corporate LANs and Intranets* by David Coleman (Prentice Hall, 1997).

7 Workflow Software

On the Web, you can take a short tutorial on workflow systems at *cne.gmu.edu/modules/workflow*. For a resource listing of workflow software, commercial products, workflow tools, and research on workflow technology, visit *www.workflowsoftware.com*. For more information, check your library or local bookstore for these books on workflow: *The Workflow Imperative* by Thomas Koulopolous (John Wiley & Sons, 1997) and *Business Process Implementation: Building Workflow Systems* by Michael Jackson and Graham Twaddle (Addison-Wesley, 1997).

8 E-mail

Today, most people realize that e-mail messages should follow basic rules of grammar and guidelines for business letter formats. For a discussion of e-mail context and contents, read "A Beginner's Guide to Effective Email" at *www.webfoot.com/advice/email.top.html*. At the Albion Cybercasting site (*www.albion.com/netiquette*) you'll find links to a netiquette quiz and excerpts from Virginia Shea's book, *The Core Rules of Netiquette*.

Did you know that you can obtain free e-mail service? Read a description of the perfect free e-mail service at *www.emailaddresses.com/guide_evolve.htm*. Then investigate any of the over 700 free e-mail services by visiting *www.emailaddresses.com/email_providers.htm*. If you change your e-mail address, you can use mail forwarding, which directs e-mail sent to your old address to your new address. That way you won't miss any e-mails when you "move." You can find a comprehensive listing of free e-mail forwarding services at *www.emailaddresses.com/email_forward.htm*.

9 Smileys

Those > symbols aren't the only ones you'll find in e-mail messages. "Smileys" such as :-) (happy face) and =|:-] (Abraham Lincoln) add some feeling and a little bit of whimsy into the otherwise stark world of electronic messaging. The classic book *Smileys* by D. Sanderson (O'Reilly, 1993) contains a collection of more than 650 smileys and answers to your deepest questions, such as "Why are smileys sideways?" You can find loads of information about smileys on the Web at sites such as the Geocities' Smiley House at *www.geocities.com/Heartland/6959/smiley.html*. To find other smiley sites, just enter the word "smiley" in any search engine.

:-)   ;-)   :-D

10 E-mail Privacy

Concerned about the privacy of your e-mail? Many of your questions are answered at the E-Mail Privacy FAQ Web page at *www.well.com/user/abacard/email.html*. At the American Civil Liberties Union site (*www.aclu.org/issues/cyber/priv/privpap.html*) you can read an excellent article on e-mail privacy. You'll find links to other excellent articles, such as "E-mail and Privacy" by Susan Butler, when you connect to the NP4 Web site. For additional information on the Pillsbury case cited in the Issue section, connect to the CyBarrister Page at *www.ssbb.com/email.html*. To read more about the Omnibus Crime Control and Safe Streets Act and the Communications Privacy Act, connect to *www.shawe.com/wf2000kb3.html*.

CHAPTER 7

CHAPTER 8

THE INTERNET

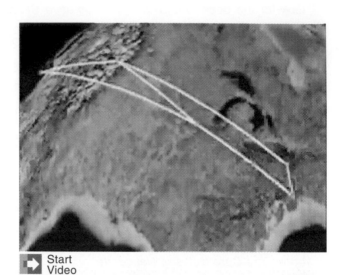

Start Video

CONTENTS

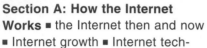
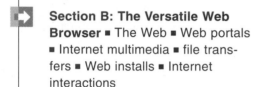
PREVIEW

Chapter 8 provides you with a look at the Internet phenomenon. In this chapter you will learn how the Internet works and you'll discover how your Web browser provides access to many different Internet services. You'll also find out how to publish your own Web pages. The *User Focus* section explains how to connect your own computer to the Internet.

When you have completed this chapter, you should be able to:

▪ Describe how you can use a dial-up connection to access the Internet

▪ Explain how an IP address, a domain name, a URL, and an e-mail address differ

▪ List Internet services that you can access using a Web browser

▪ Explain the differences between downloading a file, viewing a Web page, and playing multimedia elements on a Web page

▪ Explain how synchronous and asynchronous interactions apply to chat groups, discussion groups, and interactive gaming

▪ Explain the purpose of HTML tags and evaluate the effectiveness of a Web page design

▪ Describe how Web sites handle e-commerce

CHAPTER 8 LABS

The World Wide Web   Web Pages & HTML

CYBERSPACE

The data jack slipped smoothly into the socket just behind Kyle's ear. He flipped the switch on his computer. The power light blinked green, and the universe shifted. A moment ago, Kyle was sitting at his desk in his apartment. Now, he seems to be standing in a landscape of surrealistic terrain and fantastic buildings. Messages swirl and pulse down massive conduits, creating data links between heavily guarded corporate computing centers. The World Health Organization cube spins lazily, tipped on one of its corners. In the distance Kyle sees the towers of the Library of Congress. The golden pyramid of the Information Cartel dominates the landscape; its glowing force-field serves as a reminder that access requires security clearance.

This is **cyberspace**—a computer-generated world that exists in a hazy realm between reality and imagination. The term *cyberspace* was coined in 1984 by science-fiction writer William Gibson. Today, "cyberspace" has been popularized by journalists writing about the Internet.

No, you cannot plug your brain into a computer to prowl around in cyberspace. But your computer can provide you with access to a digital "information highway" called the Internet that winds through a landscape of useful and fascinating information, on topics as diverse as hip-hop music and military academies. In this chapter you will discover the astonishing potential of the Internet.

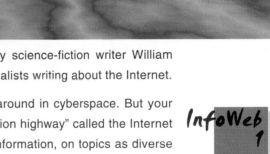

InfoWeb
1

Cyberspace

SECTION
A
HOW THE INTERNET WORKS

The Internet is a collection of local, regional, national, and international computer networks that are linked together to exchange data and distribute processing tasks. It has been evolving over the past 30 years from a fledgling experiment with four computers into a vast information network that connects millions of microcomputers, minicomputers, mainframes, and supercomputers. Why was the Internet created and how does it work? The answers to these questions will help you navigate cyberspace.

The Internet Then and Now

How did the Internet get started? The history of the Internet begins in 1957, when the Soviet Union launched Sputnik, the first artificial satellite. In response to this display of Soviet superiority, the U.S. government resolved to improve its scientific and technical infrastructure. One of the resulting initiatives was the Advanced Research Projects Agency (ARPA).

InfoWeb
2

Internet
History

ARPA swung into action with a project intended to help scientists communicate and share valuable computer resources. The **ARPANET**, created in 1969, connected computers at four universities. In 1985, the National Science Foundation (NSF) used ARPANET technology to create a similar, but larger network, linking not just a few large computers, but entire local area networks at each site. Connecting two or more networks creates an "internetwork" or "internet." The NSF network was an internet (with a lowercase "i"). As this network grew throughout the world, it became known as "The Internet" (with an uppercase "I"), as described in Figure 8-1.

FIGURE 8-1

The simple NSF network shown here and described in the 1985 video, expanded to become today's Internet, providing access to information on every continent.

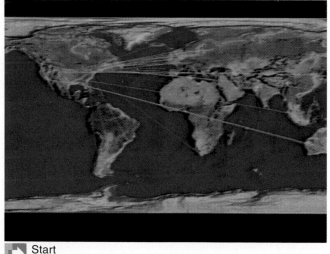

Start
Video

Early Internet pioneers—mostly educators and scientists—used primitive command-line user interfaces to send e-mail, transfer files, and run scientific calculations on Internet supercomputers. Finding information was not easy. Without search engines, Internet users relied on word of mouth and e-mail to tell colleagues "the data you need is on the Stanford computer in a file called *Chrome.txt*." In the early 1990s, software developers created new user-friendly Internet access tools, and Internet accounts became available to anyone willing to pay a moderate monthly fee. Today, the Internet connects computers all over the globe and supplies information to people of all ages and interests.

Internet Growth

Internet
Statistics

How big is the Internet? To measure the size of the Internet, you can consider how many computers are connected, how many people use it, or how much data flows through it. Regardless of which measurement you use, it is clear that the Internet is huge and continues to grow. In fact, it is so large and in such a continual state of change that most measurements of its size can be only estimates.

A computer on the Internet that provides services such as Web pages, e-mailboxes, or data routing services is referred to as an **Internet host**, a "host computer," or simply a "host." In 1969, the ARPANET consisted of four host computers. In 1986, the Internet included 2,000 host computers. By 1999, the estimated number of host computers on the Internet had mushroomed to more than 50 million worldwide (Figure 8-2).

Today, the Internet is the largest and most widely used network in the world, serving an estimated 200 million people in over 200 countries. More than one-third of U.S. households have an Internet connection. Worldwide, more than 200,000 new users sign up for Internet accounts each day. About one-half of all Internet users are females.

Internet traffic is the number of bytes transmitted from one Internet host computer to another. By 1997, Internet traffic exceeded 100 terabytes per week, roughly equivalent to the amount of information printed on the paper made from 500,000 trees or the amount of information stored in books in the U.S. Library of Congress. E-mail generates much of the traffic on the Internet. It is the most popular Internet activity—used by 63% of all Internet users—and accounts for more than 34 trillion messages sent per year in the United States alone.

Vast quantities of data are transmitted over the Internet, but how much data is actually stored on Internet computers? No one really knows. It is not currently possible to poll each computer to find out how many bytes of data are accessible. Michael Dertouzos, director of the MIT Laboratory of Computer Science, estimates that the world has 1 exabyte of data to store. An **exabyte** is 1 quintillion (10^{18}) bytes. The Internet, as large as it is, probably has a long way to go before it contains this amount of data.

FIGURE 8-2

The distribution of Internet host computers throughout the world varies from areas with a single host (represented by a red circle) to areas with 1 million hosts (represented by purple circles).

Number of Hosts

1,000,000
100,000
10,000
1,000
100
10
1

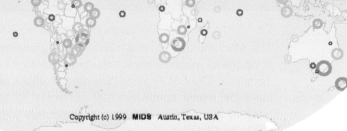

Copyright (c) 1999 **MIDS** Austin, Texas, USA

-Dc 1 1:100,000,000 Winkel Tripel projection 1999.05.12 (5 33 20)

CHAPTER 8

Internet Technology

How does data travel over the Internet? To understand how you can use the Internet to access information from a computer that is located thousands of miles away, it is helpful to have a little background on the Internet communications network. A **network service provider** (NSP), such as MCI or Sprint, maintains a series of communications links for Internet data. These links interconnect at several **network access points** (NAPs) so data can travel between NSPs.

The cables, wires, and satellites that carry Internet data form an interlinked communications network. Data traveling from one Internet host to another is transmitted from one link in the network to another, along the best possible route. If some links are overloaded or temporarily out of service, the data can be routed through different links. The major Internet communications links are called the **Internet backbone**. Figure 8-3 illustrates a layer of the Internet backbone maintained by MCI and shows, for example, that data traveling from Seattle to Dallas could be routed through Chicago, Kansas City, or San Francisco.

FIGURE 8-3

The Internet backbone in the continental U.S. provides many alternative pathways for data traveling from one computer to another.

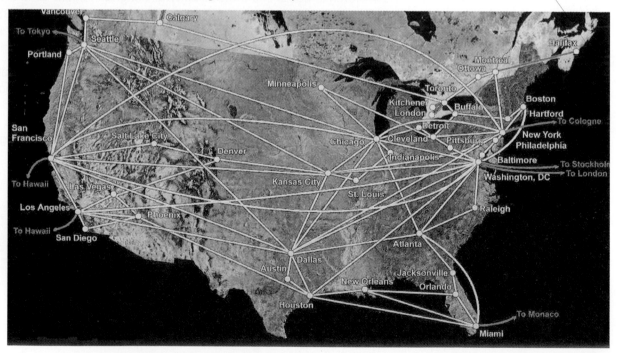

The efficient flow of data over the many communications links on the Internet requires a standard mechanism for routing data to its destination. **TCP/IP** is the acronym for Transport Control Protocol/Internet Protocol, a standard set of communications rules used by every computer that connects to the Internet. TCP/IP knits together the Internet and allows data to travel smoothly over the communications links provided by NSPs worldwide.

Internet Service Providers

Do I connect my computer to the Internet backbone? When you connect your computer to the Internet, you do not connect directly to the backbone. Instead, you connect it to an ISP that in turn connects to the backbone. An **ISP** (Internet service provider) is a company that maintains an Internet host computer providing Internet access to businesses, organizations, and individuals.

An ISP works in much the same way as your local telephone company. You arrange for service—in this case for Internet access—and the ISP charges you a monthly fee. An ISP typically provides you with a user account that includes Internet access and an e-mailbox. Most ISPs offer connections over telephone lines, but access through a cable television system or personal satellite dish is also available.

A connection that uses a phone line to establish a temporary Internet connection is referred to as a **dial-up connection**. Your computer dials your ISP's computer and establishes a connection using a phone line. Once you are connected, the ISP routes data between your computer and the Internet backbone, as shown in Figure 8-4.

FIGURE 8-4

Your computer establishes a dial-up connection to an ISP, which is connected to the Internet backbone.

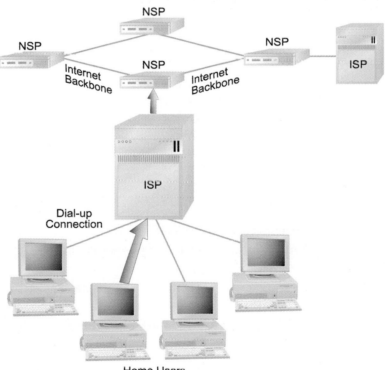

Think of your computer as an Internet visitor, rather than an Internet resident. Unlike an Internet host, which maintains a permanent connection to the Internet, your computer establishes only a temporary connection. When your computer hangs up, the connection is broken.

Internet Addresses and Domains

How does the Internet know where to send data? The Internet includes computers that perform different functions. Some computers on the Internet handle communications and route e-mail; others provide information, such as stock quotes, movie reviews, and sports scores. Regardless of its function, every computer that connects to the Internet has a unique identifying number called an **IP address**. An IP address is a set of four numbers between 0 and 255 that are separated by periods. For example, 204.146.144.253 is the IP address of the Coca-Cola Company.

Internet host computers have permanent IP addresses. In contrast, when your computer establishes a dial-up connection, it is assigned a temporary IP address from a pool maintained by your ISP. When you disconnect, your computer's temporary IP address goes back into the pool and is available for use by other dial-up users.

When data travels over the Internet, it carries the IP address of its destination. At each intersection on the backbone, a device called a **router** examines the data's IP address and then forwards the data towards its destination.

Domain
Names

Although an IP address works for inter-computer communications, people find it difficult to remember long strings of numbers. Therefore, many host computers also have an easy-to-remember name such as *cocacola.com*. The official term for this name is "fully qualified domain name" (FQDN), but most people just refer to it as a **domain name**. By convention, you should type domain names using all lowercase letters. A domain name ends with a three-letter extension that indicates its **top-level domain**. For example, in the domain name *cocacola.com*, *com* indicates that the computer is maintained by a commercial business. A top-level domain groups the computers on the Internet into the categories shown in Figure 8-5.

FIGURE 8-5	Internet Top-Level Domains
Domain	**Description**
com	Commercial businesses
edu	Four-year colleges and universities
gov	U.S. government agencies
int	Organizations established by international treaties
mil	U.S. military organizations
net	Internet administrative organizations
org	Professional and nonprofit organizations

Outside of the United States, country codes serve as top-level domains. Canada's top-level domain is *ca*. The United Kingdom's top-level domain is *uk*. Australia's top-level domain is *au*. Organizations and individuals can register a domain name for an annual fee. Although an organization called InterNIC maintains the registry, many ISPs will help you process your registration.

A computer with a domain name is popularly referred to as a **site**. A site is a metaphor for a virtual place that exists in cyberspace. For example, although you might envision *www.amazon.com* as a physical bookstore, its Web store is virtual. When you "visit" the *amazon.com* store, you're simply connecting your computer to its **Web site**—a location in a computer somewhere on the Internet.

URLs

| What is the difference between a domain name and a URL? | A Web site is

composed of a series of **Web pages** that contain information. Each page is stored as a separate file and referred to by a unique URL. Like a domain name, a **URL** (Uniform Resource Locator) is an Internet address. A URL, however, is the address of a *document* on a computer, whereas a domain name represents the IP address of a *computer*. The components of a URL include the Web protocol, the Web server name, the folder in which the page is stored, and the filename of the page.

Web page URLs begin with *http://*. The acronym **HTTP** stands for Hypertext Transfer Protocol—the protocol, or communications system, that allows Web browsers to communicate with Web servers. Many of today's Web browsers assume that all Web addresses begin with *http://*. If you are using such a browser, you can omit *http://* when you type a URL.

The next part of the URL is the Web server name. A **Web server** is a computer that uses special software to transmit Web pages over the Internet. Many Web server names are domain names prefixed with *www*. The Web server name for your favorite Chinese restaurant might be something like *www.fooyong.com*. Suppose you indicate to your Web browser that you want to access *www.fooyong.com*. By entering the Web server name, you access the site's home page. A **home page** is similar to the title page in a book. It identifies the site and contains links to other pages at the site.

The URL of a Web page reflects the name of any folder or folders in which it is stored. For example, suppose that the Chinese restaurant has a page listing its daily specials. The specials are stored in a file called *specials.html* in a folder called *information*. The URL for this page would be *www.fooyong.com/information/specials.html*. Filename extensions for Web pages are typically *.htm* or *.html*.

Some Internet computers are case sensitive. So, although a domain name is always lowercase, parts of a URL might be uppercase. When you type URLs, you should be sure to use the correct case. For example, *Information/Specials.html* is not the same as *information/specials.html*. Figure 8-6 identifies the parts of a URL.

FIGURE 8-6

A URL is the address of a Web page.

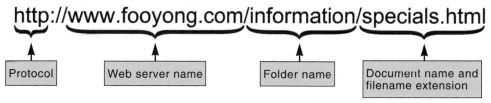

http://www.fooyong.com/information/specials.html

| Protocol | Web server name | Folder name | Document name and filename extension |

CHAPTER 8

Other Types of Internet Servers

Is the Internet the same as the Web? Although the Web is one of the Internet's most popular services, it is not the only one. Internet hosts also provide services such as e-mail, file transfers, discussion groups, and real-time chat. In Chapter 7, you learned about Internet e-mail servers that provide e-mail accounts and e-mail forwarding services. In addition, the Internet includes **FTP servers**, which maintain a collection of files that you can transfer to your own computer. These servers are particularly popular for downloading software and MP3 music files. **Usenet servers** and **IRC servers** (Internet Relay Chat servers) handle the exchange of comments among members of Internet discussion groups and chat groups.

A single Internet host can provide several services simply by running the appropriate type of server software. For example, one host computer can act as a Web server, FTP server, and Usenet server. To access Web, FTP, Usenet, IRC, and other Internet servers, your computer needs corresponding client software. Sound complicated? In the next section of this chapter, you'll find out how today's Internet provides simple access to almost all of its services.

QUICKCHECK A

1 The term _____ was originally coined by science-fiction writer William Gibson to refer to a computer-generated reality that people could experience by connecting their brain to a computer network.

2 An internetwork, also referred to as a(n) _____, is created by connecting two or more networks.

3 Internet traffic is measured in _____.

4 Typically, you would connect your home computer directly to the Internet backbone using a phone line. True or false? _____

5 All the computers on the Internet use a standard set of communications rules called _____.

6 The address *http://www.cyberspace.com* is a(n) _____.

Check Answers

SECTION B   THE VERSATILE WEB BROWSER

Lab
The World
Wide Web

In the past, you needed a separate client software program to access each type of Internet server. For e-mail, you needed an e-mail client. For FTP, you needed an FTP client. Archie, TelNet, Gopher, and Usenet clients were all part of the Internet user's software toolbox. Today, a single tool—a Web browser—has replaced this awkward collection of client software. It provides Internet users with all-purpose client software for accessing many types of servers. In Chapter 1, you learned how to start a Web browser and use a Web search engine. Now, you will find out how a browser works to display Web pages, transfer files between computers, access commercial information services, send e-mail, and interact with other Internet users.

The Web

InfoWeb
5
The Web

> How does a Web browser display a Web page?

In the mid-1960s, Ted Nelson was trying to devise a computer system that could store literary documents, link them according to logical relationships, and allow readers to comment and annotate what they read. He envisioned a set of documents, which he called a "hypertext," connected by a set of "hypertext links" that could be navigated to view additional material related to a topic (Figure 8-7). The establishment turned up its nose at his idea. Who would create all of these documents and what computer would be powerful enough to handle them? Who would be interested in following hypertext links to find information? Who, except for scholars and scientists, would be interested in communicating online? Nelson's project Xanadu never became a reality, but 25 years later his ideas resurfaced as the World Wide Web—now popularly called "the Web."

FIGURE 8-7

Ted Nelson's early sketch of project Xanadu—a distant relative of the World Wide Web—is historically interesting. Notice his use of the terms "links" and "web."

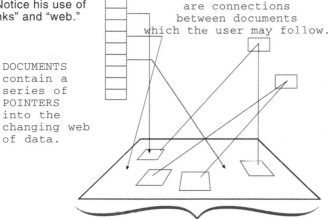

LINKS
are connections
between documents
which the user may follow.

DOCUMENTS
contain a
series of
POINTERS
into the
changing web
of data.

Expanding Tissue of Text, Data, and Graphics

The Web was born in 1990 at the European Laboratory for Particle Physics (CERN). It was an event that went virtually unnoticed, except by a few people who were really "into" computers. Within a few years, however, the Web captured the interest of the news media and the ensuing publicity created a surge of curiosity. Unlike the Internet, which is simply a mass of cables and connection points that form a communications network, the Web is an Internet service that stores and provides information.

The Web is partially responsible for the explosion of interest in the Internet. As an easy-to-use, graphical source of information, the Web opened up the Internet to millions of people who were interested in finding and exchanging information. Today, "Web surfers" (as Web users are sometimes called) can visit an estimated 800 million Web pages on more than 2.8 million Web sites, containing more than 15 terabytes of data.

The official description of the Web is a "wide-area hypermedia information retrieval initiative aiming to give universal access to a large universe of documents." The Web consists of documents—Web pages—that contain information on a particular topic. A Web page might also include one or more **links** that point to other Web pages. Links make it easy to follow a thread of related information, even if the pages are stored on computers located in different countries. Figure 8-8 shows a conceptual model of linked Web pages.

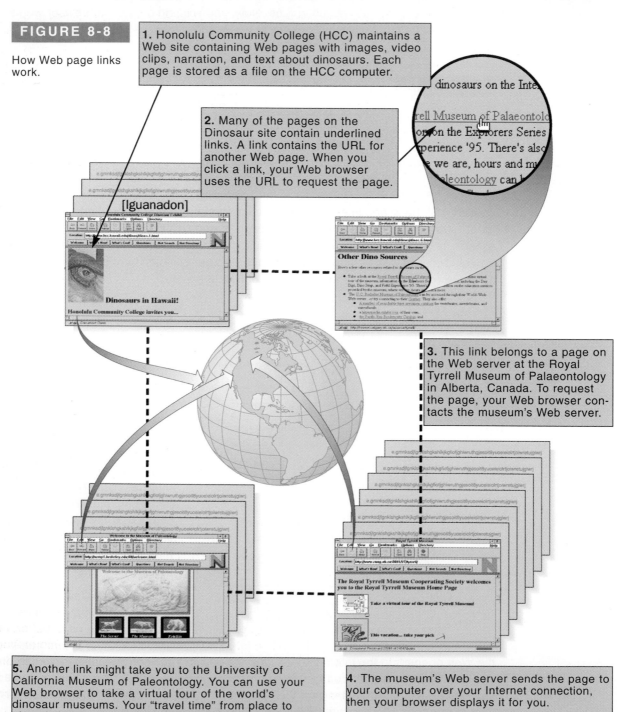

FIGURE 8-8

How Web page links work.

1. Honolulu Community College (HCC) maintains a Web site containing Web pages with images, video clips, narration, and text about dinosaurs. Each page is stored as a file on the HCC computer.

2. Many of the pages on the Dinosaur site contain underlined links. A link contains the URL for another Web page. When you click a link, your Web browser uses the URL to request the page.

3. This link belongs to a page on the Web server at the Royal Tyrrell Museum of Palaeontology in Alberta, Canada. To request the page, your Web browser contacts the museum's Web server.

5. Another link might take you to the University of California Museum of Paleontology. You can use your Web browser to take a virtual tour of the world's dinosaur museums. Your "travel time" from place to place is just the few seconds that it takes to click a link and have a page arrive at your computer.

4. The museum's Web server sends the page to your computer over your Internet connection, then your browser displays it for you.

You use a Web browser to request a Web page from a Web server. To request a page, you either type in a URL or click a Web page link. The server sends the data for the Web page over the Internet to your computer. This data includes two items: the information you want to view and a set of instructions that tells your browser how to display it. The instructions include specifications for the color of the background, the size of the text, and the placement of graphics. Additional instructions tell your browser what to do when you click a link.

The Web is constantly changing as new Web sites come online and old sites close. As a result, links are not always valid. Sometimes when you click a link nothing happens or you get an error message. If a Web server is offline for maintenance or busy from heavy traffic, you won't be able to get the Web pages that you requested, or you might receive them very slowly. If a Web page doesn't appear after 15 to 20 seconds, you can click your browser's Stop button and try to access the page later. If you receive a message that the site no longer exists, you'll need to look for information elsewhere, as shown in Figure 8-9.

FIGURE 8-9

A "page connot be found" message—sometimes called a "404 error"— indicates that a page has moved or no longer exists.

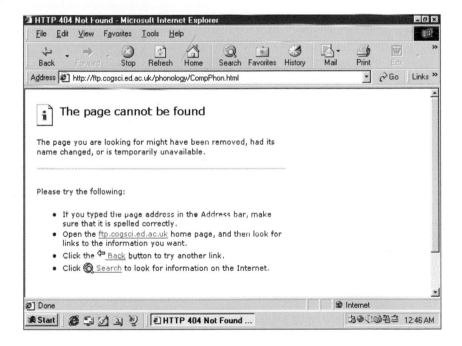

Start
Screentour

The term "home page" can refer to the main page of a Web site and it can also refer to the Web page that is displayed when your browser first starts. You can always return to your browser's home page by clicking the browser's Home button. Most browsers let you pick any Web page as your startup home page, so select one that you use often, such as your favorite search engine.

Your browser's menu and tool bars help you navigate the Web as you follow links and then retrace your steps. You'll make frequent use of the Back and Forward buttons to retrace your path through the links you've followed from one Web page to another. Your browser stores a History list of the pages that you visit during each session. It can display this list If you want to take big jumps to previously visited Web sites, instead of using the Back and Forward buttons. Your browser can also store a list of your favorite sites so that you can jump directly to them instead of entering a URL.

CHAPTER 8

Web Portals

How do I get on the Web? Your versatile browser is the gateway to millions of Web sites. Most computers include a browser, such as Microsoft Internet Explorer or Netscape Navigator. It is typically preconfigured to take you directly to a Web portal where you can start your Web journey. A **Web portal** is a Web site that provides a group of popular Web services, such as a search engine, e-mail access, chat rooms, and links to shopping, weather, news, and sports, as shown in Figure 8-10.

FIGURE 8-10

Portal sites, such as the GO Network, provide a gateway to many Web services.

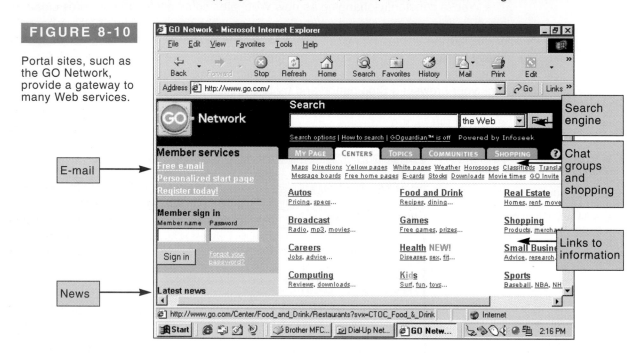

Web Portals

Popular Web portal sites include America Online (AOL), AT&T WorldNet, CompuServe, Excite, GO Network, Lycos, Microsoft Network (MSN), and Yahoo. Access to these portal sites is typically free to anyone who has access to the Internet. To connect to a portal site, simply enter its URL.

Some Web portals are maintained by **commercial information services**, which also serve as ISPs. Commercial information services typically charge a monthly membership fee of $10-$30, which includes access to dial-up connections, an e-mail account, and a personal Web page. AOL and MSN are the most popular commercial information services. You can, however, access their portal sites for free, even if you are not a member.

Your school or business might provide free Internet access. Nevertheless, many people who would like to send and receive e-mail, participate in online discussions, shop online, and have access to online information use a commercial information service.

Internet Multimedia

Can I listen to music and play videos on the Web? Today it is difficult to imagine that, prior to 1995, most Web pages contained only text. Now, Web pages include multimedia elements such as sound, animation, and video.

A media element is stored on a Web server in a file. A link for the media element would typically be displayed on a Web page that contains additional information about the topic. When you click a link to play a media element, the Web server sends a copy of the media file to your computer. This transfer can happen in one of two ways, depending on how the Web server has been set up. In one case, the Web server sends you the entire media file before starting to play it. For large video files, you might wait five minutes or more before the video begins.

A newer technology, sometimes referred to as **streaming media**, sends a small segment of the media file to your computer and begins to play it. While this first segment plays, the Web server sends the next part of the file to your computer, and so on until the media segment ends. With streaming media technology, your computer essentially plays a media file while receiving it.

As you browse the Web, you'll find multimedia elements that are displayed in place and multimedia elements that run in separate windows. Of the two, the in-place option is technologically more sophisticated. **In-place multimedia technology** plays a media element as a seamless part of a Web page. For example, an **animated GIF** like the one in Figure 8-11 uses in-place technology so that the spacecraft appears to rotate right on the Web page.

FIGURE 8-11

An animated GIF runs in place as part of a Web page. In this example, the spacecraft rotates to illustrate its operation in space.

Start
Screentour

Multimedia overlay technology adds a separate window to your screen in which multi-media elements appear. With some overlay technologies, you must manually close the window when the multimedia segment is finished. Figure 8-12 illustrates a media window that overlays a Web page.

FIGURE 8-12

Some multimedia elements play in a window that overlays the Web page.

Start
Screentour

InfoWeb
7

Plug-ins

A software module that provides your computer with the capability to view or play a specific type of file is called a **player**, **plug-in**, or **viewer**. For example, the Media Player software that is provided with Windows includes controls to play media file types such as .wav files and .avi files. Some media players work with only one type of media file. For example, the RealAudio player works with only .ra sound files. Before you can use a media element from the Web, your computer must have a corresponding media player.

Your browser maintains a list of media players that have been installed on your computer. Suppose that you're on the ZDTV site and want to view a video segment about grocery stores. ZDTV videos require a media player called RealPlayer. When you click the movie link, your Web browser checks whether RealPlayer has been installed on your computer. If the player is not present, the browser will display an error message. Most Web servers provide links to a site where you can download the necessary player.

In the context of the Web, players, plug-ins, and viewers add a feature to your browser, such as the capability to play media. Some of the most popular players include Adobe Acrobat Reader, MacroMedia Shockwave, RealNetworks RealPlayer, and Apple QuickTime.

File Transfers

Can I get a copy of a picture, sound, or video that I find on the Web? When you're viewing a Web page, it is held temporarily in the RAM of your computer but it is not stored as a file on disk. Suppose that a Web page contains a graphic, sound, or video that you would like to store on disk for later use. The process of transferring a file from a remote computer to your computer's disk drive is called **downloading**. Most Web browsers allow you to easily download Web page elements such as pictures, sounds, animations, and videos. Figure 8-13 explains how to do so.

FIGURE 8-13

You can easily download images and other Web page elements—just make sure that you respect copyright laws.

1. To download a Web page element, point to it and click the right mouse button.

2. From the shortcut menu, select "Save Picture as" to save a graphic. To save a sound or other media element, use the "Save Target As" option.

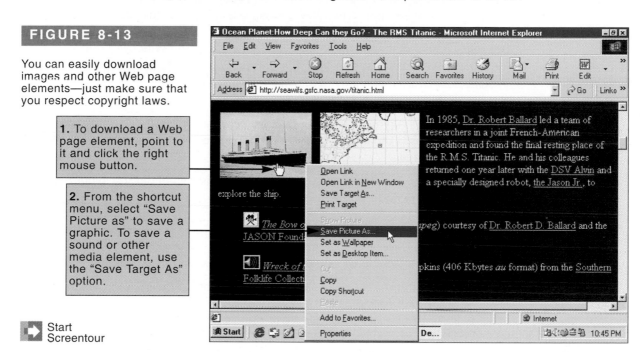

Start Screentour

Uploading is the process of sending a copy of a file from your computer to a remote computer. Suppose, for example, that a writer living in British Columbia wants to send an 8 MB file containing the manuscript for a new novel to an editor in New York. What is the best way to deliver the manuscript to the editor? The writer could copy the file containing the manuscript to a Zip disk and send it via FedEx, but that would take at least 12 hours. Another possibility would be to attach the file to an e-mail, but some e-mail systems do not accept large attachments. A third option would be to upload the file to an Internet FTP server. The editor could then download the file from the server.

InfoWeb
8

FTP
Software

Although most browsers allow you to download files, not all allow you to upload. If your browser does not have upload capabilities, you can accomplish the task using **FTP client software**, such as WinFTP (published by Ipswitch, Inc).

Many FTP servers allow people to log in and obtain downloads using "anonymous" as the user ID and their e-mail address as the password. For security reasons, however, most FTP servers provide upload capabilities only to people who have valid user accounts. To upload a file using your browser or FTP client software, you'll need to know the domain name for an FTP server on which you have an account. You must log in using your user ID and password before you can initiate the upload.

CHAPTER 8

Web Installs

How do I install software that I download from the Internet? The Internet is a terrific source of free software. On the Web, you can find sites that list thousands of downloadable shareware programs. Also, many software publishers offer free trial versions that you can download and use for a 30-day period. Typically, these sites make it easy to select software and download it to your PC.

Most downloadable software is stored as a **self-extracting file**—a single file that holds all of the modules for the software. This file is then "compressed" to reduce its size and minimize download time. When the download is complete, the file must be "reconstituted" to its original size and divided into its original modules. Then the software can be installed so that it appears on the Start menu and in the Windows Registry. A download site will typically provide you with detailed instructions on how to download and install the software that it provides. You can use the Print option on your browser's File menu to print these instructions.

InfoWeb
9

Download
Sites

Some software that you download will essentially install itself as the last phase of the download process. Otherwise, you will typically handle the installation manually by following these steps:

1. **Download the file.** Make note of the filename and remember the folder on your PC in which you stored the downloaded file.

2. **Find the file.** Use Windows Explorer to view the contents of the folder that contains the downloaded file.

3. **Open the file.** Double-click the filename of the file you downloaded.

4. **Complete the installation.** Follow the instructions on the screen.

FIGURE 8-14

It is handy to know how to download and install software from the Web so that you can take advantage of thousands of shareware, freeware, and trial versions of software.

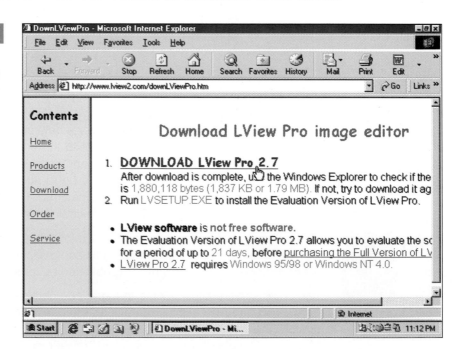

Start
Screentour

Internet Interactions

Can I interact directly with other people who are online? The most popular way to interact with other people on the Internet is with e-mail. Another possibility is to join a **discussion group** in which participants share their views on a specific issue or topic. On the Internet you'll find thousands of discussion groups on such diverse topics as snowboarding, urban policy, rave music, and William Gibson's cyberspace novels. Discussion groups take place **asynchronously**, meaning that the discussion participants are not online at the same time. For example, an English teacher might ask a question such as, "Who has had the greatest influence on the development of cyberpunk novels?" Over the next few days, other participants will post responses. When the English teacher next logs into the discussion group, he can read these responses, comment on them, or ask another question.

If you would rather interact **synchronously** with people who are online at the same time, you can join a **chat group**. To participate in a chat, you generally choose a nickname, then enter a chat room. As chat participants type, their messages appear on your screen. You'll see the messages from everyone in the chat room. Chat groups are often less focused than discussion groups as participants banter about the weather and themselves. That is not to say that serious chats never occur. On the contrary, chats can be an effective forum for professional interaction, such as when physicians in different locations use the Internet to collaborate on a diagnosis.

Recently, chat groups have come under fire because of their potential threat to personal safety and privacy. Use common sense in your chat room interactions. Don't represent yourself as something you're not. Don't provide personal information such as your name or address. Internet society, like society as a whole, has its share of deviants and rip-off experts. Most chats, however, are fairly civilized, as shown in Figure 8-15.

FIGURE 8-15

In a chat session, the participants are online at the same time, whereas discussion groups typically are asynchronous. Note, however, that in popular usage, the terms "chat group" and "discussion group" are sometimes used interchangeably.

Start
Screentour

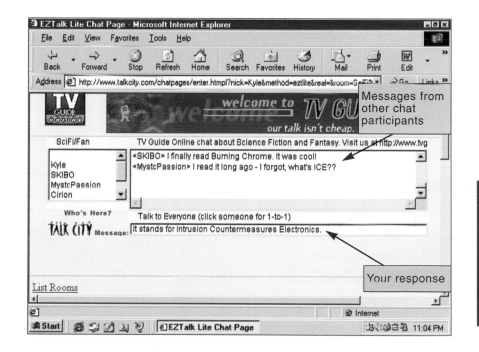

CHAPTER 8

InfoWeb 11

Games

Another aspect of Internet interaction is online **multi-player gaming**. From simple competitive word games to massive adventure games, the world of Internet gaming has it all. Imagine creating a cyber personna with the strength of a giant and the cunning of an elf. Arm yourself with your favorite weapon and venture into an imaginary world where you can defeat evil and accumulate treasure. Your fellow adventurers are people from all over the world (Figure 8-16).

FIGURE 8-16

Multi-player games give you an opportunity to play with or against, other players from all over the Internet.

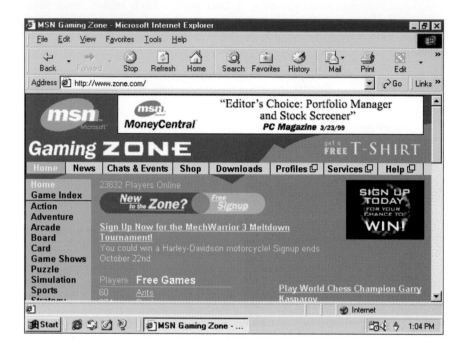

Some multi-player games are synchronous; others are asynchronous. As with chat groups, to participate in a synchronous game, you and the other players must be online at the same time. To participate in asynchronous games, you post each move to the game's referee, then pick up the results and submit new moves the next time you are online. Many multi-player games require a small fee to participate.

QUICKCHECK B

1 Your browser's _____ page is the first one you see when your browser starts.

2 A technology called _____ media essentially plays a media file while your computer receives it.

3 A(n) _____ is a software module that adds a specific feature to your browser, such as the capability to play file in RealVideo format.

4 A Web _____, such as Yahoo or AOL, provides links to a variety of information including sports, weather, and news.

5 Most commercial information services are ISPs. True or false? _____

6 To participate in a chat group, you must be online at the same time as other participants. True or false? _____

➡ Check Answers

WEB AUTHORING AND SITE MANAGEMENT

Using the Web as a source for information and interaction is great, but eventually you might want to become a Web author and publish your own pages. You might become even more ambitious and decide to create and manage your own Web site. Using today's software tools, Web authoring and publishing are not much more difficult than word processing or desktop publishing.

Why would you want to publish on the Web? You might have information that you would like to make available to the public, such as your resume or a calendar of events for your club. You might have services or products to offer that you would like people to easily obtain from any geographic location. You might want to collect information from people by using surveys or questionnaires. Web publishing will help you get your message out and collect data.

Web Publishing

What can I publish? The Web provides opportunities for publishing options ranging from a single page to an entire Web site.

A single Web page is simple to create and can publicize useful information, such as your resume or a small business fact sheet. Another use for a single Web page is to provide a list of links to sites with information on a particular topic.

A series of interlinked Web pages is essentially a mini Web site, except that it does not have its own domain name. You might publish a series of Web pages as part of a corporate site to describe the products and services offered by your department. Programmers or freelance artists might create a series of Web pages to publish examples of their work. A university instructor might publish a series of Web pages containing the syllabus, study guide, and assignments for a course.

A full Web site, with its own domain name, provides a solid point of presence on the Internet. Businesses and organizations of all types and sizes establish Web sites to provide information to customers and to sell products. With the availability of security software to protect customers' credit card numbers, online shopping has become very popular. Many online businesses try to use a recognizable domain name, such as *www.hilfiger.com*, which helps customers arrive at a site without a lengthy search.

You need only a few tools to create and publish basic pages that feature text, graphics, and links. More sophisticated Web pages might include animation, sound, video, and even interactive elements, such as questionnaires or surveys. To incorporate these sophisticated features in your Web pages, your Web server might require more elaborate publishing tools and special server software.

HTML

InfoWeb
12

HTML

What is an HTML tag? Every Web page is stored on a computer as an HTML document, which contains special instructions that tell a Web browser how to display the text, graphics, and background of that Web page. Each of these instructions, called an **HTML tag**, is inserted into the text of the document. If you look at the text of a Web page before it is displayed by a browser, you'll see the HTML tags set off in angle brackets. For example, in Figure 8-17, the sixth line contains the HTML tags <B> and </B>. The <B> tag means to begin boldfaced text. A companion tag </B> means to end the boldface. In Figure 8-17, you can examine an HTML document as it looks before and after it is displayed by a browser. See if you can figure out the purpose of the HTML tags <HR> and <IMG SRC>.

FIGURE 8-17

The HTML document (top) contains HTML tags that a browser uses to display the Web page (below).

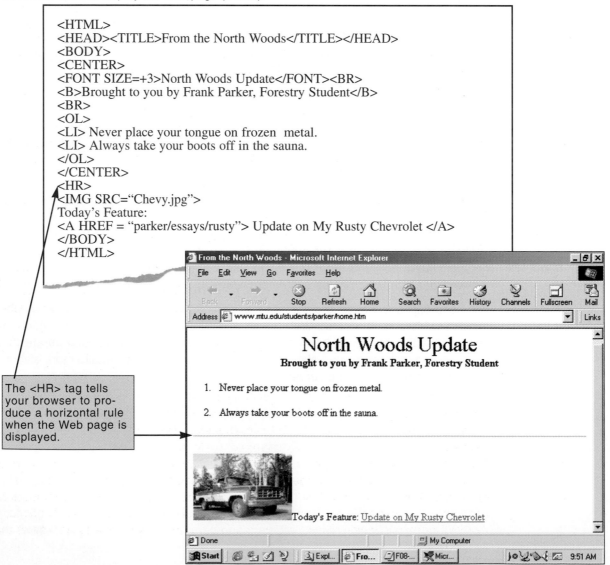

```
<HTML>
<HEAD><TITLE>From the North Woods</TITLE></HEAD>
<BODY>
<CENTER>
<FONT SIZE=+3>North Woods Update</FONT><BR>
<B>Brought to you by Frank Parker, Forestry Student</B>
<BR>
<OL>
<LI> Never place your tongue on frozen  metal.
<LI> Always take your boots off in the sauna.
</OL>
</CENTER>
<HR>
<IMG SRC="Chevy.jpg">
Today's Feature:
<A HREF = "parker/essays/rusty"> Update on My Rusty Chevrolet </A>
</BODY>
</HTML>
```

The <HR> tag tells your browser to produce a horizontal rule when the Web page is displayed.

Although you don't need to be concerned about HTML tags when you are simply viewing Web pages, a little background will help you understand how your Web browser works. A basic HTML document has two parts. The head of the document specifies a title that appears on the title bar of the Web browser when the Web page is displayed. The body of the document contains informational text, graphics, and links.

Every HTML document should begin with the tag <HTML> and end with the tag </HTML>. This point illustrates that some HTML tags work in pairs. A tag without the slash, such as <HTML>, is the opening tag. A tag with the slash, such as </HTML>, is the ending tag. Some tags do not have a corresponding end tag. For example, you need only a single <BR> tag to create a line break. Figure 8-18 lists a basic set of HTML tags that you could use to create HTML documents for Web pages.

FIGURE 8-18	Basic HTML Tags (Refer to Figure 8-17 for examples of these tags in use.)
HTML Tag	**Description and Use**
<HTML> </HTML>	Place the <HTML> tag at the beginning of a document and place the </HTML> tag at the end of the document.
<HEAD> <TITLE> ... </TITLE></HEAD>	Place immediately after the <HTML> tag. The text between the TITLE tags will appear on the title bar.
<BODY> </BODY>	Place all text and tags for the body of your Web page between the BODY tags.
<FONT SIZE=+3> ... </FONT>	To specify a font size, use a positive or negative number in place of +3.
 	The BR tag creates a line break. Use two to create a blank line.
<UL> </UL> or <OL> </OL>	UL creates a bulleted list; OL creates a numbered list. Start each list item with a <LI> tag.
<CENTER> ... </CENTER>	Text between the CENTER tags will be centered.
<B> .... </B>	Text between the B tags will appear in boldface.
<I> ... </I>	Text between the I tags will appear in italics.
<A HREF = " "> ... </A>	To create an underlined link, place the URL for the link between the quotation marks, then type the link name between the tags.
<IMG SCR=" " >	To display a graphic, place its filename between the quotation marks.
<HR>	The HR tag inserts a horizontal line.

HTML tags are basic Web page development tools and can be used successfully to create interesting Web pages. They have limitations, however, and consequently additional Web page development tools have appeared. **DHTML** (Dynamic HTML) allows elements of a Web page to be changed while the page is being viewed. **XML** (Extensible Markup Language) is a document format similar to HTML, but it allows the person who develops a Web page to define customized tags to produce effects that are not available with standard HTML. For even more flexibility, Web page developers can use **Java**, a programming language developed specially for Web applications, or **ActiveX controls**, which allow Web pages to perform software-like tasks, rather than simply displaying data.

CHAPTER 8

HTML Authoring Tools

InfoWeb
13

Authoring
Tools

Do I have to use HTML? The traditional way to create an HTML document is with a basic text editor, such as the Notepad program included with Microsoft Windows. You simply type the HTML tags and the text for your Web page, then save the file with an .htm extension. Remembering the purpose of each HTML tag, typing the tags into a document, and revising them is a fairly tedious task. Web authoring tools make it much easier to create Web pages using word processor-style interfaces, wizards, and pre-designed templates. Such tools are provided by many familiar application software packages and specialized Web authoring software.

FIGURE 8-19

Your word processing software might have a feature that converts your documents into HTML format.

Your word processing software will likely include Web authoring capabilities that allow you to create a standard document containing text and graphics, then save it in HTML format by automatically inserting HTML tags (Figure 8-19). Some spreadsheet, desktop publishing, and presentation software packages offer similar capabilities.

These familiar software tools help you create a Web page with a minimum of fuss, but they do not provide a high level of control over the final appearance of your Web page. For example, your word processor will do its best to translate your word processing document into an HTML document. Nevertheless, your word processing software is designed to create printed documents and includes features that are not available in HTML. Therefore, the exact formats and arrangement of elements that you see on your word processor's screen are not necessarily what will appear on the Web page.

As you learned in Chapter 2, Web authoring software is designed specifically to create HTML documents that will be displayed as Web pages. Popular Web authoring software titles include Microsoft FrontPage and Claris Home Page. Most of these packages provide a word processor-style interface, but allow you to implement only those features that are available in HTML. As you use Web authoring software to enter text, select type styles, and insert graphics, the software automatically inserts appropriate HTML tags.

Many Web authoring software packages also provide tools to manage an entire Web site. In addition to helping you create individual Web pages, such software maintains a map of page links and automatically tests links to pages at other sites to ensure that links are still valid. Your Web authoring software might also include Web server software so that you can test your Web site on your own computer.

Compared with using your familiar word processing software, it takes a little longer to get up and running with Web authoring software because you are learning a new package. However, if you intend to create more than an occasional Web page, such software offers greater flexibility in Web page design, and you'll save time testing and maintaining your pages.

Web Page Design Tips

How do I make a really great Web page? It is not easy to find the right balance between art and functionality that produces a really great Web page. Your skills will improve as you gain experience designing pages and as you continue to evaluate and use Web pages designed by others. The following tips can help you to avoid some of the mistakes typically made by beginning Web page designers.

InfoWeb 14

Authoring Tips

- **Plan your Web page so that it fulfills its purpose.** Determine the function of your Web page. Is its purpose to entertain, to persuade, to inform, or to instruct? A clear idea of your page's goals and functions will guide all of your design decisions. In this way, the function of your Web page will determine the form that it takes. Designs are more effective when form follows function than when form is used for form's sake.

- **Design a template to unify your pages.** A design template is a set of specifications for the location and format of all elements that you want to include on your Web pages. The purpose of a design template is to visually tie together a series of Web pages and provide a consistent interface. Your template design might include any of the following elements: background, title, text, lists, headings, subheadings, video clips, graphics, music, animations, and navigation buttons. You can get design ideas and develop a sense of style by looking at Web pages that are similar to those you plan to create.

- **Follow basic rules for good Web page design.** Viewers will lose patience and move on to other Web sites if it takes too long for your pages to appear or if the text is illegible. To make your site easy to read and use:

  - Maintain narrow line widths. Text that stretches across the entire width of the screen is more difficult to read than text in columns.

  - Make sure that you proofread your document and correct spelling errors.

  - Use contrasting colors for text and background. Black text on a white background is easiest to read.

  - Avoid drab gray as your background, but don't let background colors or graphics overpower your text.

  - Try not to use graphics files that exceed 30 KB because larger files take too long to transfer, load, and appear on a Web page.

  - Use graphics with .gif or .jpg filename extensions.

  - Present a large graphic as a small "thumbnail" with a link to the larger version of the graphic.

- **Identify your pages.** Make sure to use the <TITLE> tag on every page so that each page has a title. Also, include a way for people to contact you by including a link to your e-mail address. Place a copyright statement at the bottom of your page. The general format is the word "Copyright," followed by the year or a range of years, followed by your name: Copyright 1998 Bobby Quine.

- **Include dates.** Include a "last updated" date for the main page of your site. By also dating articles, essays, and other documents on your site, you help the reader place your information in context.

CHAPTER 8

■ **Plan your pages.** If your Web site will have multiple pages, sketch a hierarchy chart that shows how the pages will link to each other. Avoid a link plan that looks like a spider web. Although it is acceptable to have many exit links going to other pages, if possible, each page on your site should have only one entry link, as shown in Figure 8-20.

FIGURE 8-20

Sketch a plan that shows the structure of your Web site. Each box that represents a page has only one arrow pointing into the box, indicating a single entry point.

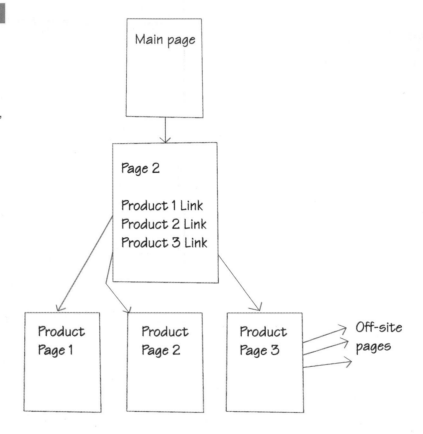

■ **Include navigation elements.** A carefully selected set of navigational buttons or links makes it easy for people to jump from page to page in a logical order. Navigation elements should be clearly visible and easy to understand. If you have multiple pages, always include a navigation element that takes the viewer back to your home page. Use the same navigation system on every page of your site.

■ **Respect the copyright and intellectual property rights of other Web sites.** If you use images and backgrounds that you have downloaded from the Web, make sure that you understand any copyright laws that apply to their reuse. Obtain permission before you use material from other Web sites and include a credit line on your page. For example, you could place a statement such as "Images courtesy of Paramount Pictures" at the bottom of your page.

Publishing Your Pages

How do I get my pages on the Internet? Creating a Web page is not the end of the publishing process. You also need to test your pages, transfer them to a Web server, and test all of your links.

1. **Test each page locally.** When you've completed the first draft of a Web page, you must test it to verify that every element is displayed correctly by a browser. You can accomplish this task without connecting to the Web by using your browser or Web authoring software. One caution: Your hard drive is much faster than a dial-up connection, so the text and graphics for your Web page will appear more quickly during your local test than they will for someone viewing your page over the Internet.

2. **Transfer pages to a Web server.** Whether you're publishing a single page, a series of pages, or an entire Web site, you must put your pages on a Web server. Although Web server software is available for your home computer, you probably will not want to leave your computer on continually with a live phone line link to the Internet. Instead, you should look for a site that will host your pages.

   Some universities allocate space for student home pages and resumes. ISPs such as America Online and AT&T also offer space for individual home pages. If you are setting up a site for your business, consider a **Web hosting service**, such as *www.highway.com*, that provides space on its Internet servers for a monthly fee.

3. **Test all links.** After you post your pages on a Web server, make sure that you test the links between your pages as well as your links to pages on other sites.

4. **Update your site to keep it current.** Periodically, you should review the information on your Web pages and verify that your links still connect to existing Web pages. You can easily change and test revised pages offline, then post them when they are completed. You might have encountered "Under Construction" signs at some Web sites, but they are typically unnecessary. You should handle your construction and revision work offline.

Building an E-commerce Site

Can I create my own online shopping site? **E-commerce** refers to buying products and services by means of the Internet. It encompasses online shopping at popular Web sites, such as Amazon.com's huge book store, MusicStreet.com's vast music CD outlet, or EddieBauer.com's online catalog of outdoor gear. E-commerce also applies to innovative online auction sites, such as *www.e-bay.com*. By 2001, e-commerce sites are expected to generate more than $17 billion in sales, with the average online shopper spending almost $800 annually.

E-commerce is not the exclusive domain of big business. Individuals can also set up e-commerce sites. Your e-commerce site could be a simple Web page that displays product information and a telephone number to call when placing an order. Alternatively, it could be an extensive online catalog that automatically takes customer orders and processes credit card information.

CHAPTER 8

InfoWeb 15

E-commerce
Construction

Many Web hosting services and portal sites offer an **e-commerce enabled Web site**, which simplifies the process of constructing an online storefront. For example, for about $35 per month, you can set up a site for as many as 12 products where shoppers use an online "shopping cart" to collect the products they want to purchase. You receive your customers' orders via e-mail and you can process them manually using standard forms provided by major credit card companies. For about $125 per month, you can establish an e-commerce site with an unlimited number of products and real-time payment processing where the Web site contacts the credit card company to automatically verify the card number and credit your bank account.

The software that runs your e-commerce site—displays your merchandise, collects orders, and processes credit cards—typically resides on the computers of your Web hosting service. As the "e-merchant" you are responsible for designing the Web pages for your site. To get your site up and running, you use your browser to access an e-commerce construction site provided by your Web hosting service. This process requires minimal technical skills, but an understanding of the Web is important. Before beginning the design process, you might find it useful to visit a variety of e-commerce sites to get ideas about how to display your merchandise, build customer confidence, simplify the order process, and create a policy for returning merchandise.

QUICKCHECK C

1 To create basic Web pages that contain only text, graphics, and _____, your Web server will not require additional software.

2 When HTML tags come in pairs, the first tag begins with a slash (/). True or false? _____

3 A basic HTML document has two parts—the head and the _____.

4 _____ software is specifically designed to create HTML documents that will be displayed as Web pages.

5 A basic Web design rule is to avoid using graphic files larger than 30 KB on your Web pages. True or false? _____

6 A careful selection of _____ buttons or links makes it easy for people to jump from page to page in a logical order.

7 When you test your pages locally, your Web pages appear more quickly than when they are viewed by a user with a dial-up Web connection. True or false? _____

8 A(n) _____ enabled Web site goes beyond simple Web pages to provide services such as online shopping carts and real-time credit card processing.

Check Answers

USER FOCUS — CONNECTING TO THE INTERNET

If your school has Internet access, your Academic Computing department has probably installed the hardware and software that you need to access the Internet from your school lab, and possibly from your dorm room. But what if you want to access the Internet from your computer at home?

To access the Internet from your home computer, you must locate an Internet service provider, set up the necessary computer equipment, install the appropriate software on your computer, and then establish your connection.

Locate an Internet Service Provider

Who will provide me with an Internet connection, and how much will it cost?

An ISP supplies you with a user account on a host computer that has access to the Internet. When you connect your personal computer to the host computer, you gain access to the Internet. Depending on your location, you might have a variety of options when it comes to selecting an ISP.

Your school might provide Internet access for students and faculty who want to use the Internet from off campus. An Internet connection provided by an educational institution is typically free.

InfoWeb
16

ISPs

Many commercial information services, such as CompuServe, AT&T WorldNet, Microsoft Network, and America Online, provide Internet access. Internet connections are also offered by some telephone companies, cable TV companies, and independent telecommunications firms. These firms charge between $10 and $40 per month for Internet access. Unlike commercial information services, they usually do not maintain their own online information, discussion groups, or downloadable software.

When selecting an ISP you should ask the following questions:

■ What is the monthly subscription rate?

■ Does the subscription rate include unlimited access?

■ Is an e-mail account included? Can you get additional e-mail accounts for other family members?

■ Does the ISP offer additional services, such as hosting personal Web pages?

■ What modem type and speed are recommended?

■ Is any additional equipment necessary (such as a network card for a connection through your cable TV provider) and who supplies it?

■ What connection speed can you expect?

■ Does the ISP require that you install any special communications software?

■ Can you access the ISP from other cities without paying for a long-distance call?

■ Can you get technical support during the hours that you're likely to be online?

CHAPTER 8

Set Up Equipment

What special equipment do I need to access the Internet? Although you can access the Internet using the cable television system, a personal satellite dish, or a cellular phone system, most people use a telephone line. The basic equipment for setting up this type of connection is a computer, a modem, and a telephone line. The equipment you use does not change the activities you can do online, but it can affect the speed at which you can accomplish these activities.

PCs and Macintosh computers can both connect to online services. A fast computer, such as a 600 MHz Pentium, speeds up some activities such as viewing graphics online. Nevertheless, the overall speed of online activities is limited by the speed of the Internet server, the speed of your modem, and the speed of your communications link.

A telephone modem (usually referred to simply as a "modem") converts the data from your computer into signals that can travel over telephone lines. It also translates arriving signals into data that your computer can store, manipulate, and display. Follow the instructions included with your modem to set it up (Figure 8-21).

FIGURE 8-21

Connect your modem to your computer, then connect it to the wall jack for your telephone. You can also connect your telephone to your modem so that you have voice as well as data communications.

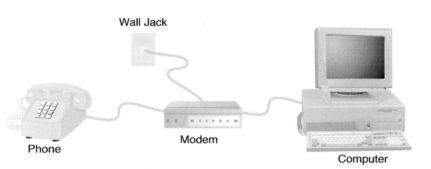

Wall Jack

Phone

Modem

Computer

A fast modem speeds up the process of sending and receiving data. Most modems today have a maximum speed of 56 kilobits per second (Kbps), although this speed is not necessarily the speed at which you will send and receive data.

FIGURE 8-22

When you are online, you can check your connection speed by double-clicking the connection icon on the Windows task bar.

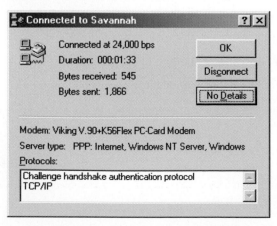

Your **connection speed** is the maximum speed at which your modem can communicate with the modems maintained by your ISP. When you dial in to your ISP, your modem and the ISP's modem negotiate a communications rate. Even if you call in using a 56 Kbps (56,000 bps) modem, your connection speed might be only 24 Kbps (24,000 bps) if your ISP has only slow modems available. You can check your connection speed when you are online by double-clicking the connection icon in the right corner of the Windows task bar (Figure 8-22).

Your **transfer rate** is the speed at which you can actually send or receive data. The quality of the phone lines in your city, the number of other people who are accessing your ISP, and the amount of traffic on the Internet can all affect transfer rate. You can be using a 56 Kbps modem and have a connection speed of 24 Kbps, but your transfer rate might be as low as 10 Kbps when traffic is high.

The telephone line that you use for voice communications is suitable for most online activities. Corporations sometimes use faster communications links such as ISDN or T1. Your telephone line, though not the speediest communications link, is certainly the least expensive.

When you are using your telephone line for online activities, you can't simultaneously use it for voice calls; while you are online, people who call you will get a busy signal. If you pick up the telephone receiver to make an outgoing call while you are online, your online connection will terminate. If you have call waiting, you should temporarily disable it while you are online because the call-waiting tone can terminate your Internet connection. Your phone company can supply you with the necessary instructions.

Install Software

Where do I get the software I need? **Internet communications software** allows your computer to transmit and receive data using the Internet's TCP/IP communications protocol. Standard TCP/IP software handles Internet communication between computers that are directly cabled to a network. **SLIP** (Serial Line Internet Protocol) and **PPP** (Point-to-Point Protocol) are versions of TCP/IP designed to handle dial-up Internet communications. When you want to access the Internet using a telephone modem, you must use PPP, SLIP, or similar communications software.

Many ISPs provide their subscribers with a complete software package that includes a browser and Internet communications software. This software is self-configuring, so that the first time you run the software, it examines your computer system and automatically selects the appropriate software settings. You have to deal with a manual installation only if your computer equipment, modem, or telephone line is not standard.

The Windows operating system also provides Internet communications software, which you can configure for your ISP, as shown in Figure 8-23.

FIGURE 8-23

If your ISP does not provide communications software, you can use the Dial-Up Networking software that is provided with the Windows operating system.

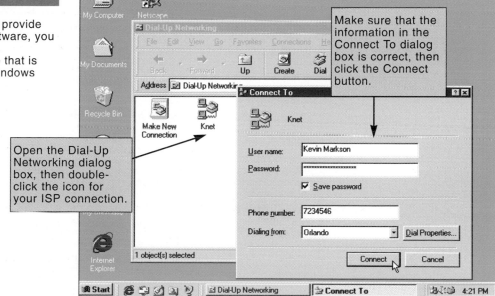

Make sure that the information in the Connect To dialog box is correct, then click the Connect button.

Open the Dial-Up Networking dialog box, then double-click the icon for your ISP connection.

Start
Screentour

CHAPTER 8

Dial In

After my hardware is set up and my software is installed, how do I dial in to the Internet? Most Internet communications software is represented by an icon on your computer's desktop or Start menu. You start the software by clicking this icon, and it automatically establishes a connection to the Internet. Figure 8-24 shows what happens when you dial in.

FIGURE 8-24

When you use a dial-up connection to access the Internet, you are essentially placing a phone call to your ISP.

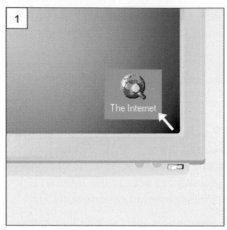

Click the Internet icon supplied by your Internet service provider.

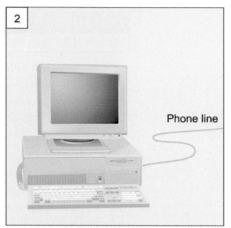

By clicking the Internet icon, you tell the computer to load your Internet communications client software, which will use SLIP, PPP, or a similar protocol to handle TCP/IP protocols as your computer transmits and receives data through your modem.

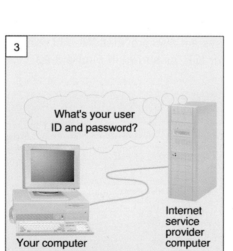

Your communications client software dials the Internet service provider. Usually, your client software has stored the ISP's telephone number, so you do not need to enter it each time that you want to connect.

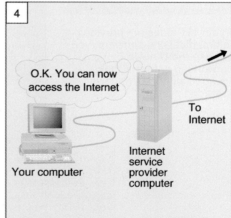

If your communications client software has stored your user ID and password, it will automatically log you in. Some people prefer to enter their password manually for better security.

ISSUE   IS THE TRUTH OUT THERE?

InfoWeb
18

Information
Quality

In an episode of the *X-Files*, Agent Scully warns Mulder about his search into the unexplored realm of extraterrestrial and paranormal phenomena: "The truth is out there, but so are lies." And so it is on the Internet, where truth mingles with lies, rumors, myths, and urban legends. The Internet is uncensored and unregulated. Anyone with a Web page or an e-mail account can rapidly and widely distribute information, which is often redistributed and forwarded like a chain letter on steroids. As an example, one e-mail message, circulated in the summer of 1999, contained this alarming first-person account: "When Zack was 2 years old, I put on the waterproof sunscreen. I don't know how, but he got some in his eyes. I called the poison control center and they told me to rush Zack to the ER now. I found out for the first time that many kids each year lose their sight to waterproof sunscreen. Zack did go blind for two days. It was horrible."

Worried parents forwarded this e-mail message to their friends, and many of them threw their sunscreen in the trash. In August of that year, members of an NBC television news team reported that they had researched the story, but failed to find evidence of any child becoming blind from sunscreen. They concluded their report by saying, "This is one of those stories that has spun out of control—touted as fact, when in reality, it's nothing more than a modern Internet myth."

The Internet has also been blamed for circulating reports that the U.S. Navy shot down TWA Flight 800. Pierre Salinger, an ex-TV reporter and a former advisor to President John F. Kennedy, made front-page headlines in November 1996 when he displayed documents that described how the Navy was testing missiles off Long Island and accidentally hit Flight 800. Although Salinger would not reveal the source of the documents, it turned out that they had been circulated on the Internet months earlier.

FIGURE 8-25

It is easy to spread conspiracy theories on the Internet, but several "watchdog" sites try to present the "facts" that dispute or confirm the theories.

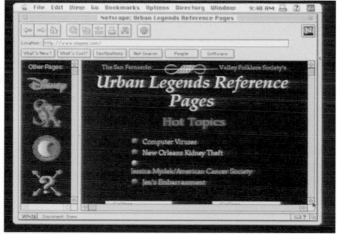

 Start
Video

The *Chicago Tribune* described Salinger's error as "merely the latest outbreak of the disturbing new information-age phenomenon of bogus news," and went on to say that "America is awash in a growing and often disruptive avalanche of false information that takes on a life of its own in the electronic ether of the Internet, talk radio, and voice mail until it becomes impervious to denial and debunking."

But is it fair to say that the Internet has a monopoly on false information? Probably not. Even well-established newspapers, magazines, and television news shows report stories that are later found to be misleading or untrue. In an article published online in *Salon*, Scott Rosenberg asks, "Who's more responsible for the spread of misinformation, the Internet or the news media? Well, ask yourself how you first heard of Salinger's memo: was it from the Net, or from a TV broadcast? The sad truth is that the old media are far more efficient disseminators of bogus news than the new."

Before the Internet became a ubiquitous part of modern life, certain "rules of thumb" helped to distinguish truth from lies and fact from fiction. In *The Truth About URLs*, Robin Raskin writes, "When printed junk mail floods our overcrowded mailboxes we have some antennae for the bogus causes and the fly-by-night foundations. We've come to expect the *New York Times* to be a credible source of information; we're not as sure about *The National Inquirer*... It takes years to establish these sorts of cultural cues for knowing whether we're getting good information or a bum steer."

Perhaps the Internet has not been around long enough for us to establish the cultural cues we need to distinguish fact from fiction in Web pages, e-mails, online chats, and discussion groups. You can, however, get some help from the Web itself. A number of sites keep track of the myths and legends that circulate on the Internet. Before you spread dire warnings about sunscreen or call a press conference to report a government coverup, you might want to check one of these sites for the real scoop.

WHAT DO YOU THINK?

1. Do older people tend to be more naïve about Internet information than young people?   ○ Yes   ○ No   ○ Not sure

2. Have you ever received e-mail chain letters or alarming messages about fake viruses?   ○ Yes   ○ No   ○ Not sure

3. Do you have your own set of rules to help you evaluate information on the Internet?   ○ Yes   ○ No   ○ Not sure

 Save Responses

CHAPTER 8 — REVIEW ACTIVITIES

INTERACTIVE SUMMARY

The Interactive Summary helps you select important concepts and facts from this chapter. Fill in the blanks to best complete each sentence. When using the NP4 CD or NP4 Web site, you can click the Check Answers buttons to automatically score your answers. Place your Tracking Disk in the floppy disk drive if you want to save your scores.

The Internet evolved from an experimental network called _____, which was developed in 1969 to help scientists communicate and share computing resources. Today, the Internet has expanded to nearly every country in the world and its traffic is measured in _____. The Internet is a communications network that uses a standard communications protocol called _____. The Web servers, FTP servers, e-mail servers, routers, and other equipment that are permanently connected to the Internet are called _____ computers. Each of these computers has a unique identifying number called a(n) _____ address, and many also have an easy-to-remember _____ name, such as *www.spiegel.com.*

One of the most popular aspects of the Internet is the World Wide Web—popularly called "the Web." Using Web _____ software, it is easy to navigate from one page of information to another by following underlined links. Web pages are stored on a Web server, and each page has a unique address called a(n) _____. Many Web pages include media elements, such as video, sound, and animation. Viewing Web page media elements typically requires a special software module called a(n) _____. Your Web browser also allows you to download data files and software from Internet sites. The software that you download has typically been stored as a(n) _____ file, so that you must "reconstitute" it and install it before you can use it.

Check Answers

A Web page is stored in _____ format that uses a series of tags, such as <B> and <HR>, to tell your browser software how to display text and graphics. It is possible to create an HTML document using a simple text editor, such as Notepad, but most word processing software provides a menu option for saving a standard document as a Web page. More sophisticated Web _____ software is designed specifically to create HTML documents and provides tools to manage entire Web sites. Web pages must be stored on a Web server so that they are available to the public. Many ISPs offer Web server space for personal Web pages; some also offer space for e-commerce sites.

Most people who access the Internet from home use a phone line to establish a temporary dial-up connection to a(n) _____, which provides Internet access for a monthly fee. A dial-up connection requires a piece of equipment called a(n) _____ and Internet communications software. The speed at which you can carry out online activities depends on several factors, including modem speed, _____ speed, and the data transfer rate.

Check Answers

INTERACTIVE KEY TERMS

Make sure that you understand all of the boldfaced key terms presented in this chapter. If you're using the NP4 CD or NP4 Web site, you can use this list of terms as an interactive study activity. First, try to define a term in your own words, then click the term to compare your definition with the definition that is presented in the chapter.

ActiveX controls, 365
Animated GIF, 357
ARPANET, 346
Asynchronously, 361
Chat group, 361
Commercial information services, 356
Connection speed, 372
Cyberspace, 345
DHTML, 365
Dial-up connection, 349
Discussion group, 361
Domain name, 350
Downloading, 359
E-commerce, 369
E-commerce enabled Web site, 370
Exabyte, 347
FTP client software, 359
FTP servers, 352
Home page, 351
HTML tag, 364
HTTP (Hypertext Transfer Protocol), 351
In-place multimedia technology, 357
Internet backbone, 348
Internet communications software, 373
Internet host, 347
Internet traffic, 347
IP address, 350
IRC servers, 352
ISP (Internet service provider), 349
Internet traffic, 347
IP address, 350
Java, 365
Links, 354
Multimedia overlay technology, 358

Multi-player gaming, 362
Network access points (NAPs), 348
Network service provider (NSP), 348
Player, 358
Plug-in, 358
PPP (Point-to-Point Protocol), 373
Router, 350
Self-extracting file, 360
Site, 350
SLIP (Serial Line Internet Protocol), 373
Streaming media, 357
Synchronously, 361
TCP/IP, 348
Top-level domain, 350
Transfer rate, 372
Uploading, 359
URL (Uniform Resource Locator), 351
Usenet servers, 352
Viewer, 358
Web hosting service, 369
Web pages, 351
Web portal, 356
Web server, 351
Web site, 350
XML, 365

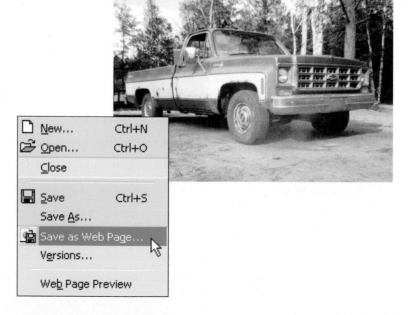

New...   Ctrl+N
Open...   Ctrl+O
Close

Save   Ctrl+S
Save As...
Save as Web Page...
Versions...

Web Page Preview

INTERACTIVE QUIZZES

Quiz yourself on important concepts from this chapter by filling in the blanks. When using the NP4 CD or NP4 Web site, you can type your answers, then use the Check Answers buttons to automatically score your responses. Place your Tracking Disk in the floppy disk drive if you want to save your scores.

1 The Internet [_____] is a series of major communications links that carry data from one NAP to another.

2 The acronym for the standard communications protocol used by all Internet computers is [_____].

3 Most people who access the Internet pay a monthly fee to a(n) [_____] that provides a dial-up connection.

4 A(n) [_____] is the address of a Web page.

5 A(n) [_____] server maintains files that you can upload and download.

6 A(n) [_____] tag, such as <CENTER>, tells a Web browser how to display a Web page.

7 Good Web page design requires the use of large graphics and banner headlines. True or false? [_____]

8 Although you can use your computer as a Web server, most people prefer to post Web pages on a Web [_____] service.

9 If you connect to the Internet using a 56 Kbps modem, you will typically be able to transfer data at that rate. True or false? [_____]

10 Dial-up Internet connections typically use SLIP or [_____] communications protocols.

 Check Answers

Enter the letter from the diagram that correctly matches each element in the list below.

1 The Internet backbone [_____]

2 A NAP or NSP [_____]

3 A dial-up connection [_____]

4 An ISP [_____]

5 A PC with a modem [_____]

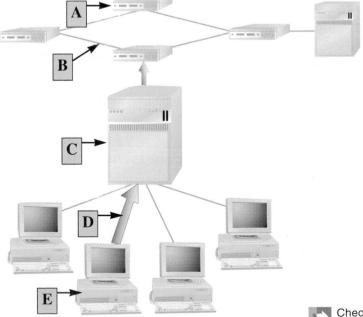

Check Answers

INTERACTIVE PRACTICE TESTS

When you use the NP4 CD or NP4 Web site, you can take practice tests that consist of 10 multiple-choice, true/false, and fill-in-the-blank questions. The 10 questions are selected at random from a large test bank, so each time you take a test, you'll receive a different set of questions. Your tests are scored immediately and you can print study guides that help you find the correct answers for any questions that you missed. If you are using a Tracking Disk, insert it in the floppy disk drive to save your test scores.

 Start Practice Test

STUDY TIPS

Study Tips help you organize and consolidate the information in a chapter by making lists, outlines, charts, and sketches. You can use paper and pencil or word processing software to complete most of the Study Tips activities.

1 Below each heading in this chapter, there is a question. Look back through the chapter and answer each of these questions using your own words.

2 Draw a conceptual diagram that shows how the Internet connects computers. Include and label the following elements: backbone, dial-up connection, host computers, router, NSP computer, NAP, ISP computer, home computer.

3 Provide an example of an IP address, a domain name, a URL, and an e-mail address. In your own words, describe the elements that each contains.

4 Make a list of the Internet services you can access using a Web browser.

5 Indicate the type of software you can use to do each of the following:
  a. Download a file.
  b. View a Web page.
  c. Play a multimedia element.

6 Describe what happens when you view a Web page and how it differs from downloading a file.

7 Describe the difference between a Web server and a Web site.

8 On the Internet, you can interact with people in discussion groups, chat groups, and interactive games. Describe the difference between synchronous and asynchronous interactions and explain how each relates to chats, discussion groups, and games.

9 Explain the tools that you can use to create HTML documents.

10 Make a photocopy of Figure 8-17. Draw arrows from the HTML document to the Web page showing which lines in the document created each element on the Web page. For example, you would draw an arrow from the line in the document that contains <HR> to the horizontal line on the Web page.

11 List the steps you would take to connect your computer at home to the Internet.

PROJECTS

A project is an open-ended activity that will help you apply the concepts you have learned. Many projects require resources in addition to your textbook, such as current magazines, library materials, or Web access. When you tackle a project, be prepared to use your critical thinking skills, logical analysis, and your creativity.

1   **Good Netiquette** The Internet, like most societies, has certain standards for behavior. What's generally acceptable online behavior in cyberspace culture? Use the Internet or your library resources to research this topic, then design a poster of netiquette rules. You can decide what audience your poster targets: children, high school students, college students, or business people. You could even select a specific business. Try to use words and images that will appeal to your target audience.

2   **No One Knows You're a Dog** In a novel called *Ender's War,* two children are catapulted to national prominence because they have innovative ideas about how to solve critical social and economic issues. No one knows they are children, however, because they communicate their ideas on a public information service, which is the central political forum in their society. This novel brings up an interesting issue, humorously alluded to in the P. Steiner cartoon.

Discuss this issue in a small group. In your discussion, address questions (a) through (d).

a. Does a communications medium that depends on the written word—rather than on videos—reduce cultural, class, ethnic, and gender bias?

b. According to pollsters, in 1980 many Americans voted for Ronald Reagan because they didn't like his opponent's Southern accent. Do you think the election would have been different if campaigning was carried out over the Internet?

c. Some evidence suggests that children who spend their free time in front of a television or computer screen tend not like to read and write. Do you think that e-mail, discussion groups, and chat groups can offset this tendency?

"On the Internet, nobody knows you're a dog."

d. Can anyone in your group relate an experience when online communications would have been preferable to face-to-face communication?

3   **Compare ISPs** When you use a dial-up line to connect to the Internet, it is preferable to make a local call rather than a long distance call. Therefore, you should pick an ISP that offers a dial-up number in your local calling area. Use the Internet, your library, and other resources to find a list of ISPs in your area. Don't forget to check commercial information services such as CompuServe, Prodigy, MSN, and AOL all the information you can about rates, reliability, quality of technical support, and services. Next, suppose that you are a reporter for your local newspaper. Write an article (about two pages, double-spaced) for the paper that compares the ISPs that offer local dial-up connections to the Internet.

CHAPTER 8

4 **Web Site Makeover** To some extent, good design is a matter of taste. When it comes to Web page design, there are usually many possible solutions that provide a pleasing look and efficient navigational tools. On the other hand, some designs just don't seem to work because they make the text difficult to read or navigate.

For this project, select a Web page that you think could use improvement. You may find the page by browsing on the Web or by looking in magazines for screen shots of Web pages. Use colored pencils or markers to sketch a plan for improving the page. Annotate your sketch by pointing out the features you have changed and why you think your makeover will be more effective than the original Web page.

5 **Design a Web Site** For this project, you'll design a Web site for yourself or for an e-commerce business (which can be fictitious). Depending on the tools you have available, you might be able to create real pages and publish them on the Web. If these tools are not available, you will still be able to complete the initial design work for this project. Your instructor will provide you with guidelines on which of the following steps to complete.

a. Write a brief description of the purpose of your Web site and your expected audience. For example, you might plan to use the site to showcase your resume to prospective employers.

b. List the elements that you plan to include on your Web site. Briefly describe any graphics or media that you want to include.

c. Make sketches of your Web site showing the structure of pages and links (like the sketch in Figure 8-20), the colors you plan to use, and the navigation elements you want to include. Annotate your sketches to describe how these elements follow effective Web page design guidelines.

d. Create a document that contains the information that you want to include for the home page of your Web site. If you have the tools, create this document in HTML format and test the page locally using your browser. Print your document or Web page.

e. If you have permission to publish your Web page on a Web server, do so. Provide your instructor with the URL for your page.

ADDITIONAL PROJECTS

Click the underlined text to link to the NP4 Web site (www.cciw.com/np4), where you can view and print additional projects for this chapter.

The Great Internet Hunt

Internet Censorship

Virtual Reality

LAB ASSIGNMENTS

Software for these labs is provided on the NP4 CD and may also be available in your school's computer lab. To start a lab, click the lab icon.

Each lab has two parts: Steps and Explore. Use the Steps first to learn and review concepts. Read the information on each page and do the numbered steps. As you work through the lab, you will be asked to answer QuickCheck questions about what you have learned. At the end of the lab, you will see a report that summarizes your answers to the QuickChecks. If your instructor wants you to turn in this report, click the Print button on the QuickCheck Report screen.

When you have completed Steps, you can click the Explore button to complete the Lab Assignments. You can also use Explore to practice the skills you learned and to explore concepts on your own.

Lab
The World Wide Web

One of the most popular services on the Internet is the World Wide Web. This lab is a Web simulator that teaches you how to use Web browser software to find information. You can use this lab whether or not your school provides you with Internet access.

1 Click the Steps button to learn how to use Web browser software. As you proceed through the Steps, answer all of the QuickCheck questions that appear. After you complete the Steps, you will see a QuickCheck Summary Report. Follow the instructions on the screen to print this report.

2 Click the Explore button on the Welcome screen. Use the Web browser to locate a weather map of the Caribbean Virgin Islands. What is its URL?

3 A Scuba diver named Wadson Lachouffe has been searching for the fabled treasure of Greybeard the pirate. A link from the Adventure Travel Web site, *www.atour.com*, leads to Wadson's Web page called "Hidden Treasure." In Explore, locate the Hidden Treasure page and answer the following questions:

   a. What was the name of Greybeard's ship?

   b. What was Greybeard's favorite food?

   c. What does Wadson think happened to Greybeard's ship?

4 In the Steps, you found a graphic of Jupiter from the photo archives of the Jet Propulsion Laboratory. In the Explore section of the lab, you can also find a graphic of Saturn. Suppose one of your friends wanted a picture of Saturn for an astronomy report. Make a list of the blue, underlined links your friend must click in the correct order to find the Saturn graphic. Assume that your friend will begin at the Web Trainer home page.

5 Enter the URL *http://www.atour.com* to jump to the Adventure Travel Web site. Write a one-page description of this site. In your paper, include a description of the information at the site, the number of pages the site contains, and a diagram of the links it provides.

6 Chris Thomson is a student at UVI and has his own Web pages. In Explore, look at the information Chris has included on his pages. Suppose you could create your own Web page. What would you include? Use word processing software to design your own Web pages. Make sure you indicate the graphics and links you would use.

Lab
Web Pages
& HTML

It's easy to create your own Web pages. As you learned in this chapter, many software tools are available to help you become a Web author. In this lab you'll experiment with a Web authoring wizard that automates the process of creating a Web page. You'll also try your hand at working directly with HTML code.

1. Click the Steps button to activate the Web authoring wizard and learn how to create a basic Web page. As you proceed through the Steps, answer all of the QuickCheck questions. After you complete the Steps, you will see a QuickCheck Summary Report. Follow the instructions on the screen to print this report.

2. In Explore, click the File menu, then click New to start working on a new Web page. Use the wizard to create a home page for a veterinarian who offers dog day-care and boarding services. After you create the page, save it on drive A or C, and print the HTML code. Your site must have the following characteristics:

   a. Title: Dr. Dave's Dog Domain

   b. Background color: Gold

   c. Graphic: Dog.jpg

   d. Body text: Your dog will have the best care day and night at Dr. Dave's Dog Domain. Fine accommodations, good food, play time, and snacks are all provided. You can board your pet by the day or week. Grooming services also available.

   e. Text link: "Reasonable rates" links to *www.cciw.com/np3/rates.htm*

   f. E-mail link: "For more information:" links to *daveassist@drdave.com*

3. In Explore, use the File menu to open the HTML document called *Politics.htm*. After you use the HTML window (not the wizard) to make the following changes, save the revised page on drive A or C, and print the HTML code. Refer to Figure 8-18 of your textbook for a list of HTML tags you can use.

   a. Change the title to Politics 2000.

   b. Center the page heading.

   c. Change the background color to FFE7C6 and the text color to 000000.

   d. Add a line break before the sentence "What's next?"

   e. Add a bold tag to "Additional links on this topic:".

   f. Add one more link to the "Additional links" list. The link should go to the site *http://www.elections.ca* and the clickable link should read "Elections Canada".

   g. Change the last graphic to display the image "next.gif".

4. In Explore, use the Web authoring wizard and the HTML window to create a home page about yourself. You should include at least a screenful of text, a graphic, an external link, and an e-mail link. Save the page on drive A, then print the HTML code. Turn in your disk and printout.

INFOWEB

The InfoWeb is your guide to print, film, television, and electronic resources. Use it to obtain updates on quickly changing technical information and to locate information for research papers. If you're using the NP4 CD, click the InfoWeb Site icon on the left side of this paragraph to access the online InfoWeb links. Otherwise, use your Web browser and type in the address of the NP4 Web site: www.cciw.com/np4. At the Web site you'll find up-to-date links to the topics covered in this chapter.

1 Cyberspace

According to *Forbes* magazine (July 7, 1997, p. 348), "Science fiction is more than an inelegant prose for pencil-necked teenagers. Businesspeople and investors looking to discover where technology is taking us would do well to pay attention to it." The article describes how science fiction can sometimes become reality. For a serious analysis of the potential effects of cyberspace on society, check your library for the book *Cyberspace: First Steps*, edited by Michael Benedikt (MIT Press, 1993). William Gibson is generally recognized as the person who coined the term "cyberspace." His novel, *Neuromancer* (Ace Books, 1995) was the first of a literary genre now called cyberpunk. At sites such as *www.georgetown.edu/irvinemj/technoculture/pomosf.html*, you can find more information about William Gibson and post-modern science fiction. At The Electronic Freedom Foundation page, *www.eff.org/pub/Publications/William_Gibson*, you'll find some links to essays and interviews. You can scope out additional links by using the Yahoo! search engine and entering "William Gibson." On the lighter side of cyberspace literature, pick up the book *Dave Barry in Cyberspace* (Fawcett Books, 1997).

2 Internet History

Many reliable sources have reported that the Internet was built because the U.S. military wanted a computer network that would survive nuclear attack. Bob Taylor, father of the ARPANET, refutes this myth in the book *Where Wizards Stay Up Late* by Hafner and Lyon (Touchstone Books, 1998). A good introduction to the Internet is the PBS site Understanding and Using the Internet at *www.pbs.org/uti/welcome.html*. It provides links to resources such as "A Beginner's Guide to the Internet," a quiz on understanding and using the Internet, and videos such as "Understanding the Internet" (PBS Home Video, 1996). Several of the people involved

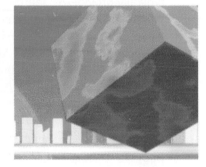

in the initial development and evolution of the Internet have written "A Brief History of the Internet" at *www.isoc.org/internet-history*. You can visit sites, such as *www.geocities.com/~anderberg/ant/history* or *www.davesite.com/webstation/net-history.shtml*, for timelines outlining the history of the Internet. Interactive timelines outlining the history of the Internet can also be found at sites such as *www.pbs.org/internet/timeline*. You'll find an on-going discussion of Internet history at the Computer Professionals for Social Responsibility's Community Memory: Discussion List on the History of Cyberspace at *memex.org/community-memory.html*.

3 Internet Statistics

It's difficult to keep track of the wild growth of the Internet. Some organizations do, however, try to gather information and make educated guesses about Internet growth. For example, Texas-based MIDs (*www.mids.org/topics/index.html*) provides not only detailed information, statistics, and maps about Internet growth, but also a link to "Internet Visualization," which is a slide presentation that helps you visualize Internet growth. For the latest market research from various sources, connect to sites such as the CyberAtlas site at *cyberatlas.internet.com*. The "Domain Survey" link at the Internet Software Consortium site, *www.isc.org*, provides statistics on the growing number of Internet hosts. Many analysts rely on information provided by Penton Media at *boardwatch.internet.com*. Georgia Institute of Technology's Graphics, Visualization, and Usability Center conducts extensive surveys of Web use. You can check out its results by connecting to *www.gvu.gatech.edu* and following the survey link for "World Wide Web Surveys." You can have some fun and make your own wild projections about the Internet using the Internet Statistic Generator at *www.anamorph.com/docs/stats/stats.html*.

4 Domain Names

If you set up your own Internet site, you'll want your own domain name. How will you know if the name you want is available? At the site *www.checkdomain.com*, you can enter a domain name such as "neuromancer.com" to see if it has already been reserved. Could you select a generic domain name such as *www.government.com*? For information on restricted domain names, tips on creating a valid domain name, and instructions on how to register a domain name, connect to the InterNIC server at *www.internic.net*. You can find additional information about Internet domain names by connecting to *www.isi.edu/in-notes/usdnr/usdom-overview.html*.

5 The Web

CERN (the European Laboratory for Particle Physics) is the birthplace of the World Wide Web. You can visit its site at *www.cern.ch* and search for "World Wide Web and CERN" to read a bit about its history. Another site for historical and archival information about the Web is maintained by the World Wide Web Consortium (W3C) at *www.w3.org/History.html*. The Web Consortium's home page at *www.w3.org* contains great links about the Web. You can also use a search engine to find information about the Web's inventor Tim Berners-Lee.

6 Web Portals

A Web portal makes a handy home page because it typically provides a search engine and links to shopping, chat, and peoplefinder sites. Some Web portals are maintained by commercial information services, such as America Online (*www.aol.com*), CompuServe (*www.compuserve.com*), Prodigy (*www.prodigy.com*), AT&T WorldNet (*www.worldnet.att.net*), and Microsoft Network (*www.msn.com*). Many of today's search engines, such as Yahoo!, Excite, Lycos, and the GO Network, are also designed to be Web portals. You can find comparisons of Web portals in computer magazines, such as the "Web Portals" article in the September 1, 1998, issue of *PC Magazine* (also online at *www.zdnet.com/pcmag/features/webportals/index.html*).

7 Plug-ins

Plug-ins provide access to audio, video, graphics, and 3-D file formats. How do you know which plug-ins you really need? You can read reviews at sites such as the NetGuide Internet Plug-ins page at *www.netguide.com/Internet/Plugins* and download plug-ins at sites like *www.download.com* (enter "plug-in" in the search box). BrowserWatch Plug-In Plaza at *browserwatch.internet.com/plug-in.html* provides links to all of the plug-ins available on the Internet. Plug-ins are one of the most quickly changing aspects of the Web, and most computer magazines periodically include one or two articles about them. At *www.pcworld.com/software/internet_www/articles/apr97/1504p110m.html*, you can read "Plunging into Plug-Ins" from the April 1997 issue of *PC World*. This article also includes download links and tells you how to remove plug-ins that you no longer want to use—something that is not as easy to do as you would hope. Books such as *Supercharged Web Browsers: A Plug-Ins Field Guide* by Cheryl Kirk and Erica Sadun (Charles River Media, 1998) provide another resource for basic information about plug-ins.

8 FTP Software

FTP (File Transfer Protocol) is probably one of the oldest, most useful, and easiest-to-use Internet applications. FTP software allows you to upload and download files from computers throughout the world. Windows 95 and 98 include FTP software, but it uses a command-line interface, so most users prefer other GUI-based FTP software such as WS_FTP Professional. You can download the shareware version from *www.ipswitch.com/Products/WS_FTP/index.html*. WinFTP is a popular Windows FTP program that you can download from *www.winsite.com/info/pc/win3/programr/winftp.zip*. File Dog at *www.edgepub.com/fd* is FTP shareware for Windows that has been highly rated by *PC Magazine*. File Dog makes a free evaluation copy available to potential users. You can read about and download an evaluation copy of another popular program, CuteFTP, at *www.cuteftp.com*. Macintosh users can look for a program called Fetch at *www.dartmouth.edu/pages/softdev/fetch.html*, which is free for users affiliated with an educational institution or nonprofit organization.

9 Download Sites

Where can you go to download the best software? The granddaddy of all download sites is maintained by Ziff-Davis at *www.zdnet.com/swlib*. At that site you'll find descriptions, ratings, and links for thousands of shareware programs. Other popular shareware sites include *www.sharewareplace.com*, *www.tudogs.com*, *www.drdownload.com*, and *www.jumbo.com*. To download commercial software, get out your credit card and connect to *www.downloadstore.com*. Of course, you can also connect to software publishers' sites, such as *www.microsoft.com/downloads*, for demos and updates.

10 Chats and Discussion Groups

To participate in discussion groups using your browser, connect to *www.dejanews.com*. Make sure that you read the rules before you begin posting comments. For interactive chats, the options seem limitless. If you log into Yahoo! chats at *www.yahoo.com* (and follow the Chat links), you'll see that often over 5,000 "chatters" are logged on at any time. Chatweb at *www.chatweb.com* has an easy-to-use interface, making it a good place to get started. If you're a member of AOL, CompuServe, MSN, or Prodigy, their members-only chat groups are also a good place to try out Internet chat. At The

WebChat Broadcasting System site, *wbs.net*, you can "just visit" or you can register (free) and participate. *Salon* magazine sponsors chats that have a reputation for being more substantive than chats at other sites. Connect to the *Salon* site at *www.salonmagazine.com* and follow the Table Talk links.

11 Games

MUDs (Multi-User Dimension or Dungeon), MOOs (MUD Object Oriented), and MUSHEs are text-based, role-playing games. These games are evolving into graphical, 3-D interactive worlds. You can visit some of these game sites with a standard Web browser. To participate at other sites, you need to download a VRML browser. If you have a vivid imagination, text-based MOOs, MUDs, and MUSHEs still exist, and you can connect to them on the Web. The Sprawl at *sensemedia.not/sprawl* is one of the longest running MOOs on the Internet. Two sites where you can find people to play traditional board games online are Gamer's Zone at *www.worldvillage.com/online/games.htm* and Microsoft's Internet Gaming Zone at *www.zone.com*. The Games Information Pages provide a good source of information about both offline and online games (*www.gamesdomain.com/gdmain.html*). At Virtual World Industry (*www.ccon.org/hotlinks/hotlinks.html*), you'll find information about and links to most of the major virtual reality game sites and browsers. It is a good launching point if you want to explore the world of virtual reality on the Web.

12 HTML

Although today's word processing software automatically produces documents in HTML format, it is handy to know a bit about what goes on behind the scenes with HTML tags. For a basic introduction on how to use HTML to create a Web page, connect to NCSA's "A Beginner's Guide to HTML" at *www.ncsa.uiuc.edu/General/Internet/WWW/HTMLPrimer.html*. Sites such as "Learning HTML by the Tags Tutorial" at *wally2.rit.edu/instruction/web/htmltags/tutorial.html* provide tutorials, links to information about graphics for the Web, and tips on how to publicize your Web site. Books, such as Sam's *Teach Yourself Web Publishing with HTML 4 in 21 Days* by Laura Lemay and Denise Tyler (Macmillan Publishing, 1999), are also helpful references. For clip art and animations, connect to Andy's Art Attack at *www.andyart.com*. Clip art on the Web is plentiful. Simply type "clip art" into your favorite search engine and follow the links. Be sure to read the permissions before using clip art from the Web.

13 Authoring Tools

Web authoring tools help you to create Web pages from within a graphical interface, generate HTML documents, and view the result in a browser window. Popular tools include Microsoft FrontPage (*www.microsoft.com/frontpage*), Adobe PageMill (*www.adobe.com/prodindex/pagemill/main.html*), and Claris Home Page (*www.filemaker.com/products/homepage3.html*). For a comparative review of HTML authoring tools, check out "HTML Editors: Find the Right Tool," at *www.cnet.com/Content/Reviews/Compare/Htmleditors/index.html*.

14 Authoring Tips

The Web contains many resources that provide suggestions, tips, and information on Web page design. Sites such as "Crafting a Nifty Personal Web Site," at *www2.hawaii.edu/jay/styleguide*, provide lots of great tips with illustrated examples. For a more serious presentation, connect to sites such as Yale's C/AIM Web Style Guide at *info.med.yale.edu/caim/manual*. You'll enjoy the Web page makeovers in the *Ziff-Davis Internet MegaSite Magazine*. Pick up a copy from your newsstand or visit online at *www.zdimag.com* and search for "makeovers." *Internet Magazine*, published by emap Business Communications in the United Kingdom, contains excellent information for Web designers. As you gain experience in Web page design, you'll find helpful tips at sites such as "WebHome Improvement: A Web Design Style Guide" at *www.htmltips.com*.

15 E-commerce Construction

Nowadays it seems that everyone is talking about it and lots of people are doing it—e-commerce, that is. According to the Computer Currents High-Tech online dictionary, e-commerce is "the use of computers and electronic communications in business transactions. E-commerce may include the use of electronic data interchange (EDI), electronic money exchange, Internet advertising, Web sites, online databases, computer networks, and point-of-sale (POS) computer systems." To find out more about e-commerce, visit the E-Commerce Project at *www.uni-muenster.de/Jurlink/ecp*, which is a comprehensive database of articles, cases, and news regarding e-commerce legal issues. Several organizations contribute to the database. For current and archival articles on e-commerce, visit sites such as *www.internetnews.com/ec-news*. To keep up with the latest information regarding e-commerce law, visit the United States Government Electronic Commerce Policy site at *www.ecommerce.gov*. If you're thinking about setting up your own e-commerce site, be sure to check out The Internet Marketing Center at *sellitontheweb.com/ezine/features.shtml* and link to e-commerce 101 and other marketing resources. You should also read about and compare the features of various e-commerce enabled Web sites offered by Internet hosting services such as Yahoo (*st0.yahoo.com/vw/feat.html*) and Hiway Technologies (*www.hiway.com/commerce*).

16 ISPs

To avoid long-distance charges when you connect to the Internet, you'll want an ISP that provides a dial-up number within your local calling area. How can you find a local ISP? CNET ISP Review at *www.cnet.com/Content/Reviews/Compare/ISP/highest.html* provides comparative reviews of ISPs and information about how to select an ISP. CNET conducts a national survey of ISPs in which national and local ISPs are rated by their subscribers. The List at *thelist.internet.com* includes over 3,006 Internet service providers from the United States, Canada, and around the world. At this site you can search for an ISP by area code or by country code. You can also search the World ISP Finder database at *www.pcworld.com/top400/isp* to find an ISP in your area code.

17 Modems

Modem technology is changing as fast as any other segment of the computer industry. In 1994, most people had 9.6 Kbps modems. Today, most computers come equipped with voice/fax modems. By 1998, 56 Kbps modems became a popular standard, replacing slower 33.3 Kbps modems. But on the Internet faster is better. What's the next step up in modems? A DSL modem? An ISDN connection? A cable modem? Your questions about modems and Internet connections are answered at Modem FAQ-Curt's High Speed Modem Page at *www.teleport.com/~curt/modems.html*. Modems, Modems, Modems at *www.rosenet.net/~costmo* has a selection of links to the home pages of modem makers, tips and troubleshooting ideas, and sources of FAQs and drivers. Popular modem makers include U.S. Robotics, which has since merged with 3Com (*www.3com.com*), Diamond MultiMedia (*www.diamondmm.com*), Zoom Telephonics (*www.zoomtel.com*), and Motorola Modems (*www.mot.com*). For a complete list of modem manufacturers, visit *www.nacs.net/~damin/test/topics/modems.html*.

18 Information Quality

Some conspiracies are now classics—the JFK assassination, Elvis sightings, and the Roswell UFO incident. New conspiracies keep popping up—the missile that shot down TWA Flight 800, the spaceship hidden behind the Hale-Bopp comet. The Disinformation Web site, which is located at *www.disinfo.com*, provides a database of information about the origins and credibility (or lack of it) of many conspiracy theories. The site includes "dossiers," which cover many sides of a given issue or topic, both pro and con. You can check out Internet-based hoaxes at the CIAC Internet Hoax Site: *www.ciac.org/ciac/CIACHoaxes.html*. The National Fraud Information Center at *www.fraud.org* helps consumers report fraud and offers helpful advice on how to avoid becoming a victim. For more information on the article mentioned in the *Issue* section, check out "Blame it on the Net" by Scott Rosenberg at *www.salon1999.com/media/media961112.html*.

CHAPTER

9 DATA SECURITY

▶ Start Video

PREVIEW

Chapter 9 focuses on threats to the data stored on computer systems—threats such as operator error, equipment failure, viruses, and computer vandalism. On a practical level, this chapter provides information on how to disinfect disks that contain viruses, make backups, and design an effective backup plan for your data. The *Issue* section takes a look at hackers, crackers, and cyberpunks.

After you have completed this chapter, you should be able to:

▪ List some of the causes for lost or inaccurate data

▪ Describe how you can protect your computer data from damage caused by power problems and hardware failures

▪ List at least five symptoms that might indicate your computer is infected by a virus

▪ Differentiate between a virus, Trojan horse, worm, logic bomb, and time bomb

▪ Describe techniques for avoiding, detecting, and eradicating computer viruses

▪ List the advantages and disadvantages of the most popular data security techniques

▪ Explain why special computer crime laws are necessary

CHAPTER 9 LAB

Data
Backup

THE TROJAN HORSE

According to legend, a war between the Trojans and the Greeks continued for more than nine years, until one of the Greek leaders conceived a brilliant plan. He ordered his men to create a huge wooden horse. When it was completed, a few soldiers hid inside and the Greek army pretended to sail away. The Trojans believed that the horse was a gift, pulled it into the city, and spent the day celebrating what they thought was a great victory. Late that night, the soldiers hidden inside the horse crept out and opened the city gates for the waiting Greek army.

What does the Trojan War have to do with computers? Like the city of Troy, modern computer users are under siege. They must do battle with computer criminals, pranksters, viruses, equipment failures, and human errors. A modern software version of the Trojan horse might even erase your data after you unknowingly bring it into your computer.

How can you protect the data on your computer from viruses? How can you prevent information that you send over the Internet from falling into the wrong hands? How do businesses, such as banks and insurance companies, protect your personal records? As you read Chapter 9, it is important that you expand your focus beyond your own computer, because as you take advantage of technology options, such as LANs and the Internet, some of your data will migrate to network servers and Web hosting services. In addition, the increasing popularity of computer communications and e-commerce means that you may be transmitting data that you don't want intercepted. Also, once this data arrives at its destination, you would like some assurance that it remains securely stored. In this chapter, you will learn how businesses protect data on their computers as well as how you can protect data on your own computer.

SECTION A   WHAT CAN GO WRONG

Today's computer users battle to avoid lost, stolen, and inaccurate data. Lost data, also referred to as missing data, consists of data that is inaccessible, usually because it was accidentally removed. Stolen data is not necessarily missing, but it has been accessed or copied without authorization. Inaccurate data consists of data that is not accurate because it was entered incorrectly, it was deliberately or accidentally altered, or it was not edited to reflect current facts.

Despite the sometimes sensational press coverage of computer criminals and viruses, the underlying cause of many data problems is simply operator error, power abnormalities, or hardware failure.

Operator Error

What's the most likely cause of lost or inaccurate data? **Operator error** refers to a mistake made by a computer user. At one time or another, everyone who has used a computer has made a mistake. A few examples will illustrate that this group is not an exclusive club:

- Working late at night, the President's press secretary finished the final revisions for the next day's speech. Intending to make a copy of the speech as a backup, he mistakenly copied the old version of the speech over the new version.

- A college student grabbed a disk without a label and, thinking it was unformatted, shoved it in the disk drive and started the formatting process. Unfortunately, the disk contained the only copy of her art history term paper.

- A clerk made a typing error and billed a patient for 555 aspirins instead of 5.

It might seem that nothing can prevent operator error. After all, mistakes do happen. Nevertheless, the number of operator errors can be reduced if users pay attention to what they're doing and establish good habits intended to help them avoid mistakes.

FIGURE 9-1

Computer software designers can help prevent operator error by designing products that anticipate mistakes that users are likely to make. For example, Microsoft Windows requests confirmation before the computer carries out any activity that might destroy data.

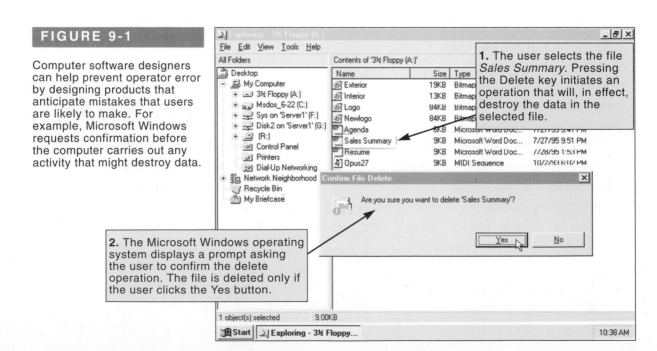

1. The user selects the file *Sales Summary*. Pressing the Delete key initiates an operation that will, in effect, destroy the data in the selected file.

2. The Microsoft Windows operating system displays a prompt asking the user to confirm the delete operation. The file is deleted only if the user clicks the Yes button.

Power Failures, Spikes, and Surges

If the power goes out, will I lose all of my data? A **power failure** is a complete loss of power to the computer system. Although you can shut off the power by accidentally bumping the computer on/off switch, a power failure is usually caused by something over which you have no control, such as a downed power line or a malfunction at the local power plant. Data stored in RAM is lost if power is not continuously supplied to the computer system. Even a brief power interruption, noticeable only as a flicker of the room lights, can force your computer to reboot and lose all of the data in RAM.

InfoWeb
1

UPS

Lightning and malfunctions at the electric company can cause spikes and surges that may damage sensitive computer components. A **power spike** is an increase in power that lasts only a short time—less than one-millionth of a second. A **power surge** lasts a little longer—a few millionths of a second. Power surges and spikes are potentially more damaging than power failures. A surge or spike can damage your computer's motherboard and the circuit boards on your disk drives, putting your computer out of action until the boards are replaced. To prevent damage from power surges and spikes, many experts recommend that you unplug your computer equipment, including your modem, during electrical storms. Unfortunately, malfunctions at your local power plant can also cause unpredictable spikes and surges, so it is a good idea to provide your computer with some protection from these "glitches."

A **UPS** (uninterruptible power supply) is the best protection against power failures, surges, and spikes. It contains a battery that provides a continuous supply of power and other circuitry that prevents spikes and surges from reaching your computer. A UPS is designed to provide enough power to keep your computer working through momentary power interruptions and to give you sufficient time to save your files and exit your programs in the event of a longer power outage. It is an essential piece of equipment for Internet and LAN servers, but it is recommended for individuals as well. The cost of a UPS for a microcomputer ranges from $100 to $600, depending on the power requirements of the computer and the features of the UPS. Most computer dealers can help you determine your computer's power requirements and recommend the appropriate size and features for a UPS that will meet your needs. Figure 9-2 shows a typical UPS.

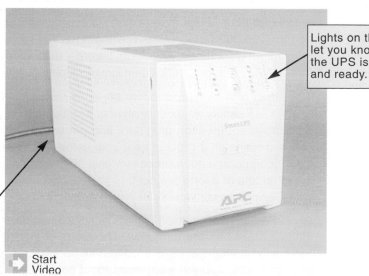

FIGURE 9-2

A UPS contains a battery that keeps your computer running for several minutes during a power failure. The battery does not supply indefinite power, so in the event of a power failure that lasts more than two or three minutes, you should save your work and turn off your computer.

To set up a UPS, plug it into a wall outlet, then plug your computer and monitor cables into the outlets on the back of the UPS.

Lights on the case let you know that the UPS is charged and ready.

Start Video

CHAPTER 9

An inexpensive device called a **surge strip** (also called a "surge suppressor" or "surge protector") can protect your computer and modem from power spikes and surges, but does not contain a battery to keep your equipment running during a power outage. If your budget doesn't cover a UPS, you should at least consider a surge strip. When you shop for a surge strip, don't make the mistake of picking out a simple power strip. A **power strip** resembles a surge strip because both contain multiple power plugs, but a power strip does not contain the electronics necessary to filter out power spikes and surges. Figure 9-3 helps you distinguish between a surge strip and a power strip.

FIGURE 9-3

A surge strip (top) typically contains the electronics necessary to prevent spikes and surges from damaging your computer. Many, but not all, surge strips also contain a place to plug the phone cable that leads to your modem. To identify a surge strip look for a silver label containing the words "transient voltage surge suppressor."

A power strip (right) simply provides multiple outlets, but cannot protect your computer and modem from power spikes and surges.

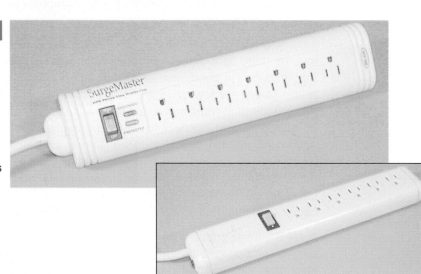

Hardware Failure

How reliable are the components of my computer system? The reliability of a computer component is expressed as its **MTBF** (mean time between failures), which is a statistic that is calculated by observing test equipment in the laboratory, then dividing the number of failures by the total hours of observation. MTBF is somewhat misleading to most consumers. For example, you might read that your hard disk drive has a MTBF of 125,000 hours, which is about 14 years. Does this MTBF mean that your hard drive will work for 125,000 hours before it fails? Unfortunately, the answer is no.

A 125,000-hour MTBF means that, *on average*, a hard disk drive like yours could function for 125,000 hours without failing. The fact remains, however, that your hard disk drive might work for only 10 hours before it fails. With this point in mind, you should plan for hardware failures, rather than simply hoping they won't happen.

The effect of a hardware failure depends on the component that fails. Most hardware failures are simply an inconvenience. For example, if your monitor fails, you can obtain a replacement monitor, plug it in, and get back to work. If a RAM chip fails, you must obtain and install a replacement chip before you can boot your computer again. Even if your computer's microprocessor chip fails, it can easily be replaced. Unless you were in the middle of a long project that you had not saved, problems with the monitor, RAM chips, or processor would not cause any data loss.

On the other hand, a hard disk drive failure can be a disaster because you might lose all data stored on the hard disk. The effect of a hard disk drive failure is considerably reduced if you have complete, up-to-date backup copies of the programs and data files on your hard disk. You will learn more about how to back up your data later in this chapter.

Fires, Floods, and Other Disasters

Should I buy some type of insurance for my computer? Computers are not immune to unexpected damage from smoke, fire, water, and breakage. Still, it is not practical to barricade your computer against every potential disaster. Many business and homeowners insurance policies provide coverage for computers. Under the terms of many standard household and business policies, a computer is treated like any other appliance. You should make sure, however, that your insurance policy covers the full cost of purchasing a new computer at current market prices.

InfoWeb
2

Computer
Insurance

Of course, replacing your damaged computer equipment will not replace your data. Some insurance companies therefore provide extra coverage for the data on your computer. This coverage would provide a sum of money to cover the time it takes to reload your data on a replacement computer. Being able to reload your data requires that you have a computer-readable backup copy of your data. Without such a backup, much of your data cannot be reconstructed. For a business, the situation is even more critical. Customer accounts, inventory, daily transactions, and financial information might be difficult, if not impossible, to reconstruct. Furthermore, a business cannot be "down" for days or weeks while data is reconstructed.

To summarize, a good insurance policy provides funds to replace computer equipment, but the only real insurance for your data is an up-to-date backup.

QUICKCHECK A

1 Inadvertently deleting a file is an example of _____ error.

2 In the event of a power failure, your computer will lose all data stored in RAM and on the hard disk. True or false? _____

3 A(n) _____ contains a battery that provides a continuous supply of power to your computer during a brief power failure.

4 A(n) _____ strip protects your computer from electrical spikes and surges, but it does not keep your computer operating if the power fails.

5 The circuitry on your computer circuit boards can be damaged by power spikes and power surges. True or false? _____

6 MTBF tells you how often an electronic device needs to be serviced. True or false? _____

7 The best insurance for your data is an up-to-date _____.

 Check
Answers

CHAPTER 9

SECTION B VIRUSES AND OTHER PESKY STUFF

Computer data can be damaged, destroyed, or altered by vandals called **hackers**, **crackers**, or **cyberpunks**. The programs that they create are colorfully referred to by various sources as "malware," "pest programs," "vandalware," or "punkware." More typically, these programs are called "viruses." What would you do if you saw the message in Figure 9-4 on your computer screen?

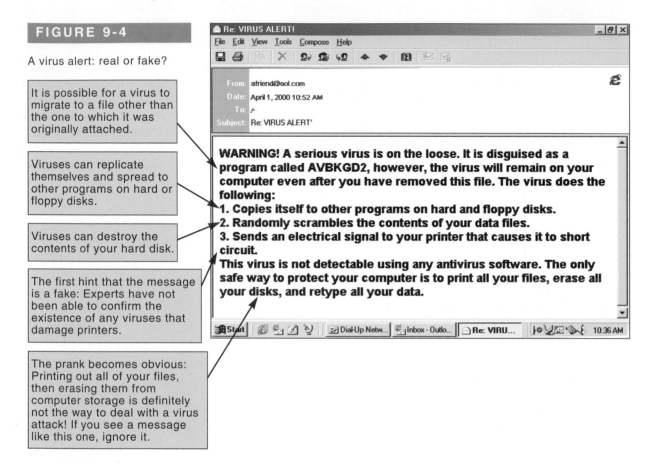

FIGURE 9-4

A virus alert: real or fake?

It is possible for a virus to migrate to a file other than the one to which it was originally attached.

Viruses can replicate themselves and spread to other programs on hard or floppy disks.

Viruses can destroy the contents of your hard disk.

The first hint that the message is a fake: Experts have not been able to confirm the existence of any viruses that damage printers.

The prank becomes obvious: Printing out all of your files, then erasing them from computer storage is definitely not the way to deal with a virus attack! If you see a message like this one, ignore it.

WARNING! A serious virus is on the loose. It is disguised as a program called AVBKGD2, however, the virus will remain on your computer even after you have removed this file. The virus does the following:
1. Copies itself to other programs on hard and floppy disks.
2. Randomly scrambles the contents of your data files.
3. Sends an electrical signal to your printer that causes it to short circuit.
This virus is not detectable using any antivirus software. The only safe way to protect your computer is to print all your files, erase all your disks, and retype all your data.

3

Viruses

The virus alert shown in Figure 9-4 is obviously a hoax, designed to frighten computer users and embarrass them when they find out that they have spread this fake virus alert to all of their friends and colleagues. Two of the most tenacious virus hoaxes are the Good Times virus and the Wobbler virus. If you receive e-mail about these or any other viruses, you should check the authenticity of the alert by connecting to one of the Web sites listed in the Viruses InfoWeb.

The term "virus" technically refers to only one of many categories of programs that can lurk on disks, in RAM, and on the Internet ready to create havoc in your computer. Other categories include Trojan horses, time bombs, logic bombs, and worms. As you'll learn in this chapter, the programs in each of these categories behave differently when attacking a computer system. Understanding how these programs work is the first line of defense in preventing such attacks.

Computer Viruses

Exactly what is a computer virus? A **computer virus** is a program that attaches itself to a file, reproduces itself, and spreads to other files. A virus can corrupt and/or destroy data, display an irritating message, or otherwise disrupt computer operations. The jargon that describes a computer virus sounds similar to medical jargon. Your computer is a "host," and it can become "infected" with a virus. A virus can spread from one computer to another. You can "inoculate" your computer against many viruses. If your computer becomes infected, you can use antivirus software to "disinfect" it.

A computer virus generally infects the files executed by your computer, such as program files with .exe extensions, the system files that your computer uses to boot up, and the macro files that automate tasks in word processing and spreadsheet applications. When your computer executes an infected program, it also executes the attached virus instructions, which replicate the virus in another file or deliver the virus payload. The term **payload** refers to the ultimate mission of a virus, which might be as harmless as displaying an annoying message or as devastating as corrupting the data on your computer's hard disk.

A virus that attaches itself to an application program, such as a game, is known as a **file virus**. One of the most notorious file viruses is Chernobyl, designed to lurk in a computer until April 26—the anniversary of the Chernobyl nuclear disaster—and then overwrite a section of your hard disk, making it impossible to access your data. Figure 9-5 illustrates how a file virus spreads.

FIGURE 9-5

How a file virus spreads.

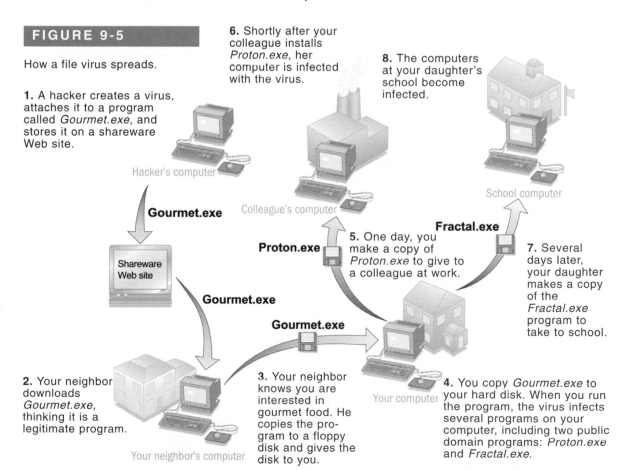

1. A hacker creates a virus, attaches it to a program called *Gourmet.exe*, and stores it on a shareware Web site.

2. Your neighbor downloads *Gourmet.exe*, thinking it is a legitimate program.

3. Your neighbor knows you are interested in gourmet food. He copies the program to a floppy disk and gives the disk to you.

4. You copy *Gourmet.exe* to your hard disk. When you run the program, the virus infects several programs on your computer, including two public domain programs: *Proton.exe* and *Fractal.exe*.

5. One day, you make a copy of *Proton.exe* to give to a colleague at work.

6. Shortly after your colleague installs *Proton.exe*, her computer is infected with the virus.

7. Several days later, your daughter makes a copy of the *Fractal.exe* program to take to school.

8. The computers at your daughter's school become infected.

Hacker's computer

Gourmet.exe

Shareware Web site

Gourmet.exe

Your neighbor's computer

Gourmet.exe

Your computer

Proton.exe

Colleague's computer

Fractal.exe

School computer

CHAPTER 9

A **boot sector virus** infects the system files that your computer uses every time you turn it on. These viruses can cause widespread damage and reoccurring problems. The old, but persistent Stoned virus infects the boot sector of floppy and hard disks, for example. In various versions of this virus, the payload can display a message, such as "Your computer is now stoned!", or it can corrupt some of the data on your computer's hard disk.

Macro Viruses

A **macro virus** infects a set of instructions called a "macro." A **macro** is essentially a miniature program that usually contains legitimate instructions to automate document and worksheet production. A hacker can create a destructive macro, attach it to a document or worksheet, and then distribute it over the Internet or on disk—often as an e-mail attachment. When anyone views the document, the macro virus duplicates itself into the general macro pool, where it is picked up by other documents. The two most common macro viruses are the Melissa virus, which attaches itself to Microsoft Word documents, and Laroux, which attaches itself to Microsoft Excel spreadsheets.

Experts estimate that more than 2,000 viruses exist. Nevertheless, most virus damage is caused by fewer than 10 viruses. Of these viruses, macro viruses account for more than 90 percent of virus attacks, as shown in Figure 9-6.

FIGURE 9-6

In today's computing environment, macro viruses are the most prolific.

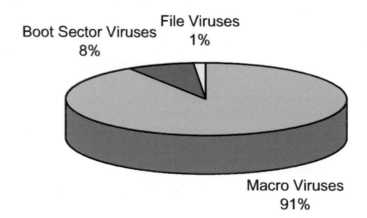

Boot Sector Viruses
8%

File Viruses
1%

Macro Viruses
91%

The symptoms of a virus infection will depend on the virus. The following symptoms *might* indicate that your computer has contracted a virus, though some of these symptoms can have other causes:

- Your computer displays vulgar, embarrassing, or annoying messages, such as "Gotcha! Arf Arf," "You're stoned!," or "I want a cookie."

- Your computer develops unusual visual or sound effects.

- You have difficulty saving files or files mysteriously disappear.

- Your computer suddenly seems to work very slowly.

- Your computer reboots unexpectedly.

- Your executable files unaccountably increase in size.

Viruses are just one category of software designed by hackers to disrupt or damage the data on computers. After considering some other categories, you'll find out how to avoid and minimize the damage they cause.

A Modern Trojan Horse

Is a Trojan horse a virus? At the beginning of this chapter, you learned about the legendary Trojan horse. A modern **Trojan horse** is a computer program that appears to perform one function while actually doing something else. A Trojan horse is not a virus, but it might carry a virus. Instead of carrying a virus, a Trojan horse can be designed to destroy data or steal passwords. For example, suppose a hacker writes a program to format hard disks and embeds this program in a file called *Sched.exe*. The hacker then distributes disks containing this Trojan horse and posts it on the Internet, where other users might assume that it is a free scheduling program. Users who download and run *Sched.exe* will discover that the program has erased all files on their hard disks. Such a Trojan horse does not harbor a virus because it does not replicate itself. Figure 9-7 shows how this type of Trojan horse program works.

FIGURE 9-7

A Trojan horse pretends to be a legitimate program.

1. The harmless-looking file called *Sched.exe* is really a Trojan horse that contains a program to format the hard drive.

2. A user innocently puts the disk containing *Sched.exe* in drive A.

3. The user tries to run the Sched program, assuming that it is a free scheduling program.

4. The command to run the Sched program activates the format program, and the contents of the hard disk are destroyed.

Another variety of Trojan horse looks just like the login screen on a network. As a user logs in, this Trojan horse collects the user's ID and password. This information is then e-mailed to a hacker or stored in a file that a hacker can access later. Armed with a valid user ID and password, the hacker can access the data stored on the network. As with the *Sched.exe* example, this type of Trojan horse does not harbor a virus because the hacker's program, which is designed to defeat network security measures, does not replicate itself.

CHAPTER 9

Time Bombs and Logic Bombs

Can a virus lurk in my computer system without my knowledge? Although a virus usually begins to replicate itself immediately upon entering your computer system, it will not necessarily deliver its payload right away. A virus or other unwelcome surprise can lurk in your computer system for days or months without discovery. A **time bomb** is a computer program that stays in your system undetected until it is triggered by a certain event in time, such as when the computer system clock reaches a certain date. A time bomb is usually carried by a virus or Trojan horse. For example, the Michelangelo virus contains a time bomb designed to damage files on your hard disk on March 6, the birthday of artist Michelangelo. The Olivia virus activates on April 10 and December 23, automatically opens the CD-ROM drive, and displays a message instructing the user to insert a music CD. After the CD begins, the virus overwrites the FAT on the hard disk and displays a message in Taiwanese. Many other time bomb attacks are keyed to dates such as Halloween, Friday the 13th, and April Fool's Day.

InfoWeb
5

Y2K Bug

Until recently, a surprising number of legitimate software programs contained a sort of time bomb that was unintentionally included by unwary programmers. The **Y2K bug** referred to a problem associated with software that did not use a four-digit date field. The programmers who wrote such software decided that dates entered as 89 instead of 1989 would save disk space and processing time. As it turns out, this decision had the potential to cause havoc with the arrival of year 2000 (Y2K). Why? Suppose a person born in 1983 applied for a driver's license in 1999. The computer uses the last two digits of the dates, subtracts 83 from 99, and determines that the applicant is 16 years old. Now suppose the same person applied for a license in the year 2000. The computer subtracts 83 from 00 and gets -83 years old! Preparing computer systems for the year 2000 required major revisions of many computer applications in business and government.

A **logic bomb** is a computer program that is triggered by the appearance or disappearance of specific data. For example, suppose a programmer in a large corporation believes that she is on the list of employees to be terminated during the next cost-cutting campaign. Her hostility overcomes her ethical judgment, and she creates a logic bomb program that checks the payroll file every day to ensure that her employment status is still active. If the programmer's status changes to "terminated," her logic bomb activates a program that destroys data on the computer.

A time bomb or logic bomb might do mischief in your computer long before the timer goes off. If the bomb is part of a virus, it could replicate and spread to other files. Meanwhile, you might also send files from your computer to other computers, not realizing that your files are infected.

Worms

Is a worm some type of virus? "At 2:28 a.m. a besieged Berkeley scientist—like a front-line soldier engulfed by the enemy—sent a bulletin around the nation: *We are currently under attack...* Thus began one of the most harrowing days of the computer age." This lead story in *The Wall Street Journal* reported the now famous Internet worm that spread to more than 6,000 Internet host computers. A software **worm** is a program designed to enter a computer system—usually a network—through security "holes." Like a virus, a worm reproduces itself. Unlike a virus, a worm does not need to be attached to a document or executable program to reproduce.

InfoWeb
6
The
Internet
Worm

The software worm that attacked the Internet entered each computer through security holes in the electronic mail system, then used data stored on the computer to, in effect, e-mail itself to other computers. The worm spread rapidly, as shown in Figure 9-8.

FIGURE 9-8

A worm attacks the Internet.

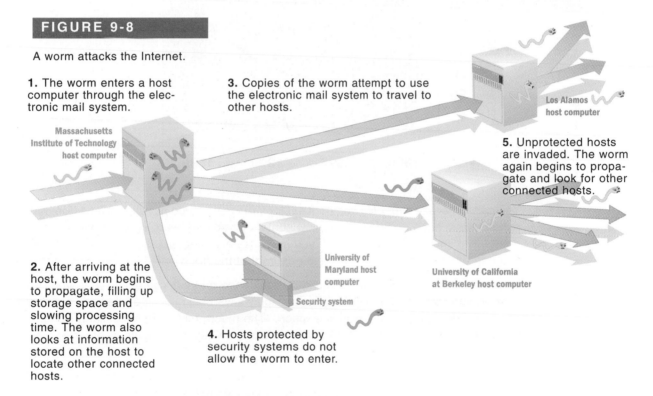

1. The worm enters a host computer through the electronic mail system.

2. After arriving at the host, the worm begins to propagate, filling up storage space and slowing processing time. The worm also looks at information stored on the host to locate other connected hosts.

3. Copies of the worm attempt to use the electronic mail system to travel to other hosts.

4. Hosts protected by security systems do not allow the worm to enter.

5. Unprotected hosts are invaded. The worm again begins to propagate and look for other connected hosts.

Massachusetts Institute of Technology host computer

University of Maryland host computer

Security system

Los Alamos host computer

University of California at Berkeley host computer

The Internet worm was not designed to destroy data. Instead, it filled up storage space and dramatically slowed computer performance. The only way to eradicate the Internet worm was to shut down the electronic mail system on the Internet hosts, then comb through hundreds of programs to find and destroy the worm, a process that took as long as eight hours for each host.

Worms are not likely to affect your personal computer because they are typically designed to attack network servers. Nevertheless, they do affect LAN and Internet users by disrupting their access to files, programs, Web pages, and other services provided by the network.

CHAPTER 9

Avoiding Viruses and Other Attacks

How can I protect my computer from viruses and other types of attacks?

Computer viruses and other types of malicious programs typically lurk on disks containing shareware or pirated software, in files downloaded from the Internet, and in e-mail attachments. A virus cannot, however, hitch a ride in a plain e-mail message. The graph in Figure 9-9 indicates the most common sources of infected files.

FIGURE 9-9

In 1999, e-mail attachments surpassed floppy disks as the most common source of infected files.

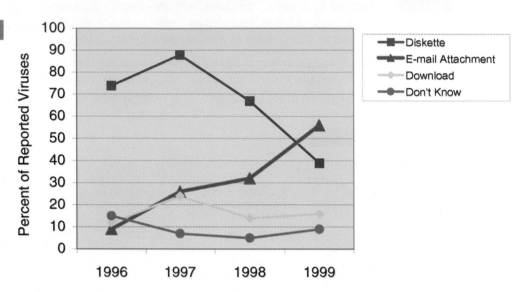

You can generally avoid file and boot sector viruses if you do not accept files from high-risk sources, such as floppy disks that contain pirated software or download sites that do not test and secure their files. If you must use a file that you suspect to be infected, you can employ antivirus software to ensure that the file is safe.

To prevent a macro virus from taking up residence on your computer, your word processing and spreadsheet software might display a warning message when you are about to open a document that includes a macro. The macro might not necessarily contain a virus, but knowing that a document has a macro can help you decide whether you want to open it.

If a document contains an infected macro but you do not open the document, the macro virus cannot spread to other documents on your computer. Therefore, if you begin to open a document that you've received from a friend, colleague, or unknown source and encounter a message indicating that the document has a macro attached, consider carefully whether the sender would have any reason to include a macro with the document. Simple letters, memos, and reports rarely call for the use of macros, so you should be suspicious of these types of documents when macros are attached.

To rid your system of a suspicious document and its macro, you must delete it. If the document exists as a file on a disk, use Windows Explorer to delete the file. If the file has arrived as an e-mail attachment, delete the e-mail message to which it is attached. Once a macro virus has established itself on your computer, you must use antivirus software to remove it.

Antivirus Software

How does antivirus software work?

InfoWeb
7

Antivirus
Software

Taking steps to avoid the sources of virus infection doesn't always work. Somehow a virus might manage to sneak into your computer. Remember, however, that many viruses lurk around for a while before doing any real damage. Therefore, catching and destroying these lurking viruses can prevent a major data disaster. **Antivirus software** (sometimes referred to as "virus detection software") examines the files stored on a disk to determine whether they are infected with a virus, then disinfects the disk, if necessary. Popular antivirus software includes Norton Antivirus, Dr. Solomon's Anti-Virus, and McAfee VirusScan.

Antivirus software uses several techniques to find viruses. As you know, a virus attaches itself to an existing program. Its presence often increases the length of the original program. The earliest antivirus software simply examined the programs on a computer and recorded their length. A change in the length of a program from one computing session to the next indicated the possible presence of a virus.

To counter early antivirus software, hackers became more cunning. They created viruses that insert themselves into unused portions of a program file without changing its length. Of course, the people who designed antivirus software fought back. They designed software that examines the bytes in an uninfected application program and calculates a checksum. A **checksum** is a number that is calculated by combining the binary values of all bytes in a file. Each time you run an application program, the antivirus software calculates the checksum and compares it with the previous checksum. If any byte in the application program has been changed, the checksum will be different, and the antivirus software assumes that a virus is present. The checksum approach requires that you start with a copy of the program that is not infected with a virus. If the original copy is infected, the virus is included in the original checksum, and the antivirus software never detects it.

Antivirus software also identifies viruses by searching your files for a virus signature. A **virus signature** is a unique series of bytes that can be used to identify a known virus, much as a fingerprint is used to identify an individual. A signature is usually a section of the virus program, such as a unique series of instructions. Most of today's antivirus software scans for virus signatures; for this reason, it is sometimes referred to as "virus scanning software."

The signature search technique is fairly quick, but it can identify only those viruses with a known signature. To detect new viruses—and new viruses seem to appear every week—you must obtain regular updates for your virus detection program that include new virus signatures.

Some viruses are specifically designed to avoid detection by one or more of these detection methods. For this reason, the most sophisticated virus protection schemes combine elements from each of these methods.

A common misconception is that write-protecting your floppy disks by opening the small hole in the corner of the disk prevents virus infection. Although a virus cannot jump onto your disk when it is write-protected, you must remove the write protection each time you save a file on the disk. With the write protection removed, your disk is open to virus attack.

Using Antivirus Software

What should I do if I think my computer has become infected? If you detect the symptoms of a virus on your computer system, you should immediately take steps to stop the virus from spreading. If you are connected to a network, alert the network administrator that you found a virus on your workstation. The network administrator can then take action to prevent the virus from spreading throughout the network. If you think that a computer has invaded your personal computer, you can find and remove it by using antivirus software. Even if you do not detect any symptoms of a virus, it is not a bad idea to use your antivirus software every month or two, just in case a virus is stealthily lurking on your hard disk.

Before you can use antivirus software, it must be installed on your computer. Many new computers come equipped with preinstalled antivirus software. Otherwise, you can buy such software from your local computer dealer, purchase it by mail order, or download a trial version from the Web. The cost of antivirus software for a microcomputer ranges between $30 and $80.

Because new viruses appear every week, it is important that your antivirus software be kept up-to-date so that it contains the information necessary to hunt for new viruses as well as old ones. Typically, the companies that publish antivirus software provide updates that you can easily download from the Internet. As a rule of thumb, you should get an update about every three months.

You run your antivirus software just as you would any program—by using the Windows Start button, then selecting the program from the Programs menu. Typically, the antivirus program will scan your computer's memory and hard disk. If it detects a virus, you will see a message indicating the name of the virus. You can then specify whether you want to try to remove it immediately. Figure 9-10 explains more about this process.

FIGURE 9-10

When your antivirus software detects a virus, it provides information about the virus and asks whether you want to remove it immediately. In most cases, you will want to use this option. Some viruses cannot be removed without destroying the host file. Unfortunately, if you don't have a pre-virus backup, it is probably too late to make one.

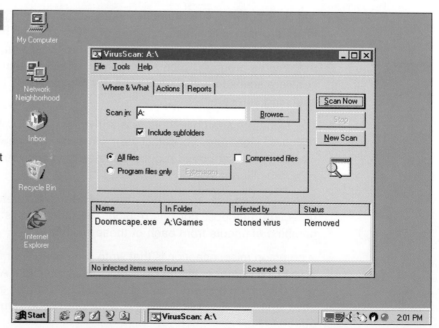

Start
Screentour

Some antivirus software stays active and watches for viruses whenever your computer is on. When operating in this mode, you do not have to remember to periodically initiate a virus scan because your antivirus software automatically checks any new programs that you install, any macros that you receive, and any files that you download from the Internet. Even if your antivirus software does not provide continuous background monitoring, you can usually set it up to automatically load and scan every time that you boot your computer. Many people like these automated features and believe that the protection they provide is worth a slight delay as the antivirus software loads and scans during the boot process.

If your antivirus software detects a virus on your computer, the infection might have spread to your backups and removable storage media, such as floppy disks, Zip disks, and removable hard disks. After removing the virus from your fixed hard disk, you should also use your antivirus software to check your removable media. If you don't remove every copy of the virus, your system will become infected again the next time you use an infected disk or restore data from an infected backup. You should also alert your colleagues, and anyone with whom you shared disks, that a virus might have traveled on those disks and infected their computer systems.

If your computer is attacked by a macro virus, you might have to manually extract the macro from each infected document. You'll find information on combating macro viruses at Microsoft's Web site and in recent editions of computer magazines.

QUICKCHECK B

1 A(n) _____ is a program that reproduces itself when the computer executes the file to which it is attached.

2 A(n) _____ virus attaches itself to documents, rather than to an .exe file.

3 A(n) _____ is a software container that might contain a virus or time bomb.

4 A(n) _____ is a program that reproduces itself without being attached to an executable file.

5 Three sources of files that should be considered a high risk for virus infection are disks brought from home, downloads, and _____.

6 Write-protecting a floppy disk is a good defense against a Trojan horse. True or false? _____

7 Many virus detection programs identify viruses by looking for a unique series of bytes called a(n) _____.

 Check Answers

CHAPTER 9

SECTION C RISK MANAGEMENT

In the story of the Trojan War, the Trojans seem so naive. Who would be so foolish as to pull such a suspicious horse into the city? In fact, many of today's computer users are just as naive about modern technology. They install programs on their computers without checking for viruses, they store massive amounts of data without backups, and they transmit sensitive data without first encrypting it. The Trojans fell for the wooden horse trick the first time, but it is a mistake they would be unlikely to repeat. Will modern computer users repeat their mistakes or learn to take precautions?

Data security involves the collection of techniques that provide protection for data. Sometimes computer users cite Jeff Richards' Laws of Data Security as tongue-in-cheek advice on how to attain foolproof security:

■ Don't buy a computer.

■ If you buy a computer, don't turn it on.

Richards' Laws emphasize the point that it is not practical to totally protect computer data from theft, viruses, and natural disasters. In most situations, providing total security is too time-consuming, too expensive, or too complex. For example, if you use your computer primarily for word processing, it might be too time-consuming to make daily backups, too expensive to keep your data in a fire-proof vault, and too complex to implement password security. On the other hand, if you take no precautions, one day you will be sorry.

InfoWeb
Risk
Management

In the context of computers, **risk management** is the process of weighing threats to computer data against the amount of data that is expendable and the cost of protecting crucial data. The steps in risk management are as follows:

1. Determine the likely threats to computer data. In the case of individual computer users, the major threats are operator error, hardware failure, and viruses.

2. Assess the amount of data that is expendable. For this assessment, you must ask yourself how much data you would have to re-enter if your hard drive was erased and how much data would be lost forever because it could not be reconstructed.

3. Determine the cost of protecting all of your data versus protecting some of it. This cost includes time as well as money.

4. Select the protective measures that are affordable, effective against the identified threats, and feasible to implement.

As you read this section of the chapter, you'll notice that many of the data security techniques mentioned apply to organizations. Understanding how an organization might protect data is important to you as an individual for three reasons. First, you will likely work with computers within an organization as part of your career, so you will share the responsibility with your coworkers for that organization's data. Second, many organizations maintain data about you, such as your credit rating, educational records, and health records. You have a vested interest in the accuracy and the confidentiality of this data. Third, you might store your own Web pages, e-commerce site, or other files on Internet or LAN computers maintained by an organization, such as a Web hosting service. The security of that data depends on the organization's security techniques.

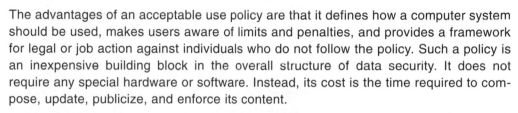

Establish Policies and Procedures

How can an organization educate its employees on the rules for acceptable computer use? In a computing environment, an **acceptable use policy** is a set of rules and regulations that specifies how a computer system should be used. This policy is most often determined by management and used by large organizations to stipulate who can access computer equipment, services, and data. For example, a company might provide e-mail accounts to its employees, but the company's acceptable use policy prohibits use of the company-owned e-mail system for non-business messages. The policy might also state that e-mail messages are not necessarily private, especially if there is reason to believe that those messages might be used for illegal or unethical transmission of data. Many employers also have specific policies prohibiting software piracy and limiting the use of company-owned computers to company business.

Acceptable
Use Policies

The advantages of an acceptable use policy are that it defines how a computer system should be used, makes users aware of limits and penalties, and provides a framework for legal or job action against individuals who do not follow the policy. Such a policy is an inexpensive building block in the overall structure of data security. It does not require any special hardware or software. Instead, its cost is the time required to compose, update, publicize, and enforce its content.

An acceptable use policy does not typically prevent operator errors that lead to lost or corrupted data. Many such operator errors can be prevented, however. Successful computer users develop habits that significantly reduce their chances of making mistakes. These habits, when formalized and adopted by an organization, are referred to as **end-user procedures**. Procedures such as the following, can help you avoid corrupted or lost data:

- Save your files frequently as you work so that you don't lose too much data if the power fails.

- When entering long columns of data, check off each item as it is entered.

- When you format a floppy disk, always view a directory of its contents first to make sure that the disk in the drive is the one you want to format.

- Use antivirus software to scan downloaded files before you open them.

- Do not open documents and spreadsheets that contain unidentified macros.

- Exercise caution when moving a file from one folder to another—rather than use the Cut button, use the Copy button to make a copy in the new destination, erasing the file from its old location only when you're sure that the file has been successfully moved to the new location.

By now, you might have figured out how policies and procedures differ. Policies are rules and regulations that apply to computer use in a general way. Procedures describe steps or activities that are performed in conjunction with a specific task. Because procedures are more specific, they generally take longer to write than policies, making them somewhat more costly for an organization to create and document.

The major advantage of procedures is that they reduce operator error. Nevertheless, procedures have two disadvantages. First, they must be updated as equipment and software change. Second, it is not possible to force people to follow them.

Restrict Physical Access to Computer Systems

If it is so easy for hackers to access data from networked computers, dial-up computers, or terminals, why keep computers locked up? In 1970, during the Vietnam War, anti-war activists bombed the Army Mathematics Research Center at the University of Wisconsin. A graduate student was killed, the building (shown in Figure 9-11) was damaged, and the computer, along with 20 years of accumulated research data, was destroyed.

FIGURE 9-11

In 1970, anti-war activists bombed the Army Mathematics Research Center at the University of Wisconsin.

One of the best ways to prevent people from damaging equipment is to restrict physical access to computer systems. If potential criminals cannot reach a computer or terminal, stealing or damaging data becomes more difficult. Here are some ways to physically protect computer equipment and data:

- Restrict access to the area surrounding the computer to prevent physical damage to the equipment.

- Keep floppy disks and data backups in a locked vault to prevent theft and protect against fire or water damage.

- Keep offices containing computers locked to prevent theft and deter unauthorized users.

- Lock the computer system unit case to prevent theft of components such as RAM and processors.

Restricting physical access to computers has some disadvantages, of course. Locks and other screening measures can make it more difficult for authorized users to access the computer system. Also, restricting physical access will not prevent a determined criminal from stealing data. Although achieving access from a remote location is more difficult, it might not be impossible. Finally, although restricting access might deter intentional acts of destruction, it will not prevent accidents.

Restrict Online Access to Data

Can people be prevented from accessing data so they can't steal it or tamper with it? Obviously, everyone should not have access to the data stored in military computers, banks, or businesses. And yet, the communications infrastructure makes it technically possible for anyone with an Internet connection to interact with these systems. In today's web of interlaced computer technologies, it has become critical to allow data access to only authorized users. The question is, How do you identify authorized users, especially those who are logging in from remote sites located thousands of miles away? The answer usually involves some sort of personal identification.

There are three methods of personal identification: something a person carries, something a person knows, or some unique physical trait. Any one of these methods has the potential to positively identify a person, and each has a unique set of advantages and disadvantages.

Identity Badges. An identity badge featuring a photo, and perhaps a fingerprint or bar code, is a popular form of personal identification in hospitals and government agencies. Designers have created high-tech identity card readers, like the one pictured in Figure 9-12, that can be used from any off-site PC.

FIGURE 9-12

A disk-shaped carrier allows a floppy disk drive to read an identity card.

Because an identity badge can be easily lost, stolen, or duplicated, it works best on-site where a security guard compares the face on the badge with the face of the person wearing the badge. Without visual verification, the use of identity badges from a remote site is not secure, unless combined with a password or PIN (personal identification number).

User IDs and Passwords. The most common way to restrict access to a computer system relies on user IDs and passwords. These items fall into the "something you know" category of personal identification. When you work on a multiuser system or network, you generally must have a user ID and password. Data security on a computer system that is guarded by user IDs and passwords depends on maintaining password secrecy. If users give out their passwords, choose obvious passwords, or write them down in obvious places, hackers can break in.

How easy is it, really, to discover someone's password? It is easier to find a password written on the bottom of a keyboard than to try to guess it from nicknames and birthdates as they always do in the movies. There is also the brute force method of trying every word in an electronic dictionary, but the success of this method decreases if a password is based on two words, a word and number, or a nonsense word that does not appear in a dictionary. Figure 9-13 shows how the composition of passwords affects the chance of unauthorized access.

FIGURE 9-13	Length and composition affect the time it takes to "break" a password (search rate = 100,000 passwords per second).		
Password Strategy	**Example**	**Number of Possibilities**	**Time to Break Password**
Any name	Ed, Christine	2,000	< 1 second using a name dictionary
Any dictionary word	tie, electrocardiogram	60,000	< 1 second using a standard dictionary
Two words joined together	batfont, funnelgum	3,600,000,000	10 hours
5 characters (a-z only)	scftw, bklpw	11,881,376	2 minutes
5 characters (a-z and 0-9)	u4got, 4ti8s	60,466,176	10 minutes
8 characters (a-z and 0-9)	ouamdaip, hitfptwp	282,110,990,7456	326 days

Biometrics

Biometrics. A third method of personal identification called **biometrics** bases identification on some unique physical characteristic, such as a fingerprint or the pattern of blood vessels in the retina of the eye. Unlike passwords, biometric data can't be lost, forgotten, or borrowed. Today biometric devices are becoming affordable technologies that could be built into personal computer systems and used instead of passwords. Biometric technologies include hand-geometry scanners, voice recognition, face recognition, and fingerprint scanners (Figure 9-14).

FIGURE 9-14

Fingerprint scanners cost less than $200 and can confirm your identity in less than two seconds, even from a pool of thousands of employees.

 Start Video

User Rights: A Second Line of Defense

What if a hacker slips past the security screening? One way to limit the amount of damage from a break-in is to assign user rights. **User rights** are rules that limit the directories and files that each user can access. When you receive an account on a computer system, the system administrator gives you rights that allow you to access only certain directories and files. For example, in your computer lab, you might have only read rights to the directories that contain software. This restriction would prevent you from deleting or changing the programs on lab computers. Most networks and host computers allow the system administrator to assign user rights such as the following:

■ Erase rights—allow you to erase files

■ Create rights—allow you to create new files

■ Write rights—allow you to save information in existing files

■ Read rights—allow you to open files and view their contents

■ File find rights—allow you to list files using a directory command

Granting users only the rights they need helps prevent both accidental and deliberate damage to data. If users are granted limited rights, a hacker who steals someone's password has only those rights granted to the person from whom the password was stolen.

Hackers occasionally gain unauthorized access to computer systems through something called a trap door. A **trap door** is a special set of instructions that allows a user to bypass the normal security precautions and enter the system. Trap doors are often created during new system development to provide system administrators with easy access to the computer for installation and testing. All trap doors should be removed before the system becomes operational.

InfoWeb
11

WarGames

In the 1983 film *WarGames*, a trap door is the key to preventing widespread nuclear destruction. A young hacker (played by Matthew Broderick) breaks into a top-secret military computer that has been programmed to deal with enemy nuclear attacks. The hacker begins to play what he thinks is a detailed computer game. The computer, however, thinks an actual attack is occurring. Soon the computer passes the stage at which it can be stopped from launching nuclear missiles, except by a trap door designed by the reclusive programmer who created the original program. The trap door provides a way for the programmer to bypass official military channels and access the computer's fail-safe program. In the exciting climax of the film, the hacker races against time to find the reclusive programmer, then gain access to the computer deep within the military installation in Cheyenne Mountain. In this fictional example, a trap door helped save the world. In general, however, if a trap door is not removed, it becomes a possible means of entry for any hacker who discovers it.

Encrypt Data

Is there any way to prevent criminals from using stolen computer data? When an unauthorized person reads data, the data is no longer confidential. Although password protection and physical security measures can be implemented to limit access to computer data, hackers and criminals still manage to gain access. Important data such as credit card accounts, bank records, and medical information should therefore be stored in encrypted format to foil hackers who break into computers. In addition, when this sort of data is transmitted over the Internet, it should be encrypted.

Encryption Methods

Encryption is the process of scrambling or hiding information so that it cannot be understood until it is decrypted, or deciphered, to change it back to its original form. Scrambling and unscrambling data requires a **key**—essentially like a decoder ring. Encryption provides a last line of defense against the unauthorized use of data. If data is encrypted, unauthorized users obtain only scrambled gibberish instead of meaningful information. Edgar Allan Poe, the American writer famous for his tales of horror, was quite interested in secret codes. He was convinced that it was impossible to design an unbreakable method of encryption. You might be familiar with simple encryption and decryption techniques, such as the one shown in Figure 9-15.

FIGURE 9-15

One of the simplest encryption methods simply substitutes a number for each letter of the alphabet.

17 21 15 20 8 20 8 5 18 1 22 5 14 14 5 22 5 18 13 15 18 5

1. This message is encrypted using a very simple substitution technique in which the number of each letter's position in the alphabet represents the letter.

2. The key to this encryption looks like this. The 17 in the encrypted message is the letter "Q," the 21 is the letter "U," and so on.

A	B	C	D	E	F	G	H	I	J	K	L	M	N	O	P	Q	R	S	T	U	V	W	X	Y	Z
1	2	3	4	5	6	7	8	9	10	11	12	13	14	15	16	17	18	19	20	21	22	23	24	25	26

Quoth the Raven "Nevermore"

3. Once you know the key, you can then decipher the message to see that it is the famous quote from Edgar Allan Poe's poem "The Raven."

Methods for encrypting computer data are far more sophisticated than the simple substitution code shown in Figure 9-15 and much more difficult to break. When a computer stores encrypted data on a local disk or tape, the program that encrypts the data can also be used to decrypt it. The encryption key needs to be known only by the encrypting computer. Encrypting transmitted data presents a different problem because the sender's computer that encrypts the data is not the same computer that decrypts the data on the recipient's end of the transmission. Somehow, transmitted data must use an encryption key that is shared by everyone, but that cannot be decrypted by everyone. Impossible as it might seem, such an encryption method exists.

Public key encryption (PKE) uses a pair of digital keys: a public key known to everyone and a private key known only to the message recipient. The public key encrypts a message. The private key decrypts a message. Suppose you want to send an encrypted message to CitiBank. You would use the CitiBank public key to encrypt the message. Once a message is encrypted, no one can use the public key to decrypt it. To decrypt the message, Citibank uses its private key. Because CitiBank does not publish its private key, no one else can decrypt the message. Figure 9-16 explains more about public key encryption.

FIGURE 9-16

Public key encryption uses two different digital keys—one to encrypt a message and one to decipher it.

Software is available to encrypt data on microcomputers, minicomputers, and mainframe computers. The cost of this software varies with its sophistication. Regardless of its cost, encryption software is virtually a necessity for some businesses—such as financial institutions that transmit and store funds electronically. Several public key encryption systems are currently available, including the popular and easy-to-use **Pretty Good Privacy** (PGP).

InfoWeb
13

Internet
Security

Internet Security

Should I have special security concerns when I'm using the Internet? When you download a file from the Internet, you can use antivirus software to ensure that the file is virus-free before you run it. But some Web sites automatically send a program to your computer and run it before you have a chance to check it for viruses. Can you just trust that this program is harmless? Unfortunately, the answer to this question is "no." While you're connected to the Internet, you could be unaware of a program that is reformatting your hard drive, getting ready to shut down your computer, making your browser hang, or scanning your hard disk for your IP address, user ID, and password. Many security problems on the Internet are the result of two technologies: Java applets and ActiveX controls.

A **Java applet** is a small program that is intended to add processing and interactive capabilities to Web pages. For example, a Java applet might total the cost of the merchandise you are purchasing online. When you access a Web page containing a Java applet, it is downloaded automatically to your computer and executed in a supposedly secure area of your computer known as a **sandbox**. In theory, the sandbox prevents Java applets from running amok and damaging files in your computer's regular RAM and disk areas. Unfortunately, some hackers have been able to breach sandbox security and create hostile Java applets that damage or steal data.

ActiveX controls, introduced in Chapter 8, provide yet another way to add processing capabilities and interaction to Web pages. Programs that use ActiveX controls are downloaded automatically to your computer. Unlike Java applets, ActiveX controls are not limited by a sandbox, so they have full access to your entire computer system. It is possible for hackers to use ActiveX controls to cause havoc.

One solution to the problem of hostile Internet programs is a **digital certificate** that identifies the author of an ActiveX control. A programmer in effect "signs" a program by attaching his or her digital certificate. Theoretically, a programmer would not sign a hostile program, so all programs with a digital certificate should be "safe." Your browser will warn you about programs that do not have a digital certificate so that you can decide whether to accept them, as shown in Figure 9-17.

FIGURE 9-17

Your browser will warn you before it accepts an unsigned Java applet or ActiveX control.

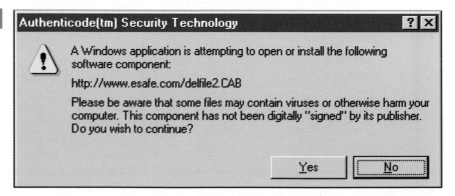

The only way to entirely avoid dangerous Java applets and ActiveX controls is to tell your browser not to accept any of them. However, many Web pages include legitimate applets and controls. If your browser doesn't accept them, you might miss some valuable features and interactions. Companies with hosts or LANs connected to the Internet often implement a **firewall** to screen out potentially hostile programs.

Secure E-commerce

Is it safe to use the Internet for online shopping and banking? The increasing popularity of online shopping has created some nervousness about the security of on-line transactions. Publicity about intercepted credit card numbers and high-tech crimes makes most consumers think twice before providing credit card numbers or other personal information over the Internet. In fact, the security of an Internet transaction is about the same as the security when you purchase merchandise by mail or by phone. As with mail and phone transactions, however, current Internet security technology does not guarantee a secure transaction. Therefore, caution is justified.

Most legitimate e-commerce sites provide their customers with a secure channel for transmitting credit card data. The secure channel is established by encrypting a customer's transmission with a security protocol such as SSL or S-HTTP. **SSL**, short for "Secure Sockets Layer," uses encryption to establish a secure connection between a customer's computer and a Web server. When a customer uses an SSL page, the URL will begin with https: instead of http:. **S-HTTP** (Secure HTTP) also encrypts data sent between a customer's computer and a Web server, but does so one message at a time, rather than by setting up an entire secure connection.

Encrypted transactions ensure that customer credit card numbers cannot be intercepted as they travel between a customer's computer and an e-commerce site. A browser usually displays an icon while accessing secure pages (Figure 9-18).

FIGURE 9-18

During secure transactions, Internet Explorer displays a lock icon and Netscape Navigator displays a key icon.

Some Web sites keep track of your visits. These sites use a "cookie" to remember the date of your last visit, your e-mail address, your last purchase, and the links you followed at the site. A **cookie** is a message sent from a Web server to your browser and stored on your hard disk. When you use a Web site that distributes cookies, it collects information such as your name, e-mail address, and the pages you visit. This information is incorporated into the cookie that the Web server stores on your computer. The next time you connect to that Web site, your browser sends the cookie to the Web server. Cookies are usually harmless, but some Web sites might ask for information that you would not want to make public.

Try to use good sense when responding to requests for personal information. Supply information, such as your address, credit card numbers, bank account numbers, and Social Security number only to sources that you're certain are reputable and that use adequate security measures to protect personal data—such as encrypting the data stored in cookies. Even though the cookies reside on your computer, they can be accessed by other cookie-like programs from disreputable sources.

Provide Redundancy

Can anything be done to minimize the damage from accidents? Accidents can destroy data and equipment. The result is **downtime**, computer jargon for the time during which a computer system is not functioning. The most dependable way to minimize downtime is to duplicate data and equipment. You will learn about duplicating *data* in the *User Focus* section of this chapter. Duplicating *equipment* simply means maintaining extra equipment that duplicates the functions critical to computing activities. This tactic is sometimes referred to as **hardware redundancy**.

Hardware redundancy is a key issue for Internet hosting services that must maintain continuous service for the hundreds of Web pages and e-commerce sites that they host. Duplicate servers, routers, and communications lines would be a key component in a hosting service's ability to maintain reliable service.

Hardware redundancy also reduces an organization's dependency on outside repair technicians. If it maintains a stock of duplicate parts, an organization can swap parts and be operational again before the manufacturer's repair technician arrives. Duplicate parts are expensive, however, and these costs must be weighed against lost revenue or productivity while repairs are under way.

QUICKCHECK C

1 _____ is the process of weighing threats to computer data against the amount of data that is expendable and the cost of protecting crucial data.

2 A(n) _____ is a rule designed to prohibit employees from installing software that has not been preapproved by the information systems department.

3 End-user procedures help reduce human errors that can erase or damage data. True or false? _____

4 If a network administrator assigns _____, users can access only certain programs and files.

5 Hackers sometimes gain unauthorized entry to computer systems through a(n) _____ that is not removed when development and testing are complete.

6 A(n) _____ is a digital message that a Web server uses to store information about your visits to its Web site.

7 _____ is computer jargon that refers to the time during which a computer system is not functioning.

8 A Web hosting service might use hardware _____ as a strategy for maintaining continuous, reliable service for its customers.

➡ Check Answers

DATA BACKUP

**Data
Backup**

A backup is a copy of a file or the contents of a disk drive. If a file is lost or damaged, you can use the backup copy to restore the data to its original working condition. Data backups probably provide the best all-round security for your data. They can protect your data from hardware failures, vandalism, operator error, and natural disasters.

Industry experts recommend that all computer users make backups. Sounds simple, right? Unfortunately, this advice tells you what to do, not how to do it. It fails to address some key questions: How often should I make a backup? How many of my files should I back up? What should I do with the backups?

To keep your data safe, you need a data backup plan tailored to your particular computing needs. To devise your data backup plan, you should consider factors such as the value of your data, the amount of data stored on your computer, the frequency with which your data changes, and the type of backup equipment you have. When these factors change, you should revise your plan. For example, the backup plan you use while in college will likely change as you pursue your career. In this section of the chapter, you will learn about the advantages and disadvantages of various backup tools and techniques, so that you can select those appropriate for your own data backup plan.

When designing your backup plan, keep the following recommendations in mind:

■ Select the right backup equipment and software.

■ Scan for viruses before you back up. If your computer is infected with a virus when you back up, your backup will also be infected.

■ Make frequent backups. You can't restore data that you haven't backed up; so if you wait a month between backups, you could lose a month's worth of data.

■ Test your backup. Before you depend on your backups, make sure that you can restore data from your backup to your hard disk. You would not want to discover that your backup files were blank because you didn't correctly carry out the backup procedure.

■ Store your backup away from your computer. If your backup is next to your computer, a fire or flood that damages your computer could also damage your backup.

Backup Equipment

Does my computer need a tape drive so I can make backups? Tape backups are the most popular microcomputer backup solution, but they are not the only option. Other backup formats, such as floppy disks, Zip disks, removable hard disks, CD-RWs, DVD-RAMs, and even paper, offer additional options. When selecting backup equipment, you should consider its capacity, speed, and reliability.

The disks and tapes that you use for backup purposes should hold your critical data, whether that data consists of only a few files or everything on your hard disk. Even if your hard disk capacity exceeds 10 GB, a backup device with 250 MB capacity might be sufficient if you've decided to back up only your data files.

The speed of a backup device indicates the length of time it will require to copy data from your hard disk. A speedy backup device will quickly back up your data so that you can resume other computing activities.

The reliability of your backup equipment determines your chances of having a usable backup when you need it. Optical media such as CDs and DVDs tend to be less prone to data loss than magnetic media, such as floppy disks, Zip disks, removable hard disks, and tape.

Tape backup has always been the first choice of businesses, and it has gained popularity with individuals as the price of tape drives has decreased. When you make a tape backup, data from the hard disk is copied to a magnetic tape. If the data on the hard disk is lost, you can restore the backup data by copying it from the tape to a functional hard disk drive. Tape backup requires tapes and a tape drive, costing less than $300. You can select an internal tape drive that fits into your computer's system unit, or an external tape drive that's ideal for a notebook computer (Figure 9-19).

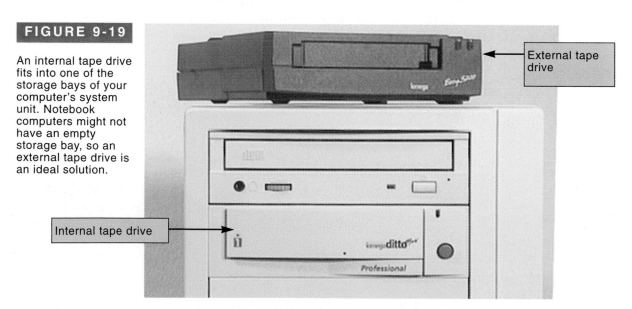

FIGURE 9-19

An internal tape drive fits into one of the storage bays of your computer's system unit. Notebook computers might not have an empty storage bay, so an external tape drive is an ideal solution.

External tape drive

Internal tape drive

Backups are typically stored in digital format, but you can also use a printout of your data for backup purposes. To restore the data from a printout, you can use a scanner or you can retype it. With either restoration method, you can introduce errors, so paper backups should be considered only as a last resort.

Considering the capacity of today's hard disks, it would be unrealistic to use floppy disks to back up all of your programs and data—a complete backup of an 8 GB hard disk would require more than 5,000 floppies! Fortunately, backing up every file is not necessary. Instead, you could back up only those folders that contain your important data files. In the event of a hard disk failure, you would reinstall all of your software from the original distribution disks or CDs, then you could copy the data files from your backups to the hard disk.

If you are using the computers in a college computer lab, you might be in a unique situation because you store most of your data on floppy disks, instead of a hard disk. An effective backup solution would be to make copies of your floppy disks using the Windows Copy Disk utility.

Zip disks provide 100 MB or 250 MB of storage, depending on the capacity of the Zip drive. As with floppy disks, Zip disk capacity is not sufficient for backing up an entire hard disk. But whereas a floppy disk has the capacity to store only a single full-screen graphic, a Zip disk can store 100 of them. A Zip disk, therefore, is a better storage option if your backup needs include graphics or other large files.

CD-RW and DVD-RAM technologies provide another option for backup equipment. CDs are the less expensive technology, but also have less capacity (650 MB) than DVDs (5 GB). A major advantage of optical technologies such as CD-RW and DVD-RAM is their reliability. CDs and DVDs are impervious to many of the factors that can destroy data on magnetic disks and tapes. Figure 9-20 summarizes the advantages and disadvantages of today's backup options.

FIGURE 9-20	Advantages and disadvantages of various backup media.		
Backup Medium	**Costs**	**Advantages**	**Disadvantages**
Floppy disks 1.44 MB	Drive: <$50 Disks (50): $10	Satisfactory for backing up a limited number of files.	Requires too many disks for a complete system backup.
Zip disks 250 MB	Drive: $199 Disks(5): $60	Reliable and especially useful for large data files.	Not practical for backing up all the programs and data on a large hard disk.
Removable hard disks 2 GB	Drive: $349 Disks (1): $125	Enough storage capacity for a full-system backup.	Potentially less reliable than floppy, Zip, or optical media.
CD-RW 650 MB	Drive: $349 Disks (1): $10	Reliable, with good storage capacity.	Slow, and not enough storage capacity for the entire contents of a large hard disk.
DVD-RAM 5 GB	Drive: $700 Disks (1): $40	Reliable, with enough capacity to back up the data typically stored on a hard disk.	Very expensive and slower than tape drives.
Tape 10 GB	Drive: $200 Tapes (1): $30	Low-cost and high capacity.	Somewhat less reliable than optical media.
Paper 1 page	Drive: None Paper: Cheap	Inexpensive backup for documents.	Information must be digitized before being restored to disk. Cannot be used to back up programs.

CHAPTER 9

Backup Software

Do I need special software to make backups?　A **backup** is essentially a copy of data. You must use software to tell the computer what to copy. There are three types of software you might use: a copy utility, a disk copy program, or backup software.

A **copy utility** is a program that copies one or more files. You can use a copy utility to copy files between a hard disk and a floppy disk, between two floppy disks of any size, from a CD-ROM to a hard disk, or from a CD-ROM to a floppy disk. A copy utility is usually included with the computer operating system.

The **Copy Disk** utility is a program that duplicates the contents of an entire floppy disk. You can use the Copy Disk utility only to copy all of the files from one floppy disk to another floppy disk of the same size. You cannot use the Copy Disk utility for files on a hard disk drive. Figure 9-21 shows how to duplicate a floppy disk.

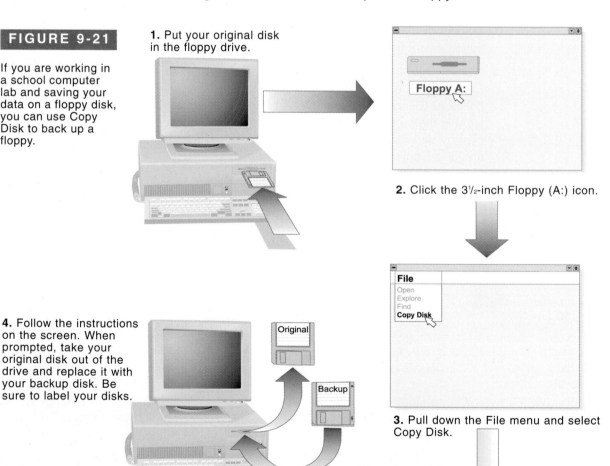

FIGURE 9-21

If you are working in a school computer lab and saving your data on a floppy disk, you can use Copy Disk to back up a floppy.

1. Put your original disk in the floppy drive.

2. Click the 3½-inch Floppy (A:) icon.

3. Pull down the File menu and select Copy Disk.

4. Follow the instructions on the screen. When prompted, take your original disk out of the drive and replace it with your backup disk. Be sure to label your disks.

Backup software is designed to manage hard disk backup to tapes or disks. When you use backup software, you can select which files you want to back up. Most operating systems include backup software, but some tape drives require special proprietary backup software. Most backup software offers automated features that allow you to schedule automatic backups and back up only those files that have changed since the last backup.

The Windows operating system presents some unique backup challenges, which can make it difficult to restore your computer system to its pre-disaster state. Consider that when you use a program, you might customize it. For example, in Microsoft Word, you might turn off the automatic grammar checking feature. You'll recall from earlier chapters that Windows stores information on all of the programs that you've installed in a file called the Registry. Most of your customization settings from software applications, such as Microsoft Word, are also stored here. In addition, the Registry contains a list of the programs that should appear on the Start menu. If you don't back up the Registry, you might be forced to reinstall all of your software, even if you are restoring from a full backup.

The problem with the Registry and a few other Windows operating system files is that these files are open when you perform a backup. Most backup software skips open files during the backup process; as a result, your "full" backups might not include the Registry. To ensure that your backup includes every file that you'll need to restore your system, make sure that you follow the directions provided by your backup software for making a copy of the Registry (Figure 9-22).

FIGURE 9-22

Microsoft Windows includes a backup utility that will make a copy of the Windows Registry.

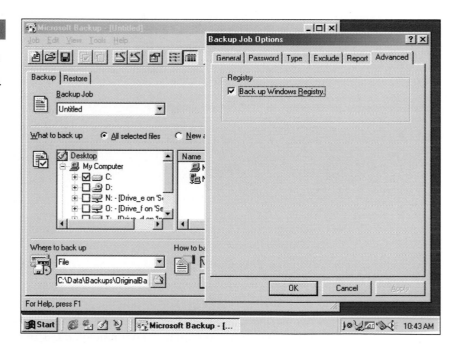

Types of Backups

> Should I back up everything on my disk?

A **full backup** is a copy of all files on a disk. It is a very safe backup method because it ensures that you have a copy of every file on the disk—every program and every data file. Because a full backup includes a copy of every file on a disk, it can take a long time to complete. While the backup is in progress, the computer generally cannot be used for other tasks. Some users consider it worth the time because this type of backup is easy to restore. You simply have the computer copy the files from your backup to the hard disk, as shown in Figure 9-23.

FIGURE 9-23

A full backup is simply a copy of all files on your hard disk.

Back up

Restore

1. Back up all files from the hard disk drive to a backup tape.

2. If the hard drive fails, you can restore all files from the backup to the hard disk drive.

Although a full backup takes a long time to complete, many backup programs let you automate the process so that the backup takes place overnight when you don't need to use your computer for other tasks.

A full backup of your computer's hard disk is likely to consist of many megabytes of data. Make sure that you have purchased a tape backup device and backup tapes with enough capacity to hold all of the data on your hard disk. You are likely to eventually fill your hard disk to capacity, so if it holds 8 GB of data, for example, you should consider a backup system with equal capacity.

A **differential backup** is a copy of the files that have changed since the last full backup. You use a differential backup in conjunction with a full backup. First, you make a full backup of all files on your system. Then, at regular intervals, you make a differential backup. It takes less time to make a differential backup than to make a full backup, but restoring data from a differential backup is a little more complex—you first restore data from the last full backup, then restore the data from the last differential backup, as shown in Figure 9-24.

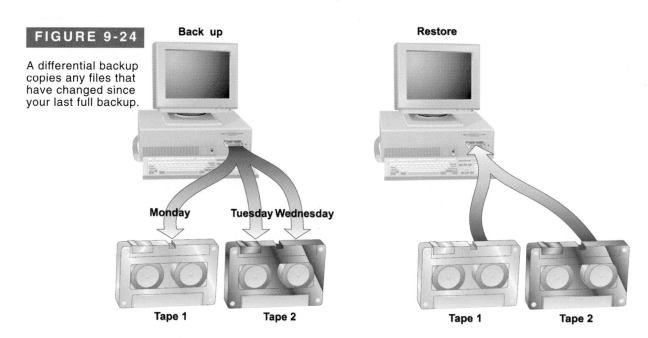

FIGURE 9-24

A differential backup copies any files that have changed since your last full backup.

Back up   **Restore**

Monday   Tuesday Wednesday   Tape 1   Tape 2

Tape 1   Tape 2

1. Make a full backup on Monday evening.

2. On Tuesday evening, use a different tape to back up only the files that have been changed since the full backup.

3. On Wednesday evening, back up only the files that have been changed since the full backup. These files include the ones you changed or created on Tuesday and Wednesday. Put these files on the same tape you used for Tuesday's backup.

4. Suppose the hard disk fails. To restore your data, first load the full backup onto the hard disk. This step restores the files as they existed on Monday evening.

5. Next, load the data from the differential backup tape. This step restores the files you changed on Tuesday and Wednesday.

Differential backups are probably the most popular type of backups because they are easy to create. If you are using tapes for your backup, you need only two tapes: one for the full backup and one for the differential. Take care to label your tapes so that you know which one contains the full backup and which one contains the differential files.

An **incremental backup** is a copy of the files that have changed since the last back-up—not necessarily the files that have changed from the last *full* backup, but the files that have changed since *any* backup. When you use incremental backups, you must have a full backup and maintain a series of incremental backups. The incremental backup procedure is similar to the differential backup procedure, but there's a subtle difference. With a *differential* backup, you maintain one full backup and one differential backup. The differential backup contains any files that have changed since the last full backup. With an *incremental* backup procedure, you maintain a full backup and a series of incremental backups. Each incremental backup contains only those files that have changed since the last incremental backup.

To restore the data from a series of incremental backups, you restore the last full backup, then sequentially restore each incremental backup. Figure 9-25 illustrates the backup and restore process for an incremental backup.

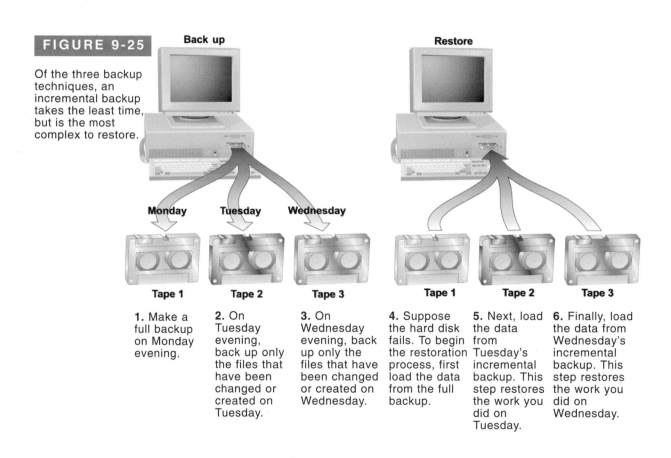

FIGURE 9-25

Of the three backup techniques, an incremental backup takes the least time, but is the most complex to restore.

Back up   Restore

Monday   Tuesday   Wednesday

Tape 1   Tape 2   Tape 3   Tape 1   Tape 2   Tape 3

1. Make a full backup on Monday evening.

2. On Tuesday evening, back up only the files that have been changed or created on Tuesday.

3. On Wednesday evening, back up only the files that have been changed or created on Wednesday.

4. Suppose the hard disk fails. To begin the restoration process, first load the data from the full backup.

5. Next, load the data from Tuesday's incremental backup. This step restores the work you did on Tuesday.

6. Finally, load the data from Wednesday's incremental backup. This step restores the work you did on Wednesday.

Incremental backups take the least time to create and provide a little better protection from viruses than other backup methods, because your backup contains a series of copies of your files. On the other hand, they are the most complex type of backup and require good recordkeeping. You must make sure that you accurately label the tape used for each incremental backup. Otherwise, you might not be able to restore the tapes in the correct order.

Backup Schedule

How frequently should I make a backup? Any data backup plan is a compromise between the level of protection and the amount of time devoted to backup. To be absolutely safe, you would need to back up your data every time you change the contents of a file, which would seriously reduce the amount of work you could complete in a day. More realistically, you should make backups at regular intervals. The interval between backups will depend on the value of your data—what that data is worth to you or your employer in terms of time and money.

An individual using a personal computer might not be particularly worried about the consequences of data loss. Data backup for such an individual should be quick, easy to complete, and reduce some of the inconvenience of data loss. However, it would not necessarily restore all data or programs. A backup schedule that offers this minimal amount of protection would require a once-a-week backup of those data files that have changed since the last full backup (including the Registry), as shown in Figure 9-26.

FIGURE 9-26

A basic backup plan for a typical individual would require weekly differential backups.

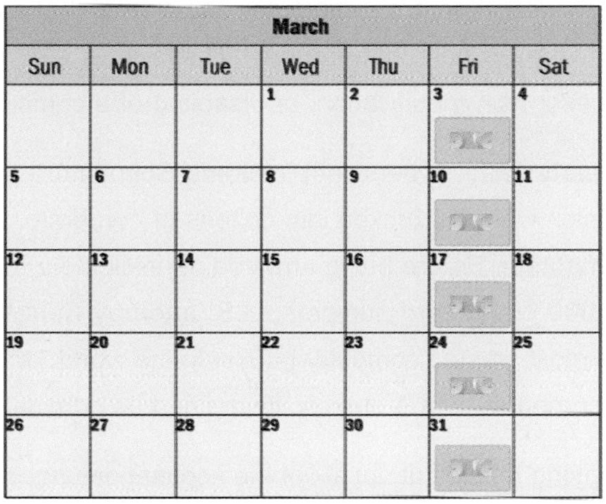

March

Sun	Mon	Tue	Wed	Thu	Fri	Sat
			1	2	3	4
5	6	7	8	9	10	11
12	13	14	15	16	17	18
19	20	21	22	23	24	25
26	27	28	29	30	31	

In the event of a hard disk drive failure, an individual who uses this backup plan would have to reinstall all software from original disks and restore all data from the backup disks. The data entered or changed since the last backup would be lost. If the last backup was made at the end of the day on Monday and the hard disk failed on Thursday, the data from Tuesday, Wednesday, and Thursday would be lost.

A more rigorous backup plan would be required for more valuable data, particularly if the data was produced by an application, such as an accounting system or payroll program, that operates on a weekly or monthly cycle. Every time you use an accounting system, for example, you do not use all files that contain your data. Therefore, a file could be damaged by a virus or disk error, but you might not know it for several days or weeks until you try to access the file. In the meantime, you might have made backups that contain the damaged file. A more sophisticated backup procedure—one that you might use with an accounting system—would typically combine daily, weekly, and monthly backups to allow you to reconstruct data at any point before the file damage occurred.

CHAPTER 9

IS IT A CRIME?

The accounting firm Ernst & Young estimates that computer crime costs individuals and organizations in the United States between $3 billion and $5 billion each year. Some "old-fashioned" crimes that take a high-tech twist because they involve a computer can be prosecuted using traditional laws. For example, a person who attempts to destroy data by setting fire to a computer might be prosecuted under traditional arson laws.

Traditional laws do not, however, cover the range of possibilities for computer crimes. Suppose a person unlawfully enters a computer facility and steals backup tapes. That person might be prosecuted for breaking and entering. But would breaking and entering laws apply to a person who uses an off-site terminal to "enter" a computer system without authorization? And what if a person copies a data file without authorization? Has that file really been "stolen" if the original remains on the computer?

Many countries have computer crime laws that specifically define computer data and software as personal property. These laws also define as a crime the unauthorized access, use, modification, or disabling of a computer system or data.

In early 1995, cybersleuth Tsutomu Shimomura tracked down a hacker named Kevin Mitnick who had broken into dozens of corporate, university, government, and personal computers. Before being arrested, Mitnick stole thousands of data files and more than 20,000 credit card numbers. U.S. attorney Kent Walker commented, "He was clearly the most wanted computer hacker in the world." Mitnick's unauthorized access and use of computer data are explicitly defined as criminal acts by computer crime laws.

Denying many, but not all, of the accusations against him, Mitnick claimed, "No way, no how, did I break into NORAD. That's a complete myth. And I never attempted to access anything considered to be classified government systems." Although vilified in the media, Mitnick had the support of many hackers, who believed that the prosecution had grossly exaggerated the extent of his crimes. Nonetheless, Mitnick was sentenced to 46 months in prison and ordered to pay restitution in the amount of $4,125 during his three-year period of supervised release. The prosecution was horrified by such a paltry sum—an amount that was much less than its request for $1.5 million in restitution.

Forbes reporter Adam L. Penenberg took issue with the 46-month sentence imposed by Judge Marianne Pfaelzer, and wrote, "This in a country where the average prison term for manslaughter is three years. Mitnick's crimes were curiously innocuous. He broke into corporate computers, but no evidence indicates that he destroyed data. Or sold anything he copied. Yes, he pilfered software—but in doing so left it behind. This world of bits is a strange one, in which you can take something and still leave it for its rightful owner. The theft laws designed for payroll sacks and motor vehicles just don't apply to a hacker."

Unfortunately for Mitnick, the jail term and $4,125 fine were, perhaps, the most lenient part of his sentence. Mitnick, who had served most of his jail term while awaiting trial, was scheduled for a supervised release soon after sentencing. The additional conditions of Mitnick's supervised release include a ban on access to computer hardware, software, and any form of wireless communication. He is prohibited from possessing any kind of passwords, cellular phone codes, or data encryption devices. And just to make sure that he doesn't get into any trouble with technologies that are not specifically mentioned in the terms of his supervised release, Mitnick is prohibited from using any new or future technology that performs as a computer or provides access to one. Perhaps worst of all, he cannot obtain employment with a company that has computers or computer access on its premises.

The Mitnick case illustrates our culture's ambivalent attitude toward hackers. On the one hand, they are viewed as evil cyberterrorists who are set on destroying the glue that binds together the Information Age. From this perspective, hackers are criminals who need to be hunted down, forced to make restitution for damages, and prevented from creating further havoc.

From another perspective, hackers are viewed more as Casper, the friendly ghost in our complex cybermachines—as moderately bothersome entities whose pranks are tolerated by the computer community, along with software bugs and hardware glitches. Seen from this perspective, a hacker's pranks are part of the normal course of study that leads to the highest echelons of computer expertise. "Everyone has done it," claim devotees, "even Bill Gates (founder of Microsoft) and Steve Jobs (founder of Apple computer)."

InfoWeb 14
Computer Crime

Which perspective is right? Before you make up your mind about computer hacking and cracking, you might want to further investigate the Mitnick case and similar cases by following the Computer Crime InfoWeb links.

WHAT DO YOU THINK?

1. Should it be a crime to steal a copy of computer data, while leaving the original data in place and unaltered?   ○ Yes   ○ No   ○ Not sure

2. Was Mitnick's sentence fair?   ○ Yes   ○ No   ○ Not sure

3. Should hackers be sent to jail if they cannot pay restitution to companies and individuals who've lost money as a result of a prank?   ○ Yes   ○ No   ○ Not sure

Save Responses

CHAPTER 9

CHAPTER 9 REVIEW ACTIVITIES

INTERACTIVE SUMMARY

The Interactive Summary helps you select important concepts and facts from this chapter. Fill in the blanks to best complete each sentence. When using the NP4 CD or NP4 Web site, you can click the Check Answers buttons to automatically score your answers. Place your Tracking Disk in the floppy disk drive if you want to save your scores.

Operator error and equipment failure are two of the leading causes of lost data. Equipment failure is sometimes caused by short power _____ or longer power surges. Either a UPS or a(n) _____ strip can protect computer equipment from these power problems. A brownout or power failure can cause a computer to lose the data in _____. A(n) _____ provides battery power for several minutes—enough time to save data, close files, and shut down Windows normally. It is possible to obtain insurance coverage for computer equipment, but the best insurance for the data that is stored on a computer is an up-to-date _____.

Computer data is also threatened by computer _____ that attach to a file, reproduce themselves, and spread to other files. A(n) _____ is a sort of software container that can harbor a variety of programs, such as one to steal a password. A software _____ is typically designed to enter a network and reproduce itself, and replicates itself without being attached to an executable program. The best protection for such "malware" is _____ software.

▶ Check Answers

As part of a risk management strategy, many organizations create a(n) _____ use policy that specifies how a computer system should be used. An organization may also create end-user _____ that describe the way computer tasks should be performed. To limit physical access to its computer facility and restrict online access to data, an organization might use identity badges, passwords, or some type of _____ identification device, such as a fingerprint scanner. If these security measures are breached, user _____ may limit the directories and files that can be accessed. Also, if data has been _____, unauthorized users obtain only scrambled gibberish, instead of meaningful information.

Computers that access the Internet are vulnerable to hostile _____ applets and ActiveX controls. Most browser software displays a warning message when you attempt to download programs without a signed digital _____. An organization can also set up _____ software to prevent hostile programs from entering LANs and servers. The security of Internet transactions can be increased by using _____ to establish a secure connection between a client computer and a Web server, or by using S-HTTP to encrypt individual messages. In the event of an equipment failure, an operator error, or a virus attack, a data backup is essential. The most popular backup medium is _____, but it is also possible to back up to floppy disks, Zip disks, removable hard disks, CDs, DVDs, or paper. When using the Windows operating system, it is important to make sure that full backups contain a copy of the Windows _____.

▶ Check Answers

INTERACTIVE KEY TERMS

Make sure that you understand all of the boldfaced key terms presented in this chapter. If you're using the NP4 CD or NP4 Web site, you can use this list of terms as an interactive study activity. First, try to define a term in your own words, then click the term to compare your definition with the definition that is presented in the chapter.

Acceptable use policy, 407
Antivirus software, 403
Backup, 420
Backup software, 421
Biometrics, 410
Boot sector virus, 398
Checksum, 403
Computer virus, 397
Cookie, 415
Copy Disk, 420
Copy utility, 420
Crackers, 396
Cyberpunks, 396
Data security, 406
Differential backup, 423
Digital certificate, 414
Downtime, 416
Encryption, 412
End-user procedures, 407
File virus, 397
Firewall, 414
Full backup, 422
Hackers, 396
Hardware redundancy, 416
Incremental backup, 424
Java applet, 414
Key, 412
Logic bomb, 400
Macro, 398
Macro virus, 398
MTBF (mean time between failures), 394
Operator error, 392
Payload, 397
Power failure, 393

Power spike, 393
Power strip, 394
Power surge, 393
Pretty Good Privacy (PGP), 413
Public key encryption (PKE), 413
Risk management, 406
Sandbox, 414
S-HTTP (Secure HTTP), 415
SSL (Secure Sockets Layer), 415
Surge strip, 394
Time bomb, 400
Trap door, 411
Trojan horse, 399
UPS (uninterruptible power supply), 393
User rights, 411
Virus signature, 403
Worm, 401
Y2K bug, 400

CHAPTER 9

INTERACTIVE QUIZZES

Quiz yourself on important concepts from this chapter by filling in the blanks. When using the NP4 CD or NP4 Web site, you can type your answers, then use the Check Answers buttons to automatically score your responses. Place your Tracking Disk in the floppy disk drive if you want to save your scores.

1 MTBF specifies the amount of time your computer will run on a UPS. True or false?

2 A(n) _____ virus infects .exe files, whereas a(n) _____ virus is attached to documents and spreadsheets.

3 Because a virus might lurk in a computer for some time before delivering its payload, a periodic virus scan might be able to prevent a data disaster. True or false? _____

4 Antivirus software searches through your data looking for a virus _____.

5 A five-character password is harder to break than a password made from two dictionary words joined together. True or false?

6 A(n) _____ created to bypass regular security during installation should be removed when the installation is complete.

7 Data that is scrambled using _____ key encryption can be deciphered only by using a special private key.

8 A(n) _____ is stored on your computer and contains information about you that has been collected at a Web site that you visited.

Check Answers

Fill in the blanks based on the illustration.

1 The illustration depicts the process of making a(n) _____ backup.

2 Tape 1 should contain a(n) _____ backup.

3 Tape 2 and Tape 3 contain data that has changed since the last backup of any sort. True or false? _____

4 To restore this backup, you would first restore tape number _____.

5 With this type of backup, you must make sure to accurately _____ each tape.

Back up

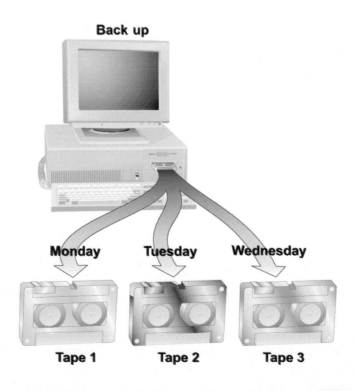

Monday   Tuesday   Wednesday

Tape 1   Tape 2   Tape 3

Check Answers

INTERACTIVE PRACTICE TESTS

When you use the NP4 CD or NP4 Web site, you can take practice tests that consist of 10 multiple-choice, true/false, and fill-in-the-blank questions. The 10 questions are selected at random from a large test bank, so each time you take a test, you'll receive a different set of questions. Your tests are scored immediately and you can print study guides that help you find the correct answers for any questions that you missed. If you are using a Tracking Disk, insert it in the floppy disk drive to save your test scores.

 Start Practice Test

STUDY TIPS

Study Tips help you organize and consolidate the information in a chapter by making lists, outlines, charts, and sketches. You can use paper and pencil or word processing software to complete most of the Study Tips activities.

1 Use your own words to answer the questions that appear under each section heading in this chapter.

2 Create a chart to review the factors that cause data loss or misuse. List the factors you learned about in this chapter in the first column. Then place an X in the appropriate column to indicate whether that factor leads to data loss, inaccurate data, stolen data, or intentionally damaged data. Some factors might have more than one X.

3 Complete the following chart to summarize what you have learned about viruses, Trojan horses, time bombs, logic bombs, and software worms.

Type	Infects	Spreads by	Triggered by
File virus			
Boot sector virus			
Macro virus			
Trojan horse			
Worm			
Time bomb			
Logic bomb			

4 Make a checklist of steps to follow if you suspect that your computer is infected with a virus.

5 List the four steps in the risk management process.

6 List the data security techniques discussed in the *Risk Management* section. Then indicate the advantages and disadvantages of each technique.

7 Use your own words to write descriptions of full, incremental, and differential backup procedures. Make sure that your descriptions clearly explain the difference between incremental and differential backups.

8 On a sheet of paper, list all of the reasons you can think of for making a backup of computer data.

PROJECTS

A project is an open-ended activity that will help you apply the concepts you have learned. Many projects require resources in addition to your textbook, such as current magazines, library materials, or Web access. When you tackle a project, be prepared to use your critical thinking skills, logical analysis, and your creativity.

1 **Lost Data: What's Your Experience?** Describe a situation in which you or someone you know lost data stored on a computer. What caused the data loss? What steps could have been taken to prevent the loss? What steps could you or the other person have taken to recover the lost data?

2 **Risk Management: A Personal Perspective** Assess the risk to the programs and data files stored on the hard disk of your computer by answering the following questions:

a. What threats are likely to cause your data to be lost, stolen, or damaged?

b. How many data files (not program files) do you have?

c. If you add up the size of all of your files, how many megabytes of data do you have?

d. How many of these files are critical and would need to be replaced if you lost all of your data?

e. What would you need to do to reconstruct the critical files if the hard disk drive failed and you did not have any backups?

f. What measures could you use to protect your data from the threats you identified in the first question? What is the cost of each measure?

g. Balancing the threats to your data, the importance of your data, and the cost of protective measures, what do you think is the best plan for the security of your data?

3 **Word Macro Viruses** In this chapter, you learned that a Word document can harbor a macro virus.Using library or Internet resources, find a list of symptoms for the Word macro viruses that are currently circulating. Check your disks to see whether you have any of these viruses.

Write a one-page report describing what you learned about Word macro viruses and their presence on, or absence from, the documents you have on your disks.

4 **The Internet Worm** The Internet worm created concern about the security of data on military and research computer systems, and it raised ethical questions about the rights and responsibilities of computer users. Select one of the following statements and write a two-page paper that argues for or against it. You might want to use the Internet or library resources to learn more about each viewpoint. Be sure to include the resources you used in a bibliography.

a. People have the "right" to hone their computing skills by breaking into computers. As a computer scientist once said, "The right to hack is held higher than the right of someone to tell you not to. It's an inalienable right."

b. If problems exist, it is acceptable to use any means to point them out. The computer science student who created the Internet virus was perfectly justified in claiming that he should not be convicted because he was just trying to point out that security holes exist in large computer networks.

c. Computer crimes are no different from other crimes, and computer criminals should be held responsible for the damage they cause by paying for the time and cost of replacing or restoring data.

5 **Understanding an Acceptable Use Policy** Obtain a copy of your school's student code or computer use policy, then answer the following questions. If your school does not have such a policy, create one that addresses these questions.

a. To whom does the policy apply—students, faculty, staff, community members, others?

b. What types of activities does the policy specifically prohibit?

c. If a computer crime is committed, would the crime be dealt with by campus authorities or by state law enforcement agents?

d. Does the policy state the penalties for computer crimes? If so, what are they?

6 **Lost Weekend: Full, Incremental, and Differential Backups** Assume that your hard disk drive fails on a Friday afternoon. Explain how you would restore your data over the weekend if you had been using each of the following backup systems:

a. A full backup every Friday evening

b. A full backup every Friday evening with a differential backup on Wednesday evening

c. A full backup every Friday evening with an incremental backup Monday through Thursday evenings

7 **Hoax!** Most Internet users have received panicked e-mail about the GoodTimes virus. It turns out that this virus does not exist—it is a hoax. How can you tell the difference between a real virus alert and a hoax? The best policy is to check a reliable site. You can easily locate sites that list hoaxes by entering "hoax" in any Internet search engine such as Yahoo! Sites with reliable reports include *www.nonprofit.net/hoax/hoax.html*, *www.urbanlegends.com*, and *ciac.llnl.gov/ciac/CIACHoaxes.html*.

Visit at least one of these sites and find the descriptions of five hoaxes. Write a one-page summary that includes the name and description of each hoax, the way in which the hoax is spread, and reasons why people might believe the hoax.

ADDITIONAL PROJECTS

Click the underlined text to link to the NP4 Web site (www.cciw.com/np4), where you can view and print additional projects for this chapter.

Antivirus Software

Cyber Crime

Biometrics

CHAPTER 9

LAB ASSIGNMENTS

Software for this lab is provided on the NP4 CD and may also be available in your school's computer lab. To start the lab, click the lab icon.

The lab has two parts: Steps and Explore. Use the Steps first to learn and review concepts. Read the information on each page and do the numbered steps. As you work through the lab, you will be asked to answer QuickCheck questions about what you have learned. At the end of the lab, you will see a report that summarizes your answers to the QuickChecks. If your instructor wants you to turn in this report, click the Print button on the QuickCheck Report screen.

When you have completed the Steps, you can click the Explore button to complete the Lab Assignments. You can also use Explore to practice the skills you learned and to explore concepts on your own.

Data Backup

The Data Backup Lab gives you an opportunity to make tape backups on a simulated computer system. Periodically, the hard disk on the simulated computer will fail, which gives you a chance to restore the data from your simulated backups and assess the convenience and efficiency of different backup procedures.

1 Click the Steps button to learn how to use the simulation. As you work through the Steps, answer all of the QuickCheck questions that appear. After you complete the Steps, you will see a QuickCheck Summary Report. Follow the directions on the screen to print this report.

2 Click the Explore button. Create a full backup every Friday using only Tape 1. At some point in the simulation, an event will cause data loss on the simulated computer system. Use the simulation to restore as much data as you can. After you restore the data, print the Backup Audit Report.

3 In Explore, create a full backup every Friday on Tape 1 and a differential backup every Wednesday on Tape 2. At some point in the simulation, an event will cause data loss on the simulated computer system. Use the simulation to restore as much data as you can. Print the Backup Audit Report.

4 In Explore, create a full backup on Tape 1 every Monday. Make incremental backups on Tapes 2, 3, 4, and 5 each day for the rest of the week. Continue this cycle, reusing the same tapes each week. At some point in the simulation, an event will cause data loss on the simulated computer system. Use the simulation to restore as much data as you can. Print the Backup Audit Report.

5 Photocopy a calendar for next month. On the calendar, indicate your best plan for backing up data. In Explore, implement your plan. Print out the Backup Audit Report. Write a paragraph or two discussing the effectiveness of your plan.

INFOWEB

InfoWeb Site
Chapter 9

The InfoWeb is your guide to print, film, television, and electronic resources. Use it to obtain updates on quickly changing technical information and to locate information for research papers. If you're using the NP4 CD, click the InfoWeb Site icon on the left side of this paragraph to access the online InfoWeb links. Otherwise, use your Web browser and type in the address of the NP4 Web site: www.cciw.com/np4. At the Web site, you'll find up-to-date links to the topics covered in this chapter.

1 UPS: Uninterruptible Power Supplies

Using an uninterruptible power supply (UPS) is the best way to avoid the problems that power outages can cause. Periodically, computer magazines feature articles about the latest UPS technology. For example, in the *PC Computing* article, "Usability Test: Call for Backup" by David Gerding (*www4.zdnet.com/pccomp/features/excl0897/zap/zap.html*), you can read about several of the latest UPS devices and the companies that make them. *Information Week*'s "Keep the Power On" by Logan Harbaugh at *www.techweb.com/se/directlink.cgi?IWK19970414S0050* will fill you in on why you need a UPS and how to evaluate various models. You can also check the CDW's Buyer's Zone at *www.buyerszone.com/ups/bg.html* for a buyer's guide to power supplies. The major UPS vendors are American Power Conversion (*www.apcc.com*), Best Power Technology, Inc. (*www.bestpower.com*), Deltec Electronics Corporation, which has joined with Powerware (*www.powerware.com*), MGE UPS Systems (*www.mgeups.com*), and Tripp Lite (*www.tripplite.com*).

2 Computer Insurance

Does your homeowner's insurance policy cover your desktop computer? Your notebook computer? You might want to check with your insurance agent. You might want to first read some articles, such as "Computer Insurance: What to Ask Your Agent" (*www.insure.com/home/compq.html*) from the Insurance News Network, which provides eight simple questions to ask your insurance agent. Some insurance companies offer special coverage for computer equipment, and Safeware at *www.safeware-ins.com* is one of them. Safeware publishes an annual report on computer theft losses, "Safeware's 1998 Loss Study," that you can read at its Web site,

www.safeware-ins.com/lprindex.html. "Crime Statistics That Will Surprise You" at the PC Guardian site, *www.pcguardian.com/facts-crst.html*, is interesting reading about hardware and information theft. Once you've read this article, you'll want to learn about computer security products at vendors such as Computer Security Products (*www.computersecurity.com/index.html*).

3 Viruses

To learn more about viruses, what they are, and how they work, you might read "Frequently Asked Questions on Virus-L/comp.virus" at *www.bocklabs.wisc.edu/~janda/virl_faq.html.* You'll find additional virus FAQs and many practical tips in the *Windows* magazine online article, "WinFAQ: PC Viruses—Here's What You Need to Know About Viruses-and How to Keep Your System Safe" by Lenny Bailes (*www.techweb.com/se/directlink.cgi?WIN19980101S0101*). You can find information about the latest viruses, including descriptions of specific virus payloads at Symantec's AntiVirus Research Center at *www.symantec.com/avcenter/index.html* and at Network Associates' Virus Information Center at *vil.nai.com/villib/alpha.asp.* The ICSA Lab publishes an annual survey of virus attacks. The 1999 survey is available at *www.icsa.net/99survey.* For a taste of the virus problems that face network managers, check out the article "Trend InterScan Secures Top Virus-Protection Spot" by Jeffrey H. Rubin and Timothy M. O'Shea in the April 5, 1999, issue of *Network Computing* magazine (also on the Web at *www.techweb.com/se/directlink.cgi?NWC19990405S0018*). Some virus reports are hoaxes. Check the site *www.nonprofit.net/hoax/hoax.html* before you panic and spread information about a fake virus. You can also connect to the Data Fellows site at *www.datafellows.com/virus-info*, which maintains a database of viruses and up-to-date information on virus hoaxes.

4 Macro Viruses

Macro viruses are some of the most prolific threats. By attaching themselves to macros in documents or spreadsheets, these viruses are transmitted over networks and with e-mail attachments by users who might not even be aware that their documents are infected. For up-to-date information on combating macro viruses, your first stop should be Microsoft's site, *www.microsoft.com.* At the Microsoft site, use the Search button and key phrase "macro virus" to locate the list of articles about macro viruses. At *officeupdate.microsoft.com/articles/macroalert.htm*, you'll find a good explanation of the Concept virus that infects Word macros. TechWeb at *www.techweb.com* is another good source of information if you search using the key phrase "macro virus."

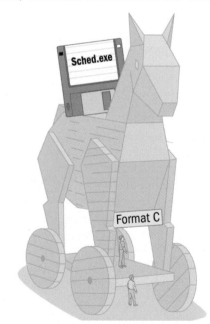

5 Y2K Bug

Did we experience a rash of computer glitches, errors, and outages when the year 2000 arrived? The "year 2000 problem," sometimes called the "year 2000 time bomb" or "Y2K bug," was real. Programmers feverishly worked to correct hardware and software before the stroke of midnight, January 1, 2000. To find out more about Y2K—before and after—visit sites with links to articles, press releases, user groups, vendors, and FAQs, such as *www.year2000.com.* You can enter "Y2K" in any Web search engine to find loads of articles, such as Peter de Jager's "You've Got to Be Kidding!" (*www.year2000.com/y2kkidding.html*). A number of computer industry analysts made predictions about the extent of the Y2K problem. It is interesting to read their predictions in light of what actually happened. You might, for example, check out Gary North's Y2K Links and Forums at *www.garynorth.com/* or Ed Yourdon's Web site at *www.yourdon.com/index.htm.*

6 **The Internet Worm**

In November 2, 1988, Robert Morris, a computer science graduate student at Cornell and the son of the chief scientist at the National Computer Security Center, launched a worm that invaded thousands of Internet computers. "A Tour of the Worm" at *www.mmt.bme.hu/~kiss/docs/opsys/worm.html*, written by Donn Seeley of the Department of Computer Science at the University of Utah, presents a chronology and a detailed description of the internal workings of the Internet worm. You'll find additional information and a good set of links if you connect to the About.com Guide to Internet/Network Security (*netsecurity.miningco.com/library/blworm.htm*). Is it ethical to release a harmless worm on the Internet? Visit sites on computer ethics, such as the one found at North Carolina State University's *www2.ncsu.edu/eos/info/computer_ethics*. Search on key phrases "Internet worm and computer ethics" and link to various articles that analyze the ethics of computer hacking.

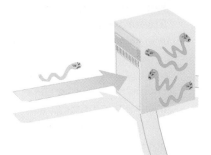

7 **Antivirus Software**

Many antivirus software packages are available—some commercial, some shareware, and some even freeware. The two most highly rated companies that make antivirus software are Symantec (*www.symantec.com*) and McAfee (*www.mcafee.com*), now a division of Network Associates. Their products will protect your computer from virus attacks of all sorts. If you purchase and use their software, make sure you download the updates regularly so that new viruses don't slip by.

8 **Risk Management**

For some tips on how to secure your data, connect to the CNET article "Keeping Pying Eyes at Bay" (*www.cnet.com/Content/Features/Howto/Protect/ss04.html*). One of the best ways to protect yourself from data loss is to always keep a backup of important data. The Internet offers new ways to provide data backup and data warehousing. Panorama Software Corporation at *www.pansoft.com/index.html* is one of many companies that offer products that allow corporations to back up their large computer systems over the Internet. To learn more about risk management analysis, services, and products, check out IBM's Risk Management Web pages at *www.brs.ibm.coml*. If you would like to read about some of the latest computer incidents, connect to the Risks Digest at *www.csl.sri.com/~risko/risks.txt*.

9 **Acceptable Use Policies**

Have you ever thought about starting a word processing business using the computers in one of your school's computer labs? Could you operate such a business from your dorm room using your own computer? Can you use your company's e-mail for personal business? You can find the answers to these questions in your school's or company's acceptable use policy. For an example of an acceptable use policy, check out Creighton University's "NSFNet Acceptable Use Policy" at *www.creighton.edu/nsfnet-aup.html*. This AUP identifies what is acceptable as well as unacceptable use. You might also look at Mountainview Computer Technology's Acceptable Use Policy, located on the Web at *www.new-hampshire.net/aup.htm*, which list rules for its Internet customers. The article, "Developing a School or District Acceptable Use Policy for Student and Staff Access to the Internet"(*www.etdc.wednet.edu/aup/index.html*), discusses guidelines and a philosophy for developing an acceptable use policy for K-12 school districts. This Web site also includes links to a PowerPoint slide presentation; samples of policies, consent forms, and letters to parents; an article that reviews Internet case law; and other resources on legal aspects of acceptable use and the Internet.

CHAPTER 9

10 **Biometrics**

The *New York Times* article, "Use of Recognition Technology Grows in Everyday Transactions," at *www.nytimes.com/library/cyber/week/082097biometrics.html* provides a good introduction to new technologies that are making computers more secure. To learn about the future of biometrics, visit *www.tech.purdue.edu/search* and use the key phrase "biometric technology" to search for the latest news on biometrics. If you are just beginning to explore biometrics, a great basic article is "The Body as a Password" by Ann Davis (*Wired* magazine, July 1997).

What about commercial products? The article "You Can't Forget This Password: Hint: It's Your Face, Iris, Fingerprint" at *www.usnews.com/usnews/issue/990517/17biom.htm* provides a basic overview of biometrics. Read about face recognition software developed by Miros, Incorporated, at *www.miros.com*. Biometrics Identification is one of several companies that make fingerprint verification equipment. You can learn more about its products at *www.biometricid.com*. For links to other biometrics sites, enter "biometrics and computer security" in any search engine.

11 **WarGames**

In the 1983 film *WarGames*, a young boy with an amazing grasp of computers accidentally engages a secret government supercomputer in what he thinks is a game. Unfortunately, the supercomputer, which controls the U.S. nuclear armaments, believes it is involved in a real World War III engagement with Russia. To learn more about this film, check out its page at the Internet Movie Database at *us.imdb.com/M/title-exact?WarGames+(1983)*, where you can find a plot summary, cast list, trivia information, and more. For a Web-based, Java-enabled taste of what the film is like, check out WarGames Logon at *www-public.rz.uni-duesseldorf.de/~ritterd/wargames/logon.htm*. At this Web site, you can view pictures from the film, listen to sound clips, play some games, take a tour of a decommissioned missile silo, and engage in some nostalgia for the 1980s.

12 **Encryption Methods**

You can learn about encryption at Netsurfer Focus on Cryptography and Privacy at *www.netsurf.com/nsf/v01/03/nsf.01.03.html*. This Web site presents an introduction to cryptography, information about key certification, a discussion of e-mail issues, e-commerce issues, and other resources. One of the most popular and well-publicized encryption methods is Pretty Good Privacy (PGP). You can learn all about PGP at "Getting Started with Encryption: An Introduction to PGP" at *www.cs.uchicago.edu/~cbarnard/pgptalk/index.html*. This Web site is an online PGP tutorial that was presented at the Computer Professionals for Social Responsibility conference in October 1995. The MIT distribution site for PGP at *web.mit.edu/network/pgp.html* includes information on how to integrate PGP with mail programs, a link to frequently asked questions, and links to Internet information on PGP, in addition to a link through which you can download a copy of the program.

Interesting books on encryption include *Building in Big Brother: The Cryptographic Policy Debate* by Lance J. Hoffman (Springer Verlag, 1995), *The Computer Privacy Handbook: A Practical Guide to E-Mail Encryption, Data Protection, and PGP Privacy Software* by Andre Bacard (Peachpit Press, 1995), and *Internet Cryptography* by Richard E. Smith (Addison-Wesley, 1997).

The Spartans of ancient Greece might have been the first to use military cryptography, perhaps as early as the fifth century B.C. Since then, cryptography has been used to keep secrets, provide mental exercise, and amuse those who appreciate mathematics and analysis, as well as to preserve and protect military secrets. Are there coded messages in the works of Francis Bacon and Shakespeare? Find out by reading "Cryptology in the 16th and 17th Centuries" at *home.att.net/~tleary/cryptolo.htm*. Did the poet Edgar Allan Poe really dabble with cryptography? You can learn the answer when you read "The Legend of Poe the Cryptographer," written by Daniel W. Dukes at *www.nadn.navy.mil/EnglishDept/poeperplex/cryptop.htm*. If you're interested in trying your hand at cryptograms, check out Today's Cryptogram and Contest at *www.mindspring.com/~fmnshare/today.html*. You might also venture over to the Magic Decoder Game at *raphael.math.uic.edu/~jeremy/crypt/cgi-bin/magic-gateway.cgi*.

13 Internet Security

The site *www.consensus.com/security/ssl-talk-sec02.html* features a good set of FAQs on security. The well-known Web site for AntiOnline is loaded with tips and solid advice on security. Check it out at *www.antionline.com*.

Many of the digital certificates you'll see on the Web have been registered with VeriSign. You can read about the certification process at *www.verisign.com*. Cylink, a network security firm, provides an excellent summary of digital certificates at *www.cylink.com/library/white/digitalsig.htm*. To find out whether your browser maintains the security of your Internet mail address, connect to *www.helie.com/BrowserCheck*. Want to find out more about cookies? Check out Marc Slayton's Geek Talk column at *www.hotwired.com/webmonkey/webmonkey/geektalk/96/45/index3a.html*, which explains how cookies work and how you can read the cookie files on your computer.

Personal firewall software provides some protection against Web-borne vandalism. Cybermedia's firewall named Guard Dog is designed to protect your computer from Internet intruders, such as viruses, cookies, and Trojan Horses, that can damage data on your hard disk or steal private files. Read all about Guard Dog at *www.mcafee.com/about/press_releases/pr04169901.asp*. eSafe Protect creates a secure sandbox for Internet files. At the eSafe Web site (*www.esafe.com*), you can link to a quick tour of the eSafe Protect software, then download it. You can view simulations of vandal software that might be transmitted over the Internet and take a "test" to find out how your computer security rates. A third product, SurfinShield, is published by Finjan Software. You can download a product demo at *www.finjan.com*, experience an attack, and link to some excellent articles about the Internet and security-related issues.

14   Computer Crime

Computer crime law is a double-edged sword. We need laws that protect us from computer crimes, yet we also need to make sure that computer crime laws are not so broad and sweeping that they infringe on our civil liberties and constitutional rights. Mitchell Kapor addresses this issue in "Civil Liberties in Cyberspace: When Does Hacking Turn from an Exercise of Civil Liberties into Crime?" at *www.eff.org/pub/Legal/cyberliberties_kapor.article*. The Electronic Frontier Foundation at *www.eff.org* was founded by Kapor and others to protect civil liberties as technology changes the way people work and do business. At the EFF Web site, you can find articles about computer crime, civil liberties, computer searches and seizures, and other topics related to computers and the law. At the Laws and Crime site, *www.blkbox.com/~guillory/comp4.html*, you can find a directory that includes links to U.S. federal and state computer crime laws, computer crime sentencing guidelines, and computer crime categories. At the National Security Institute (*nsi.org*), you can read "Computer Security and the Law" (*nsi.org/Library/Compsec/cslaw.txt*), an article that provides information for lawyers on the legal aspects of computer security. *Computer Crime: A Crime Fighter's Handbook* by David Icove, Karl Seger, and William VonStorch (O'Reilley, 1995) is a highly regarded book about computer crime. You can read a synopsis and review of this book at *www.ora.com/catalog/crime/desc.html*.

For information on the Mitnick case that was discussed in the *Issue* section of this chapter, read the *WiredNews* article, "Mitnick Could Go Free in January" written by Douglas Thomas, at *www.wired.com/news/news/polkitics/story/21197.html*, then connect to Adam Penenberg's short, but fascinating interview with Kevin Mitnick at *www.forbes.com/tool/html/99/apr/0405/feat.htm*. For the hacker/cracker viewpoint on the Mitnick case and on general matters of messing around with computers, check out the Crypt Newsletter at *sun.soci.niu.edu/~crypt*.

ADDITIONAL TIPS

Tip 1: Pace Yourself

In Chapters 10–15, the focus shifts to a somewhat more business-oriented and technical view of computers, which you're likely to find relevant to your career and to any advanced courses in computing that you might take. When you read these chapters, remember that they are divided into sections A, B, C, and so on. Consider reading one section at a sitting, rather than trying digest an entire chapter all at once.

Tip 2: Tracking Disk

If you are using a Tracking Disk to record your scores, you should make sure that you have a backup copy of it. You can copy the files from your tracking disk to a folder on the hard disk of your home computer or you can follow the instructions on page 420 to make a duplicate copy of your Tracking Disk.

Tip 3: NP4 Web Site

The NP4 Web site provides an alternative to your CD for selected content from your textbook. Use the Internet Explorer Web browser to connect to *www.cciw.com/np4* where you can access the following:

- Chapter Preview videos
- Chapter Previews
- Table of Contents for each chapter
- Chapter Introduction
- Interactive Summary
- Interactive Key Terms
- Interactive Quizzes
- Practice Tests and Study Tips
- Projects
- Lab Assignments (but not the lab activities)
- InfoWebs

You can use your Tracking Disk at the Web site, just as you can from your CD.

CHAPTER
10 DATA REPRESENTATION

CONTENTS

PREVIEW

The information in this chapter will help you understand why your files are stored in different formats and the significance of file extensions such as .pcx, .tif, .wmf, .mid, and .wav. You will learn how to use compression software to shrink the size of your files and save storage space on your disks.

When you have completed this chapter, you should be able to:

■ Explain how information theory applies to the data representation codes used by computers

■ Determine how many bits are needed to represent a given number of messages

■ Define the key characteristics of ASCII, ANSI, EBCDIC, and Unicode

■ Explain the difference between bitmap and vector graphics

■ Calculate the storage space required for a monochrome, grayscale, or color bitmap graphic

■ Explain the difference between waveform audio and MIDI music

■ List the advantages and disadvantages of data compression

■ Use the file extension to identify the type of data that a file contains

CHAPTER 10 LABS

Binary Numbers

Data Representation

ONE IF BY LAND

It was April 18, 1775, the eve of the American Revolution. The Massachusetts Minutemen were huddled around a plank table planning a defense strategy against well-armed and professionally trained British troops. If the Minutemen sent a scout to collect information on the British route of attack, how would he communicate what he had learned? The Minutemen solved this problem by using the plan recounted in Longfellow's poem about Paul Revere's famous ride:

One if by land, and two if by sea;
And I on the opposite shore will be,
Ready to ride and spread the alarm
Through every Middlesex village and farm.

The Old North Church tower was visible for miles. As a signal for Paul Revere, either one or two lanterns would be lit in the church tower. One lantern meant that the British were coming by land. Two lanterns meant that the British were coming by sea. But what if some of the British troops arrived on land and others arrived by sea? Would the Minutemen need another lantern for this third possibility? The answer to this question is clear when you understand information theory and data representation, the topics of this chapter.

InfoWeb
1
Paul Revere

In Chapter 5, you were introduced to the use of binary numbers, ASCII, and EBCDIC to represent data. In Chapter 10, you will pursue the subject of data representation in more depth and discover how computers store graphical, video, and sound data, in addition to text-based data. Have you ever wondered why so many file formats and filename extensions exist? Why, for example, does your computer store some music as WAV files, but other music in MIDI files or MP3 files? Why are there so many file formats for graphics? Should you use the JPEG, GIF, or BMP format for your Web graphics? You'll find answers to these questions and more in this chapter.

SECTION A: INFORMATION THEORY

InfoWeb
2

Information Theory

The Minutemen could have positioned 20 or 30 lanterns on a hillside to spell out the words "LAND" or "SEA." Instead, if we accept Longfellow's account of the historical evening in 1775, Paul Revere and the Minutemen used a simple code in which one light meant "by land" and two lights meant "by sea." It seems that the Minutemen selected a fairly efficient way to convey information. Was there an even more efficient way? To answer this question, you need to understand **information theory**, the study of the most efficient way to represent or encode information. Information theory is an important concept for computer and software design. If information is represented efficiently, it can be stored in a small amount of space and transmitted quickly.

Using information theory, computer scientists have designed various ways of encoding and storing information. The way in which information is encoded and stored in a computer is referred to as a **file format**. A computer stores the data for your documents in a file format different from the one it uses to store your graphics data, video data, or audio data. In this chapter, you'll learn about different ways of encoding data and the file formats that this encoding produces.

Efficiently Storing and Transmitting Information

Could the Minutemen have sent their message with fewer than two lanterns?

Some methods for storing and transmitting information are more efficient than others. Using information theory, you can evaluate the efficiency of the Minutemen's code. Then you can apply what you learn to understanding the efficiency with which computers store and transmit information.

The Minutemen had two possible messages to convey. We'll refer to these possible messages as "units of information." One of these units of information represented the message "by land." The other unit of information represented the message "by sea," as shown in Figure 10-1.

FIGURE 10-1

Paul Revere's code used lanterns to convey messages.

One lantern in the church tower signaled that the British were coming by land.

Two lanterns signaled that the British were coming by sea.

CHAPTER 10

Information theory tells us that the Minutemen could have used a more efficient code, using one lantern instead of two. Figure 10-2 shows that with one lantern, it is possible to convey as many as two units of information; the lantern can be on or off, representing messages, such as "yes" or "no," "land" or "sea," or "true" or "false."

FIGURE 10-2

One lantern can convey as many as two units of information.

In the "on" state, the lantern indicates that the British are coming by land.

In the "off" state, the lantern indicates that the British are coming by sea.

How do the Minutemen and their lanterns apply to computers? As you learned in Chapters 4 and 5, a computer is an electronic device that stores and manipulates electrical currents that represent bits—0s and 1s. Think of a bit as the equivalent of one lantern. A bit can be a 1 or a 0, just as a lantern can be on or off. The "on" state of the lantern corresponds to a 1 bit, and the "off" state corresponds to a 0 bit. A computer can use a single bit (one lantern) to store and convey two units of information: a 1 bit might correspond to "yes" and a 0 bit might correspond to "no"; a 1 bit might correspond to "land" and a 0 bit might correspond to "sea"; and so forth.

You might think that it is not a good idea to use an unlit lantern to convey the message "by sea." A dark church tower could mean many things. For example, the church might have been locked, so that no one could get to the tower to place the lantern. Or, maybe the lantern burned out. In either of these cases, the church tower would be dark and would convey the message that the British are arriving by sea, even though they are really arriving by land.

The point is that information theory tells you that it is *theoretically* possible for the Minutemen to convey either "by land" or "by sea" using only one lantern. However, it might not have been *practical* to do so. As you will see in Chapter 11, information theory can be extended to account for potential problems that might occur when data is actually transmitted.

Representing Information

How can we code more complex messages? A computer uses a bit as the building block for more complex messages, which are constructed with a series of bits. One bit can convey two units of information. If a computer uses two bits (two lanterns) or three bits (three lanterns) how many different units of information can it convey? Figure 10-3 shows that two bits can convey four units of information, each unit representing a different message.

FIGURE 10-3

Two bits or two lanterns can convey four different units of information, representing four messages.

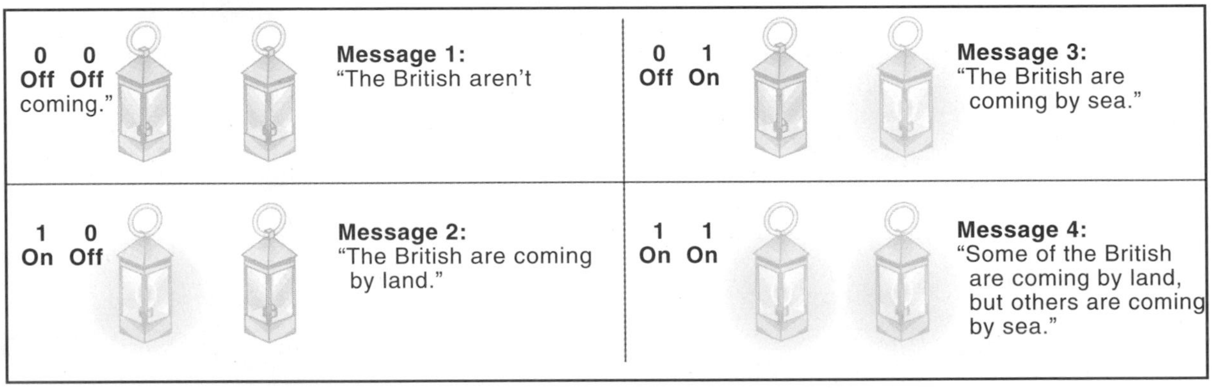

```
0   0          Message 1:              0   1          Message 3:
Off Off        "The British aren't     Off On         "The British are
coming."                                                 coming by sea."


1   0          Message 2:              1   1          Message 4:
On  Off        "The British are         On  On        "Some of the British
               coming by land."                        are coming by land,
                                                        but others are coming
                                                        by sea."
```

The number of units of information that you can convey is simply the number of different combinations you can make with a given number of bits. There is a pattern here. With one bit, you can convey two units of information. With two bits, you can convey four units of information. With three bits, you can convey eight units. The pattern is 2, 4, 8; these numbers are all powers of 2, as shown in Figure 10-4.

FIGURE 10-4

Powers of 2.

$$2^0 = 1$$
$$2^1 = 2$$
$$2^2 = 2 \times 2 = 4$$
$$2^3 = 2 \times 2 \times 2 = 8$$
$$2^4 = 2 \times 2 \times 2 \times 2 = 16$$
$$2^5 = 2 \times 2 \times 2 \times 2 \times 2 = 32$$
$$2^6 = 2 \times 2 \times 2 \times 2 \times 2 \times 2 = 64$$
$$2^7 = 2 \times 2 \times 2 \times 2 \times 2 \times 2 \times 2 = 128$$
$$2^8 = 2 \times 2 \times 2 \times 2 \times 2 \times 2 \times 2 \times 2 = 256$$

You now have a rule about conveying information: The maximum number of different units of information you can convey with n bits is 2^n. For example, if you use four bits (or four lanterns), the exponent n is 4. The maximum number of units you can convey is 2^4 or $2 \times 2 \times 2 \times 2$, which is 16. So, if you use four bits, you can convey a maximum of 16 different units of information. Figure 10-5 summarizes this rule.

FIGURE 10-5

The maximum number of different units of information you can convey with n bits is 2^n.

When you use one bit (one lantern)...	...you can convey two (2^1) units of information.	0 1
When you use two bits (two lanterns)...	...you can convey four (2^2) units of information.	00 01 10 11
When you use three bits (three lanterns)...	...you can convey eight (2^3) units of information.	000 100 001 101 010 110 011 111
When you use four bits (four lanterns)...	...you can convey sixteen (2^4) units of information.	0000 0100 1000 1100 0001 0101 1001 1101 0010 0110 1010 1110 0011 0111 1011 1111

If you have a certain number of bits (or lanterns), you can use the rule illustrated in Figure 10-5 to determine how many different messages you can send. Now turn the rule around. If you know how many messages you might want to convey, how can you determine the minimum number of bits you need? Suppose that Paul Revere knew a spy in the British army who was going to signal information about the month when British reinforcements would arrive. How many bits (lanterns) would the spy need to convey any month between January (month 1) and December (month 12)? You can determine this number by figuring out what power of 2 provides an adequate number of messages. What power of 2—what exponent—would provide at least 12 different messages?

Suppose the spy uses three lanterns. The exponent would be 3 and the spy could send 2^3 messages (8 messages)—not enough to report 12 months. Four lanterns would provide 2^4 messages (16 messages). The spy would need at least four lanterns to send 12 different messages.

Representing Numbers

What if the Minutemen wanted to send a message about the number of British troops in the advance force? Suppose the person in the church tower knew that the British advance force had 50 troops. You know that this information could be sent using fewer than 50 lanterns! Information theory tells us that the Minutemen could use only six lanterns to convey the message that 50 British troops would attack. Which of the lanterns would be off and which would be on to send this message?

Lab
Binary Numbers

Although the Minutemen, like the rest of us, are accustomed to working with the decimal number system (base 10), the binary number system (base 2) would provide a more efficient way for the Minutemen to transmit numbers to Paul Revere. The binary number system uses only two digits, 0 and 1, which correspond to the "off" and "on" states of a lantern. If you need to review the binary number system, take a few minutes to work with the Binary Numbers Lab, using the icon on the left side of this page.

The decimal number 50 is 110010 in binary. To convey the number 50, the Minutemen would arrange six lanterns as follows: on-on-off-off-on-off, as shown in Figure 10-6.

FIGURE 10-6

Six lanterns represent the number 50.

Binary digits	1	1	0	0	1	0
Place value	2^5 thirty-twos	2^4 sixteens	2^3 eights	2^2 fours	2^1 twos	2^0 ones
Binary to decimal conversion	1×32 +	1×16 +	0×8 +	0×4 +	1×2 +	0×1 = 50 (decimal)

Computers can use on and off bits to store decimal numbers in binary format. Information theory tells us, however, that the binary number system has limitations. For example, many early microcomputers had only an 8-bit word size. What is the largest decimal number that one of these computers could store in binary format? If your answer is 255, you are correct. If you assign 1s to all eight bits, you have the binary number 11111111, which is equivalent to the decimal number 255.

InfoWeb
3
Binary Numbers

Using the binary number system, an 8-bit computer could not work with numbers greater than 255 or less than 0. Such a computer would not be very useful, so computer scientists devised alternative ways to use "on" and "off" bits to represent large numbers. Because these alternatives use the binary digits 0 and 1, they are referred to as **binary codes**. If computing is your major, you will learn about these binary codes in your more advanced courses.

You have now seen how the Minutemen could have used lanterns to represent numbers and how a computer can use a series of 1s and 0s to represent a number. Next, you'll learn how computers store letters and punctuation symbols.

Representing Characters

> How many lanterns would the Minutemen need to send messages composed of words?

Character representation refers to the way non-numeric data, such as a letter of the alphabet or a punctuation mark, is represented by a series of bits. A **character representation code**, also referred to simply as a "code," is a series of bits that represents a letter, symbol, or numeral. Don't confuse these "codes" with encryption and secret codes. The codes used to represent data on computers are public and must remain that way so computers can share data.

Data
Representation

Suppose that you want to represent each of the 26 characters in the alphabet. How many lanterns or bits would you need? Although it might seem that five bits are enough to represent the 26 characters in the alphabet, written English uses uppercase and lowercase versions of each letter of the alphabet and a variety of symbols for punctuation and abbreviations, such as $ # @ & +. If you count these letters, symbols, and the numerals 0 through 9, at least 95 different characters need to be represented.

As computers evolved from the primitive number crunchers of the 1940s and 1950s, several standard character representation codes emerged. Today, the most widely used character representation codes are ASCII and EBCDIC, which were introduced in Chapter 5. A third code, ANSI, is a variation of the ASCII code. A fourth code, Unicode, has been proposed for future worldwide use.

ASCII (American Standard Code for Information Interchange) is the most widely used coding scheme for character data. A file of data encoded using ASCII is referred to as an **ASCII file** or as "a file in ASCII format." The standard ASCII code uses seven bits to represent 2^7 symbols (128 symbols), including uppercase and lowercase letters, special control codes, numerals, and punctuation symbols. Figure 10-7 shows you how to use a matrix to find the ASCII code for the lowercase letter "a."

FIGURE 10-7

A table or matrix is often used to provide a compact reference to the ASCII code.

1. Locate the lowercase letter "a" in the matrix.

2. Look at the top of the column to find the binary digits for the three leftmost bits.

3. Look across the row to find the binary digits for the four rightmost bits.

4. Combine the binary digits from the top of the column and the side of the row. The ASCII code for "a" is 110001.

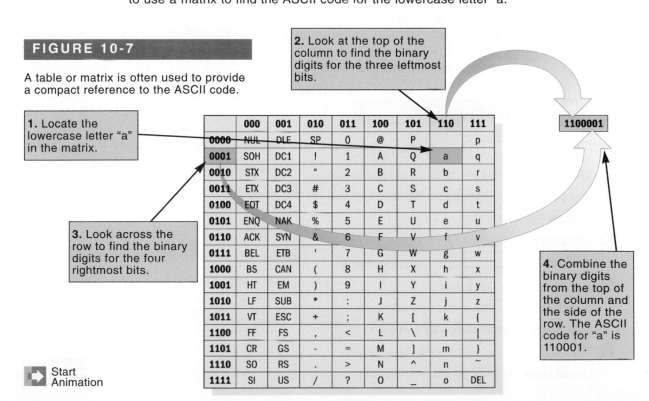

	000	001	010	011	100	101	110	111
0000	NUL	DLE	SP	0	@	P		p
0001	SOH	DC1	!	1	A	Q	a	q
0010	STX	DC2	"	2	B	R	b	r
0011	ETX	DC3	#	3	C	S	c	s
0100	EOT	DC4	$	4	D	T	d	t
0101	ENQ	NAK	%	5	E	U	e	u
0110	ACK	SYN	&	6	F	V	f	v
0111	BEL	ETB	'	7	G	W	g	w
1000	BS	CAN	(	8	H	X	h	x
1001	HT	EM	)	9	I	Y	i	y
1010	LF	SUB	*	:	J	Z	j	z
1011	VT	ESC	+	;	K	[	k	{
1100	FF	FS	,	<	L	\	l		
1101	CR	GS	-	=	M	]	m	}
1110	SO	RS	.	>	N	^	n	~
1111	SI	US	/	?	O	_	o	DEL

1100001

Start Animation

The **ANSI** (American National Standards Institute) code uses eight bits to represent each character. The 8-bit ANSI code can convey a maximum of 2^8 (that is, 256) units of information, so it can be used to code 256 letters and symbols. The first 128 characters of the ANSI code are the same as those defined by the ASCII code, but with an additional zero as the leftmost bit. For example, the letter "a" is represented by the ASCII code 1100001 and by the ANSI code 01100001. In addition to the 128 characters represented by the ASCII code, the ANSI code represents 128 other characters, such as the copyright symbol ©, the pound sterling symbol £, and European language characters such as á, ê, and æ.

EBCDIC (Extended Binary Coded Decimal Interchange Code) is an 8-bit character representation code developed by IBM for its mainframe computers. EBCDIC does not use the same code as ASCII or ANSI for the initial 128 characters. For example, the letter "a" is represented by 10000001 in EBCDIC.

Standard ASCII defines 128 characters, which is sufficient for the numbers, letters, and punctuation marks used in English. ANSI represents all of these characters plus many of the characters used in European languages. EBCDIC represents the standard alphabet and an assortment of control codes. However, none of these coding schemes supports alternative character sets such as Hebrew, Cyrillic, or Arabic. These coding schemes also do not support languages such as Japanese or Chinese, which require thousands of different symbols.

InfoWeb
4
Unicode

Unicode is a 16-bit code that can represent more than 65,000 different characters. Theoretically, Unicode can represent characters in every language used today, as well as characters from languages that are no longer used. Such a code would be very useful in international business and communications, where a document might need to contain sections of text in Japanese, English, and Chinese. Unicode also facilitates the **localization** of software—that is, the modification of software for use in specific countries. With Unicode, a software developer can modify a computer program to display on-screen prompts, menus, and error messages in different languages for use in specific countries or regions. Both Microsoft and Apple have announced plans to add Unicode support to their operating systems.

QUICKCHECK A

1 [＿＿＿＿＿＿] is an area of research that describes how the amount of information you can convey depends on the way that you encode the information.

2 To convey nine units of information, you need a minimum of [＿＿＿＿＿＿] lanterns.

3 If you code data using the [＿＿＿＿＿＿] number system, 255 is the largest number with which an 8-bit computer can work.

4 The [＿＿＿＿＿＿] code uses seven bits to represent 128 symbols, including uppercase letters, lowercase letters, control codes, and punctuation symbols.

5 [＿＿＿＿＿＿] is a 16-bit code used to represent characters in every language used today.

6 When a software developer modifies a computer program to display prompts, menus, and error messages in different languages, it is referred to as [＿＿＿＿＿＿] of software.

Check Answers

SECTION B REPRESENTING GRAPHICS AND VIDEO

InfoWeb
5
Graphics Formats

Graphics, such as photographs and drawings, are quite different from documents that contain numbers and text. Obviously, computers cannot store and transmit graphics using character representation codes such as ASCII. Nevertheless, they must somehow encode graphics as 1s and 0s to store and transmit them electronically. How does this process work?

There are two very different approaches to encoding graphics for computer systems: bitmap and vector. The differences between these two graphical coding schemes affect the image quality, the amount of space required to store the image, the amount of time required to transmit the image, and the ease with which you can modify the image.

Bitmap Graphics

How does a computer store graphical data? Computers store bitmap images, such as digital photos, using a code that indicates the state of each individual dot, or pixel, displayed on the screen. Bitmap graphics range from simple black-and-white images to full-color photographic-quality images. The simplest bitmap image is a **monochrome graphic**, which contains only the colors white and black. To understand how a computer codes monochrome graphics, think of a grid superimposed on a picture. The grid divides the picture into cells, each of which is equivalent to a pixel on the computer screen. With monochrome graphics, each cell, or pixel, can be colored either black or white. If the section of the photo in a cell is black, the computer represents it with a 0 bit. If the section of the photo in a cell is white, the computer represents it with a 1 bit. Each row of the grid is represented by a series of 0s and 1s, as shown in Figure 10-8.

FIGURE 10-8

A computer stores a monochrome graphic using a 0 to represent a black pixel and a 1 to represent a white pixel.

The original picture

The bitmap

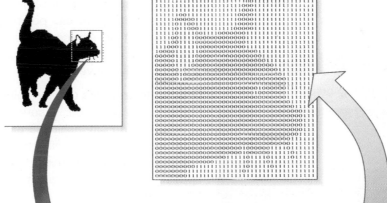

The computer examines each cell in the matrix. If the cell is white, it is coded as a 1. If the cell is black, it is coded as a 0. This pattern of 0s and 1s is stored on disk to represent the graphic.

The computer divides the picture into a matrix equivalent to the resolution of the screen. Here you see only a small part of the entire matrix.

With monochrome graphics, the number of bits required to represent a full-screen picture is the same as the number of pixels on the screen. The number of *bytes* required to store the image is the number of bits divided by 8. To see how this process works, study the calculation in Figure 10-9.

FIGURE 10-9

Calculating the size of a monochrome bitmap graphic.

640 pixels

480 pixels

1. Multiply the horizontal by the vertical resolution of the screen:

640 × 480 = 307,200 pixels

The result is the number of pixels on the screen. Because a monochrome graphic uses only one bit to represent each pixel, this result is also equal to the number of *bits* needed to store the graphic.

2. It is more conventional to measure storage requirements in bytes rather than in bits. Because there are eight bits in a byte, divide the total number of bits by 8 to calculate the number of *bytes* required for the graphic:

307,200 ÷ 8 = 38,400 bytes

As you saw in Figure 10-9, a monochrome graphic displayed at 640 x 480 resolution requires 640 × 480 or 307,200 bits. With eight bits per byte, the graphic requires 38,400 bytes, a relatively small amount of storage space. However, monochrome graphics are seldom used because their two-dimensional appearance is not very realistic.

FIGURE 10-10

A 256-grayscale bitmap graphic.

Grayscale graphics display a bitmap image using shades of gray or "gray scales." Whereas a monochrome graphic is similar to an old-fashioned paper cut-out silhouette, a grayscale graphic is similar to a black-and-white photo. The more gray shades used, the more realistic the image appears. To represent a grayscale graphic, like the one in Figure 10-10, a computer uses a more complex coding scheme than it uses to represent monochrome graphics.

A computer typically represents grayscale graphics using 256 shades of gray. How many bits are required for a 256-grayscale picture? You can answer this question by applying information theory. In a 256-grayscale graphic, each pixel can be white, black, or one of 254 shades of gray—a total of 256 different possibilities. How many bits are needed to convey 256 units of information? The answer is eight: 2^8 is 256. Therefore, a 256-grayscale graphic requires eight bits (one byte) for each pixel. A full-screen 256-grayscale graphic at 640 x 480 resolution requires 307,200 bytes, as shown by the calculation in Figure 10-11.

FIGURE 10-11

Calculating the size of a 256-grayscale graphic.

Multiply the horizontal by the vertical resolution of the screen:

640 × 480 = 307,200

The result is the number of pixels on the screen. A 256-grayscale graphic uses one byte to represent each pixel, so this result is also the number of *bytes* needed to store the graphic.

640 pixels

480 pixels

For more realism, computers can display color images. A computer represents color graphics using either 16 colors, 256 colors, or 16.7 million colors. For a **16-color graphic**, each pixel can have one of 16 colors. To represent these 16 different units of information, you need only four bits of storage space for each pixel. A full-screen 16-color graphic at 640 x 480 resolution requires 153,600 bytes of storage space.

A **256-color graphic** requires eight bits (one byte) for each pixel. A full-screen 256-color graphic at 640 x 480 resolution requires 307,200 bytes—twice as much storage space as a 16-color image, but the same amount as a 256-grayscale graphic.

A photographic-quality graphic can display as many as 16.7 million colors and is called a **24-bit** or **true-color graphic**. To represent 16.7 million colors requires 24 bits (three bytes) for each pixel. Is there a difference in the image quality of 16-, 256-, and true-color graphics? You can judge for yourself by comparing the appearance of the graphics in Figure 10-12.

FIGURE 10-12

A 16-color graphic is quite easy to distinguish, but the difference between a 256-color graphic and a true-color graphic is very subtle.

Files that contain graphics can be quite large, as you have seen. Such large files also require lengthy transmission or download times. For example, it could take half a minute or longer to download a 256-color, 640 x 480 bitmap image from an Internet site to your computer at home. A 16-color graphic would take only half as long to download.

Three techniques are used to decrease graphics storage space and transmission time. First, making an image physically smaller by shrinking it or cropping it will decrease the number of pixels required to represent the graphic. Second, the size of a graphics file can be reduced by a technique known as compression, which is discussed later in this chapter. Third, a technique called dithering reduces file size by reducing the number of colors in a graphic.

Dithering uses patterns composed of two or more colors to produce the illusion of additional colors and shading, relying on the human eye to blend colors and shapes. For example, an area of solid orange on a 256-color image can be dithered into a pattern of yellow and red dots in a 16-color image. Dithering is a popular technique for reducing the size of graphics on Web pages. Suppose you have a 256-color graphic of Stonehenge that you want to use on a Web page. You would like to reduce the time that a Web browser requires to display the image, so you need to reduce the number of bytes used to represent the image. If you simply convert the file to a 16-color graphic, the colors of the resulting graphic are quite different from those of the original. If you dither the 256-color graphic, the result is a graphic composed of 16 colors that appears much more similar to the original. You can see the difference in Figure 10-13.

FIGURE 10-13

A dithered image simulates colors. The orange sky is simulated by a pattern of yellow and red dots.

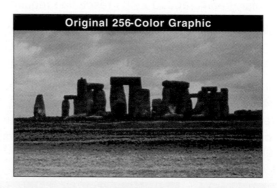

Original 256-Color Graphic

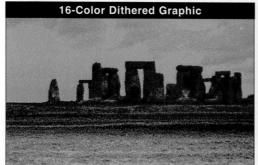

16-Color Dithered Graphic

16-Color Non-dithered Graphic

CHAPTER 10

Scanned photos and other realistic images are typically saved as bitmap graphics. The filename extensions .bmp, .pcx, .tif, .jpg, and .gif typically indicate files that contain bitmap images. Filename extensions are often used as the name of the file format; a file with a .gif extension (pronounced "Jiff" or sometimes "Giff") is usually called a "GIF file."

Because bitmap graphics are coded as a series of bits that represent pixels, you can modify or edit this type of graphic by changing individual pixels. To modify a bitmap graphic, you use bitmap graphics software, sometimes referred to as "photo editing software" or "paint software." Software packages such as Microsoft Paint, PC Paintbrush, Adobe Photoshop, or Micrografx Picture Publisher let you zoom in on a section of a picture so that you can modify individual pixels more easily. Because making large-scale changes pixel by pixel can be tedious, bitmap graphics software provides additional tools to cut, copy, paste, and change the color of sections of a picture.

Bitmap graphics software gives you the capability to modify photographic-quality images. For example, you can retouch or repair old photographs, modify recent photos (see Figure 10-14), and design eye-catching new pictures using images that you cut and paste from several photos.

FIGURE 10-14

Using bitmap graphics software, you can edit images pixel-by-pixel. For example, the pixels for the woman in this photo are being erased using the circle-shaped tools supplied by the software.

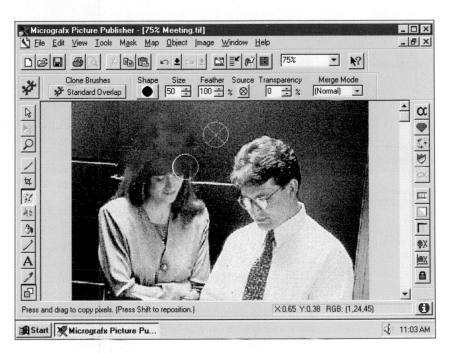

 Start
Screentour

Vector Graphics

What is the difference between vector graphics and bitmap graphics? As explained in Chapter 2, a vector graphic consists of a set of instructions that recreates a picture. When you create a vector graphic, you draw lines and shapes in various colors. The computer then translates these lines and shapes into a set of instructions that can recreate your graphic. It stores the instructions instead of the actual picture. Vector graphics typically do not look as realistic as bitmap images, as you can see by comparing the images in Figure 10-15.

FIGURE 10-15

Vector graphics, such as the one pictured at left, generally look less realistic than bitmap graphics, such as the one pictured on the right.

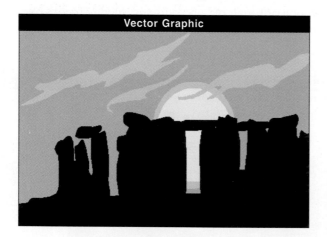

Vector Graphic

Bitmap Graphic

Vector graphics have several advantages, which make them an important tool for simple illustrations and diagrams that might be displayed and printed at various sizes. You can think of the parts of a vector graphic as separate objects that you can individually stretch, shrink, distort, color, move, or delete. For example, a vector graphic might contain a sun that you created with a yellow circle. You could easily move the sun to a different location in the picture, enlarge it, or change its color. When you shrink or enlarge a vector graphic, the objects shrink proportionally and maintain their smooth edges. Whereas a circle in a bitmap image might appear to have jagged edges after it is enlarged, a circle in a vector graphic will appear to be a smooth curve at any size.

A vector graphic also requires much less storage space than a bitmap image. The storage space requirements reflect the complexity of the graphic. Each instruction requires storage space, so the more lines, shapes, and fill patterns present in the graphic, the more storage space it requires. The vector graphic shown in Figure 10-15 requires only 4,894 bytes of storage. Vector graphic files typically have filename extensions such as .wmf, .dxf, .mgx, .eps, and .cgm. Vector graphics software is referred to as "drawing software," and it is sometimes packaged separately from the paint software used to produce bitmap graphics. Popular vector graphics software packages include Micrografx Designer and CorelDRAW.

CHAPTER 10

When you use vector graphics software to draw a picture, you work with drawing tools to create shapes or objects. For example, you can use the filled circle tool to draw a circle that is filled with a solid color. The data for creating the circle is recorded as an instruction such as CIRCLE 40 Y 200 150, which means create a circle with a 40-pixel radius, color it yellow, and place the center of the circle 200 pixels from the left of the screen and 150 pixels from the top of the screen.

Using drawing tools, you can create geometric objects such as filled rectangles or circles. You can also create irregular shapes by connecting points to create the outline of a shape. Objects that you create with the drawing tools can be assembled into a picture by changing the position, size, and color of the objects. The drawing software adjusts the instructions accordingly. For example, if you move the circle to the right side of the image, the instruction that the computer stores for the circle changes to CIRCLE 40 Y 500 200. Figure 10-16 shows how to use drawing tools to create a vector graphic.

FIGURE 10-16

To draw a circle, select the filled circle tool, then drag the mouse pointer to indicate the location and size of the circle. A color palette at the bottom of the window allows you to select the circle color. Once you've created the circle object, you can move it and change its size or color. You can draw irregularly shaped objects, such as clouds, by connecting short line segments.

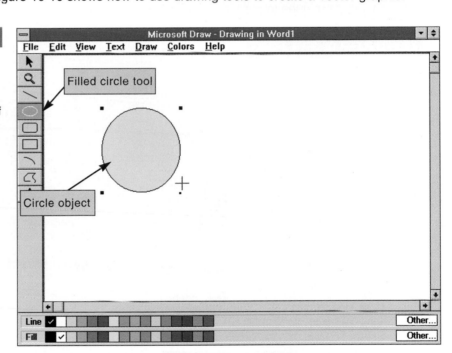

 Start
Screentour

The clouds are created as a series of short line segments and filled with color.

The sun is a series of filled circles, each a different shade of yellow or orange.

The background is a filled rectangle.

Stonehenge is created as a series of short line segments and filled with black.

Digital Video

How do computers store video data? A video is composed of a series of frames. Each frame is essentially a still picture, which could be stored as a bitmap graphic. However, a video displays 30 frames per second, which means that a digital video requires tremendous storage capacity.

As you have seen, a full-screen 256-color image at 640 x 480 resolution requires 307,200 bytes of storage space. Multiply this number by 30 to calculate how many bytes are needed for each second of video—that's 9,216,000 bytes, or about 9 megabytes, for 1 second of video (Figure 10-17). A 2-hour movie would require 66,355,200,000 bytes, more than 66 gigabytes! It would be only marginally possible to play back such a digitally recorded video, even using the most powerful supercomputer. As you will learn later in this chapter, video data requires some special coding techniques to produce a video file of manageable size.

FIGURE 10-17

If this 4-second video was as large as a 640 x 480 screen, it would require about 36 megabytes of storage space.

Start Video

QUICKCHECK   B

1 A(n) [_____] graphic is represented using a code that indicates the state of each pixel displayed on the screen.

2 A 256-grayscale graphic requires [_____] bit(s) for each pixel.

3 A technique called [_____] reduces a 256-color graphic to a 16-color graphic and is frequently used to reduce the size of graphics files stored on the Internet.

4 [_____] graphics are stored as a series of instructions on how to recreate the objects in the picture.

5 Bmp, .wmf, .dxf, and .tif are bitmap filename extensions. True or false? [_____]

6 A 3-gigabyte hard drive can easily store the digital data for a full-length movie. True or false? [_____]

Check Answers

CHAPTER 10

SECTION C REPRESENTING SOUND

Computers can record, store, and play back sounds such as voices and music. Sound or audio data can be represented in two very different ways: as a waveform or as MIDI music. The difference between the two is much like the difference between a tape recording and a player-piano roll.

InfoWeb
6

Digital Audio

Waveform Audio

How do computers store music? **Waveform audio** is a digital representation of sound. Music, voice, and sound effects can all be recorded as waveforms. To digitally record sound, samples of the sound are collected at periodic intervals and stored as numeric data. Figure 10-18 shows how a computer digitally samples a sound wave.

FIGURE 10-18

Sampling a sound wave.

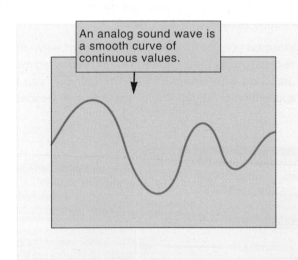

An analog sound wave is a smooth curve of continuous values.

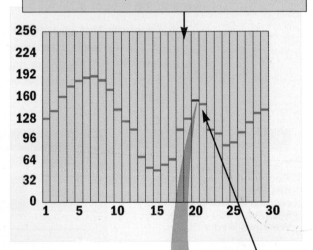

To digitize a wave, it is sliced into vertical segments, called samples. For purposes of illustration, this one-second sound wave has been sliced into 30 samples.

The height of each sample is converted into a binary number and stored. The height of sample 20 is 155 (decimal), so it is stored as its binary equivalent, 10011011.

Sample	Sample Height (Decimal)	Sample Height (Binary)
1	130	10000010
2	140	10001100
3	162	10100010
4	175	10101111
5	185	10111001
6	188	10111100
7		
12	115	01110011
13	68	01000100
14	50	00110010
15	45	00101101
16	60	00111100
17	66	01000010
18	115	01110011
19	129	10000001
20	155	10011011
21	153	10011001
22	115	01110011

Sampling rate refers to the number of times per second that the sound is measured during the recording process. It is expressed in hertz (Hz). One thousand samples per second is expressed as 1,000 Hz or 1 KHz (kilohertz). Higher sampling rates increase the quality of the sound recording but require more storage space than lower sampling rates.

The height of each sample can be saved as an 8-bit number for radio-quality recordings or as a 16-bit number for high-fidelity recordings. The audio CDs you buy at your favorite music store are recorded at a sampling rate of 44.1 KHz, which means a sample of the sound is taken 44,100 times per second. Sixteen bits are used for each sample. To achieve stereo effects, you must take two of these 16-bit samples. Therefore, each sample requires 32 bits of storage space. When you sample stereo CD-quality music at 44.1 KHz, you can store only 8 seconds of music on a 1.44 MB floppy disk. Forty-five minutes of music—the length of a typical rock album—requires about 475 MB.

To conserve space, applications that do not require such high-quality sound use much lower sampling rates. Voice is often recorded with a sampling rate of 11 KHz or 11,000 samples per second. This rate results in lower-quality sound, but the file is about one-fourth the size of a file for the same sound recorded at 44.1 KHz.

The waveform files you record and store on your computer generally have .wav, .mod, .au, or .voc filename extensions. To record or play back waveform files, you need music software. Such software is usually included with sound cards. Alternatively, you can use the Windows Sound Recorder application or Media Player applications, described in Figure 10-19.

FIGURE 10-19

The Windows Sound Recorder, shown here, is designed for playing and recording WAV files. To play MIDI files, you can use the Windows Media Player.

Start
Screentour

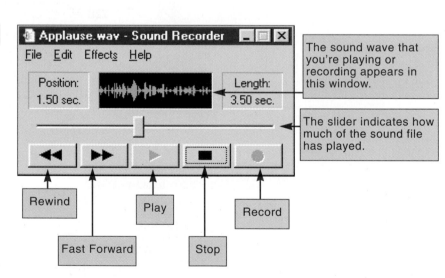

The sound wave that you're playing or recording appears in this window.

The slider indicates how much of the sound file has played.

Rewind

Fast Forward

Play

Stop

Record

MIDI Music

Can I use MIDI to store voice and music data? **MIDI** (Musical Instrument Digital Interface) files contain the instructions that MIDI instruments and MIDI sound cards use to recreate or synthesize sounds. MIDI files store and recreate musical instrument sounds, but not speaking or singing voices. MIDI files are much more compact than waveform files. Three minutes of MIDI music requires only 10 *kilo*bytes of storage space, whereas three minutes of waveform music requires 15 *mega*bytes.

MIDI is a music notation system that allows computers to communicate with music synthesizers. The computer encodes the music as a sequence and stores it as a file with a .mid, .cmf, or .rol filename extension. A **sequence** is analogous to a player-piano roll that contains punched information indicating which musical notes to play. A MIDI sequence contains instructions specifying the pitch of a note, the point at which a note begins, the instrument that plays the note, the volume of the note, and the duration of the note, as shown in Figure 10-20.

Most of today's computers include a MIDI-capable sound card. You can download MIDI music files from the Internet and play them on your computer. You can also plug a MIDI instrument, such as an electronic keyboard, into the sound card's MIDI/joystick port to record your own MIDI tunes.

FIGURE 10-20

A MIDI sequence is stored as a series of tracks. Each track represents an instrument. When you compose MIDI music, you can assign an instrument to each track, write the notes the instrument should play, and indicate the volume and sound quality.

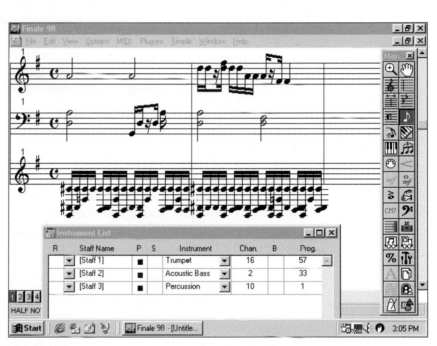

Start
Screentour

Q U I C K C H E C K   C

1 _____ audio is analogous to bitmap graphics, whereas _____ music is analogous to vector graphics.

2 The _____ rate refers to the number of times per second that a sound is measured during the recording process.

3 A MIDI sequence is a digital recording of human speech. True or false? _____

4 Human speech should be recorded at a higher sampling rate than music. True or false? _____

5 Ten minutes of music stored in WAV format would require more storage space than ten minutes of music stored in a MIDI file. True or false? _____

Check
Answers

InfoWeb
7

Data
Compression

Despite the use of information theory to design effective coding schemes for representing characters, graphics, and sounds, the files that contain such data can be quite large. As you learned earlier in this chapter, one second of video requires 9 MB, a full-screen bitmap graphic requires 307,200 bytes, and a 45-minute waveform sound file might be as large as 475 MB. Large files need lots of storage space, require lengthy transmission times, and easily become fragmented, thereby reducing the efficiency of your computer's hard disk drive. If you could reduce the size of a file without losing any of the data it contains, you would be able to minimize these problems.

Data compression is the general term used to describe the process of recoding data so that it requires fewer bytes of storage space. The process is similar in concept to condensing and reconstituting orange juice. To condense orange juice, water is removed. To compress a file, bytes are removed, which reduces the file size. Data compression is reversible. Just as water can be added to reconstitute orange juice, bytes that were previously removed from a file can be restored so that the data can be returned to its original form. The process of reversing data compression is sometimes referred to as **uncompressing**, **decompressing**, **extracting**, or **expanding** a file.

When data is compressed, the size of the file that holds the data shrinks. The amount of shrinkage is referred to as the **compression ratio**. A compression ratio of 20:1, for example, means that a compressed file is 20 times smaller than the original file. Data compression techniques can be applied to text, graphics, sound, and video data. Some techniques require specialized computer hardware, whereas others are implemented entirely by software. The hardware or software routine that compresses and uncompresses text, graphics, sound, or video files is technically referred to as a **codec** (COmpressor/DECompressor). There are two types of data compression: disk compression and file compression.

Disk Compression

Does Windows include compression software? With some versions of Windows, Microsoft provides disk compression utility software called DriveSpace. **Disk compression** shrinks your files and places them in a special volume on your hard disk. A **disk volume** is a disk or an area of a disk that has a unique name and is treated as a separate disk. Disk compression creates a **compressed volume** containing data that has been recoded to use storage space more efficiently. A compressed volume is treated essentially as a separate drive, usually with its own device letter. When you want to use a file from the compressed volume of the disk, the computer automatically expands the file to its regular size. When you store a file on the compressed volume, the computer automatically shrinks it.

The advantage of disk compression is that you gain storage space without having to purchase additional hardware. Under optimal circumstances, you can effectively double the capacity of a hard disk. More typically, you can expect to gain about one-third more storage space when you use a disk compression utility.

Disk compression has two potential drawbacks. First, if you decide that you no longer want a compressed volume on your drive, you must have enough drive space to hold all of the files in their uncompressed state. Many users, taking advantage of the extra storage space provided by disk compression, would not have this space available. Second, a file error in the compressed volume could mean the loss of all of the data in that volume. Regular backups are important for compressed disks.

CHAPTER 10

File Compression

| Can I compress just a single file? | Yes. **File compression** shrinks one or more files into a single smaller file, as illustrated in Figure 10-21. Unlike disk compression, which creates a disk volume, file compression creates a compressed file. You cannot use this compressed file until it has been uncompressed. PKZIP and WinZip are popular shareware programs that compress and uncompress files. Typically, these programs produce compressed files with .zip extensions. In computer jargon, compressing a file with this software is sometimes called **zipping**; uncompressing a file is called **unzipping**. You can zip program files or data files. The advantage of file compression is that zipped files can fit on a single floppy disk more easily and take less time to upload or e-mail. The disadvantage is that typically you must manually unzip the files before you use them.

FIGURE 10-21

File compression software shrinks one or more files into a single file that requires less storage space than the original files.

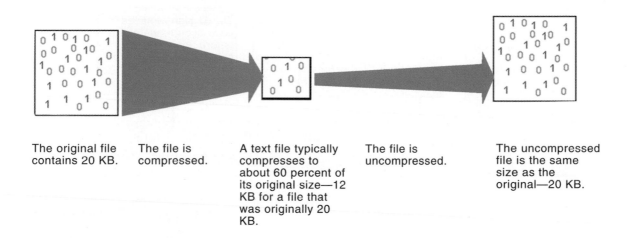

The original file contains 20 KB. The file is compressed. A text file typically compresses to about 60 percent of its original size—12 KB for a file that was originally 20 KB. The file is uncompressed. The uncompressed file is the same size as the original—20 KB.

A twist on the traditional file compression model is the self-extracting file (introduced in Chapter 8), which contains compressed data and the software necessary to uncompress it. These files have an .exe extension, which means that you can run them. When you run a self-extracting executable file, it automatically uncompresses the data that it contains. This process saves you the time of launching your compression utility, locating the file you want to uncompress, and running the uncompression routine. Because self-extracting files contain the program code necessary to carry out the decompression, they are somewhat larger than their non-self-extracting counterparts. Typically, self-extracting files contain programs, not data files.

Using a file compression utility, you can shrink text and .bmp files by as much as 70 percent. However, some other types of files hardly shrink at all because they are already stored in a compressed format. Next, you will learn about several techniques that compression utilities use to shrink text, graphics, video, and music files. You'll find out why some files become considerably smaller when you compress them, but other files do not seem to change size at all.

Text File Compression

How does a compression utility shrink my document files? Text files contain many repeating patterns of words and spaces, so compression utilities can shrink text files to less than half of their original size using compression techniques such as adaptive pattern substitution and pointers.

Adaptive pattern substitution is a compression technique designed specifically to compress text files. It scans the entire text and looks for patterns of two or more bytes. When it finds such a pattern, it substitutes a byte pattern that is not used elsewhere in the file and makes a "dictionary" entry. Let's look at a simple example.

How does adaptive pattern substitution work to compress a phrase such as "the rain in Spain falls mainly on the plain"? The uncompressed phrase is 44 bytes long, including spaces and punctuation. Look at Figure 10-22 to see how adaptive pattern substitution compresses this phrase to 29 bytes.

FIGURE 10-22

Text compression: adaptive pattern substitution.

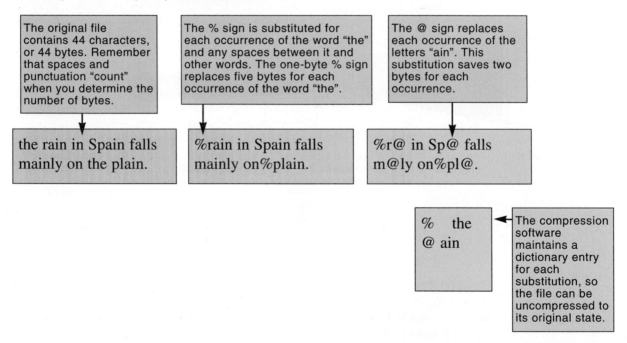

The original file contains 44 characters, or 44 bytes. Remember that spaces and punctuation "count" when you determine the number of bytes.

The % sign is substituted for each occurrence of the word "the" and any spaces between it and other words. The one-byte % sign replaces five bytes for each occurrence of the word "the".

The @ sign replaces each occurrence of the letters "ain". This substitution saves two bytes for each occurrence.

the rain in Spain falls mainly on the plain.

%rain in Spain falls mainly on%plain.

%r@ in Sp@ falls m@ly on%pl@.

| % | the |
| @ | ain |

The compression software maintains a dictionary entry for each substitution, so the file can be uncompressed to its original state.

The symbols used for the substitution in Figure 10-22 are actual characters and are used only for the purpose of an example. Obviously, in a real document, these characters could not be used because they might occur in the document. You would not want the computer to replace the e-mail address coco@canine.com with cocoaincanine.com!

The effectiveness of adaptive pattern substitution depends on the content of the document. Compression will work best in documents that contain large chunks of repeating information. Longer documents are more likely to contain repetitions, so they usually compress at a better ratio than documents shorter than one page.

Another text compression technique scans a file and looks for repeated words. When a word occurs more than once, the second and all subsequent occurrences of the word are replaced with a number. The number acts as a "pointer" to the original occurrence of the word, and a dictionary entry is not needed. Figure 10-23 shows how pointers can be used to compress a text file.

FIGURE 10-23

Text compression: using pointers to compress a file.

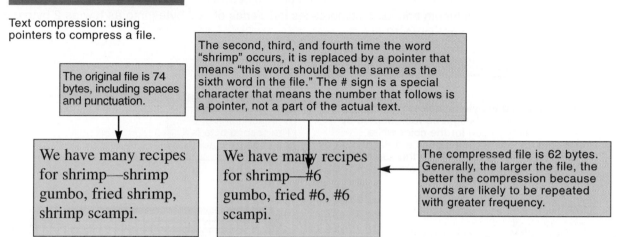

The original file is 74 bytes, including spaces and punctuation.

The second, third, and fourth time the word "shrimp" occurs, it is replaced by a pointer that means "this word should be the same as the sixth word in the file." The # sign is a special character that means the number that follows is a pointer, not a part of the actual text.

We have many recipes for shrimp—shrimp gumbo, fried shrimp, shrimp scampi.

We have many recipes for shrimp—#6 gumbo, fried #6, #6 scampi.

The compressed file is 62 bytes. Generally, the larger the file, the better the compression because words are likely to be repeated with greater frequency.

Remember that you must uncompress a file before you can use it. If you tried to open a compressed file using your word processing software, the document would appear as an illegible scramble of letters and symbols, as shown in Figure 10-24. More typically, your word processing software would not even open the file and would instead display an error message indicating that the file type—with the .zip extension—cannot be opened. Such a message would be your cue to unzip the file before you try again to open it.

FIGURE 10-24

Although most word processing software will not open a compressed document, the Notepad software, shipped with Windows is an exception. Notepad will open a compressed file, but the text will appear as an illegible scramble of letters and symbols. The file is not damaged—it simply needs to be unzipped before you try again to open it.

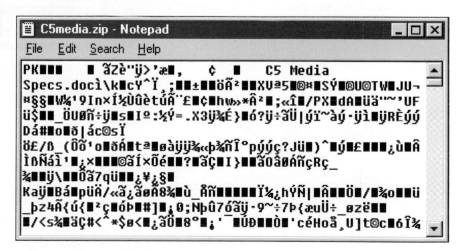

Graphics File Compression

Can I use a compression utility to shrink a graphics file? Uncompressed bitmap graphics files are very large; however, they often contain repetitious data, such as large blocks of the same color, that can be compressed. **Run length encoding** is a compression technique that looks for patterns of bytes and replaces them with a message that describes the pattern. As a simple example, suppose a section of a picture has 167 consecutive white pixels and each pixel is described by one byte of data. The process of run length encoding compresses this series of 167 bytes into as few as 2 bytes, as shown in Figure 10-25.

FIGURE 10-25

In an uncompressed file, each pixel of a 256-color bitmap requires one byte to indicate its color. For example, a white pixel might be represented by 11111111, a binary code for the color white. Run length encoding compresses graphical data by recoding series of pixels that are the same color.

2. The next five pixels are coded "00000101 00000000." The first byte is the binary representation of 5. The second byte is the code for black.

1. The data for the first 167 white pixels can be compressed as "10100111 11111111." The first byte is the binary representation of 167. The second byte is the code for white.

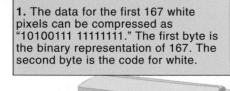

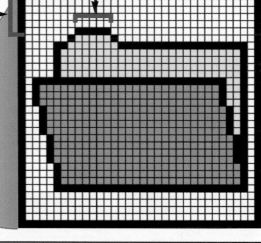

3. Without compression, the first nine rows of the graphic require 288 bytes of file space because there are 288 pixels. With compression based on run length encoding, only 30 bytes—the binary numbers in columns 2 and 4 of this table—are required for this section of the graphic.

Number of Repetitions (Decimal)	Number of Repetitions (Binary)	Pixel Colors	Pixel Colors (Binary)
167	10100111	White	11111111
5	00000101	Black	00000000
26	00011010	White	11111111
1	00000001	Black	00000000
5	00000101	Yellow	10100000
1	00000001	Black	00000000
23	00010111	White	11111111
2	00000010	Black	00000000
7	00000111	Yellow	10100000
18	00010010	Black	00000000
5	00000101	White	11111111
1	00000001	Black	00000000
25	00011001	Yellow	10100000
1	00000001	White	11111111
1	00000001	Black	00000000

CHAPTER 10

Files with .bmp filename extensions usually contain bitmap images that have not been compressed. When you use PKZIP or WinZip to compress a .bmp file, the result is typically a dramatically smaller graphics file.

Graphics files with .tif, .pcx, .gif, and .jpg filename extensions contain bitmap images that have already been stored in compressed formats. The graphics software that you use to open and save these files contains the program code necessary to compress and decompress them. This process usually goes unnoticed because it happens automatically.

Compressed graphics file formats use one of two categories of compression: lossy or lossless. **Lossy compression** "throws away" some of the original data for the graphic; in theory, the human eye won't miss the lost information. The **JPEG** (Joint Photographic Experts Group) format uses lossy compression. **Lossless compression** provides the means to reconstitute all of the original data in a graphics file. The **TIFF** (Tag Image File Format), **PCX** (PC Paintbrush), and **GIF** (Graphics Interchange Format) formats employ lossless compression.

When you save a graphic, most graphics software allows you to select a file format. Graphics that are already stored in a compressed format, such as TIFF, JPEG, GIF, and PCX typically cannot be further compressed by using a file compression utility such as PKZIP. Graphics stored in an uncompressed format, such as BMP, will shrink considerably when you use compression software.

Video File Compression

Is there a way to compress large video files?   You learned earlier in this chapter that video is composed of a series of frames, each of which is essentially a bitmap image. You also learned that noncompressed video requires huge amounts of storage space. The feature-length movie, *Toy Story*, was generated entirely by computers (Figure 10-26).

FIGURE 10-26

The full-length film *Toy Story* was generated entirely by computers and requires the equivalent of 1,200 CD-ROMs of storage space.

InfoWeb
8
Toy Story

Digital Video

It is possible to display video on your personal computer by reducing the number of frames displayed per second, reducing the size of the video window, or coding only the changes that take place from one frame to the next.

Video for Windows, **QuickTime**, and **MPEG** are popular formats used to encode, compress, store, and play back digitized video. You can recognize Video for Windows files by their .avi filename extension. QuickTime files have a .mov filename extension. MPEG (Moving Picture Experts Group) is technically a compression method, rather than a file format, although it creates files with an .mpg filename extension. Originally, MPEG required specialized hardware for compression and uncompression. With today's fast computers it is possible to play MPEG videos without such special hardware. However, specialized hardware is still required for the compression process. MPEG can compress a two-hour video into a few gigabytes. Figure 10-27 compares features of today's three major video formats.

FIGURE 10-27	Video File Formats				
Format	**Filename Extension**	**Frames/ Second**	**Resolution**	**Color Palette**	**Sound**
Video for Windows	.avi	30	320 x 240	8-bit	8-bit mono
QuickTime	.mov	10-12	320 x 240	8-bit	8-bit mono
MPEG-1	.mpg	30	352 x 240	24-bit	16-bit stereo
MPEG-2	.mpg	60	720 x 480 or 1280 x 720	24-bit	16-bit stereo

The number of frames per second directly affects the perceived smoothness of the video. High-quality video displays 30 frames per second. Lower-quality video displays only 10–15 frames per second; that video might appear jerky but is acceptable for some computer applications, such as training videos or animated product catalogs.

Another technique that makes video display possible on a microcomputer is reducing the image size. Displaying an image on one-quarter of your screen requires only one-fourth of the data required to display a full-screen image, so most desktop videos use only a small window on your computer screen.

Video files shrink if you compress each frame using a standard graphics compression technique such as JPEG. Called **intraframe compression**, this technique produces compression ratios between 20:1 and 40:1, depending on the data in the frame.

Yet another technique requires the computer to evaluate the difference between two frames and store only the data that has changed. Suppose you have a video segment that doesn't change very much from one frame to the next. A "talking head" is a good example; the mouth and eyes change from frame to frame, but the background remains fairly stable. Instead of recording all data for each frame, a technique called **motion compensation** stores only the data that changes between one frame and the next. Depending on the data, motion compensation can produce compression ratios of 200:1.

CHAPTER 10

MP3 Music Compression

Can I compress music and sound files? Although it is possible to use compression utilities, such as WinZip and PKZIP, to shrink WAV and MIDI files, the compression ratio is typically unsatisfactory. **MP3** is a popular format for compressing musical data. It is a variation of MPEG compression, technically called "MPEG Audio Layer 3." MP3 is a lossy compression technique because it filters out audio data that is outside of normal human hearing. Additional compression routines then apply a fairly complex compression algorithm to the remaining data. MP3 compression preserves a high degree of sound quality, while reducing file size by a factor of 12.

InfoWeb
10

MP3

You can find thousands of MP3 music files with their characteristic .mp3 filename extensions at various Web sites, easily download your selections, and play them using **MP3 player** software. MP3 players can be downloaded from the Web. You can also play MP3 files using the most recent version of the Windows Media Player.

You can create your own MP3 files from your favorite music CDs. The first step is to use **MP3 ripper** software (sometimes called a "CD grabber") to convert the songs on your CD into WAV files. These WAV files are huge, so the next step is to compress them into MP3 format using software called an **MP3 encoder**. Once they are in MP3 format, you can use your MP3 player to listen to the files on your computer.

Suppose that you want to send a large WAV music file as an e-mail attachment. Would you compress the WAV into a ZIP file or into an MP3 file? That depends on the software you would expect on the e-mail recipient's computer. Just about every Windows computer has the ability to play WAV files, and a high percentage of people have installed WinZip or PKZIP to compress document and graphics files. Fewer people have MP3 players. MP3, however, would provide the best sound quality in the smallest file size. Most experts would suggest that you use the MP3 format and, if your e-mail recipient does not have an MP3 player, direct him or her to a download site.

QUICKCHECK   D

1 Data _____ is a technique for recoding data so it requires fewer bytes of storage space.

2 Disk compression creates a compressed _____ on your hard disk.

3 Compression utilities, such as PKZIP and WinZip, typically produce files with _____ filename extensions.

4 A technique called _____ compresses text files by substituting a small byte pattern for a reoccurring sequence of characters.

5 JPEG files have been compressed using a(n) _____ compression technique that loses some of the data from the original image.

6 One technique for reducing the size of video files is to reduce the number of frames displayed per second. True or false? _____

7 An MP3 _____ compresses WAV files into MP3 format.

 Check Answers

USER FOCUS: USING A COMPRESSION UTILITY

InfoWeb 11

Compression Utilities

WinZip is a popular file compression utility that you can obtain by mail from a share-ware distributor, download from the Internet, or purchase from a local computer store. This software effectively reduces the size of text and BMP files. Let's take a specific example to see how you might use this software. Suppose you have a 1.8 megabyte file called *Clients.doc* on your hard disk (drive C) in a folder called Reports. The file contains information about the customers for a mail-order business that you want to give to your coworker. You want to put this file on a single 1.44 MB floppy disk that you inserted in drive A. Because *Clients.doc* requires 1.8 MB, it will not fit on a single floppy disk in its uncompressed state.

Compressing a File with WinZip

> How do I use WinZip to compress a file?

Before you can compress the file for your coworker, you'll need to have the WinZip software installed on your computer. You should be able to locate it on the Programs menu after you click the Windows Start button. To compress a file, you would first specify the name that you want to assign to the compressed file—*Clients.zip*, for example. Next, you tell WinZip which file you want to compress—*Clients.doc*, for example.

After selecting *Clients.doc*, WinZip compresses the file to make a smaller file on drive A called *Clients.zip*. Figure 10-28 shows you the basic steps for compressing a file.

FIGURE 10-28

After you compress a file, your compression software will display information about the size of the compressed file.

1. Use the New button to begin the compression procedure.

2. Enter the name that you want assigned to the compressed file.

3. Select the file that you want to compress.

Start Screentour

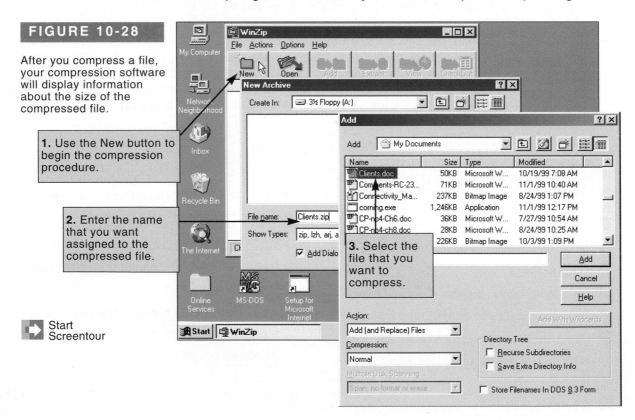

Unzipping a File

Does my coworker need to uncompress the file before using it? Because it is not possible to use a compressed file directly, your coworker must uncompress the *Clients.zip* file. To do so, your coworker must start the WinZip program, then indicate which file to uncompress. WinZip will also want to know where to put the uncompressed file. Figure 10-29 shows WinZip uncompressing the *Clients.zip* file and storing the uncompressed file on drive C in the Documents folder as *Clients.doc*.

FIGURE 10-29

WinZip uncompresses *Clients.zip* from drive A and places the uncompressed file *Clients.doc* on drive C in the Documents folder.

Start
Screentour

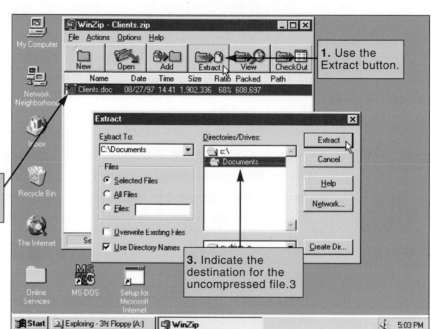

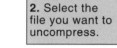

2. Select the file you want to uncompress.

1. Use the Extract button.

3. Indicate the destination for the uncompressed file.3

Compressing E-mail Attachments

How do I compress a file before I attach it to an e-mail? E-mail attachments provide you with the flexibility to send text, graphics, and sound files, but your friends won't be happy if you send huge, uncompressed files that take forever to download from the e-mail server. You should make it a rule to compress any file that exceeds 100 KB before you attach it to an e-mail. The process is simple:

1. Launch your compression software. Use PKZIP or WinZip for document and graphics files; use your MP3 encoder for WAV files.

2. Compress the file. Use your compression software and make sure that you remember where you store the file—you might want to use a separate folder to hold any files that you compress for e-mail attachments.

3. Close your compression software.

4. Create an e-mail message and attach the compressed file. Refer back to page 331 for a Screentour on sending e-mail attachments. It is helpful for the recipient if you indicate which software you used to compress the file.

5. Send the e-mail.

ISSUE WOULD YOU PAY TO USE A FILE FORMAT?

Most people understand that Web-based documents, graphics, videos, music, and other media enjoy the same copyright protection as their non-Web counterparts. Using copyrighted media requires permission, and sometimes the copyright holder charges a fee for its use. Nevertheless, many Internet users and Web site developers were dismayed when rumors spread throughout the online community that use of the popular GIF format would require substantial licensing fees. Users were wondering if they now needed to pay a fee every time that they stored a graphic in GIF format. Were these rumors about GIF licensing fees based on fact, or were they just the latest addition to a growing collection of urban legends cropping up on the Internet? A little background will set the stage for the answer to this question.

As you know from reading this chapter, bitmap graphics are stored in various file formats, including BMP, TIFF, JPEG, PCX, and GIF. The two most popular file formats for Web-based graphics are JPEG and GIF. JPEG's lossy compression technique works well for photographic images but is not really suitable for animations, diagrams, and line art. In contrast, the GIF file format uses a lossless compression technique called LZW (Lempel Ziv Welch) that works especially well for animations and many other types of graphics.

In the June 1984 issue of IEEE's *Computer* magazine, LZW developer Terry Welch described the LZW compression algorithm in enough detail for implementation by most programmers. LZW compression seemed to be just the ticket for Internet-based graphics. In 1987, programmers at the huge CompuServe information service used it as a key element of a new graphics file format called GIF. Touted as a free, nonproprietary graphics file format, GIF quickly became one of the most popular formats on the Internet, supported by virtually every browser and graphics software package.

In December 1994, after GIF was in circulation for seven years, CompuServe dropped the GIF bombshell. Although CompuServe had led the online community to believe that GIF was a nonproprietary file format, it issued a statement explaining that the LZW compression algorithm used in the GIF file format was patented technology owned by Unisys. CompuServe had agreed to pay licensing fees to Unisys. Other developers would also have to obtain a license from Unisys to use LZW compression. This announcement was interpreted by some members of the computing community as a sort of usage tax that would be slapped on every file saved in GIF format. Users were horrified by the prospect of paying to use a file format or switching to the less acceptable JPEG format.

Speculation on GIF usage fees gave birth to a flurry of furious e-mail messages and prompted software developer Hakan Andersson to post a message to the comp.graphics discussion group that began, "People, people, CALM DOWN! This all originates from a

CHAPTER 10

huge misunderstanding!" As e-mail poured into Unisys, its public relations department found it expedient to circulate an open letter to the online community that began, "The concerns, inquiries, and some apparent confusion that have resulted from the December CompuServe advisory clearly indicate that we need to clarify our policy concerning the use of the Unisys Lempel Zev Welch (LZW) patent by software developers for the major on-line services." The letter went on to explain that license fees were required for any software that *created* GIF files, but no additional fees would be required for the *use* of images created by that software. So, for example, CompuServe could supply its subscribers with Web page construction software that provided the capability to create and save graphics in GIF format. CompuServe would be required to pay a licensing fee to Unisys, but CompuServe's subscribers would not have to pay any additional fees to create a GIF image.

The facts eventually prevailed, and the GIF issue seemed to be settling peacefully on the horizon. Today's most popular graphics software, such as Adobe Photoshop, Micrografx Picture Publisher, and CorelDRAW, include the capability to create GIF files. The companies that publish this software pay licensing fees to Unisys for the LZW compression technology that creates GIF files. Yet, in 1999, the controversy roared back to life when the Web crackled with the news that Unisys would to start prosecuting Web sites that were displaying GIF images without paying an expensive licensing fee. In reality, Unisys was targeting Web sites that displayed GIF graphics created with non-licensed software. Primarily at risk were users of certain freeware graphics software whose publishers had failed to obtain a license from Unisys to include LZW compression routines for the GIF format. Those Web developers who used commercial graphics software to create the GIF graphics posted on their sites had nothing to fear. What are the ramifications of this issue for Web developers and Internet users? Before you answer the "What Do You Think?" questions, you might want to refer to some of the resources listed in the GIF Controversy InfoWeb.

InfoWeb
12

GIF
Controversy

WHAT DO YOU THINK?

1. Would you be willing to pay a fee to save
files in GIF format?   ◉ Yes   ○ No   ○ Not sure

2. Did CompuServe act irresponsibly by leading
people to believe that the GIF format was
public?   ◉ Yes   ○ No   ○ Not sure

3. Would it be easy to replace GIF with a different file format?   ◉ Yes   ○ No   ○ Not sure

 Save
Responses

CHAPTER 10

CHAPTER 10 REVIEW ACTIVITIES

INTERACTIVE SUMMARY

The Interactive Summary helps you select important concepts and facts from this chapter. Fill in the blanks to best complete each sentence. When using the NP4 CD or NP4 Web site, you can click the Check Answers buttons to automatically score your answers. Place your Tracking Disk in the floppy disk drive if you want to save your scores.

Computer scientists have used information _____ to design various ways of efficiently encoding and storing information. Beginning with the idea that a bit can have two states, represented by 0 and 1, the rule for conveying information says that the maximum number of different units of information you can convey with _____ bits is 2^n. Therefore, with four bits, you can convey _____ different units of information. This rule can be applied to a number of data representations schemes for text, sound, and graphical data. For example, the ASCII code uses _____ bits to represent the 128 basic uppercase letters, lowercase letters, numerals, and punctuation marks in the English language. EBCDIC and ANSI codes, which contain 256 symbols, require _____ bits. Unicode, which can represent more than 65,000 symbols, is a(n) _____ bit code. ASCII, EBCIDC, ANSI, and Unicode are all character codes, used to represent text in file formats such as TXT, DOC, and RTF.

Information theory also helps computer scientists devise ways to encode and store graphical information. For example, a(n) _____ graphic is composed of a gridwork of pixels. By applying information theory, you can determine that each pixel in a 256-color graphic requires _____ bits and each pixel in a true-color graphic requires _____ bits. As an alternative to storing a graphic pixel-by-pixel, _____ graphics are stored as a series of instructions that the computer can use to reconstruct an image.

▶ Check Answers

Like graphics, sounds can be represented in two fundamentally different ways. _____ audio digitally represents a sound as a series of samples, which are then converted into binary numbers. The alternative method for encoding and storing sound, called _____, is a notation system that allows a computer to synthesize or reconstruct the notes made by a variety of musical instruments.

The data in a file can be _____ or recoded so that it requires fewer bytes of storage space. Disk compression uses compression utility software, such as DriveSpace, to create a compressed _____, which can contain an entire hard disk's worth of files in compressed format. _____ compression utilities, such as PKZIP and WinZip, shrink one or more files into a single, smaller file suitable for such uses as e-mail attachments. Compression utility software allows computer users to compress selected drives or files, but files can be compressed in other ways, too. Some graphics and sound file formats include automatic compression routines. Files that have been stored in formats such as TIFF, JPEG, PCX, GIF, MPEG, and MP3 are already compressed and are not likely to shrink significantly if you also use compression utilities, such as PKZIP and WinZip.

▶ Check Answers

INTERACTIVE KEY TERMS

Make sure that you understand all of the boldfaced key terms presented in this chapter. If you're using the NP4 CD or NP4 Web site, you can use this list of terms as an interactive study activity. First, try to define a term in your own words, then click the term to compare your definition with the definition that is presented in the chapter.

INTERACTIVE QUIZZES

Quiz yourself on important concepts from this chapter by filling in the blanks. When using the NP4 CD or NP4 Web site, you can type your answers, then use the Check Answers buttons to automatically score your responses. Place your Tracking Disk in the floppy disk drive if you want to save your scores.

1 According to information theory, 3 bits can convey [＿＿＿＿] units of information.

2 ASCII, ANSI, EBCDIC, and Unicode are [＿＿＿＿] representation codes.

3 A monochrome graphic requires [＿＿＿＿] bit(s) to represent each pixel.

4 24-bit graphics are also called [＿＿＿＿] color graphics.

5 A(n) [＿＿＿＿] graphics file contains a digital representation of each pixel in an image.

6 A(n) [＿＿＿＿] file is essentially the musical version of a vector graphic because it stores instructions for recreating a sound.

7 Both PKZIP and WinZip create a compressed disk volume that acts as a separate hard disk. True or false? [＿＿＿＿]

8 The popular MP3 format is a compressed version of a MIDI file. True or False? [＿＿＿＿]

9 JPEG uses a(n) [＿＿＿＿] compression technique, whereas GIF uses a(n) [＿＿＿＿] compression technique.

Check Answers

Identify each type of graphic by placing its letter in the correct box below.

1 Monochrome [＿＿＿＿]

2 Grayscale [＿＿＿＿]

3 Dithered 16-color [＿＿＿＿]

4 256-color [＿＿＿＿]

5 True-color [＿＿＿＿]

6 Vector [＿＿＿＿]

Check Answers

A

B

C

D

E

F

INTERACTIVE PRACTICE TESTS

When you use the NP4 CD or NP4 Web site, you can take practice tests that consist of 10 multiple-choice, true/false, and fill-in-the-blank questions. The 10 questions are selected at random from a large test bank, so each time you take a test, you'll receive a different set of questions. Your tests are scored immediately and you can print study guides that help you find the correct answers for any questions that you missed. If you are using a Tracking Disk, insert it in the floppy disk drive to save your test scores.

Start Practice
Test

STUDY TIPS

Study Tips help you organize and consolidate the information in a chapter by making lists, outlines, charts, and sketches. You can use paper and pencil, or word processing software to complete most of the Study Tips activities.

1 Use your own words to answer the questions under each of the section headings.

2 Complete the following chart to show how many units of information you can convey with a given number of bits:

Number of Bits	1	2	3	4	5	6	7	8
Number of Units of Information								

3 Perform the calculations necessary to complete the following table:

Screen Width in Pixels	640	640	640	640	1024
Screen Height in Pixels	480	480	480	480	768
Graphics Type	Monochrome	16-color	256-color	True-color	True-color
Number of Bytes Required					

4 List the characteristics of the ASCII, ANSI, EBCDIC, and Unicode character representation codes.

5 A monochrome graphic with two colors per pixel requires one bit to represent each pixel. A color graphic with 16 colors per pixel requires four bits to represent each pixel. How many bits per pixel are required for a color graphic with four colors per pixel?

6 Describe the difference between bitmap graphics and vector graphics.

7 Describe the difference between waveform audio and MIDI music.

8 Define the terms "codec" and "compression ratio."

9 Describe the difference between disk compression and file compression.

10 Make a list of the filename extensions mentioned in this chapter, then for each extension on your list indicate the type of data it contains (text, graphics, sound) and whether the data in the file is stored in a compressed format.

P R O J E C T S

A project is an open-ended activity that will help you apply the concepts you have learned. Many projects require resources in addition to your textbook, such as current magazines, library materials, or Web access. When you tackle a project, be prepared to use your critical thinking skills, logical analysis, and your creativity.

1 **Your Own Bitmap Graphics** Make a photocopy of the grids below or make two 8 x 8 grids on graph paper. Using the first grid, fill in the pixels on the grid to reconstruct an 8-pixel x 8-pixel one-bit monochrome graphic from the following binary codes: 00100000, 01010000, 10001010, 10001111, 11111010, 10001000, 10001000, 10001000. Using the second grid, create your own graphic, then convert it into binary format.

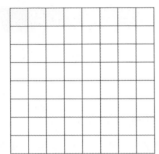 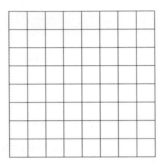

2 **Try Your Hand at Text Compression** One way to compress text is to replace repeated occurrences of words with a pointer to the first occurrence of that word. Using a # symbol and a number as your pointer, write out the compressed form of the following paragraph:

A computer system is composed of a computer and peripheral devices, such as a printer. The components of a computer system that you can see and touch are referred to as hardware. Software refers to the nonphysical components of a computer system, particularly the programs, or lists of instructions, that are needed to make the computer perform a specific task.

3 **Modern, Classical, and Rock** Use your library and Internet resources to find more information and write a two- to three-page report about MIDI music. You might want to address questions such as the following: To what extent do musicians use computer-generated music today? Which modern, classical, and rock composers or performers make extensive use of computer-generated music? How has computer-generated music enhanced the sound quality, creativity, or appeal of modern music?

4 **Graphics Software** Software publishers produce a variety of graphics software packages that differ based on the type of graphics supported and the tools they provide to manipulate graphics. Use current computer magazines to research graphics software packages. Write a paper describing three of the software packages. Indicate the key features, the graphics formats supported, and the price of each package. Finally, explain which package you would purchase and why.

5 **Another Picasso?** You learned that bitmap graphics require quite a lot of storage space. You can create your own bitmap image and see for yourself. Use Microsoft Paintbrush (Windows 3.1), Microsoft Paint (Windows 95, 98 and 2000), or any available paint software to create a simple graphic. Store the graphic on a floppy disk in BMP format. Print your graphic. Don't forget to sign your original work of art! To find the size of your graphic file, you will probably need to use File Manager or Windows Explorer. Write the file size on your printout.

6 **Unzip It** You learned that PKZIP and WinZip are popular compression utilities. The *User Focus* section of this chapter describes how to use WinZip. Using PKZIP is similar. For this project, you must download and unzip the file *Mystery.zip* from *www.cciw.com/np4/project10-6.html*. If your computer does not have PKZIP or WinZip, you'll need to download this software from one of the sites listed in InfoWeb 11. Make sure that you abide by the license agreement when you use this software. After you download and unzip the *Mystery.zip* file, follow the instructions in the *Readme.txt* file to complete the project.

7 **Globalization, Localization, and Unicode** Current trends in the globalization of communications and business require the use of computers. Much of the data, such as financial transactions, is usable regardless of the local language. However, the programs that manipulate data are generally most effective if they are localized so that users do not have to translate screen prompts and error messages. Using your library resources, write a two- to three-page paper on software localization and how it contributes to globalized communications and business.

8 **Converting Binary to Decimal to Hexadecimal** Although today's computer users rarely need to deal with binary, octal, or hexadecimal numbers, the Windows calculator provides a quick and easy way to convert numbers if you need to do so. For this project, complete (a) through (e), then fill out the table in (f).

a. On a computer with the Microsoft Windows operating system, look for the Windows Calculator program. In Windows 3.1, it is in the Applications program group. In Windows 95 use the Start button, select Programs, then select Accessories. If you can't find the Calculator program, ask your technical support person for help.

b. Start the Windows Calculator.

c. Click the View menu, then click Scientific.

d. To convert from decimal to binary, make sure that the Decimal button is selected. Enter a decimal number such as 255. Click the Binary button and the calculator will show the binary equivalent—in this case, 11111111.

e. To convert from binary to decimal, make sure that the Binary button is selected, then enter a binary number such as 101. Click the Decimal button to show the decimal equivalent—in this case, 5.

f. Fill in the following table:

Decimal	Binary	Octal	Hexadecimal
10			
	10		
32			
			FE
	111011		

ADDITIONAL PROJECTS

Click the underlined text to link to the NP4 Web site (www.cciw.com/np4), where you can view and print additional projects for this chapter.

MP3 Compression Standard

Explore the GIF Controversy

LAB ASSIGNMENTS

Software for these labs is provided on the NP4 CD and may also be available in your school's computer lab. To start a lab, click the lab icon.

Each lab has two parts: Steps and Explore. Use the Steps first to learn and review concepts. Read the information on each page and complete the numbered steps. As you work through the lab, you will be asked to answer QuickCheck questions about what you have learned. At the end of the lab, you will see a report that scores your answers to the QuickChecks. If your instructor wants you to turn in this report, click the Print button on the QuickCheck Report screen.

When you have completed Steps, you can click the Explore button to complete the Lab Assignments. You can also use Explore to practice the skills you learned and to explore concepts on your own.

Computers process and store numbers using the binary number system. Understanding binary numbers helps you recognize how a digital computer works by simply turning electricity on and off. It also helps you understand the basics of information theory. In this lab, you learn about the binary number system—how to convert numbers from —binary to decimal and from decimal to binary.

1 Click the Steps button to learn about the binary number system. As you proceed through the steps, answer all of the QuickCheck questions. After you complete the steps, you will see a report that summarizes your performance on the QuickChecks. Follow the instructions on the screen to print the QuickCheck report.

2 Click the Explore button, then click the Conversions button. Practice converting binary numbers into decimal numbers. For example, what is the decimal equivalent of 00010011? Calculate the decimal value on paper. To check your answer, enter the decimal number in the decimal box, and then click the binary boxes to show the 1s and 0s for the number you are converting. Click the Check It button to see if your conversion is correct.

Convert the following binary numbers into decimal numbers:

a. 00000101	d. 10010010
b. 00010111	e. 11111110
c. 01010101	f. 10001100

3 In Explore, click the Conversions button. Practice converting decimal numbers into binary numbers. For example, what is the binary equivalent of 82? Calculate the binary value on paper. To check your answer, enter the decimal number in the decimal box, and then click the binary boxes to show the 1s and 0s for its binary equivalent. Click the Check It button to see if your conversion is correct.

Convert the following decimal numbers into binary numbers:

a. 77	d. 117
b. 25	e. 214
c. 92	f. 64

4 In Explore, click the Binary Number Quiz button. The quiz provides you with 10 numbers to convert. Make each conversion and type your answer in the box. Click the Check Answer button to see if you are correct. When you have completed all 10 quiz questions, follow the instructions on the screen to print your quiz results.

CHAPTER 10

Lab

Data Representation

A computer stores many types of data—text, graphics, sound, animation, and video. Digital computers, such as the microcomputers you use, store these different types of data as the electronic equivalent of 1s and 0s. How is it possible to reduce a long document or complex graphic to a series of 1s and 0s? In this lab, you'll find out.

1 Click the Steps button to learn how text, monochrome graphics, color graphics, and vector graphics are stored. As you proceed through the Steps, answer all of the QuickCheck questions that appear. After you complete the Steps, you will see a QuickCheck Summary Report. Follow the instructions on the screen to print this report.

2 Click the Explore button, then click the Text button. Suppose you are a computer and you need to sort the list below containing words, numbers, and symbols. Look up the ANSI representation for the first character of each item on the list. Then, sort the list according to this ANSI code. The item with the lowest ANSI code should be first in the list. The list is as follows:

broom
3
Tree
]
Bottle
03
10

3 Using Explore's Text button, find the ANSI code for your first and last name. Write it on paper. Then write the decimal equivalent to the ANSI code for your first and last name.

4 Suppose you are a computer, and you receive the following 1s and 0s from your modem. Using Explore's Text button, convert these 1s and 0s into the letters, numerals, and symbols that would be displayed on the screen.

01010100	01101000	01100101
00100000	00110100	00100000
01101111	01100110	00100000
01001000	01100101	01100001
01110010	01110100	01110011

5 Suppose you are a computer, and you receive a monochrome graphics file containing a string of 1s and 0s. Using Explore's Monochrome graphics button, create this graphic, then print it.

```
00010000
00111000
01111100
11111110
11101110
01000100
00000000
```

6 Using Explore's Monochrome graphics button, convert the following decimal numbers into a monochrome graphic, then print it.

8, 12, 254, 255, 254, 12, 8, 0

7 Suppose you are a computer, and you must send a monochrome graphic to another computer over a local area network. Using Explore's Monochrome graphics button, convert the following graphic into 1s and 0s, then print it.

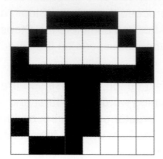

8 Suppose you are a computer, and you receive a 16-color graphics file containing a string of 1s and 0s. Using Explore's Color graphics button, recreate this graphic, then print it.

```
11111111    11001111    11001111    11001111
00000000    11000100    01000100    11001111
11111111    11001100    01001100    11001111
00000000    11111100    11001100    11111111
11111111    11111111    00101111    10101111
00000000    11111111    00101010    10101111
11111111    11111111    00101010    11111111
00000000    11111111    00101111    11111111
```

9 Using Explore's Vector graphics button, recreate a vector graphic from the following set of instructions. Print your completed graphic.

Shape	Color	Top	Left	Width	Height
Circle	red	73	212	50	50
Circle	yellow	137	212	50	50
Circle	green	202	212	50	50
Rounded rectangle	black	39	200	73	241

CHAPTER 10

INFOWEB

InfoWeb Site
Chapter 10

The InfoWeb is your guide to print, film, television, and electronic resources. Use it to obtain updates on quickly changing technical information and to locate information for research papers. If you're using the NP4 CD-ROM, click the InfoWeb Site icon on the left side of this paragraph to access the online InfoWeb links. Otherwise, use your Web browser and type in the address of the New Perspectives Web site: www.cciw.com/np4. At the Web site, you'll find up-to-date links to the topics covered in this chapter.

1 Paul Revere

If you want to know whether the British came by land or by sea, you can read Longfellow's poem, *Paul Revere's Ride*. But reader beware: Longfellow used poetic license and played a bit with the facts. To learn the real story, read the poem, and listen to an interpretive reading, visit the River Cities site created by Ross School students at *ross.pvt.k12.ny.us/boston/revere.htm*. For more facts about the events of April 18, 1775, check out *www.city-net.com/~davekle/revere.htm*. And if you'd like to read a parody about the real hero that night, read "The Midnight Ride of William Dawes" written by Helen Moore at *www.colorpro.com/wmdawes/theride.html*.

2 Information Theory

How is it that you can scratch a CD-ROM and yet it still plays without error? Chalk it up to Claude Shannon's information theory. You can read Warren Weaver's easy-to-understand introduction to Claude Shannon's 1949 classic, "The Mathematical Theory of Communication" (you'll find excerpts at *darkwing.uoregon.edu/~felsing/virtual_asia/info.html*).

If your major is mathematics or computer science, you might be interested in Web sites that provide technical background about information theory. Using any search engine to look for "Claude Shannon" or "information theory," you should find a good selection of interesting Web sites, such as David J. C. MacKay 's online course at *131.111.48.24/pub/mackay/info-theory/course.html*. Visit *www.wfu.edu/Academic-departments/Speech-Communication/infot/infop1.html*, then link to the diagram for a visual approach to information theory.

3 Binary Numbers

John Selvia has a great site on binary numbers. He says "I learned how to interpret binary from reading Michael Crichton's *Andromeda Strain* in college. Now, you gotta understand that for an artistic, creative type like myself, suddenly understanding how binary works was a big deal, worthy of running out of the bathroom stall where I was reading the book and yelling Eureka!" Selvia's site at *www.dnaco.net/~ivanjs/binary.html* includes a clear explanation of binary numbers and instructions on binary finger counting. Learn how cavepeople could have counted up to 1,023 on their fingers, instead of counting only to 10! Other good sources of information on binary numbers can be found by searching for "binary" at the PC Webopaedia site *www.webopaedia.com*. You might also connect to online courses, such as *spectra.eng.hawaii.edu/Courses/EE150/Book/chap1/subsection2.1.2.1.html*. For an alternative explanation of how computers use binary numbers, check your local library for *The Electronic Cottage* by J. Denkin (New York: Bantam Books, 1981) and refer to Chapter 3. The author uses a unique bucket-and-hose analogy to explain how computers communicate.

4 Unicode

The Unicode standard is of special interest to countries and ethnic groups with written languages that use characters other than those in the Latin alphabet. You can learn all about the Unicode standard and the languages it supports at sites such as the Arabic Scientific Alliance Web page (*www.asca.com/unicode.html*). Interesting articles about Unicode have been written, including one at the Chinese Software Digest site, *www.gy.com/www/ww1/ww2/unne.htm*. For the most up-to-date information on Unicode, visit the Unicode Consortium Web page at *www.unicode.org*.

5 **Graphics Formats**

With the increasing popularity of digital art and Web-based graphics, it is useful to understand the advantages and disadvantages of the many graphics formats, such as TIFF, GIF, JPEG, BMP, and PCX. A good source of links to pages and FAQs about graphics formats is the Graphics File Formats Page at *www.dcs.ed.ac.uk/~mxr/gfx/utils-hi.html*. Bryan Chamberlain has written an excellent article, "Understanding Image File Formats" at *www.zdjournals.com/tma/9508/tma95801.htm*. Chamberlain's article is packed with practical advice, comparative tables, and descriptions of the most popular graphics formats. Check your library for the definitive reference on file formats, *Encyclopedia of Graphics File Formats,* second edition. by James Murray and William VanRyper (O'Reilly, 1996).

The Wide Area Communications Web site, located at *www.widearea.co.uk/designer/compress.html* contains an excellent basic introduction to Web graphics. The Bandwidth Conservation Society page, *www.infohiway.com/way/faster*, provides links to useful information on graphics formats, such as the tutorial titled "GIF Tips and Tricks," which includes a quick guide to color palettes. *PC Magazine* has a great article about Web graphics at *www.zdnet.com/pcmag/issues/1512/pcmg0015.htm*. The Web version of the Louvre Art Museum is so popular that special Internet sites called "mirror sites" have been set up all over the world to accommodate the more than 200,000 weekly cybervisitors. Check out this site for art of all types at *www.sunsite.unc.edu/wm*.

6 **Digital Audio**

One of the most comprehensive sound links on the Web is sponsored by Oxford University at *www.comlab.ox.ac.uk/archive/audio.html*. An extensive Webring index, called Sound-Ring, at *sr.webring.org/cgi-bin/webring?ring=sr;id=33;prev5*, has links to hundreds of music sites. You can find a good set of basic FAQs on sound file formats at *home.sprynet.com/~cbagwell/audio.html*. You'll also find a good discussion of audio formats in Zap's MUSIC-ON-THE-NET Tutorial at *www.lysator.liu.se/~zap/tutorial/formats.html*.

You can take a comprehensive tutorial on MIDI music and file formats by Jim Heckroth by connecting to *kingfisher.cms.shu.ac.uk/midi/main_p.htm*. You'll find lots of links to MIDI information and sample MIDI files and products at the MidiWebTM site, *www.midiweb.com*. Can your sound card make a difference in sound quality? You can compare sound quality at the Wavetable sound card test drive site, *pubweb.nwu.edu/~jll544/sndsmpl.html*.

7 **Data Compression**

You can find everything you wanted to know about data compression in a series of FAQs at *www.cis.ohio-state.edu/hypertext/faq/usenet/compression-faq/top.html*. You can read about two of the most popular compression programs at *cnet.com/Content/Reports/Shootouts/Zip0721*. Wavelet compression is a relatively new technique for compressing graphics and videos. The Compression Engines site at *www.cengines.com* provides you with details about wavelets. At the Codec Central Web site, *www.terran-int.com/CodecCentral/geninfo.html*, you can learn about the compression and decompression (codec) algorithms that make desktop video and video over the Web possible. You also can read about multimedia technology, view sample multimedia movies, and peruse a glossary of digital video terms.

8 **Toy Story**

The film *Toy Story*, a coproduction of Walt Disney Pictures and Pixar, is the first completely computer-animated feature film in the history of motion pictures. It took more than 800,000 machine-hours to render the final frames. Find out more about *Toy Story* at *pixar.com/feature/toystory/toystory.html*. Be sure to follow the link "Sun Microsystems on the nitty gritty" for a detailed description of the computing power behind the film.

9 Digital Video

To learn more about digital video, start at *www.ividea.com/dvmpeg.htm* for an overview of digital video formats and discussion of MPEG. You can also connect to New Frontiers in Learning at *ibis.nott.ac.uk/guidelines/ch62/chap6-2-6.2.4.2.html* for an excellent overview of digital video formats. These formats are categorized as (1) those formats that require additional computer hardware and (2) formats that are software-only. For in-depth information on the Video for Windows AVI format, link to John McGowan's site at *www.rahul.net/jfm/avi.html*. McGowan's site gets top honors for its wealth of information on file formats and data compression—don't miss this site! MPEG is an important part of DVD movie technology. Read more about it at *www.mpeg.org/index.html/starting-points.html*. Apple Computer hosts the definitive site for QuickTime video information, samples, links, and plug-ins at *www.quicktime.apple.com*. For example, you'll find a clear description of the QuickTime format at *www.apple.com/quicktime/information/index.html*. For updates on video codecs, you might check out Web sites such as Codec Central, located at *www.terran.com/CodecCentral/index.html*.

10 MP3 Compression

What exactly is MP3 technology? For an explanation, use any of your favorite online resources, such as *webopedia.internet.com/TERM/M/MP3.html* or *www.dailymp3.com/how1.html*. The articles in the August 1999 issue of *Wired* magazine titled "I Want My MP3" provide background information about MP3 technology, including compression, an analysis of the various MP3 players, a timeline charting the digital game plans of the recording industry, as well as addresses for popular MP3 Web sites. For current articles about MP3 technology, visit sites such as *www.wired.com/news/news/mpthree* and link to articles that interest you. What controversy swirls around MP3? Read about "The Great MP3 Wars" at *www.zdnet.com/yil/content/mag/9904/mp3-4.html*. Some major record labels are afraid that customers are "stealing" their music. Find out how the major label companies have adjusted to MP3 technology by reading articles such as *www.wired.com/news/news/politics/mpthree/story/21944.html*. Read "EFF: Piracy Not the Problem" at *www.wired.com/news/news/politics/mpthree/story/21645.html* to understand the reaction of the Electronic Frontier Foundation to the recording industry's lack of enthusiasm for MP3 technology. For a comprehensive list of resources and/or links to resources and visit sites such as *www.mpeg.org/MPEG/mp3.html* and *www.mp3.com*. These sites include links to such favorites as FAQs about MP3, MP3 search engines, and public domain MP3s.

11 Compression Utilities

The two most popular compression utilities for Windows are PKZIP and WinZip. You can visit the PKWARE site at *www.pkware.com* and download a trial copy of PKZIP. If you would like to download an evaluation version of WinZip, visit *www.winzip.com*.

12 GIF Controversy

CompuServe's 1995 announcement that Unisys owned the patent for the LZW compression routine used in GIF files sparked a controversy that continues today. A fine summary of the issues is provided in the article "The GIF Controversy: A Software Developer's Perspective" by Michael C. Battilana, available online at *www.cloanto.com/users/mcb/19950127giflzw.html*. You can read official information about LZW licensing at *www.unisys.com/unisys.lzw*. A good set of FAQs about the issue can be found at *www-dse.doc.ic.ac.uk/~nd/surprise_95/journal/vol2/hml/article2.imag4.html*. To find out about recent developments in the GIF controversy, read the article detailing the 1999 GIF "scare" at the LinuxWorld site (*www.linuxworld.com/linuxworld/lw-1999-09/lw-09-vcontrol_3.html*). It also presents information about the PNG file format, which was designed to replace GIF as a nonproprietary file format. For more about the PNG standard, refer to Greg Roelofs' book, *PNG: The Definitive Guide* (O'Reilly and Associates, 1999). You can also enter "GIF," "LZW," or "PNG" in any Web search engine to locate additional articles and information.

CHAPTER 11

COMMUNICATIONS SYSTEMS

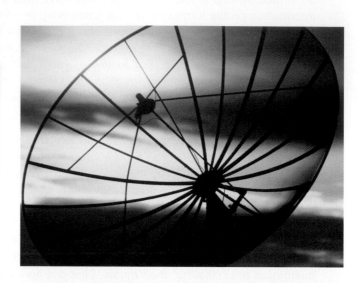

CONTENTS

PREVIEW

In this chapter you will learn the basic terminology of data communications and some technical details about how modems and LANs transport data. You will learn how to access the Internet using the telephone system, the cellular phone system, the cable TV system, and satellites. You will also learn how to set up a simple local area network for data communications.

When you have completed this chapter, you should be able to:

- Explain Shannon's communications system model
- Define bandwidth and discuss how it affects data communications
- Discuss the advantages and disadvantages of Internet access over telephone, cellular phone, cable TV, and satellite systems
- Describe how packet switching differs from circuit switching
- Describe today's popular LAN access methods and LAN communications protocols
- Explain the differences between collision handling on Ethernet and Token Ring networks
- Understand how to set up a simple Ethernet network

CHAPTER 11 LAB

Building a
Network

CANS AND STRING

"Communications" means getting information from point A to point B. Communications technology can be simple or sophisticated. Link two cans together with string and you have a simple "telephone." Link two computers using modems, telephone lines, cellular towers, satellites, and fiber-optic cables and you have a sophisticated communications system.

We are surrounded by data, which is transmitted over a communications infrastructure made up of telephone lines, cable television lines, satellites, computer networks, and transmitters for microwave, radio, and television signals. Although most of the systems in this communications infrastructure were originally designed for other purposes, such as carrying voice communications, they are being pressed into service to transport computer data. Today, individuals and organizations are taking advantage of this vast communications infrastructure to gather, transmit, and locate computer-based information.

The purpose of this chapter is to explain how the cables and transmitters that form a worldwide communications infrastructure provide pathways for transporting computer-generated information. The chapter begins with an overview of useful data communications terminology. The focus then shifts to ways that current telephone, cellular phone, cable TV, Internet, and local networks provide an infrastructure for computer data communications. This chapter ends with a lesson on building a low-cost computer network—it's easier than you think!

SECTION A   DATA COMMUNICATIONS

InfoWeb 1

Communications
Terminology

Data communications is the process of transmitting and receiving data in an orderly way so that data arriving at its destination is an accurate duplication of the data that was sent. When data travels a short distance, the communication is referred to as **local communications**. When data travels a long distance, the communication is referred to as **telecommunications**; the prefix "tele" is derived from a Greek word that means "far" or "far off."

The difference between a short distance and a long distance is somewhat arbitrary. For example, when your computer sends data to a printer in the next room, it is regarded as local communications. However, phoning the person in the next room would be regarded as telecommunications because you are transmitting data over a telecommunications device. Because the same basic communications concepts apply to both local communications and telecommunications, in this chapter it is not necessary to further distinguish between the two.

Basic data communications concepts are the building blocks for understanding how data travels on a communications system. These concepts come in handy when you install, configure, or upgrade a local area network. In addition, they help you set up modems, fax machines, Internet access, and cellular data transfers.

A **communications system** is the combination of hardware, software, and connecting links that transport data. In 1949, Claude Shannon, an engineer at the prestigious Bell Labs, published an article that described a communications system model. In this model, data from a source is encoded and sent over a communications channel where it is decoded by a receiver. According to Shannon, effective communication depends on the efficiency of the coding process and the channel's resistance to interference called **noise**. Study Figure 11-1 for an overview of Shannon's communications system model.

FIGURE 11-1

Shannon's communications system model diagrams the flow of data from a source to a receiver.

Noise
5. Noise, such as electrical interference, sometimes disrupts a transmission. The message can become garbled unless the communications system has the capability to check for errors and correct them.

Source → Encode → Channel → Decode → Receiver

1. The source originates or initiates the communication. The source might be a person, a computer, or another communications device.

2. The message, represented here by a folder, is the information that the source wants to communicate to the receiver. The message might be a document, picture, sound, or numeric data.

3. The message is encoded by changing its format into one that can be transmitted over telephone lines, broadcast by radio waves, or transmitted as light waves.

4. The encoded message travels by means of a channel or communications link. A communications link might include telephone wiring, fiber-optic cable, microwaves, or satellites.

6. The message is decoded at the end of the transmission. Decoding usually means reversing the coding process that occurred before the message was sent.

7. The receiver is the destination for the message. The receiver can be a person, a computer, or another communications device.

CHAPTER 11

Communications Signals

Exactly what is transmitted when I send a message? When you use a modem to send a document from your computer to another computer or fax machine, symbols such as "A" and "!" don't magically squirt through the phone cables. Instead, most of today's communications systems transmit messages and data in the form of electromagnetic signals. You can think of these signals as waves that ripple through cables or through the air.

Like ocean waves, electromagnetic waves are characterized by their size and their spacing. The height of an electromagnetic wave is referred to as its **amplitude** (Figure 11-2). Waves with higher amplitudes are more powerful (louder in the case of sound waves) than waves with low amplitudes. The distance between waves is referred to as **wavelength**.

FIGURE 11-2

Electromagnetic waves are characterized by their wavelength and amplitude.

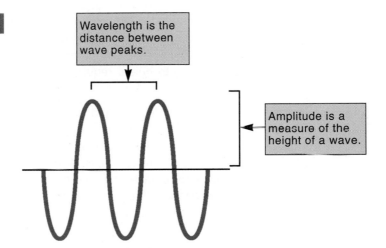

Wavelength is the distance between wave peaks.

Amplitude is a measure of the height of a wave.

Frequency is the number of times per second that the wave cycle repeats or "oscillates." Shorter wavelengths produce higher frequencies because when the waves are closer together, more of them will occur during each second. Signal frequency is measured in hertz (Hz), kilohertz (KHz), megahertz (MHz), or gigahertz (GHz). One hertz is equal to one "wave" or oscillation per second. For example, a tuning fork that produces the note A above middle C vibrates at a frequency of 440 Hz. A radio broadcast at 101 MHz means that the radio wave is oscillating 101,000,000 times per second.

The sound signals that travel over phone lines have frequencies between 300 Hz and 3,000 Hz. Computer communications carried out using telephone company equipment use the same frequencies that are allocated to voice transmissions. For example, when the communication involves sending a string of 1s and 0s for an ASCII code, a 0 could be transmitted at 1,070 Hz and a 1 could be transmitted at 1,270 Hz.

Although you usually see a wave depicted as a smooth curve, waves can have different shapes. These shapes are referred to as **waveforms** or "wave patterns." Analog signals typically represent an unlimited range of values and, therefore, have a smooth, curved waveform. Digital signals, on the other hand, represent discrete values within a limited range and, therefore, have a square or "stepped" wave pattern. Compare the analog and digital wave patterns shown in Figure 11-3 on the next page.

FIGURE 11-3

Analog waveforms are curved, whereas digital waveforms are squared, or "stepped."

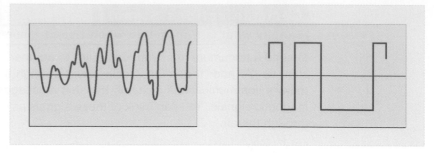

Analog wave pattern   Digital wave pattern

It is possible to convert analog signals into digital signals, and vice versa. For example, as you learned in Chapter 10, the process of sampling a sound wave creates a digital version of an analog sound. Also, your computer modem converts the digital signal from your computer into an analog signal that can be sent over phone lines. What is the advantage of a digital signal? Compared to analog signals, digital transmissions are usually less susceptible to noise, require simpler circuitry, and are easier to "clean" before boosting.

What is the significance of "cleaning" a wave? Remember that a digital transmission is in the form of 1s and 0s, whereas an analog transmission is composed of a continuous range of values. Suppose that a digital transmission uses different voltages to transmit 0s and 1s. A "perfect" 0 is sent as 0 volts. A "perfect" 1 is sent as +5 volts. What if during transmission some interference changes the frequency of a "perfect" 1 to +4 volts? When the signal is received, the receiving device can recognizes the +4 volt signal as a 1 and can "clean" the signal by reestablishing its voltage to +5.

In contrast, suppose that interference changes a 1,200 Hz wave in an analog transmission to a 1,233 Hz wave. The receiving device cannot determine if the 1,233 Hz signal is an error or if it is just one of the many analog values that was originally sent. Determining whether this signal needs to be cleaned and determining how it should be cleaned becomes more difficult because it is analog. The 1,233 Hz signal therefore remains part of the transmission, resulting in static or erroneous data bits.

Communications Channels and Media

What technology options are available for carrying communications signals?

A **communications channel** is a physical path or frequency for a signal transmission. Some channels, such as telephone cables, provide a physical path for analog audio signals. Other channels might be a frequency or range of frequencies, rather than a physical cable. For example, a television channel, such as Channel 12, is a specific frequency used to broadcast audio-visual data for a television station.

A **communications medium** carries one or more communications channels and provides a link between transmitting and receiving devices. The media most frequently used in today's communications systems include twisted-pair cable, coaxial cable, and fiber-optic cable. Section B of this chapter provides additional details on today's popular communications channels and media.

Bandwidth

Why do some communications channels have a higher capacity than others?

Bandwidth

Just as a four-lane freeway can carry more traffic than a two-lane street, some communications systems can carry more data than others. The capacity of a communications system depends on the bandwidth of the channels it uses. **Bandwidth** is the transmission capacity of a communications channel. Typically, a channel with high bandwidth can carry more data than a channel with low bandwidth. For example, the channels that make up the Internet backbone have a higher bandwidth than your home telephone line. High-bandwidth communications systems, such as cable TV, are sometimes referred to as **broadband**, whereas systems with less capacity, such as the telephone system, are referred to as **narrowband**. The bandwidth of a digital signal is usually measured in bits per second (bps). In contrast, the bandwidth of an analog signal is expressed in hertz (Hz), as shown in Figure 11-4.

FIGURE 11-4

The bandwidth of this analog channel is 4 Hz.

This 4 Hz bandwidth can carry four frequencies.

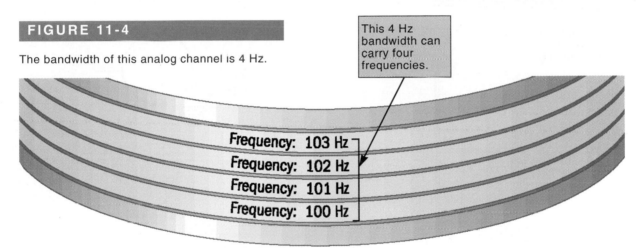

Frequency: 103 Hz
Frequency: 102 Hz
Frequency: 101 Hz
Frequency: 100 Hz

Data Transfer Rate

How fast can computer data travel over a communications channel? Although bandwidth is a measure of the capacity of a communications channel, it does not necessarily coincide with the actual speed at which you can transmit your data. Many communications channels work something like an airport conveyor belt that delivers luggage. The conveyor belt moves at a constant speed. If you have three pieces of luggage and you are the only person on the plane, your bags will arrive one right after another. However, if you have just arrived on a full 747, your bags will be intermixed with those of hundreds of passengers, and it will take longer for you to get them. The messages that you send over a communications channel are like pieces of luggage. When a communications channel is busy, it takes longer to send and receive data.

Most communications take place serially: one piece of information follows another. For a computer, **serial transmission** means that a byte is broken down into individual bits that are transmitted one after another over the communications medium. Faster data transfer can be achieved by **parallel transmission**, in which all of the bits for an entire byte are sent at the same time. Serial transmission is typically used for modem and network communications. Parallel transmission is typically used for sending data to a printer.

Communications System Topologies

How are various communications channels connected? A communications system is composed of many channels that must connect to each other to transmit data. For example, your telephone would be useless if the line from your house simply ended at the telephone pole. Your telephone line becomes part of a communications system because it connects to your local phone company's switching station so that your calls can be routed to their destination.

The pattern or path of the interconnections in a communications system is referred to as its **topology**. A communications system, such as a network, can use a single topology, or it can contain a mixture of topologies. Commonly used topologies include star, bus, and ring (Figure 11-5).

FIGURE 11-5

Communications system topologies include star, bus, and ring.

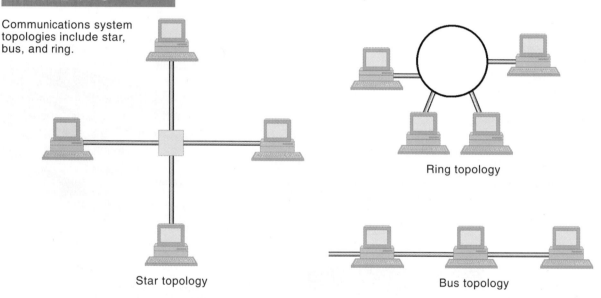

Ring topology

Star topology

Bus topology

In a **star topology**, like the one used to connect telephone lines to the phone company's switching station, communications lines fan out from a central location and each line provides essentially a private link to a centralized hub. The advantage of the star topology is that every connection is dedicated to one user and that particular user gets use of the full bandwidth of the channel. Its disadvantage is the high cost of the media and equipment needed to supply individual connections.

A **bus topology** provides a common or shared communications pathway. This topology is typically used by cable TV companies, which string cables from one house to the next in a long chain. A bus topology can supply the same signal to multiple users, as is the case with cable TV signals. If each user or device on a bus wants different signals, however, the bandwidth must be divided and no one will get to use the full bandwidth of the channel.

A **ring topology** connects devices in a continuous loop—it is essentially a bus topology in which the ends of the bus are connected. A signal leaves the sending device, travels in sequence to each of the devices connected to the loop, then returns to the sending device. Ring topologies are used in some local area networks.

Communications Protocols

How does a communications channel deal with interference? In Shannon's communications system model, noise sometimes interferes with transmissions. Suppose that you send a message to a business colleague, "Let's meet at the exhibition hall at 5:00 P.M." As the sequence of bits for the word "hall" travels across the communications channel, some interference changes a single bit. The "a" in the word "hall," which was transmitted as 01100001, arrives at its destination as 01101001, which is the ASCII code for the letter "i." When "hall" is changed to "hill," the meaning of the message has been altered.

To ensure that the data you transmit is not altered by noise, both the sending and the receiving computers must strictly follow a set of protocols. A **communications protocol** is a set of rules that ensures the orderly and accurate transmission and reception of data. When two devices communicate, they must agree on protocols for starting and ending a transmission, recognizing transmission errors, sending data at the correct speed, and formatting or packaging the data.

Computers use error-checking protocols to ensure accurate delivery of data. One error-checking protocol uses a **parity bit** to describe the number of 0s or 1s in a sequence of data. Using the **even parity** protocol, the number of 1 bits, including the parity bit, must be an even number. With the **odd parity** protocol, the number of 1 bits must be an odd number. For example, under even parity, would you add a 0 or 1 parity bit to 01000001? The sequence of bits already contains an even number of 1 bits, so you would add a 0 parity bit. Study Figure 11-6 to see how parity works.

FIGURE 11-6

Parity helps a communications system determine whether data has been corrupted during transmission.

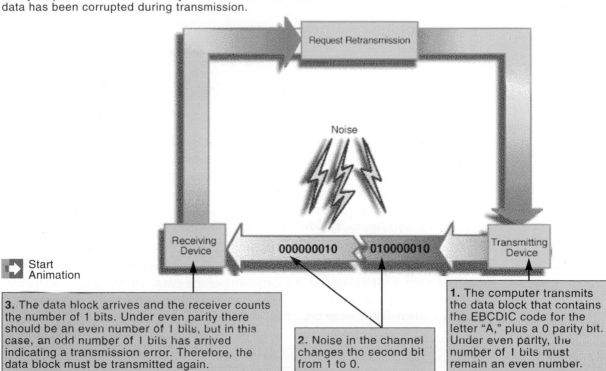

Request Retransmission

Noise

Receiving Device   000000010   010000010   Transmitting Device

Start Animation

3. The data block arrives and the receiver counts the number of 1 bits. Under even parity there should be an even number of 1 bits, but in this case, an odd number of 1 bits has arrived indicating a transmission error. Therefore, the data block must be transmitted again.

2. Noise in the channel changes the second bit from 1 to 0.

1. The computer transmits the data block that contains the EBCDIC code for the letter "A," plus a 0 parity bit. Under even parity, the number of 1 bits must remain an even number.

Synchronous and Asynchronous Protocols

How does the receiving computer know when the transmission begins and ends? A major challenge with serial communications is coordinating the transmission and the reception. The transmitting computer sends a series of bits, but if the receiving computer misses the first three bits of a serial transmission, the message would be hopelessly garbled, as shown in Figure 11-7.

FIGURE 11-7

Without start and stop bits, a transmission can become garbled.

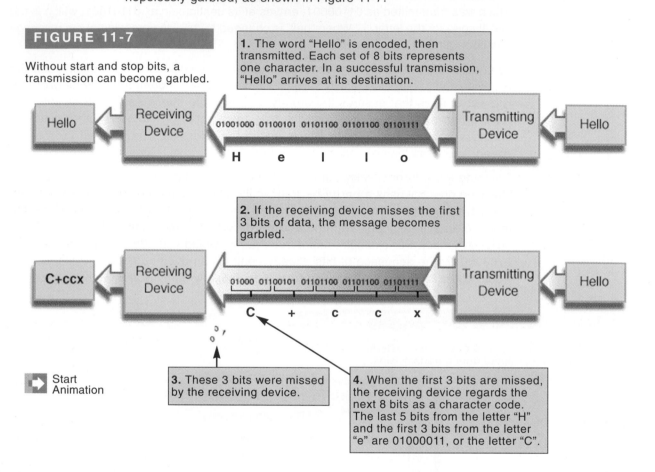

1. The word "Hello" is encoded, then transmitted. Each set of 8 bits represents one character. In a successful transmission, "Hello" arrives at its destination.

2. If the receiving device misses the first 3 bits of data, the message becomes garbled.

Start Animation

3. These 3 bits were missed by the receiving device.

4. When the first 3 bits are missed, the receiving device regards the next 8 bits as a character code. The last 5 bits from the letter "H" and the first 3 bits from the letter "e" are 01000011, or the letter "C".

There are two ways to coordinate serial communications, referred to as synchronous and asynchronous protocols. Using a **synchronous protocol**, the sender and the receiver are synchronized by a signal called a clock. The transmitting computer sends data at a fixed rate, and the receiving computer expects the incoming data at the same fixed rate. Much of the communication that takes place on the main circuit board of a computer is synchronous; however, communication between two microcomputers rarely uses the synchronous protocol.

Computer modems typically use an **asynchronous protocol**, in which one modem transmits a **start bit** to indicate the beginning of the data. The modem then transmits the data as a series of one or more bytes, called a **block**. The end of each block is indicated by transmitting a **stop bit**, as shown in Figure 11-8 on the next page.

FIGURE 11-8

Asynchronous protocol requires start and stop bits.

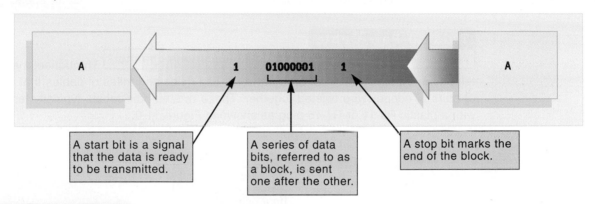

A start bit is a signal that the data is ready to be transmitted.

A series of data bits, referred to as a block, is sent one after the other.

A stop bit marks the end of the block.

Signal Direction

Do all channels send and receive data? Different communications channels, protocols, and devices provide different capabilities for sending and receiving data. For example, you use a CB radio differently from the way you use the telephone—with a CB radio, you must press a button when you are ready to send and release the button when you want to receive. In contrast, with a telephone you don't have to take any action to switch between talking and listening.

Simplex communication allows communication in only one direction. A radio transmitter uses simplex communication—it can transmit, but it cannot receive signals.

Half-duplex communication allows you to send or receive, but not to do both at the same time. A CB radio is an example of half-duplex transmission. The CB radio is in receive mode until you press the "talk" button.

Full-duplex communication allows you to send and receive at the same time. A telephone line is an example of full-duplex communication; most computer communications take place in this mode.

Some communications are sent and then echoed back to the sender as a means of checking accuracy. This type of communication is referred to as **echoplex communication**. Echoplex is useful in situations when it is important to be absolutely certain that data was transmitted accurately.

QUICKCHECK   A

1 _____, such as electrical interference, can disrupt data communications.

2 _____ is the transmission capacity of a communications channel.

3 The telephone system typically uses a(n) _____ topology; cable TV systems use a(n) _____ topology.

4 Communications _____ are rules that ensure the orderly and accurate transmission and reception of data.

5 A computer using _____ parity would need to add a 1 bit to 11011100 before sending it.

6 Most data communications are asynchronous. True or false? _____

 Check Answers

COMMUNICATIONS CHANNELS

You use a communications channel, sometimes referred to as a "link," to transport data to and from your computer to other communications devices. Communications channels have different characteristics that affect their reliability and data transport speed.

Twisted-Pair Cable

What's the most typical type of communications channel? Throughout the world, telephone systems and local area networks use miles and miles of cables that consist of pairs of copper wire twisted together. These twisted-pair cables typically terminate with a plastic RJ-11 or RJ-45 plug as shown in Figure 11-9.

FIGURE 11-9

When twisted-pair cable is used for data communications, the cable terminates with a plastic RJ-45 connector, which plugs into a hub or a wall outlet that leads to a communications system. Twisted-pair cable used for telephones has a smaller RJ-11 connector.

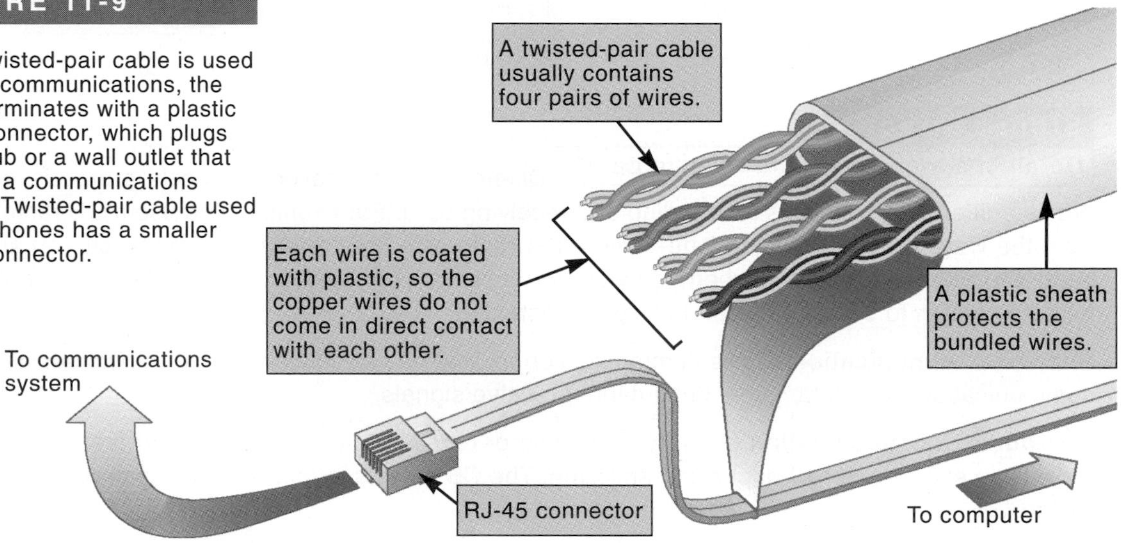

A twisted-pair cable usually contains four pairs of wires.

Each wire is coated with plastic, so the copper wires do not come in direct contact with each other.

A plastic sheath protects the bundled wires.

To communications system

RJ-45 connector

To computer

As explained in Chapter 7, there are two main types of twisted-pair cable. In a shielded twisted-pair (STP) cable, the wire pairs are coated with a foil shield, which reduces signal noise that might interfere with data transmission. Unshielded twisted-pair (UTP) cable contains no shielding. It is less expensive than shielded cable, but more susceptible to signal noise.

Twisted-pair cables are classified into five categories based on their transmission capacity. Category 1 cable is unshielded and recommended only for analog voice communications. Category 2 is a better grade of unshielded cable that is suitable for voice and digital data communications at rates up to 1 Mbps (megabit per second). Shielded or unshielded Category 3, 4, and 5 cables are suitable for communications at 16 Mbps, 20 Mbps, and 100 Mbps, respectively. Category 1 cable is considered **voice-grade cable**, which means that it is recommended for transmitting voice, but not data signals. In contrast, a **data-grade cable** is considered suitable for data transmissions.

When you purchase a cable to connect a modem to a telephone wall outlet, your choice will typically be limited to inexpensive Category 1 voice-grade "patch" cables with pre-installed RJ-11 connectors. This type of cable is sufficient for the quality and speed that you can expect when using the telephone system. In contrast, when you purchase a cable to connect your network interface card to a network hub, you should select a Category 5 unshielded or shielded cable with RJ-45 connectors.

Coaxial Cable

What about other popular cable options? Coaxial cable, often called "coax cable" (pronounced "co-ax"), is a high-capacity communications cable consisting of a copper wire conductor, a non-conducting insulator, a foil shield, a woven metal outer shielding, and a plastic outer coating, as shown in Figure 11-10.

FIGURE 11-10

Coaxial cable contains shielding, which helps increase its bandwidth.

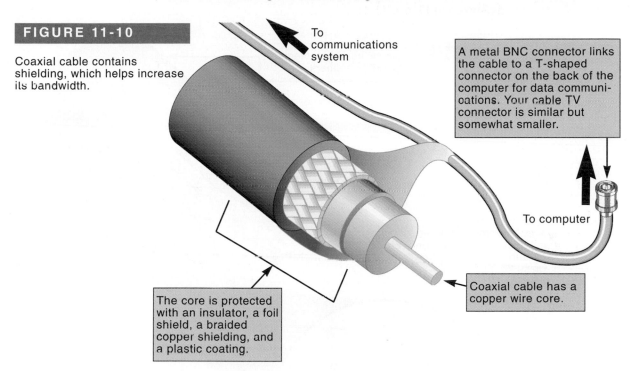

To communications system

A metal BNC connector links the cable to a T-shaped connector on the back of the computer for data communications. Your cable TV connector is similar but somewhat smaller.

To computer

The core is protected with an insulator, a foil shield, a braided copper shielding, and a plastic coating.

Coaxial cable has a copper wire core.

Coaxial cable is typically used to carry cable television signals because its high capacity allows it to carry signals for more than 100 television channels simultaneously. It also provides good capacity for data communications and is used in situations where twisted-pair cable is not adequate to carry the required amount of data.

Coaxial cable is sometimes called a "Category 6 cable" and has a bandwidth that exceeds 100 Mbps. Of the two types of coax cable, thin coax is 3/16-inch in diameter and typically found in local area network installations and home cable TV wiring. Thick coax cable is 3/8-inch thick and is found in older local area networks and in cable TV trunk lines.

Although it has excellent bandwidth, coaxial cable is less durable, more expensive, and more difficult to work with than twisted-pair cable. Coaxial cable was once the most widely used type of cable for connecting computers in local area networks, but today it is being replaced by twisted-pair cable. For situations where high bandwidth is required, however, both coaxial cable and twisted-pair cable are being replaced by fiber-optic cable.

Fiber-Optic Cable

What's so special about fiber-optic cable? **Fiber-optic cable** is a bundle of extremely thin tubes of glass. Each tube, called an **optical fiber**, is much thinner than a human hair. A fiber-optic cable usually consists of a strong inner support wire; multiple strands of optical fiber, each covered by a plastic insulator; and a tough outer covering, as shown in Figure 11-11.

FIGURE 11-11

A fiber-optic cable contains hundreds of tiny glass tubes, which carry data.

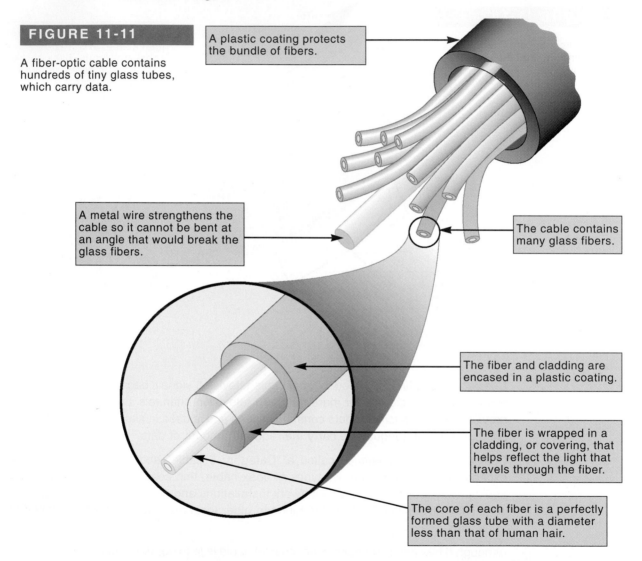

A plastic coating protects the bundle of fibers.

A metal wire strengthens the cable so it cannot be bent at an angle that would break the glass fibers.

The cable contains many glass fibers.

The fiber and cladding are encased in a plastic coating.

The fiber is wrapped in a cladding, or covering, that helps reflect the light that travels through the fiber.

The core of each fiber is a perfectly formed glass tube with a diameter less than that of human hair.

The use of optical fibers for communications is a relatively new development. Early researchers had determined that optical-fiber transmissions would be severely limited if the glass contained traces of water and metals. It was not until the 1970s that glassmakers became able to manufacture fibers of acceptable purity. By the 1980s, they had developed a process to create glass of such purity that if the ocean was as pure, you would be able to see through it to the floor of the 32,000 foot deep Mariana Trench.

Unlike twisted-pair and coaxial cables, fiber-optic cables do not conduct or transmit electrical signals. Instead, miniature lasers send pulses of light that represent data through the fibers. Electronics at the receiving end of the fiber convert the light pulses back into electrical signals. Each fiber is a one-way communications channel, which means that at least two fibers are required to provide a two-way communications link. Figure 11-12 illustrates how signals travel through fiber-optic cable.

FIGURE 11-12

A laser sends up to 1.7 billion pulses of light per second down the hollow core of a glass tube. The cladding reflects the light to keep it in the tube.

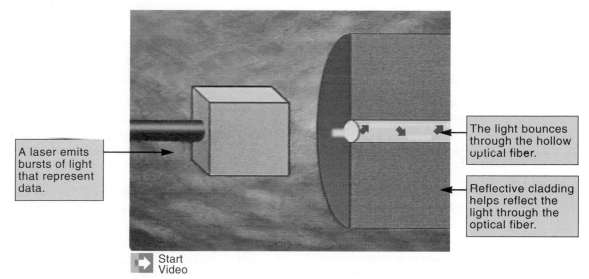

A laser emits bursts of light that represent data.

The light bounces through the hollow optical fiber.

Reflective cladding helps reflect the light through the optical fiber.

Start
Video

One advantage of fiber optics is that light signals encounter very little resistance when moving through the glass cable. Whereas twisted-pair and coaxial cable signals need an electrical "boost" after traveling less than a mile, light signals can travel very long distances over optical fiber. Researchers have been able to send signals as far as 5,000 miles without a boost.

Fiber-optic cable is sometimes referred to as Category 7 cable. Two types of fiber-optic cable exist. **Single-mode cable** has a very narrow core, usually less than 10 microns. Light can take only a single path through this cable, which results in transmission speeds that can exceed 50 gigabytes per second. **Multi-mode cable** has a relatively wide, 50 to 100 micron core. This width gives a light beam room to bounce around, causing signal distortion and reducing bandwidth. However, multi-mode cable is easier to install, and new technologies keep increasing its transmission speed, making it the optical cable of choice for most computer networks.

Many telephone and cable companies are upgrading their main trunk lines to fiber-optic cable. Usually, however, the connection from the utility pole to your house remains twisted-pair or coax cable because it is less expensive, easier to install, and more durable. As a result, the fiber-optic cable increases the bandwidth of the entire *system*, but the bandwidth for an individual user might not have increased.

Radio and Infrared Links

Don't some data communications use wireless links? It is possible to communicate without using wires. We do so when we speak to each other face to face, but what about data communications? Data communications can take to the airwaves using radio, infrared, or microwave signals. In this section you'll find out about radio and infrared communications. You'll learn about microwaves in the next section.

Radio waves provide wireless transmission for mobile communications, such as cellular telephones, and for stationary communications where it is difficult or impossible to install cabling, such as in remote, geographically rugged regions. Radio wave networks operate in frequencies between 1 MHz and 3 GHz. Before you can use a frequency for communications, it must be licensed from the Federal Communications Commission (FCC).

A radio communications link uses a **transmitter** to send a signal at a particular frequency or group of frequencies. A **receiver** at the other end of the transmission picks up the signal. Wireless communications channels are generally slower than cables. They are also susceptible to signal interference, eavesdropping, and jamming.

Infrared transmissions use a frequency range just below the visible light spectrum to transport data. An FCC license is not required for infrared transmission. Infrared transmission is an example of **line-of-sight communication**, in which the transmitter that sends the signal must have an unobstructed path to the receiver for the transmission to work.

You're probably familiar with infrared devices, such as hand-held remote controls for televisions. Infrared can also provide a communications link for transferring data between a computer and peripheral devices. In Figure 11-13, for example, you can see the infrared sensor in the lower-left corner of the printer; the notebook computer has an infrared port built into the back of the case, making it possible to send data to the printer without using a cable.

FIGURE 11-13

By pointing the infrared port of the computer at the printer's infrared sensor, you can send data to the printer without using a cable.

Start
Video

Microwave and Satellite Links

How do communications satellites fit into the picture?

InfoWeb

Satellites

A **microwave** is an electromagnetic wave with a frequency of at least 1 gigahertz (GHz). Data converted into microwaves can be sent over a microwave link. **Microwave transmission** sends a high-frequency signal from a transmitting station to a receiving station. Microwave transmitting and receiving stations cannot be more than 25 or 30 miles apart because at farther distances, the curve of the earth blocks the line-of-sight transmission path. To avoid this problem, many communications systems transmit microwave signals between a land-based **ground station** and a communications satellite.

First-generation communications satellites were placed in geosynchronous orbits 22,282 miles above the earth. A satellite in a **geosynchronous orbit** (GEO) stays above the same part of the earth by orbiting at the same speed as the earth's rotation. A GEO satellite provides continuous coverage over a particular area, but because of the distance between the satellite and earth it requires about 0.24 second to transmit data. Many of the most recent communications satellites have been launched into **low-earth orbit** (LEO) about 1,000 miles above the earth. Because they are closer to the earth's surface, LEO satellite transmission times decrease to only a few hundredths of a second. A LEO satellite does not remain above the same earth location as it orbits, however, so a LEO communications system requires a web of satellites, like the one shown in Figure 11-14.

FIGURE 11-14

A low-earth orbit communications system requires a web of satellites to provide continual coverage over an area such as North America.

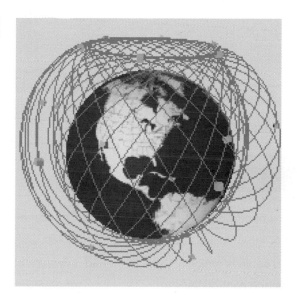

Start
Animation

A telecommunications satellite contains a **transponder** that receives a signal on one frequency, amplifies the signal, then retransmits the signal on a different frequency. The transponders in today's satellites typically transmit at one of seven frequency ranges, referred to as "bands." Of these seven frequency bands, three are typically used for data communications: C-band, with frequencies between 3.7 and 6.4 GHz; Ku-band, with frequencies between 11.7 and 17.8 GHz; and Ka-band, with frequencies between 18 and 31 GHz.

Transmissions from a satellite transponder are sent to satellite dishes. A familiar site in many communities, a **satellite dish** "catches" satellite transmissions on its parabolic surface, then reflects these signals to a feedhorn. The **feedhorn** contains a small metal probe that is a microwave antenna. The feedhorn funnels signals to a device called a low noise block (LNB) downconverter, which converts the microwave signal into an electrical current, amplifies it, and lowers its frequency. The downconverted signal is conveyed by cable to the indoor receiver. Figure 11-15 illustrates the major parts of a satellite dish.

FIGURE 11-15

A satellite dish can be used to receive data as well as cable TV signals.

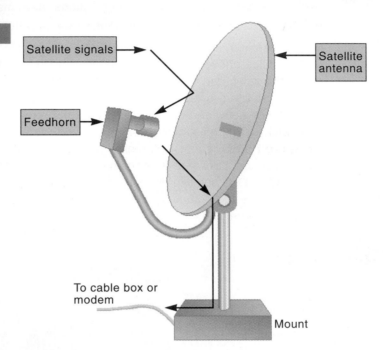

Satellite signals

Satellite antenna

Feedhorn

To cable box or modem

Mount

Q U I C K C H E C K   B

1 UTP has the highest bandwidth of any cable you can buy. True or false? [_____]

2 [_____] cable is typically used for local area networks and cable television.

3 Twisted-pair and coaxial cables transmit [_____] signals, whereas fiber-optic cables transmit pulses of [_____].

4 The highest-capacity fiber-optic cable is called [_____] cable.

5 Wireless communications channels are generally slower than cables. True or false? [_____]

6 Satellites send a high-frequency [_____] signal to a ground station or satellite dish.

➡ Check Answers

SECTION C — COMMUNICATIONS SYSTEMS

Cables, satellites, transmitters, and receivers are the building blocks of today's communications systems, which evolved from early courier services, such as the Pony Express and Wells Fargo. Technology began to shrink the globe, so to speak, in 1844, when Samuel Morse sent the first telegraph message. By the turn of the century, more than 1 million miles of telegraph lines linked cities and continents. The telegraph was soon upstaged by a new communications system based on the telephone. Riding on the coattails of the telephone system came the cellular phone system. At the same time, cable television companies began stringing thousands of miles of cable to deliver "pay TV." In addition to these commercial communications systems, many businesses established local area networks (LANs) and a decentralized communications structure called the Internet grew rapidly into a worldwide link for computer communications. The rest of this section explains how individuals and organizations use communications systems to connect to the Internet and exchange computer data.

The Telephone System

What are the advantages and disadvantages of using the telephone system to communicate computer data? Looking back, a marriage between telephones and computers seemed inevitable. Computers provide lightning-fast data processing and tremendous capacity for storing data. The telephone network provides a pipeline for sending that data throughout the world.

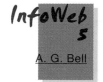

InfoWeb
5

A. G. Bell

In 1876, Alexander Graham Bell transmitted the first telephone message (Figure 11-16). Over the next century his company, now known as AT&T, built a communications empire that established much of the communications technology that the telephone network uses today.

FIGURE 11-16

This picture is an excerpt from a re-enactment of the first telephone message. Alexander Graham Bell spilled acid on his trousers while testing a new liquid transmitter. When he called to his assistant, "Mr Watson, come here—I want you!" his voice was transmitted to the receiver in the next room.

Start
Video

The telephone network uses **circuit switching** technology, which temporarily connects one telephone to another for the duration of a call. This type of switching provides callers with a direct pipeline over which streams of voice data can flow. You can also use this pipeline to access your Internet service provider. As you'll see later in this chapter, other communications systems use different types of switching when carrying information that is not formatted as a constant stream.

InfoWeb
6

The Phone
System

The telephone communications system uses a tiered network to transport calls. At each level of the network, a switch creates a connection so that a call eventually has a continuous circuit to its destination. The first tier of this network physically connects each telephone in a city to a local switch in what's called a central office. As explained earlier in the chapter, these connections use a star topology, which provides each house with a dedicated, but low-bandwidth data pathway. The second tier links several local offices. Connections then fan out to switches maintained by many different local and long-distance telephone companies. Figure 11-17 illustrates how you would use the telephone network to make a long-distance voice call or to access Internet data.

FIGURE 11-17

Using the telephone system (blue arrows), you can place voice calls and connect to your ISP.

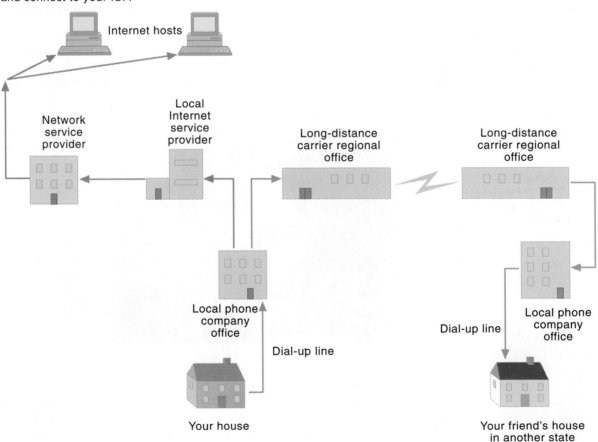

The telephone network offers a variety of services for voice and data communications. Originally, telephones communicated using analog audio signals, and that type of service continues to connect most homes and many businesses to the central office. This analog service, sometimes referred to as **POTS** for "plain old telephone service," is characterized by a dial-up connection that is created when you dial, then destroyed when you hang up. When you want to send digital computer data over a POTS line, you must use what is technically referred to as a **voiceband modem** to convert digital pulses into analog audio tones. These devices are usually simply called "modems."

The term "modem" is derived from the words "modulate" and "demodulate." In communications terminology, **modulation** means changing the characteristics of a signal, as when a modem changes a digital pulse into an analog signal. **Demodulation** means changing a signal back to its original state, as when a modem changes an audio signal back to a digital pulse. Modulating a digital signal allows computers, fax machines, and other digital devices to use POTS lines for data transport.

Inexpensive access is the primary advantage of the telephone system for computer communications. Most people have telephone service, so an inexpensive modem is all that's required to set up data communications. Computer communications are virtually indistinguishable from voice communications, and as a result service charges are the same as for voice calls. Using the latest modem technology, POTS lines have a maximum data transport capacity of about 52 Kbps per second. Therefore, a 56 Kbps modem provides more theoretical bandwidth than your telephone connection actually supports.

Some applications, such as high-quality videoconferencing, require more capacity than is provided by POTS lines. Telephone companies are scrambling to offer higher-capacity digital services, which can transport voice and computer data using a digital sampling technique similar to the way a computer digitizes music in WAV format. When you send computer data over a digital line, your computer must have a device called a **DSU** (data service unit) that places the data in the proper format for transmission. A DSU is similar to a modem in some respects, but instead of converting analog to digital, a DSU simply changes data from the digital format used in your computer to a digital format that is suitable for transport over the digital telephone line. In North America, the telephone network offers digital services including ISDN, ADSL, T1, and T3. European and Asian telephone networks offer a slightly different variety of digital services.

ISDN service (Integrated Services Digital Network) transports data digitally over dial-up or dedicated lines. A **dedicated line**, also called a "leased line," is a permanent connection between two locations. Phone companies offer two grades of ISDN service: a basic service with 64 Kbps capacity and an enhanced service with 128 Kbps capacity. **ADSL service** (Asymmetric Digital Subscriber Line) supports data rates up to 9 Mbps when receiving data and up to 640 Kbps when sending data. Both ISDN and ADSL are typically affordable for individuals as well as businesses. Businesses sometimes opt for more costly communications options that provide higher bandwidth. **T1 service** provides 1.5 Mbps send and receive capacity over a dedicated line. **T3 service** uses fiber-optic cables to provide service with a capacity of 45 Mbps over a dedicated line.

For data communications applications, the telecommunications infrastructure is only as good as its weakest link. For example, suppose a law firm wants to have a videoconference between its home office in Chicago and a Nashville hotel, where one of the firm's lawyers is staying. If the Chicago office has ISDN service but the hotel has only POTS lines, the POTS line would limit the speed of data transmission. At both sites, the video images would appear as a series of still images instead of full-motion video.

The Cellular Phone System

Can I use a computer with a cellular phone? The cellular phone system is based on wireless technology and provides mobile communications facilities that you can carry with you. As with the telephone system, the cellular phone system was originally designed to carry voice communications, but has been pressed into service for data communications as well.

InfoWeb 7

Mobile Computing

The advantage of data communications on the cellular phone system is mobility. Police can access local and national law enforcement computer databases while on patrol. Sales representatives can check their computerized schedulers and read e-mail while traveling. Investors can access stock quotes over the Internet while at lunch.

The disadvantages of cellular communications include high cost, reliability problems, and lack of security. Cellular communications charges are considerably higher than those for the regular telephone system. Usually, you pay for air time—the number of minutes you are connected—whether you dial a call or answer an incoming call. In addition, you must pay long-distance charges and surcharges for roaming calls placed outside of your local calling area.

Cellular transmissions are susceptible to more interference than communications that travel over cables. Overloaded cellular channels are noisy with transmissions that sometimes spill over from other calls and with static caused by electrical equipment and other transmitting devices. Channel noise is especially troublesome for transmitting data. If there's too much channel noise, a data transmission becomes unreliable.

Communications signals over the cellular system are literally floating in the air and can be easily intercepted with the right equipment. When transmitting sensitive or confidential data over a cellular phone system, it is advisable to encrypt it.

A cellular phone uses FM radio waves to send voice and data communications to a base station tower. A tower is located in the middle of a 10-square-mile geographical area called a cell. Each cell provides 50 to 70 radio channels, one for each simultaneous call within the cell. To see how this system works, study Figure 11-18, which depicts each cell as a hexagon and represents groups of channels by a color.

FIGURE 11-18

The towers in adjacent cells of a cellular phone network cannot use the same radio channels.

Each color represents a range of frequencies broadcast within a cell.

Adjacent cells must broadcast different frequencies.

Each cell contains a tower to send and receive signals.

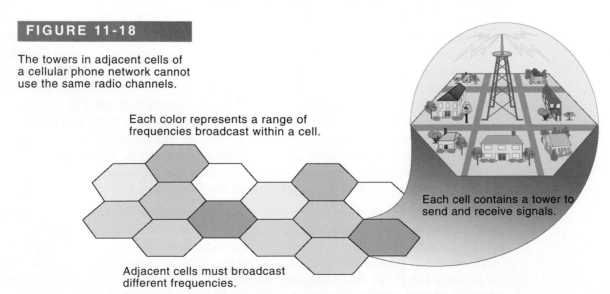

The cellular phone system handles data transmission in the same way that it handles voice calls. Suppose that you have a computer in your car and you want to access the Internet. Figure 11-19 traces the path of your cellular Internet access.

FIGURE 11-19

When you use your cellular phone to call an Internet service provider, your call is routed to the nearest cell tower. From the tower, you are connected to your ISP by land lines. Your ISP then provides access to the Internet, just as if you were using your home phone.

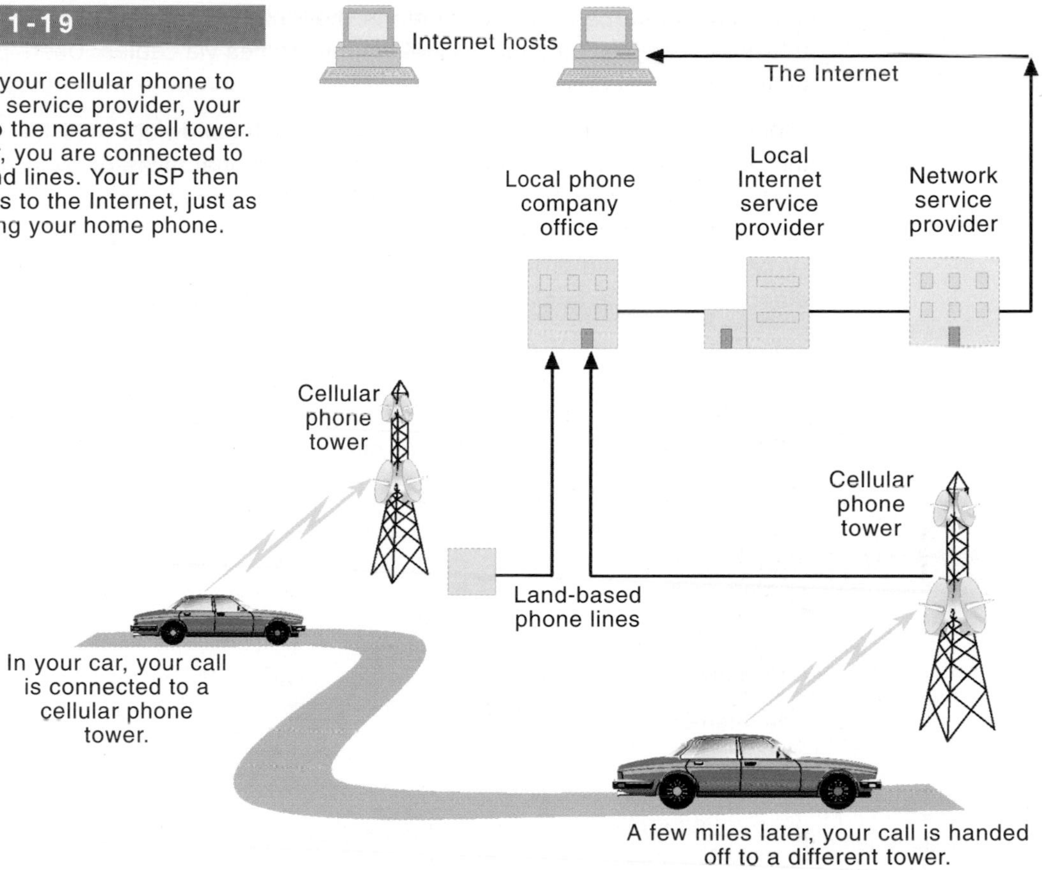

Internet hosts

The Internet

Local phone company office

Local Internet service provider

Network service provider

Cellular phone tower

Cellular phone tower

Land-based phone lines

In your car, your call is connected to a cellular phone tower.

A few miles later, your call is handed off to a different tower.

You can send and receive data over the cellular phone system using a number of devices, including cellular phones and specialized transmit/receive modems. Most cellular phones provide a connection point for a **cellular modem**, which is similar to a voiceband modem, but functions in the cellular environment. Cellular modems are available as PCMCIA cards for notebook computers and in external or internal configurations for desktop computers. Finding the right combination of phone, modem, and cable can be tricky, however, so most experts recommend that you seek the help of a technician from your cellular phone company. Once you have the necessary equipment, you can simply plug the modem into the appropriate expansion slot or port of your computer, then use the cable to connect the modem to your cellular phone.

As an alternative to a cellular phone, you can use a device that combines a modem with a transmitter and receiver. The transmitter/receiver handles the actual data transmission. These devices are typically available from wireless communications companies and require that you subscribe to their communications services.

Whatever equipment you use, transmitting data over the cellular phone system is slow—less than 14.4 Kbps—and much less reliable than using land lines. Some experts recommend that you try to access the Internet only when you are stationary, such as when your car is parked. As a result, today's cellular phone system is one of the least attractive data communications options for the general computing public.

The Cable Television System

Does the cable television system offer any facilities for computer data communications? In the past 20 years, cable television has become available to an estimated 65 percent of the homes in the United States. Cable TV stations receive broadcasts via satellite, then funnel them to homes via cables. Users pay a fee for this service, depending on the number and type of channels to which they subscribe.

Cable TV companies have installed miles of high-bandwidth (400 MHz) coaxial cables and are currently in the process of adding additional miles of even higher-bandwidth (700 MHz) fiber-optic cable. These cables, which are connected to every subscriber's home, have a carrying capacity far in excess of the capacity of POTS lines, so cable TV bandwidth could provide quick transmission for computer-based video, audio, and teleconferencing in addition to a variety of television programs.

Today, many cable TV companies have become Internet service providers, but most offer Internet service only to their TV customers, so you'll probably have to subscribe to a package that includes television programming as well as Internet service. Figure 11-20 illustrates how the cable television system transmits television shows and provides Internet access.

FIGURE 11-20

Your local cable TV office receives television programs from a satellite, then transmits them over a cable to all its subscribers. To provide Internet access, your cable company must also have a connection to the Internet and make some provision for you to send data as well as receive it.

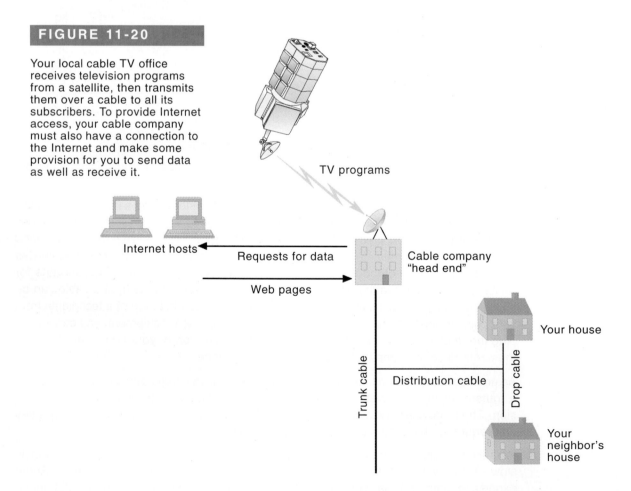

Cable
Modems

To access the Internet, your computer needs a cable modem and an Ethernet card—the same network interface card you would use to connect your computer to a local area network. A **cable modem** is a device designed to demodulate a signal from the cable and translate it back into Internet data. Your cable company will provide you with the type of cable modem that works with its equipment. Figure 11-21 illustrates how to connect your computer and your TV to the cable TV communications infrastructure.

FIGURE 11-21

The incoming coaxial cable provided by your cable TV service can be split to accommodate a cable modem in addition to a television set.

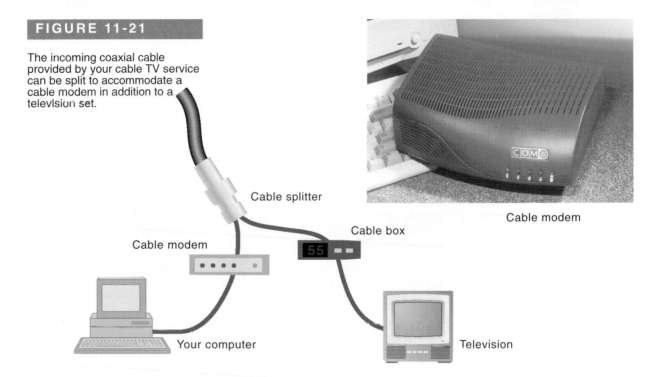

Cable splitter

Cable modem

Cable box

Cable modem

Your computer

Television

A cable modem has a theoretical capacity of 30 Mbps (30 million bits per second)—much faster than a 52 Kbps (52 thousand bits per second) POTS line. As it turns out, however, 30 Mbps is not the entire story. Although the capacity of a cable modem may be 30 Mbps, data transfer speeds more typically average about 1.5 Mbps.

Remember that most cable TV systems use a bus topology. You and your neighbors all share the bandwidth. In neighborhoods with many cable modem users, the cable can quickly become clogged as users access Internet sites, transfer files, and download large graphics files.

U.S. and Canadian cable companies first offered Internet access in 1997 and attracted about 25,000 subscribers. By 2000, cable modem service was available to about 25 million customers and more than 1 million of these customers had installed cable modems. How many more of these customers will abandon their voiceband modems is anyone's guess. Stay tuned to see if cable TV can challenge the telephone system's dominant role in computer communications.

Direct Satellite Service

Can I use a satellite to access the Internet? **Direct satellite service** (DSS) uses a geosynchronous or low-earth orbit satellite to send television, voice, or computer data directly to a satellite dish owned by an individual. Initially pioneered for broadcasting television programs, in 1997 this technology was first used commercially to transmit Internet data directly to homes and offices.

One of the first Internet DSS services, DirecPC transmits Internet data directly to your private 21-inch satellite dish. The 400+ Kbps bandwidth provides lightning-fast display of Web pages and streaming video.

DirecPC satellites transmit in only one direction, referred to as **downstream**, meaning from the satellite to you. How, then, can you transmit information **upstream**—from your computer to Web servers? For example, suppose you click a Web page link or type in a URL. Somehow that information must be transmitted from your computer to the Web, so that the page you've requested can be located and sent via satellite. DirecPC requires a standard modem and phone line for upstream transmission. The entire system is illustrated in Figure 11-22.

FIGURE 11-22

DirecPC sends Internet data downstream, but uses a conventional phone line for upstream requests.

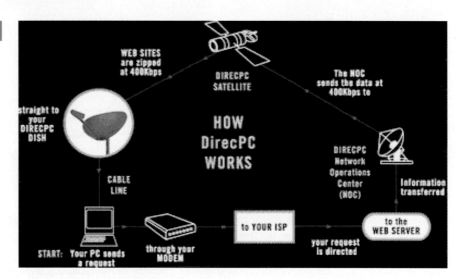

With current technology, upstream data transfer rates differ from downstream rates. A typical downstream rate of 400 Kbps means that your computer will receive data fairly quickly—Web pages should appear on the screen almost instantly and file transfers will be completed in a fraction of the time required on a POTS line. In contrast, upstream data transfer rates are limited by the speed of a conventional voiceband modem and will realistically be about 24–48 Kbps.

The Internet and Intranets

How do data networks differ from phone, cellular, and cable TV networks?

The Internet has become the hub of data communications. As you have discovered, most communications systems provide some way to access the Internet and use it to transport data. The Internet is rapidly replacing other data communications technology, such as private WANs (wide area networks) and dial-in computer bulletin boards.

Some organizations have employed Internet technology for smaller networks. An **intranet** uses TCP/IP protocols and Internet software to handle data communications within an organization. In a sense it is a mini-Internet, providing Internet services such as Web pages and Internet mail. An intranet, however, is designed for access primarily from the employees within a particular organization, rather than the general public.

As you know, a LAN is a network that serves users in a limited local area. The distinction between a LAN and an intranet is a bit fuzzy. A LAN might use TCP/IP protocols, but will also use other protocols such as Novell NetWare's IPX. Figure 11-12 summarizes the characteristics of the Internet, intranets, and LANs.

FIGURE 11-23	The Internet, Intranets, and LANs		
	Internet	**Intranet**	**LAN**
Operated by	Consortium	Private company	Private company
Coverage area	Worldwide	Within the company	Within the company
Protocol	TCP/IP	TCP/IP	TCP/IP, IPX/SPX, NetBIOS/NetBEUI
Services	Web, Internet e-mail, FTP	Access to company-specific Web pages, access to Internet	File sharing, printer sharing, local e-mail
Number of servers	Millions	Typically 1-5	Typically 1-5

The Internet, intranets, and LANs were all specifically invented and designed for efficient digital data transmission. Contrast this goal with that of the telephone and cellular phone systems, which were originally optimized for voice communications, or the cable TV system, which was originally optimized for visual data. Basic differences between these systems result from the nature of the "stuff" that is transmitted. Phone conversations and television broadcasts are continuous and sequential events that seem, intuitively, to require some sort of continual circuit. Therefore, it is logical that these communications systems use circuit switching technology to create a continuous connection for communications.

It would seem unlikely that chopping a phone conversation into little chunks and then reassembling it could somehow make the communication more efficient. Data communications, on the other hand, are not necessarily continuous. Because they are more like a letter than a phone conversation, it is conceivable that you could chop up a data message and then send the pieces to their destination, where they would be reassembled into the original message.

Unlike the telephone network that uses circuit switching technology, the Internet employs **packet switching** technology that divides a message into smaller units called **packets**. Each packet in one message is addressed to the same destination, but one packet can travel a different route over the network than other packets. At the receiving end of the transmission, all of the packets are gathered together, and then reassembled. Packets can be routed to avoid congested or inoperable communications links (Figure 11-24).

FIGURE 11-24

Sending data as packets.

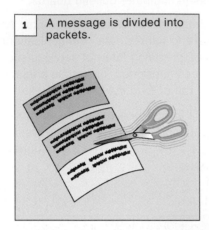

1 A message is divided into packets.

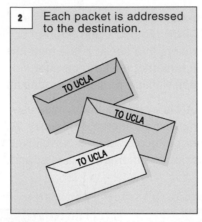

2 Each packet is addressed to the destination.

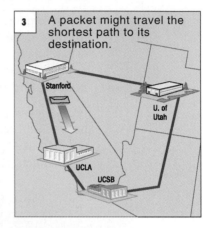

3 A packet might travel the shortest path to its destination.

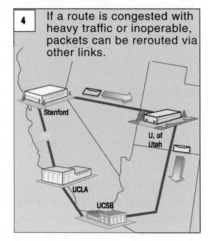

4 If a route is congested with heavy traffic or inoperable, packets can be rerouted via other links.

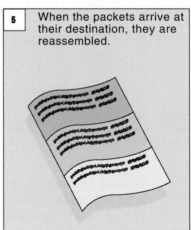

5 When the packets arrive at their destination, they are reassembled.

 Start Animation

The advantage of packet switching is its efficient use of available bandwidth. Packets from many different messages can share a single communications circuit. Packets are shipped over the circuit on a "first come, first served" basis. If some packets from a message are not available, the system does not need to wait for them. Instead, the system sends whatever packets are ready, regardless of the message to which they belong. Contrast this approach with a circuit-switched network such as the telephone system. Suppose someone is "on hold." No communication is taking place, yet the circuit is reserved and cannot be used for other communications.

InfoWeb 11
Packet Switching

Even though packet switching provides an efficient and dependable protocol for data communications, most experts agree that the Internet in its current form will not meet the data transport needs of a growing population of users, especially for graphics, audio, video, or teleconferencing applications. Network service providers are continually adding bandwidth to the Internet backbone by increasing the number and capacity of their communications channels.

Ethernet and Token Ring LANs

How do local area networks handle data communications? | Local area networks are a popular type of small communications system. Most LANs use packet switching technology, as does the Internet. Therefore, studying how LANs handle data communications can add to your understanding of how communications systems handle data packets. Network data communications are directed on one level by hardware components and on another level by software components.

InfoWeb
12
Network
Access
Methods

As explained in Chapter 7, each computer on a network requires a network interface card to establish a data pathway between it and the network communications channel. A network interface card plugs into an expansion slot in the computer main board or into a PCMCIA slot. In turn, a cable plugged into the interface card connects the computer to the rest of the network. A network interface card supports a particular network access method. A **network access method** is a set of specifications that defines how data will be physically transmitted from one network node to another. From a user's perspective, the network access method is determined by the type of network interface card and cables that connect the network nodes. Devices on a network must use the same network access method to communicate and share the network resources. Today, the most popular network access methods include Ethernet and Token Ring.

Ethernet, first introduced in Chapter 7, is the most popular network access method and transmits data at 10 or 100 Mbps. Ethernet nodes are arranged in a bus topology or in a star topology with a centralized hub. There are several variations of Ethernet, each of which is characterized by data transport speed and the type of cable that connects the workstations. Figure 11-25 describes some variations of the Ethernet access method.

FIGURE 11-25	Ethernet Technologies			
Ethernet Type	**Cable Type**	**Maximum Cable Length**	**Topology**	**Speed**
10Base5 "Thick Ethernet"	Thick coax	1,640 ft	Bus	10 Mbps
10Base2 "Thin Ethernet"	Thin coax	607 ft	Bus	10 Mbps
10BaseT	Twisted-pair	328 ft	Star	10 Mbps
100BaseTX	Twisted-pair	328 ft	Star	100 Mbps
100BaseFx	Fiber-optic	1.2 mi	Star	100 Mbps

On an Ethernet network, before a network interface card sends a packet, it checks to see whether the network is busy. If another network interface card is sending a packet, it waits and tries again later. If the network is not busy, the network interface card broadcasts the packet to every device on the network. Every device receives the packet, but it is accepted only by the device to which it is addressed.

Sometimes, two devices on an Ethernet network simultaneously check the network and see that it's not busy. These two devices then send packets at the same instant. When two packets are sent at the same time, it's called a **collision**. Ethernet networks use a method called **CSMA/CD** (carrier sense multiple access with collision detection) to deal with collisions.

When messages collide, both devices stop sending and wait for a random period of time before attempting to send again. You can probably see why it is essential that both devices wait a random period of time. If the devices were designed to wait for a specific period of time, both would wait and then try again at the same time, resulting in another collision. They would continue to wait and collide, wait and collide, and never send the message. Figure 11-26 shows how packets are transmitted on an Ethernet network.

FIGURE 11-26

How Ethernet works.

1. One of the workstations checks the network to make sure that it is not busy, then broadcasts a packet. The packet is addressed to workstation #21, but all the workstations receive it. Every workstation examines the address of the packet, but only the workstation to which it is addressed reads it.

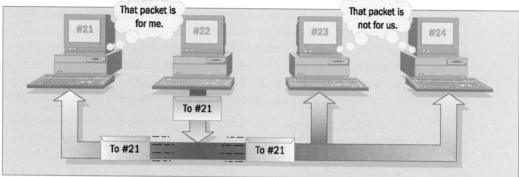

2. If two workstations simultaneously check the network, find it is not busy, and send packets at the same time, a collision occurs.

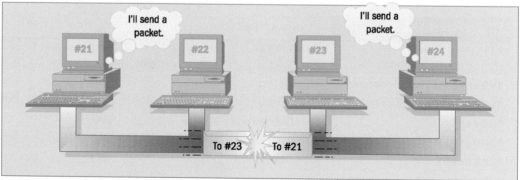

3. When a collision occurs, a special signal travels over the network to indicate that it is "jammed." This signal lasts a fraction of a second, then the network is again ready for traffic. The two workstations that had sent simultaneous packets each wait for a random length of time before trying to send their packets again.

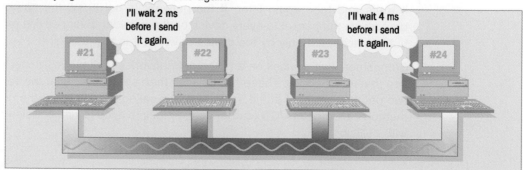

Introduced in Chapter 7, Token Ring—the second most popular network access method—transmits data at either 4 or 16 megabits per second over twisted-pair wire. As its name suggests, the cable arrangement for a Token Ring network is based on a ring topology. It uses a special message called a **token** to prevent collisions. The token travels around the network carrying a signal to indicate whether the network is busy or available to carry a data packet, as shown in Figure 11-27.

FIGURE 11-27

How token passing works.

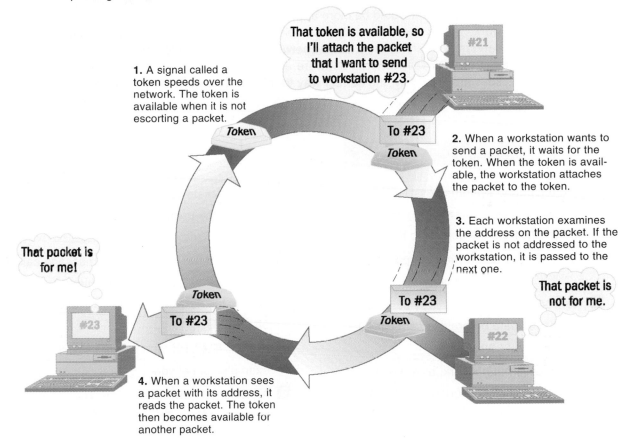

A network access method specifies the hardware that a network uses to transport data, but additional data transport specifications are handled by software. Regardless of whether a network is based on Ethernet or Token Ring technology, it requires some sort of **network communications protocol**, which specifies the structure of the packets. This protocol is controlled by software.

You are familiar with the TCP/IP communications protocol used by the Internet and intranets. TCP/IP is also a popular protocol for Ethernet and Token Ring LANs. Other popular LAN protocols include IPX/SPX and NetBIOS/NetBEUI. **IPX/SPX** (internetwork packet exchange/sequenced packet exchange) is the protocol used by Novell NetWare, the most popular stand-alone microcomputer network software. **NetBIOS/NetBEUI** (NetBIOS Extended User Interface) is a Microsoft network protocol, shipped with the Windows operating system.

What is interesting and somewhat counterintuitive is the fact that a single network can use more than one communications protocol. For example, an Ethernet network might use both TCP/IP and IPX/SPX protocols. TCP/IP could provide the protocol for data that is traveling to the Internet, whereas IPX/SPS would provide the protocol for data that is traveling to and from a local file server. Protocol determinations are typically made by a network specialist when the network is constructed, but network users might need to select one or more protocols when setting up an Internet connection.

Another potentially confusing aspect of networks is that people sometimes refer to their network by the server type, rather than by the network access method. You might, for example, hear someone refer to a "Novell network" or a "Windows NT network," when actually it would be more appropriate to refer to the network as an "Ethernet network." As is the case with protocols, a single network can have several types of servers. Therefore, the Ethernet network in an organization might have one file server that runs Novell NetWare software and one file server that runs Windows NT server software. Typically, the correct way to refer to a network is by its access method.

QUICKCHECK   C

1 The telephone system uses _____ switching technology to route calls from the sender to the receiver.

2 Ethernet and Token Ring are popular network _____ methods.

3 Network _____ packages and addresses data before it is sent over the network.

4 On an Ethernet network, a packet is broadcast to all network devices, not just the device to which it is addressed. True or false? _____

5 When packets collide on an Ethernet network, the packet with the highest address goes first. True or false? _____

6 On some networks, a special message called a(n) _____ continuously travels around the network picking up and dropping off packets.

7 TCP/IP, IPX/SPX, and NetBIOS/NetBEUI are examples of network _____.

8 An Ethernet network requires TCP/IP and Novell NetWare. True or false? _____

 Check Answers

USER FOCUS: BUILDING A LOW-COST LAN

Data communications networks are not the exclusive property of large corporations, huge government agencies, and giant telecommunications companies. You can have your own computer network. In fact, if you already have two or three computers (maybe counting your friends' or coworkers' computers), your network will cost less than $200!

When you've built your network, you can use it to share data, collaborate on computer projects, and try out some multiplayer games.

Lab
Building a
Network

What You'll Need

| What do I need to set up my network? | First, you'll need some computers—at least two. To make it easy, all of the computers you'll connect to your network should run Windows 95, Windows NT, Windows 98, or Windows 2000. These versions of Windows include built-in networking software that will handle the network protocols.

You'll need one network interface card for each computer. For the simplest and least expensive network, look for 10BaseT Ethernet cards. These cards cost between $20 and $100. You can get a dependable basic card for about $25.

The next item on your shopping list is a 10BaseT hub. Look for a hub with five ports so that you can connect as many as five devices to your network. Even if you don't have five computers that you want to connect, a five-port hub provides room for expansion. Five-port hubs range in price from $60 to $200. For a basic network, one of the low-cost hubs should suffice (Figure 11-28).

FIGURE 11-28

An inexpensive five-port 10BaseT hub is a good choice for a small network.

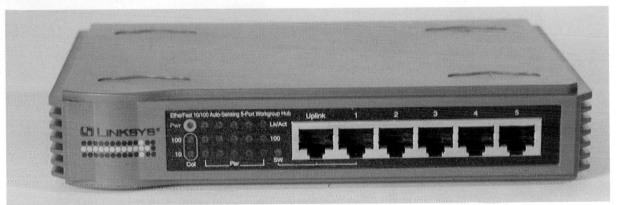

You'll also need 10BaseT cables. These cables, which are sometimes referred to as **network patch cables**, are sold in various lengths with RJ-45 plugs at each end. They're suitable for distances up to 100 feet. For each computer, you'll need a cable long enough to reach the hub. Look for Category 5 UTP (unshielded twisted-pair) cables. A 20-foot cable costs about $15.

Finally, make sure you have a Philips-head screwdriver handy.

Install Network Cards

| What do I do with all this stuff? | Your first step is to put a network card in each

computer. To do so, follow the manufacturer's instructions for opening the computer's system unit. Usually, you'll need to unscrew a few screws on the back of the case.

Before you touch any components inside the case, it is a good idea to "ground" yourself to release static electricity that might damage components on the motherboard. Computer technicians use special grounding straps that attach to their wrists. If you don't have a grounding strap, touch some metal before you reach into the computer case.

FIGURE 11-29

Installing a network card.

Locate an unused expansion slot on the main board of your computer and carefully plug in the network card, as shown in Figure 11-29.

If you're a gambler, you can refasten the system unit case now. However, if things don't go exactly right, you might have to access the network card to troubleshoot the problem. It's probably prudent to reassemble the system unit after your network is up and running smoothly.

Install the Cables and Hub

Where do I attach the cables? The cables are meant to connect each computer to the hub. Plug one end of a cable into the network card that you just installed in the computer. Plug the other end into any one of the ports in the hub. You'll see why 10BaseT topology is referred to as a star—the cables branch out from the hub sort of like the points of a star.

Your hub needs electrical power. Follow the manufacturer's directions for plugging your hub into a wall outlet or UPS (uninterruptible power supply). In case of a power failure, you'd like your network connections to remain intact until you can save your files and shut down the system gracefully.

Activate Network Software

How will the computers on my network know how to communicate? Now you can turn on the computers. Windows should automatically detect the network cards you have just installed. A Windows wizard will display a series of dialog boxes to guide you through the rest of the installation process. For your first network, you should select the Client for Microsoft Networks protocol and indicate to the wizard that you want to share files and printers, as shown in Figure 11-30.

FIGURE 11-30

Use the Windows Network dialog box to select Client for Microsoft Networks, then select File and Print Sharing.

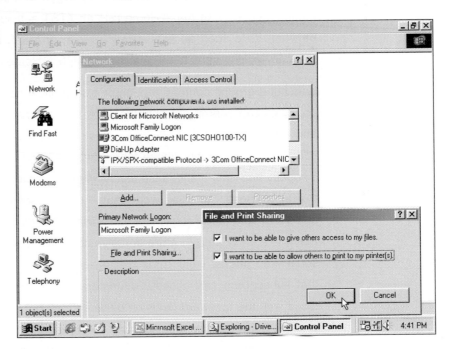

 Start
Screentour

With file and printer sharing activated, your network should be operational. You might want to use the Network Neighborhood icon to map drive letters and printers.

IS "OPEN ACCESS" IMPORTANT?

Today, most Internet surfers access the Internet using telephone lines and voiceband modems that provide average access speeds of 30–40 Kbps. In the deregulated telephone industry of the United States, dial-up consumers have a wide choice of phone companies for basic phone service and of ISPs for Internet access. Many cable TV companies now offer cable modems, which provide a high-speed (1.5 Mbps) alternative to dial-up Internet access. Cable modem users, however, do not have the variety of options that are available to dial-up customers because cable television companies typically enjoy a monopoly within any given community. As a result, most consumers who want cable TV have no choice of provider, nor do they have a choice if they want to access the Internet using cable modems.

Consumer advocates warn that cable company monopolies over high-speed Internet access could have a negative effect on what the Supreme Court has called "the most participatory form of mass speech yet developed." What is specifically troubling is the trend for cable companies to require Internet subscribers to use the cable company's ISP. For example, AT&T, which in 1998 merged with cable giant TCI, bundles its cable modem access with the @Home ISP, an AT&T subsidiary. Instead of having a choice between ISPs such as AOL, CompuServe, or MSN, AT&T's cable subscribers automatically gain access to the Internet through @Home.

Watchdog groups contend that cable monopolies increase the probability that a cable company can control not only the price that you pay for access, but also the amount and kind of content that you can access on the Internet. According to an organization called No Gatekeepers, these fears have some basis in fact. For example, one cable company has issued a warning that its Internet service cannot be used for any business-related purpose, including work-related e-mail. Some cable subscribers also limit the amount of data that a subscriber can download each month. From here, many critics see that it is a short step to more intrusive controls, such as censoring the content of personal Web pages, limiting the discussion topics in chat rooms, and limiting the sites that subscribers can access. Ultimately, these critics suggest, consumers might be faced with the awkward decision between fast, but censored access via cable modem or slow, but uncensored access via dial-up connections. Many consumer groups and ISPs are demanding that the government adopt an "open access" policy, in which cable companies would be forced to allow competing ISPs, such as AOL, to use their cables.

In a CNET news article, reporter Corey Rice points out that "The cable industry is vehemently opposed to open access, saying the billions of dollars companies have invested in upgrading cable networks would be for naught if ISPs were simply allowed to piggyback on networks they don't own." This sentiment is echoed by C. Michael Armstrong, Chairman and CEO of AT&T: "It's not fair. It's not right. Worse, it will inhibit industry

CHAPTER 11

growth and competition. No company will invest billions of dollars to become a facilities-based broadband services provider if competitors who have not invested a penny of capital nor taken an ounce of risk can come along and get a free ride on the investments and risks of others."

Cable companies also offer responses to charges of operating irresponsible monopolies and limiting data access. They point out that cable monopolies exist because city council members throughout the country bought into the idea that it would not be economically feasible for more than one company to install cables to every home in a community and then compete for customers. Upgrading the cable infrastructure to support Internet access might have similar economic limitations. Furthermore, as most people realize, the cable TV infrastructure does not have unlimited bandwidth. Many companies limit data downloads to prevent a few subscribers from "hogging" most of the bandwidth.

Some experts, such as public policy consultant Blair Levin, believe that there exists a low risk that cable Internet access providers would be able to control consumers' free access to Web sites and content. Consumers speak with their wallets and will not tolerate censored Web access. The FCC has taken a "wait-and-see" attitude toward the issue. In the words of FCC chairman William Kennard, "The best policy for now is watchful restraint." In contrast, the Canadian government now requires open access.

InfoWeb 14

Open Access

The controversy over open access has many facets and important implications for future telecommunications policies. You can explore the issue in detail by following the links provided by the Open Access InfoWeb.

WHAT DO YOU THINK?

1. If you had to choose between a fast, but censored Internet connection over cable and a slow, but uncensored dial-up connection, would you select the cable connection? ○ Yes ○ No ○ Not sure

2. Should cable companies be forced to allow open access to competing ISPs? ○ Yes ○ No ○ Not sure

3. Do you think that 1.5 Mbps cable modem access is worth $30 per month when 56 Kbps dial-up service is available for $20 per month? ○ Yes ○ No ○ Not sure

 Save Responses

CHAPTER 11 REVIEW ACTIVITIES

INTERACTIVE SUMMARY

The Interactive Summary helps you select important concepts and facts from the chapter. Fill in the blanks to best complete each sentence. When using the NP4 CD or NP4 Web site, you can click the blue buttons to automatically score your answers. Place your Tracking Disk in the floppy disk drive if you want to save your scores.

In a communications system, a(n) [＿＿＿＿] encodes a message, which is sent as a wavelike signal over a communications [＿＿＿＿] to a receiver. [＿＿＿＿] signals may represent an unlimited range of values and have a smooth, curved waveform. [＿＿＿＿] signals, which have a square wave pattern, represent discrete values and typically are less susceptible to distortion from noise. Communications channels can be characterized by their speed and by their capacity, which is referred to as [＿＿＿＿]. [＿＿＿＿] channels, such as coaxial cable, have more capacity than [＿＿＿＿] channels, such as telephone lines. Whether a channel is transmitting analog or digital signals, [＿＿＿＿] along the channel can sometimes cause interference. Therefore, communications systems use a set of rules called communications [＿＿＿＿] that ensure the orderly and accurate transmission of data.

Today, computer communications, including Internet access, take place over a variety of communications systems, some of which were originally designed for other purposes. The telephone system, originally intended to carry analog voice data, uses [＿＿＿＿] switching technology, which creates a continuous circuit from sender to receiver for the duration of a call. To access the Internet over the telephone system, typically a(n) [＿＿＿＿] modem changes the digital pulses generated by a computer into an analog signal that can be treated as a voice transmission. The cellular phone system can also be used for data communications, but its costs are higher than those for conventional telephone service and its transmission speeds are far slower. ➡ Check Answers

Cable TV companies typically offer Internet access by means of a(n) [＿＿＿＿] modem that allows customers to connect their computers to the coaxial cable that also supplies television programming. Direct satellite service can provide Internet access as well. Satellites, however, typically transmit only in the [＿＿＿＿] direction, meaning from the satellite to a computer. Transmitting data in the other direction requires a standard modem and phone line.

Networks designed for computer data typically use packet [＿＿＿＿] technology, in which a message is divided into small units, called packets, and each packet is addressed to the same destination. The method for creating packets, sending packets from one device to another, and preventing packets from colliding depends on the network access method and communications protocol. The two most popular network access methods are [＿＿＿＿] and Token Ring. Popular network communications protocols include the Internet standard [＿＿＿＿], Novell NetWare's [＿＿＿＿], and Microsoft's [＿＿＿＿]. ➡ Check Answers

INTERACTIVE KEY TERMS

Make sure that you understand all of the boldfaced key terms presented in this chapter. If you're using the NP4 CD or NP4 Web site, you can use this list of terms as an interactive study activity. Try to define a term in your own words, then click the term to compare your definition with the definition that is presented in the chapter.

INTERACTIVE QUIZZES

Quiz yourself on important concepts from this chapter by filling in the blanks. When using the NP4 CD or NP4 Web site, you can type your answers, then use the Check Answers buttons to automatically score your responses. Place your Tracking Disk in the floppy disk drive if you want to save your scores.

1 Signal [＿＿＿＿＿] is measured in hertz, kilohertz, megahertz, or gigahertz.

2 It is easier to eliminate noise from a digital signal than from an analog signal. True or false? [＿＿＿＿＿]

3 Most computer communications take place in full-[＿＿＿＿＿] mode, in which data can be sent and received at the same time.

4 A(n) [＿＿＿＿＿] bit can be added to transmitted data as part of the error-checking protocol.

5 Fiber-optic cable provides a higher bandwidth than coaxial cable. True or false? [＿＿＿＿＿]

6 An analog, voiceband network will tend to use [＿＿＿＿＿] switching, whereas a digital data network will use [＿＿＿＿＿] switching.

7 When referring to the type of LAN in your school or business, you should use the name of the network [＿＿＿＿＿] method, rather than the name of the software that runs on the network servers.

8 A consumer movement to force cable TV companies to allow competing ISPs to use their cables for Internet access is often referred to as [＿＿＿＿＿] access.

Check Answers

Enter the letter of the picture that best matches each description below.

1 BNC connector [＿＿＿＿＿]

2 Ring topology [＿＿＿＿＿]

3 RJ-45 connector [＿＿＿＿＿]

4 Windows networking icon [＿＿＿＿＿]

5 Analog waveform [＿＿＿＿＿]

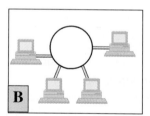
A

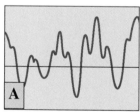
B

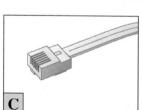
C

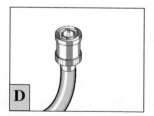
D

E

Check Answers

INTERACTIVE PRACTICE TESTS

When you use the NP4 CD or NP4 Web site, you can take practice tests that consist of 10 multiple-choice, true/false, and fill-in-the-blank questions. The 10 questions are selected at random from a large test bank, so each time you take a test, you'll receive a different set of questions. Your tests are scored immediately and you can print study guides that help you find the correct answers for any questions that you missed. If you are using a Tracking Disk, insert it in the floppy disk drive to save your test scores.

 Start Practice
Test

STUDY TIPS

Study Tips help you organize and consolidate the information in a chapter by making lists, outlines, charts, and sketches. You can use paper and pencil, or word processing software to complete most of the Study Tips activities.

1 Arrange the boldfaced terms in this chapter into the following categories: communications services, communications protocols, communications devices, communications channels, and miscellaneous.

2 Without looking back in this chapter, sketch out Shannon's communications system model and add appropriate labels.

3 List and describe some of the services offered by telephone companies for data communications.

4 Describe how you could use the cellular phone system to access the Internet.

5 List the advantages and disadvantages of cable modems for Internet access.

6 Design a poster illustrating how packet switching works.

7 This chapter provided an example of simplex (radio), half-duplex (CB radio), and full-duplex (telephone) communications. Describe at least one more example of each.

8 Suppose you are a computer that is packaging data for transmission and you must assign a parity bit. Given each of the following bytes and the required parity, fill in the table to indicate whether you would add a 1 or a 0 as the parity bit.

Byte	Parity	Parity Bit (0 or 1)
10000011	Even	
11100100	Even	
00000000	Even	
10011001	Odd	
10000111	Odd	

9 Make a list of the communications links in the *Communications Channels* section and note the advantages and/or disadvantages of each.

10 Associate the following terms with either a network access method, a network communications protocol, or a network topology:

Star	Ethernet	CSMA/CD	Ring	
Token Ring	Bus	Token	TCP/IP	IPX/SPX

PROJECTS

A Project is an open-ended activity that will help you apply the concepts you have learned. Many projects require resources in addition to your textbook, such as current magazines, library materials, or Web access. When you tackle a project, be prepared to use your critical thinking skills, logical analysis, and your creativity.

1 **Communications Archeologist** Using information from this chapter, from your library, and from the Internet, make a list of important artifacts (objects) in the evolution of communications systems. Make sure that you can associate a date with each of these artifacts. Now suppose it is the year 2500 and you are an archeologist newly arrived from another planet. You see these artifacts in a museum. How would you use them to explain the evolution of communications systems on planet Earth? Write a report detailing your theories about the evolution of Earth's communications systems, using diagrams, timelines, and other visual elements.

2 **Phone, Cable, or Satellite?** You can access the Internet using telephone, cable, or satellite systems. Which one would be best for you? Research the Internet access options that are available in your area, then answer the following questions:

a. If available, what is the cost of ISDN service from your local phone company?

b. Does your cable TV company offer Internet access? If so, what is the cost of the equipment you'll need? What are the charges for Internet access?

c. Is direct satellite service available in your area for Internet access? If so, what is the cost of equipment and access?

d. Which system would you prefer for accessing the Internet? Why?

3 **2001 Today** In 1945, Arthur C. Clarke, a young British engineer and aspiring writer (who later wrote the science fiction classic, *2001: A Space Odyssey*), conceived the idea of artificial satellites that would orbit the earth in geosynchronous orbit. It was not until 1960 that the United States launched an inflatable satellite called Echo I, which transmitted and received voice, music, and data from Earth. Satellite technology opened up new horizons in communications, now incorporated in telephone and cable TV systems. Use your library and Internet resources to learn more about satellite technology. Then create a brief informational brochure describing satellite technology. You can select your target audience (elementary school children, college students, seniors, science club members, and so on). Your instructor might specify that you should use word processing or desktop publishing software to produce your brochure.

4 **The Scoop on Data Communications** Suppose you are a news reporter for your student newspaper. What do you think other students would like to know about using their computers for data communications? Write a two-page article about student use of the communications infrastructure available at your school.

5 **Communications in the Workplace** Your career field probably makes extensive use of communications technologies. To prepare for your career, you should understand which technologies are used and how to use them. Research and write a paper describing how communications technologies are used in your career field. At the end of the paper, include a list of these technologies. Check off those that you currently know how to use.

6 **Communications Tour** Arrange to tour an office at your school or a local business. As part of the tour, interview your tour guide about technologies used for internal and external communications. Don't forget low-tech options such as U.S. mail. Create a diagram to illustrate what you learned about the flow of communications into and out of the office you toured.

7 **Alexander Graham Bell** Many of today's communications technologies are based on Bell's research and inventions. Born in Scotland, Bell emigrated to the United States, but lived much of his life in Canada. When he married, his wedding present to his wife was all but 10 of his shares in his newly formed company, Bell Telephone. Use the Internet and the library to find out more about Bell's life and research, then write a brief biographical sketch describing his effect on today's communications systems.

8 **The Worldwide Wait** As more and more people use the Internet for communications, the more difficult it becomes to provide the necessary bandwidth for fast access. Use the Internet and your library to find information on the Internet bandwidth problem. Make sure that you use references less than 12 months old, because Internet technology is changing very rapidly. Write a summary describing the current Internet bandwidth and recent proposals to increase it. Your instructor will provide guidelines on the length and format for your paper.

9 **Is It Shrinking?** We've all heard people exclaim that communications are shrinking the globe. It's an understandable image for a world in which you can pick up a telephone and call someone in Singapore or watch television images of events taking place right now in virtually any country in the world. But how does this technology affect people? What are the advantages and the disadvantages of instant access and worldwide communications? Make a list of at least 10 advantages and disadvantages. Then do a little research to find out what the experts think. Write an essay that presents your opinion about how society can best deal with the effects of new and planned communications technologies. Your instructor will give you guidelines for the essay's length and format.

ADDITIONAL PROJECTS

Click the underlined text to link to the NP4 Web site (www.cciw.com/np4), where you can view and print additional projects for this chapter.

Communications Across the Globe

Building a Home Network

Claude Shannon

CHAPTER 11

LAB ASSIGNMENTS

Software for this lab is provided on the NP4 CD and may also be available in your school's computer lab. To start the lab, click the lab icon.

A lab has two parts: Steps and Explore. Use the Steps first to learn and review concepts. Read the information on each page and complete the numbered steps. As you work through the lab, you will be asked to answer QuickCheck questions about what you have learned. At the end of the lab, you will see a report that scores your answers to the QuickChecks. If your instructor wants you to turn in this report, click the Print button on the QuickCheck Report screen.

When you have completed the Steps, you can click the Explore button to complete the Lab Assignments. You can also use Explore to practice the skills you learned and to explore concepts on your own.

Building a Network

Here's your chance to become a computer lab manager and see if you can please all of the students who use your labs. In the Building a Network Lab, you control a simulated computer network that provides services to student computer labs and to students dialing in from home. By monitoring usage and installing new equipment, see if you can make all of your students happy!

1. Click the Steps button to learn how to use the simulation to monitor and configure the network. As you work through the Steps, answer all of the QuickCheck questions that appear. After you complete the Steps, you will see a report that summarizes your performance on the QuickChecks. Follow the directions on the screen if you would like to print this report.

2. Use a photocopier to make several copies of the Network Statistics table shown on the next page. In Explore, use File/Open to set up the network configuration stored as *msu.net*. Record the statistics for one day on a copy of the Network Statistics table, then answer questions (a) through (e).

    a. How many hours during the day are more than 25 percent of the lab users without computer access?

    b. Are remote users satisfied with the level of dial-in service?

    c. Would you characterize the printer load as high or low?

    d. Does the current demand exceed the capacity of the file server?

    e. What should you do to improve the network to meet demand?

3. In Explore, install a network hub and a file server in the Tech Room. Install a print server with an attached printer in Lab 1. Install another print server and attach a printer in Lab 2. Install three workstations in Lab 1 and five workstations in Lab 2. Record the statistics for one day on a copy of the Network Statistics table, then answer questions (a) through (e).

    a. How many hours during the day are more than 25 percent of the lab users without computer access?

    b. Are remote users satisfied with the level of dial-in service?

    c. Would you characterize the printer load as high or low?

    d. Does the current demand exceed the capacity of the file server?

    e. What should you do to improve the network to meet demand?

4 In Explore, use File/Open to set up the network configuration stored as *wfcc.net*. Use no more than 30 devices to construct what you think is an optimal network for the students in the simulation. (*Hint:* Don't forget to save your network frequently on your floppy disk as you are working on it.) Make sure that you test your network for at least five days. The percentage of students unable to access workstations and modems should rarely exceed 25 percent. Server and printer loads should never reach 100 percent. After you are satisfied with your network, print out your network configuration report.

	Network Statistics			
Time	**Lab Users Without Workstations**	**Remote Users Without Workstations**	**File Server Load**	**Printer Load**
8:00				
9:00				
10:00				
11:00				
Noon				
1:00				
2:00				
3:00				
4:00				
5:00				
6:00				
7:00				
8:00				
9:00				
10:00				
11:00				

CHAPTER 11

INFOWEB

InfoWeb Site Chapter 11

The InfoWeb is your guide to print, film, television, and electronic resources. Use it to obtain updates on quickly changing technical information and to locate information for research papers. If you're using the NP4 CD, click the InfoWeb Site icon on the left side of this paragraph to access the online InfoWeb links. Otherwise, use your Web browser and type in the address of the New Perspectives Web site: www.cciw.com/np4. At the Web site you'll find up-to-date links to the topics covered in this chapter.

1 Communications Terminology

Although communications have become an integral part of computing, many computer dictionaries do not yet include the most current communications terms. On the Internet you'll find several good sources that explain communications terminology. For basic definitions, connect to the General Communications Glossary at *www.mendonet.com/telecom/glossary/index.html*. You'll find another basic glossary at the Sprint Web site, *www.sprint.com/sprint/annual/is_96/GLOSS/p_42main.html*. If you can't find what you need at those sites, you'll find a great set of links to other technical glossaries and dictionaries in Alex's Giant Glossary Listing at *www.iserv.net/~alexx/glossary.htm*. A good glossary of cable TV terms is found at *videotron.ab.ca/Technology/glossary.html*, the Web site hosted by Videotron Communications Ltd. Finally, for those difficult-to-find definitions of satellite communications terms, check out *www.gl.umbc.edu/~cellis3/gloss2.html*.

2 Bandwidth

The number of devices transmitting data over cables and the airways is multiplying at an astounding rate. Is there enough bandwidth for all of these transmissions? A chronic problem on the Internet is lack of bandwidth, which causes delays in data transmission and translates to slow response from a Web site. Read about the evolution of Internet bandwidth in the article "Internet Pipe Schemes" by connecting to *www.internetworld.com/print/monthly/1996/10/schemes.html*. According to George Gilder, bandwidth will replace computing power as the driving force in twenty-first century technology. You can read about his ideas in a series of articles that were first published in *Forbes* magazine by visiting *www.seas.upenn.edu/~gaj1/ggindex.html*. Indeed, bandwidth is shaping up to be the key computing and communication issue of the late twentieth and early twenty-first centuries. You can read more about bandwidth issues by visiting *www.digital.com/rcfoc/980309.htm*. You can see some interesting visualizations of weekly Internet traffic and bandwidth usage on academic servers at one institution, visit *yggdrassil.meirion-dwyfor.ac.uk/uccuwww/mrtg* and then link to Academic server FS 1 or FS 2. For information about bandwidth associated with specific lines, such as ISDN or T1 lines, visit *boardwatch.internet.com/isp/summer99/bandwidth.html*.

3 Fiber Optics

An important part of the telecommunications infrastructure that supports voice and data transmission is fiber-optic cable. With fiber-optic cable, data travels as light wave transmissions, rather than as digital or analog electrical transmissions. What exactly is fiber-optic cable, and how does it work? For a basic overview of fiber optics, visit *oak.cats.ohiou.edu/~sl302186/fiber.html*. For additional information, visit Lascomm Fiber Optic Data and Video Communications at *www.lascomm.com/toc.htm*, which has tutorials on fiber-optic cables, articles on a variety of fiber-optic topics, a glossary of industry terms, and case stories of innovative uses of fiber optics. For a discussion of how sound is transmitted over fiber-optic cables, the history of fiber-optics in telecommunications, and a description of how fiber-optic cables work, visit *www.att.com/technology/forstudents/brainspin/fiberoptics*. To learn about the fiber-optic industry and fiber-optic manufacturers, check out The Fiber Optic Marketplace at *fiberoptic.com*.

4 Satellites

How do satellites work? Visit Web sites such as *octopus.gma.org/surfing/satellites/satellite.html* or *www.atek.com/satellite/work.html* for easy-to-understand discussions of the basics, including geo-synchronous, medium, and low-earth orbiting satellites. You can find more information on satellite orbits at *www.np.ac.sg/~chw/orbits.html*. For an excellent overview of satellite technology, read the November 1997 issue of *BYTE* (*www.byte.com/art/9711/sec5/art1.htm*). You can view some interesting satellite images at Dundee Satellite Receiving Station, *www.sat.dundee.ac.uk*, a satellite receiving installation in the United Kingdom. You can interact with some fascinating satellite simulations at *www.cea.berkeley.edu/Education/lessons/indiv/dataflow/animation.html*—a wonderful set of Web pages designed by Eric Olson.

5 Alexander Graham Bell

Perhaps more than any other invention, the telephone has changed the fabric and texture of our society. In fact, without the telephone, the Internet probably would not exist. Alexander Graham Bell was only 29 years old when he invented the telephone, and it was only one of many inventions and contributions that he made to our society. In addition to the telephone, Bell invented a type of telegraph that could transmit more than one message at a time and a device called a photophone, which transmitted sound on a beam of light. He also worked on the phonograph, aerial vehicles, hydroairplanes, and the selenium cell. In addition, he founded the National Geographic Society. Several excellent books about Bell have been written. You might visit your local library and request a copy of *Bell: Alexander Graham Bell and the Conquest of Solitude* by Robert Bruce (Boston: Little, Brown, 1973, 1990) and the more recent biography *Alexander Graham Bell: Making Connections* by Naomi Pasachoff (Oxford University Press, 1998).

Alexander Graham Bell's Path to the Telephone, at *cti.itc.virginia.edu/~meg3c/albell/homepage.html*, reconstructs the path Bell took when he invented the telephone. It includes a detailed cognitive map that shows the inspiration for Bell's work and discusses some of the sources of his ideas in the work of other scientists and inventors. You can also view excerpts from Bell's original notebooks. At The Telephone History Web Site, *www.cybercomm.net/~chuck/phones.html*, you can find links to Web pages with telephone history, photographs of antique telephones, histories of U.S. and international telephone companies, telephone history articles, and lots more. You might also find it interesting to visit AT&T's Web site, at *www.att.com/technology/history/chronolog/1876telephone.html*, where you can watch a Quick Time movie of Bell and Watson if your computer system has the proper movie player.

6 The Phone System

You probably use it at least once a day, but have you ever wondered how the plain old telephone system works? How does your voice get from your kitchen telephone to your Aunt Belinda's living room 2,000 miles away? At *www.att.com/technology/forstudents/brainspin/routing*, you can find the basics of how local and long-distance calls are routed. An interactive exercise at this site provides some insight into the tasks that switching computers perform. POTS (plain old telephone system) is just one facet of today's telephone network. Pacific Bell provides a user's guide to ISDN at its Web site, *gw2.pacbell.com/products/business/fastrak/networking/isdn/info/isdn-guide/index.html* that can help you learn more about this type of high speed telephone line. Look up ADSL at *www.webopaedia.com*, then follow the links provided to find information about this emerging technology.

7 Mobile Computing

For a general introduction to cellular technology, take a look at the article, "What Is Cellular?" at *www.internet-connections.net/web2/cellrone/whatiscelular.html*. For an excellent technical introduction to the topic of mobile computing, read "Mobile Computing and Disconnected Operation: A Survey of Recent Advances" at *www.cis.ohio-state.edu/~jain/cis788-95/mobile_comp/index.html*. For more general articles, ranging from reviews of new products to advice about choosing a cellular telephone, avoiding injury while traveling, or protecting your equipment from theft, read *Mobile Computing Online* magazine at *www.mobilecomputing.com*. Using the cellular phone network for Internet access can be a bit tricky. 3Com provides a helpful overview at *www.3com.com/carrier/nsd/technology/30201.html*.

Suppliers of mobile computing products and services include Bell Atlantic Mobile (*www.bam.com*), Cellular One (*www.cellularone.com*), Aironet Wireless Communications (*www.aironet.com*), and Fujitsu Personal Systems (*www.fpsi.com*).

8 Cable Modems

During 1997, people started referring to something called the World Wide Wait, previously known as the World Wide Web. Why change "Web" to "Wait"? Increases in the number of online users and in the use of graphics and multimedia on Web sites have created a traffic jam on the Information Highway. Cable modems are one possible solution to the Internet traffic jam. Make sure that you read the C/NET news article "Cable Modems Burn Up the Wires," which you can find on the Web at *www.cnet.com/Content/Features/Techno/Cablemodems/index.html*. You might take a look at "How a Cable System Works" at *www.geocities.com/SiliconValley/Park/3254/cabletv.htm*. You'll also find an encyclopedia of information on the cable TV industry at *www.catv.org/index.html*.

9 DSS

Several new companies are poised to bring satellite-powered telecommunications to consumers and businesses. Among them are Teledesic, Hughes Network Systems, Voice Span, CyberStar, Odyssey, and M-Star. The Satellite Broadcasting & Communications Association Web site, which is located at *www.sbca.com/consumer.html* features information for consumers on direct-to-home satellite, including its history, a timeline, and a glossary of terms. You can also find information here on how to locate a satellite specialist in your area. Telesat DirecPC (Canada) has a good explanation of how DirecPC works and how fast it is, as well as success stories about DirecPC. The main Web site for DirecPC is at *www.direcpc.com*, then link to DirecPC at Home. The article, "How Satellites from Outer Space Will Save the Web," at *www5.zdnet.com/anchordesk/story/story_914.html*, is from ZDNet's Anchordesk and provides an overview of the anticipated effect of satellite telecommunications on the Web as well as links to several articles about the satellite telecommunications industry. Tune into "Satellite Communications in the 21st Century," a speech by Steven D. Dorfman, through Dbs-Online's satellite industry news at *www.hughes.com/speeches/century21.html*. This speech provides a perspective on where the satellite industry was in 1995 and where it hopes to be in the twenty-first century.

10 Intranets

By 1997, "intranet" was a popular buzz word in corporate America and had spawned a several-billion-dollar industry. At the complete intranet resource, *www.intrack.com/intranet*, you can learn about the basics of intranets, calculate the cost of implementing an intranet, view intranet demos, read articles about intranets, and read intranet case studies. The *Intranet Journal* at *www.intranetjournal.com* presents interviews with experts, advice on building intranets, and special reports about the use of intranets. Be sure to visit *www.cio.com/forums/intranet* for answers to frequently asked questions about intranets. Netscape and Microsoft are two of the biggest providers of intranet software solutions. You also can read case studies of intranets at *www.cio.com/forums/intranet* and at Microsoft's Intranet Solutions Center site, *www.microsoft.com/technet/intranet*.

11 Packet Switching

Packet switching is a technique that divides a message into smaller units, sends those packets to their destination by the best route available, and reassembles the packets at the receiving end. This technology made the Internet possible. In "Economic FAQs about the Internet" by Jeffrey K. MacKie-Mason and Hal R. Varian at *www.sims.berkeley.edu/resources/infoecon/FAQs/FAQs.html*, you can read the section on Internet Technology that explains how packet switching works, how it differs from circuit switching, and why data networks use packet switching. The Packet Switching Web site at *www.erg.abdn.ac.uk/users/gorry/eg3561/intro-pages/ps.html* includes diagrams that make the packet switching process easy to understand, along with a discussion of the details. If you find it easier to understand and retain information that you listen to, as opposed to read, Circuit Switching versus Packet Switching at *www.seas.upenn.edu/~ross/lectures/over/cs_vs_ps.htm* includes an audio file of a 15-minute lecture.

12 Network Access Methods

The major network access methods include Ethernet, Token Ring, ARCNET, FDDI, and ATM. Visit "Networking: A Primer" at *www.baynetworks.com/Products/Papers/wp-primer.html* for background information on LANs, reviews of all major network protocols, and discussions of hubs, bridges, routers, and switches. To learn more about Ethernet, check out Lantronix's Ethernet Tutorial at *www.lantronix.com/technology/tutorials*. Lantronix has produced Ethernet and Fast Ethernet products since 1989. Charles Spurgeon's Ethernet Web Site at *wwwhost.ots.utexas.edu/ethernet* displays a drawing of the first Ethernet system and includes links to technical papers, a list of vendors, FAQs, configuration guides, and Ethernet Usenet groups. For a comprehensive presentation of Token Ring technology, visit the High-Speed Token Ring Web site at *www.hstra.com*, where you can find news articles, white papers, case studies, and related links. You can find ARCNET features and benefits, a resource guide, and a list of companies with example applications at the ARCNET Trade Association's Web site at *www.arcnet.com*. Cisco Systems presents a thorough discussion of Fiber Distributed Data Interface (FDDI) at *www.cisco.com/univercd/cc/td/doc/cisintwk/ito_doc/fddi.htm*. The Cell Relay Retreat at *cell-relay.indiana.edu/cell-relay* has links to documents that will help you get started with ATM, including a FAQ list, dictionary, acronyms list, and tutorials, among many other resources. To learn more about the ATM standard, you can connect to the Asynchronous Transfer Mode Tutorial at *www.npac.syr.edu/users/mahesh/homepage/atm_tutorial*.

13 TCP/IP

For a good overview of TCP/IP, including figures, visit *www.cisco.com/warp/public/535/4.html* or visit *oac3.hsc.uth.tmc.edu/staff/snewton/tcp-tutorial/index.html*. When you use a dial-up line to access the Internet, you need a special version of TCP/IP, such as SLIP, or PPP. For an explanation of the differences between PPP and SLIP, visit *www.ccsi.com/survival-kit/slip-vs-ppp.html*. The Windows 95 Page: Configuring Dial-Up Internet Access at *www.halcyon.com/cerelli/dialup.htm* provides step-by-step directions on how to add a dial-up networking adapter to the Windows 95 control panel and how to add and configure the TCP/IP protocol. Articles at *www.windows95.com/howto* set out to make dial-up networking easy. The articles include detailed, step-by-step, illustrated instructions on establishing PPP, SLIP, and PPP Dial-back connections.

14 Open Access

The controversy over open access appears to be heating up, as more telecommunications companies bring cable Internet access online. The professional organization, Computer Professionals for Social Responsibility, has published a short, but interesting article on this controversy, available at *www.cpsr.org/cpsr/nii/cyber-rights/web/current-highbandwidth.html*. Another good summary of the case for open access is available from the Consumer Federation of America at *www.consumerfed.org/broadbandaccess.pdf*. You can find additional information at the No Gatekeepers Web site, *www.nogatekeepers.org*. For the other side of the issue, you might connect to *news.cnet.com/news/0-1004-200-852114.html* and read the CNET News article, *Groups Bristle at FCC Report on High-Speed Net*. You can also find the text of a speech by AT&T chairman C. Michael Armstong that addresses the open access issue at *www.att.com/speeches/98/981102.maa.html*. For current updates, enter "open access" or "AT&T TCI" into any search engine.

CHAPTER 12

INFORMATION SYSTEMS IN ORGANIZATIONS

PREVIEW

As you read this chapter, you should think about the relationships among people, organizations, and information. Consider the ways you interact with organizations: You make purchases from sales organizations, you are a student in an educational organization, you will probably have a career as an employee of an organization—you might even create your own organization. The information you learn in this chapter will help you interact with organizations as a client, customer, employee, or founder.

When you have completed this chapter, you should be able to:
■ Describe the activities that take place in a typical business
■ Provide examples of the computer's role in TQM, employee empowerment, rightsizing, BPR, and e-commerce
■ Describe the information needs of executives, managers, and workers
■ Provide examples of office automation that make significant improvements in ways that organizations operate
■ Describe the transaction processing systems that are typically used in businesses
■ Differentiate between an MIS and a DSS
■ Explain how an expert system works

FROM HOBBITS TO COMPUTERS

In J. R. R. Tolkien's classic adventure novel, *The Hobbit*, an eccentric wizard sends a hobbit named Bilbo Baggins on a dangerous expedition in search of a fabulous treasure guarded by a cranky old dragon. Bilbo bustles off without a hat, walking stick, money, or (as he suddenly realizes) any handkerchiefs! "Don't worry," says one of his fellow adventurers, "you will have to manage without pocket-handkerchiefs, and a good many other things, before you get to the journey's end."

In contrast to Bilbo's pitifully equipped departure, most modern expeditions are carefully orchestrated events requiring high-tech gear, ranging from deep-water submersible vessels to freeze-dried ice cream.

Abercrombie & Livingston Outfitters, Ltd., has provisioned hundreds of expeditions that challenge human skill, knowledge, and endurance. In addition to supplies, A&L provides highly respected expertise on appropriate gear for any terrain or climate. A&L's main offices are located in London. Branch outlets are spread across the globe in Telluride, Katmandu, Geneva, Lima, Guatemala City, and Dar es Salaam.

InfoWeb
1
Hobbits

A&L relies on a computerized information system to conduct business efficiently and effectively. An **information system** collects, maintains, and provides information to people. Today, most information systems are computerized. A computerized information systems can be defined as the computers, peripheral devices, programs, data, people, and procedures that work together to record, store, process, and distribute information. In this chapter, the terms "information system" and "computer information system" are used interchangeably to refer to information systems that are computerized. This chapter describes how computer systems like the one at A&L Outfitters—a fictitious company—help businesses and organizations function effectively.

According to Peter Drucker, one of today's most influential writers about business and management, "the purpose of an organization is to enable ordinary people to do extraordinary things." Organizations have accomplished amazing feats such as sending astronauts into space, building a huge communications network, and inventing freeze-dried ice cream.

An **organization** is a group of people working together to accomplish a goal. You are probably a member of an organization, such as a student club, a fraternity or sorority, a sports team, or a political party. You also deal with many organizations every day: your school, stores, banks, and government agencies. Many organizations use computers to operate more effectively, gather information, and accomplish tasks. In this section, you'll review some basic concepts about organizations and businesses. These concepts give you a foundation for understanding how computers and related technologies enhance organizational activities.

Types of Organizations

What's the difference between an organization and a business? You've learned that an organization is a group of people working together toward a goal. Any organization that seeks profit by providing goods and services is called a **business**. A&L Outfitters is an example of a business that was formed to make a profit selling expedition equipment. Some organizations are formed to accomplish political or charitable goals that do not include amassing personal profit. These organizations are known as nonprofit organizations.

Every organization has a mission—a goal or plan. All activities that take place in an organization, including those activities that involve computers, should contribute to this mission. The written expression of an organization's mission is called a **mission statement**. A mission statement describes not only an organization's goals, but also the way in which those goals will be accomplished. For example, the mission of A&L Outfitters is to make a profit by providing high-quality equipment and services for professional expeditions in mountain, jungle, and polar environments. Companies publish their mission statements in corporate reports and on the Web, as shown in Figure 12-1.

FIGURE 12-1

At Course Technology's corporate Web site, you can find the company's mission statement.

Organizational Activities

Are there activities that most organizations have in common? Computer and communications technologies help organizations carry out many activities—some are specific to a particular organization, whereas others are common to many organizations. It is useful to look at some of the broad categories of organizational activities where information systems are applied. Most organizational activities can be classified into the four functional groups shown in Figure 12-2.

FIGURE 12-2

Most organizational activities can be classified into four functional groups.

Operations	Financial Management
Sales and Marketing	Human Resources Management

The primary activities of an organization are called **production** or **operations**. Different organizations carry out different production activities. For example, a university educates students. An automobile manufacturer makes cars. A hospital provides health care. A&L Outfitters sells expedition equipment and provides expedition support services.

In addition to production, every organization must manage its money. A university tracks tuition payments, payroll, and maintenance expenses. An automobile maker tracks manufacturing costs, payroll expenses, and income from sales. A hospital tracks patient bills, insurance payments, staff wages, and medication expenses. A&L Outfitters tracks the cost of the equipment it sells, customer payments, and expenses for salaries, rents, and business taxes. Tracking the flow of money through an organization is referred to as **accounting** or **financial management**.

Most organizations need to promote their activities. A university needs to let prospective students know what educational services it provides. An automobile manufacturer must advertise its products to potential buyers. A hospital needs to convince patients that it can best serve their health care needs. A&L Outfitters advertises its products and services in specialized mountaineering and expedition magazines. Advertising and promoting an organization are the jobs of **sales and marketing**, or **public relations**.

Organizations are made up of people. University faculty, staff, and administrators; automotive workers and managers; and health care workers in a hospital must be hired, evaluated, and supervised. A&L Outfitters hires sales associates, experienced expedition consultants, purchasing agents, shippers, maintenance workers, and managers. It must keep track of these employees' salaries and benefits, evaluate how well they perform their jobs, and plan how to best use each employee's skills and talents. Keeping track of employees in an organization is referred to as **human resources management**.

Computers increasingly provide assistance with tasks in all four of these functional groups. You'll read about some specific examples later in this chapter.

Trends and Challenges

Could an organization function without computers? Computers are certainly an important aspect of organizational activities. Organizations exist in a rapidly changing and competitive environment where opportunities and threats abound. A well-known business analyst, Michael Porter, created the Five Forces model, shown in Figure 12-3, to illustrate the interaction between these opportunities and threats.

FIGURE 12-3

Michael Porter's Five Forces model.

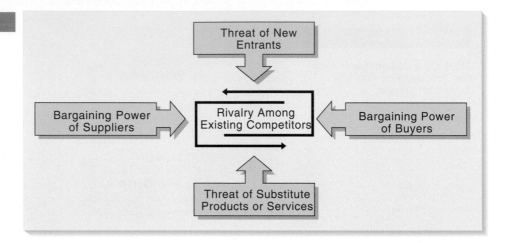

InfoWeb
5

Competition

To be successful in its mission, an organization must respond effectively to opportunities and threats. But what is an effective response? An organization has a choice of three fundamental strategies. First, it can become better at what it does—for example, by lowering costs and prices, by improving its products or services, or by offering better customer service. A second response is to change the structure of an industry. For example, unable to compete effectively with bookstore chains, such as Barnes & Noble, Amazon.com pioneered the idea of selling books on the Web. As a third response, an organization can create a new product or service. The music industry responded to pirated music tapes by promoting difficult-to-copy audio CD technology.

Business analysts continuously devise new techniques for responding to opportunities and threats, such as automation, downsizing, total quality management, re-engineering, "just in time" inventory, employee empowerment, and e-commerce. Let's look at how A&L has responded to some of the challenges it faced throughout the years.

A&L was founded in 1892. At first it had only one office, located in the heart of London. Business was conducted in person and by mail until A&L installed a new and revolutionary technology, the telephone. The telephone enhanced communications among A&L, its customers, and its suppliers, but it did nothing to change the basic way employees processed and shipped customer orders—everything was done manually.

In the 1950s, "automation" was fashionable. A&L installed a system of pneumatic tubes to transport order forms quickly from the salesroom to the warehouse. **Automation** is the use of electrical or mechanical devices to improve manufacturing or other processes.

A&L added branch outlets in the 1970s and took a big step into **computerization** by purchasing a minicomputer and hiring information system staff to write programs to process orders and track inventory. The computer system was a success—A&L managers always knew what was in stock and could place timely orders to restock the warehouse.

In the 1980s, despite the computerized inventory system, customers were defecting to competitors that promised faster delivery. A&L tried a technique called TQM to increase customer satisfaction by decreasing shipping times. **TQM** (total quality management) is a strategy in which an organization makes a commitment to analyzing and improving the quality of its products or services. A&L used computers to track the entire shipping process. Managers analyzed this data and then devised a plan to streamline shipping operations. Shipping operations were made even more efficient by distributing some warehousing operations to the outlets. Each outlet now kept its own stock of frequently ordered products, ready for immediate delivery. Employees were empowered to make more decisions, such as what to stock for their local markets. **Employee empowerment** means giving employees the authority to make business decisions.

A&L's centralized minicomputer system was not designed for this distributed inventory structure, so in 1992 the company's managers decided to move to a new computerized inventory system. They decided to "rightsize" by moving inventory management from the minicomputer to networked microcomputers. **Rightsize** means to find the most effective configuration for human and computer resources. It often means moving operations from a mainframe computer system to a network of smaller computers.

To further improve the company, A&L managers considered **business process redesign** (BPR), which requires radical changes to existing business practices to achieve improvements in performance. They considered, but rejected, **just-in-time inventory management**, which would reduce inventory costs if merchandise was ordered from A&L's suppliers only when a customer ordered an item from A&L.

In 1999, A&L once again took a look at its computer system to figure out how to provide an e-commerce Web site with up-to-date inventory information that would let customers know exactly what was in stock at the time they placed an order.

Techniques for improving organizations fade in and out of popularity. What's important is that organizations continually strive to improve their products and services.

QUICKCHECK A

1 A(n) [_____] system collects, maintains, and provides information to people.

2 All activities that take place in an organization should contribute to the organizational [_____].

3 Organizations must successfully respond to opportunities and [_____], or they will cease to exist.

4 [_____] is the use of electrical or mechanical devices to improve manufacturing and other business processes.

5 [_____] is a strategy in which an organization makes a commitment to analyzing and implementing ways to improve the quality of its products and services.

6 Some companies [_____] by moving operations from a mainframe computer to a microcomputer network.

 Check Answers

PEOPLE, DECISIONS, AND INFORMATION

Every organization requires people. To coordinate the activities of its employees, most organizations have an organizational structure that arranges employees in ascending order of authority and pay. An organizational chart, such as the one in Figure 12-4, depicts the pyramid-shaped hierarchy of employees in an organization such as A&L Outfitters.

FIGURE 12-4

At the top of most organizations is a single individual. As you progress down the organizational chart, each level fans out to encompass more employees.

InfoWeb
8

Organizational
Charts

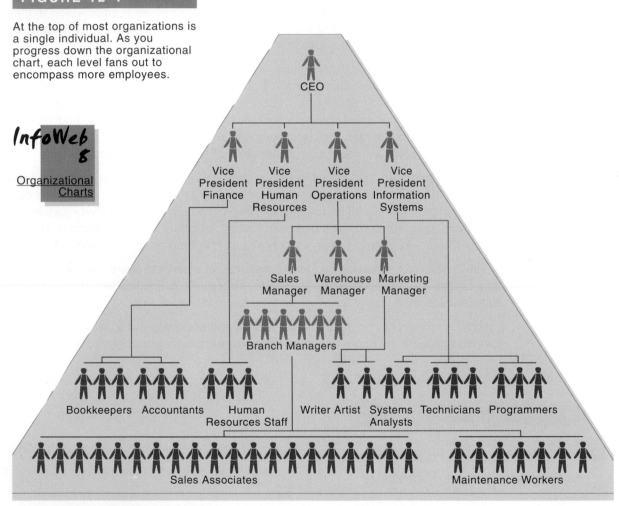

People in the organizational pyramid can be classified as either workers or managers. **Workers** are the people who carry out the organization's mission. For example, they assemble cars, write newspaper articles, sell merchandise, answer telephones, lay bricks, cut trees, or fix engines. Workers are usually supervised by managers.

Managers determine organizational goals and plan what steps to take to achieve those goals. They approve new products, authorize new construction, and supervise workers.

Workers and managers all perform activities that contribute to the success of an organization. In the course of their work, both workers and managers are required to make decisions. To appreciate the significance of an information system, it's useful to understand the types of decisions made by people at each level of the organizational pyramid.

Workers

Do workers use information systems? In today's workplace, a high percentage of workers use information systems and other computer or communications technologies. The technology available to a worker depends on what the organization provides and what is needed to do the job. Every worker's situation is unique, but it is possible to make some generalizations about the technology that workers use by looking at worker classifications. Some business experts classify workers as information workers, service workers, or goods workers. These workers are the foundation of the organizational pyramid, as shown in Figure 12-5.

FIGURE 12-5

Worker classification in the organizational pyramid.

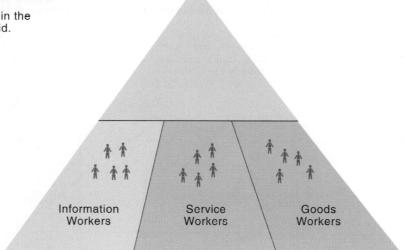

Information Workers   Service Workers   Goods Workers

Information workers produce and manipulate information. Examples of information workers include architects, writers, computer programmers, secretaries, and accountants. These workers often make extensive use of information systems. A computer is one of the information worker's most important tools.

Service workers are employees whose primary activity is delivering services to customers. Examples of service workers include sales associates, taxi drivers, nurses, and receptionists. Service workers often use information systems, but their main focus is person-to-person interaction.

Goods workers create and manipulate physical objects. Examples of goods workers include farmers, construction workers, assembly-line workers, miners, mechanics, and plumbers. Goods workers sometimes use computerized equipment and robots to manipulate and analyze physical objects.

A&L employees include information workers and service workers. Like many of today's businesses, A&L does not have goods workers because it does not manufacture any products. According to the U. S. Department of Labor, less than 20 percent of the labor force in the United States is employed as goods workers. England, Canada, France, and Germany have work forces with similar compositions. Figure 12-6 on the next page describes the jobs of A&L service and information workers.

FIGURE 12-6

A&L workers.

Accountants and bookkeepers are information workers. They keep track of cash flowing in and out of the business. Bookkeepers are typically responsible for sending customer bills and recording customer payments. They also make sure that A&L promptly pays its own bills for inventory, phone, electricity, and so on.

The human resources staff consists of secretarial and clerical information workers. They continually monitor employee contracts, insurance policies, and other benefit programs.

Sales associates are service workers who help customers by taking orders and recommending products.

Information system staff members are information workers such as programmers, systems analysts, and Web designers who use computers to plan and implement changes to A&L's information system.

A&L's technicians are service workers who install, move, and repair in-house computers.

A&L's in-house writer and artist are information workers. The writer produces advertising copy and product descriptions, assisted by the artist, who supplies graphics. Both use computers to produce their work, and they make extensive use of the Web for ideas.

Managers

What managerial tasks are enhanced by information systems? Just as there are different types of workers, so there are different types of managers, with different responsibilities in an organization. Managers are classified as executive managers, middle managers, or supervisors, as shown in Figure 12-7.

FIGURE 12-7

Managerial levels of the organizational pyramid.

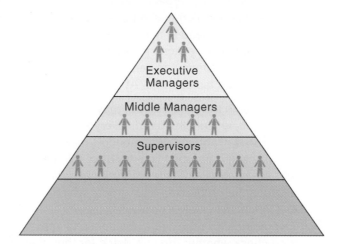

Executive managers, sometimes referred to as "senior managers," set long-range goals for an organization. They are typically entrepreneurs who create new businesses under the expectation that they will be a long-range success. They create the mission statement for an organization. They also cultivate business relationships with bankers, politicians, and other industry leaders in case their influence is needed in the future. This emphasis on long-range and future goals is referred to as **strategic planning**.

A&L's founder stated the company's mission as "providing the highest-quality expedition equipment and exceptional customer service." Today, A&L's chief executive officer is trying to anticipate market changes in the next 5 to 10 years. He is using A&L's information system to assist with this planning effort.

Middle managers are responsible for designing ways to achieve the plans laid out by executive managers. In general, middle managers decide how to deploy human, financial, and natural resources to achieve organizational goals. This type of action planning is referred to as **tactical planning**.

At A&L, middle managers are responsible for figuring out how to achieve the founder's mission of providing high-quality equipment and exceptional customer service. Several years ago, a group of managers made plans to create a quality assurance lab to test new products. The managers used data from A&L's information system to identify financial resources for the new test lab. Using these financial resources, they found a suitable location and hired employees to staff the lab.

Supervisors are managers who deal primarily with day-to-day operations. They schedule and monitor workers and processes. Scheduling and monitoring are sometimes referred to as **operational planning**. At A&L, the quality assurance lab supervisor receives a list of new products. Using computerized scheduling capabilities provided by A&L's information system, the supervisor assigns each product to a tester and schedules the test date. After testing is complete, results are stored in the information system so that they can be accessed by sales associates who are consulting with customers.

Problems and Decisions

How do workers and managers use information systems? One of the major functions of an information system is to help people make decisions in response to problems. Problems occur at all levels of an organization and require strategic, tactical, or operational solutions and decisions. According to Herbert Simon, who is well known for his insights into organizational behavior and for his pioneering role in artificial intelligence, the decision-making process has three phases. First, a person must recognize a problem or a need to make a decision. Next, he or she must devise and analyze possible solutions or actions to solve the problem. Finally, the person selects an action or solution. Sometimes, the decision-making phases are clear-cut, objective, standardized, and based on factual data. At other times, decision making is more intuitive.

All problems are not alike, but they can be classified into three types: structured, semi-structured, and unstructured. Everyday, run-of-the-mill, and routine problems are called **structured problems**. When people make decisions in response to structured problems, the procedure for obtaining the best solution is known, the objective is clearly defined, and the information necessary to make the decision is easy to identify. An example of a structured problem is figuring out which customers should receive overdue notices. The information for this decision is usually stored in a file cabinet or in a computer system. The method for reaching a solution is to look for customers with outstanding balances, then check whether the due dates for their payments fall before today's date.

Semi-structured problems are less routine than structured problems. When solving a semi-structured problem, the procedure for arriving at a solution is usually known; however, it might involve some degree of subjective judgment. Also, some of the information regarding the problem might not be available, might lack precision, or might be uncertain. An example of a semi-structured problem at A&L is how to respond to last year's increase in the number of rain forest expeditions. Should A&L stock more warm-weather gear? Should it increase advertising in ecology publications? Managers at A&L can use data on last year's sales, last year's advertising, and projected advertising budgets to make the decision. However, there is no firm data about how many rain forest expeditions will actually take place. Therefore, the decision involves some degree of uncertainty.

Unstructured problems require human intuition as the basis for finding a solution. Information relevant to the problem might be missing, and few, if any, parts of the solution can be tackled using concrete models. An example of an unstructured problem at A&L would be whether to decrease inventory levels of cold-weather equipment in response to global warming trends. Inventory and sales information on cold-weather equipment exists for past years. Information on global warming, though it exists, is not definitive. To determine future inventory levels of cold-weather equipment, someone at A&L must make an educated guess based on historical inventory data and inconclusive information on climactic changes.

Computer information systems help people solve structured, semi-structured, and even unstructured problems. The degree of assistance that an information system provides will vary with the problem. Traditionally, computers have contributed most to solving structured problems. Although some computer tools can be applied to semi-structured and unstructured problems, these problems are still often resolved based on someone's "gut feeling."

Information and Information Analysis Tools

Where do computers get the information that they supply to the workers and managers who make decisions? Information systems are designed to collect information that workers and managers need to make decisions. This information comes from both internal and external sources. Organizations generate **internal information** about inventory levels, cash flow, personnel, customers, orders, sales, and so on. Today, this internal information is increasingly generated with the help of computerized input devices such as terminals, bar-code readers, and personal computers. Once it is generated, the information is stored in an information system.

Organizations collect **external information** from outside sources. External information, unlike internal information, is typically not stored permanently in an organization's information system. Instead, it is collected when needed for a specific purpose, then erased later when it is no longer needed.

Using Internet resources and other communications capabilities, it is becoming increasingly easy to collect external information about competitors' products, pricing, finances, and plans. Such information is often available from a company's Web site or from sites housing business publications or analyses. Organizations can also collect external information, such as mailing lists and credit reports, about potential customers. Other readily available external information includes patent information, demographics, labor statistics, maps, and government documents. Figure 12-8 illustrates one popular Web site for gathering external information on business competitors.

FIGURE 12-8

The Zacks Web site provides competitive information and news about businesses.

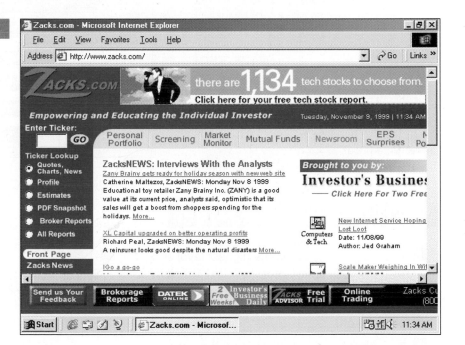

Information systems supply workers and managers with reports and information analysis software tools to manipulate information. Most information systems periodically produce a fixed set of reports, such as daily cash receipts or monthly sales summaries. In addition, some information systems allow users to customize their own reports to provide the right information in the right format for making a decision.

Information analysis tools help people model problems, then find a logical path to a solution or decision. Information analysis tools include spreadsheets, flowcharts, and special-purpose analysis software, such as the package shown in Figure 12-9.

FIGURE 12-9

When using Criterium DecisionPlus to select a college, you define criteria such as cost and academic program. After you provide weights for each criterion, the software displays a graph ranking each school.

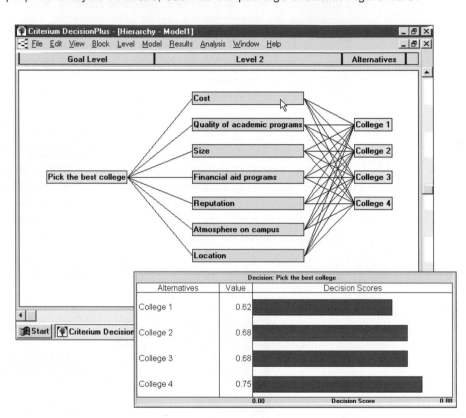

Start
Screentour

Q U I C K C H E C K   　　B

1 [　　　　　　] is the highest level of management in the organizational pyramid.

2 Less than 20 percent of the U.S. labor force consists of [　　　　　　] workers.

3 The managerial activity that emphasizes long-range and future goals is called [　　　　　　] planning.

4 Middle managers are typically responsible for [　　　　　　] planning.

5 [　　　　　　] problems require human intuition as the basis for decision making.

6 [　　　　　　] information is generated by the organization itself, whereas [　　　　　　] information is collected from sources outside the organization.

Check
Answers

SECTION C — INFORMATION SYSTEMS

The purpose of an information system is to improve the effectiveness of an organization by providing useful, accurate, and timely information. For example, a computerized information system helps A&L Outfitters improve the effectiveness of its operations by providing data communications among outlets, tracking orders from customers, scheduling shipments to expedition base camps, and tracking inventory at each branch outlet

An information system might have one or more of the following components or subsystems: an office automation system, a transaction processing system, a management information system, a decision support system, and an expert system. Let's take a closer look at each of these systems.

Office Automation

Can an information system automate routine office tasks? As its name suggests, an **office automation system** "automates," or computerizes, routine office tasks. Word processing, spreadsheet, scheduling, databases, and e-mail software are integral parts of most office automation systems. LANs, intranets, and the Internet also play important roles in office automation by providing communications between workers and centralized storage for documents, reports, memos, and other data.

InfoWeb

Office Automation

A&L's office automation system uses electronic mail to overcome the problem of communicating between outlets in seven time zones. Word processing software helps with routine correspondence, such as responses to inquiries from potential customers, congratulatory messages to successful expeditions, and letters to suppliers. In the London office, scheduling software maintains appointment calendars for A&L sales agents and executives.

Transaction Processing

How does an organization collect information on production or operations?

In an information system context, a **transaction** is an event that requires a manual or computer-based activity. When you order a product at a Web site or buy merchandise in a store, you are involved in a transaction. When you make a phone call or pay your phone bill, you are also involved in a transaction. Most transactions require a sequence of steps. For example, to pay your phone bill, you must receive the bill, write a check for the amount, and place the check in the mail. Then, the post office must deliver your payment to the phone company, and the phone company must record the payment. For the transaction to be successful, all steps of the transaction process must be completed. If even one step fails, the entire transaction has failed.

The production activities of an organization usually involve one or more transactions. A **transaction processing system** (TPS) keeps track of the transactions for an organization by providing a way to collect, store, display, modify, or cancel transactions. Examples of transaction processing systems that are found in businesses today include the following:

■ A **point-of-sale (POS) system** that records items purchased at each cash register and calculates the total amount due for each sale. Some POS systems automatically verify credit cards, calculate change, and identify customers who have previously written bad checks.

InfoWeb 10

Transaction Processing

- An **order-entry/invoice system** that provides a way to input, view, modify, and delete customer orders. It helps track the status of each order, and it creates invoices.

- A **general accounting system** that records the financial status of a business by keeping track of income, expenses, and assets.

- An **e-commerce system** that collects online orders and processes credit card payments.

The data that is used by a transaction processing system is typically stored in files or databases and can be used to produce a regularly scheduled set of reports, such as monthly bills, weekly paychecks, annual inventory summary, daily manufacturing schedules, or periodic check registers. Figure 12-10 diagrams the processes that take place in a typical transaction processing system.

FIGURE 12-10

Characteristics of a transaction processing system.

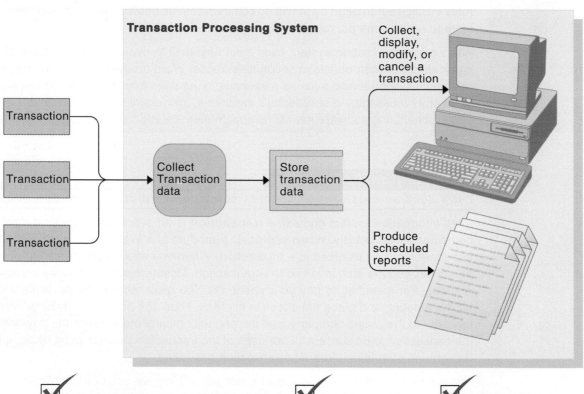

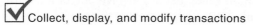

☑ Collect, display, and modify transactions   ☑ Store transactions   ☑ List transactions

Transaction processing systems at A&L Outfitters computerize order entry, invoicing, inventory control, and general accounting. Study Figure 12-11 to learn how A&L's current order entry system processes transactions for customer orders.

FIGURE 12-11

A&L's transaction processing system.

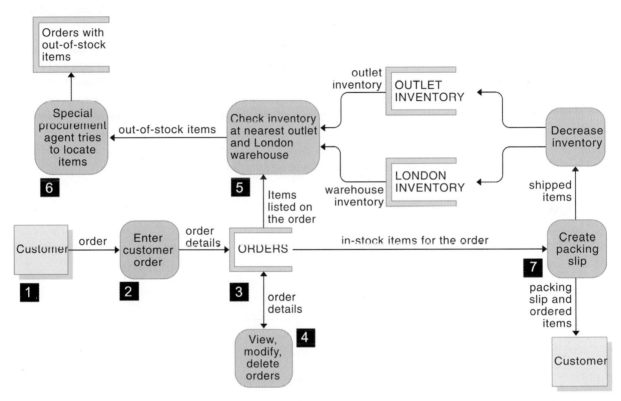

1 A customer wants to order equipment and supplies.

2 A sales representative takes an order from a customer by entering the customer's selections on a microcomputer connected to A&L's network. Occasionally, A&L agents are dispatched to remote locations, where they take orders on a notebook computer, then send the completed order to the London office using a modem.

3 The order is stored on the network file server.

4 Sales associates can modify an order if a customer wants to add or change items. If an expedition is canceled, the order can be deleted.

5 Each item on the order is checked against the existing inventory. If it is not in stock at the local outlet, a telecommunications link to London checks whether the item is available from the central warehouse.

6 Ordered items that are not in stock locally or in the central warehouse are tracked down by a special procurement agent.

7 A list of available items becomes the packing slip that accompanies the shipment to the customer.

A&L's e-commerce Web site currently runs as a stand-alone application, not linked to the transaction processing system. A&L analysts are currently trying to determine the feasibility of providing the company's e-commerce customers with information about merchandise availability. Would this feature require fundamental changes in A&L's transaction processing system? One possibility would be to create a new e-commerce application that ties into step 2 of the transaction shown in Figure 12-11. Customer orders could be transferred to the TPS, which would check merchandise availability before finalizing the order.

Management Information Systems

How can the data collected by a transaction processing system be presented in a format that is more conducive to decision making? A transaction processing system is designed mainly for use by clerical personnel to record transactions. Most transaction processing systems generate a limited number of reports that provide a basic record of completed transactions. However, managers need more sophisticated reports to help them understand and analyze data. These reports are usually created by a management information system.

The term "management information system" is used in two contexts. It can be a synonym for the term "information system," or it can refer to a specific category or type of information system. We'll use the term **management information system** (MIS) in this second context, to refer to a type of information system that uses the data collected by a transaction processing system but manipulates that data to create reports that managers can use to make routine business decisions in response to structured problems. As Figure 12-12 shows, an MIS is characterized by the production of routine reports that managers use for structured and routine tasks.

FIGURE 12-12

Characteristics of a management information system.

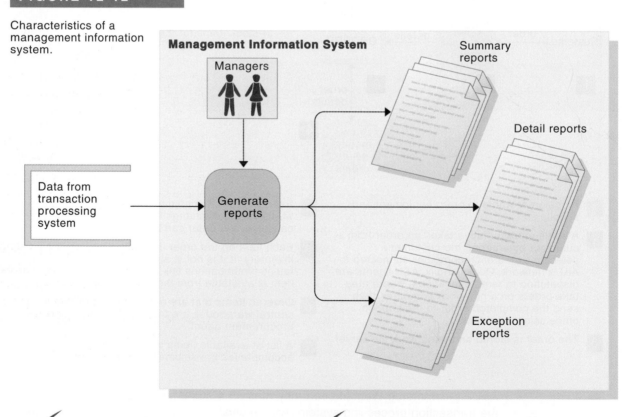

Management Information System

Managers

Data from transaction processing system → Generate reports → Summary reports / Detail reports / Exception reports

☑ Produce routine and on-demand reports

☑ Increase efficiency of managerial activity

☑ Provide information for managerial activities

☑ Provide information for structured, routine decisions

One of the major goals of an MIS is to increase the efficiency of managerial activity. As you learned earlier in this chapter, different levels of management have different information needs. In response to these different needs, a management information system produces several types of reports. A **detail report** is an organized list—for example, a report of inventory items alphabetized by product name. Such reports are suitable for some supervisory activities, but they are rarely used for tactical or strategic planning. A **summary report** combines or groups data and often shows totals. For example, a summary report might show the total annual sales for the past five years. Summary reports are useful in tactical and strategic planning. An **exception report** like the one in Figure 12-13 contains information that is outside of normal or acceptable ranges, such as a reorder report showing low-stock items in inventory.

FIGURE 12-13

Exception reports help managers take action, such as reordering inventory. Managers also use exception reports to analyze potential problems, such as continued inventory shortages or large numbers of customers making late payments.

Low Stock Inventory — London			
Item#	**Description**	**QOH**	**Vendor**
00876543	Qualo-fil Sleeping bag	3	REI
00887654	Sm. Alum. Backpack - red	10	Sierra
01456788	Waterproof matches	23	Striker

The A&L management information system supplies managers of branch outlets with many reports, produced on a daily, weekly, or monthly basis. Once a day, the managers at each branch outlet receive a summary report showing the number of orders filled, the total amount due for the orders, the number of payments received, and the total amount of all payments. On a weekly basis, the inventory manager of each branch outlet receives a report that lists inventory items that need to be reordered. Every month, each branch outlet manager receives a summary report of total income and expenses for the branch. Also on a monthly basis, the Vice President of Sales in the London office receives a summary report showing income and expenses for all branches, along with the total profit for the entire company.

To create these reports, the MIS extracts, sorts, and totals the data from the transaction processing system. The specifications for most of these reports were created by A&L's information systems department when the MIS was designed. Managers at A&L can also request customized reports if the standard reports do not meet their needs. However, they can request reports based only on the data collected by the TPS and MIS systems. To incorporate data from external information systems or to create data models of "what-if" scenarios, A&L's managers would need to use a decision support system.

Decision Support Systems

Can managers and workers get information relevant to problems that weren't anticipated when the information system was designed? A **decision support**

InfoWeb
11
DSS

system (DSS) allows users to manipulate data directly, to incorporate data from external sources, and to create data models of "what-if" scenarios. A DSS is designed to help managers and workers make non-routine decisions, such as solving a semi-structured problem in which the decision might be based on imprecise data or might require "guesstimates." Decision makers use a DSS to design decision models and make queries. A **decision model** is a numerical representation of a realistic situation, such as a cash-flow model of a business that shows how income adds to cash accounts and expenses deplete those accounts. A **decision query** is a question or set of instructions describing the data that needs to be gathered to make a decision.

A decision support system derives its name from the fact that it "supports" the decision maker; that is, it provides the tools the decision maker needs to examine the data. However, a DSS does not make decisions—that task remains the responsibility of the human decision maker.

A DSS typically includes modeling tools, such as spreadsheets, so managers can create a numerical representation of a situation and explore "what-if" alternatives. A DSS also typically includes statistical tools so that managers can study trends before making a decision. In addition, a DSS usually includes data from the organization's transaction processing system and it might include or access external data such as stock market reports, as shown in Figure 12-14.

FIGURE 12-14

Characteristics of a decision support system.

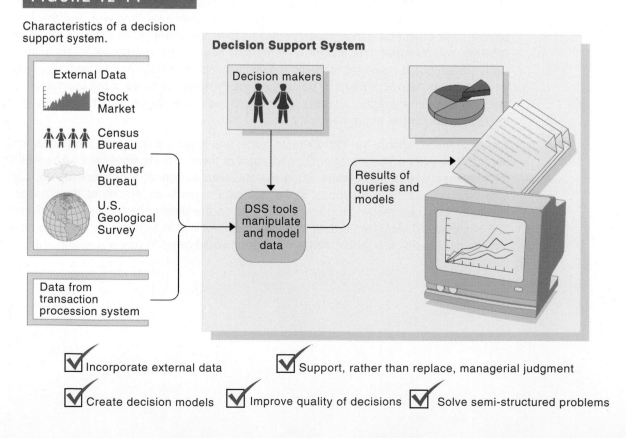

✓ Incorporate external data   ✓ Support, rather than replace, managerial judgment

✓ Create decision models   ✓ Improve quality of decisions   ✓ Solve semi-structured problems

The managers at A&L Outfitters use their DSS to tackle diverse problems because it contains a good selection of decision support tools. For example, one A&L branch outlet manager is using the DSS to project next year's sales of cold-weather camping equipment. To make this projection, he first retrieves from the A&L transaction processing system the data on the past two years' sales of each item of cold-weather camping equipment. He then transfers the data into a spreadsheet so that he can manipulate it and examine several "what-if" scenarios. He uses the DSS link to a commercial information service to filter through articles about camping, recreation, and weather. For example, the manager discovers that weather systems last year were especially intense. Because of the bad weather, expeditions to cold climates were not advisable and sales of cold-weather equipment declined.

Next, the manager uses the DSS to search through an A&L database that contains information on all expeditions sent out during the past five years. The DSS helps him create a graph showing that expeditions to cold regions declined last year after a steady increase for the previous three years. Should he gamble and assume that last year was an unusual deviation in a steadily increasing cold-weather equipment market? By manipulating the data in the spreadsheet, the manager looks at best- and worse-case scenarios and decides that it is not too risky to order 5 percent more cold-weather camping equipment.

InfoWeb 12

Expert Systems

Expert Systems and Neural Networks

Do information systems ever make decisions? You've just seen how a DSS helps a manager manipulate the data necessary to make a decision. The DSS does not make a decision, however. Instead, the manager must analyze the data and reach a decision. The DSS does not substitute for the judgment of the manager, which is appropriate in situations where trained professionals are making decisions. On the other hand, in many organizations, it would be useful if every decision did not need to be made by a highly paid expert.

An **expert system**, sometimes referred to as a "knowledge-based system," is a computer system designed to analyze data and produce a recommendation or decision. An expert system is a computerized expert, as explained in Figure 12-15.

FIGURE 12-15

An expert system encapsulates the knowledge of a human expert within a narrowly defined area, such as spectral analysis, medical diagnosis, or geological formations.

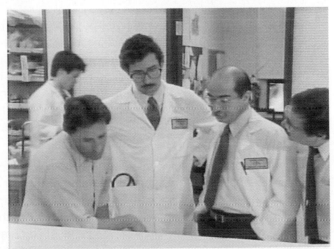

Start
Video

To create an expert system, the knowledge of an expert about a particular type of decision is captured in a set of facts and rules called a **knowledge base**. A knowledge base is stored in a computer file and then manipulated by software called an **inference engine**. When it is time to make a decision, the inference engine begins analyzing the available data by following the rules in the knowledge base. If the expert system needs additional data, it checks external databases, looks for the data in a transaction processing system, or asks the user to answer questions, as shown in Figure 12-16.

FIGURE 12-16

Characteristics of an expert system.

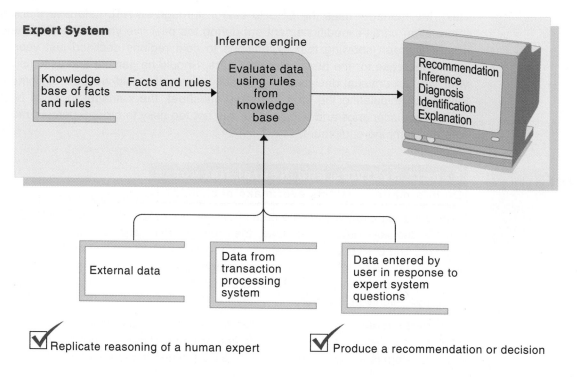

An expert system is not a general-purpose problem solver or decision maker. Each expert system is designed to make decisions in a particular area or "domain." For example, an expert system created for use at the Campbell Soup Company captured the knowledge of an expert cooking-vat operator to help less experienced employees troubleshoot problems that might arise as the soup cooks. Other expert systems have been developed to locate mineral deposits, diagnose blood diseases, evaluate corporate financial statements, underwrite complex insurance policies, and recommend stock purchases.

Expert systems are sometimes created by using a computer programming language, but more often they are created by using an expert system shell. An **expert system shell** is a software tool that helps in developing expert system applications. It is an expert system without any rules. The shell contains the inference engine and a method for entering the rules for the knowledge base. To create the expert system, you use the shell to enter the rules, then use the inference engine to test the rules and make certain that the decisions they produce are correct.

Expert systems are often designed to deal with data that is imprecise or with problems that have more than one solution. Using a technique called **fuzzy logic**, an expert system can deal with imprecise data by asking for a level of confidence. For example, suppose an expert system is helping you identify a whale you spotted off the coast of Hawaii. The expert system asks, "Did you see a dorsal fin?" You're not sure. You think you saw one, but it could have been a wave. If the expert system is using fuzzy logic, it will let you respond with something like "I'm 85 percent certain I saw a dorsal fin." Based on the confidence level of your answers to this and to other questions, the expert system might be able to tell you that it is "pretty sure," maybe 98 percent confident, that you saw a gray whale.

InfoWeb
13

Neural
Networks

An expert system begins with a set of facts and rules. But what if the rules are not known? Can a computer "learn" how to make decisions based on hundreds or thousands of lightning-fast attempts at trial and error? A **neural network** uses computer circuitry to simulate the way in which a brain might process information, learn, and remember. For example, a neural network could be connected to a digital projector that displays photos of people's faces. Which faces are males and which are females? The neural network begins with a list of criteria with no values attached. "Hair length" might be one criteria, but the neural net is not programmed to expect that females usually have longer hair than men. Based on the evidence, the neural network begins to establish its own criteria—its own rules—about the data. Neural networks have been successfully implemented in many business and financial applications where identification and trend analysis are important.

QUICKCHECK   C

1 Word processing software is likely to be part of a(n) _____ system.

2 An information system that collects information when customers purchase merchandise is a point-of-sale system that would be classified as a(n) _____ processing system.

3 A(n) _____ system is characterized by the production of regularly scheduled reports that managers use for structured and routine tasks.

4 A(n) _____ report contains information that is outside of normal or acceptable ranges, such as a reorder report showing inventory items that need to be restocked.

5 A(n) _____ system provides users with the ability to manipulate data directly, create data models, and incorporate external data.

6 A(n) _____ system is designed to capture the knowledge of a specialist in the form of rules. These rules are the basis for the computer to make a decision in response to a problem.

7 A(n) _____ contains an inference engine and a method for analyzing data, but does not contain any rules.

8 A(n) _____ uses computer circuitry to simulate the way in which the brain processes, learns, and remembers information.

Check Answers

CHAPTER 12

USER FOCUS   CREATING EXPERT SYSTEM FACTS AND RULES

What's really fascinating about an expert system is its ability to make inferences based on the rules and data in a knowledge base. This ability essentially means that an expert system can "think for itself" to draw conclusions from a set of facts.

You might have read J. R. R. Tolkien's fantasy novels about the adventures of Frodo and Bilbo Baggins. Tolkien's books are populated with an extensive cast of characters from several generations of hobbits. A genealogy chart would be useful to understand the family tree. For example, read through the facts in Figure 12-17 about the Baggins family and see if you can determine how Linda and Bungo are related.

FIGURE 12-17

Baggins family knowledge base.

> Linda is a female, her mother is Laura, her father is Mungo, and she is married to Bodo.
>
> Bilbo is a male, his mother is Belladonna, his father is Bungo, and he is single.
>
> Belba is a female, her mother is Laura, her father is Mungo, and she is married to Rudigar.
>
> Bungo is a male, his mother is Laura, his father is Mungo, and he is married to Belladonna.

InfoWeb 14

Rules

You were probably able to infer from these facts that Linda and Bungo are siblings—sister and brother, actually. What could a computer do with these facts? Computers, as you have probably heard, know only the facts they have been given. If you want a computer to know that Linda and Bungo are siblings, you have to explicitly enter this fact. This requirement was true until expert systems and logic programming were developed. Now, however, we can give an expert system the set of facts in Figure 12-17 and a general rule about siblings, such as "If two people have the same mother and father, they are siblings." The expert system can then use this rule to infer that Linda and Bungo are siblings.

Because the sibling rule is generic—because it doesn't mention any specific people—the expert system can use it to make inferences about other people in the knowledge base who are siblings. Suppose for a moment that you are the expert system's inference engine. Using the sibling rule, can you find any other siblings in the knowledge base shown in Figure 12-17?

Knowing that the purpose of an expert system is to use rules to make inferences based on a series of facts, you can see that the core activity for creating an expert system is writing facts and rules for the knowledge base. Let's take a closer look at the characteristics of facts and rules.

Facts

| How do I write the facts for a knowledge base? | A fact is a basic building block of a knowledge base. You can think of a fact as a statement or simple sentence. For example, here is a knowledge base with three simple facts:

> Belladonna is a female.
> Bilbo is a male.
> Belladonna is Bilbo's mother.

Once the facts are in a knowledge base, you can ask questions, and the expert system will search through the facts to produce an answer. For example, you might ask, "Is Bilbo a male?" and the expert system would respond with the answer "Yes." Or, you might ask, "Who is Bilbo's mother?" and the expert system would answer, "Belladonna." These answers seem obvious to you because you have seen the relevant rules in the knowledge base. However, in a realistic situation, the knowledge base might contain hundreds of facts about the Baggins family. You could ask, "Who was Balbo's wife?" The expert system could tell you that Balbo Baggins was married to Berylla.

The way you write the facts for a knowledge base depends on the development tool you use. With an expert system shell, you might be able to type the facts as simple sentences, such as "Belladonna is a female." If you use a programming language, such as Prolog, to construct your expert system, you might use a shorthand notation called **predicate logic**. Suppose that you want to enter a fact about Bilbo's parents. Instead of entering a rule like "Bilbo's mother is Belladonna and his father is Bungo," you can use the following predicate logic shorthand: parents('Bilbo', 'Belladonna', 'Bungo'). Using predicate logic, you put facts into the framework described in Figure 12-18.

FIGURE 12-18

Expressing facts using predicate logic.

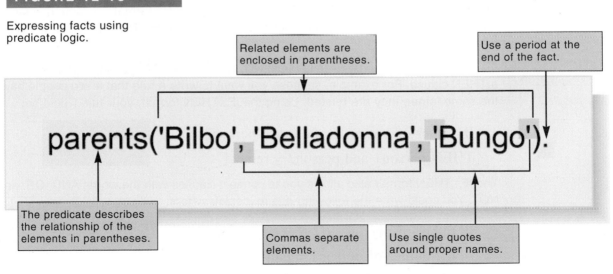

Related elements are enclosed in parentheses.

Use a period at the end of the fact.

parents('Bilbo', 'Belladonna', 'Bungo').

The predicate describes the relationship of the elements in parentheses.

Commas separate elements.

Use single quotes around proper names.

At the beginning of this *User Focus* section, you looked at a series of facts that described the Baggins family. Figure 12-19 shows these facts written in predicate logic.

FIGURE 12-19

Baggins facts in predicate logic format.

person('Linda', female, 'Laura', 'Mungo', 'Bodo').

person('Bilbo', male, 'Belladonna', 'Bungo', single).

person('Belba', female, 'Laura', 'Mungo', 'Rudigar').

person('Bungo', male, 'Laura', 'Mungo', 'Belladonna').

Rules

Can I use predicate logic for rules? As with facts, the way in which you enter the rules for an expert system depends on the development tool you use. You'll be disappointed to learn that most development tools do not allow you to enter rules in free-form English. Even though you might think of the siblings rule as "Any two people who have the same mother and father are siblings," you will not be able to use this wording when you enter the rule. The reason most expert system development tools do not accept free-form English rules is that such rules are often too ambiguous for the computer to use in making inferences. Therefore, a more structured format for writing rules is required. In general, a development tool requires you to use IF...THEN format or predicate logic to write rules.

IF...THEN format requires rules to begin with an IF clause. The IF clause is followed by a THEN clause. For example, suppose you want to write a rule that if two people have the same father, they are related. Using the IF...THEN format, your rule would be:

IF father-of-person1 = father-of-person2

THEN person1 and person2 = related

The IF...THEN format also allows you to connect clauses with the words AND, OR, and NOT. You could write the following rule to identify sisters:

IF father-of-person1 = father-of-person2

AND mother-of-person1 = mother-of-person2

AND person1=female

AND person2=female

THEN person1 and person2 = sisters

The format for predicate logic rules is a little more abstract, but it's fun to figure out how this shorthand works. First, think of the rule as the *outcome* followed by a series of facts that would make the outcome true. For example, you would think about the siblings rule as "Person A and Person B are siblings *if* Person A has a mother and father *and* Person B has the same mother and the same father."

Now take each clause, beginning with "Person A and Person B are siblings." How would you express this idea in predicate logic? You would write siblings(PersonA, PersonB). You make PersonA one word to show that it is one thing. If you wrote it "Person A" (with a space), the computer might think it was two things: one Person and some other thing called A. You must capitalize PersonA. Although it seems backward, the capitalization tells the computer that you're not referring to someone named "PersonA," such as a man named "Mr. PersonA." Instead, PersonA means any person, and the computer needs to figure out that person's name.

Next, how would you express "Person A has a mother and father" in predicate logic format? You would write person(PersonA, Mother, Father). Again, you capitalize Mother and Father to tell the computer that it needs to substitute some real mother and father names here. Can you guess how to express the clause, "Person B has a mother and father?"

When you write the clause person(PersonB, Mother, Father), how does it imply that Person B has the *same* mother and father as Person A? In the rule for Person B, you used "Mother" and "Father," just as you did in the rule for Person A. If you had written person(PersonB, Ma, Pa), you would be implying that Person A has different parents from Person B.

Now you need to join these clauses together. You use the symbols :– for "if". You use a comma to represent the word "and". Your completed rule is shown in Figure 12-20.

FIGURE 12-20

The siblings rule expressed in predicate logic.

siblings(PersonA, PersonB):-	Person A and Person B are siblings if
person(PersonA, Mother, Father),	Person A has a Mother and Father and
person(PersonB, Mother, Father).	Person B has [the same] Mother and [the same] Father.

As you can see, creating the facts and rules for an expert system exercises your mind. In everyday activities, you probably don't think about how you think. How did you look at the facts about the Baggins family and infer which hobbits were siblings? You "just did it," right? But when you write facts and rules for an expert system, you have to become aware of your own mental processes—how you analyze information and make decisions. The people who create expert systems have a job that is sometimes complex and often introspective. Their goal, however, is to create an expert system in which all of the details of a decision are hidden from the user. Therefore, using an expert system is much easier than creating one.

ISSUE   DO COMPUTER MODELS WORK?

In Tolkien's book *The Hobbit*, Bilbo Baggins, alone and lost in a dark tunnel, gropes about in the dark, finds a small ring, and drops it in his pocket. That seemingly insignificant incident set in motion events that would plunge the Hobbits' world into chaos.

InfoWeb
15

Chaos

According to some scientists, our world—the real world—is already chaotic. **Chaos theory**, more formally known as the "theory of complex dynamical nonlinear systems," is the study of unstable behavior in complex systems. The theory was first introduced by meteorologist Edward N. Lorenz. In 1960, Lorenz was trying to create a computer model to predict the weather. He noticed that just a small change in the initial conditions of his model would drastically alter its long-term weather predictions. This discovery came to be known as the Butterfly Effect and is described by Ian Stewart, author of *Does God Play Dice? The Mathematics of Chaos*, as follows: "The flapping of a single butterfly's wing today produces a tiny change in the state of the atmosphere. Over a period of time, what the atmosphere actually does diverges from what it would have done. So, in a month's time, a tornado that would have devastated the Indonesian coast doesn't happen. Or maybe one that wasn't going to happen, does."

Maybe you've played the popular computer game SimCity. This game simulates a complex system—a city populated with little "simmies" or simulated people who go to work, have kids, build houses, pile up garbage, and grumble when the electric company builds a nuclear power plant next door. In the game, you become the city planner and try to keep the simmies happy. What you soon discover is that a seemingly insignificant event might set in motion other events that can turn your once-thriving city into a ghost town. That insignificant event is an element of chaos.

How does chaos theory apply to information systems in organizations? An organization is a complex system. The members of an organization—managers, stockholders, and employees—typically want it to succeed, and they depend on computers to gather and analyze data that can be used to plan strategic improvements. Most current computer models, however, do not account for the possible effects of chaotic events. Therefore, despite powerful computer information systems, it is difficult to accurately predict the future and to understand whether organizational changes—new products, new markets, and so on—will succeed. This bleak outlook for computer models is summarized by Crossan, White, Lane, and Klus in a 1996 issue of *Organizational Dynamics*: "No matter how much we know..., no matter how powerful the computers are, specific long-range predictions are not feasible. We can know, but we cannot predict...."

It would seem that chaos theory essentially invalidates strategic planning and makes computer models obsolete. "Not so," say a hardy group of researchers who are trying to incorporate chaotic elements into computer models. They suggest that although a system might be complex, much of the complexity results from a huge number of inter-actions between essentially simple entities. Chris Meyer, who heads the Ernst & Young Center for Business Innovation, provides a colorful example: "Suppose you come down from Mars and you see taxicabs working the streets of New York. You want to simulate that. Each yellow car has a simple brain following a few simple rules: Stop for anything that waves. Go where it says." Meyer suggests that a model containing these simple rules will closely simulate what actually happens as taxis buzz around Times Square.

Researchers are working on such simulations. For example, programmers at the accounting firm of Coopers & Lybrand have developed a computer program designed to predict whether a new music CD will become a hit. The program contains 50,000 simulated people—simmies—who are fad-following music fans and whose record-buying habits have been determined from market research. For example, some of the simmies are programmed to run right out and buy any CD produced by their favorite musician, others wait until they've heard the song a few times on the radio, while others have "random" purchasing habits. After requesting some background information on the current popularity of the musician, the program sets the simulated music fans in action to see how many purchase the CD. Managers can use the simulation to make decisions about which new CDs to include in their product line.

Some experts believe that these simulations are accurate representations of a complex system and that they incorporate the Butterfly Effect—that in fact, every interaction could cause the Butterfly Effect. Other experts argue that we can never verify with cer-tainty that a computer model represents the world because we don't know whether it includes all possible factors or takes into account all possible starting values.

WHAT DO YOU THINK?

1. Does your intuition tell you that chaos theory
   is valid?   ○ Yes   ○ No   ○ Not sure

2. Does chaos theory invalidate deterministic
   tools, such as spreadsheet "what-if" analysis?   ○ Yes   ○ No   ○ Not sure

3. Is it possible to create a computer model
   that is an accurate representation of a
   complex system?   ○ Yes   ○ No   ○ Not sure

 Save Responses

INTERACTIVE SUMMARY

The Interactive Summary helps you select important concepts and facts from this chapter. Fill in the blanks to best complete each sentence. When using the NP4 CD or NP4 Web site, you can click the Check Answers buttons to automatically score your answers. Place your Tracking Disk in the floppy disk drive if you want to save your scores.

Computer [   ] systems play a key role in helping organizations achieve their goals, which are set forth in a(n) [   ] statement. These computer systems are used to record and improve organizational activities such as production, financial management, sales, and human resources management. Computers can be used by people at all levels of the organizational [   ]. [   ] workers use computers to produce and manipulate information. [   ] workers, such as wait staff and receptionists, mainly focus on person-to-person interaction, but often access computers to enter orders, schedule appointments, and track customer transactions. [   ] workers typically create and manipulate physical objects, sometimes using computerized equipment and robots. Managers depend on information systems to supply information that is essential for long-term [   ] planning and shorter-term tactical planning.

Office [   ] systems computerize routine tasks, such as producing form letters and tracking employee schedules. Transaction [   ] systems provide an organization with a way to collect, display, modify, or cancel transactions. These systems encompass activities such as general accounting and e-commerce.

 Check Answers

[   ] information systems typically build on the data collected by a TPS to produce reports that managers use for the business decisions needed to solve routine, structured problems. These reports might include a(n) [   ] report that lists transactions or other data, a(n) [   ] report that provides totals for grouped data, and a(n) [   ] report that contains information that is outside of normal or acceptable ranges.

A decision [   ] system helps workers and managers make non-routine decisions by constructing a decision model that includes data collected from internal and external sources. These models are designed to numerically represent real-world scenarios and allow users to explore a variety of [   ] alternatives. A(n) [   ] system is designed to analyze data and produce a recommendation or decision based on a set of facts and rules called a(n) [   ] base. These facts and rules can be created using an expert system shell or a logic programming language, such as Prolog. A(n) [   ] engine evaluates the facts and rules to produce answers to questions that have been posed to the system. Using a technique called [   ] logic, these systems can deal with imprecise data and with problems that have more than one solution.

 Check Answers

INTERACTIVE KEY TERMS

Make sure that you understand all of the boldfaced key terms presented in this chapter. If you're using the NP4 CD or NP4 Web site, you can use this list of terms as an interactive study activity. First, try to define a term in your own words, then click the term to compare your definition with the definition that is presented in the chapter.

INTERACTIVE QUIZZES

Quiz yourself on important concepts from this chapter by filling in the blanks. When using the NP4 CD or NP4 Web site, you can type your answers, then use the Check Answers buttons to automatically score your responses. Place your Tracking Disk in the floppy disk drive if you want to save your scores.

1 Michael Porter's Five Forces model specifies the five types of information systems that typically exist in an organization. True or false? _____

2 A spreadsheet would be considered one of many information _____ tools provided by an information system.

3 Many businesses today are adapting their _____ processing systems to accommodate e-commerce.

4 A decision model is a computer system designed to analyze a collection of facts and rules, then produce a recommendation or decision. True or false? _____

5 A(n) _____ network uses computer circuitry to simulate the way a brain might process information, learn, and remember.

6 If you create an expert system using Prolog, you will enter facts and rules using _____ logic.

7 According to _____ theory, seemingly insignificant changes in the starting parameters for a computer model can cause drastic changes in the model's predictions.

Check Answers

Study the diagram, then fill in the blanks to complete each statement below.

1 The diagram depicts a(n) _____ processing system.

2 A(n) _____ report would list the transactions stored in the area labeled "Orders."

3 The procurement agent could use a(n) _____ report to see which inventory items are out of stock.

4 A(n) _____ system could collect online orders from the customers shown on the diagram.

5 _____ workers would typically access the information in this system.

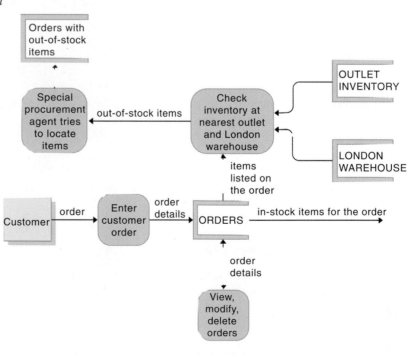

Check Answers

INTERACTIVE PRACTICE TESTS

When you use the NP4 CD or NP4 Web site, you can take practice tests that consist of 10 multiple-choice, true/false, and fill-in-th-blank questions. The 10 questions are selected at random from a large test bank, so each time you take a test, you'll receive a different set of questions. Your tests are scored immediately and you can print study guides that help you find the correct answers for any questions that you missed. If you are using a Tracking Disk, insert it in the floppy disk drive to save your test scores.

 Start Practice
Test

STUDY TIPS

Study Tips help you organize and consolidate the information in a chapter by making lists, outlines, charts, and sketches. You can use paper and pencil or word processing software to complete most of the Study Tips activities.

1 Divide a sheet of paper into four quadrants labeled Operations, Sales and Marketing, Human Resources, and Financial Management. In each quadrant, list at least five examples of a specific organization's activities. For example, in the Operations quadrant, you might list "A computer manufacturer assembles microcomputers."

2 Refer to Michael Porter's Five Forces model in Figure 12-3. For each of the following events, indicate whether it would be classified as bargaining power of suppliers, threat of new entrants, bargaining power of buyers, threat of substitute products or services, or rivalry among existing competitors.

   a. The value of the dollar falls in world markets, making Japanese car imports very expensive.

   b. Luxury-car makers move into the utility vehicle market, offering upscale competition to the once-popular Jeep Cherokee.

   c. 3½-inch disk drives become popular with computer users.

   d. Fighting in the Middle East results in serious oil shortages.

   e. Cable TV companies offer two-way communications links for sending computer data.

3 Without looking back in this chapter, draw an organizational pyramid showing the three levels of management and the three categories of workers.

4 Classify the following as information workers, goods workers, or service workers:

Secretaries	Miners	Construction workers
Electricians	Dock workers	Cashiers
Beauticians	Actors	Writers
Scientists	Welders	Chefs

5 List the three fundamental strategies that an organizational can use to respond to threats or take advantage of opportunities.

6 Create a summary table or grid to illustrate the differences between structured, semi-structured, and unstructured problems.

7 Create a chart or table that summarizes the characteristics of transaction processing systems, management information systems, decision support systems, and expert systems.

8 Look at the following knowledge base expressed in predicate logic format. Does the rule at the end identify brothers, sisters, friends, or cousins? If an expert system uses this knowledge base, what will it infer? (Careful, it's tricky!)

male(sam).

male(charlie).

male(linus).

male(pat).

male(george).

female(lucy).

female(lynn).

female(amanda).

female(gretchen).

parents(linus, amanda, sam).

parents(lynn, amanda, sam).

parents(pat, gretchen, george).

brothers(X,Y):–
    male(X),
    parents(X, Mother, Father),
    male (Y),
    parents(Y, Mother, Father).

PROJECTS

A project is an open-ended activity that will help you apply the concepts you have learned. Many projects require resources in addition to your textbook, such as current magazines, library materials, or Web access. When you tackle a project, be prepared to use your critical thinking skills, logical analysis, and your creativity.

1 **Mission, Threats, and Opportunities** Suppose that you are a management consultant for one of the following well-known companies. The company needs to produce a mission statement, and it is your job to help. The company also wants to know what factors might influence its business in the future. Pick one of the companies. Use library or Internet resources to find some background information on the company. Write a mission statement for your company, then use Michael Porter's Five Forces model as the basis for listing five factors that you think are likely to affect your company's business in the next year or two.

Ziff-Davis

Nike

Black & Decker

Harley-Davidson

Mattel

Intel

Royal Caribbean Cruise Line

2 Organizational Activities Think of any real or hypothetical business or nonprofit organization. Assume that the organization is divided into four departments—operations, financial management, sales and marketing, and human resources management. Write a one-paragraph summary of the types of activities that would be handled by each of the four departments.

3 Responding to a Threat Assume that you are the manager of a bookstore, located in a mall. Business seems to be declining as increasing numbers of your previous customers shop at online bookstores. Write a short paper explaining how you would deal with this threat and keep the bookstore profitable.

4 Taking Advantage of Opportunities Assume that you are the manager of a medium-sized snowmobile company. Jet skis are just becoming popular. Write a short paper explaining why you think your company should or should not get into the jet ski business.

5 Evaluating Strategies Assume that you are the president of a national fast-food chain. The board of directors has proposed that you empower the employees at the local outlets by allowing them to make decisions about menu items, restaurant decor, and general operations. List three possible advantages to this approach. List three possible disadvantages to this approach.

6 Researching Decision Support Systems Assume that you are the Information Systems Director for a manufacturer of office furniture. The president of the company has asked you to learn more about decision support systems. Use the library or the World Wide Web to search for information about current decision support systems. Make a list of ten DSS resources and write a one-sentence description of each.

7 The Russian Royal Family Your organization is preparing a Web site containing genealogical information on royal families from around the world. You have been asked to collect information on the Russian czars. Use your library or the Internet to find the full name, mother's name, father's name, spouse's name, and siblings for each of the last three Russian czars. Record this information as if you were going to use it in a knowledge base. Use the predicate logic syntax you learned in the *User Focus* section.

ADDITIONAL PROJECTS

Click the underlined text to link to the NP4 Web site (www.cciw.com/np4), where you can view and print additional projects for this chapter.

Neural Networks

Chaos Theory

INFOWEB

The InfoWeb is your guide to print, film, television, and electronic resources. Use it to obtain updates on quickly changing technical information and to locate information for research papers. If you're using the NP4 CD, click the InfoWeb Site icon on the left side of this paragraph to access the online InfoWeb links. Otherwise, use your Web browser and type in the address of the New Perspectives Web site: www.cciw.com/np4. At the Web site you'll find up-to-date links to the topics covered in this chapter.

1 Hobbits

If you haven't read J. R. R. Tolkien's books, you've missed out on a really great adventure. Start with *The Hobbit* and then move directly to the trilogy *Lord of the Rings*. Tolkien has a dedicated following on the Web. Try the Grey Havens site at *tolkien.cro.net*, where you'll find maps of Middle Earth, original art, songs, and discussion groups. At *www.geocities.com/Area51/Vault/7882/tolkiennav.html,* you'll find more information about hobbits and the Tolkien universe, along with lots of links to other sites. For the latest facts and rumors about the *Lord of the Rings* movie, visit sites such as *www.xenite.org/faqs/lotr_movie/index.html* or *fandom.com/ringbearer*. By the way, "hobbit" is also a somewhat obscure computer term that refers to the high-order bit—that's the leftmost bit in a sequence of 1s and 0s.

2 Peter Drucker

Peter Drucker is known as a somewhat unorthodox analyst of business, economics, politics, and society. He is extensively quoted and has written 28 books that have been translated into more than 20 languages. One of his most recent books, *Managing in a Time of Great Change* (Plume, 1998), includes some insights on how information systems can help a business succeed in the emerging global market. His book *Management Challenges for the 21st Century* (Harperbusiness, 1999) is a must-read as the new century begins. You'll find a short biography of Drucker at *www.cgu.edu/drucker* hosted by the Peter F. Drucker Graduate School of Management at Claremont Graduate University. You can get a quick overview of the Peter F. Drucker Foundation for Nonprofit Management by visiting *www.pfdf.org*, and don't miss the *Wired* magazine interview with the "arch-guru of capitalism" at *www.wired.com/wired/archive/1.03/drucker.html*.

3 Business: Terminology and Magazines

Information systems are one of the building blocks of modern businesses and organizations. If you're thinking about a career in computer information systems, it will pay to be familiar with current terms and trends in the corporate world. The Management and Technology Dictionary at *www.euro.net/innovation/Management_Base/Mantec.Dictionary.html* bills itself as the "largest Internet dictionary on management and technology. Yogesh Malhotra's award-winning site at *www.brint.com* contains a superb collection of information on many aspects of business and technology. *Outlook* (*www.ac.com:80/overview/Outlook/6.98/over_currentf1.html*) is an electronic magazine on "changing for success," from Andersen Consulting. The popular print magazine, *Upside*, has a Web counterpart at *www.upside.com*, where you can read about the latest trends in business technology. Another business magazine, *Forbes*, also has a companion Web site at *www.forbes.com*. For a more academic perspective, you might connect to the Technology Review from MIT at *www.techreview.com*.

4 Mission Statements

You can read the mission statements for a variety of businesses by entering "mission statement" in any Web search engine. You'll find information on how to develop a mission statement in the online SOHO Guidebook at *www.toolkit.cch.com/Text/P03_4001.htm*. It's not a new idea, but many business consultants suggest that in addition to a mission statement, a business should have a "story." Read about the benefits of a business story in Edward O. Welles's timeless article, "Why Every Company Needs a Story." You'll find this article at *www.inc.com/articles/details/0,6378,ART1658_CNT53,00.html*. Vist *www.wiley.com/products/subject/business/forbes/forbes.html* to download sample material from *Forbes Greatest Business Stories of All Times* (John Wiley & Sons, 1997).

5 Competition

Business and competition go hand-in-hand in today's marketplace. Michael Porter's Five Forces model illustrates how competitive forces shape a business. You'll find a visualization of the Five Forces model at *www.infonortics.com/archives/1997agsiconference/moffett/sld012.htm* and a slide show presentation at *www.mgt.smsu.edu/cbppt/mgt487_3/ppframe.htm*. Porter's book *Competitive Advantage: Creating and Sustaining Superior Performance* (Free Press, 1998) contains a full discussion of competitive theory. Strategic information systems help companies succeed in an increasingly competitive market. Read how one company, ChemQuest, employs Porter's Analysis Model to determine the sustainability of profits by visiting *www.chemquest.com/sustain.htm* and using the Next button to navigate the site. Roger Clarke has written a superb summary of classic business theory relating to strategic information systems. You'll find his article, "The Path of Development of Strategic Information Systems Theory," at *www.anu.edu.au/people/Roger.Clarke/SOS/StratISTh*.

6 TQM

The American Society for Quality promotes quality concepts, principles, and techniques. Its Web site at *www.asq.org* includes FAQs and a glossary. Good books on the topic include *The Deming Route to Quality and Productivity: Road Maps and Roadblocks* (WWS, 1986) and *Deming's Road to Continual Improvement* (SPC Press, 1991), both by William W. Scherkenbach. In the United States, something of a national frenzy erupted over "quality" in the 1980s and as a result, the U.S. Congress created a 1988 law establishing the Malcolm Baldrige National Quality Award. You can read about it at *www.quality.nist.gov/law.htm* and *www.asq.org/abtquality/awards/baldrige.html*.

One derivative of quality management is called "benchmarking." The American Productivity and Quality Center hosts a Web site at *www.apqc.org/best* that provides links to benchmarking sites. You'll find a good executive summary of benchmarking by Peter Griffin at *www.quality.co.uk/benchadv.htm*. Japanese corporations are widely envied for their exacting quality control. The NASA Web pages at *mijuno.larc.nasa.gov/dfc/kai.html* provide information about a Japanese quality technique called "Kaizen."

7 BPR

The classic definition of BPR is a six-step approach to radical redesign of business processes. For a summary of this six-step approach, visit *www.abs.uci.edu/depts/facil/renovate/bpi_what.html*. At *www.brint.com/papers/bpr.htm*, you'll find an excellent overview of business process redesign written by Yogesh Malhotra. The U.S. Department of Defense has an online course about BPR at *www.dtic.mil/c3i/bprcd/0113.htm*.

8 Organizational Charts

It's interesting to look at the organizational charts for a variety of businesses. You can do so easily by entering "organizational chart" as the search term in any search engine. Software available today, such as Visio, makes creating an organizational chart easy and efficient. Find out more about Visio by visiting *www.visio.com* and searching for "Organizational Chart Wizard." For an example of an Internet organizational chart based on the Malcolm Baldrige National Quality Program, visit *www.orgchart.net*.

9 Office Automation

What is office automation? Read a definition and overview of the electronic workplace at *www.dcs.uwaterloo.ca/~marj/officeauto.html*. Visit *www.wwhr.hq.dla.mil/library/standards/GS326.htm* for the government's description of office automation positions. Guidelines for office automation security can be found at *www-08.nist.gov/secpubs/ncsc_oa.txt*. You might also be interested in "The Failed Promise of E-Interaction" at *www.zdnet.com/zdnn/content/inwk/0507/287785.html*. For additional references related to office automation, check out the Groupware links in the Chapter 7 InfoWeb section.

10 Transaction Processing

Transaction processing might seem like old technology. Most information systems have gone beyond simply tracking transactions to offering more flexible reporting and information management capabilities. Is there anything new in transaction processing? You'll find some insightful comments on this question by reading Christopher Avram's article on "New Paradigms for Transaction Processing" at *www.ct.monash.edu.au/~cavram/papers/tp/tr94-02h.html*. For additional information on transaction processing, connect to the site of the granddaddy of all transaction processing systems, IBM, at *www.ibm.com* and search using the keywords "transaction processing." The search results will include links to sites such as the "Transaction Processing Facility Family of Products" and "E-business Transaction Processing". At the CICS site, *www.hursley.ibm.com/cics*, you'll find links to articles about transaction processing technology and industry solutions.

11 DSS

Daniel Power provides an excellent online overview of decision support systems at *dss.cba.uni.edu/isworld/dss.html*. At *www.uky.edu/BusinessEconomics/dssakba/periodcl.html*, you'll find an extensive list of links to DSS Web sites maintained by Clyde Holsapple and Andrew Whinston, authors of the excellent textbook, *Decision Support Systems: A Knowledge-based Approach* (The West Group, 1996). Another excellent text, available in many university libraries, is *Decision Support Systems and Intelligent Systems* by Efraim Turban and Jay E. Aronson (1998). Many Web sites are actually decision support systems that you can use to make real-life decisions. If you are trying to make a career decision, check out *careeragent.computerworld.com/~start/career_success.htm*, *Computerworld*'s CareerAgent site. If you are trying to figure out a low-cost, yet healthy diet, connect to The Diet Problem at *www.mcs.anl.gov/home/otc/Guide/CaseStudies/diet*. Thinking of moving? The Homebuyer's Fair at *www.homefair.com/index.html* helps you compute equivalent salaries, calculate the cost of your move, and rate cities based on crime, schools, environment, and so on. For travel decisions, connect to Microsoft's online "travel agent" at *www.expedia.com*.

12 Expert Systems

For a quick overview of expert systems, connect to *www.ghgcorp.com/clips/ExpertSystems.html* or to MultiLogic's site at */multilogic.com/software*, where you can select a link to test-drive some simple expert system examples. For additional information and links, jump to the site maintained by *PC AI* magazine at *www.primenet.com/pcai*. Acquired Intelligence, also has Web-based demos, such as an expert system that is designed to help you identify whales, at *www.aiinc.ca/demos/whale.html*.

13 Neural Networks

Bernard Widrow carried out the pioneering research for neural networks at Stanford University in the 1950s. This technology requires massive computer capacity and, for that reason, practical applications have been limited. However, neural networks are fascinating. Imagine computers that function the way scientists think the brain functions! "An Introduction to Neural Networks" by Leslie Smith at *www.cs.stir.ac.uk/~lss/NNIntro/InvSlides.html* provides a good place to begin exploring this technology. At *www.cacs.usl.edu/~manaris/ai-education-repository/neural-n-tutorial.html*, you'll find tutorials on neural networks. You can, of course, enter "neural network" in any search engine to find additional information.

14 Rules

In the *User Focus* section, you learned how to create predicate logic rules for a knowledge base. The syntax for those rules is modeled on Prolog, a programming language popular for developing expert systems. For more information on the syntax of these rules, use your favorite Web search engine to search for "Prolog." A good source of information is the Amzi! site at *www.amzi.com*. At this site, you can click the "Automated Site Guide" link to use an expert system that interprets information you provide to determine which articles about Prolog it should recommend. You'll especially like two of the articles at this site. The first, "White Paper on Rules, Prolog, and Logic Server Technology" (*www.amzi.com/prolog.htm*), provides a quick overview and examples of how to use rules. A second article, "Exploring Prolog" (*www.amzi.com/profun.htm*), describes how to use Prolog to write an adventure game. The classic book on Prolog is *Programming in Prolog*, fourth edition by Clocksin and Mellish (Springer-Verlag, 1994). Another popular book is *The Art of Prolog: Advanced Programming Techniques* by Leon Sterling and Ehud Shapiro (editor) (MIT Press, 1994).

15 Chaos

The place to begin is the ChaosForum site at *www.chaosforum.com*. Here you'll find a broad range of links to topics such as a quick introduction to chaos theory, a set of interesting FAQs, and a bibliography. Next, check out the chapter, "Thinking Past the Obvious" in Joseph O'Connor's book, *The Art of Systems Thinking: Essential Skills for Creativity and Problem Solving* (Thorsons, 1998). For a really cool article on how to apply chaotic software to manufacturing processes, read "The Man from CHAOS" by William Green at *www.fastcompany.com/online/01/chaos.html* . You'll find more details on the Coopers & Lybrand simulation in the Forbes article, "Playing the Game of Life," which is posted online at *www.forbes.com/forbes/97/0407/5907100a.htm*. The Santa Fe Institute is the "mecca" for computational approaches to complex systems. Don't miss the online demos of chaos simulations at *www.santafe.edu/projects/swarm/examples/index.html*. For some perspective on the entire chaos movement, connect to *foxnet.cs.cmu.edu/people/spot/nab/perplexity.html* and read "From Complexity to Perplexity." You'll find additional links about chaos theory, the Butterfly Effect, and Edward N. Lorenz at the ThinkQuest online library by searching for "chaos."

CHAPTER 12

CHAPTER 13 DEVELOPING EFFECTIVE INFORMATION SYSTEMS

CONTENTS

PREVIEW

In this chapter you'll find out how to create or upgrade an information system—how to determine what needs to be done, how to design and construct the system, how to test the system to make sure it works correctly, and how to maintain the system. The *User Focus* section introduces you to an important development tool, data flow diagrams.

When you have completed this chapter, you should be able to:

■ Describe the system development life cycle

■ Explain the roles of a project team and a systems analyst

■ Understand the difference between a problem statement and a solution

■ Use the PIECES framework to identify problems in an information system

■ Explain how data flow diagrams, data dictionaries, and process specifications document the way in which an information system works

■ Understand the difference between system requirements and application specifications

■ Explain the purpose of unit testing, integration testing, system testing, and acceptance testing

■ Explain the advantages and disadvantages of direct conversion, parallel conversion, phased conversion, and pilot conversion when switching to a new system

CHAPTER 13 LAB

System
Testing

TO THE NORTH POLE

Three men sat around a kitchen table in Oslo, Norway. "So we'll try it!" one said, and they all agreed. It was the beginning of a daring attempt to cross 413 nautical miles of shifting ice, snow drifts, and frigid water between Canada and the North Pole without assistance from sled dogs, snowmobiles, or resupply flights. Each man would pull a specially designed Kevlar and fiberglass sled containing food, water, and fuel. Each sled would weigh 265 pounds when fully loaded.

The expedition members knew that their success depended on having the right gear and provisions. They looked at Web sites and e-commerce sites for a number of expedition outfitters, concluding that Abercrombie & Livingston Outfitters would provide the best selection of equipment and the most personalized service.

Several items needed by the expedition were not in stock at A&L's Telluride store—the location closest to the expedition's staging area in Resolute, Canada. The team couldn't wait for the back-ordered items to arrive with the next scheduled inventory shipment, so an A&L employee, referred to as a "special procurement agent," contacted other A&L outlet stores. The agent found the items at the Geneva outlet and had them shipped to the Telluride store. The team received the necessary equipment in time, but the process required significant effort on the part of the special procurement agent. Could A&L's computer system be improved to automatically search other stores for out-of-stock products?

InfoWeb
1

Expeditions

Information systems grow and change to reflect the evolving needs of an organization. An outdated information system might be replaced with a totally new system. A major component, such as an expert system or an e-commerce site, might be added to an existing information system. An information system is also likely to require many small modifications in response to changing government regulations, customer demands, employee suggestions, and management requests. A&L would like to improve its existing information system so that a product that is out of stock in one store could be easily located at another store. This chapter describes the process that A&L used to plan and implement this improvement.

SYSTEMS ANALYSIS

InfoWeb
2
Mythical
Man-Month

The computer industry abounds with tales of information systems, developed at great expense, that didn't meet expectations because they didn't work correctly, were too complex to use, or weren't flexible enough to meet changing business needs. As Frederick Brooks observes in his book *The Mythical Man-Month*, "One can expect the human race to continue attempting systems just within or just beyond our reach, and software systems are perhaps the most intricate and complex of all man's handiwork."

Creating an information system can be compared to building a house. You don't just grab a hammer and start nailing pieces of wood together. It is important to have a plan. The process of planning and building an information system is referred to as **systems analysis and design**.

InfoWeb
3
Methodologies

Whether you are part of a team that is developing a complex corporate information system or you are developing a small information system for your own use, you will be more likely to succeed if you analyze the purpose of the information system, carefully design the system, test it thoroughly, and document its features. The methodology that you use to develop an information system depends on the type of system and the company for which you work. Systems analysis and design methodologies include structured analysis, joint application development (JAD), rapid application development (RAD), and object-oriented development.

A **system development life cycle** (SDLC) is an outline of a process that helps develop successful information systems. The SDLC is divided into phases, with each phase including a number of tasks. Although several variations of the SDLC exist, most of them include phases similar to those shown in Figure 13-1.

FIGURE 13-1

The system development life cycle (SDLC) outlines a series of steps, or phases, that occur during the life span of an information system.

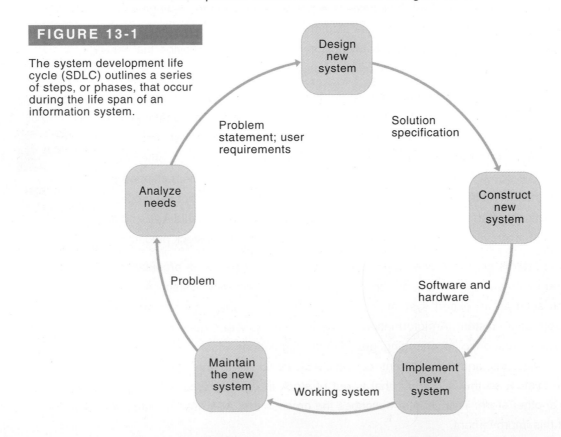

Analyze Needs

What's the beginning of the life cycle?

The motivation for a new information system usually emerges from a serious problem with the current system. If the current system is manual, it might not be cost-effective or competitive. Computerized systems can become obsolete when, for example, the hardware is out of date or when the software no longer meets the needs of the business mission.

The first phase of the SDLC is to analyze needs. This phase requires several activities, listed in Figure 13-2.

FIGURE 13-2

Analysis activities.

Select the Project Team

Who participates in the process of building an information system? Typically, a team of employees, managers, and technicians participates in the process of building an information system, under the supervision of the information systems department. An **information systems department**, or "IS department," is the wing of a business or organization responsible for developing and maintaining the computers, data, and programs for an information system.

IS Departments

Historically, IS departments were part of the finance component because computers were initially deployed in businesses for accounting and inventory management functions. As computers spread and began to assist with a wider variety of business tasks, some organizations changed their organizational charts to make the IS department a separate entity reporting directly to the chief executive officer or president. This reorganization provided IS departments with more autonomy to make budget decisions and to prioritize projects. In addition, it provided more interaction with employees and managers from other departments.

Most IS departments are headed by a **chief information officer** (CIO). IS managers and team leaders report to the CIO. They supervise the technicians and computer professionals who develop new systems and operate the computer equipment.

Systems Analysts

In many organizations, computer professionals called **systems analysts** are responsible for analyzing information requirements, designing new information systems, and supervising their implementation. Systems analysts also create specifications for application software for the new system and then give those specifications to computer programmers, who in turn create software to meet those specifications.

Increasingly, managerial and clerical employees outside the IS department participate in the development of information systems. For example, A&L's special procurement agent has expertise that will be needed to improve the system's ability to search other A&L stores for out-of-stock merchandise. She and a systems analyst from A&L's information systems department have formed a project team to initiate work to update the system.

CHAPTER 13

InfoWeb
6

Project
Teams

A **system development project team**, or "project team" for short, is a group of people who are assigned to analyze and develop an information system. The composition of a project team depends on the scope of the project. Larger and more complex projects tend to have large project teams, with a majority of the people on the team being systems analysts or other computer professionals. Smaller projects tend to have fewer members on the project team, and a higher percentage of the team members are likely to be users rather than computer professionals. Figure 13-3 contains some excerpts from the first meeting of A&L's project team, as the special procurement agent explains what she calls the "cross-shipping problem."

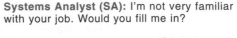

FIGURE 13-3

Excerpts from the first project
team meeting.

Systems Analyst (SA): I'm not very familiar with your job. Would you fill me in?

Special Procurement Agent (SPA): As you probably know, when a customer walks into one of our outlets and places an order, the order is usually filled with items from the local outlet's inventory. If an item is out of stock at that outlet, the computer checks to see whether it is available in the London warehouse.

SA: Yes, I know how that works. And if the item is in stock in London, we ship it from London to the outlet.

SPA: Right. But if the item is not in the outlet or the London warehouse, the order comes to me and I try to hunt down the out-of-stock item at other A&L outlets. If I find the item, I have to decide whether it is feasible to "cross-ship" the item to the outlet where it was ordered.

SA: By "cross-ship," do you mean that one outlet ships the item to another outlet?

SPA: Exactly.

SA: But why do you have to decide whether it is feasible to ship an item?

SPA: We have stores all over the world. Shipments between some of our outlets can be very expensive and take weeks to arrive. It requires a fair amount of time for me to check the inventories, check shipping rates, and decide which outlet can supply the item the most quickly and least expensively.

SA: I see.

SPA: It's costing the company a lot of money to deliver some of these items, especially considering the time I spend and the possible delay experienced by the customer.

Define the Problem

How does the project team begin to analyze an information system? The first activities in the analysis phase are to define the problem and create one or more problem statements. A **problem statement** is a sentence that identifies what needs to be improved or fixed. Here are some examples of well-defined problem statements for information systems:

- In a garden supply store, the price tags frequently fall off items—especially the plants—so customers have to wait at the registers while an employee checks the price.

- In a police car, officers do not have access to out-of-state arrest warrants, so they might stop a motorist for a minor violation but fail to make an arrest on a more serious charge.

A common pitfall in the analysis phase is stating a solution, rather than a problem. Solutions are not appropriate at this stage of the SDLC because the project team should not consider solutions until team members understand more about the problem with the current system. Although the following statements might sound reasonable, they are solutions, not problems:

- The garden supply store needs a bar-code reader so that cashiers can determine the price of an item even if it doesn't have a price tag.

- Police cars should be equipped with computers that can access a national database of outstanding arrest warrants.

James Wetherbe's **PIECES framework** helps identify problems in an information system. Each letter of PIECES stands for a potential problem, as shown in Figure 13-4.

FIGURE 13-4

PIECES help identify problems that might exist in an information system.

Performance
A performance problem means that an information system does not respond quickly enough to users or takes too long to complete processing tasks.

Information
An information problem means that users don't receive the right information at the right time, in a usable format.

Economics
An economics problem means that the system costs too much to use.

Control
A control problem means that information is available to unauthorized users or that authorized users are not given the authority to make decisions based on the information they receive.

Efficiency
An efficiency problem means that too many resources are used to collect, process, store, and distribute information.

Service
A service problem means that the system is too difficult or inconvenient to use.

At A&L Outfitters, the special procurement agent classified the procurement problem as an efficiency problem. Too many resources—that is, too many hours of her time—are devoted to choosing the best location from which to cross-ship items. The special procurement agent and systems analyst at A&L Outfitters therefore created the following problem statement:

> If a customer orders an item that is out of stock, the current procedures are not efficient for determining whether other outlets have the item in stock and from which outlet the item could be cross-shipped most cost-effectively.

Study the Current System

Is it really important to understand the current system before planning a new system? Typically, a new information system is designed to replace a system or process that is already in place. It is essential to study the current system carefully and to understand its strengths and weaknesses before planning the new system. Systems analysts create data flow diagrams, data dictionaries, and process specifications to document the way in which a system works.

A **data flow diagram** (DFD) graphically illustrates how data moves through an information system. You can think of a DFD as a map that traces the possible paths for data traveling from entities (such as customers) to processes (such as printing), or to storage areas. In DFD terminology, an **external entity** is a person, organization, or device outside the information system that originates or receives data. A **data store** is a filing cabinet, disk, or tape that holds data. A **process** is a manual or computerized routine that changes data by performing a calculation, updating information, sorting a list, and so on. Arrows called **data flows** indicate how data travels from entities to processes and data stores. Figure 13-5 uses a DFD to document how an order is processed by A&L's information system.

FIGURE 13-5

On this DFD, the data moving through an information system is represented by arrows. The rounded rectangles represent processes that affect the data. Inventory is a data store. The Customer box represents an external entity.

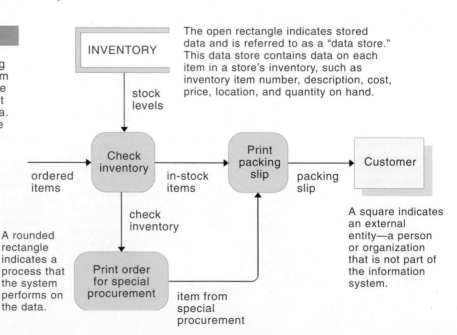

The open rectangle indicates stored data and is referred to as a "data store." This data store contains data on each item in a store's inventory, such as inventory item number, description, cost, price, location, and quantity on hand.

A square indicates an external entity—a person or organization that is not part of the information system.

A rounded rectangle indicates a process that the system performs on the data.

 Start Animation

A DFD illustrates an overview of a system, but how does a systems analyst describe the details? For example, one of the arrows on the DFD in Figure 13-5 is labeled "ordered items." Does the data for "ordered items" include the retail price of the item? Systems analysts use a **data dictionary** to document detailed descriptions of the data that flows through an information system and data that is stored by that system. Read the data dictionary description for "ordered items" in Figure 13-6.

FIGURE 13-6

The data dictionary description of the "ordered items" data from the DFD in Figure 13-5.

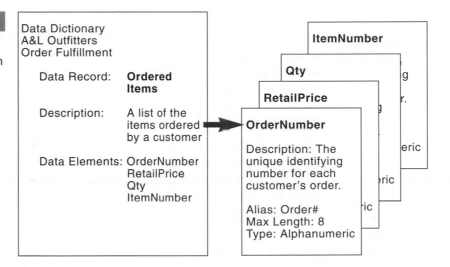

A **process specification** explains what happens to data within a process. For example, A&L's DFD includes a process called "Check inventory." What exactly does this process entail? What is the information system supposed to do when it checks the inventory? A process specification would describe in detail exactly what the information system accomplishes in this process.

Systems analysts often use **structured English** to concisely and unambiguously explain the logic of a process. Structured English differs from standard English because it limits the words you can use to those defined in the data dictionary and to specific logical terms such as "if...then." Figure 13-7 provides an example of process specifications written in structured English.

FIGURE 13-7

This process specification, written in structured English, describes the current Check Inventory process shown on the DFD in Figure 13-5.

```
Check inventory

If the QuantityOnHand at the nearest Outlet >= Qty
    then print the item information on packing slip
    otherwise, if QuantityOnHand at the London
    warehouse >= Qty
        then print item information on packing slip
        otherwise, print the order for the special
        procurement agent.
```

Data flow diagrams, data dictionaries, and process specifications are valuable tools for analyzing information systems. These tools help systems analysts produce documentation that is also useful in the design and maintenance phases. It can be difficult, however, to keep the diagrams, dictionaries, and specifications for an information system up to date. For example, if the IS department at A&L decided to rename Qty to QtyOrdered, several revisions would be needed in the data dictionary and the process specification. It might be easy to miss one of the changes, which could lead to errors and bugs in the information system.

InfoWeb
7

CASE Tools

To make it easier to maintain data flow diagrams, process specifications, and data dictionaries, many systems analysts use CASE tools. CASE stands for "computer-aided software engineering." A **CASE tool** is a software application that is designed for summarizing system requirements, diagramming current and proposed information systems, scheduling development tasks, preparing documentation, and developing computer programs.

CASE tools automate many of the routine housekeeping tasks required by the systems analysis and design process. For example, if the project team wants to use the label "QtyOrdered" instead of "Qty," a CASE tool would make appropriate revisions on every DFD and data dictionary entry. Figure 13-8 shows a screen from a CASE tool called PowerDesigner.

FIGURE 13-8

PowerDesigner CASE tool.

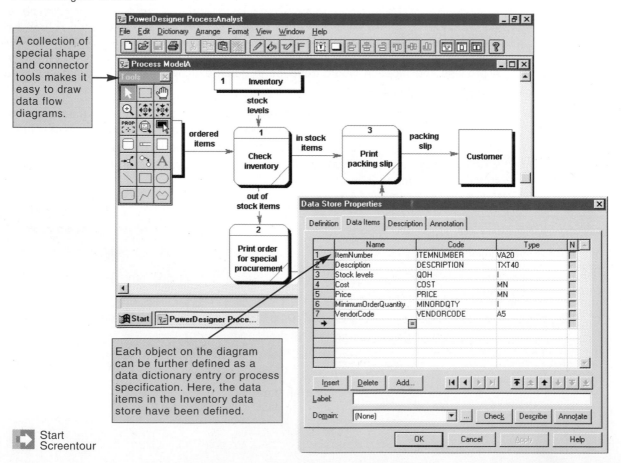

A collection of special shape and connector tools makes it easy to draw data flow diagrams.

Each object on the diagram can be further defined as a data dictionary entry or process specification. Here, the data items in the Inventory data store have been defined.

Start
Screentour

Determine System Requirements

How does the project team determine what the new system should do? **System requirements** are the criteria for successfully solving the problem or problems that have been identified in an information system. These requirements guide the design and implementation for a new or updated information system. They also serve as an evaluation checklist at the end of the development project, so they are sometimes called **success factors**. A new or updated information system should meet the requirements defined by the project team.

An analyst determines requirements by interviewing users and studying successful information systems that solve problems similar to those found in the current system.

The special procurement agent at A&L Outfitters created the following list of requirements:

- The system should be able to solve cross-shipping problems without any human intervention.

- When the information system fills an order, it should check stock in all outlets, then determine the best outlet from which to ship each item.

- The system should be easy to maintain. When shipping rates or shipping times between outlets change, it should be a simple task to change that information in the system.

Another way to determine requirements is to construct a prototype. A **prototype** is an experimental or trial version of an information system. Often the prototype is not a fully functioning system because it is designed to demonstrate only selected features that might be incorporated into a new information system. A systems analyst shows the prototype to users, who evaluate which features of the prototype are important for the new information system.

CHAPTER 13

Q U I C K C H E C K   A

1 The _____ is an outline of a process that helps develop effective information systems.

2 _____ are often responsible for analyzing information requirements, designing a new information system, and supervising the new system implementation.

3 A(n) _____ is a sentence that identifies what needs to be improved or fixed in an information system.

4 A(n) _____ tool is software that is designed for drawing diagrams of information systems, writing process specifications, and maintaining data dictionaries.

5 _____ are the criteria for successfully solving a problem or problems.

6 A(n) _____ is an experimental or trial version of an information system that is under development.

 Check Answers

SECTION B   SYSTEM DESIGN

FIGURE 13-9

Design activities.

In the design phase, alternative solutions are identified and evaluated, hardware and software are selected, and the specifications for constructing the system are developed, as noted in Figure 13-9.

Identify Potential Solutions

How does the team come up with solutions?

There might be more than one way to solve the problem and meet the requirements that were specified in the analysis phase of the SDLC. Some potential solutions might be better than others—more effective, less costly, or less complex. Therefore, it is not a good idea to proceed with the first solution that comes to mind. The project team should, instead, identify several potential solutions by "brainstorming" and researching case studies on Web sites and in computer magazines.

An information system includes people, procedures, data, hardware, and software. When identifying potential solutions, the project team must consider whether alternatives are available for any of these areas. For example, the team might consider software alternatives such as using an application development tool, writing custom software, or purchasing a commercial program.

An **application development tool** is essentially a type of software construction kit that contains building blocks that can be assembled into a software product. Application development tools include expert system shells, 4GLs, and component objects. A **4GL**, or fourth-generation language, is a programming language that contains built-in commands for complex tasks such as sorting data and creating columnar reports. A **component object** is a pre-programmed module such as a menu bar that a programmer can insert into a program.

Application development tools usually produce applications more quickly than traditional programming languages can. As an analogy, consider baking a cake. You can sift the flour with the salt, mix the sugar, eggs, shortening, and milk, then combine the dry and wet ingredients, and so forth to create a cake "from scratch." This process is analogous to creating a software application using a programming language. Another way to bake a cake is to use a cake mix. You just add water and eggs, mix, and bake. An application development tool is the programmer's "cake mix" and provides a quicker, easier way to construct an application.

Creating an information system using a programming language can take many months or years and is very costly. An application development tool reduces the time and cost somewhat, although application development remains a major effort. Another possibility would be to purchase a commercial software application and customize it where possible to fit with the way that the organization works. Commercial software is available for many business functions, including accounting, inventory management, and e-commerce. In summary, there are often three alternative software solutions: (1) build the application using an application development tool; (2) create the application using a programming language; or (3) buy a commercial software application.

InfoWeb
8
<u>Solutions</u>

Evaluate Solutions and Select the Best

| How does the team choose the best solution? | After listing alternative solutions, the project team can evaluate each one based on its advantages and disadvantages. A&L's team is considering three possible software solutions: writing a module from scratch with a programming language, purchasing commercial software, and using an application development tool.

The first software solution would require a small team of programmers to write a custom module that determines when and where to cross-ship items. The advantage of this solution is that a custom program can be designed to exactly meet the procurement agent's requirements. The disadvantage of this solution is that it requires the services of one or more programmers. Considering the backlog of upgrade requests in the IS department, the module would probably not be available for 18 months.

Another potential software solution for A&L is to purchase a commercial software application that already includes the ability to determine when and where to cross-ship items. The advantage of this solution is that commercial applications have already been well tested and could be installed very quickly. It might be difficult, however, to locate a commercial application that would work with A&L's current transaction processing system. Many commercial applications are designed to interact only with other modules purchased from the same vendor. Except for the cross-shipping problem, A&L is happy with its current transaction processing system and doesn't intend to switch to an entirely new system just to add cross-shipping capability.

The third software solution is to use an application development tool such as an expert system shell. An advantage of this solution is that the special procurement agent can play an active role in the development process. Disadvantages include the time that the special procurement agent will have to spend participating in the system development and the possible trouble that she and the systems analyst might encounter in integrating the expert system with the rest of the transaction processing system. To evaluate the three software solutions, the project team creates a list of evaluation criteria:

- The solution must run on A&L's current hardware.

- The software application for the solution must integrate with the current transaction processing system.

- The solution must be in place within six months.

- The solution must meet the requirements delineated in the analysis phase.

- Support for the solution must be available from a vendor, software publisher, manufacturer, or the A&L information systems department.

After evaluating the alternatives, the project team decides that the best solution is to use an expert system shell to create a cross-shipment module that would work with the current transaction processing system. Custom programming would take too long, and the team was unable to locate an appropriate commercial application that would work with A&L's current information system.

The project team takes its proposal to management. In most organizations, management approval is necessary for modifications or additions to an information system. Management approval is also necessary for equipment purchases, software purchases, and time commitments for personnel resources, such as the time that it takes to design, create, test, and maintain an information system.

CHAPTER 13

Purchase Hardware and Software

Once the team selects a solution, how does the development process begin?

InfoWeb
9

RFPs &
RFQs

Once the team selects a solution and management clears the project to proceed, the next activity is to purchase the hardware and software needed to implement the solution. Typically, more than one vendor sells the hardware and software necessary for the new system, so an organization often has a choice of vendors.

The method for selecting the hardware, software, and vendor depends on the project team's understanding of what is required for the solution. If the team members do not know exactly what hardware and software are needed, they can describe the problem and ask vendors how they would solve it. If the project team members know exactly what they want, they just need to find a reputable vendor who sells the equipment at a reasonable price.

A **request for proposal** (RFP) is a document that describes the information system problem and the requirements for the solution. The RFP essentially asks vendors to recommend hardware and software for the solution and to describe their qualifications for implementing the solution. A project team usually issues an RFP when a vendor's knowledge and experience in the solution area is more comprehensive than that of the team members. Look at the sample RFP in Figure 13-10.

FIGURE 13-10

An RFP describes the problem and asks the vendor to suggest a solution.

Abercrombie & Livingston Outfitters, Ltd.
23 Baker Street, London, PL2 3BB England
Telephone (0752) 506102/Fax (0752) 506398

Request for Proposal

Abercrombie & Livingston Outfitters, Ltd., is an international supplier of expedition equipment. Inventory and order fulfillment are performed using the Summit order entry and inventory control system running on a DEC VAX 4000-600 computer system.

The current Summit order entry and inventory control system does not allow for automated cross-shipment of goods that are out of stock at a local outlet. Orders for items that are out of stock locally are referred to the Special Procurement Agent, who checks whether the item is in stock in any other S&L outlet. If the item is in stock elsewhere, the Special Procurement Agent must determine the best location from which to ship the item, and request a cross-shipment to the required location.

We would like to automate this process. If your company has prior experience with projects of this sort, we invite you to prepare a proposal as outlined below:

1.   Company information

2.   Similar project experience: Include information on similar projects undertaken by your company, with names and telephone numbers of contacts at those projects

3.   Proposal summary: Briefly explain how you would resolve the problem

A **request for quotation** (RFQ) is a request for a formal price quotation on a list of hardware and software. A project team submits an RFQ when it knows the make and model of the equipment and the titles of the software packages needed, but wants to compare prices from different vendors. Compare the RFQ in Figure 13-11 with the RFP in Figure 13-10.

FIGURE 13-11

An RFQ asks the vendor for a price on specific hardware or software items.

Abercrombie & Livingston Outfitters, Ltd.
23 Baker Street, London, PL2 3BB England
Telephone (0752) 506102/Fax (0752) 506398

Request for Quotation

Please return this form showing your current price for the following item(s) by June 30:

Item	Description	Quantity	Price	Delivery Date
1.	XpertPro development	1		

The A&L project team members explore a variety of expert system development tools. Eventually they select a product called XpertPro, an expert system shell that has been used successfully in many companies in Europe and North America. They selected XpertPro because it runs on their current hardware, it is compatible with Windows operating systems, it will integrate with the current transaction processing system, and it appears to provide the necessary capabilities. Because the special procurement agent knows exactly what she wants, she asks the A&L purchasing department to send RFQs to vendors that sell XpertPro. When the vendors return the RFQs, the purchasing agent at A&L looks for the vendor that offers the most competitive price and then orders XpertPro from that vendor.

Develop Application Specifications

How does the project team make sure that the information system solves the problem? **Application specifications** describe the way that an application should interact with the user, store data, process data, and format reports. The specifications are similar to an architectural blueprint that shows the detailed plan for constructing a building. For large information systems, a systems analyst develops the specifications after interviewing users to determine their information needs. The specifications are then given to a programming team or application developer, who creates the application. In a small information systems project, you as the user might develop your own specifications. Then you might give the specifications to a programmer or, if you have the expertise, you might create the application yourself.

Whether the system under development is large or small, it requires detailed specifications so that the final system solves the problem defined during the analysis phase. At A&L, the specifications for the expert system define the rules for the knowledge base. The project team develops the following rules for the cross-ship expert system:

- If the ordered item is in stock at the outlet nearest the destination of the order, then deliver the item from that outlet.

- If the ordered item is not in stock in any outlet, then send the order to the special procurement agent.

- If the ordered item is in stock at only one outlet, then cross-ship the item from that outlet.

- If the ordered item is in stock in more than one outlet, then cross-ship it from the outlet with the lowest shipping cost and fastest delivery time.

QUICKCHECK   B

1 In the _____ phase, a systems analyst identifies several potential solutions, evaluates these solutions, and then selects the one that offers the most benefits at the lowest cost.

2 A(n) _____ is essentially a software construction kit that contains building blocks that you can assemble into a software product.

3 A(n) _____ is a document sent to vendors that describes the problem and the requirements for the solution.

4 The project team would send out a(n) _____ if it knows exactly what hardware and software are needed.

5 _____ specifications describe the way that an application should interact with the user, store data, process data, and format reports.

Check
Answers

SYSTEM CONSTRUCTION

In the construction phase, new hardware and software are installed, applications are created to meet the specifications developed during the design phase, and the new system is tested, as noted in Figure 13-12.

FIGURE 13-12

Construction activities.

✓ Install hardware &
  software

✓ Create applications

✓ Test applications

Install Hardware and Software

What's the first step in the construction phase? Installing hardware and software is the first step in the construction phase. The expert system for A&L Outfitters does not require any new hardware. In many development projects, however, new hardware is required and would be installed during the construction phase. New hardware can either replace old equipment or be connected to existing equipment. In either case, it must be tested to ensure that it operates correctly. Problems with new hardware or connections to other equipment must be corrected during the construction phase so they do not disrupt the implementation phase.

Many information systems require new software such as a commercial application, a programming language, an application development tool, or an expert system shell. This software must be installed and tested to ensure that it works correctly. Software testing can reveal problems that result from incompatibilities with the existing hardware or an incorrect installation of the software. These problems must be corrected before continuing with system construction activities. Some problems might result from bugs (that is, errors) in the software and must be corrected by the software publisher.

A&L's project team installs and tests the expert system development shell, XpertPro. At this stage, the team is only testing the *development tool* to verify that it runs on the computer without generating error messages—the rules for the expert system have not yet been entered, so the team is not testing the cross-shipping rules. When the team members are sure that the expert system shell operates correctly, they continue with the construction process.

Create Applications

After the project team installs the new hardware and software, what's the next step in the construction phase? The next step in the construction phase depends on the software tools that have been selected for the project. So far, you have seen that information systems can be constructed using tools such as a programming language, an application development tool, or commercial software. Figure 13-13 outlines the construction process for some commonly used construction tools.

FIGURE 13-13	Construction techniques depend on the tool.
Construction Tool	**Construction Technique**
Programming language	1. Install the programming language. 2. Write software modules using programming language. 3. Test software modules separately and with other modules.
Component objects	1. Install the component objects. 2. Use the components as building blocks to construct modules. 3. Test each module separately and with other modules.
Expert system shell	1. Install the expert system shell. 2. Enter facts and rules to create the knowledge base. 3. Test the expert system to make sure that the rules are correct.
Commercial software	1. Install the commercial software. 2. Customize the software to meet specifications, if possible. 3. Test to make sure that the customization reflects the specifications.

When the software for an information system is created using a programming language or application development tool, the process is referred to as **programming** or **software engineering**.

When an information system is constructed using commercial application software, the software has been written and tested by the software publisher. Nevertheless, it sometimes needs to be customized. **Software customization** is the process of modifying a commercial application to reflect the needs of the users. Customization might include changing the appearance of the user interface, enabling or disabling the mouse, selecting the menus that appear on screen, and designing forms or reports. The extent to which a commercial application can be customized depends on the options available in the application. For example, some commercial applications provide options for customizing report formats while other commercial applications do not.

The process of designing, entering, and testing the rules in an expert system is referred to as **knowledge engineering**. Because the members of the A&L project team have decided to use an expert system shell to construct the cross-ship module, their major construction activities are to enter and test the facts and rules for the expert system. Like any application, the A&L expert system must meet the design specifications and go through a rigorous testing process to ensure that the facts and rules produce the expected results.

Test Applications

How can the team ensure that a new information system works? A rigorous testing process is the only way to make sure that a new information system works. Different types of testing during the construction phase help identify and fix problems before the information system is incorporated into day-to-day business activities.

Application testing is the process of trying out various sequences of input values and checking the results to verify that the application works correctly. Application testing is performed in three ways: unit testing, integration testing, and system testing.

As each application module is completed, it undergoes **unit testing** to ensure that it operates reliably and correctly. When all modules have been completed and tested, **integration testing** is performed to ensure that the modules operate correctly together. Unit testing and integration testing are usually performed in a test area. A **test area** is a place where software testing can occur without disrupting the organization's regular information system. A test area might be located in an isolated section of storage on the computer system that runs the organization's regular information system, or it might be located on an entirely separate computer system. When problems are discovered during unit testing or integration testing, the team must track down the source of the problem and correct it. Unit testing and integration testing are then repeated to make sure that the problem is corrected and that no new problems were introduced when the original problem was fixed (Figure 13-14).

FIGURE 13-14

The results of unit and integration testing must be examined carefully to make sure that the application processes data reliably and accurately.

After unit and integration testing are completed, **system testing** ensures that all hardware and software components work together correctly. If an existing information system is modified, system testing is performed when the new or modified units are combined with the rest of the existing system. In a completely new information system, system testing is performed to simulate daily work loads and to make sure that processing speed and accuracy meet the specifications. Ideally, system testing is performed in a test area. If an organization does not have the hardware resources to duplicate its existing information system for testing purposes, system testing must be performed on the "live," or production, system. This technique can cause some disruption in the normal functions of the organization.

A&L's project team has one application module to test: the expert system. As part of its testing effort, the project team places a series of sample orders. The results of the test are examined to see whether the expert system completes the orders as expected. In most cases, the expert system works, but the team discovers that two orders do not go through correctly. On examining these two orders, the A&L team notices that in both cases, the item was in stock in two locations that had the same shipping cost and the same shipping time. No rule had been entered that told the system which location to select under these circumstances. The A&L team adds the following rule:

> If more than one outlet has the item in stock and the shipping cost and the shipping time are the same, then ship from the outlet that has more of the items in stock.

After adding this rule, the team tests the expert system again. This time, all of the test orders are processed correctly.

The A&L project has only one module, so integration testing is not necessary. For system testing, the project team loads the expert system and a copy of the order system into a test area. The purpose of this testing session is to verify that the order data is communicated correctly between the existing order entry system and the new expert system. The system test goes smoothly, and so it is time for the project team to schedule implementation of the new system.

QUICKCHECK   C

1 _____ is the process used to create a program using a programming language or application development tool.

2 The process of designing, entering, and testing the rules in an expert system is referred to as _____.

3 _____ testing verifies correct operation of a particular software module.

4 _____ testing verifies correct operation of multiple modules working together.

5 A(n) _____ is a place where software testing can occur without disrupting the existing information system.

6 _____ testing ensures that all hardware and software components work together correctly.

▶ Check Answers

IMPLEMENTATION STRATEGIES

In the implementation phase, the information system is placed into operation. This phase requires careful planning and preparation. The activities that occur in the implementation phase are shown in Figure 13-15.

Train Users

How do employees learn how to use the new information system? A&L's expert system works behind the scenes, so it doesn't require any user interaction or training. For many new information systems, however, users need extensive training on hardware operation, data entry, and backup procedures. If user training is required, the project team typically organizes training sessions.

InfoWeb
11

Training

Training sessions can be conducted by members of the project team or by professional trainers. During these training sessions, users learn how to interact with the interface, how to use the new system to perform their day-to-day tasks, and how to find additional information in their user manuals or procedure handbooks. A **procedure handbook** contains the step-by-step instructions for performing a specific task. It often takes the place of a lengthy user manual because in a large organization, an employee in a particular department usually performs specific tasks and does not need to know how all features of the system work.

FIGURE 13-15

Implementation activities.

- ✓ Train users
- ✓ Convert data
- ✓ Convert to new system
- ✓ Acceptance testing

Convert Data

What happens to the data from the old system? The data that's required by A&L's new expert system is taken directly from the transaction processing system, so it is not necessary to convert any data before implementing the new system. Nevertheless, implementation of many new information systems requires data to be converted from a manual or existing computer system for use in the new system. For example, suppose that a local building inspector's office has a manual system for issuing and renewing construction permits. It has more than 8,000 permits on record. If this office computerizes its operations, it will need to convert these 8,000 records into an electronic format that can be accessed by the new computerized system.

When converting data from a manual system to a computer system, the data can either be typed or scanned electronically into the appropriate storage media. Some organizations have a lot of data that must be converted, and the conversion process can take a long time, require extra personnel, and be quite costly.

When converting data from an existing computer system to a new system, a programmer typically writes **conversion software** to read the old data and convert it into a format that is usable by the new system. Without such software, users would be forced to manually re-enter data from the old system into the new system.

Convert to New System

How does a business switch from the old system to the new system?

System conversion refers to the process of deactivating an old information system and activating the new one. It is also referred to as "cutover" or "go live." There are several strategies for converting to a new system.

A **direct conversion** means that the old system is completely deactivated and the new system is immediately activated. Direct conversion usually takes place during non-peak hours to minimize disruption to normal business routines. Direct conversion is risky, however, because if the new system does not work correctly, it might need to be deactivated and undergo further testing. In the meantime, the old system must be reactivated and the transactions that were entered into the new system need to be reentered into the old system so that business can continue.

A **parallel conversion** avoids some of the risk of direct conversion because the old system remains in service while some or all of the new system is activated. Both the old and the new systems operate in parallel until it can be determined whether the new system is performing correctly. Parallel conversion often requires that all entries be made in both the new and old systems, which is costly in terms of time, computer resources, and personnel. Parallel conversion is fairly safe, but often not practical because of the cost and duplication of effort.

Phased conversion works well with larger information systems that are modularized. In a **phased conversion**, the new system is activated one module at a time. After it has been determined that one module is working correctly, the next module is activated, and so on, until the entire new system is operational. In a phased conversion, each module of the new system must work with both the old system and the new system, which greatly increases the complexity and cost of the conversion.

A **pilot conversion** works well in organizations with several branches that have independent information processing systems. The new information system is activated at one branch. After it has been determined that the system works correctly at one branch, it is activated at the next branch. During a pilot conversion, some method must be developed to integrate information from branches using the new system with information from branches still using the old system.

A&L Outfitters has decided on a direct conversion for the following reasons:

- The added expense of a parallel conversion is probably unnecessary because the expert system has been extensively tested and is likely to work correctly.

- A pilot conversion is not possible because all branch outlets access the same information system.

- Phased conversion would not be feasible because there is only one module.

Acceptance Testing

What about the people who are buying or will be using the system? Do they get a chance to make sure it is working correctly? A new or upgraded information system undergoes a final test called acceptance testing. **Acceptance testing** is designed to assure the purchaser or user of the new system that the system does what it is supposed to do. The procedures for acceptance testing are usually designed by the users and systems analysts, and they often include the use of real data to verify that the system operates correctly under normal and peak data loads. Acceptance testing might occur at the end of the construction phase or during the implementation phase, depending on the organization's implementation plan.

At A&L Outfitters, the special procurement agent has allotted a week's time to observe the expert system in operation and make sure that it is working acceptably. If the week passes and no major problems appear, the project team will consider the implementation phase complete.

QUICKCHECK D

1 A(n) [_____] contains step-by-step instructions for performing a specific task.

2 [_____] is often used to convert data from an old information system into a format that is usable by the new system.

3 Data conversion refers to the process of converting data, whereas [_____] refers to the process of switching from the old system to the new system.

4 [_____] conversion means the old system is completely deactivated and the new system is immediately activated.

5 In a(n) [_____] conversion, both the new system and the old system remain operational—entries are made in both systems until it is determined that the new system is performing correctly.

6 In a(n) [_____] conversion, one module of the new system is activated at a time.

7 In a(n) [_____] conversion, the new system is activated in a single branch or location, where it is thoroughly tested before being activated in the rest of the organization.

8 [_____] testing is designed to assure the purchaser or user of the new system that the system does what it is supposed to do.

▶ Check Answers

SECTION E   SYSTEM MAINTENANCE

FIGURE 13-16

Maintenance activities.

- ✔ Follow daily backup procedures
- ✔ Monitor system performance
- ✔ Identify and fix problems
- ✔ Modify system to meet changing needs

InfoWeb 12

Maintenance

After an information system is implemented, it remains in operation for a period of time. During this time, maintenance activities ensure that the system functions as well as possible. Figure 13-16 shows the major maintenance activities for a typical information system.

In an information system that is centered around a mainframe computer or minicomputer, the task of operating the computer on a day-to-day basis is typically the responsibility of the **system operator**, also called the "computer operator." The system operator performs system backups and data recovery, monitors system traffic, and troubleshoots operational problems. Additional responsibilities might include installing new versions of the operating system and software applications; but in some organizations, these responsibilities are delegated to a systems programmer. A **systems programmer** is the operating system guru, whose responsibilities include installing new versions of the operating system and modifying OS settings to maximize performance.

In an information system that is centered on a microcomputer network, a network manager or network specialist is typically responsible for day-to-day operations and system maintenance. Some maintenance activities might also fall on the shoulders of individual users, who are often charged with the responsibility of backing up their workstations and performing workstation installations of new software.

Maintaining the computer hardware and operating system is only a small part of the overall maintenance picture. Modifications to application software require a significant share of IS department resources to fix bugs, add new features, and deal with new versions of commercial applications. Some organizations spend as much as 80 percent of their information systems budget on software maintenance. As shown in Figure 13-17, maintenance tasks follow a U-shaped curve—an information system requires the most maintenance at the beginning and at the end of its life cycle.

FIGURE 13-17

An information system requires the most maintenance during the beginning and the end of its useful life span.

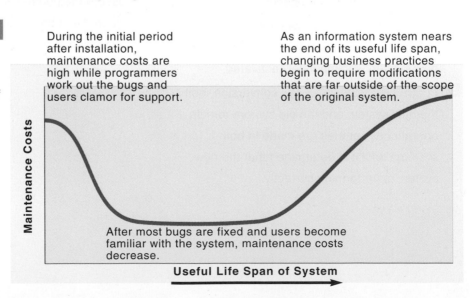

During the initial period after installation, maintenance costs are high while programmers work out the bugs and users clamor for support.

As an information system nears the end of its useful life span, changing business practices begin to require modifications that are far outside of the scope of the original system.

After most bugs are fixed and users become familiar with the system, maintenance costs decrease.

Maintenance Costs

Useful Life Span of System

Another maintenance activity that requires extensive IS department resources is end-user support. Even after in-depth training, employees sometimes forget procedures or have difficulty when they encounter a new set of circumstances. These employees turn to the IS department for help. Many organizations have established a **help desk** to handle end-user problems. The help desk is staffed by a support technician who is familiar with the application software. The support technician keeps records of problems and solutions, and routes bug reports to the appropriate programming group.

The maintenance phase continues until the information system is no longer cost-effective or until changes in the organization make the information system obsolete. It is not unusual for an information system to remain in operation for 20 years. Consequently, the maintenance phase of the SDLC is the most expensive because it lasts for the entire life of the information system. Eventually an information system's useful or cost-effective life nears a close. It is then time to begin the system development life cycle again.

A&L's new expert system will be maintained along with the transaction processing system. Information systems personnel will make sure that it is backed up regularly. They will also monitor system performance to ensure that the expert system does not create a bottleneck and slow down the rest of the system. The special procurement agent has a copy of the expert system that she can use to make modifications in response to changing conditions, such as shipping rates.

QUICKCHECK E

1 _____ activities include backing up the system, monitoring the system for correct performance, and modifying the system in response to changing conditions.

2 Some organizations spend as much as _____ percent of their information systems budget on software maintenance.

3 In the early stages of a new information system, much of the maintenance effort deals with _____ .

4 An information system is typically used until it is no longer _____ or until it is made obsolete by changes in the organization.

5 The maintenance phase of the _____ is typically the most expensive.

 Check Answers

CHAPTER 13

USER
FOCUS

USING DATA FLOW DIAGRAMS

DFDs are one of the most important tools in a systems analyst's toolbox. It is much easier to get an overview of an information system by studying a DFD than by reading a lengthy description. Before you learn about DFD details, look at the DFD in Figure 13-18 and see if you can figure out whether it represents A&L's transaction processing system, MIS, DSS, or expert system.

FIGURE 13-18

Does this DFD represent A&L's transaction processing system, MIS, DSS, or expert system?

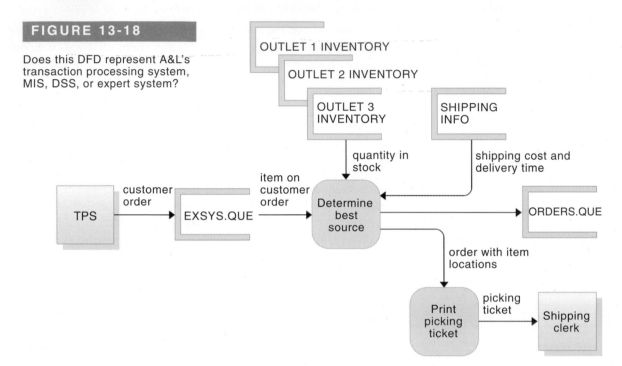

As you have probably recognized, the DFD in Figure 13-18 depicts A&L's new expert system. The purpose of this system is to figure out the best source for each item ordered by a customer. Obviously, if an item is in stock at the local outlet, that outlet is the best source. However, if the item is not in stock locally, the expert system will search the inventory of other A&L outlets. If it finds the item at one or more other outlets, the expert system will analyze shipping prices and times to select the best source. The system then prints a picking ticket at the appropriate outlet. A picking ticket is a list of inventory items and their locations that shipping clerks use to find the items to be packed in an order.

DFD Symbols

What is the significance of the different symbols on a DFD? The symbols shown in Figure 13-19 are the basic building blocks for a DFD.

The square box represents an external entity—an outside source or destination for data. An external entity might be a customer who places an order, a supplier from which a business receives inventory items, or another computer system that provides data. You should label external entities with a singular noun such as "Customer" or "Supplier."

The DFD in Figure 13-18 on the previous page shows two external entities: TPS (transaction processing system) and Shipping clerk. The cross-ship expert system receives data from the A&L transaction processing system and sends data to a shipping clerk.

FIGURE 13-19

Data flow diagram symbols.

External entity

Process

Data store

Data flow

A rounded rectangle, called a "process box," represents an activity such as "Print picking ticket," "Remove duplicates," or "Sort by last name." A process box label usually begins with a verb, such as "Print" or "Sort," to show that a process does something to the data. The DFD for A&L's system in Figure 13-18 contains two processes. You can see from the labels on these processes that this system determines which outlet is the best source for an item that a customer ordered. It also prints a picking ticket.

An open-ended rectangle represents a data store. It shows data at rest, such as when data is stored in a file on a hard disk. You can label data stores with the name of the file that contains the data. The DFD in Figure 13-18 contains several data stores. EXSYS.QUE holds customer orders while they are waiting to be processed. Each OUTLET INVENTORY data store represents the inventory data maintained by one of A&L's branch outlets. The SHIPPING INFO data store contains the shipping rates and times for delivery services, such as FedEx, UPS, and the postal service. ORDERS.QUE is a file that contains customer orders and, importantly, the nearest A&L outlet that has the item in stock.

An arrow represents a data flow—data that will be processed or stored by the information system. Arrows at the end of a data flow indicate what happens to the data—whether it is headed for a process, data store, or external entity. A double-ended arrow indicates that data moves in both directions. You should label data flow lines with the name of a record, such as "order form," or with a field name, such as "lastname." The DFD for the A&L system in Figure 13-18 shows that the data in this system is a customer order. A customer order contains the customer name and address, as well as the items ordered by the customer.

CHAPTER 13

Interpreting a DFD

How should I read a DFD so that I can understand the information system it represents? You can begin to understand a DFD if you first look at the external entities to find out where the data originates and where it is ultimately headed. Next, you can trace the path of the data by following the arrows. To find out how the data is processed, you can read the labels on the process boxes.

It is important to recognize that the data you are tracing is not the only data in the system. To process the data that you are tracing, the information system often requires other data. For example, to determine which outlet is the best source for items on a customer order, the information system needs to look at data stored in OUTLET INVENTORY and SHIPPING INFO. The annotated DFD in Figure 13-20 highlights some of the important points you can discover from the DFD of A&L's expert system.

FIGURE 13-20

Annotated A&L DFD.

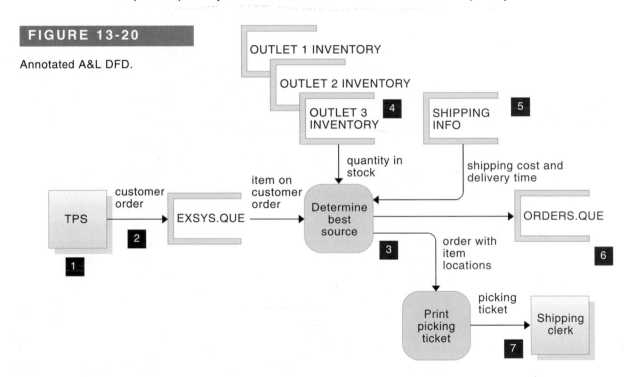

1 Data originates from the A&L transaction processing system and ends up in the hands of a shipping clerk and in the ORDERS.QUE data store.

2 The data originates as a record called "customer order."

3 The system carries out two processes: It determines the best source for an ordered item, and it prints a picking ticket.

4 To determine the best source for an inventory item, the system checks inventory using data from a series of data stores called OUTLET INVENTORY. Each data store contains the inventory for one A&L outlet store.

5 The system uses the data from the SHIPPING INFO data store if the item is not in stock at the local outlet.

6 After the system determines the best source, it has a customer order that contains a list of ordered items and the outlet from which each item can be shipped. This data is stored in ORDERS.QUE, where it can be accessed by A&L's other information systems. The order data is further processed by being printed as a picking ticket.

7 The order is filled by the shipping clerk based on information gathered by the cross-ship expert system.

Accuracy and Completeness

How can I tell whether a DFD is accurate? If someone shows you a DFD, it is likely that your feedback is needed on the completeness and accuracy of the data flows and processes. After you have interpreted the DFD and have an overview of the system it depicts, think carefully about each process. Examine the data that enters the process and the data produced by the process. Is the data that enters the process sufficient to produce the data that leaves the process? For example, suppose that the OUTLET INVENTORY data store was missing from A&L's expert system DFD. Without this data, how could the "Determine best source" process take an order item and produce the name of the outlet that has the item in stock? If OUTLET INVENTORY was omitted, the DFD would not be accurate.

You can also check the DFD for black holes and miracles. A **black hole** is a process that has no output. A process that just "does something" to data, but doesn't put that data anywhere, is useless. A **miracle** is a process that has no input. It is an aptly named mistake—like a wizard trying to conjure a bouquet of flowers from thin air, it is impossible for an information system to process data it doesn't have. The black holes and miracles you see in Figure 13-21 would be errors if you found them on a DFD.

FIGURE 13-21

Black holes and miracles.

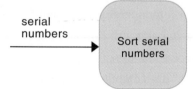

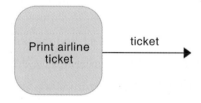

A popular video circulating on the Internet depicts a husky office worker in shirtsleeves, tapping tentatively at his keyboard and peering with puzzlement at the computer screen. Suddenly, he begins to bang on the keyboard. In frustration, he then swings the keyboard at the monitor, sending it crashing to the floor. Columnist Nick Wingfield reported on the video in the Wall Street Journal Interactive Edition, "The video, called Badday, has captivated thousands of Internet users as a vivid document of mankind's frustration with machines, a powerful reminder of the violent impulses nearly everyone has felt at one time or another when a monitor goes dark, a keyboard clunks out, or a word processing document simply disappears."

Today's computerized information systems require software, and much of the systems analysis and design process focuses on software development. Why is it, then, that computers and computer software are so often characterized as being difficult to use? How is it that one of the new words in the computer lexicon is "techno-rage"? What prompts comments like, "My machine sometimes makes me think I'm an idiot!"

Programmer and user-interface designer Alan Cooper offers an explanation and solution in his book, *The Inmates are Running the Asylum*. The book's title is a metaphor for what Cooper perceives as the current state of information system design and development. The "inmates" are computer programmers and the "asylum" is the frustrating, seemingly demented world of computer technology with its cryptic error messages, puzzling user manuals, and inscrutable "modes" of operation. According to Cooper, programmers don't intentionally create bad technology products. "Programmers aren't evil. They work hard to make their software easy to use. Unfortunately, their frame of reference is themselves, so they only make it easy to use for other software engineers, not for normal human beings." Cooper suggests that it is possible to create intuitive, easy-to-use technology products by devoting more time during the SDLC to developing detailed product specifications with the assistance of an "interactive designer" who is familiar with the psychology and habits of a typical computer user.

Paul Somerson, writing in *PC Computing* magazine asserts, "You shouldn't have to plod through manuals, or spend hours waiting on support lines just to get your work done. This stuff is way, way too hard and overcomplicated." Somerson offers a 10-point User's Bill of Rights that begins, "1. All computers should be forced to work the way people do, rather than the other way around."

The first point of Somerson's Bill of Rights echos the last point of another User's Bill of Rights, developed by Clare-Marie Karat, a psychologist and IBM researcher: "10. The user should be the master of software and hardware technology, not vice-versa. Products should be natural and intuitive to use."

Karat agrees with Cooper's comments about programmers being unable to understand the people who use their software. She says, "The profile of the people who use systems has changed, while the system, and the culture in which they have developed, have not adjusted... The engineers and computer scientists who design hardware and software know little about the needs and frustrations of consumers."

BusinessWeek columnist Stephen H. Wildstrom published Karat's Bill of Rights and asked for reader feedback. The response was overwhelming and led Wildstrom to comment in a follow-up article, "The computer industry has a lot of baffled, frustrated, and unhappy customers." Surprisingly, a number of readers disagreed with the tenets of the Bill of Rights. For example, Jef Raskin, one of the Macintosh computer interface designers pointed out that "the mouse was not intuitive. A person seeing one for the first time had no idea how to use it."

Until we are able to implant some kind of "instant computer genius" chip at birth, it might be that people will just have to invest some time learning how to use a computer. "It shouldn't take a Ph.D. to understand that a few hours invested in learning about the computer and its software will make subsequent products intuitively usable," wrote one *BusinessWeek* reader. Other readers questioned how much simplicity one could really expect from a computer. A computer that is as simple to use as a toaster would seem unlikely. As readers pointed out, a toaster is designed to do only one thing, whereas a computer essentially changes from one machine to another, depending on the software that it is using to perform a task.

InfoWeb
14

Techno-rage

Who is right? Can technology be simplified, yet remain powerful enough to accomplish complex tasks? The Techno-rage InfoWeb link provides more food for thought on this issue.

WHAT DO YOU THINK?

1. Can you identify with the frustration depicted in the Badday video? ○ Yes ○ No ○ Not sure

2. Is it possible to make information systems significantly easier to use? ○ Yes ○ No ○ Not sure

3. Would you agree that programmers do not understand the viewpoint of a typical computer user and consequently produce bad software? ○ Yes ○ No ○ Not sure

⬛➡ Save Responses

CHAPTER 13

CHAPTER 13 REVIEW ACTIVITIES

I N T E R A C T I V E   S U M M A R Y

The Interactive Summary helps you select important concepts and facts from this chapter. Fill in the blanks to best complete each sentence. When using the NP4 CD or NP4 Web site, you can click the Check Answers buttons to automatically score your answers. Place your Tracking Disk in the floppy disk drive if you want to save your scores.

The process of planning and building information systems is referred to as systems [_____] and design. Several methodologies exist for this process. The one that you use will depend on the type of system that you are constructing. In general, however, system development follows a system development [_____] cycle (SDLC), which consists of a number of steps, or "phases." The first phase of the SDLC is to [_____] needs. Typically, this task is performed by a project [_____], which interviews users, studies the current system, devises a(n) [_____] statement, and determines system requirements (also called [_____] factors).

In the [_____] phase of the SDLC, the project team identifies potential solutions, evaluates those solutions, and then selects the best one. The solution is then refined into a series of [_____] specifications that describe the way that the new information system should interact with the user, store data, process data, and format reports. To find the right hardware and software to implement the solution, the project team might send out a request for [_____], asking vendors to recommend a solution and specify hardware and software requirements. As an alternative, when team members know exactly what hardware and software they need for the solution, they can send out a request for [_____] that simply asks for vendor prices. ➡ Check Answers

During the [_____] phase of the SDLC, the project team supervises the technicians who set up new hardware, install programming languages and other application [_____] tools, create and test applications, and customize software. In this phase, three types of testing help ensure that new software works correctly. [_____] testing is performed on each module, then [_____] testing is performed to make sure that all of the modules work together correctly. [_____] testing ensures that all of the hardware and software components work together.

In the [_____] phase of the SDLC, data is converted from the old system to the new one, users are trained, and the new system goes live. During this phase, the information system undergoes a final test called [_____] testing, designed to assure the system's owner that the new system works as specified.

After installation, an information system enters the [_____] phase of its life cycle. During this phase, a(n) [_____] operator typically performs backups, monitors system utilization, and troubleshoots operational problems. As users discover bugs, programmers must fix them. Ongoing user support from a help [_____] might also be required. ➡ Check Answers

INTERACTIVE KEY TERMS

Make sure that you understand all of the boldfaced key terms presented in this chapter. If you're using the NP4 CD or NP4 Web site, you can use this list of terms as an interactive study activity. First, try to define a term in your own words, then click the term to compare your definition with the definition that is presented in the chapter.

CHAPTER 13

INTERACTIVE QUIZZES

Quiz yourself on important concepts from this chapter by filling in the blanks. When using the NP4 CD or NP4 Web site, you can type your answers, then use the Check Answers buttons to automatically score your responses. Place your Tracking Disk in the floppy disk drive if you want to save your scores.

1 Computer professionals called systems [   ] are often responsible for identifying problems with an information system, designing new systems, and supervising system development and installation.

2 According to the PIECES framework, an information system has a(n) [   ] problem if it does not respond quickly enough to users or it takes too long to complete processing tasks.

3 Project teams often use [   ] English to describe the logic of a process that takes place within an information system.

4 A(n) [   ] tool is specialized software that members of a project team can use to plan and document an information system.

5 A 4GL would be most useful during the analysis phase of the SDLC. True or false? [   ]

6 During a(n) [   ] conversion, the old information system is totally deactivated and replaced by a new system.

7 The [   ] phase of the SDLC is typically the most costly.

 Check Answers

Refer to the diagram and enter the correct answer into each box.

1 The diagram is called a(n) [   ].

2 The diagram includes [   ] processes.

3 [   ] is the label given to the external entity.

4 The arrows on the diagram are referred to as data [   ].

5 The box labeled "INVENTORY" is called a data [   ].

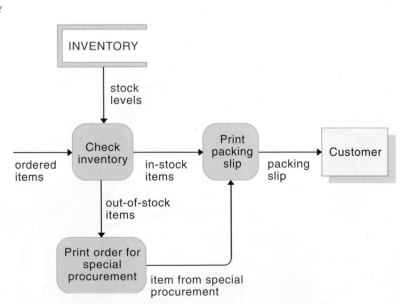

Check Answers

Check Answers

INTERACTIVE PRACTICE TESTS

When you use the NP4 CD or NP4 Web site, you can take practice tests that consist of 10 multiple-choice, true/false, and fill-in-the-blank questions. The 10 questions are selected at random from a large test bank, so each time you take a test, you'll receive a different set of questions. Your tests are scored immediately and you can print study guides that help you find the correct answers for any questions that you missed. If you are using a Tracking Disk, insert it in the floppy disk drive to save your test scores.

 Start Practice
Test

STUDY TIPS

Study Tips help you organize and consolidate the information in a chapter by making lists, outlines, charts, and sketches. You can use paper and pencil, or word processing software to complete most of the Study Tips activities.

1 Write a short explanation of the types of activities that occur in each of the five phases of the system development life cycle.

2 Indicate whether each statement describes a problem or a solution.

a. The desk clerks at a hotel need access to the central reservations database so they can find out whether rooms are available due to cancellations.

b. Notebook computers should be purchased for the salespeople so they can prepare quotations without returning to the main office.

c. When a customer calls and orders an item that is not in stock, the order clerks cannot find out when the item is expected to be back in stock.

d. The clerk in accounting needs a Zip drive.

e. It takes too long to print the current daily reports.

3 Create a table that shows the differences between unit testing, integration testing, system testing, and acceptance testing. Your table should show the purpose of the test, what is tested, and the phase of the SDLC in which it is tested.

4 For each of the problem descriptions, use the PIECES framework to indicate whether each should be classified as a performance, information, economics, control, efficiency, or service problem.

a. When an employee quits, sometimes the network manager is not notified and the ex-employee continues to have access to company data by using the Internet.

b. Customers at the Department of Motor Vehicles must wait while sales clerks walk to computer terminals located in the back of the office, check records, then return.

c. When order entry clerks complete an order, they must wait 10 seconds while the computer stores the order. During this time, they cannot enter other orders.

d. When patients are admitted to a hospital, the admitting clerk writes information on a paper form. This information is then sent to data entry, where it is entered into the hospital computer system. The data entry clerks are backlogged, so patient data is not available in the computer system for at least 12 hours.

5 Suppose you want to diagram the data flowing into a mail room. The data comes from the post office and ends up in employee mailboxes. The diagram should have one process, in which each item is sorted according to its address. Draw a DFD of the mail-sorting system. Label each symbol on the diagram.

PROJECTS

A project is an open-ended activity that will help you apply the concepts you have learned. Many projects require resources in addition to your textbook, such as current magazines, library materials, or Web access. When you tackle a project, be prepared to use your critical thinking skills, logical analysis, and your creativity.

1 **Evaluating Possible Solutions** Rodney Watson is a systems analyst for U-Fix-It hardware stores. U-Fix-It installed bar-code readers at each register to speed checkouts and improve inventory control. Unfortunately, the clerks are complaining that the bar-code labels are falling off many of the items. When this problem happens, the clerk must call for someone to manually check the price of the item. Rodney has identified four possible solutions.

   a. Switch to a bar-code label that has better adhesive on the back so the labels are less likely to fall off.

   b. Modify the system so that clerks can check the current price of an item on a computer price list from their terminals.

   c. Print weekly price lists and place them at each register so the clerks can check the price of any item.

   d. Hire additional workers to check prices so that customers don't have to wait so long for a price check.

Explain which of these solutions you would select and why. If you need additional information before making a decision, describe the information that you need.

2 **Problems and Solutions** Jennifer Aho works in the circulation department of *Cycle*, a magazine dedicated to bicycle and triathlon enthusiasts. The magazine's IS department prints a monthly report showing the current number of *Cycle* subscribers in each ZIP code. Jennifer calculates the total number of subscribers for the current month and enters this total in a worksheet. She then creates a line chart showing the increase or decrease in total subscribers for the current year. It takes Jennifer four hours each month to calculate the total number of subscribers, enter the total on her worksheet, and print the latest copy of the chart.

   a. Define the problem.

   b. Think of two possible solutions to this problem. Describe each solution.

   c. Which solution would you select? Why?

3 **Request for Proposal** Use your Web browser to search the Web for an actual request for proposal. You can use the search function at *www.lycos.com* or any other Internet search engines. Try the phrase "request for proposal" as the search string.

Select a request for proposal from the list and write a brief summary of the proposal that includes the following:

   a. The URL of the proposal

   b. The organization or business that submitted the proposal

   c. A brief summary of the problem that the organization is trying solve

4 **Cool CeeDees** Assume that you are the manager of a music store called Cool CeeDees. You have defined the following problem: "The current cash register and checkout system does not keep track of the titles of the CDs we sell. It takes too much time to manually count the number of copies of each CD remaining in stock to determine which CDs must be reordered." Write a one-page request for proposal, asking vendors to recommend a solution to this problem.

5 **CASE Tools** CASE tools are one of the most important items in a systems analyst's toolkit. Suppose you have been recently hired as a systems analyst, and your supervisor asks you to find and evaluate three CASE tools. Browse the Web and look in computer trade journals to find three CASE tools. Write a memo to your supervisor reporting on your progress. In the memo include the name of each CASE tool, its publisher, its price, and a short description of its purpose and features.

6 **Purchase Process** Most businesses purchase equipment, supplies, or inventory from various vendors. For example, the publisher of Barnett newspapers purchases supplies and equipment for its staff of reporters, editors, advertising agents, and production crew. Suppose a reporter needed a new notebook computer to take on field assignments. Use the data flow diagram below to discover how Barnett would track this reporter's purchase order. Write a one-page description of this process.

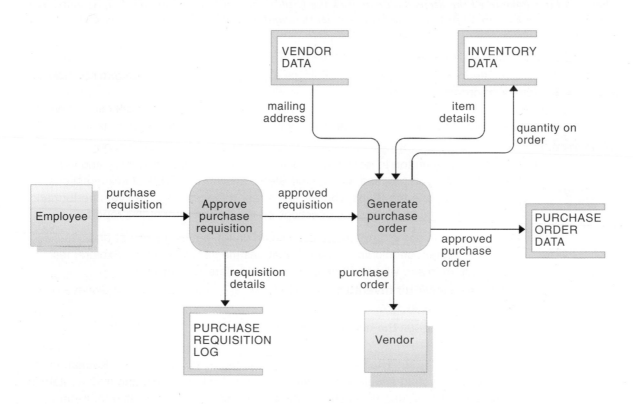

ADDITIONAL PROJECTS

Click the underlined text to link to the NP4 Web site (www.cciw.com/np4), where you can view and print additional projects for this chapter.

<u>**Systems Analysis Methodologies**</u>

<u>**Information Systems Department Careers**</u>

LAB ASSIGNMENTS

Software for this lab is provided on the NP4 CD and may also be available in your school's computer lab. To start the lab, click its blue icon.

Each lab has two parts: Steps and Explore. Use the Steps first to learn and review concepts. Read the information on each page and complete the numbered steps. As you work through the lab, you will be asked to answer QuickCheck questions about what you have learned. At the end of the lab, you will see a report that scores your answers to the QuickChecks. If your instructor wants you to turn in this report, click the Print button on the QuickCheck Report screen.

When you have completed the Steps, you can click the Explore button to complete the Lab Assignments. You can also use Explore to practice the skills you learned and to explore concepts on your own.

In the System Testing Lab, you are responsible for testing the expert system designed for A&L Outfitters. You will discover whether the expert system correctly determines how to cross-ship orders from one A&L outlet to another. If you do all of the Lab Assignments in order, you will thoroughly test the system. Your instructor might select only one or two of these assignments, however; in that case, you'll get a flavor of the system testing process.

1. Click the Steps button to learn how to place test data in A&L's inventory and to place test orders. As you proceed through the Steps, answer the QuickCheck questions. After you complete the Steps, you will see a report that summarizes your performance on the QuickChecks. Follow the directions on the screen to print this report.

2. When an item is not in stock at the destination outlet, but is in stock at *one* other outlet, the system should find the outlet that has the item in stock. In Explore, test A&L's system to see whether it processes such orders correctly:

   a. Use the **View/Edit Inventory** dialog box to make sure that only the Geneva outlet has item 3002 in stock.

   b. Place an order on the queue for item 3002 with Katmandu as the destination outlet.

   c. Process the order. The item is not in stock at the destination outlet, Katmandu, so the expert system should search the inventory of other outlets and find the item in Geneva. The picking ticket should show Ship From: Genv and Ship to: Katm.

   d. Design a test plan that tests at least one order from each outlet and that tests at least one order for each of the five inventory items. Carry out your test plan and record the results. Does the system correctly process orders for an item that is not in stock at the destination outlet, but is in stock at one of the other A&L outlets? If not, explain what the system does wrong, and how it should work.

3. When an item is not in stock at the destination outlet, but is in stock at *two or more* other outlets, the system should find the outlet with the lowest shipping cost. In Explore, conduct the following tests to see whether such orders are processed correctly:

   a. Use the **View/Edit Inventory** dialog box to make sure that only the Geneva and Telluride outlets have item 3002 in stock.

   b. Place an order for item 3002 with Katmandu as the destination outlet.

   c. Process the order. The item is not in stock at the destination outlet, Katmandu, but it is available in Geneva and Telluride. The expert system should select the outlet with the lowest shipping cost.

d. Click the View Shipping Info button to check the shipping information. Click Katmandu, the destination outlet, to view the cost per pound and the time in days to ship an item to that outlet from each of the other outlets. Of the two outlets where this item is available (Geneva and Telluride), Geneva's shipping cost is lowest. The picking ticket should show Ship From: Genv.

e. Design a test plan of five tests to further test how the system handles orders that are in stock at two or more outlets other than the destination outlet. Carry out your test plan and record the results. Did the system correctly process the orders in your test plan? If not, explain what the system did wrong, and how it should work.

4 When an item is in stock at two outlets with the same shipping cost, the system should find the outlet with the fastest shipping time. In Explore, conduct the following tests to see if such situations are processed correctly.

a. Click the **View Shipping Info** button, then click **Guatemala City** as the destination outlet. Notice that items shipped to Guatemala City from Lima and Geneva have the same shipping cost—$26 per pound. Also notice that items shipped from Lima will arrive more quickly—shipping takes two days from Lima, but three days from Geneva. Therefore, if an out-of-stock item is needed in Guatemala City, but it is in stock in Geneva and Lima, the expert system should select Lima. Let's test this feature.

b. Make sure that item 3004 is in stock *only* in Lima and Geneva, then order item 3004 with Guatemala City as the destination.

c. Process the order. Because the shipping cost is the same from Lima and Geneva, the expert system should select the outlet with the fastest shipping time. The picking ticket should show Ship From: Lima.

d. Shipping rates are also the same from Telluride and Guatemala City to Geneva. Set up a test in which item 3005 needs to be shipped to Geneva, but is in stock only in Telluride and Guatemala City.

e. Does the system correctly process an order for an item that is in stock at two outlets with the same shipping cost? If not, explain what the system does wrong, and how it should work.

5 In Explore, test the following scenario: If an item is not in stock in the destination outlet, but is in stock at two other outlets with the same shipping cost and the same shipping time, the system should find the outlet that has the highest quantity of the item in stock.

a. There is one situation in which an item can be in stock in two outlets with the same shipping cost and the same shipping time: if an item is in stock in Telluride and Guatemala City and is to be shipped to Katmandu. Make sure that Telluride has two of item 3005 in stock, and Guatemala City has five of item 3005 in stock. Also, make sure that item 3005 is not in stock in any other outlets.

b. Place an order on the queue for item 3005 with Katmandu as the destination outlet.

c. Process the order. Because there are more of item 3005 in stock in Guatemala City, the picking ticket should show Ship From: Guatemala City.

d. Does the system correctly process an order for an item that is in stock in two outlets with the same shipping cost and the same shipping time? If not, explain what the system does wrong, and how it should work.

CHAPTER 13

INFOWEB

The InfoWeb is your guide to print, film, television, and electronic resources. Use it to obtain updates on quickly changing technical information and to locate information for research papers. If you're using the NP4 CD, click the InfoWeb Site icon on the left side of this paragraph to access the online InfoWeb links. Otherwise, use your Web browser and type in the address of the NP4 Web site: www.cciw.com/np4. At the Web site you'll find up-to-date links to the topics covered in this chapter.

1 Expeditions

The Norwegian expedition to the North Pole is based on a true story chronicled by Borge Ousland in a March 1991 *National Geographic* article, "The Hard Way to the North Pole." If expeditions interest you, you can connect to *www.nationalgeographic.com/andes/index.html* to read about the National Geographic resident explorer's expedition to the Indes in Search of Inca Secrets. At the Web site, you can link to the expedition or to a virtual autopsy of a teenage Inca girl who was sacrificed in an ancient Inca ritual. At another Web site (*outside.starwave.com/places/africa*), you can read "Outside Online: Kilimanjaro Climb for Care" and listen to RealAudio broadcasts that were made during the climb. The University of California Research Expeditions Program at *shanana.berkeley.edu/urep* provides information about field research expeditions that are open to public participation. The range of expeditions is broad, from studies of biodiversity to studies of archaeological sites. Expedition sites are located in Yosemite National Park, Ireland, Costa Rica, Kenya, Brazil, Hawaii, Ecuador, and other places around the world.

2 Mythical Man-Month

Frederick P. Brooks' book, *The Mythical Man-Month* (Addison-Wesley, 1995), is among the classics of information systems literature. The book describes why information systems are so difficult to develop. First published in 1975, it was revised in 1995 and several new chapters were added. You can read reviews of this new edition at *daffy.robelle.com/smugbook/manmonth.html*. Another source of reviews is the Amazon online bookstore at *www.amazon.com*. After you connect to the site, enter "Mythical Man-Month." Brooks received the Bower award and Prize in Science (*sln.fi.edu/inquirer/brooks.html*).

3 Methodologies

Different systems analysis and design methodologies offer a variety of approaches to the process of creating an information system. The classic methodology, structured analysis, was pioneered by Gane, Sarson, and Yourdon. Yourdon's book, *Modern Structured Analysis* (Yourdon Press, 1991), summarizes this approach. The University of Missouri at St. Louis has an excellent systems analysis site with links to many related topics at *www.umsl.edu/~sauter/analysis/analysis_links.html*. Andersen Consulting has spent many years refining a systems analysis methodology referred to as METHOD/1. Because Andersen is one of the largest single-source employers of information systems personnel, it pays to become familiar with its methodology. Connect to the Andersen Web site at *www.ac.com:80/services/foundation/foun_prod.html*, and scroll down to "Method/1." Joint application development (JAD) emphasizes the requirements of a new information system, rather than an extensive analysis of the old one. Users provide input to analysts during JAD sessions. The book *Joint Application Development*, second edition, by Jane Wood and Denise Silver (John Wiley, 1995) provides a good overview of JAD methodology. On the Web, you'll find a quick introduction to JAD at *www2.computerworld.com/home/print9497.nsf/All/SL47jad*.

An alternative to JAD, rapid application development (RAD), uses extensive prototyping to churn out software within a compressed timeframe. The book to read on this topic is *Rapid Development: Taming Wild Software Schedules* by Steve McConnell (Microsoft Press, 1996). You'll find excerpts on the Web at *www.construx.com/stevemcc/rdexcrpt.htm*. You can learn about object-oriented analysis and design methodologies in *Object-Oriented Analysis* by Peter Coad and Edward Yourdon (Yourdon Press, 1991). The Web site *quepasa.cs.tu-berlin.de/~bg/dipl2om/section1_6_0_1.html* has a nice discussion and diagrams of how object-oriented analysis fits into the SDLC.

4 IS Departments

Information systems departments are relatively new arrivals on the corporate organizational chart. In some organizations, IS is a separate organizational branch; in others, it is under the organizational umbrella of the finance department. Within the IS department, employees were traditionally arranged in a hierarchy that included high-level managers, middle managers, and technicians. You can see examples of some IS department organizational charts if you enter "IS department organizational chart" in any Web search engine. Recently, the trend is to flatten this hierarchy by removing middle managers. You can read an interesting online article about this trend in "Dotted Lines and Crooked Arrows" by Mitch Betts at *www2.computerworld.com/home/print9497.nsf/All/Slorg214AD6*. A similar *ComputerWorld* article called "Rebuilding the IS Organization" by Robert Zawacki can be found at *www.computerworld.com/home/online9697.nsf/all/951101SL9511lead*. What's it like to work in an IS department? Connect to *www2.computerworld.com/home/online9697.nsf/All/971006path* to read "Choosing Your Career Path" by Lina Fafard.

5 Systems Analysts

At *ComputerWorld*'s online careers site, *www.computerworld.com/car/index.html*, you can find current and archived articles on important career issues, a salary survey, a special report on IS education, a skills survey, and a list of the 100 best places to work. The Computer Museum's Careers in Computing section at *www.tcm.org/html/resources/cmp-careers/cnc-sysanalyst.html* has a detailed description of what systems analysts do, where they are likely to work, and what the career outlook for this profession is. In addition, this Web page provides links to other Internet resources for systems analysts, including the Institute of Electronic and Electrical Engineers, The Computer Society, and the International Programmers Guild. You might also want to visit the High Tech Workforce Resource Center at *www.techworkforce.org* for a description of information technology careers, including systems analyst.

6 Project Teams

The trend in most organizations is toward teamwork. For a general definition of teamwork, a description of the characteristics of successful teams, tips on team building, and more, visit *home.nycap.rr.com/klarsen/learnorg/index.html*. More specific information about IS project teams can be found in university course outlines at sites such as *www.mce.be/events/740.htm* or *www.infosys.utas.edu.au/courses/units/BSA302.html*. Information about building a project team—specifically, what to look for when selecting IS personnel, consultants, and business participants—can be found at *www.itmweb.com/methd03a.htm*. The article "It's a Brand-New Ballgame as Business Workers Fill IS Jobs" (*www.idg.net/crd_business_9-52581.html*) provides insight into team building when business managers join an IS project team. NASA Headquarters Library has an extensive reading list pertaining to project teams and teamwork at *www.hq.nasa.gov/office/hqlibrary/ppm/ppm5.htm*. Items on the list range from articles in *Fortune* magazine to books from the late 1980s and early 1990s, when corporations first began to recognize the importance of teamwork for successful project development.

7 CASE Tools

CASE software automates, manages, and simplifies the development of information systems by providing tools to summarize system requirements, diagram old and proposed systems, schedule development tasks, prepare documentation, and develop program code. You'll find a good, though lengthy discussion of CASE tools and applications in "The Effective Use of Automated Application Development Tools" by P. J. Guinan, J. G. Cooprider, and S. Sawyer at *www.research.ibm.com/journal/sj/361/guinan.html*. A really terrific CASE site is hosted by Applied Information Science at *www.aisintl.com*. At the AIS site, you'll find nonbiased product reviews of CASE tools and a detailed bibliography (*www.aisintl.com/case/biblio.html*) of CASE book and articles. In addition, you can locate information about the major CASE software products at vendor sites such as CASEwise (*www.casewise.com*), PowerDesigner (*www.sybase.com/products/powerdesigner*), Designer/2000 (*www.oracle.com*), WinA&D (*excelsoftware.com*), and System Architect (*www.popkin.com*).

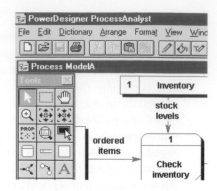

8 Solutions

One way to come up with solutions is to look at how other organizations have solved similar problems. Microsoft Solution Product Guides at *www.microsoft.com/industry/sql7* presents articles that describe how Microsoft's information technology products provide business solutions in industries as diverse as accounting, education, engineering, health care, manufacturing, retail, and public safety. IBM Business Solutions at *www.ibm.com/Solutions* has descriptions of how IBM products provide solutions for both small businesses and multinational corporations. Some of the industries include banking, finance, and securities; insurance; telecommunications and media; travel and transportation; and utility and energy services. You can find similar discussions of information technology solutions for businesses at Digital Products and Solutions, *www.compaq.com/products/messaging.html*, and Sun Products & Solutions, *www.sun.com/products-n-solutions*.

9 RFPs & RFQs

RFPs and RFQs can become fairly lengthy documents because organizations like to "cover all the bases" to make sure that a vendor is legitimate and will supply an accurate price quote. Before you create your own RFP or RFQ, it pays to look at those created by other organizations. Use the Lycos search engine (*www.lycos.com*) and enter "RFP" or "RFQ" as the search term. The Nova Scotia Department of Finance site at *www.gov.ns.ca/finance/ptns/tocompl.htm* illustrates in great detail all of the steps and documents that can be used in a request for proposal process. Looking at these Web pages should give you a good idea of the steps in the RFP process in a government agency and the various documents that need to be prepared. An RFQ typically provides a client with a price quote on equipment, software, or services. Some companies provide clients with a standard RFQ form—often available on the Web—which helps to streamline the RFQ process. Examples include Cleveland Circuits at *www.libertycontrolsales.com/rfq.htm*; DFS International, Inc., Request for Quotation at *www.dfsintl.com/rfiquote.html*; and Mission Electronics Corporation Request for Quotation at *www.dram.com/ndex.htm* (then click "QuickQuote").

10 System Testing

A good set of testing FAQs is available at *www.faqs.org/faqs/software-eng/testing-faq*. At the STORM site (*www.mtsu.edu/~storm*) hosted by Middle Tennessee State University, you'll find some handy links to testing information. The classic article "Bug Bounty Hunters" from *Byte* magazine (*www.byte.com/art/9711/sec17/art3.htm*) emphasizes three important points about testing: (1) the cost of debugging software increases as you move through the software development process, (2) to ensure high-quality products, testing needs to include validation and verification throughout the entire development process, and (3) testing costs a lot of money and can delay release of a product to market. The article offers automated software testing tools as a partial solution to these problems and describes how they work.

11 Training

Training employees to use a new information system can become a logistical nightmare. Imagine training thousands of employees on a system they have to begin using tomorrow. *Datamation* and *ComputerWorld* magazines frequently include articles about employee training. For example, "The Right Formula for Training" by Lauren Gibbons Paul provides an overview of training options, including computer-based and Web-based training (*www.datamation.com/entap/09jit.html*). Another article, "Choose the Right Training Strategy" by Peter Katz and Cynthia Katz, provides a framework for evaluating training methods (*www.datamation.com/roi/ChoosetheRight.html*). One analyst maintains that "Eighty of every $100 of IS training is a complete waste." Joseph Maglitta's poetically titled article "Train in Vain?", located at *www2.computerworld.com/home/print9497.nsf/All/SL0825jm*, explains why training often fails to provide employees with the skills they need to effectively use a new information system.

12 Maintenance

Two approaches to the high cost of maintaining an information system include outsourcing and restructuring. The *Datamation* article, "Outsource Your Maintenance Migraines" by Deborah Ashbrand (*www.datamation.com/servc/06out.html*), explains why and how it can be cost-effective to outsource information system maintenance tasks. Another *Datamation* article, "Death by Development" by Peter Vogel (*www.datamation.com/netmg/Thinkwrap_960315.html*), explains why it might be advantageous to rethink the division between IS development and maintenance personnel. Many maintenance responsibilities fall on the shoulders of the systems operator. To find out if you might like this job, connect to *stats.bls.gov/oco/ocos128.htm* or *www.tcm.org/html/resources/cmp-careers/cnc-operator.html*. For an overview of how maintenance activities fit into the overall IS department, connect to *www.blackmagic.com/ses/bruceg/sysadm.html* and read "Sample System Administrator Manual" by Bruce C. Gabrielson.

13 DFDs

A data flow diagram is one of the many diagramming tools in the systems analyst's toolbox. For a quick overview of DFDs, connect to the Applied Information Science site at *www.aisintl.com/case/dfd.html*. DFDs were suggested as early as 1977 in the now classic text, *Structured Systems Analysis* by Gane and Sarson (Prentice-Hall, 1977). An alternative approach using a slightly different symbol set was proposed by Tom De Marco in *Structured Analysis and Systems Specifications* (Yourdon, Inc., 1979). You'll find a sample set of DFDs at Professor Sauter's site, *www.umsl.edu/~sauter/analysis/dfd/dfd.htm*.

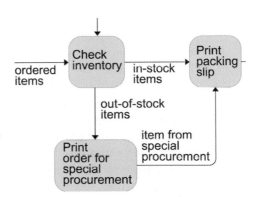

14 Techno-rage

The pace at which technology has improved does not seem to be keeping pace with the rate at which it is invading our lives. As technology proliferates, more and more "nontechnical" people are called upon to use technology-driven devices, from ATMs to in-car mapping programs. Techno-rage, like road rage, seems to be an underlying current in many work environments. You can view the Badday video, learn its history, and read some interesting commentary by searching for "Badday" or connecting to sites such as *www.visi.com/~rico/badday2.html*. Nick Wingfield's *Wall Street Journal* article about the video is on the Web at *www.download.net/misc/badday.txt*. Paul Somerson's User's Bill of Rights is online at *www.zdnet.com/pccomp/opinion/opin0498/paul0498.html*. *BusinessWeek's* online archives contain Stephen Wildstrom's interesting article, "A Computer User's Manifesto" (*www.businessweek.com/1998/39/b3597037.htm*), which features Clare-Marie Karat's User's Bill of Rights, and "Computer Users Are Mad as Hell" (*www.bsinessweek.com/1998/42/b36000052.htm*). You can also use any search engine to look for the term "techno-rage." Check your local library, bookstore, or your favorite online bookstore for Alan Cooper's book, *The Inmates Are Running the Asylum*.

CHAPTER 14 MANAGING DATABASES

PREVIEW

Chapter 14 begins with an overview of the terminology associated with databases. It then presents several models for structuring the data in a database. Next, the chapter turns to more practical matters, including database software and database management tasks. The *User Focus* section describes how to use Boolean logic to search for information in disk-based and Web-based databases.

When you have finished this chapter, you should be able to:

■ Explain the difference between a flat file and a database

■ Define the term "data independence" and explain how it applies to file management systems and database management systems

■ Differentiate between a record type and a record occurrence

■ Describe the distinguishing characteristics of the four major database models

■ Recommend whether to use custom software, file management software, database management software, or object-oriented tools to solve a data management problem

■ List six major database management activities

■ Use Boolean logic to construct SQL and Internet search engine queries

CHAPTER 14 LAB

SQL
Queries

HOT LIPS

*M*A*S*H*, a "two thumbs up" film made in 1970, depicted the hijinks of doctors and nurses in a Mobile Army Surgical Hospital (M.A.S.H.) during the Korean War. The film quickly was recast for television and became a hit series. Millions of viewers tuned in to catch the exploits of two irreverent doctors, John McIntyre and Hawkeye Pierce; a clever procurement officer named Radar O'Reilly; and an officious head nurse, Margaret "Hot Lips" Houlihan.

It was during the Korean War that the first commercial electronic computer predicted the outcome of the 1952 presidential election. At that time, some experts predicted that only five or six of these machines would be sufficient to satisfy the world's data processing needs. Using computers to maintain data in a M.A.S.H. unit was unthinkable then. Today, however, computers are deployed with U.S. troops all over the world. Computers are also standard equipment in virtually every hospital and medical clinic.

Our society is becoming increasingly dependent on information stored in medical, law enforcement, financial, and government databases. In Chapter 3, you learned some basic, practical database skills. The emphasis in Chapter 14 provides a more technical perspective on databases, presenting information that is especially useful to anyone who might be setting up databases in a school or office.

InfoWeb
1

M*A*S*H

FILE AND DATABASE CONCEPTS

The term *data file* has several meanings within the context of computing. You might think of a data file as a file that contains any type of data, including text, numbers, graphics, sounds, and even software modules. Alternatively, you might think of a data file as any file that is not an executable or program file. Both are valid definitions, but the term *data file* might also refer to a structured file or database, such as an e-mail address book, which contains information that has been organized in a uniform format.

Database Concepts

Because the term *data file* has multiple definitions, when you see it in a computer magazine or documentation, you might have to use clues from the context of the article to decide exactly what it means. In this chapter, "data file" refers to a file that holds a collection of information that is organized in a uniform format. Such a data file could hold the information for a simple address book, an inventory list, a student roster, an airline's flight schedules, and so on.

The tasks associated with maintaining and accessing the data stored in a data file are often referred to as **data management**. In this chapter, you will learn about data management concepts by using data about the employees who work at Midtown General Hospital. The people who work in the Midtown Human Resources department use some of this data to maintain basic information about each employee, track absenteeism, examine gender equality, and make staffing projections. The payroll department also uses some of the data to generate employee paychecks. The Midtown data is stored in a series of data files. Each data file has a **file structure** that describes the way in which the data is stored in that file. Figure 14-1 shows some of the data in Midtown's Employee file and provides a review of basic file terminology.

FIGURE 14-1

A file contains records that are made up of fields.

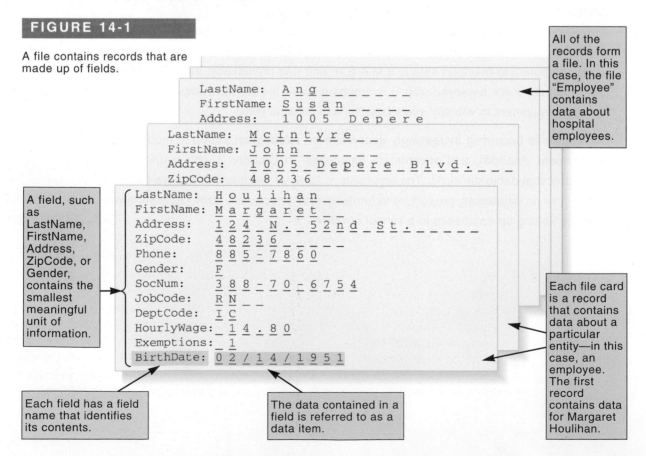

All of the records form a file. In this case, the file "Employee" contains data about hospital employees.

```
LastName:    A n g _ _ _ _ _ _ _
FirstName:   S u s a n _ _ _ _ _
Address:     1 0 0 5   D e p e r e

LastName:    M c I n t y r e _ _
FirstName:   J o h n _ _ _ _ _ _
Address:     1 0 0 5 _ D e p e r e _ B l v d . _ _ _
ZipCode:     4 8 2 3 6

LastName:    H o u l i h a n _ _
FirstName:   M a r g a r e t _ _
Address:     1 2 4 _ N . _ 5 2 n d _ S t . _ _ _ _ _ _
ZipCode:     4 8 2 3 6 _ _ _ _ _
Phone:       8 8 5 - 7 8 6 0
Gender:      F
SocNum:      3 8 8 - 7 0 - 6 7 5 4
JobCode:     R N _ _
DeptCode:    I C
HourlyWage:  _ 1 4 . 8 0
Exemptions:  _ 1
BirthDate:   0 2 / 1 4 / 1 9 5 1
```

A field, such as LastName, FirstName, Address, ZipCode, or Gender, contains the smallest meaningful unit of information.

Each field has a field name that identifies its contents.

The data contained in a field is referred to as a data item.

Each file card is a record that contains data about a particular entity—in this case, an employee. The first record contains data for Margaret Houlihan.

Fields

What is the basic building block for a data file? As you saw in Figure 14-1, a **field** contains the smallest unit of meaningful data, so you might call it the basic building block for a data file. Each field has a **field name** that describes its contents. For example, the field name BirthDate might describe a field containing an employee birth date.

A field can be either variable-length or fixed-length. A **variable-length field** is like an accordion—it expands to fit the data you enter, up to some maximum limit. A **fixed-length field** contains a predetermined number of characters (bytes). The data that you enter in a fixed-length field cannot exceed the allocated field length. Moreover, if the data you enter is shorter than the allocated length, blank spaces are automatically added to fill the field. All of the fields in Figure 14-1 are fixed length. The underscores indicate the number of characters that are allocated for each field.

Data Types

Are there any special rules about the data I can enter in a field? The data that you can enter into a field depends on the field's data type. From a technical perspective, the **data type** specifies the way the data is represented on the disk and in RAM. From a user perspective, the data type determines the way you can manipulate the data. Every field in a file is assigned a data type.

The two most common data types are numeric and character. A **numeric data type** is assigned to fields containing numbers that you might want to manipulate mathematically by adding, averaging, multiplying, and so forth. As an example, the HourlyWage field in Figure 14-1 is a numeric field, so the data in this field can be multiplied by the number of hours worked to calculate an employee's pay. There are two main numeric data types: real and integer. The data in the HourlyWage field is a **real number** because it contains a decimal point. The data in the Exemptions field is a whole number or **integer**.

The **character data type**, which is also referred to as the "string data type," is assigned to fields containing data that does not need to be mathematically manipulated. Examples of character data include names, descriptions, cities, state abbreviations, telephone numbers, and Social Security numbers.

Some of the data we call "numbers" does not require a numeric data type. A Social Security "number" is an example of data that looks numeric but would not be mathematically manipulated. Social Security numbers, therefore, are usually stored as character data. Other examples of "numbers" that are generally stored as character data include phone numbers and ZIP codes.

Some file and database management systems provide additional data types such as date, logical, and memo. You would use the **date data type** when you want to manipulate dates, such as when you want to store 10/15/01 but display "October 15, 2001." The **logical data type** is used to store true/false or yes/no data using minimal storage space. For example, you might want to store data in a field to indicate whether an employee has a CPR certificate. You could use a logical field called CPRCert in which you would enter either Y or N. A **memo data type** usually provides a variable-length field into which you can enter comments. For example, a human resources manager might use a memo field to store comments about an employee's job performance.

Records

What is the relationship between an entity and a record? An **entity** is a person, place, thing, or event about which you want to store data. A **record** contains fields of data about one entity. For example, one of the records for Midtown employees contains data about the entity Margaret Houlihan.

The **record length** is a measure of the maximum number of bytes that a record is designed to hold. A data file with fixed-length fields will have fixed-length records; therefore, the same amount of storage space is required for each record. For example, every record in the Midtown Employee file contains the same number of characters. You might wonder how this is possible if the data in the fields is different for each record. What if an employee has a very long last name—shouldn't that record be longer than one for an employee with a short last name? The answer is no. Recall that blanks are added to fields that contain data with less than the maximum allocated bytes. Therefore, including the blanks, each of the records contains the same number of bytes.

Calculating a file's record length is important because it helps determine storage needs. Suppose that you want to store a data file on a 1.44 MB floppy disk. You have approximately 1,440,000 bytes of storage space available. Could you fit 10,000 of the Midtown employee records on this disk? To answer this question, study Figure 14-2, which explains how to calculate the size of one employee record and then, from that calculation, determine the number of records that will fit on a disk.

FIGURE 14-2

Calculating record size and storage requirements.

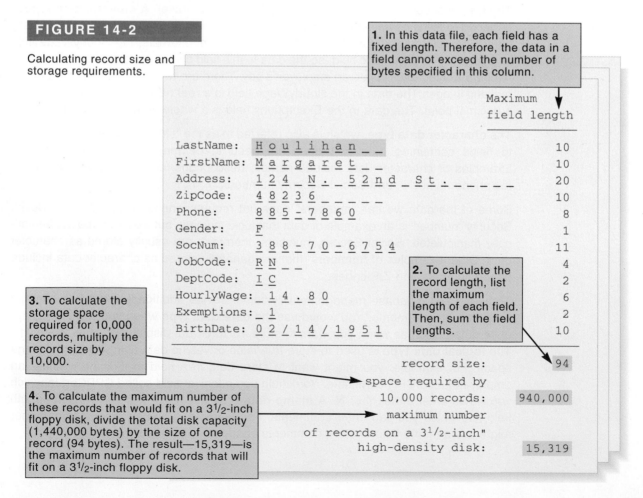

1. In this data file, each field has a fixed length. Therefore, the data in a field cannot exceed the number of bytes specified in this column.

Maximum field length

Field	Value	Maximum field length
LastName:	Houlihan _ _	10
FirstName:	Margaret _ _	10
Address:	1 2 4 _ N . _ 5 2 n d _ S t . _ _ _ _ _	20
ZipCode:	4 8 2 3 6 _ _ _ _ _	10
Phone:	8 8 5 - 7 8 6 0	8
Gender:	F	1
SocNum:	3 8 8 - 7 0 - 6 7 5 4	11
JobCode:	R N _ _	4
DeptCode:	I C	2
HourlyWage:	_ 1 4 . 8 0	6
Exemptions:	_ 1	2
BirthDate:	0 2 / 1 4 / 1 9 5 1	10

2. To calculate the record length, list the maximum length of each field. Then, sum the field lengths.

3. To calculate the storage space required for 10,000 records, multiply the record size by 10,000.

4. To calculate the maximum number of these records that would fit on a 3 1/2-inch floppy disk, divide the total disk capacity (1,440,000 bytes) by the size of one record (94 bytes). The result—15,319—is the maximum number of records that will fit on a 3 1/2-inch floppy disk.

record size: 94

space required by 10,000 records: 940,000

maximum number of records on a 3 1/2-inch" high-density disk: 15,319

Record Types and Record Occurrences

Who specifies the fields that a record contains? The person who creates the file structure for a data file defines the fields it will contain. This task is similar to designing a blank form for a manual record-keeping system or card file. The record structure is referred to as a **record type**. Once you've entered data into a record, it is referred to as a **record occurrence**. Midtown has record occurrences for Margaret Houlihan and other employees.

The number and names of the fields in a record depend on the data that the records will contain. Different record types are needed for different data. An organization or business will typically need a number of different record types for storing data. For example, Midtown has defined four record types for storing human resources data:

■ Employee information is stored using a record type called Employee.

■ Job classifications are stored using a record type called Job.

■ Department descriptions are stored using a record type called Department.

■ Payroll history is stored using a record type called Timecard.

Look at Figure 14-3 to get a general idea of the record types maintained by Midtown.

FIGURE 14-3

Midtown maintains record types for employees, job classifications, department descriptions, and employee timecards in four record ʼ

Job

```
JobTitle:     _ _ _ _ _ _ _ _ _ _ _ _ _ _ _ _ _ _ _
JobCode:      _ _ _ _
PayGrade:     _ _
Description: _ _ _ _ _ _ _ _ _ _ _ _ _ _ _ _ _ _ _
             _ _ _ _ _ _ _ _ _ _ _ _ _ _ _ _ _
```

Employee

```
LastName:    _ _ _ _ _ _ _ _ _
FirstName:   _ _ _ _ _ _ _ _ _
Address:     _ _ _ _ _ _ _ _ _
ZipCode:     _ _ _ _ _ _ _ _
Phone:       _ _ _ _ _ _ _
Gender:      _
SocNum:      _ _ _ _ _ _ _ _ _
JobCode:     _ _ _ _
DeptCode:    _ _
HourlyWage: _ _ _ _ _ _
Exemptions: _ _
BirthDate:   _ _ _ _ _ _ _ _ _
```

Department

```
DepartmentName: _ _ _ _ _ _ _ _ _ _ _ _ _ _ _
DeptCode:       _ _
OfficeNumber:   _ _ _ _
Phone:          _ _ _ _ _ _ _ _
```

Timecard

```
PayPeriod:    _ _  _ _ _ _ _ _ _
HoursWorked: _ _
SocNum:       _ _ _ _ _ _ _ _ _ _
```

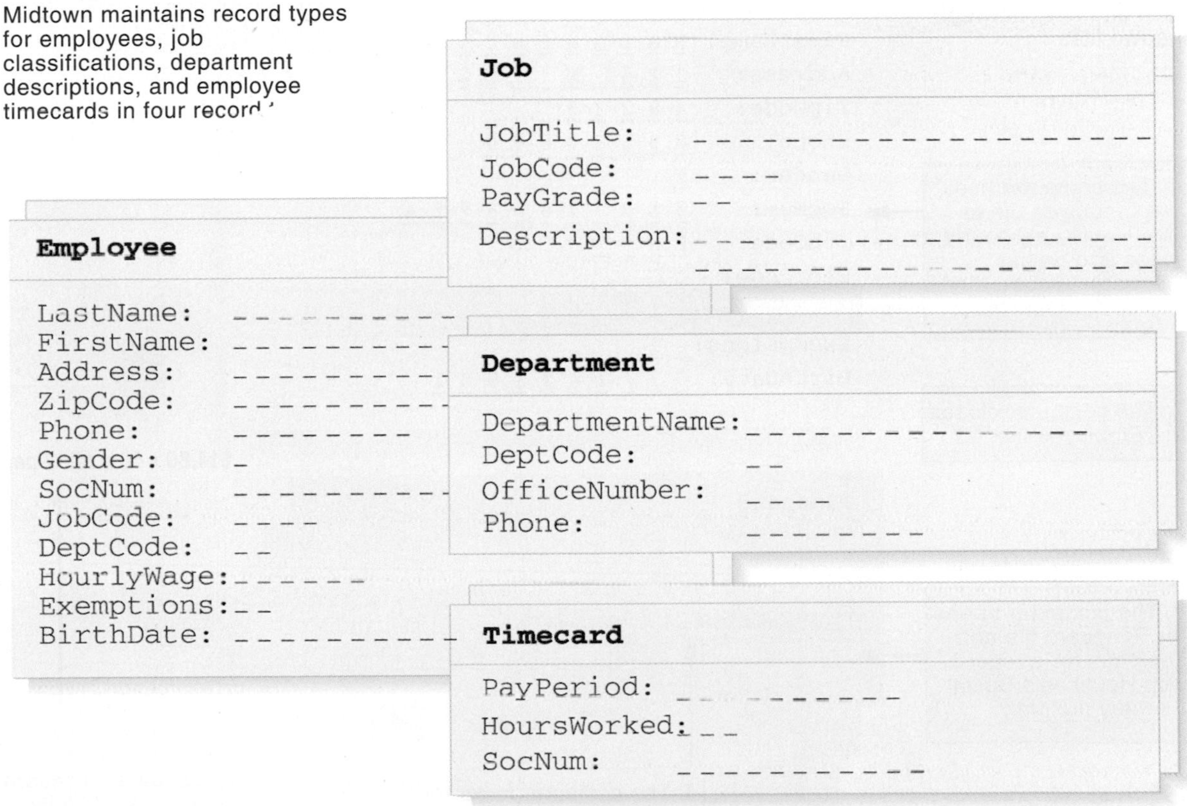

Flat Files

Do all of the records in a data file contain the same fields? As you learned in Chapter 2, the term *flat file* is sometimes used to refer to a data file in which all of the records have the same field names, field lengths, and data types. You could also say that a flat file is a single *record type*.

People use the term *flat file* primarily when they want to distinguish between a single file and a database. The Employee data file that you saw in Figure 14-1 is a flat file because all of the records are the same record type—they have the same fields, field lengths, and data types.

Flat files are not particularly efficient for complex data management tasks. Suppose, for example, that Midtown stored employee data in one file and timecard data in another file. Margaret Houlihan's hourly wage is stored in the Employee file, but the number of hours she worked is stored in the Timecard file. To calculate Houlihan's paycheck, the computer has to first open the Employee file to get the hourly wage, then close this file. Next, it must open the Timecard file, find Houlihan's timecard, and find the hours she worked. Finally, it must perform the multiplication, as shown in Figure 14-4.

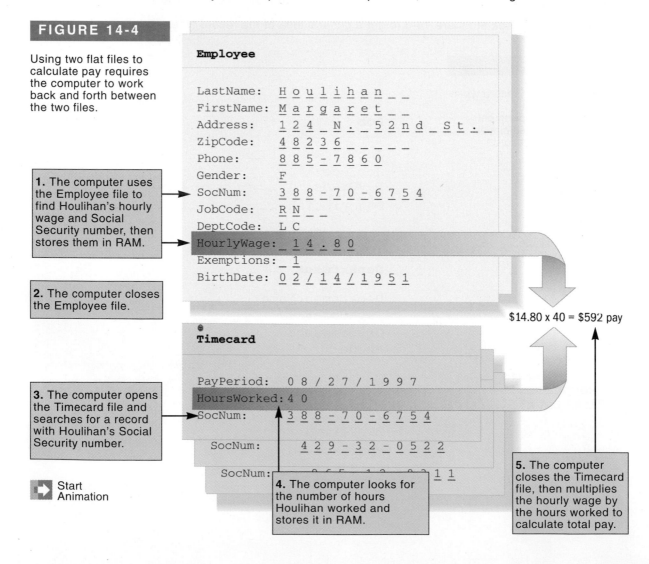

FIGURE 14-4

Using two flat files to calculate pay requires the computer to work back and forth between the two files.

Employee

```
LastName:    H o u l i h a n _ _
FirstName:   M a r g a r e t _ _
Address:     1 2 4 _ N . _ 5 2 n d _ S t . _
ZipCode:     4 8 2 3 6 _ _ _ _ _
Phone:       8 8 5 - 7 8 6 0
Gender:      F
SocNum:      3 8 8 - 7 0 - 6 7 5 4
JobCode:     R N _ _
DeptCode:    L C
HourlyWage:  _ 1 4 . 8 0
Exemptions:  _ 1
BirthDate:   0 2 / 1 4 / 1 9 5 1
```

1. The computer uses the Employee file to find Houlihan's hourly wage and Social Security number, then stores them in RAM.

2. The computer closes the Employee file.

$14.80 x 40 = $592 pay

Timecard

```
PayPeriod:   0 8 / 2 7 / 1 9 9 7
HoursWorked: 4 0
SocNum:      3 8 8 - 7 0 - 6 7 5 4
   SocNum:      4 2 9 - 3 2 - 0 5 2 2
      SocNum:                      1 1
```

3. The computer opens the Timecard file and searches for a record with Houlihan's Social Security number.

4. The computer looks for the number of hours Houlihan worked and stores it in RAM.

5. The computer closes the Timecard file, then multiplies the hourly wage by the hours worked to calculate total pay.

Start Animation

Databases

Does a database offer flexibility for using more than one file? "Database" is one of those terms that has no single definition. It is sometimes used loosely to describe any data file made up of records and fields. This usage, however, does not distinguish between a flat file and a database, so it is not completely accurate from a technical perspective. It is more accurate to define a **database** as a variety of different record types that are treated as a single unit. This definition implies that several flat files or record types can be consolidated or related in such a way that they can be used as essentially one unit—a database.

To use Midtown's four record types as essentially one unit, they must be consolidated into a database. After creating this database, you can combine the data from more than one record type. For example, you could combine the Employee and Timecard record types so that you could access the HourlyWage data and the HoursWorked data without opening and closing multiple files. As you examine the process for calculating employee pay in Figure 14-5, contrast it with the more complex process required if the data is stored in flat files (Figure 14-4).

FIGURE 14-5

When a computer uses related record types from a database to calculate pay, it can combine two records (Employee and Timecard) to temporarily create a record that contains the data from both files. The computer then simply multiplies the HourlyWage by the HoursWorked.

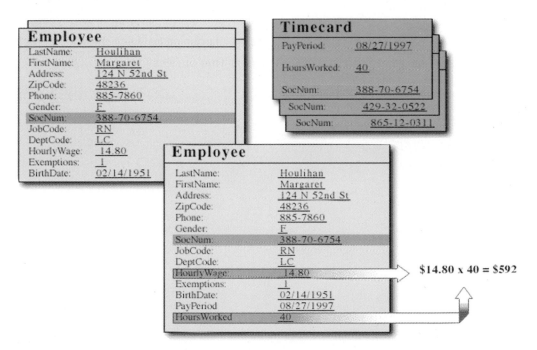

Start
Animation

InfoWeb
3

<u>Database Administrator</u>

Although a database provides more flexibility than a flat file, a database is typically more difficult to design and maintain. In businesses and organizations with substantial data management needs, a **database administrator** generally supervises database design, development, testing, and maintenance. In many respects, the database administrator performs tasks similar to those carried out by a systems analyst, but the emphasis is on data collection, manipulation, and reporting. As a career, database administration provides opportunities to work with many aspects of a business and interact with employees, managers, and executives.

QUICKCHECK   A

1 A(n) _____ field expands as you enter data.

2 You should use a(n) _____ data type for a field that contains Social Security numbers.

3 Real numbers and integers can be entered into fields that have been defined as a(n) _____ data type.

4 The abstract or general description of the Midtown employee file is called a record _____, whereas a record that contains the data for John McIntyre is called a record _____.

5 All of the records in a(n) _____ file are the same record type.

6 A database would be better than a flat file for data that requires different record types, but has relationships between the various record types. True or false? _____

Check Answers

A **data model** is a description of the way that data is stored in a database. When a database is constructed using an efficient data model, data can be entered, located, and manipulated in ways that provide useful information for a business or organization. When you are designing the structure for a database, a data model helps you understand the relationships between entities and helps you create the most efficient structure to hold your data.

Entity Relationships

InfoWeb
4

Data
Modeling

How does a data model describe data? In Section A, you learned that a record represents an entity and is structured into a series of fields. A **relationship** is an association between entities. For example, at Midtown a relationship exists between an employee entity and a timecard entity. You could describe this relationship by saying "an employee has a timecard." A data model lets you describe relationships between entities and define them as relationships between record types when you create the structure for a database.

Database designers graphically depict data models using diagramming techniques, such as entity-relationship diagrams, Bachman diagrams, and data structure diagrams. For example, the diagram in Figure 14-6 shows the relationship between an employee and a timecard.

CHAPTER 14

FIGURE 14-6

This entity-relationship diagram shows that "an Employee has a Timecard."

A data diagram can also show **cardinality**—that is, the number of occurrences that can exist between two record types. There are three possible types of cardinality: one-to-one, one-to-many, and many-to-many, as shown in Figure 14-7.

FIGURE 14-7

Diagramming cardinality.

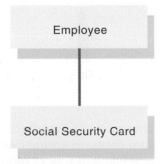
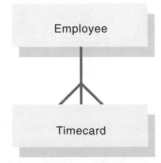
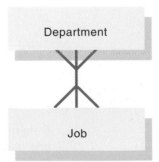

A one-to-one relationship is shown by using a single line to connect the boxes that represent record types.

A one-to-many relationship is shown by adding a "crow's foot" to the end of the line next to the record type with many occurrences.

A many-to-many relationship is shown by adding a "crow's foot" to both ends of the connecting line.

A **one-to-one relationship** means that one record in a particular record type is related to only one record of another record type. For example, each employee has one Social Security card. Also, a particular Social Security card is assigned to only one person.

A **one-to-many relationship** means that one record in a particular record type may be related to more than one record of another record type. For example, one employee can have many timecards, one job title can be held by many employees, or one department can have many employees.

A **many-to-many relationship** means that one record in a particular record type can be related to many records in another record type, and vice versa. For example, a department might require personnel with many job descriptions, such as nurses, technicians, and physicians. At the same time, a particular job might be required in more than one department; for example, nurses might be required in the intensive care department and in obstetrics. The data diagram in Figure 14-8 shows the relationships between Midtown record types.

FIGURE 14-8

A data diagram for Midtown General Hospital shows relationships and cardinality between entities.

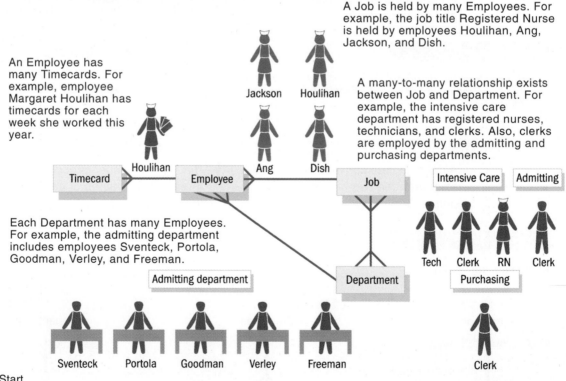

An Employee has many Timecards. For example, employee Margaret Houlihan has timecards for each week she worked this year.

A Job is held by many Employees. For example, the job title Registered Nurse is held by employees Houlihan, Ang, Jackson, and Dish.

A many-to-many relationship exists between Job and Department. For example, the intensive care department has registered nurses, technicians, and clerks. Also, clerks are employed by the admitting and purchasing departments.

Each Department has many Employees. For example, the admitting department includes employees Sventeck, Portola, Goodman, Verley, and Freeman.

Start Animation

Data models help database designers create the most efficient structure for a database and decide which database model will provide the most effective database environment. There are four major **database models**, each of which has a different way of representing the relationships between entities. Although each database model is described using slightly different terminology, the concepts of record types, fields, and relationships are useful for understanding all of the models.

Hierarchical Database Model

What is the simplest database model?   The simplest database model arranges record types as a hierarchy. In a **hierarchical database**, a record type is referred to as a **node** or "segment." The top node of the hierarchy is referred to as the **root node**. Nodes are arranged in a hierarchical structure as a sort of upside-down tree. A **parent node** can have more than one child node. A **child node**, however, can have only one parent node. The relationship between a parent node and a child node must be one-to-many. Study Figure 14-9 for an overview of the hierarchical database model.

FIGURE 14-9

In this hierarchical database model, Department, Job, Employee, and Timecard are nodes.

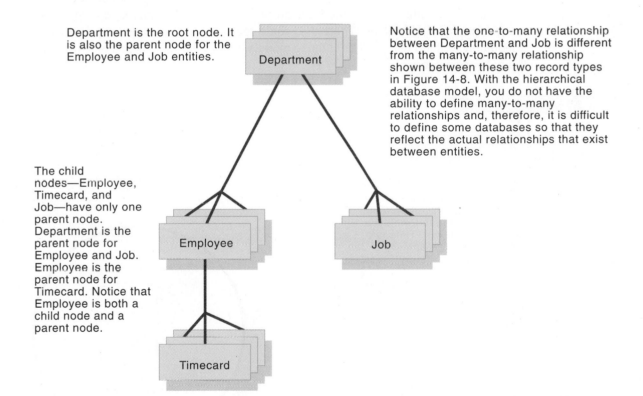

Department is the root node. It is also the parent node for the Employee and Job entities.

Notice that the one-to-many relationship between Department and Job is different from the many-to-many relationship shown between these two record types in Figure 14-8. With the hierarchical database model, you do not have the ability to define many-to-many relationships and, therefore, it is difficult to define some databases so that they reflect the actual relationships that exist between entities.

The child nodes—Employee, Timecard, and Job—have only one parent node. Department is the parent node for Employee and Job. Employee is the parent node for Timecard. Notice that Employee is both a child node and a parent node.

In a hierarchical database, the relationships between records are established by creating physical links between the stored records. This physical linking means that each record is stored on the disk medium with a set of pre-defined access paths to other records. A hierarchical database is effective for data that has fairly simple relationships and when data access is routine and predictable. Hierarchical databases are less effective for data with complex relationships and in situations that require flexible or "on the fly" data access, because the relationships are physical links defined at the time the database is created. If you want to add a record type or define a new relationship, you must redefine the database and then store it in its new form.

CHAPTER 14

Network Database Model

Which database model allows record types to have more than one parent?

In a **network database**, related record types are referred to as a **set**. A set contains an **owner**, which is similar to a parent record in a hierarchical database. It also includes one or more **members**, which are roughly equivalent to the child records in a hierarchical database. Only one-to-many relationships are allowed in the network database model.

The network and hierarchical database models are similar in many respects. Like the hierarchical model, the network model is a collection of physically linked records. The physical link is created when the data is stored on tape or disk. Both models allow only one-to-many relationships between entities. The major difference between the two models is that a network database permits member records to have more than one owner, whereas a hierarchical database limits a child to only one parent. Consequently, a network database model provides more flexibility for defining relationships between records. Unfortunately, neither the hierarchical nor the network database model allows many-to-many relationships. Therefore, some real-world data relationships cannot be adequately defined using either of these models. Figure 14-10 provides an overview of the network database model.

FIGURE 14-10

The network database model allows a record to have more than one owner.

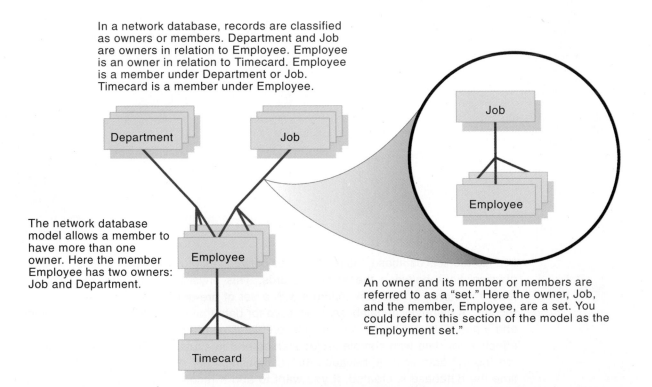

In a network database, records are classified as owners or members. Department and Job are owners in relation to Employee. Employee is an owner in relation to Timecard. Employee is a member under Department or Job. Timecard is a member under Employee.

The network database model allows a member to have more than one owner. Here the member Employee has two owners: Job and Department.

An owner and its member or members are referred to as a "set." Here the owner, Job, and the member, Employee, are a set. You could refer to this section of the model as the "Employment set."

Relational Database Model

What if I need more flexibility to define relationships? A relational database is perceived by its users to be a collection of **tables** (also called "relations"), which are roughly equivalent to a collection of record types. A row of the table is called a **tuple** and is equivalent to a record. The columns in the table are called **attributes** and are equivalent to fields. Today's microcomputer databases are most often created using the relational database model because it offers great flexibility for defining relationships.

InfoWeb 5

Relational Databases

The strategy for defining relationships in the relational model is fundamentally different from that employed in the hierarchical or network models. In the relational model, records are related by the data stored jointly in the fields of records in two files. For example, Margaret Houlihan's Employee record is related to her Timecard records because the data in the SocNum fields is the same. The significance of the relational database model is that the tables seem to be essentially independent, but they can be related in many flexible ways. Furthermore, because the tables are a conceptual aid, the user does not need to deal with a physical storage plan for the data on disk. Figure 14-11 provides an overview of relational database structure and terminology.

FIGURE 14-11

The relational database model is based on a series of tables.

The data for each record type is stored in a table. A relational database for the Midtown General Hospital would have four tables: Employee, Timecard, Job, and Department.

Data from the two tables can be combined by matching the data in two fields. For example, the data in the Employee and the Timecard tables can be joined by matching the data in the SocNum field.

Table: Employee

LastName	FirstName	Address	SocNum
Ang	Susan	99 Lake Shore Dr.	453-78-2311
Houlihan	Margaret	124 N. 52nd St.	388-70-6754
McIntyre	John	1005 Depere Blvd.	475-66-6245

Table: Timecard

PayPeriod	HoursWorked	SocNum
05/26/1997	45	453-78-2311
05/26/1997	40	388-70-6754
05/26/1997	49	475-66-6245
06/02/1997	40	453-78-2311
06/02/1997	40	388-70-6754
06/02/1997	43	475-66-6245

Table: Job

JobTitle	JobCode	PayGrade	Description
Registered Nurse	RN	5	A registered...
Staff Physician	SMD	9	A Staff...

Table: Department

DepartmentName	DeptCode	OfficeNumber	Phone
Intensive Care	IC	S0502	885-7070
Emergency Room	ER	B100	885-1222
Obstetrics	OB	S0301	885-1344

CHAPTER 14

Object-Oriented Database Model

Do other data models exist? The object-oriented data model provides an alternative to the hierarchical, network, and relational models. An **object-oriented database model** treats an entity as an **object** defined by attributes, which are equivalent to data fields. An object can be manipulated using **methods**. Objects with similar attributes can be grouped into a **class**. An analogy will explain the meaning of class, object, attribute, and method.

InfoWeb 6

Object-oriented model

Suppose you have a class of things called "fasteners" that includes objects such as screws and nails. Each object has attributes. A nail has a point, and it has a flat head. A screw has a point, a grooved head, and spiral ridges on its shaft. What method do you apply to a nail? You pound it with a hammer. What method do you use with a screw? You twist it with a screwdriver.

How does this idea apply to the data at Midtown? A Midtown employee can be described as an *object* with *attributes* such as a last name, first name, and Social Security number. Employee objects are grouped by *class:* registered nurse, clerk, staff physician, and so on. The *method* for paying an employee depends on the class to which an employee object belongs. Registered nurses and clerks are paid by the hour. Staff physicians are paid a salary. Figure 14-12 shows an object-oriented approach to Midtown data.

FIGURE 14-12

An object-oriented database model defines data as objects that can be manipulated individually or as a class.

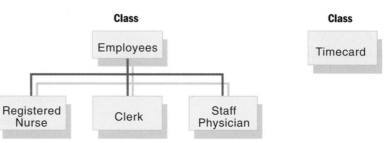

Objects that share common characteristics are grouped into a class. The class Employees includes the objects Registered Nurse, Clerk, and Staff Physician. The Timecard object is a separate class.

Objects

RN

LastName:_____
FirstName:_____
Address:_____
SocNum:_____
HourlyWage:_____

Clerk

LastName:_____
FirstName:_____
Address:_____
SocNum:_____
HourlyWage:_____

MD

LastName:_____
FirstName:_____
Address:_____
SocNum:_____
Salary:_____

All objects in the Employees class share attributes, such as LastName, FirstName, Address, and so on. Unique attributes can also be assigned to a particular object. Here Staff Physicians (MDs) have a Salary attribute, whereas RNs and Clerks have an HourlyWage attribute.

Methods to calculate weekly pay

Find hours worked on Timecard and multiply by HourlyWage

Divide annual salary by 52

The method CalculateWeeklyPay calculates the weekly pay for RNs and Clerks by multiplying the HourlyWage attribute by the HoursWorked attribute from the Timecard object. For Staff Physicians, the CalculateWeeklyPay method divides the Salary attribute by 52 because there are 52 weeks in a year.

Using an object-oriented database for Midtown data provides a structure capable of defining complex data relationships. It also offers flexibility in creating variations of a single record type. For example, in the hierarchical, network, and relational models, all of the employee records have the same structure, which includes a field for hourly wage. To use these models for salaried employees, you would need to design a new record type such as SalaryEmployee. With the object-oriented database, the record type for salaried employees would be a variation of Employee and therefore would not require a separate series of commands.

In the past, mainframe databases often followed the hierarchical or network model. During the 1980s, the relational model gained popularity. Databases that companies and individuals maintained on microcomputers typically followed the relational model, primarily because this model was supported by most microcomputer database management software. The object-oriented model has been becoming more popular on both mainframe and microcomputer platforms.

Q U I C K C H E C K ▕ B

1 A data ▢ describes the way that data is stored in a database.

2 In addition to relationships, a data diagram can show ▢, the number of occurrences that can exist between two record types.

3 For the Midtown data, the Employee and Timecard record types would be diagrammed as a(n) ▢-to-many relationship.

4 The simplest database model is a(n) ▢ model.

5 If member records have more than one owner, it is best to use a hierarchical database model. True or false? ▢

6 The ▢ database model is structured as a collection of tables.

7 If you want to assign methods to your data, you should use an object-oriented database. True or false? ▢

➡ Check Answers

CHAPTER 14

SECTION C DATA MANAGEMENT SOFTWARE

Data management software helps you create an efficient hierarchical, network, relational, or object-oriented collection of data. It helps you enter and manipulate data, format data into reports, and interact with data on the Web. The software you select for these tasks depends on your data model, the flexibility you require for manipulating your data, and the resources you can devote to maintaining your data. This section describes the advantages and disadvantages of custom software, file management software, database management systems, object-oriented tools, and Web-enabled database tools.

Custom Software

Because every database is unique, do I need to write my own custom file management software? Historically, file management tasks were often accomplished using **custom software**, which was built "from scratch" using a programming language. An organization with many different data files would require many custom programs to manipulate the data in those files, as shown in Figure 14-13.

FIGURE 14-13

In the custom program approach, each file requires its own set of programs. Notice that many of the programs for the Employee file are similar in function to programs for the Timecard file.

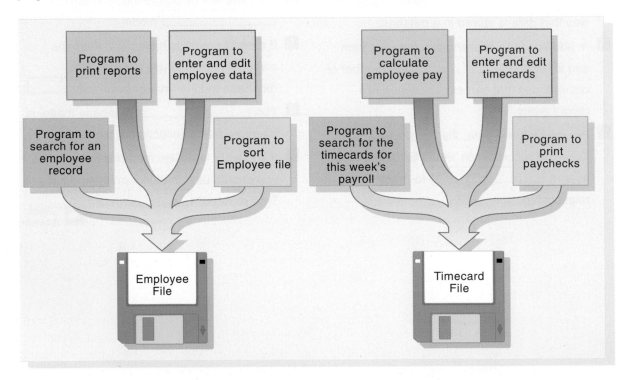

It is possible to create custom software to accommodate hierarchical, network, relational, and object-oriented models. Custom data management software has the advantage of being tailored to the exact needs of a business or organization. Today, this type of software is assembled using programming languages and specially designed database components, which maximize flexibility and minimize development time.

File Management Software

Can commercial file management software adapt to my data management needs? You can purchase commercial **file management software** that allows you to specify field names, select data types, and designate field lengths for each file you create. You can then use standard features provided by the software for basic data management tasks such as entering, changing, organizing, displaying, locating, and printing data. Figure 14-14 illustrates how file management software handles the data management tasks that are common to a number of data files.

FIGURE 14-14

File management software provides a standard set of programs that handle basic data management functions for any file. If needed, custom programs, such as one to calculate employee pay, can be used to supplement the standard set of file management programs.

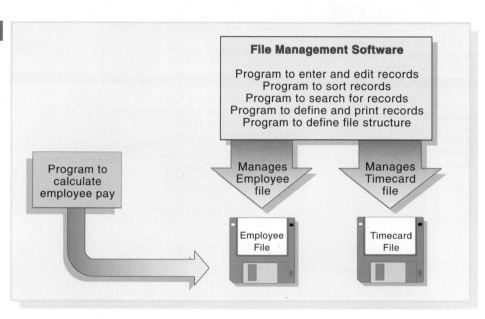

File management software adapts to different files as a result of a concept called data independence. **Data independence** refers to the separation of data from the programs that manipulate the data. For example, if you change the file structure by adding a field, the programs that manipulate the data should continue to function. File management software promotes data independence because it is not tied to a particular data file.

File management software is not part of a data file; in fact, you might say that it is external to the data. If you don't like the software you used to create your data files, you can typically switch to different file management software and use it with your existing data files.

In some situations, the basic file management features provided by commercial file management software are not sufficient for the needs of an organization—perhaps the software does not allow enough flexibility in designing reports, or perhaps it does not provide a way to graph the data. If the file management software's basic features are inadequate, you might require a customized program, which you would typically use in addition to the commercial file management software.

File management software, which is generally considered the easiest and least expensive data manipulation tool, does have some limitations. It creates and manipulates only flat files, opens only one file at a time, and does not allow you to specify relationships between entities.

Database Management Systems

Can I buy commercial software that will let me work with data in more than one file at a time? A **database management system** (DBMS) is application software that helps you manage the data in more than one file at a time. A DBMS performs the same functions as a file management system does, but in addition it allows you to work with more than one file by defining relationships among record types, as shown in Figure 14-15.

FIGURE 14-15

A database management system provides the programs necessary to manage the data in all of the record types of a database. It also helps you define relationships between record types and allows you to write custom programs to handle additional data.

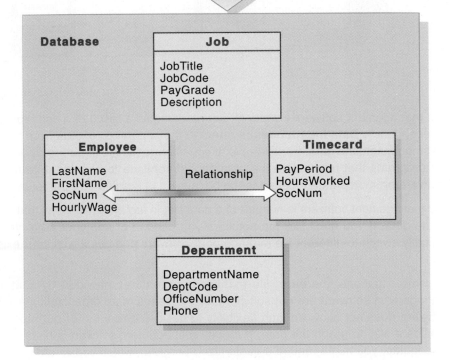

A DBMS typically provides a way to create custom programs for data management tasks that you perform frequently. For example, every two weeks you might want to locate all of the timecards for the current pay period, then find the hourly wage from each employee's Employee record, and finally calculate total pay. You could use the built-in functions of the database software to perform each of these operations, one by one. Alternatively, by creating a custom program for this task, you could tell the DBMS to "do payroll" and it would automatically perform all of the necessary operations.

Many of today's database management systems provide an option for client/server operation. Using a client/server DBMS on a network, DBMS server software runs on the network server. This software processes requests for data searches, sorts, and reports that originate from the DBMS client software running on individual workstations. For example, you might want to search an aircraft database for a list of the planes used by commercial airlines worldwide. Your DBMS client would refer this request to the DBMS server. The server would search for the information and sends it over the network to your workstation. Once at your workstation, you can sort the list and create your own customized report. In this way, client/server operations distribute data processing tasks. If your DBMS did not have client/server capability, the entire database would be copied to your workstation and your software would search for the requested data—a process that would typically take much longer than if the data was processed with the help of the server.

It would be possible to create a database management system using a programming language. Because a DBMS is quite complex, however, most users elect to purchase a commercial DBMS package. The cost of a database management system can be a worthwhile investment, especially for an organization with many record types and databases to maintain. Figure 14-16 shows one popular DBMS software.

FIGURE 14-16

Microsoft Access is one of the most popular database management systems for microcomputers.

Object-Oriented Tools

Can I use a DBMS to create an object-oriented database? File management systems and database management systems operate on a passive data set in which the data simply waits for a program to process it. In contrast, an object-oriented database often includes methods that perform actions on the data. To construct an object-oriented database, you should use an **object-oriented DBMS** (OODBMS) or a programming language, such as **Smalltalk**, that is designed to manipulate objects and define methods.

With the object-oriented approach, the only programs that must operate external to the database are those that you use to define the objects, methods, and classes for the database. These programs are usually provided by the object-oriented database software, although they do not become part of the database itself. Figure 14-17 illustrates the object-oriented approach.

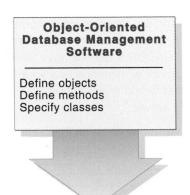

InfoWeb 8

OODBMS Tools

FIGURE 14-17

An OODBMS provides a way to define objects, methods, and classes. Most other data management activities, such as sorting, searching, and calculating, are performed by methods incorporated in the database.

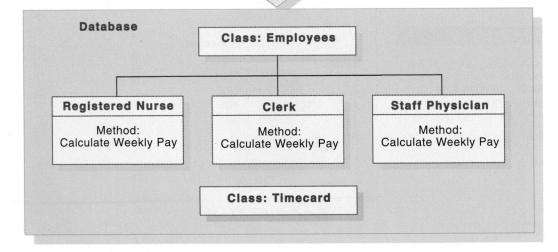

Object-Oriented Database Management Software

Define objects
Define methods
Specify classes

Database

Class: Employees

Registered Nurse	Clerk	Staff Physician
Method: Calculate Weekly Pay	Method: Calculate Weekly Pay	Method: Calculate Weekly Pay

Class: Timecard

Web-Enabled Database Tools

Is it difficult to design a database that can be accessed over the Web?

InfoWeb
9

DB Web
Tools

Web-enabled databases allow you to access a database over the Internet by using a standard Web browser. As an example, suppose that you're designing a Web-based bookstore. You want customers to connect to your Web site and type in an author name or book title. You then want to display a list of matching books that you have in stock, along with information on each book, such as its title, author, publisher, publication date, and price. The results of a customer's search depend on what the customer is seeking and what you have in stock. Because HTML pages are static, it would seem impossible to create a series of Web pages that would provide results for any customer's search. Also, because you have all of the data already stored in a database, it would be very inefficient to re-enter it as HTML-formatted Web pages. Instead, you would like your database to automatically generate a Web page of books in response to a customer's search.

To interact with a Web-based database, it is necessary to pass requests from the browser software to the database, and then pass the results back to the browser. Programs written to the **CGI** (Common Gateway Interface) provide this capability. These programs can be written in programming languages such as Perl, C, and Visual Basic. High-performance alternatives to CGI include proprietary interfaces such as **ISAPI** and **NSAPI**. A high-speed, but nonproprietary tool is **Active Server Page**, a Web page that contains programming code designed to interact with a database. Specialized Web database development tools such as Cold Fusion provide a way to link HTML pages to a database without programming. Web database development tools are also included with many popular database packages, such as Microsoft Access and IBM DB2.

Using any of these Web database development tools, you can set up a bookstore site—for example, one in which a customer enters a book title or author name such as "John Grisham." The customer's search is sent to your Web server, where your database software searches for any books by John Grisham. Your Web server then uses the data in your database to generate a Web page listing all of Grisham's books available from your bookstore and sends the page back to the customer's browser.

CHAPTER 14

QUICKCHECK C

1 Historically, file management tasks were often accomplished by [_____] software designed to hold data and to manipulate that data.

2 File management software adapts to different files as a result of a concept called [_____].

3 File management software is external to a data file, but the methods that manipulate data are internal in a(n) [_____] database.

4 File management software works with only one file at a time; if you want to define relationships between data in two or more files, you must use [_____] software.

5 A(n) [_____] DBMS distributes data processing tasks between a workstation and a network server.

6 You can create a Web-enabled database using standard HTML tags. True or false? [_____]

Check
Answers

DATABASE MANAGEMENT TASKS

A "data management environment" refers to the software or program that you use to design and manage data, whether you use custom software, file management software, database management systems, object-oriented tools, or Web-enabled tools. Regardless of the data management environment you use, many data management tasks remain the same. In this section, you will learn more about specific data management tasks.

Designing the File Structure

Where do I begin? The key to an effective file or database is the initial design of its structure. With a good structure, the data can be flexibly manipulated to provide timely, meaningful, and accurate information for decision making. Suppose that you are a database administrator faced with the task of designing an effective way to store and manage your organization's data. How do you proceed?

The first step is to determine what data needs to be collected and stored. In other words, you must decide what fields to include. To do so, you might begin by listing the information that is available, as well as any additional information that is necessary to produce the on-screen output or printed reports required by your organization. Each piece of information on your list is a candidate for a data field. If you are designing a file or database for the human resources department, for example, you would probably recognize the need for information such as employee name, address, phone number, job code, and birth date.

The second step in the design process is to organize the information into fields so that it can be used flexibly. For example, would it be better to store an employee name as a single field or to specify separate fields for the first name and the last name? If you would like to print mailing labels with the name in the format "Margaret Houlihan" and also print an employee list with the names in the format "Houlihan, Margaret" you would need to have separate fields for the first and the last names. If you did not use separate fields, "Margaret Houlihan" would be entered into a single field. It would then be very difficult to devise a way to separate the first name from the last name and reverse them if you wanted to output the name as "Houlihan, Margaret."

Next, you must decide on the data type for each field. As you learned earlier in this chapter, most data management environments let you select from character, numeric, date, logical, and memo data types. Remember that data for calculations should be defined as numeric. After you specify the data type, you should decide on the format and valid range for each field. The **field format** provides a template for the way data is displayed on the screen and printed. For example, if you specify a field format of XX/XX/XXXX, the entry 10152001 appears as 10/15/2001. On the other hand, if you specify the format XX-XX-XXXX, the entry 10152001 appears as 10-15-2001. In addition to dates, other commonly used field formats are shown in Figure 14-18.

FIGURE 14-18	A series of 9s indicates a numeric field; Xs indicate data in a character field.
Currency	$9,999.99
Social Security number	XXX-XX-XXXX
Telephone number	(XXX)XXX-XXXX
ZIP code	XXXXX-XXXX

Many data management environments allow you to use a **range check** to specify what constitutes the range of valid entries in each field and, thereby, decrease errors. For example, you might specify that the HourlyWage field can contain values from $0.00 to $50.00. If a user enters $150 instead of $15, the database will not accept the entry.

Your ability to define field formats and range checks depends on the particular data management environment that you use. The programming languages used to create custom software generally provide the commands necessary to create a section of your program that will display and print fields based on your specifications. With the object-oriented approach, you would define field formats and range checks as methods. Not all file and database management systems provide a way to define field formats and range checks. You might need to refer to the documentation to find out if a particular environment supports these two features.

The next step in database design is deciding how to group the fields. Each group that you create becomes a record type; if you are using an object-oriented model, each group becomes an object and the objects may further be grouped into classes. You should structure the groups to reduce storage space requirements and to provide the level of access and flexibility required by the people who use the data.

In an object-oriented environment, you can also define methods that process the data in each object. A careful consideration of which objects inherit each method will help you to produce an efficient object-oriented database.

When you group fields into record types, you essentially make the choice between using a flat file and a database. If you arrange all fields in a single record type, you are using a flat file structure. If you arrange the fields into more than one record type, you are using a database structure. Let's look at an example.

Suppose that the information systems manager of Midtown wants to keep track of computer equipment in case it needs to be replaced or repaired. Would it be best to maintain a flat file or a database? Figure 14-19 shows a flat file, which would keep track of computer equipment and provide the information necessary to send it to a repair center.

FIGURE 14-19

With a flat file structure, all of the equipment data is placed in a single file.

Item	Serial Number	Date Purchased	Repair Center	Repair Center Phone	Repair Center Address
Computer	458876	02/12/1995	Epson	415-786-9988	93 Torrance Blvd.
Computer	433877	03/03/1996	IBM	913-559-5877	2 Bradhook Ave.
Printer	6855200	03/03/1996	Epson	415-786-9988	93 Torrance Blvd.
Computer	884411	01/21/1995	Epson	415-786-9988	93 Torrance Blvd.
Modem	B7654D	01/21/1995	High Tech	509-776-7865	4109 Highway 56
Computer	5544998	01/21/1995	IBM	913-559-5877	2 Bradhook Ave.

CHAPTER 14

Using a flat file for the equipment data is not very efficient. The problem with this structure becomes evident when you look at the repair center data. The Epson repair center name, address, and phone number are repeated on many records. If the repair center moves to a different location, a data entry clerk will have to change the address in many records.

Repetition of data is referred to as **data redundancy** and is very undesirable because it makes inefficient use of storage space and makes updating cumbersome. In a well-structured database, the data is stored non-redundantly.

Normalization

The process of analyzing data to create the most efficient database structure is referred to as **normalization**. There are five normalization procedures, the first of which is to eliminate data redundancy by removing the repeating fields and grouping them as a new record type, as shown in Figure 14-20.

FIGURE 14-20

You can eliminate much of the redundant equipment data by creating a second record type that holds data about each repair center. Only the repair center name is retained in the Equipment record type. It can be used to link the two records.

Record type: Equipment

Item	Serial Number	Date Purchased	Repair Center
Computer	458876	02/12/1995	Epson
Computer	433877	03/03/1996	IBM
Printer	6855200	03/30/1996	Epson
Computer	884411	01/21/1995	Epson
Modem	B7654D	01/21/1995	High Tech
Computer	5544998	01/21/1995	IBM

Record type: RepairCenter

Repair Center	Repair Center Phone	Repair Center Adress
Epson	415-786-9988	93 Torrance Blvd.
IBM	913-559-5877	2 Bradhook Ave.
High Tech	509-776-7865	4109 Highway 56

Start Animation

The other normalization procedures can further streamline a database. You will learn more about normalization if you take a database course that covers advanced topics.

You might wonder why the computer can't search for each record that you want to change and automatically make the update. This operation, of course, is possible. However, every time data is entered, the possibility of an error creeps in. If an entry clerk enters "Epsom" instead of "Epson," the software will not find this record as part of the search and will not make the update. Errors of this sort have a way of increasing over time, eventually leaving the database with many inaccuracies.

Adding Records

When can I enter my data? When you specify the database structure, you essentially design a blank form that will hold data. After the form is complete, you can begin to enter data. As you enter each record, it is assigned a **record number**. The first record you enter becomes record #1, the second record you enter becomes record #2, and so forth. In an object-oriented database, each object receives a unique **object ID number**, which is similar to a record number. The computer uses record numbers and object IDs to keep track of the data that you enter.

Consistency is important for data entry because it affects the efficiency of your searches. Suppose that you're entering employee data for registered nurses and you enter "RN" as the job code for some employees, but "NURS" for other employees who hold the same position. If you later want the database software to print a list of all nurses and you ask for all RNs, the employees you identified with NURS will not be included on the list.

Another issue related to consistent data entry is case sensitivity. **Case sensitivity** means that uppercase letters are not equivalent to their lowercase counterparts. In a case-sensitive database, the state abbreviation MI is not the same as the abbreviation Mi. Not all data management environments are case sensitive. You must read the documentation to determine whether a particular data management environment is case sensitive.

Database designers try to minimize inconsistent input by using input lists whenever possible. An **input list** contains all valid choices for a field. Instead of typing data into a field, a user selects one of the items from the list (Figure 14-21), thereby avoiding the possibility of a typographical error.

FIGURE 14-21

Using an input list reduces typographical errors and data inconsistencies.

Instead of typing a state name or abbreviation, clicking the field displays an input list.

When you select a state, the database software enters the state abbreviation in the field so that you avoid typing the wrong abbreviation or making a typographical error.

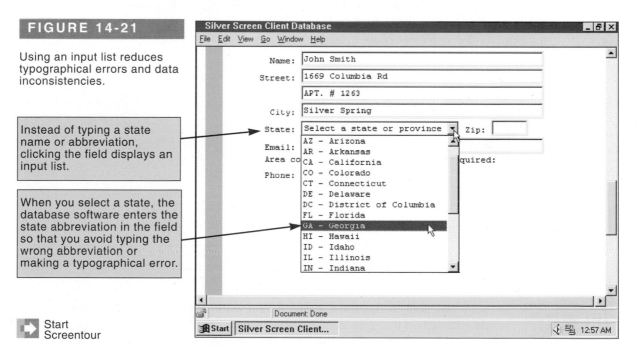

Start
Screentour

Searching

How do I find a particular record once it is entered? A real file or database may contain hundreds or thousands of records. If you want to find a particular record or a particular group of records, scrolling through every record is too cumbersome. Instead, you can enter search specifications called a **query**, and the computer will quickly locate the records you seek.

Queries can be simple or complex. An example of a simple query would be if you want a list of everyone who has "Jones" as a last name. A more complex query might be to find anyone in the database with a last name of "Jones" who works as an "LPN" and was hired after "01/01/97" but before "01/01/98."

InfoWeb
11
SQL

As you learned in Chapter 3, most database management systems have a special query language, which provides a set of commands for locating and manipulating data. **SQL** (Structured Query Language) is a popular query language for microcomputers, minicomputers, mainframes, and even supercomputers.

As an alternative to a query language, many data management environments allow you to query by example. As you learned in Chapter 3, query by example provides you with a blank record into which you enter examples or specifications of the records you want to find. Figure 14-22 shows how you might use query by example on a form for the Midtown employee records.

FIGURE 14-22

Query by example makes it relatively simple to locate a particular record.

You specify the query by typing in examples of the records that you want to find. Here, the query specifies all female RNs who make more than $10 per hour.

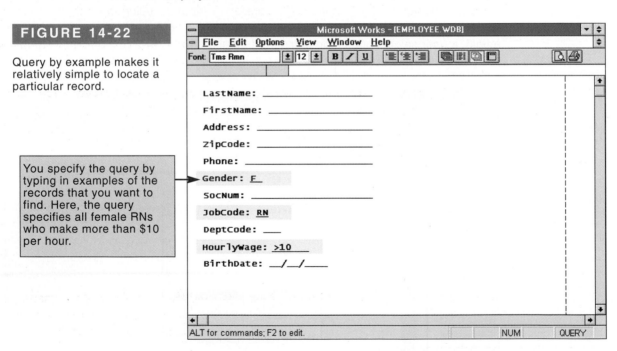

InfoWeb
12
Data
Warehouses

In many respects, a database is like a vast warehouse of data from which you can locate information that provides you with insights about the status of a business or the success of an organization. The similarity between databases and warehouses has given rise to the terms *data warehousing* and *data mining*. **Data warehousing** means collecting vast amounts of data—usually at least 10 GB. **Data mining** means combing through that data to discover patterns and relationships important to decision making.

Updating Information

What if I want to change some of the data? Often the reason that you search for a particular record is to update it—that is, to change it or delete it. The typical process is to enter a query so that the computer finds and displays the record you want to update. Next, you make the changes and, if necessary, indicate that you want to save the record in its changed format.

Different data management environments have different ways of saving updated records. With many environments, changes are saved automatically as soon as you move to the next record. With other environments, you must issue an explicit command to save the changes that you make. To learn the specific procedures for your data management environment, refer to the software documentation or online Help.

In addition to carrying out individual changes, computers make it easy to perform **global updates** that change the data in more than one record at a time. Consider the Employee file in the Midtown General Hospital database. A number of employees are working at $5.15 per hour. Suppose that Midtown General Hospital wants its employees to make at least $6.00 per hour. Instead of searching for each employee with an hourly wage of $5.15 and manually changing the numbers to $6.00, you could enter a command such as:

UPDATE EMPWAGE SET HourlyWage = 6.00 WHERE HourlyWage <6.00

Let's see how this command performs a global update. The UPDATE command means that you want to change the data in some or all of the records. EMPWAGE is the name of the file that contains the data you want to change. SET HourlyWage = 6.00 tells the DBMS to change the data in the HourlyWage field to 6.00. WHERE HourlyWage <6.00 tells the DBMS to change only those records in which the current hourly wage is less than $6.00.

Organizing Records

Can I organize my data in different ways? It is easier to use information if it is presented in a sequence related to the way in which the information will be used. For example, if you want to view a list of employees and you are looking for a specific employee by name, it is handy to have the employee records alphabetized by last name. If, on the other hand, you want to view a list of employees to compare hourly wages, it is useful to have the records in numeric order according to the number in the HourlyWage field.

A **sort key** is the field used to arrange records in order. Suppose Midtown managers want employee records arranged alphabetically by last name. The sort key would be LastName. Alternatively, if they want the records arranged by hourly wage, the sort key would be HourlyWage.

There are two ways to organize records in a file: you can sort them or you can index them. If you change the order of the file itself, by essentially rearranging the sequence of the records on the disk, you are **sorting**. Because the records are rearranged, each record receives a new record number to indicate its new position in the file. Sorting is an acceptable procedure for smaller files in which the time to sort the records is minimal. Sorting is not acceptable for files that you want organized in multiple ways.

CHAPTER 14

An alternative way to organize records is by indexing. **Indexing** leaves the records in their original order and retains the original record numbers but creates additional files, called **index files**. You can think of an index file as being similar to the index of a book. The index of a book contains topics in alphabetical order, which allows you to find a topic in the index list easily. Next to the topic is a page number that points to the location of the actual information about the topic. Figure 14-23 shows how an index file lists the contents of the LastName field in alphabetical order, then uses the record number as a pointer to the corresponding record number in the original file.

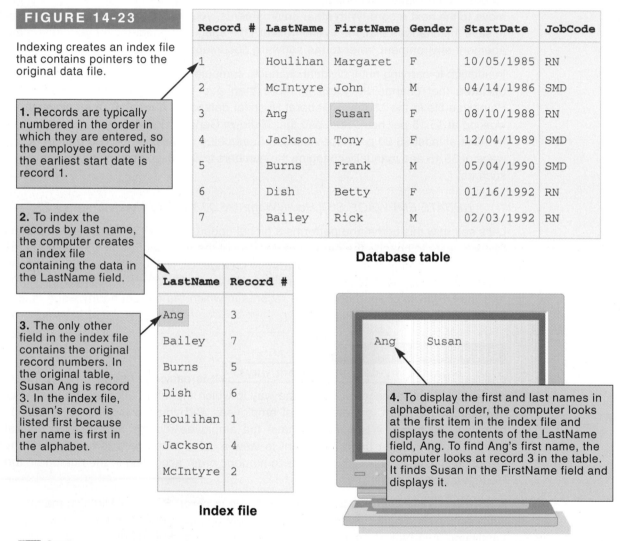

FIGURE 14-23

Indexing creates an index file that contains pointers to the original data file.

1. Records are typically numbered in the order in which they are entered, so the employee record with the earliest start date is record 1.

2. To index the records by last name, the computer creates an index file containing the data in the LastName field.

3. The only other field in the index file contains the original record numbers. In the original table, Susan Ang is record 3. In the index file, Susan's record is listed first because her name is first in the alphabet.

Record #	LastName	FirstName	Gender	StartDate	JobCode
1	Houlihan	Margaret	F	10/05/1985	RN
2	McIntyre	John	M	04/14/1986	SMD
3	Ang	Susan	F	08/10/1988	RN
4	Jackson	Tony	F	12/04/1989	SMD
5	Burns	Frank	M	05/04/1990	SMD
6	Dish	Betty	F	01/16/1992	RN
7	Bailey	Rick	M	02/03/1992	RN

Database table

LastName	Record #
Ang	3
Bailey	7
Burns	5
Dish	6
Houlihan	1
Jackson	4
McIntyre	2

Index file

Ang   Susan

4. To display the first and last names in alphabetical order, the computer looks at the first item in the index file and displays the contents of the LastName field, Ang. To find Ang's first name, the computer looks at record 3 in the table. It finds Susan in the FirstName field and displays it.

Start Animation

What makes indexing so flexible is that you can have multiple index files for each data file. Most DBMSs provide an indexing feature. You should be aware, however, that not all data management environments differentiate between the terms "sort" and "index." For example, Microsoft Access uses the term "sort" for procedures that organize data *without* rearranging records.

Generating Reports

How can I produce a professional-looking report based on the data in a data file? The output from a data file presents information in a format that facilitates making a decision, preparing an analysis, or taking some action. Traditionally, output has been presented as words and numbers in reports, but it can also assume other formats such as Web pages, graphs, graphics, and sound.

In response to a query, your data management environment might display a list of records that match your search criteria. This simple list shows the information you need, but it might not provide it in the optimal format. The list might include some unnecessary fields, it might not include a title or page numbers, it might not display subtotals or totals, and the column headings might not be as descriptive as you would like. If the list is not adequate, you can design a screen-based or printed report that conveys information more effectively. A database report is the formatted output of some or all of the data from a database.

The part of a data management environment that provides you with the ability to design reports is called a **report generator**. Usually a report generator helps you to create a report template. A **report template** does not contain any data. Instead, it holds the outline or general specifications for a report, including such things as what to title the report, which fields to include, which fields you want to subtotal or total, and how the report should be formatted. For example, you might create a report template called Midtown Employees, which specifies the following:

■ The title of the report is Midtown General Hospital Employees.

■ The report contains six columns with data from the LastName, FirstName, SocNum, Gender, StartDate, and JobCode fields.

■ The headings for the columns are Last Name, First Name, Social Security #, Gender, Start Date, and Job Code.

■ The report is arranged alphabetically by last name.

This template would be used to produce a report similar to the one shown in Figure 14-24.

FIGURE 14-24

A report arranged in columns.

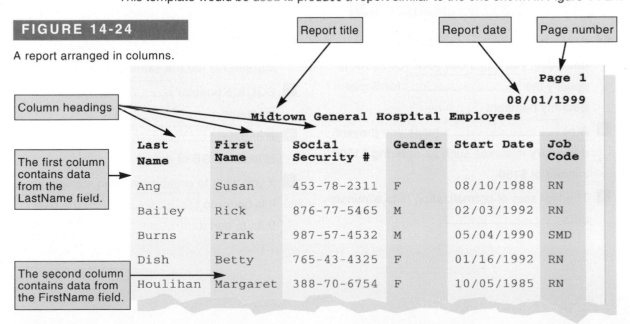

Report title   Report date   Page number

Column headings

The first column contains data from the LastName field.

The second column contains data from the FirstName field.

```
                                                           Page 1
                                                        08/01/1999
                     Midtown General Hospital Employees

    Last         First      Social          Gender  Start Date   Job
    Name         Name       Security #                           Code

    Ang          Susan      453-78-2311     F        08/10/1988   RN

    Bailey       Rick       876-77-5465     M        02/03/1992   RN

    Burns        Frank      987-57-4532     M        05/04/1990   SMD

    Dish         Betty      765-43-4325     F        01/16/1992   RN

    Houlihan     Margaret   388-70-6754     F        10/05/1985   RN
```

After you use a report generator to design a template for a report, you can produce the report at any time. When you produce the actual report, it is based on the data currently contained in the file. For example, the report in Figure 14-24 was produced on August 1, 1999. This report includes employees who are listed in the database as of that date. Now suppose that on September 1 Midtown hires several new employees who are added to the database. You then use the Midtown Employee report template to print a report on September 2. This report will follow the same format as the previous report, but will include the new employees.

The reports that you create using a report generator can be displayed, printed, saved as a file, or output as Web pages. Some data management software also provides tools to output data as a graph, sound, or graphics. Whatever format you select for your output, you can effectively present information by observing the following guidelines:

- Present only the amount of information needed. Too much information can make it difficult to identify what is essential.

- Present information in a usable format. For example, if subtotals are necessary for making a decision, include them. Users should not have to make additional manual calculations.

- Information should be timely. Reports must arrive in time to be used for effective decision making. Some decisions require periodic information—for example, monthly sales reports. Other decisions require ongoing information that will be best satisfied by a continuous display—for example, stock prices.

- Information should be presented in a clear, unambiguous format. Make sure that you include necessary titles, page numbers, dates, labels, and column headings.

- Present information in the format most appropriate for its audience. In many cases, a traditional report organized in rows in columns is most appropriate. In other cases, graphs might be more effective.

QUICKCHECK   D

1 When designing the structure for a file or database, you might use XXX-XX-XXXX to specify the _____ for Social Security numbers.

2 A(n) _____ helps you prevent data entry mistakes such as entering $1500 instead of $150.

3 The first step of normalization is to eliminate data _____.

4 In a(n) _____ database, Margaret is not the same as margaret.

5 SQL is a popular _____ language.

6 A data _____ typically contains at least 10 GB of data.

7 If you want to organize a file in multiple ways, it is better to _____ the data than to sort it.   ➡ Check Answers

USER FOCUS: USING BOOLEAN LOGIC IN QUERIES

InfoWeb 13
Boolean

Suppose that you're using a search engine to locate information in a Web database. You decide to use the "advanced" search feature, but the instructions tell you to enter something called a "Boolean string" or a "Boolean expression." What should you do? In the context of a search engine or database, a **Boolean string** or "Boolean expression" is a sequence of keywords, field names, and logical operators that specify a query. For example, the Boolean string "meteor and Russia not Connery" might help you find information about the meteor that crashed into the Russian countryside, but screen out Web sites pertaining to an old science fiction movie about meteors starring Sean Connery.

FIGURE 14-25

George Boole defined the logic that is today used to search for information in databases and on the Web.

The mathematician George Boole (Figure 14-25) is responsible for defining a system of logic now called Boolean logic or Boolean algebra, which uses three **Boolean operators**: NOT, AND, and OR. Elements of Boole's system of logic have been universally adopted by database query languages such as SQL and are used to enter queries into search engines that help you find information on the Web.

According to experts such as Alan Cooper, who claims that, "Users don't understand Boolean," some people have difficulty using Boolean logic for search specifications. It is easy to confuse the meaning of Boolean AND and OR, because in casual speech we often use these words in exactly the opposite sense from the way that Boole defined them. Nevertheless, the use of Boolean logic in query languages for databases and Web searches is so pervasive that it is important for computer users to understand Boole's meanings for AND and OR.

Set Theory

So what is the difference between AND and OR? To understand the difference between AND and OR, it is useful to think about set theory. Set theory is a simple way of depicting what happens when you combine, select, or exclude elements from a group. Imagine a group of things. In set theory, all of the things in your group are called "the universe." Graphically, you represent this universe with a rectangle. Now suppose that some of the things in your universe are electronic gizmos. You can represent these gizmos with a circle, as shown in Figure 14-26.

FIGURE 14-26

A circle represents the electronic gizmos in your universe.

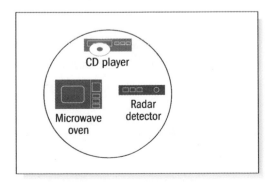

CD player

Microwave oven

Radar detector

Your universe might also contain car parts, such as tires, hood ornaments, steering wheels, CD players, and radar detectors. As you might expect, you can draw another circle in the universe to represent car parts. The catch is that some car parts are also electronic gizmos (CD players and radar detectors, for example). You show this idea by overlapping the circles in your universe. Study Figure 14-27 and make sure that you understand the four categories of things in your universe.

FIGURE 14-27

Adding car parts to your universe requires a second circle.

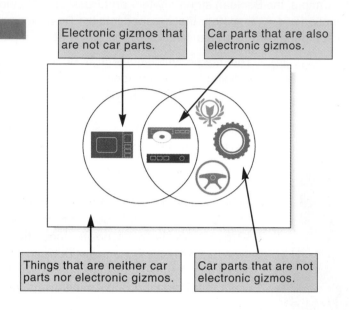

Electronic gizmos that are not car parts.

Car parts that are also electronic gizmos.

Things that are neither car parts nor electronic gizmos.

Car parts that are not electronic gizmos.

Now, here's the part that many people find tricky. Which things in your universe are *electronic gizmos AND car parts*? According to Boole, they are CD players and radar detectors. AND means a thing must fit *both* criteria: It must be both an electronic gizmo and also a car part.

To show this idea on your diagram, only the overlapping part of the circles is colored, as shown in Figure 14-28.

FIGURE 14-28

Using Boolean logic, electronic gizmos AND car parts are found in the area where the two circles overlap.

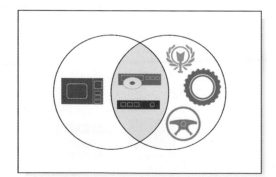

Now, what about the things that are *electronic gizmos OR car parts*? OR means a thing fits *either* criterion. So tires, radar detectors, CD players, hood ornaments, steering wheels, and microwave ovens fit the bill. To show this idea in your universe, both circles are colored, as shown in Figure 14-29.

FIGURE 14-29

Using Boolean logic, electronic gizmos OR car parts include any of the items in the circles.

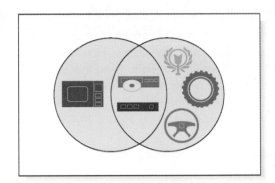

NOT means to select the opposite. For example, what things in your universe are *NOT car parts*? Everything not in the car parts circle. What things are *NOT (car parts OR electronic gizmos)*? To figure this statement out, first do the OR in parentheses. What in your universe is car parts OR electronic gizmos? All of the things in the circles. The NOT is what's left—everything outside the circles, as shown in Figure 14-30.

FIGURE 14-30

Using Boolean logic, NOT (car parts OR electronic gizmos) includes only those items that are not in the circles.

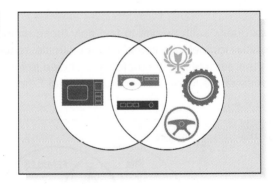

To summarize: AND means that a thing must meet both criteria. It is restrictive—it includes only the overlapping area of the two circles. OR means that a thing must fit either criterion. It is more inclusive—it includes anything in either circle. NOT means "the other things"—those things not in either circle.

CHAPTER 14

Boolean Queries

How does set theory apply to database queries? When you use a query to locate data in a database, it tells the DBMS what you want to find. Most popular query languages, such as SQL, use command words, expressions, relational operators, and Boolean operators to formulate a query.

Simple queries are usually constructed by using a command word such as FIND and an expression such as LastName = 'Houlihan'. A simple **expression** usually has a field name on the left and the specific thing that you want to find on the right. The query that you use to locate the record for an employee with the last name Houlihan, for example, is *FIND LastName = 'Houlihan'*. You can create expressions using **relational operators** such as =, >, <, >=, <=, and <>. Figure 14-31 provides a quick review of these operators.

FIGURE 14-31	Relational operators.
Operator	**Description**
=	Equal to
>	Greater than
<	Less than
>=	Greater than or equal to
<=	Less than or equal to
<>	Not equal to

A complex query, such as one to find only those employees who are registered nurses, have Houlihan for their last name, and are female, requires the use of Boolean operators. Let's use the sample set of employees, shown in Figure 14-32, to visualize the results from queries of the Midtown General Hospital Employee database.

FIGURE 14-32

Visualizing a diagram of Midtown employees can help you understand complex queries.

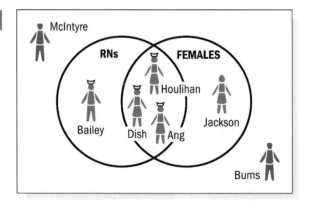

When used in a query, the logical operator AND connects two expressions, both of which must be true to match the search criteria. For example, the search criteria *JobCode = 'RN' AND Gender = 'F'* requests only those records for female registered nurses. If Margaret Houlihan is a female and a registered nurse, her record would match the search criteria. Figure 14-33 shows the results of such a search.

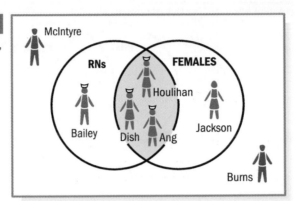

FIGURE 14-33

JobCode = 'RN' AND Gender = 'F'

The logical operator OR connects two expressions, only one of which needs to be true to match the search criteria. The search criteria *JobCode = 'RN' OR Gender = 'F'* would produce all records for females, regardless of their job code. The search would also produce all records for registered nurses of either gender.

The logical operator NOT precedes a simple or complex expression and, in a search specification, produces the records that do not match the expression. For example, the expression *NOT JobCode = 'RN'* would produce records for any employees who are not registered nurses. What about the expression *NOT (JobCode = 'RN' AND Gender = 'F')*? Think of it this way: The computer will locate the records for all employees who are registered nurses and female, but it will not produce these records. Instead, it will produce all of the other records. The parentheses help to specify the order for the AND, OR, and NOT operations. The part of the expression in parentheses should be evaluated first. Will the search *NOT (JobCode = 'RN' AND Gender = 'F')* produce the record for Rick Bailey? Yes, it will, and Figure 14-34 shows why.

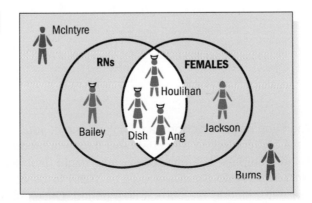

FIGURE 14-34

NOT (JobCode = 'RN' AND Gender = 'F')

CHAPTER 14

What about using NOT and OR, as in the search criteria *NOT (JobCode = 'RN' OR Gender = 'F')*? This time, the computer essentially eliminates any records for registered nurses. It also eliminates any records for female employees. Figure 14-35 provides a conceptual diagram of this query.

FIGURE 14-35

Not (JobCode = 'RN' OR Gender = 'F')

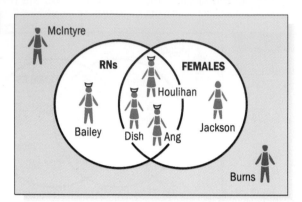

Search criteria can become quite complex. You might, for example, want to search the employee table in Figure 14-36 to find the salaries of only those female employees who started working after August 1, 1988, but before August 1, 1990, as registered nurses or staff physicians (SMD). The search criteria would be:

Gender = 'F' AND (StartDate > 08/01/1988 AND StartDate < 08/01/1990) AND (JobCode = 'RN' OR JobCode = 'SMD')

FIGURE 14-36

Midtown employee table.

LastName	FirstName	Gender	StartDate	JobCode
Ang	Susan	F	08/10/1988	RN
Bailey	Rick	M	02/03/1992	RN
Burns	Frank	M	05/04/1990	SMD
Dish	Betty	F	01/16/1992	RN
Houlihan	Margaret	F	10/05/1985	RN
Jackson	Tony	F	12/04/1989	SMD
McIntyre	John	M	04/14/1986	SMD

When you need to perform a complex search, you might want to experiment with parts of the search first, to be certain that the parts produce what you expect. For example, in the complex search above, you might first test the expression *(StartDate > 08/01/1988 AND StartDate < 08/01/1990)* to be certain that it retrieves records with start dates during the correct time period. Once you have tested parts of your query, you can combine them to create your complete query. To try some SQL queries, use the SQL Lab on the NP4 CD.

ISSUE   HAS PRIVACY DISAPPEARED?

You might be astonished by the amount of information stored about you in computer databases. Your bank has information on your financial status, credit history, and the people, organizations, and businesses to which you write checks. School records indicate something about your ability to learn and the subjects that interest you. Medical records indicate the state of your health. Credit card companies track the places you shop and what you purchase in person, by mail, or on the Web. Your phone company stores your phone number, your address, and a list of the phone numbers you dial. The driver's license bureau has your physical description. Your Internet cookies track many of the Web sites that you frequent. By compiling this data—a process sometimes referred to as "profiling"—an interested person or company could guess some very private things about you, such as your political views or even your sexual orientation.

Glen L. Roberts operates a Web site that he describes as "Stalking—Privacy—Spying —Snooping!" He sums up the current status of privacy by saying, "The information is there! It's available to ANYONE who wants to ACCESS it for whatever their PURPOSE may be! Good or Evil! The information is here [on the Web], it is quick to access, it is free, and from anywhere in the world you can learn about people anywhere in the USA!"

When records were stored on index cards and in file folders, locating and distributing data constituted a laborious process that required hand transcriptions or photocopies of sheaves of papers. Today, this data appears in electronic format and is easy to access, copy, sell, ship, consolidate, and alter. Privacy advocates point out the potential for misusing data that has been collected and stored in computer databases. A University of Miami law professor, A. Michael Froomkin, writes, "The most important part of the emerging database phenomenon, however, arises from the combination of the growth in computer processing power with the likelihood that routine personal data collection will soon become nearly ubiquitous. As the cost of data storage plummets, these trends will make it possible to assemble an individual data profile of extraordinary detail by cross-referencing multiple, extensive, databases. These profiles have uses in commerce, in law-enforcement; some applications are benign, some less so."

Privacy advocates are encouraging lawmakers to restrict the sale and distribution of information about individuals. One proposal would require your permission before information about you could be distributed. Privacy legislation in the United States has been slow to emerge. For example, the Consumer Internet Privacy Act of 1997 was referred to the Subcommittee on Telecommunications, Trade, and Consumer Protection in the same year that it was introduced but had not yet come up for vote by the end of 1999.

The issue of online privacy is not simple. Information about you is not necessarily "yours." Although you might "reveal" information about yourself on an application form, other information about you is collected without your direct input. For example, suppose that you default on your credit card payments. The credit card company has accumulated information on your delinquent status. Shouldn't it have the freedom to distribute this information, for example, to another credit card company?

Furthermore, many individuals knowingly let companies gather profiling information so as to get free products. A trend that developed in 1999 was to swap a free PC or other merchandise for permission to collect information on a person's "clickpaths"—the Web sites that they visit, their online spending habits, and so on. For one such offer, recipients of a free PC were required to agree to the terms of a lengthy contract, which included the following section on profiling: "The Free-PC System will monitor your use of the Free-PC System, and will construct personal profiles about your interests and characteristics from the information supplied directly or indirectly to us, whether from your use of the Free-PC System, the Internet or otherwise as well as through the use of data harvesting and mining techniques. Such collected information may be used for our marketing or promotional purposes, for providing services to you, and in administering the Free-PC System and our relationship with you."

Many Web surfers appreciate the shortcuts offered by intelligent agents that assemble a customized profile so as to recommend books, CD, videos, news articles, and other targeted goods or services. These users may willingly give up some measure of privacy for the convenience afforded by these agents.

Privacy

Databases that contain personal information do provide positive benefits. For example, the LEXIS-NEXIS database has been used for a number of socially beneficial activities, such as locating heirs to estates, reuniting family members, finding pension beneficiaries, and tracing the influence of personal donations in politics. The electronic privacy issue appears to be heading toward some type of compromise between strict privacy and wholesale collection/distribution of personal data. Check out the privacy InfoWeb for more information on the issue, as well as tips and computer programs that you can use to protect your privacy online.

WHAT DO YOU THINK?

1. Do you think that data about you should be distributed only after your permission has been obtained?   ◉ Yes   ○ No   ○ Not sure

2. Can you identify an actual incident when you discovered that data about you had been distributed without your approval?   ◉ Yes   ○ No   ○ Not sure

 Save Responses

CHAPTER 14 REVIEW ACTIVITIES

INTERACTIVE SUMMARY

The Interactive Summary helps you select important concepts and facts from this chapter. Fill in the blanks to best complete each sentence. When using the NP4 CD or NP4 Web site, you can click the Check Answers buttons to automatically score your answers. Place your Tracking Disk in the floppy disk drive if you want to save your scores.

In a data file, a(n) _____ contains the smallest unit of data and can be assigned a data _____, such as character, numeric, date, or memo. A(n) _____ contains data about one _____, which could be a person, place, thing, or event. The term _____ is used to refer to a file in which all of the records have the same record type. The term _____ refers to a variety of record types that are treated as a single unit.

A data model is a description of the way that data is stored in a database. A data model diagram can show the _____ between entities, such as when an employee entity clocks in with a time-card entity. These diagrams also show _____, the number of occurrences that can exist between two record types. On the conceptual level, the structure of a database can follow one of four models. The _____ database model organizes entities as parents and children, but allows a child entity to have only one parent. The _____ database model organizes entities into owners and members, but allows members to have more than one owner. The _____ database model is the most popular option; it organizes data into tables that can be joined in many flexible ways. The _____ database model organizes entities into classes of objects that can be manipulated by _____.   ➡ Check Answers

Files and databases can be implemented using a variety of software tools. _____ software allows a programmer to create a file "from scratch," along with the programs that will manipulate the data in those files. This approach to data management is often costly and difficult to reuse for other projects. _____ management software allows you to create flat files and use built-in utility programs to sort, search, display, and print data. A(n) _____ management system helps you manipulate the data in more than one file at a time. For building object-oriented databases, you can use an object-oriented database management system or programming _____, such as Smalltalk.

Database management tasks include designing the file structure, adding records, searching for information, updating information, organizing records, and generating reports. When designing a file structure, it is important to look ahead to the way that the data will be used. A careful selection of fields will allow the data to be used flexibly—for example, printing names in the format Margaret Houlihan or Houlihan, Margaret. Eliminating data _____ as part of the normalization process will make it easier to update a file, and specifying a(n) _____ check to limit the range of valid entries will make it more difficult for data entry errors to occur.

 Check Answers

INTERACTIVE KEY TERMS

Make sure that you understand all of the boldfaced key terms presented in this chapter. If you're using the NP4 CD or NP4 Web site, you can use this list of terms as an interactive study activity. First, try to define a term in your own words, then click the term to compare your definition with the definition that is presented in the chapter.

Active Server Page, 625
Attributes, 627
Boolean operators, 645
Boolean string, 645
Cardinality, 623
Case sensitivity, 639
CGI (Common Gateway Interface), 635
Character data type, 617
Child node, 625
Class, 628
Custom software, 630
Data independence, 631
Data management, 616
Data mining, 640
Data model, 623
Data redundancy, 638
Data type, 617
Data warehousing, 640
Database, 621
Database administrator, 622
Database management system (DBMS), 632
Database models, 624
Date data type, 617
Entity, 618
Expression, 648
Field, 617
Field format, 636
Field name, 617
File management software, 631
File structure, 616
Fixed-length field, 617
Global updates, 641
Hierarchical database, 625
Index files, 642
Indexing, 642
Input list, 639
Integer, 617
ISAPI, 635
Logical data type, 617
Many-to-many relationship, 624
Members, 626
Memo data type, 617
Methods, 628
Network database, 626
Node, 625

Normalization, 638
NSAPI, 635
Numeric data type, 617
Object, 628
Object ID number, 639
Object-oriented database model, 628
Object-oriented DBMS, 634
One-to-many relationship, 624
One-to-one relationship, 624
Owner, 626
Parent node, 625
Query, 640
Range check, 637
Real number, 617
Record, 618
Record length, 618
Record number, 639
Record occurrence, 619
Record type, 619
Relational operators, 648
Relationship, 623
Report generator, 643
Report template, 643
Root node, 625
Set, 626
Smalltalk, 634
Sort key, 641
Sorting, 641
SQL (Structured Query Language), 640
Tables, 627
Tuple, 627
Variable-length field, 617
Web-enabled databases, 635

INTERACTIVE QUIZZES

Quiz yourself on important concepts from this chapter by filling in the blanks. When using the NP4 CD or NP4 Web site, you can type your answers, then use the Check Answers buttons to automatically score your responses. Place your Tracking Disk in the floppy disk drive if you want to save your scores.

1 A record [＿＿＿＿＿＿] is similar to a blank form, whereas a record [＿＿＿＿＿＿] is like a completed form.

2 Hierarchical and network databases require a physical link between related records. True or false? [＿＿＿＿＿＿]

3 "Tuple," "table," "relation," and "attribute" are all terms associated with the [＿＿＿＿＿＿] database model.

4 Data [＿＿＿＿＿＿] refers to the separation of data and the programs that manipulate that data.

5 A Web-enabled database must be stored in HTML format. True or false? [＿＿＿＿＿＿]

6 If you format a Social Security number field as XXX-XX-XXXX, the series of Xs indicates that the field type is [＿＿＿＿＿＿].

7 A(n) [＿＿＿＿＿＿] key is the field used to arrange records in alphabetical or numeric order.

8 A(n) [＿＿＿＿＿＿] file helps organize the records in a file without changing their physical order.

9 [＿＿＿＿＿＿] operators include AND, OR, and NOT.

Check Answers

Refer to the file structure information at right and use a calculator to correctly fill in the following blanks.

1 Number of fields [＿＿＿＿＿]

2 Record length [＿＿＿＿＿]

3 Space required by 500 records [＿＿＿＿＿]

4 Number of records that will fit on a 1.44 MB floppy disk [＿＿＿＿＿]

5 Any evidence of data redundancy? [＿＿＿＿＿]

6 999999 would be the field format for which field? [＿＿＿＿＿]

Employee Record Structure

Field	Length	Data Type
LastName	10	Character
FirstName	10	Character
Address	20	Character
ZipCode	10	Character
Phone	13	Character
SocNum	11	Character
Hourly Wage	6	Numeric
Bonus points	6	Numeric
DateHired	10	Date

Check Answers

CHAPTER 14

INTERACTIVE PRACTICE TESTS

When you use the NP4 CD or NP4 Web site, you can take practice tests that consist of 10 multiple-choice, true/false, and fill-in-the-blank questions. The 10 questions are selected at random from a large test bank, so each time you take a test, you'll receive a different set of questions. Your tests are scored immediately and you can print study guides that help you find the correct answers for any questions that you missed. If you are using a Tracking Disk, insert it in the floppy disk drive to save your test scores.

 Start Practice
Test

STUDY TIPS

Study Tips help you organize and consolidate the information in a chapter by making lists, outlines, charts, and sketches. You can use paper and pencil, or word processing software to complete most of the Study Tips activities.

1 Create a chart that summarizes the terminology used as synonyms for the terms "record type," "record," and "field" in hierarchical, network, relational, and object-oriented databases.

2 List the steps you should follow to design a flat file or a database.

3 Draw a hierarchy diagram showing the relationships among the following terms: file, program file, data file, free-form data file, structured data file, flat file, database, relational database, hierarchical database, network database, object-oriented database.

4 Complete the chart below to summarize the characteristics of data management software:

	Custom	File Management	Database Management	Object-Oriented
Files manipulated with	A custom program			
Promotes data independence (Y/N)	N			
File support		One at a time		
Allow relationships (Y/N)		N		

5 Explain the difference between a record occurrence and a record type.

6 For each of these pairs of record types, draw a data structure diagram showing whether the relationship is one-to-one, one-to-many, or many-to-many.

Author   Book

Musician   CD

Person   Social Security number

House   Mailbox

7 Suppose you have a universe that contains overlapping circles for pilots and CIOs (chief information officers). Draw diagrams showing each of the following:

a. NOT (Pilots AND CIOs)

b. NOT (Pilots)

c. (NOT Pilots) AND (NOT CIOs)

d. NOT (Pilots OR CIOs)

P R O J E C T S

A project is an open-ended activity that will help you apply the concepts you have learned. Many projects require resources in addition to your textbook, such as current magazines, library materials, or Web access. When you tackle a project, be prepared to use your critical thinking skills, logical analysis, and your creativity.

1 Gourmet Gallery Suppose that you are the database administrator for a large gourmet supply store. You're working with the inventory manager to define an effective record format for your inventory file. The inventory manager gives you a sample of the index cards now being used to keep track of the inventory.

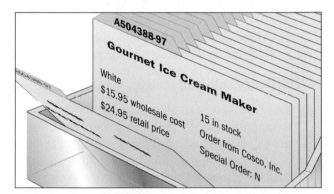

Use this card to design an effective record format for the inventory data file by doing the following:

a. List each field that the inventory record should contain. Your field names should be descriptive, contain no more than 10 characters, and be only one word. For example, use "PARTNUMBER," not "PN." Remember to think about how the data might be used for output—the fields you define might not be exactly the same as the fields on the index card.

b. Assign a data type to each field. You may use the following data types: character, numeric, date, and logical.

c. Define the length of each field. You might have to make some intelligent guesses about the field length because you do not know what all of the data looks like. For example, you can see from the example that some part numbers are at least 10 characters long, but you might guess that some part numbers will be longer—use your best judgment. Be careful about the length of fields that contain dollar values. Do not leave a space for the $ sign, but do provide a space for the decimal point.

d. Where appropriate, indicate the input or output format for a field—for example, you would use 9999.99 for currency fields.

2 Central State University Suppose that you work on the staff at Central State University and you have the following data:

The Management Department (phone: 455-9800) has three graduate faculty: Professor Sharon Smith (office: BA 502, phone: 455-9897), Associate Professor Rico Gomez (office: BA 510, phone: 455-9888), and Associate Professor Ariel Headly (office: BA 402, phone: 455-9776). S. Smith teaches Quantitative Analysis (course ID: MM525) on Tuesday and Thursday, 7–9 P.M., in room BA 10. She also teaches the Graduate Seminar (course ID: MM698) on Monday, 7–10 P.M., in room BA 21. R. Gomez teaches Personnel Management (course ID: MM560) on Monday and Wednesday, 7–9 P.M., in room BA 20. A. Headly teaches Leadership in Organizations (course ID: MM610) on Thursday, 6–9 P.M., in room BA 20.

continued on the following page

CHAPTER 14

a. Draw a data structure diagram showing how you would arrange this data in a hierarchical data-base, then draw the specific occurrence of the data described here.

b. R. Gomez decides to help A. Headly teach the Leadership in Organizations course. Now this course has two instructors. Redraw your data structure diagram using a network model to show this relationship. Also, redraw your diagram showing an occurrence of the data.

c. Diagram the tables you would use if you were to structure this data as a relational database.

3 **Indexing** Suppose that you have a small file with the records about computer books shown at right.

a. Manually create an index file that will organize the records in alphabetical order according to author last name.

b. Create another index table to organize the records by publication date from most recent to oldest.

Record Number	Author	Title	Publication Date
1	Norton, Peter	Programmer's Guide to the IBM PC	1985
2	Craig, John Clark	Visual Basic Workshop	1991
3	Minsky, Marvin	Society of Mind	1986
4	Nelson, Theodore	Literary Machines	1987
5	Wodasky, Ron	Multimedia Madness	1992
6	Waite, Mitchell	UNIX Primer Plus	1983

4 **The Boolean Web** Most Web search engines allow you to formulate "advanced" searches using Boolean operators. By using these operators, you can specify a very precise search that, in many cases, will help you pinpoint the information you need without having to wade through thousands of potential site links. To complete this project, find the answers to questions (a) through (e) using the Boolean search capabilities of a Web browser, such as *www.lycos.com*, *www.altavista.com*, or *www.infoseek.com*. In addition to writing out the answers, indicate the Boolean search you used to find the answer.

a. What did Albert Einstein think about socialism?

b. Where can you find information about the dogs that the Soviets launched into space?

c. Where can you find a quote from Confucius about learning?

d. How many sites contain information about the Magna Carta or about netserfs?

e. Where would you find information about what netserfs think of the Magna Carta?

5 **Normalization** Take the first step in the normalization process by eliminating the data redundancy in the Invoice file below. If necessary, create new record types. Assume you are working with a relational database model.

Invoice Number	Customer Name	Address	Date	Item Number	Item	Price	Number Purchased
0010	Jack Wei	503 S. HWY 7	09/01/1994	56887	B&D Hammer	17.69	1
0010	Jack Wei	503 S. HWY 7	09/01/1994	67433	Sand Paper–Fine	4.98	2
0010	Jack Wei	503 S. HWY 7	09/01/1994	2230B	CTR Sink	2.49	1
0011	Sally Zachman	834 N. Front St.	09/01/1994	56887	B&D Hammer	17.69	1
0012	Brad Koski	2910 52nd St.	09/02/1994	56887	B&D Hammer	17.69	2
0012	Brad Koski	2910 52nd St.	09/02/1994	4311A	9-inch Brush	7.89	1

ADDITIONAL PROJECTS

Click the underlined text to link to the NP4 Web site (www.cciw.com/np4), where you can view and print additional projects for this chapter.

Toy Store

LAB ASSIGNMENTS

Software for this lab is provided on the NP4 CD and may also be available in your school's computer lab. To start the lab, click the lab icon.

The lab has two parts: Steps and Explore. Use the Steps first to learn and review concepts. Read the information on each page and do the numbered steps. As you work through the lab, you will be asked to answer QuickCheck questions about what you have learned. At the end of the lab, you will see a report that scores your answers to the QuickChecks. If your instructor wants you to turn in this report, click the Print button on the QuickCheck Report screen.

When you have completed the Steps, you can click the Explore button to complete the Lab Assignments. You can also use Explore to practice the skills you learned and to explore concepts on your own.

Lab
SQL Queries

To query many relational databases, you use SQL (usually pronounced by saying the letters of the acronym, "S Q L"). IBM developed SQL in the mid-1970s for use in mainframe relational database products such as DB2. In 1986, the American National Standards Institute (ANSI) adopted SQL as the standard relational database language. It is now used extensively on microcomputer databases as well. Understanding how to use SQL is an important skill for many data management jobs. In this lab, you will get a taste of this powerful and flexible database language. To gain further expertise, you should refer to the course offerings at your school.

1 Click the Steps button to learn how to formulate SQL queries. As you proceed through the steps, answer the QuickCheck questions. After you complete the Steps, you will see a report that summarizes your performance on the QuickChecks. Follow the instructions on the screen to print the QuickCheck report.

2 In Explore, use the scroll bar to browse through the database to find the answers to the following questions:

   a. What are the names of the staff physicians? (*Hint:* The JobCode for staff physicians is SMD.)

   b. How many LPNs are in the database?

   c. Who makes more than $20 per hour?

   d. What is Ralph Smith's job?

   e. When was Tony Jackson hired?

3 In Explore, try the following queries and indicate whether each accomplishes the result listed:

   a. **QUERY:** SELECT * FROM Employee order by Hourlywage

      RESULT: Displays employees beginning with the person who is the lowest paid

   b. **QUERY:** SELECT * FROM Employee where Gender = 'F' AND Jobcode = 'SMD'

      RESULT: Displays all female staff physicians

   c. **QUERY:** SELECT * FROM Employee where LastName between 'C' and 'M'

      RESULT: Displays all employees with last names that begin with a C, D, E, F, G, H, I, J, K, L, and M

   d. **QUERY:** SELECT * FROM Employee where Gender = 'M' or Hourlywage > 20.00

      RESULT: Displays only men who make more than $20 per hour

   e. **QUERY:** SELECT * FROM Employee where DeptCode <> 'OB' order by BirthDate

      RESULT: Displays all of the obstetricians' birthdays

4 In Explore, suppose that the database contains thousands of records and it is not practical to browse through all of them using the scroll bar. Write down the queries you would use to do the following:

a. Find the record for Angela Peterson.

b. Find the records for all RNs.

c. Find all employees who work in Intensive Care (IC).

d. Find all employees who make less than $15 per hour.

e. Find all employees who do not work in obstetrics (OB).

5 In Explore, suppose that the database contains thousands of records and it is not practical to browse through all of them using the scroll bar. Write down the queries you use to do the following:

a. Find the name of the oldest employee.

b. Find the departments that have female employees.

c. Find out how many employees work in Intensive Care.

d. Find the last names of the female employees who make between $10 and $15 per hour.

e. Get an alphabetized list of male employees who work as RNs or LPNs.

6 Circle the errors in the following SQL queries:

a. SELECT * FROM Employee where DeptCode <> OB order by BirthDate

b. SELECT * FROM Employee where Wages between 10 and 50

c. SELECT * FROM Employee where order = LastName

d. SELECT * FROM Employee where DeptCode <> 'OB' and Hourly Wage > '$10.00' order by LastName

e. SELECT * FROM Employee where FirstName like T*

INFOWEB

Chapter 14

The InfoWeb is your guide to print, film, television, and electronic resources. Use it to obtain updates on quickly changing technical information and to locate information for research papers. If you're using the NP4 CD, click the InfoWeb Site icon on the left side of this paragraph to access the online InfoWeb links. Otherwise, use your Web browser and type in the address of the NP4 Web site: www.cciw.com/np4. At the Web site you'll find up-to-date links to the topics covered in this chapter.

1 M*A*S*H

*M*A*S*H* was both a movie and a television series that captured the attention and hearts of Americans from 1970, when the movie was released, through 1983, when the last television episode was broadcast. *M*A*S*H* was written by Richard Hooker (Pocket Books, 1968). The movie was directed by Robert Altman and distributed by 20th Century Fox. At the M*A*S*H 4077th home page (*www.netlink.co.uk/users/mash*), you can read profiles of the characters and actors, learn where the cast members are now, take a tour of the camp, take a trivia challenge, and more. Mobile Army Surgical Hospitals did not go away with the end of the Korean War. At the 807th MASH Operations Desert Shield and Operation Desert Storm site, *www.iglou.com/law/mash.htm*, you can read a diary that runs from December 8, 1990, to June 29, 1991, detailing the experiences of the Army medical corps during a more recent war.

1952 was an election year. The Korean War depicted in *M*A*S*H* contributed to a close race between Dwight Eisenhower and Adlai Stevenson. As a promotional gimmick, CBS used the new UNIVAC computer to predict the election results. Did CBS trust the results of that first computer prediction of election outcomes? Read *The IEEE Computer Society Events in the History of Computing* at *www.computer.org/50/history/1952.htm* to find out.

2 Database Concepts

Database Design for Mere Mortals: A Hands-On Guide to Relational Database Design by Michael J. Hernandez (Addison-Wesley, January 1997) provides an introduction to relational database design concepts that's easy to understand and apply. On the Web, head for the University of Massachusetts Database Systems Laboratory Database site, *www-ccs.cs.umass.edu/db/databasesites.html*, where you can find links to database textbooks, research journals, bulletins, bibliographies, technical reports, books, and database-related discussion groups.

Popular database magazines include *Datamation* at *www.datamation.com* and *Data and Intelligent Enterprise* at *www.intelligententerprise.com/dbframe.shtml*, where you can find Database Programming and Design archives as well as DBMS archives and Oracle View archives. In addition, you can find links to articles on database technology and software at ZDNet's AnchorDesk (*www.zdnet.com/anchordesk*), and then search using the key term "database".

The Data Management Association International (DAMA) at *www.dama.org* is the leading organization for professionals in database management. Other professional associations include the Information Resources Management Association at *www.hbg.psu.edu/Faculty/m1k/IRMA.html*, the International Data Warehousing Association at *www.idwa.org*, and the Society for Information Management at *www.simnet.org*.

CHAPTER 14

3 Database Administrator

What does a database administrator do? How is a database administrator's job different from a systems analyst's job or a database manager's job? A good place to start looking for answers to these career questions is the Bureau of Labor Statistics Occupational Outlook Handbook section on the Computer Scientists and Systems Analysts site, *stats.bls.gov/oco/ocos042.htm*. You can find more information about database-oriented careers by visiting the Boston Computer Museum's Careers in Computing site, *www.tcm.org/html/resources/cmp-careers/cnc-data.html*. Using a Web search engine and the search phrase "database administrator," you'll find articles such as the April 1997 issue of *ComputerWorld*, which contains an article called "DB Dandies." This article gives you an idea of which database skills are the most highly valued and some of the qualities that managers look for in job candidates (*www2.computerworld.com/home/print9497.nsf/All/SLcar0421a*). When considering any career, it is worthwhile to consider what your starting salary will be and what salary increases will be like over the course of your career path. DataMaster's 1999 Computer Industry Salary Survey at *www.datamasters.com/dm/survey.html* provides a list of IS/IT positions with salary information (median low, region median, median high) organized by region of the country. The article "Are Your Pay Scales Right?" at *www.datamation.com/staff/07mba.html* discusses the idea of establishing pay scales based on benchmark information. This article includes a list of IT jobs with brief descriptions, including database manager, and includes links to *Datamation*'s very extensive salary survey. From *Computerworld*'s 11th Annual Salary Survey at *www2.computerworld.com/home/online9697.nsf/All/970901survey*, you can get an idea of the kind of salary increases you can expect from a database-related career.

4 Data Modeling

One of the most highly recommended books on data modeling is *Data Modeling Essentials* by Graeme Simsion (The Coriolis Group, 1996). For a quick online introduction to data modeling techniques, connect to the Applied Information Science site at *www.aisintl.com/case/method.html*. Another online article, "Building a Logical Data Model" at *www.dbmsmag.com/9506d16.html* from DBMS Online, by George Tillmann, provides a basic definition of data modeling, discusses the various elements of a data model (for example, objects, entities, relationships, and attributes), and describes how they relate to each other. The article is based on his book *A Practical Guide to Logical Data Modeling* (McGraw-Hill, 1993) and uses the entity-relationship approach to data modeling. The Canadian Ministry of Forests at *www.for.gov.bc.ca/isb/datadmin/s7_mdl12.htm* provides one of the best online sites for data modeling. By searching the Web for "data modeling," you can find other excellent data modeling sites, such as the one hosted by CERN at *www.cern.ch/Adamo/guide/Chapter-2.html*. Data modeling software such as Embarcadero Technologies' ER/Studio (*www.embarcadero.com*) help database designers build easy-to-manipulate graphical data models, then turn them into production databases.

5 Relational Databases

Edgar F. Codd invented the relational database. In his article "A Relational Model of Data for Large Shared Data Banks," which first appeared in *Communications of the ACM*, Vol. 13, No. 6, June 1970, Codd describes the 12 characteristics of a relational database system. Search the Intelligent Enterprise site (*www.intelligententerprise.com*) for commentary and discussion on the original 1970 article as well as on other articles by Codd. For additional insight into relational databases, refer to Codd's classic reference book, *The Relational Model for Database Management* (Addison-Wesley, 1990) in which he expands on his earlier work and defines 333 characteristics of a "pure" relational database system.

In "Overview of the Relational Model" at *www.utexas.edu/cc/dbms/utinfo/relmod/index.html* from the University of Texas at Austin's Database Management Services, you can find a simple explanation of the relational model and reasons why you might need to understand it. The Web-based document discusses the relational data structure, including notation, properties of relational tables, relational keys, and data integrity; manipulation of relational data; and normalization. There are also a brief reading list and links to other database resources on the Internet.

C. J. Date is one of the most prolific writers on the topic of databases. Through his extensive teaching, training, and writing activities, Date has explained the relational model to thousands of software engineers, software designers, educators, students, journalists, and end users. In a 1994 interview, Date talked about the future of the database industry and integrating object-oriented database concepts with relational concepts. Date's classic book on databases is now in its sixth edition: *An Introduction to Database Systems* (Addison-Wesley, 1999).

6 Object-Oriented Database Model

According to the article "So What the Hell is OODBMS?", the key difference between a relational database and an object-oriented database lies in the way that an object-oriented database stores data and manages the relationships among data elements. Is an object-oriented database best suited for use with complex data? Can it describe simple relationships or complex relationships? Are object-oriented databases particularly good at handling certain kinds of data? Are object-oriented databases beginning to replace other kinds of databases in the business world? This article, which you can find at *www2.computerworld.com/home/print9497.nsf/All/SL1106rev,* will help you answer these questions and understand the key differences between object-oriented databases and relational databases.

The classic book, *Object Databases: The Essentials*, by Dr. Mary E. S. Loomis (Addison-Wesley, 1995), can help you understand the differences between object-oriented databases and relational databases. It explains the basic concepts of object-oriented databases, compares OODBMS features with relational database management system features, and illustrates how to use an OODBMS on a project. The end of the book has a more technical emphasis because it describes using object-oriented languages such as Smalltalk and C++ to program an OODBMS. You can read a DBMS Online interview with Dr.

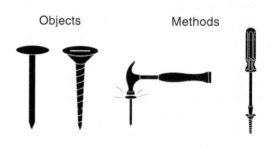

Objects   Methods

Loomis at *www.dbmsmag.com/int9412.html,* where she explains what an object-oriented database is, discusses the differences in philosophy between traditional database systems and object databases, and describes some of the differences between relational database models and object-oriented models.

"Object DBMSs: Now or Never," at *www.dbmsmag.com/9707d13.html* from DBMS Online, can give you a less technical view of the differences between traditional databases and object-oriented databases. It vividly describes an example of a database that contains image, audio, and animation data and contrasts this information with the typical transaction data found in traditional databases.

7 DBMS Software

When this textbook went to press, the most popular microcomputer DBMS software included Lotus Approach (*www.lotus.com/home.nsf/welcome/approach*), Claris FileMaker Pro (*www.claris.com*), Microsoft Access (*www.microsoft.com/office/access/default.htm*), Oracle (*www.oracle.com*), and Sybase PowerBuilder (*www.sybase.com/products/powerbuilder*). You can learn more about these software packages by visiting their Web sites. Another route is to enter the search term "database software" at *www.ask.com*, then use the pull-down list to view the names of popular database software and link to their sites. At *www.zdnet.com/pcmag/features/suites/ft-db.htm*, you'll find comparative reviews of popular DBMS software

8 OODBMS Tools

An overview of OODBMS is available at *www.dacs.dtic.mil/techs/oodbms2/Overview.html*. For more information on OODBMS products, visit vendor sites: Computer Associates, the world's third-largest software publisher produces an OODBMS called Jasmine (*www.cai.com/products/jasmine.htm*). Objectivity publishes the Objectivity OODBMS (*www.objectivity.com*). The popular Versant OODBMS is published by Versant Object Technology (*www.versant.com/us/index.html*).

Object-oriented databases are still struggling to gain a foothold in corporate data management. One of the problems has been reconciling the object model with the relational model. David Linthicum discusses this problem in "Objects Meet Data" (*www.dbmsmag.com/9609d16.html*), and includes a list of object-to-relational products and vendors. A comprehensive list of object-oriented CASE tools from the July 1997 issue of DBMS Online can be found at *www.dbmsmag.com/9707d161.html*.

9 DB Web Tools

ZDNet provides excellent information for Web database developers at the Web site *www.zdnet.com/devhead*. There, you can follow links to articles about older technologies, such as CGI and Perl scripts, as well as the up-and-coming Web database tool, Active Server Page (ASP).

At WWW Database Tools, *www.gov.nb.ca/hotlist/wwwdbase.htm*, you can find an extensive list of annotated links to the Web sites of companies that are producing products designed to link databases with the Web. Popular Web database tools include Oracle Web Developer Suite at *www.oracle.com*; Borland Intrabuilder at *www.borland.com*; Microsoft Visual InterDev, Active Server Page technology, and Web Assistant at *www.microsoft.com*; Netscape Visual JavaScript at *www.netscape.com*; Sybase's PowerBuilder Enterprise and NetImpact Dynamo at *www.sybase.com*; Allaire Cold Fusion at *www.allaire.com*; and IBM's Net.Data at *www.ibm.com*.

10 Normalization

You can find a basic definition of the concept of normalization at PCWebopedia's normalization page (*www.pcwebopedia.com/normalization.htm*). For more information, detailed examples, and tips, read "Normalization" at *www.troubleshooters.com/littstip/ltnorm.html*. At The Software Developer's Handbook site (*www.mtjeff.com/~calvin/devhbook/databasedesign.html*), you can read an article about normalization, which includes the rules of normalization and detailed examples illustrating how the rules are used. At the end of the article, you'll find information on other database resources, including a list of books and links to other normalization resources on the Web.

11 SQL

In exploring the area of query languages, you can start with PCWebopedia's basic definition of "query languages" or "SQL" at *www.pcwebopedia.com/SQL.htm*. At the end of the definition, you'll find links to additional Web resources.

The SQL Tutorial at *w3.one.net/~jhoffman/sqltut.htm* begins with a basic definition of SQL and then provides a detailed description of how to use SQL queries. There is also a helpful section of commonly asked questions, such as "Why can't I just ask for the first three rows in a table?" and "Aren't database tables just files?" Allen Taylor's series of three articles, "What Is SQL, and Why Should I Care?" at *www.computerbits.com/archive/19960500/sql1.htm*, is as entertaining as it is informative.

12 Data Warehouses

The basic definition of data warehouse at *www.cait.wustl.edu/cait/papers/prism/vol1_no1* introduces the concept and provides a concise explanation of why it is important to organizations. According to the article "Data Warehousing Fundamentals" at *www.broughton-sys.com/Bsihtml/Data_ware.html*, data warehousing isn't just a way of storing historical data about an enterprise—it is a unifying and coherent method for organizing information systems. In "The Wiser, Gentler Data Warehouse" at *www.sunworld.com/swol-05-1997/swol-05-datawarehouse.html*, SunWorld presents a step-by-step guide to developing a successful data warehouse. The Data Warehouse Research Center site, *www.cio.com/CIO/rc_dw.html*, provides general resources on data warehousing that range from articles, case studies, a glossary, and white papers to a list of vendors that sell data warehousing applications.

Once you have an organization's data stored and accessible in a data warehouse, how do you extract information from it? The answer is data mining. You'll find information about data mining by digging into the article "Digging into Data Mining," located at *www.dbmsmag.com/9710d05.html*. The article "Data Mining Today" at *www.dbmsmag.com/9702d16.html* reviews the most current data mining technologies, and you can find information about vendors of data mining tools at the Data Warehousing Information Center site, *pwp.starnetinc.com/larryg/index.html*. Two organizations, the Data Mining Group (*www.dmg.org*) and the Data Mining Institute (*www.datamining.org*), promote a broader understanding of data mining and work to establish standards for its use.

13 Boolean

George Boole is a luminary of mathematics and logic whose work shows the practicality of these fields. Using his basic definitions of AND, OR, and NOT, individuals can wade through piles of irrelevant data in minutes to find the one piece of information they need. To learn more about Boole, read the brief essay "George Boole" at *www.advbool.com/Misc/boole.html*. At the end of the essay, you will find a short reading list that points to sources of additional material on George Boole's life. For a longer biographical sketch and to see a portrait of Boole, you might visit the George Boole site at *www-groups.dcs.st-andrews.ac.uk/~history/Mathematicians/Boole.html*. At "The Calculus of Logic," *www.maths.tcd.ie/pub/HistMath/People/Boole/CalcLogic/CalcLogic.html*, you can read an essay that Boole wrote to describe his "application of a new and peculiar form of Mathematics to the expression of the operations of the mind in reasoning." Computer Logic, at *www.ort.org/edu/itweb/itcourse.htm* hosted by ORTnet, presents a tutorial on basic Boolean logic as it is implemented in computers.

14 Privacy

A. Michael Froomkin's article mentioned in the Issue section is called "Flood Control on the Information Ocean: Living with Anonymity, Digital Cash, and Distributed Databases" and is available at *www.law.miami.edu/~froomkin/articles/ocean.htm*. Glen Roberts' "The Stalker's Home Page" is online at *www.glr.com/stalk.html*. The links at this site are truly awesome and essential armament for protecting your privacy in this age of electronic databases. The John Marshall Law School (Chicago) has compiled the Cyberspace Law Subject Index. Check out its "privacy" links by connecting to *www.jmls.edu/cyber/index/privacy.html*.

You might want to read "The War Over Your Personal Privacy Is Over. You Lost!" By Angela Gunn in the *Seattle Weekly* (July 8, 1999) (*www.seattleweekly.com/features/9927/features-gunn.shtml*). If you're concerned about Web cookies, turn to "How Web Servers' Cookies Threaten Your Privacy" at *www.junkbusters.com/ht/en/cookies.html*. The Privacy.net home page (*www.privacy.net*) does an excellent job of categorizing privacy issues. If you are concerned about who has access to your personal data, such as medical records and credit reports, you can check the Consumer Action Organization (*www.consumer-action.org/Library/English/Pubs-Privacy_FN.html*), where you'll find some sage advice about your Social Security number. Note that you can retain some degree of anonymity on the Internet by using the Anonymizer site *www.anonymizer.com/3.0/index.shtml*. At the Privacy Rights Clearinghouse (*www.privacyrights.org*), you'll find information about additional ways to safeguard your privacy and prevent identity theft.

CHAPTER 14

CHAPTER 15 COMPUTER PROGRAMMING

PREVIEW

In this chapter, you'll learn how programmers specify, code, and test a computer program. Understanding these steps in the programming process will be useful if you become involved in software development as a programmer or as a computer user.

When you have completed this chapter, you should be able to:

■ Describe the difference between a systems analyst and software engineer

■ Describe the difference between a "small" program and a "large" program using the Department of Defense standards

■ Identify the assumptions and known information in a problem statement

■ Describe the relationships among algorithms, pseudocode, and program code

■ List at least four ways to express an algorithm

■ Identify control structures in a simple program

■ Describe the difference between syntax errors and logic errors

■ Explain the purpose of program documentation, remarks, and user reference

■ List today's most popular computer programming languages and the major characteristics that differentiate them

CHAPTER 15 LAB

Visual
Programming

THE PIZZA PROGRAM

It's Tuesday night. Your study group is pulling an all-nighter just before final exams when the munchies strike. Pizza sounds really good, but your group has a grand total of $24.63— not much to feed eight hungry students. You all agree to call several pizza places to compare prices. One of your friends, looking up from her financial management text, says, "Maximize pizza, minimize cost!"

You call VanGo's Pizzeria first and find out that it sells an 8-inch round pizza with two toppings for $8.99. Your friends call a pizza place named The Venice and discover that it has a 10-inch square pizza for $11.99. Which one is the better deal? You search for a calculator but can't find one. Your friend with the pocket protector offers to let you use his notebook computer so that you can write a program to compare pizza prices. Now what?

This chapter is an introduction to **computer programming**, the process of writing instructions that direct the computer to carry out a specific task. The basic concepts of computer programming include problem statements, algorithms, coding, control structures, testing, and documentation. Additional chapter topics cover the characteristics of computer programming languages and brief descriptions of today's most popular programming languages. This chapter is a steppingstone for programming activities, such as the Visual Programming Lab.

SECTION A SOFTWARE ENGINEERING

Software engineering is the systematic approach to the development, operation, maintenance, and retirement of software. Software engineers are responsible for designing and creating software that is used in an information system. The jobs of the systems analyst and the software engineer overlap, but they are not the same. A systems analyst plans an entire information system, including hardware, software, procedures, personnel, and data. A software engineer focuses on the software component of an information system: on software design, programming, and testing.

InfoWeb
1

Software
Engineering

What is the point of learning about software engineering and computer programming if you do not plan to become a programmer? There are several reasons for taking this step. First, you are likely to use many computer programs during your career, and when you realize that your word processing program contains 750,000 lines of code, you will understand how a few bugs might exist. You will also understand that you would not want to undertake the task of writing a word processing program on your own—that it is a project best left to professional programming teams. Finally, although you would not typically write the productivity software you use, it is possible that you might have the opportunity to develop or participate in the development of software applications that are specific to your needs. Your understanding of computer programming and software engineering will help you plan constructively and participate productively in the development process.

Computer Programs

Is it difficult to write a computer program? Compared to the commercial applications you use, the programs that you'll work with in this chapter are relatively "tiny." By the Department of Defense's standards, a "small" program is one with fewer than 100,000 lines of instructions. A "medium-sized" program is one with 100,000 to 1 million lines. A "large" program is one with more than 1 million lines. Research has shown that, on average, one programmer completes only 20 lines of code per day. It is not surprising, then, that most commercial programs are written by teams of programmers and take many months, or years, to complete.

In Chapter 2, you learned that a computer program is a set of detailed, step-by-step instructions that tell a computer how to solve a problem or carry out a task. Although we speak of "writing a computer program," it is not exactly the same process as writing a letter. When you write a letter, you are not particularly concerned about its structure or efficiency, as long as you communicate your message.

People can tolerate some degree of ambiguity when they communicate. Suppose that you write your friend a letter that includes the following statement: "Remember to water my plants and lock the doors. Oh, and don't forget to feed the fish." You assume your friend knows which plants to water and how much water to use, you hope your friend remembers what to feed the fish, and you assume that your friend will feed the fish before leaving the house and locking the door. Computers are less able than people to deal with ambiguity. So, when you give your computer a set of instructions, you need to be more explicit than you would be with a person. You must think of computer programming as a process that is more structured, more precise, and less ambiguous than writing a casual letter to a friend. Computer programming begins with a problem statement, which is the basis for an algorithm. An algorithm, in turn, is the basis for program instructions. Section A provides an overview of problem statements, algorithms, and program instructions.

The Problem Statement

What's a good problem statement for the pizza program? Problems that you might try to solve using a computer often begin as questions—for example, "Which pizza place has the best deal?" But this question is not stated in a way that helps you devise a way for the computer to arrive at an answer. The question is vague. It does not tell you what information is available for determining the best deal. Do you know the price of several pizzas at different pizza places? Do you know the sizes of the pizzas? Do you know how many toppings are included in each price? The question "Which pizza place has the best deal?" does not explain what "best deal" means: Is it merely the cheapest pizza? Is it the pizza that gives you the most toppings for the dollar? Is it the biggest pizza you can get for the $24.63 that you and your friends managed to scrape together? Study Figure 15-1 and see if you can pose a problem statement that is better than the initial vague question, "Which pizza place has the best deal?"

FIGURE 15-1

Which pizza place has the best deal?

You were first introduced to problem statements in Chapter 13 within the context of systems analysis and design. In the context of programming, a problem statement defines certain elements that must be manipulated to achieve a result or goal. A good problem statement for a computer program has three characteristics:

- It specifies any assumptions that define the scope of the problem.
- It clearly specifies the known information.
- It specifies when the problem has been solved.

In a problem statement, an **assumption** is something that you accept as true so as to proceed with the program design. For example, with the pizza problem, you can make the assumption that you want to compare two pizzas. Furthermore, you can assume that some pizzas are round and others are square. To simplify the problem, you might make the additional assumption that none of the pizzas is rectangular—that is, none will have one side longer than the other. This assumption simplifies the problem because you need to deal only with the "size" of a pizza, rather than the "length" and "width" of a pizza. A fourth assumption for the pizza problem is that the pizzas you compare have the same toppings. Finally, you assume that the pizza with the lowest cost per square inch is the best buy.

The **known information** in a problem statement is the information that you supply to the computer to help it solve a problem. For the pizza problem, the known information includes the prices, shapes, and sizes of pizzas from two pizza places. The known information is often included in the problem statement as "givens." For example, a problem statement might include the phrase, "given the prices, the shapes, and the sizes of two pizzas... ."

After identifying the known information in a problem statement, you specify how to determine when the problem has been solved. Usually this step means specifying the output you expect. Of course, you cannot specify the answer in the problem statement—you won't know, for example, whether VanGo's Pizzeria or The Venice has the better deal before you run the program. But you can specify that the computer should output which pizza is the better deal.

Suppose that the best deal means getting the biggest pizza at the lowest price; in other words, the best deal is the pizza that has the lowest price per square inch. In this case, pizza that costs 5¢ per square inch is a better deal than pizza that costs 7¢ per square inch. The problem is solved, therefore, when the computer has calculated the price per square inch for both pizzas, compared the prices, and printed a message indicating which one has the lower price per square inch. You could write this part of the problem statement as "The computer will calculate the price per square inch of each pizza, compare the prices, then print a message indicating whether Pizza 1 or Pizza 2 has the lower price per square inch."

After thinking carefully about the problem, you have a list of assumptions, a list of known information, and a description of what you expect as output. The complete problem statement for the pizza program is:

Assuming that there are two pizzas to compare, that both pizzas contain the same toppings, and that the pizzas could be round or square; and given the prices, the shapes, and the sizes of the two pizzas; the computer will calculate the price per square inch of each pizza, compare the prices, then print a message indicating which pizza has the lower price per square inch.

This problem statement is rather lengthy. The following format for the problem statement is easier to understand:

ASSUMPTIONS:
There are two pizzas to compare, Pizza 1 and Pizza 2
The pizzas have the same toppings
A pizza is either round or square
Neither of the pizzas is rectangular
The pizza with the lower cost per square inch is the "best buy"
GIVEN:
The price of each pizza in dollars
The shape of each pizza (round or square)
The size of each pizza in inches
COMPUTE:
The price per square inch of each pizza
COMPARE PRICES AND DISPLAY:
"Pizza 1 is the best deal" if Pizza 1 has the lower price per square inch
"Pizza 2 is the best deal" if Pizza 2 has the lower price per square inch
"Neither is the best deal" if both pizzas have the same price per square inch

Algorithms

How do I formulate an algorithm for the pizza problem? An **algorithm** is a set of steps for carrying out a task, which can be written down and implemented. For example, the algorithm for making a batch of macaroni and cheese is a set of steps that includes boiling water, cooking the macaroni in the water, and adding cheese. The algorithm is written down, or expressed, as instructions in a recipe. You can implement the algorithm by following the instructions.

Algorithms

An important characteristic of a correctly formulated algorithm is that by carefully following the steps, you are guaranteed to accomplish the task for which the algorithm was designed. If the recipe on a macaroni package is a correctly formulated algorithm, by following the recipe, you should be guaranteed a successful batch of macaroni and cheese.

An algorithm for a computer program is the set of steps that explains how to begin with the known information specified in a problem statement and how to manipulate that information to arrive at a solution. An algorithm for a computer program is typically first written in a format that is not specific to a particular programming language. As a result, the software engineer focuses on formulating a correct algorithm, rather than on expressing the algorithm using the commands of a computer programming language. In a later phase of the software development process, the algorithm is translated into instructions written in a computer programming language so that it can be implemented by a computer.

The steps in an algorithm are the conceptual building blocks that form the foundation for a computer program. When you are just beginning to write computer programs, the amount of detail required to express an algorithm might seem unclear. For example, you might wonder whether an algorithm needs to specify the steps necessary to do addition—do you need to explain how to "carry"? The detail necessary for the algorithm's "building blocks" depends on the computer language you intend to use to write the program. As you become familiar with the commands that a language contains and the function of each command, you will gain an understanding of the level of detail required. For the pizza problem, let's suppose that you will use the BASIC computer language. Study Figure 15-2 to understand the level of detail that would be appropriate for the algorithm building blocks that you might use as the basis for a BASIC program.

CHAPTER 15

FIGURE 15-2	Algorithm building blocks.
Algorithm Task	**Example**
Assign a value to a variable	Size = 10
Evaluate an expression or "solve an equation"	SquareInchPrice = Price / SquareInches
Ask for information (input) from the user	Enter the price of a pizza
Display or print the results of calculations	Display the SquareInchPrice
Make decisions	If the pizza is square, calculate SquareInches by multiplying the Size * Size
Repeat some instructions	Repeat the price calculations for as many pizzas as the user wants

To design an algorithm, you might begin by recording the steps that you take to solve the problem yourself. If you take this route, remember that to solve the pizza problem you have to obtain initial information on the cost, size, and shape of each pizza. The computer also needs this initial information, so part of your algorithm must specify how the computer gets it. When the pizza program runs, it should ask the user to enter the initial information needed to solve the problem. Your algorithm might begin like this:

Ask the user for the shape of the first pizza and hold it in RAM as Shape1.
Ask the user for the price of the first pizza and hold it in RAM as Price1.
Ask the user for the size of the first pizza and hold it in RAM as Size1.

Next, your algorithm should specify how to manipulate this information. You want the computer to calculate the price per square inch, but an instruction like "Calculate the price per square inch" neither specifies how to do the calculation nor deals with the fact that you must perform different calculations for square and round pizzas. A more appropriate set of instructions is shown in Figure 15-3.

FIGURE 15-3

An algorithm for calculating the price per square inch.

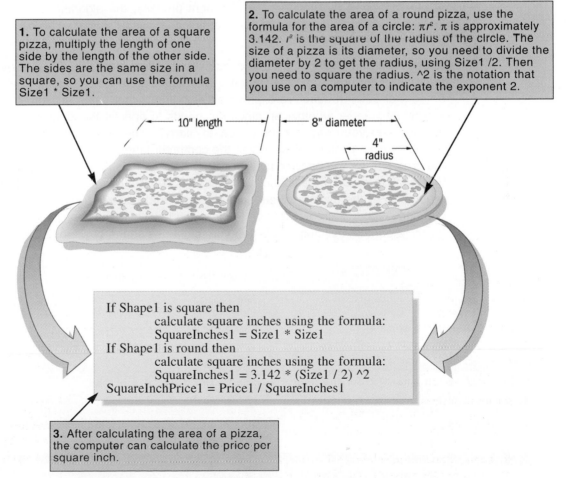

1. To calculate the area of a square pizza, multiply the length of one side by the length of the other side. The sides are the same size in a square, so you can use the formula Size1 * Size1.

2. To calculate the area of a round pizza, use the formula for the area of a circle: πr^2. π is approximately 3.142. r^2 is the square of the radius of the circle. The size of a pizza is its diameter, so you need to divide the diameter by 2 to get the radius, using Size1 /2. Then you need to square the radius. ^2 is the notation that you use on a computer to indicate the exponent 2.

```
If Shape1 is square then
        calculate square inches using the formula:
        SquareInches1 = Size1 * Size1
If Shape1 is round then
        calculate square inches using the formula:
        SquareInches1 = 3.142 * (Size1 / 2) ^2
SquareInchPrice1 = Price1 / SquareInches1
```

3. After calculating the area of a pizza, the computer can calculate the price per square inch.

So far, the algorithm calculates the price per square inch of one pizza. It should specify a similar process for calculating the price per square inch of the second pizza.

Finally, the algorithm should specify how the computer decides what to display as the solution. You want the computer to display a message telling you which pizza has the lowest square-inch cost, so your algorithm should include something like the following:

If SquareInchPrice1< SquareInchPrice2 then display the message "Pizza 1 is the best deal."
If SquareInchPrice2 < SquareInchPrice1 then display the message "Pizza 2 is the best deal."

But don't forget to indicate what you want the computer to do if the price per square inch is the same for both pizzas:

If SquareInchPrice1 = SquareInchPrice2 then display the message "Both pizzas are the same deal."

The complete algorithm for the pizza problem is shown in Figure 15-4.

FIGURE 15-4

The algorithm for the pizza problem has five main sections.

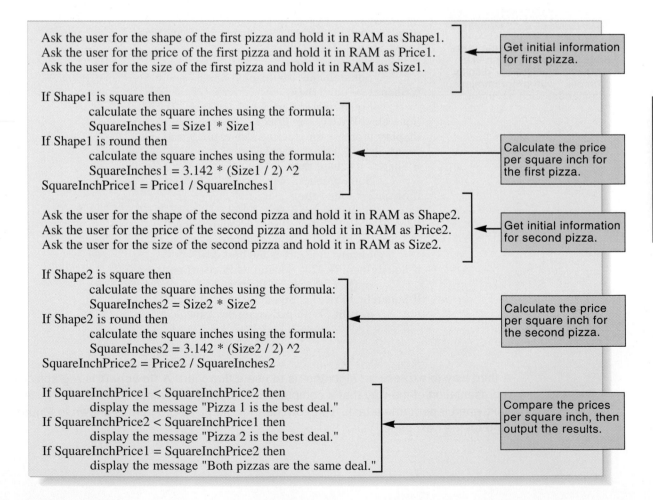

Ask the user for the shape of the first pizza and hold it in RAM as Shape1.
Ask the user for the price of the first pizza and hold it in RAM as Price1.
Ask the user for the size of the first pizza and hold it in RAM as Size1.
— Get initial information for first pizza.

If Shape1 is square then
      calculate the square inches using the formula:
      SquareInches1 = Size1 * Size1
If Shape1 is round then
      calculate the square inches using the formula:
      SquareInches1 = 3.142 * (Size1 / 2) ^2
SquareInchPrice1 = Price1 / SquareInches1
— Calculate the price per square inch for the first pizza.

Ask the user for the shape of the second pizza and hold it in RAM as Shape2.
Ask the user for the price of the second pizza and hold it in RAM as Price2.
Ask the user for the size of the second pizza and hold it in RAM as Size2.
— Get initial information for second pizza.

If Shape2 is square then
      calculate the square inches using the formula:
      SquareInches2 = Size2 * Size2
If Shape2 is round then
      calculate the square inches using the formula:
      SquareInches2 = 3.142 * (Size2 / 2) ^2
SquareInchPrice2 = Price2 / SquareInches2
— Calculate the price per square inch for the second pizza.

If SquareInchPrice1 < SquareInchPrice2 then
      display the message "Pizza 1 is the best deal."
If SquareInchPrice2 < SquareInchPrice1 then
      display the message "Pizza 2 is the best deal."
If SquareInchPrice1 = SquareInchPrice2 then
      display the message "Both pizzas are the same deal."
— Compare the prices per square inch, then output the results.

CHAPTER 15

Expressing an Algorithm

What's the best way to express an algorithm? You can express an algorithm in several different ways, including structured English, pseudocode, flowcharts, and object definitions. These tools are not programming languages, and they cannot be processed by a computer. Their purpose is to provide a way for you to document your ideas for program design.

As you learned in Chapter 13, structured English is a subset of the English language with a limited selection of sentence structures that reflect processing activities. Refer back to Figure 15-4 to see how you can use structured English to express the algorithm for the pizza problem.

InfoWeb
3

Pseudocode
& Flowcharts

Another way to express an algorithm is with pseudocode. **Pseudocode** is a notational system for algorithms that has been described as "a mixture of English and your favorite programming language." Pseudocode is less formalized than structured English, so the structure and wording are left up to you. Also, when you write pseudocode, you are allowed to incorporate command words and syntax from the computer language that you intend to use for the actual program. Compare Figure 15-4 with Figure 15-5 and see if you can pick out some of the differences between structured English and pseudocode.

FIGURE 15-5

The pseudocode for the pizza program mixes English-like instructions, such as "display prompts," with programming commands, such as "input."

```
display prompts for entering shape, price, and size
input Shape1, Price1, Size1
if Shape1 = square then
        SquareInches1 ← Size1 * Size1
if Shape1 = round then
        SquareInches1 ← 3.142 * (Size1 / 2) ^2
SquareInchPrice1 ← Price1 / SquareInches1
display prompts for entering shape, price, and size
input Shape2, Price2, Size2
if Shape2 = square then
        SquareInches2 ← Size2 * Size2
if Shape2 = round then
        SquareInches2 ← 3.142 * (Size2 / 2) ^2
SquareInchPrice2 ← Price2 / SquareInches2
if SquareInchPrice1 < SquareInchPrice2 then
        output "Pizza 1 is the best deal."
if SquareInchPrice2 < SquareInchPrice1 then
        output "Pizza 2 is the best deal."
if SquareInchPrice1 = SquareInchPrice2 then
        output "Both pizzas are the same deal."
```

A third way to express an algorithm is to use a flowchart. A **flowchart** is a graphical representation of the way that a computer should progress from one instruction to the next when it performs a task. The flowchart for the pizza program is shown in Figure 15-6 on the next page.

FIGURE 15-6

The pizza program flowchart illustrates how the computer will proceed through the instructions in the final program.

Key to Flowchart Symbols

- Start or end
- Input or output
- Decision
- Calculation
- • Connector
- ⟶ Flow line

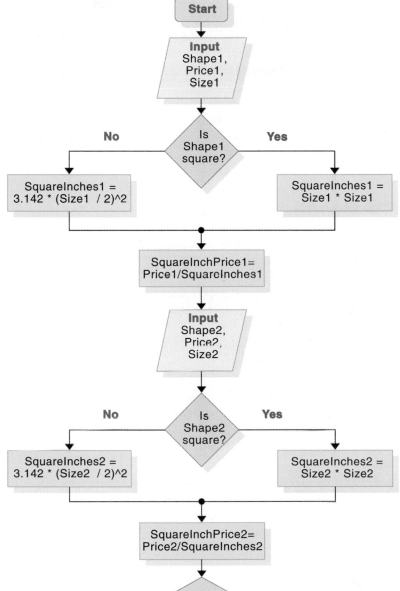

Start

Input
Shape1,
Price1,
Size1

Is Shape1 square?
No → SquareInches1 = 3.142 * (Size1 / 2)^2
Yes → SquareInches1 = Size1 * Size1

SquareInchPrice1 = Price1/SquareInches1

Input
Shape2,
Price2,
Size2

Is Shape2 square?
No → SquareInches2 = 3.142 * (Size2 / 2)^2
Yes → SquareInches2 = Size2 * Size2

SquareInchPrice2 = Price2/SquareInches2

Is SquareInchPrice1 < SquareInchPrice2?
Yes → Output "Pizza 1 is the best deal."

No → Is SquareInchPrice1 > SquareInchPrice2?
No → Output "Both pizzas are the same deal."
Yes → Output "Pizza 2 is the best deal."

End

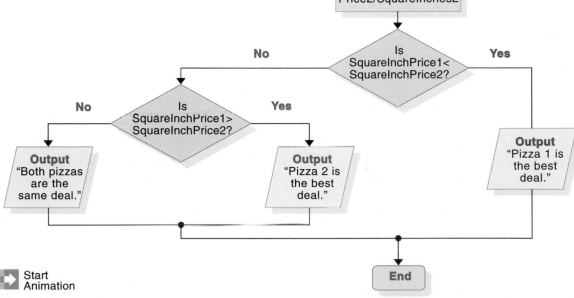

▶ Start Animation

Another way to express an algorithm is to define objects that the computer must manipulate, then specify the method for manipulating each object. This way of expressing an algorithm is useful for designing object-oriented programs, which you will learn more about later in this chapter. Figure 15-7 provides a description of one of the objects for the pizza program.

FIGURE 15-7

A description for the "calculate Best Deal" button object in the pizza program.

> **Object: Calculate Best Deal**
> Type: Button
> Appearance:　　　［ **Calculate Best Deal** ］
>
> Method:
> IF Shape1 = "square" THEN SquareInches1 = Size1 * Size1
> IF Shape1 = "round" THEN SquareInches1 = 3.142 * (Size1 / 2)^2
> SquareInchPrice1 = Price1/SquareInches1
> IF Shape2 = "square" THEN SquareInches2 = Size2 * Size2
> IF Shape2 = "round" THEN SquareInches1 = 3.142 * (Size1 / 2)^2
> SquareInchPrice2 = Price2/SquareInches2
> IF SquareInchPrice1 < SquareInchPrice2 THEN BestDeal = "Pizza 1 is the best deal."
> IF SquareInchPrice2 < SquareInchPrice1 THEN BestDeal = "Pizza 2 is the best deal."
> IF SquareInchPrice1 = SquareInchPrice2 THEN BestDeal = "Both pizzas are the same deal."

QUICKCHECK　　　A

1 If you have a job as a(n) _____, you would focus on the software component of an information system.

2 The U.S. Department of Defense defines a "large" program as one that has about 100,000 line of code. True or false? _____

3 Before you write a computer program, you should write a(n) _____ to define the elements that must be manipulated to achieve a result or goal.

4 A(n) _____ is a set of steps for carrying out a task or solving a problem.

5 "A mixture of English and your favorite programming language" is the description of _____.

6 A(n) _____ is a graphical representation of the way that a computer should progress from one instruction to the next when it performs a task.

▶ Check Answers

SECTION B — CODING COMPUTER PROGRAMS

InfoWeb
4

Programming
Careers

A problem statement and an algorithm are often combined into a document called the **program specification**, which is essentially a blueprint for a computer program. When the program specification is complete, it is time to begin coding the program. **Coding** is the process of using a computer language to express an algorithm. A person who codes or writes computer programs is called a **computer programmer**.

With many computer programming languages, the coding process means entering commands. With other computer programming languages, you enter or select the characteristics of objects, or you enter descriptive statements about the objects.

To code the pizza algorithm using the BASIC computer language, you type a list of commands. Look at the completed program in Figure 15-8 and study the callouts to get a general understanding of the elements of a computer program.

FIGURE 15-8

The pizza program is written as a list of steps. The computer executes the steps starting at the top of the list.

Command words are shown in blue.

Remarks that begin with REM explain each section of the program.

Data is stored in variables, or memory locations, in RAM. The variable Shape1$ stores text, such as the word "round." The $ indicates a text variable. Other variables, such as Price1 and Size1, store numbers; they do not include $ as part of the variable name.

```basic
REM  The Pizza Program
REM  This program tells you which of two pizzas is the best deal
REM  by calculating the price per square inch of each pizza.
REM Collect initial information for first pizza.
INPUT "Enter the shape of pizza one:"; Shape1$
INPUT "Enter the price of pizza one:"; Price1
INPUT "Enter the size of pizza one:"; Size1
REM  Calculate price per square inch for first pizza.
REM  If the first pizza is square, calculate square inches by multiplying one side by the other.
IF Shape1$ = "square" THEN SquareInches1 = Size1 * Size1
REM  If the first pizza is round, calculate the number of square inches where
REM  pi = 3.142, size / 2 = radius, and (size / 2) ^2 = radius squared:
IF Shape1$ = "round" THEN SquareInches1 = 3.142 * (Size1 / 2) ^2
SquareInchPrice1 = Price1 / SquareInches1
REM Collect initial information for second pizza.
INPUT "Enter the shape of pizza two:"; Shape2$
INPUT "Enter the price of pizza two:"; Price2
INPUT "Enter the size of pizza two:"; Size2
REM Calculate price per square inch for second pizza.
IF Shape2$ = "square" THEN SquareInches2 = Size2 * Size2
IF Shape2$ = "round" THEN SquareInches2 = 3.142 * (Size2 / 2) ^2
SquareInchPrice2 = Price2 / SquareInches2
REM Decide which pizza is the best deal and display results.
IF SquareInchPrice1 < SquareInchPrice2 THEN Message$ = "Pizza 1 is the best deal."
IF SquareInchPrice2 < SquareInchPrice1 THEN Message$ = "Pizza 2 is the best deal."
IF SquareInchPrice1 = SquareInchPrice2 THEN Message$ = "Both pizzas are the same deal."
PRINT Message$
END
```

CHAPTER 15

Program Sequence

How do I tell the computer the sequence that it should follow to perform instructions? **Sequential execution**, in which the computer performs each instruction in the order in which they appear, is the normal pattern of program execution. That is, the first instruction in the program is executed first, then the second instruction, and so on through the rest of the instructions in the program. Here is a simple program written in the QBASIC computer language that outputs `This is the first line.`, then outputs `This is the second line.`

```
PRINT "This is the first line."
PRINT "This is the second line."
```

Although most modern programming languages do not use line numbers, older programming languages, such as the original version of BASIC, required programmers to number each instruction like this:

```
100 PRINT "This is the first line."
200 PRINT "This is the second line."
```

If the lines in a program are numbered, a computer begins executing the instruction with the lowest number, then proceeds to the instruction with the next highest number, and so on. The flowchart in Figure 15-9 represents a simple sequential execution of commands.

FIGURE 15-9

Sequential program execution means that the computer performs the instructions one after the other.

Start
Animation

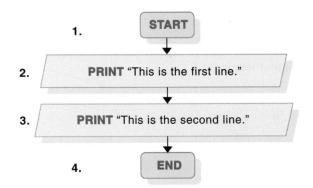

Some algorithms specify that a program must execute instructions in an order different from the sequence in which they are listed, skip some instructions under certain circumstances, or repeat instructions. **Control structures** are instructions that specify the sequence in which a program is executed. There are three types of control structures: sequence controls, selection controls, and repetition controls.

Sequence Controls

GOTO

Is there a way to have the computer follow a different sequence? A **sequence control structure** changes the sequence, or order, in which instructions are executed by directing the computer to execute an instruction elsewhere in the program. In the following simple QBASIC program, the GOTO command tells the computer to jump directly to the instruction labeled "Widget." By performing the GOTO statement, the program will never execute the command PRINT "This is the second line."

```
PRINT "This is the first line."
GOTO Widget
PRINT "This is the second line."
Widget: PRINT "All Done!"
END
```

The flowchart in Figure 15-10 shows how the computer follows a series of sequential commands, then "jumps" past other commands as the result of a GOTO command.

FIGURE 15-10

Executing a GOTO command directs the computer to a different part of the program.

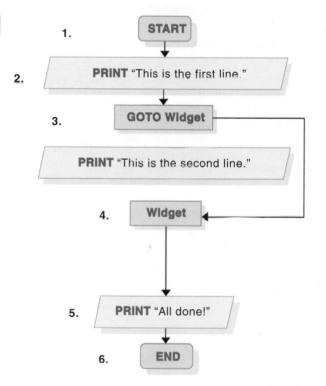

Start
Animation

Although it is the simplest control structure, the GOTO command is rarely used by skilled programmers because it can lead to programs that are difficult to understand and maintain. In 1968, the journal *Communications of the ACM* published a now-famous letter from Edsger Dijkstra, called "Go To Statement Considered Harmful." In his letter, Dijkstra explained that injudicious use of the GOTO statement in programs makes it difficult for other programmers to understand the underlying algorithm, which in turn means that such programs are difficult to correct, improve, or revise.

Experienced programmers prefer to use sequence controls other than GOTO to transfer program execution to a subroutine, procedure, module, or function. A **subroutine**, **procedure**, **module**, or **function** is a section of code that is part of a program, but is not included in the main sequential execution path. A sequence control structure directs the computer to the statements they contain, but when these statements have been executed, the computer neatly returns to the main program. Figure 15-11 shows the execution path of a program that uses the GOSUB command to transfer execution to a subroutine.

FIGURE 15-11

Executing a GOSUB command directs the computer to a different section of the program.

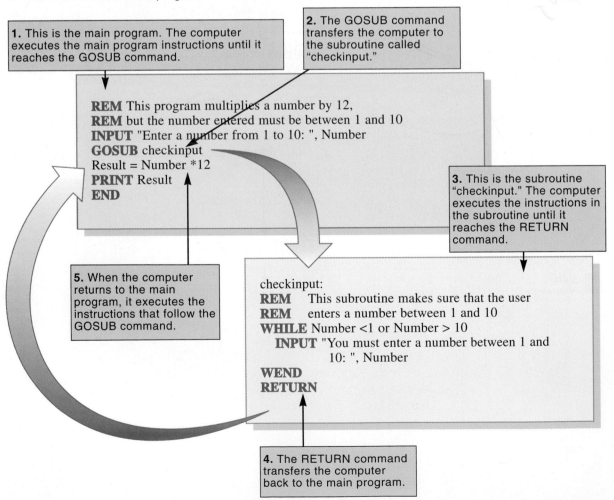

1. This is the main program. The computer executes the main program instructions until it reaches the GOSUB command.

2. The GOSUB command transfers the computer to the subroutine called "checkinput."

```
REM This program multiplies a number by 12,
REM but the number entered must be between 1 and 10
INPUT "Enter a number from 1 to 10: ", Number
GOSUB checkinput
Result = Number *12
PRINT Result
END
```

3. This is the subroutine "checkinput." The computer executes the instructions in the subroutine until it reaches the RETURN command.

5. When the computer returns to the main program, it executes the instructions that follow the GOSUB command.

```
checkinput:
REM    This subroutine makes sure that the user
REM    enters a number between 1 and 10
WHILE Number <1 or Number > 10
    INPUT "You must enter a number between 1 and
            10: ", Number
WEND
RETURN
```

4. The RETURN command transfers the computer back to the main program.

Selection Controls

Can the computer make decisions while it executes a program? A **selection control structure**, also referred to as a "decision structure" or "branch," tells a computer what to do, based on whether a condition is true or false. A simple example of a selection control structure is the IF..THEN..ELSE command. The following program uses this command to decide whether a number entered is greater than 10. If the number is greater than 10, the computer prints "That number is greater than 10!" If the number is not greater than 10, the program performs the ELSE instruction and prints "That number is 10 or less."

```
INPUT "Enter a number from 1 to 10:", Number
IF Number > 10 THEN PRINT "That number is greater than 10"
ELSE PRINT "That number is 10 or less."
END
```

Figure 15-12 uses a flowchart to illustrate how a computer follows commands in a decision structure.

FIGURE 15-12

The computer executes a decision indicated on the flowchart by the question in the diamond shape.

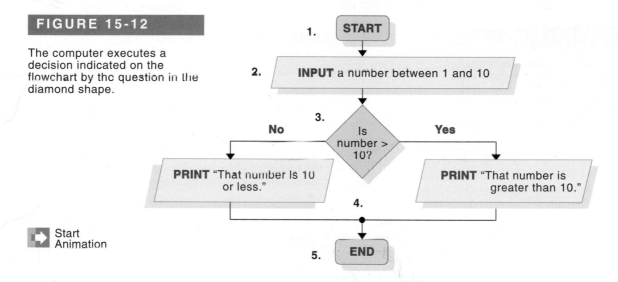

Start Animation

Repetition Controls

Can a computer automatically repeat a series of instructions? A **repetition control structure**, also referred to as a "loop" or "iteration," repeats one or more instructions until a certain condition is met. In QBASIC, the most frequently used loop commands are FOR..NEXT and WHILE..WEND.

The command words FOR or WHILE mark the beginning of a loop. The commands NEXT and WEND (which means "while ends") mark the end of the loop. The following simple QBASIC program uses the FOR..NEXT command to print a message three times:

```
FOR N = 1 TO 3
   PRINT "There's no place like home."
NEXT N
END
```

Follow the path of program execution in Figure 15-13 to see how a computer executes a series of commands in a repetition structure.

FIGURE 15-13

To execute a loop, the computer repeats one or more commands until some condition indicates that the looping should stop.

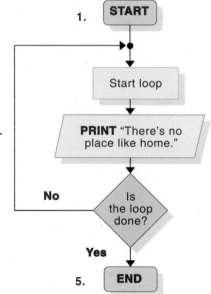

1. START
2. 3. 4.   Start loop
   PRINT "There's no place like home."
   Is the loop done?   No   Yes
5. END

Start Animation

To get a better idea of how a FOR..NEXT loop works, pretend that you're the computer executing the FOR..NEXT instructions below. You can use the box labeled N in the margin as a RAM location. As the computer, you would also have a screen on which to display output—use the Screen Output box. Now, let's walk through the loop.

```
FOR N = 1 TO 3
   PRINT "There's no place like home."
NEXT N
END
```

N

Screen Output

1. As the computer, the first time you see the instruction FOR N = 1 TO 3, you set N equal to 1. To do so, write the number 1 in the N box in the margin.

2. You would then execute the next instruction, PRINT "There's no place like home." To do so, write the phrase "There's no place like home." in the Screen Output box.

3. The instruction NEXT sends you back to the command FOR N = 1 TO 3. Because this occasion is the second time you have executed this statement, put a 2 in the N box in the margin (you can erase the 1 that was there previously).

4. You need to check whether the value in box N is greater than 3. Why do this? Because the command FOR N = 1 TO 3 means you can continue to loop only if N is 3 or less. Well, N is only 2, so you can proceed.

5. Go to the next instruction, which is PRINT "There's no place like home." Write this sentence again in the Screen Output box.

6. Moving on, you reach the NEXT statement again, which sends you back to the FOR statement.

7. Continue by changing the value in the N box to 3. Check the N box to make sure it does not contain a value greater than 3. It doesn't, so continue.

8. The next line instructs you to PRINT "There's no place like home." Write this sentence again in the Screen Output box. The NEXT statement sends you back to the FOR statement. Increase the value in the N box to 4. This time when you check whether the value in N is greater than 3, it is. That means the loop is complete and you should jump to the statement past the end of the loop.

9. The next statement is END, so you've completed the program.

QUICKCHECK   B

1 _____ is the process of using a computer language to express an algorithm.

2 A(n) _____ control structure changes the order in which instructions are executed by transferring program execution to instructions elsewhere in the program.

3 A(n) _____ control structure tells a computer what to do, depending on whether a condition is true or false.

4 A(n) _____ control structure repeats one or more instructions until a certain condition is met.

Check Answers

CHAPTER 15

SECTION C DEBUGGING AND DOCUMENTING

As you are coding a program, you must test each section of your code to make sure that it works correctly. This process is referred to as **debugging** because the process "gets the bugs out" so that they don't cause errors when you use the program. As you are coding, you should also write **documentation** as a permanent record that explains how your program works.

Testing a Program

How do I know whether my program will function correctly? A computer program must be tested to ensure that it works correctly. Testing often consists of entering test data to see whether the program produces correct results. If testing does not produce the expected results, the programmer must examine the program for errors, correct the errors, and test the program again. The process can get a bit frustrating at times, as shown in the video associated with Figure 15-14. Nevertheless, testing is a crucial step in the programming process.

FIGURE 15-14

A video created by Stanford students in 1967 depicts a programmer's frustration with the coding, testing, and debugging process.

➡ Start
Video

To test the pizza program, for example, you could run the program and enter data for which you have already calculated the results. Using a calculator, you could determine that $.08 is the price per square inch of a 15-inch square pizza that costs $18.50. One way to test the program is to run it and enter "square" for the shape, $18.50 for the price, and 15 for the size. The program should produce the result $.08 for the price per square inch of this pizza. If it doesn't, you know that your program contains an error and that you must correct it.

Testing a single set of values is not enough, however. At a minimum, you should test every statement at least once, and you should test every decision branch. The pizza program has two possible decision branches for calculating the price per square inch. One branch is for square pizzas; the other branch is for round pizzas. Even if you enter a set of test data for a square pizza and the program provides the correct result, you cannot assume that the program is working correctly until you also test it with data for a round pizza.

When you find an error, or bug, in a program, it could be a syntax error or a run-time error. A **syntax error** occurs when an instruction does not follow the syntax rules, or grammar, of the programming language. For example, when you want to print a message, you need to use the PRINT command. The command `IF AGE = 16 THEN` `"You can` `drive."` will produce a syntax error because the command word PRINT is missing. The correct version of the command is `IF AGE = 16 THEN PRINT` `"You can` `drive."`

Syntax errors are very easy to make, but they are typically easy to detect and correct. A syntax error can be caused by omitting a command word, misspelling a command word, or using incorrect punctuation, such as using a colon (:) where a semicolon (;) is required. Many of today's programming languages detect and point out syntax errors when you are in the process of coding each instruction. Because these languages identify syntax errors when you type each line of code, you typically will have few syntax errors when you test programs written with these languages.

The other type of program bug is a **run-time error**, which, as its name indicates, shows up when you run a program. Run-time errors can be caused by a typing error that results in the correct syntax but does not produce the intended result. For example, suppose that you erroneously use the < symbol in the following command for the pizza problem:

```
IF SquareInchPrice1 < SquareInchPrice2 THEN PRINT "Pizza 2 is a
better deal than Pizza 1."
```

The command produces the wrong output as a result of the error you introduced when you used the < sign instead of the > sign.

Other run-time errors are classified as logic errors. A **logic error** is an error in the logic or design of the program. Logic errors can be caused by an inadequate definition of the problem or by an incorrect or incomplete solution specified by the flowchart or pseudocode. Logic errors are usually more difficult and time-consuming to identify than syntax and run-time errors.

Program Documentation

Why do I need to document my programs? A computer program inevitably must be modified because needs change. Modifying a program is much easier if the program has been well documented. For example, suppose VanGo's Pizzeria and The Venice both add a new rectangular pizza to their menus. In that case, you and your friends would want to modify the pizza program so that you can enter the dimensions of a rectangular pizza. First, you need to understand how the current program works. Although this step might seem like a fairly easy task for the short pizza program, imagine trying to understand a 50,000-line program that calculates income tax, especially if you weren't the person who wrote the original program. You might want some additional information to explain the logic behind the program and the formulas that the programmer devised to perform calculations.

Program documentation explains how a program works and how to use it. The documentation that you create should be useful to other programmers who need to modify your code and to people who use your program. Typically, program documentation takes two forms: remarks inserted into the program code and "written" documentation.

CHAPTER 15

Remarks are explanatory comments inserted into a computer program along with the lines of code. They are ignored by the computer when it executes the program, but for programmers who must modify the program, these remarks can prove very handy. To revise a computer program, a programmer reads through the original program to find out how it works, then makes revisions to the appropriate sections of code. It is easier to understand the original program if the person who wrote it has placed remarks in the program. A well-documented program contains initial remarks that explain its purpose. These remarks contain essentially the same information as the problem statement. For example, the pizza program contains the following initial remarks:

```
REM    The Pizza Program
REM    This program tells you which of two pizzas is the best deal
REM    by calculating the price per square inch of each pizza.
```

Remarks should also be added to the sections of a program in which the purpose of the code is not immediately clear. For example, in the pizza program, the purpose of the expression 3.142*(size/2)^2 might not be immediately obvious to a programmer reading the code. Therefore, it would be helpful to have a remark preceding the expression, like the following:

```
REM The program calculates the number of square inches
REM in a round pizza where
REM pi = 3.142, size/2 = radius, and (size/2)^2 = radius squared:
SquareInches = 3.142*(size/2)^2
```

There is no hard and fast rule about when you should include a remark in a program. If you were to work with a group of programmers on a project, your group might develop guidelines to ensure that remarks are used consistently throughout the code for the project. As you gain experience writing programs, you will develop a sense for using remarks appropriately.

Written documentation is external to a program and contains information about the program that is useful to programmers and the people who use the program. Written documentation can be paper-based or in electronic format. Because documentation serves two audiences—the programmers and the users—there are two broad categories of written documentation for computer programs: program manuals and reference manuals, summarized in Figure 15-15.

Figure 15-15	Different types of documentation have different characteristics.	
	Program Manual	**Reference Manual**
Audience	Programmers	Users
Major focus	Problem statement Algorithm	How to install the program How to start the program How to use each feature
Writing style	Technical, using structured English, pseudocode, flowcharts	Nontechnical prose
Additional material	Printout of program code	Troubleshooting tips Diagrams of screens and menus

A **program manual** contains any information about the program that might be useful to programmers, including the problem statement and algorithm. Because a program manual is a software development and maintenance tool, it is used by programmers, not users. A reference manual, which you learned about in Chapter 1, contains information that helps users learn to use a computer program. A computerized version of the user reference is usually supplied as online Help.

InfoWeb
6

Technical
Writing

Programmers are generally responsible for documenting their code and contributing to the program manual, but the trend is to hire professional technical writers to author user reference manuals. A **technical writer** specializes in explaining technical concepts and procedures, often by simplifying complex concepts for a nontechnical audience. Many colleges and universities offer technical writing courses, and some also offer technical writing degrees. Experienced technical writers are in demand as contract, part-time, and full-time employees in the computer industry.

QUICKCHECK   C

1 Entering known data to see whether a program produces the correct results is part of the _____ process.

2 If you ignore the rules or grammar of a programming language, you are likely to get a(n) _____ error.

3 Suppose that you run the pizza program and the output indicates that Pizza 2 is the best deal. Your test data, however, shows that Pizza 1 is the best deal. Because this error appeared when you ran the program, it would be classified as a(n) _____ error.

4 _____ errors are usually the most difficult and time-consuming errors to identify.

5 Programmers insert _____ into programs to explain how the program works and to make it easier for other programmers to modify the program.

6 A(n) _____ manual is documentation used by programmers, whereas a(n) _____ manual is documentation designed for the people who use the program.

 Check Answers

CHAPTER 15

SECTION D — PROGRAMMING LANGUAGE CHARACTERISTICS

Hundreds of programming languages have emerged over the last 40 years. Some languages were developed to make the programming process more efficient and less error-prone. Other languages were developed to provide an effective command set for specific types of programs, such as business programs or scientific programs. Still other languages were created specifically as teaching tools.

Programming languages have characteristics that describe how they work and provide information about the types of computing tasks for which they are appropriate. For example, Pascal can be described as a high-level, procedural, compiled language. When you need to select a language to use for a program, it is useful to understand some of the general characteristics of programming languages and the advantages or disadvantages of these characteristics.

Procedural

Was the pizza program written using a procedural language? Languages with procedural characteristics create programs composed of a series of statements that tell the computer how to perform the processes for a specific task. Languages with procedural characteristics are called **procedural languages**. BASIC, the language that you used for the pizza program, has procedural characteristics. The instructions tell the computer exactly what to do: display a message on the screen asking the user to enter the shape of the pizza; display a message asking for the price of the pizza; display a message asking for the size of the pizza; if the shape is square, calculate the square-inch price with the formula SquareInchPrice = Price/Square Inches, and so forth.

As you might guess, procedural languages are well suited for programs that follow a step-by-step algorithm. Programs created with procedural languages have a starting point and an ending point. The flow of execution from the start to the end is essentially linear—that is, the computer begins at the beginning and executes the prescribed series of instructions until it reaches the end, as shown in Figure 15-16.

FIGURE 15-16

A computer executes a procedural language sequentially, with an occasional diversion to a subroutine or procedure.

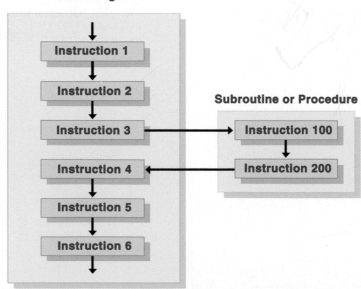

Main Program

Instruction 1
Instruction 2
Instruction 3 → **Subroutine or Procedure** → Instruction 100
Instruction 4 ← Instruction 200
Instruction 5
Instruction 6

Declarative

Do all languages require the programmer to specify the exact procedure for the solution? A **declarative language** lets a programmer write a program by specifying a set of statements and rules that define the conditions for resolving a problem. Such a language has a built-in method for considering the rules and determining a solution. Describing a problem and the rules that lead to a solution places an emphasis on words rather than on mathematical formulas. For this reason, declarative languages are useful for programs that manipulate ideas and concepts, rather than numbers.

Unlike a program that is created using a procedural language, a program created with a declarative language does not tell the computer how to solve a problem. Instead, it describes the problem. For example, Figure 15-17 contains a short program written in the Prolog language that describes several people and the condition for determining which of these people have a sister in the list.

FIGURE 15-17

A Prolog program is based on a declarative language.

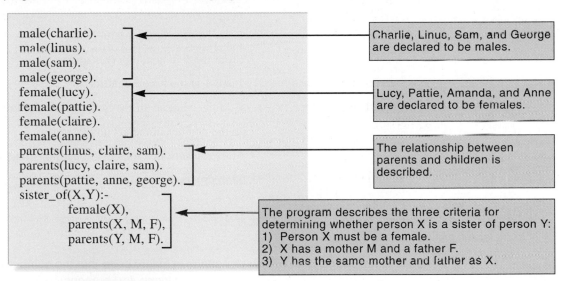

```
male(charlie).
male(linus).
male(sam).
male(george).
female(lucy).
female(pattie).
female(claire).
female(anne).
parents(linus, claire, sam).
parents(lucy, claire, sam).
parents(pattie, anne, george).
sister_of(X,Y):-
        female(X),
        parents(X, M, F),
        parents(Y, M, F).
```

Charlie, Linus, Sam, and George are declared to be males.

Lucy, Pattie, Amanda, and Anne are declared to be females.

The relationship between parents and children is described.

The program describes the three criteria for determining whether person X is a sister of person Y:
1) Person X must be a female.
2) X has a mother M and a father F.
3) Y has the same mother and father as X.

Scripting

Is HTML a language? HTML is generally classified as a scripting language. A **scripting language** defines a task in the form of a script. Scripts require a host application to run and cannot be run as stand-alone applications. For example, you use HTML tags to specify a script for how to display a Web page. This script is interpreted by a Web browser. The Web browser is the host application—without it, the HTML script cannot run.

Scripting languages, such as Visual Basic for Applications, are available for many software applications, including word processing, spreadsheet, and database software. You can use such scripting languages to automate tasks and create macros within the applications. Scripting languages are typically easier to use than other types of programming languages, but have fewer features and control options. They are a good choice for non-programmers who want to automate and customize the tasks performed by their application software.

Low-Level

> The pizza program used commands like PRINT and END. Don't computers understand only ones and zeros?

A **low-level language** requires a programmer to write instructions for the lowest level of the computer system—that is, for specific hardware elements, such as the processor, registers, and RAM locations. A low-level language is useful when a programmer needs to directly manipulate what happens at the hardware level. Programmers typically use low-level languages to write system software, such as compilers, operating systems, and device drivers.

Each instruction in a low-level language usually corresponds to a single instruction for the processor. In Chapter 5 you saw how an instruction, such as MMR M1 REG1, tells a computer to move a number from a RAM location into a register. With a low-level language, several instructions are necessary to tell the computer how to perform even simple operations, such as adding two numbers together. Figure 15-18 shows a section of a program, written in a low-level language, that adds two numbers together.

FIGURE 15-18

Low-level, assembly language instructions.

Assembly Language Instructions	Explanation of Instructions
LDA 5	Load 5 in the accumulator
STA Num1	Store the 5 in a memory location called Num1
LDA 4	Load 4 in the accumulator
ADD Num1	Add the contents of memory location Num1 to the number in the accumulator
STA Total	Store the sum in a memory location called Total
END	Stop program execution

A **machine language** is a low-level language in binary code that the computer can execute directly. Machine languages are very difficult for humans to understand and manipulate. They were primarily used in the earliest days of computer development, when other programming languages were not available.

High-Level

> What's the alternative to using a low-level language?

A **high-level language** allows a programmer to use instructions that are more like human language, such as the BASIC command PRINT "Please wait..." When high-level languages were originally conceived in the 1950s, computer scientists thought they would eliminate programming errors. This was not to be the case—syntax, run-time, and logical errors are possible even with high-level languages. Nevertheless, high-level languages significantly reduce programming errors and make it possible to write programs in less time than when using low-level languages. Programs written in high-level languages must be translated into instructions that the computer can execute. Therefore, a high-level language must be "compiled" or "interpreted" by the computer.

Compiled

How does a high-level language produce machine-executable instructions?

A **compiler** translates a program written in a high-level language into low-level instructions before the program is executed (Figure 15-19). The commands that you write in a high-level language are referred to as **source code**. The low-level instructions that result from compiling the source code are referred to as **object code**.

When you use a **compiled language**, you must compile your program to produce executable program code. Therefore, if you write, compile, and run a program, but then discover that it contains a bug, you must fix your program, then recompile it before you test it again. Once your compiled version is bug-free, you can run the program again and again without recompiling it.

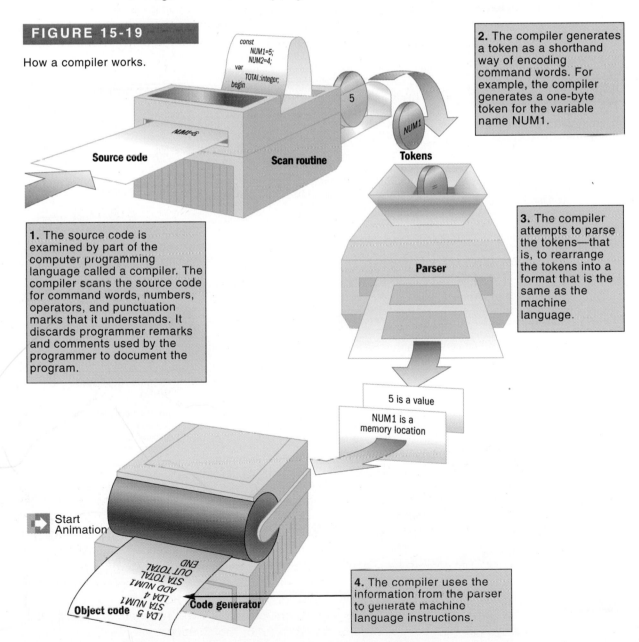

FIGURE 15-19

How a compiler works.

2. The compiler generates a token as a shorthand way of encoding command words. For example, the compiler generates a one-byte token for the variable name NUM1.

Source code   **Scan routine**   **Tokens**

1. The source code is examined by part of the computer programming language called a compiler. The compiler scans the source code for command words, numbers, operators, and punctuation marks that it understands. It discards programmer remarks and comments used by the programmer to document the program.

3. The compiler attempts to parse the tokens—that is, to rearrange the tokens into a format that is the same as the machine language.

Parser

5 is a value

NUM1 is a memory location

Start Animation

Object code   **Code generator**

4. The compiler uses the information from the parser to generate machine language instructions.

CHAPTER 15

Interpreted

How does an interpreter differ from a compiler? An **interpreted language** uses an interpreter instead of a compiler to create code that the computer can execute. When you run a program that is written in an interpreted language, the language's **interpreter** reads one instruction and converts it into a machine language instruction, which the computer executes. After the instruction is executed, the interpreter reads the next instruction, converts it into machine language, and so forth. Programs written in interpreted languages take longer to execute because the computer must translate every instruction as it is executed. A program with many loops is especially inefficient in an interpreted language because the instructions contained in the loop are translated multiple times, once for each time that the loop is executed.

What is the advantage of an interpreted language over a compiled language? With an interpreted language, you do not need to wait for your program to compile, so the testing process seems to take less time. Figure 15-20 illustrates the concept of a language interpreter.

FIGURE 15-20

A programming language interpreter.

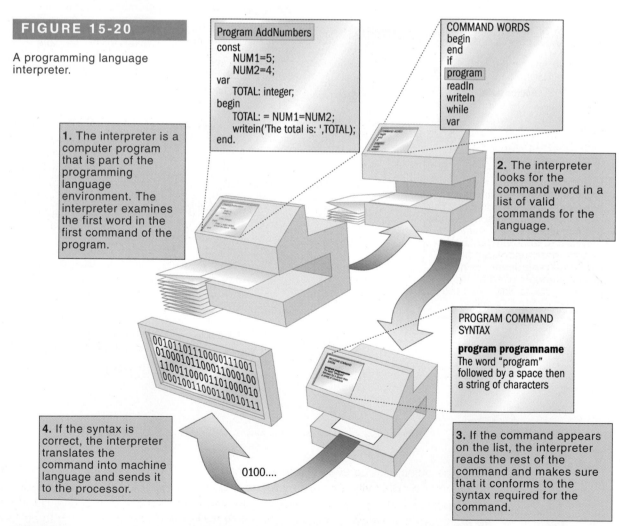

```
Program AddNumbers
const
    NUM1=5;
    NUM2=4;
var
    TOTAL: integer;
begin
    TOTAL: = NUM1=NUM2;
    writein('The total is: ',TOTAL);
end.
```

COMMAND WORDS
begin
end
if
program
readln
writeln
while
var

1. The interpreter is a computer program that is part of the programming language environment. The interpreter examines the first word in the first command of the program.

2. The interpreter looks for the command word in a list of valid commands for the language.

PROGRAM COMMAND SYNTAX

program programname
The word "program" followed by a space then a string of characters

4. If the syntax is correct, the interpreter translates the command into machine language and sends it to the processor.

0100....

3. If the command appears on the list, the interpreter reads the rest of the command and makes sure that it conforms to the syntax required for the command.

001011011100001111001
010001011000011001
110011000011000100
001001100011001011

Start
Animation

Object-Oriented

How do objects figure into computer programming? **Object-oriented languages** are based on an approach to programming that uses objects. An object is an entity or "thing" that a program manipulates. For example, a button—a rectangular icon on the screen—is an object. You are familiar with the way you can click a button using the mouse. A programmer can use an object-oriented language to define a button object in a program and display the button when the program runs.

OOP

An object belongs to a class, or group, that has specific characteristics. A common example is the object class called *window*. All window objects, including application windows, belong to the class called *window* and share certain characteristics, such as a title bar and a close button. When a programmer creates a new window object, it acquires, or "inherits," the characteristics and capabilities of the *window* class. Each specific instance of a window object may also have its own unique characteristics, such as its title, size, or location on the screen. Figure 15-21 shows several objects from an object class.

FIGURE 15-21

Two objects on the screen are in the class "window": the Document - WordPad window and the Save As window. All windows are rectangular and have a title bar. You can open and close windows, and you can move them around on the screen.

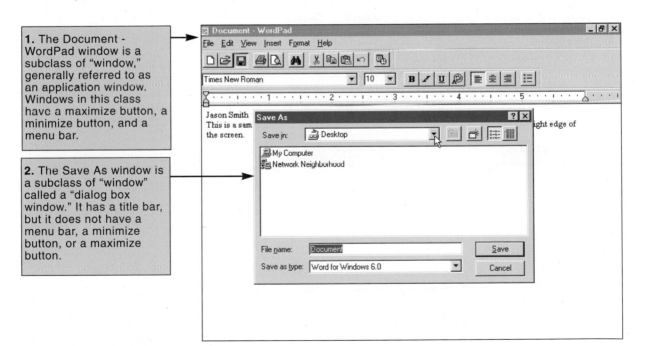

1. The Document - WordPad window is a subclass of "window," generally referred to as an application window. Windows in this class have a maximize button, a minimize button, and a menu bar.

2. The Save As window is a subclass of "window" called a "dialog box window." It has a title bar, but it does not have a menu bar, a minimize button, or a maximize button.

The same object can be used in many different programs, thus significantly enhancing programmer productivity. For example, many software applications provide users with a way to save a file, save a file under a new name, open a file, and print a file. If you were programming such applications, it would be handy to have an object to perform these tasks. Anytime you wrote a program that needed to perform these tasks, you could simply use this object and avoid "recreating the wheel."

Visual
Programming

Event-Driven

Do all programs follow a set sequence of actions? A **program event** is an action or occurrence, such as a key press or mouse click, to which a program might respond. An **event-driven language** helps programmers easily create programs that constantly check for and respond to a set of events. Most programs that use graphical user interfaces are event-driven—they display controls, such as menus, on the screen and take action when the user activates one of the controls. Because of the many visual elements that a programmer must manipulate, creating event-driven programs is sometimes referred to as "visual programming." You can learn more about this type of programming by working with the Visual Programming Lab.

To create an event-driven program, lines of program code are attached to graphical objects, such as command buttons and icons. Users manipulate an object to generate an event—for example, clicking a button labeled "Continue." The click event causes the instructions attached to that object to be executed. Figure 15-22 shows a screen from an event-driven program and the program code attached to one of the events.

FIGURE 15-22

In an event-driven program, users manipulate objects, which cause the computer to execute the corresponding lines of program code.

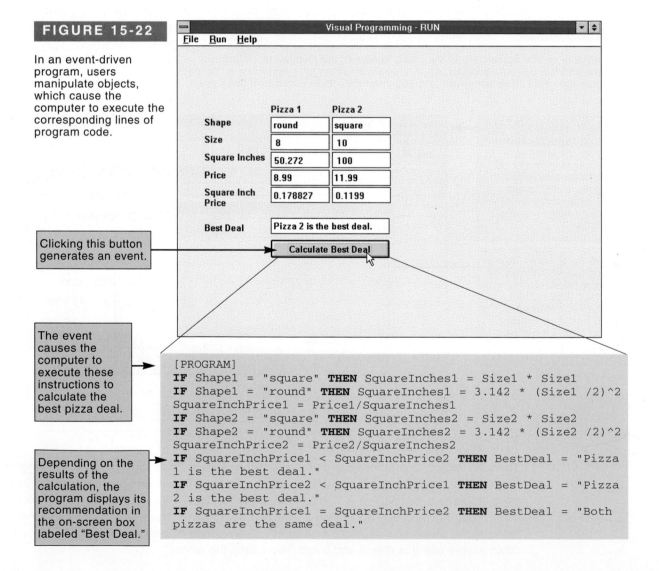

Clicking this button generates an event.

The event causes the computer to execute these instructions to calculate the best pizza deal.

Depending on the results of the calculation, the program displays its recommendation in the on-screen box labeled "Best Deal."

```
[PROGRAM]
IF Shape1 = "square" THEN SquareInches1 = Size1 * Size1
IF Shape1 = "round" THEN SquareInches1 = 3.142 * (Size1 /2)^2
SquareInchPrice1 = Price1/SquareInches1
IF Shape2 = "square" THEN SquareInches2 = Size2 * Size2
IF Shape2 = "round" THEN SquareInches2 = 3.142 * (Size2 /2)^2
SquareInchPrice2 = Price2/SquareInches2
IF SquareInchPrice1 < SquareInchPrice2 THEN BestDeal = "Pizza
1 is the best deal."
IF SquareInchPrice2 < SquareInchPrice1 THEN BestDeal = "Pizza
2 is the best deal."
IF SquareInchPrice1 = SquareInchPrice2 THEN BestDeal = "Both
pizzas are the same deal."
```

Components

Who creates the objects that I use in my programs? In practice, object-oriented and event-driven programs contain many objects that were created by the program designer. However, programmers can also purchase objects called components or libraries. **Components** are prewritten objects that programmers can customize and add to their own programs. They are available commercially for a few of today's most popular programming languages. Using components is often referred to as **component programming**.

For example, suppose that you have been hired by a city government to write software to track recyclables. The engineers want to generate graphs periodically to compare the amounts of glass, paper, aluminum, and other recyclable materials. A graphing component will help you provide this function in your software. You simply attach the graphing component to the rest of your program code. The engineers also need to fill in government forms. You can purchase a forms component, customize it for the government forms, and attach it to your recycling software.

Programmers can select from a wide array of components that provide a variety of functions, such as spreadsheet-like rows and columns, database management, expert systems, report generation, online Help, data acquisition, text editing, scientific imaging, and 3-D graphics. Components are advertised in programming language magazines, such as *Visual Basic Programmer's Journal*.

QUICKCHECK   D

1 A(n) ☐ language creates programs that are composed of a series of statements that tell a computer how to perform the processes for a specific task.

2 A(n) ☐ language lets a programmer construct a program by specifying a set of rules that defines the conditions for resolving a problem.

3 A(n) ☐ language requires a programmer to write instructions for the lowest level of the computer system—that is, for the specific hardware elements, such as the processor, registers, and RAM locations.

4 In a compiled language, ☐ code is compiled, or translated, into object code, which the computer can execute.

5 Some computer programming languages use a(n) ☐ to convert instructions to machine language one line at a time when the program is executed.

6 In a(n) ☐ language, program code is attached to objects and executed when something happens to that object.

7 ☐ are prewritten objects designed to be customized and added to programs.

8 A(n) ☐ is an action, such as a key press or mouse click, to which a program might respond.

Check Answers

USER FOCUS — SELECTING A PROGRAMMING LANGUAGE

Usually, more than one programming language is suitable for a task. So, when you select a language for a project, keep in mind the following questions:

- Do the characteristics of the programming language fit the task at hand?
- Is the language currently used for other applications in the organization?
- Does the organization have expertise using the language?

If the answers to all these questions are "yes," then the language that you are considering should be a good choice for the project. The descriptions of popular programming languages in this section will help you answer the first question.

8086 assembly language is a low-level language consisting of short mnemonic commands that the computer can easily translate into machine language. The 8086 assembly language instruction set is specific to the Intel 8086 microprocessor. Programs written in this language can be executed only by computers with microprocessors from the x86 family. Today, 8086 assembly language is used primarily for programs or segments of programs that must be made as short as possible or that must run as quickly as possible. Professional programmers use 8086 assembly language for the sections of application programs that need to execute quickly and for system software that controls computer hardware.

Visual Basic

BASIC and Visual Basic are probably the most popular programming languages because they are easy to use and available for almost every type of computer system. Since BASIC (Beginner's All-purpose Symbolic Instruction Code) was introduced in 1964, many popular versions of this language have been created, including GW-BASIC shipped with the original IBM PCs, Microsoft's QBASIC, and Visual Basic for Applications. BASIC is a high-level, procedural language. Most versions of BASIC are interpreted languages, although some versions provide compiling capabilities.

Early versions of BASIC were regarded as too limited for the development of sophisticated commercial programs, but newer versions, such as Microsoft's Visual Basic (VB), are comprehensive and powerful programming languages suitable for use in professional programming projects. Visual Basic is especially useful for creating event-driven programs that have a graphical user interface. Visual Basic for Applications (VBA) is a subset of Visual Basic that creates macros for Microsoft applications, such as Word, Excel, Access, and PowerPoint.

C is a compiled procedural language that provides both high-level commands and low-level access to hardware. This duality gives the programmer significant flexibility in writing programs. As a result, experienced C programmers can make their programs very fast and efficient. Unfortunately, this flexibility can make C programs difficult to understand, debug, and maintain.

C++

C++ is an object-oriented version of C. Many people believe that the object-oriented nature of C++ can make programmers more productive. However, object-oriented programming requires a significantly different mental perspective from that of procedural programming. Therefore, many programmers experience difficulty incorporating the object-oriented features of C++ in their programs.

COBOL (COmmon Business-Oriented Language) is the language most typically used for transaction processing on mainframe computer systems. Developed in 1960, COBOL is a high-level, procedural, compiled language used by thousands of professional programmers to develop and maintain complex programs in large organizations and businesses. COBOL instructions tend to be rather long, but they are easy to understand, debug, and maintain. This functionality is particularly important in situations where critical programs must be maintained and modified by many different programmers over a period of years.

FORTRAN (FORmula TRANslator), developed in 1954, is the oldest high-level computer programming language still in use, although it has undergone several revisions since its creation. FORTRAN was designed by scientists and is often used to create scientific, mathematical, and engineering programs on mainframes and minicomputers.

InfoWeb
10
Java,etc.

Java and **J++** are high-level, object-oriented programming languages based on C++ but optimized for Web applications. Java and J++ programs are typically used to create animated graphics on a Web page or to create an application, called an **applet**, that contains customized Web page controls such as buttons, check boxes, or text input boxes. When a browser connects to a Web page that has an associated Java or J++ program, the program code is downloaded and runs on your computer. Because the program runs on your computer instead of the Web server, you'll avoid the transfer time for sending your input and for receiving a response.

Java and J++ differ in one significant respect. Java is a platform-independent language, which means that Java programs will run on a Macintosh or UNIX computer as well as on a PC. J++, on the other hand, provides programmers with tools to call upon specific Windows features. By using these tools, a programmer can produce faster, more efficient applications. If a programmer uses these tools, however, the program will run only on a computer that uses the Windows operating system.

JavaScript, not to be confused with Java, is a scripting language that provides a subset of Java features. JavaScript code is embedded in a Web page just like HTML tags. It is interpreted by your Web browser when it receives a Web page. The primary use of JavaScript is to create Web pages with interactive forms.

Pascal was designed in 1971 to help students learn how to program computers. Pascal is a high-level, procedural, compiled language. The design of the language encourages a structured approach to programming. Despite its structured design, Pascal is not typically used for professional and commercial applications.

Prolog and LISP (LISt Processor) are declarative languages, often used to develop expert systems. These languages, which were developed in 1971 and 1960, respectively, have not gained as much popularity as procedural languages, probably because early computer applications were designed to handle tasks that required simple and repetitious calculations—tasks that procedural languages could handle effectively. Tasks that require a computer to perform complex logical operations on character data are better handled by declarative languages.

SQL (Structured Query Language) was developed to provide a standard language for defining and manipulating a database. SQL is a high-level declarative language that allows programmers and users to describe the type of information that they want to derive from a database. Although a database can also be manipulated by a procedural language such as COBOL, SQL is generally regarded as more effective because SQL commands are tailored to database activities.

CHAPTER 15

ISSUE WHAT ARE PROFESSIONAL ETHICS?

When discussing ethical issues, we often do so from the perspective of the victim. We imagine how it might feel if someone else—an employer, the government, cyberpunks, and so on—pilfered our original art work from a Web site, read our e-mail, or stole our credit card number from an e-commerce site. It is quite possible, however, that at some time in your career you will encounter situations in which you could become the perpetrator—the copyright violator, the snoop, or the thief.

Every day, computer professionals must cope with ethical dilemmas, in which the right course of action is not entirely clear or in which the right course of action is clear, but the consequences—such as getting fired from work—are not easy to face.

Suppose, for example, that you have just been hired to manage a local area network in a prestigious New York advertising agency. On your first day of work, your employer hands you a box containing the latest upgrade for Microsoft Office and asks you to install it on all the computers in the organization. When you ask if the agency owns a site license, your boss responds, "No, do you have a problem with that?" What would you reply? Would you risk your job by insisting that the agency order enough copies for all the computers before you installed it? Or, would you go ahead and install the software, assuming that your boss would take responsibility for this violation of the software license agreement?

Now imagine that you've been hired as a programmer for a local public school system. One day, the Superintendent of Schools calls you into her office and asks if you can write software that will monitor online access and provide reports to management. From your understanding of the school's network and Web access, you realize that it would be easy to write such monitoring software. You also realize, however, that the Superintendent could use the software to track individual teachers and students as they visit Web sites. You ask the Superintendent if faculty and students would be aware of the monitoring software, and she replies, "What they don't know won't hurt them." Should you write the program? Should you write the program, but spread a rumor that monitoring software is being used to track faculty and student Web access? Should you pretend that it would be technically impossible to write such software?

A Code of Ethics is designed to help computer professionals thread their way through a sometimes tangled web of ethical decisions. Published by many professional organizations, such as the Association for Computing Machinery, the British Computer Society, the Australian Computer Society, and the Computer Ethics Institute, each code varies in detail, but supplies a similar set of overall guiding principles for professional conduct. One of the shortest codes is published by the Computer Ethics Institute:

1. Thou shalt not use a computer to harm other people.
2. Thou shalt not interfere with other people's computer work.

3. Thou shalt not snoop around in other people's files.

4. Thou shalt not use a computer to steal.

5. Thou shalt not use a computer to bear false witness.

6. Thou shalt not use or copy software for which you have not paid.

7. Thou shalt not use other people's computer resources without authorization.

8. Thou shalt not appropriate other people's intellectual output.

9. Thou shalt think about the social consequences of the program you write.

10. Thou shalt use a computer in ways that show consideration and respect.

These 10 guidelines are short and to the point, but have drawn fire from critics, such as Dr. N. Ben Fairweather, the Centre for Computing and Social Responsibility's resident philosopher and research fellow, who states, "It is easy to find exceptions to the short dos and don'ts of the 'ten commandments' ...The ease with which these can be found, described and repeated gives rise to the possibility of generally good guidance falling into unwarranted disrepute: indeed, every time such a short code of ethics falls into unwarranted disrepute, the whole idea of acting morally is brought into disrepute too." Dr. Fairweather seems to be suggesting that hard and fast rules may not apply to all situations.

Not all Codes of Ethics are short and snappy. For example, the ACM's Code of Ethics and Professional Conduct contains 21 guidelines, including "ACM members must obey existing local, state, province, national, and international laws unless there is a compelling ethical basis not to do so." But it goes on to say, "...sometimes existing laws and rules may be immoral or inappropriate and, therefore, must be challenged. Violation of a law or regulation may be ethical when that law or rule has inadequate moral basis or when it conflicts with another law judged to be more important. If one decides to violate a law or rule because it is viewed as unethical, or for any other reason, one must fully accept responsibility for one's actions and for the consequences."

InfoWeb 11

Professional
Ethics

CHAPTER 15

WHAT DO YOU THINK?

1. Would you follow your boss's orders to install unlicensed software?   ○Yes ○ No ○ Not sure

2. If you went ahead and installed the software, but it was later discovered by the software publisher, do you think that you would be held responsible?   ○Yes ○ No ○ Not sure

 Save Responses

CHAPTER 15 REVIEW ACTIVITIES

INTERACTIVE SUMMARY

The Interactive Summary helps you select important concepts and facts from this chapter. Fill in the blanks to best complete each sentence. When using the NP4 CD or NP4 Web site, you can click the Check Answers buttons to automatically score your answers. Place your Tracking Disk in the floppy disk drive if you want to save your scores.

Software _____ is the systematic approach to the development, operation, maintenance, and retirement of software. Computer _____ is the process of coding and testing the instructions that direct a computer to carry out a specific task. A computer program begins with a problem statement that contains (1) _____ that are accepted as true so as to proceed with the program design, (2) _____ information—sometimes called "givens," and (3) a description of what you expect as the output. After the problem statement is complete, a programmer formulates a(n) _____, which specifies the general process for solving the problem. Only after preliminary planning should the programmer begin _____ the program by using a computer language to specify the instructions that the computer will use to carry out a task. Procedural computer languages, such as BASIC, COBOL, and C, are composed of instructions that the computer executes in a sequence that is determined by the _____ controls provided by the programming language. For example, a(n) _____ control causes the computer to execute a decision and, based on that decision, to proceed to a particular branch of the program. A(n) _____ control causes the computer to repeat one or more instructions until a specified condition is met. ➡ Check Answers

A computer program is not complete until it has been thoroughly tested and the "bugs" have been eliminated. During the testing process, a programmer might identify _____ errors that are caused when an instruction does not follow the rules or grammar of the programming language. A(n) _____ error shows up when the program runs, even though all of the program syntax is correct. A program with a(n) _____ error will typically run, but the results will be incorrect due to a problem in the program's overall design. In addition to testing a program, a programmer should create _____, which allows other programmers to read, understand, and modify the program code.

Today's computer languages provide a wide variety of options for selecting the best programming tool for a particular task. Although procedural languages have traditionally dominated for number-crunching tasks, _____ languages are useful for programs that manipulate ideas and concepts. _____ languages, such as HTML and Visual Basic for Applications, are good choices for non-programmers who want to design Web sites or automate the tasks performed by their application software. High-level, low-level, compiled, interpreted, object-oriented, and event-driven languages all offer advantages and disadvantages that should be considered before a language is selected for a particular project. ➡ Check Answers

INTERACTIVE KEY TERMS

Make sure that you understand all of the boldfaced key terms presented in this chapter. If you're using the NP4 CD or NP4 Web site, you can use this list of terms as an interactive study activity. First, try to define a term in your own words, then click the term to compare your definition with the definition that is presented in the chapter.

Algorithm, 671
Applet, 697
Assumption, 669
Coding, 677
Compiled language, 691
Compiler, 691
Component programming, 695
Components, 695
Computer programmer, 677
Computer programming, 667
Control structures, 678
Debugging, 684
Declarative language, 689
Documentation, 684
Event-driven language, 694
Flowchart, 674
Function, 680
High-level language, 690
Interpreted language, 692
Interpreter, 692
Known information, 670
Logic error, 685
Low-level language, 690
Machine language, 690

Module, 680
Object code, 691
Object-oriented languages, 693
Procedural languages, 688
Procedure, 680
Program documentation, 685
Program event, 694
Program manual, 687
Program specification, 677
Pseudocode, 674
Remarks, 686
Repetition control structure, 682
Run-time error, 685
Scripting language, 689
Selection control structure, 681
Sequence control structure, 679
Sequential execution, 678
Software engineering, 668
Source code, 691
Subroutine, 680
Syntax error, 685
Technical writer, 687
Written documentation, 686

INTERACTIVE QUIZZES

Quiz yourself on important concepts from this chapter by filling in the blanks. When using the NP4 CD or NP4 Web site, you can type your answers, then use the Check Answers buttons to automatically score your responses. Place your Tracking Disk in the floppy disk drive if you want to save your scores.

1 Prior to coding, an algorithm can be expressed using structured English, pseudocode, or a(n) _____.

2 Sequence controls typically transfer program execution to a(n) _____, procedure, module, or function.

3 A repetition control is also referred to as a(n) _____ or iteration.

4 In a BASIC program, REM stands for _____.

5 If you misspell a command word in a program, you have made a(n) _____ error.

6 A(n) _____ translates an entire program into object code before the program is executed.

7 In the context of programming, a mouse click would be considered a program _____.

8 A(n) _____ is a prewritten object that is designed to be incorporated into a computer program.

9 LISP, Prolog, and Pascal are declarative languages. True or false? _____

➡ Check Answers

Refer to the program at right and enter the correct line number in the boxes below.

1 The beginning of the loop _____

2 The end of the loop _____

3 The remark _____

4 The calculation _____

5 The beginning of the subroutine _____

6 The last line that the computer executes _____

7 The line that produces printed output _____

8 The last line of the subroutine _____

```
100 REM This program lets you enter a number between 1 and 10,
        then multiplies it by 12.
110 INPUT "Enter a number from 1 to 10: ", Number
120 GOSUB checkinput
125 Result = Number *12
130 PRINT Result
140 END
150 checkinput
170 WHILE Number <1 or Number > 10
180 INPUT "You must enter a number between 1 and 10: ", Number
190 WEND
200 RETURN
```

 Check Answers

INTERACTIVE PRACTICE TESTS

When you use the NP4 CD or NP4 Web site, you can take practice tests that consist of 10 multiple-choice, true/false, and fill-in-the-blank questions. The 10 questions are selected at random from a large test bank, so each time you take a test, you'll receive a different set of questions. Your tests are scored immediately and you can print study guides that help you find the correct answers for any questions that you missed. If you are using a Tracking Disk, insert it in the floppy disk drive to save your test scores.

 Start Practice Test

STUDY TIPS

Study Tips help you organize and consolidate the information in a chapter by making lists, outlines, charts, and sketches. You can use paper and pencil or word processing software to complete most of the Study Tips activities.

1 Describe how the job of a systems analyst differs from the job of a software engineer.

2 Is there a difference between an algorithm and a computer program? Why or why not?

3 Give an example of a sequence control structure, a selection control structure, and a repetition control structure.

4 Explain the difference between a syntax error and a logic error.

5 Explain the difference between program remarks and written documentation.

6 Which lines in the program below contain branch or loop control structures?

```
INPUT "Employee Name:"; EmpName$
WHILE EmpName$ <> "EOF"
    INPUT "Hours Worked "; HoursWk
    INPUT "PayRate      "; PayRate
    GrossPay = HoursWk * PayRate
    IF GrossPay > 50 THEN
        Tax = GrossPay *.12
    ELSE
        Tax = 0
    END IF
    NetPay = GrossPay - Tax
    PRINT "Gross Pay "; GrossPay
    INPUT "Employee Name"; EmpName$
WEND
PRINT "Payroll complete."
END
```

7 Fill in the following table to summarize the characteristics of today's popular programming languages. Most languages will have more than one characteristic.

Language	Procedural	Declarative	Low-level	High-level	Compiled	Interpreted	Object-oriented	Component	Event-driven	Scripting
BASIC										
Visual Basic										
COBOL										
FORTRAN										
Pascal										
C										
C++										
Prolog/LISP										
SQL										
Java										
HTML										

CHAPTER 15

PROJECTS

A project is an open-ended activity that will help you apply the concepts you have learned. Many projects require resources in addition to your textbook, such as current magazines, library materials, or Web access. When you tackle a project, be prepared to use your critical thinking skills, logical analysis, and your creativity.

1 **What Information Do You Need?** In this chapter, you learned that problem solving requires information. List the known information required to solve the following problems:

a. Calculate the square footage of a rectangular room.

b. Calculate the amount of gasoline required to drive your car from New York City to San Francisco.

c. Calculate how much it costs to ship a box of books from Dallas, Texas, to Portland, Oregon.

d. Calculate how much it would cost to purchase new carpeting for your living room.

e. Calculate your tuition for next semester.

2 **Assumptions and Known Information** To grasp a problem, you must understand the assumptions on which the problem is based and the known information you can use to solve the problem. To practice identifying assumptions and known information, study the following problem. Think about the information you would need to solve the problem yourself. Identify the assumptions and known information.

Problem: Two tourists are planning a walking tour of a city. Starting at their hotel, they plan to visit a bookstore, a science museum, a Thai restaurant, and a craft market. A city map shows the location of each place. According to the legend on the map, one-half inch on the map is a one-mile walk. The tourists want to know how far they will walk on their tour.

3 **Writing an Algorithm** The algorithm is the key to writing an effective computer program. If you as the programmer understand the steps that efficiently carry out a task or solve a problem, you should be able to translate your algorithm into a workable computer program. To try your hand at writing an algorithm, use the problem statement in Project 2. Write an algorithm for determining the total distance that the tourists will walk. *Hint:* Think about the steps you would take to solve this problem using the map, a calculator, and a ruler.

4 **Find the Errors** A friend has written a BASIC program to calculate the number of tanks of gas her car will require to go a specified number of miles. Unfortunately, the program doesn't work correctly. She shows you a printout of the program (see below) and asks for your help.

A syntax error and a logic error prevent the program from working correctly. Examine the program code carefully to locate the two errors, then write the corrected lines.

```
REM This program calculates the number of tanks of gas
REM required to drive my car a specified number of miles.
MilesPerGallon = 22.5
GallonsPerTank = 12
INPUT "Enter the number of miles to drive:", MilesToDrive
GallonsRequired is MilesToDrive / MilesPerGallon
TanksRequired = GallonsRequired / GallonsPerTank
PRINT "This trip will require:"
PRINT MilesPerGallon
PRINT "tanks of gas."
END
```

5 Imagine You're a Computer To understand a computer program or to debug program code, computer programmers have a trick. They imagine that they are the computer executing the code. By following exactly what the computer should do at each step in a program, a programmer can discover how a program works or which instructions cause problems. Try a simple example. Imagine you are a computer instructed to execute the following BASIC program. Indicate the values of A and Y after you execute each instruction. At the beginning of the program, A and Y are each assigned a value of 0.

```
REM Sample program
A = 10
Y = A * 3
A = A * Y
END
```

6 Documentation—Good or Bad? Writing documentation is not an easy task. Many programs have hundreds of features. Organizing these features into a useful reference format and describing the features so that even a beginner can understand them requires good logical and writing skills. How good is the documentation for programs you use? Describe the documentation for a computer program that you have used. Discuss what you like or do not like about the documentation, and indicate how you think it can be improved.

7 Batting Averages A baseball player's batting average is calculated by dividing the number of times the player hit the ball by the number of times the player was at bat, minus the number of times the player "walked," as in the formula, Hits / (TimesAtBat – Walks). Write the specifications for a program that calculates a baseball player's batting average. Be sure to include the assumptions, known information, formula for calculation, and output description. Also, create a flowchart to express the algorithm.

8 The Card Shark Assume you are talking to a friend on the phone. You know your friend has three cards and they are all in the same suit. For example, your friend might have the two of clubs, the five of clubs, and the eight of clubs. Furthermore, assume that the cards are shuffled so they are in no particular order. You need to tell your friend how to sort the cards so the lowest-numbered card is first and the highest-numbered card is last. You cannot see the cards, however, and your friend cannot communicate with you except to say OK. You need to give your friend general instructions, such as "Take the first two cards and compare the numbers on them." Write out the instructions, or algorithm, for sorting the three cards.

9 Computing Careers What are the job prospects for computer programmers? Looking at employment ads is one way to find out. To research the employment opportunities in a large city of your choice, look in the classified ad section of a printed or Web-based newspaper. Write a summary of your research by answering the following questions:

a. What were your sources of information?

b. How many computer programming jobs were available?

c. What was the average salary offered?

d. What were the educational requirements for entry-level positions?

e. What programming languages seem to be in greatest demand?

ADDITIONAL PROJECTS

Click the underlined text to link to the NP4 Web site (www.cciw.com/np4), where you can view and print additional projects for this chapter.

Computer Languages

Grading Computer Literacy Exams

CHAPTER 15

LAB ASSIGNMENTS

Software for this lab is provided on the NP4 CD and may also be available in your school's computer lab. To start the lab, click the lab icon.

The lab has two parts: Steps and Explore. Use the Steps first to learn and review concepts. Read the information on each page and complete the numbered steps. As you work through the lab, you will be asked to answer QuickCheck questions about what you have learned. At the end of the lab, you will see a report that scores your answers to the QuickChecks. If your instructor wants you to turn in this report, click the Print button on the QuickCheck Report screen.

When you have completed the Steps, you can click the Explore button to complete the Lab Assignments. You can also use Explore to practice the skills you learned and to explore concepts on your own.

In the Visual Programming Lab, you'll use an event-driven, object-oriented programming environment to create simple programs. This lab provides a "taste" of what it would be like to program in a visual language such as Visual Basic.

1. Click the Steps button to learn how to create a graphical user interface containing buttons, labels, and text boxes. As you work through the Steps, answer all of the QuickCheck questions. After you complete the Steps, you will see a QuickCheck Summary Report of your answers. Follow the directions on the screen to print this report.

2. In Explore, create a program to calculate the total cost of carpeting a room. Test your program, then print it showing the cost of $12.99/sq. yd. carpeting for a 10 x 14 foot room.

   Assume that the room is rectangular. The known information is the length and width of the room, and the price of a square yard of carpet. You must calculate:

   - The square feet of carpet needed (length * width of room)
   - The square yards of carpet needed (square feet/9)
   - Total price of the carpet (price per square yard * square yards needed)

   Your user interface should look like the following screen:

Visual Programming - EDIT

File Run Help   Button

| [Button] | **AB** | **abl** | Current Program | [trash] Please dispose of |
| Button | Label | Text Box | SOL2.VPG | objects properly! |

Carpeting Calculator
This program calculates the cost
of carpeting a rectangular room.

Instructions: Enter the dimensions   Length: [____]
of the room and the price per   Width: [____]
square yard of the carpet, then   Price per square yard: [____]
click the Calculate Cost button.

                                          [Calculate Cost]

            The square footage of the room is: [____]
              Square yards of carpet needed: [____]
           The total price of carpeting will be $: [____]

3 Suppose that you like to shop from catalogs. Your favorite catalog is having a sale—selected merchandise is discounted 10%, 20%, 30%, or 40%. You want to know how much you'll save if you buy some of the merchandise. In Explore, create a program to calculate savings. Test your program, then print it showing the savings for an $863 item at 30% discount.

Assume that the items you purchase will be discounted and that there is no additional charge for shipping. The known information is the original price of the item and its discount—10%, 20%, 30% or 40%. Calculate how much you will save. (For example, for a 10% discount, multiply the original cost by .1.) Your user interface should look like the following screen:

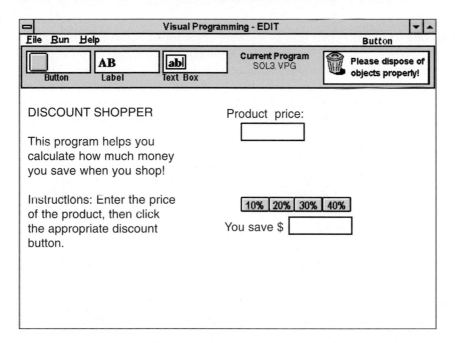

4 In your recording studio, studio musicians are paid by the hour, but your sound technicians are salaried. You started to make a program to calculate weekly paychecks, but it doesn't seem to work.

Your assumption is that some employees are salaried and some are hourly. You know the annual salary for each salaried employee. You know the hourly wage and the hours worked each pay period by each hourly employee. You want to calculate the weekly pay for salaried employees (Wages / 52) and the weekly pay for hourly employees (Wages * Hours).

In Explore, open the program PAY.VPG and test it. For a salaried employee who makes $32,240 per year, enter 32240 in the Wages box, then click the Salaried button. The output should be 620, which is the annual salary divided by 52 pay periods per year. Next, for an hourly employee who makes $8 per hour and works a 40-hour week, enter 8 in the Wages box and 40 in the Hours box. Click the Hourly button. The output should be 320. Find what's wrong with this program and correct it. Print your solution.

INFOWEB

The InfoWeb is your guide to print, film, television, and electronic resources. Use it to obtain updates on quickly changing technical information and to locate information for research papers. If you're using the NP4 CD, click the InfoWeb Site icon on the left side of this paragraph to access the online InfoWeb links. Otherwise, use your Web browser and type in the address of the NP4 Web site: www.cciw.com/np4. At the Web site you'll find up-to-date links to the topics covered in this chapter.

1 Software Engineering

Mickey Williamson provides an in-depth overview of software engineering in the CIO magazine article, "Software Development" (*www.cio.com/archive/041596_devenpor_content.html*). You might pay particular attention to the last page, which lists the habits of highly effective developers. The Software Engineering Institute (SEI) at Carnegie Mellon University publishes research results and guidelines about effective software development. The SEI Web site at *www.sei.cmu.edu* is definitely worth a visit. Similar activities take place at the NASA/Goddard Space Flight Center Software Engineering Laboratory (SEL) at *sel.gsfc.nasa.gov*.

One of the most practical books about programming is Steve McConnell's *Code Complete* (Microsoft Press, 1993). It is full of practical tips that will help you complete your programming projects on time, within budget, and with minimal bugs. You'll find a series of software development checklists excerpted from Steve's book at the Construx Software Builder's site (*www.construx.com/chk.htm*). The Programmer's Vault Web site (*chesworth.com/pv*) includes tutorials for programmers of various skill levels. At this site, you can learn the basic methods for programming computer games or delve into the technical world of matrix transformations. A terrific site for information on programming languages, programming tips, and job listings is *www.itmweb.com*.

Are you curious about the books that famous programmers have on their bookshelves? If so, scroll and link to Gregory Wilson's article, "Great Books," published in the Fall 1997 issue of *Dr. Dobb's Journal* (*www.ddj.com/ddj/1997/1997.careers2/wils.htm*). Many programmers subscribe to *Dr. Dobb's Journal*, which must be one of the first computer magazines ever published (*www.ddj.com*). Another favorite is *American Programmer*, edited by the renowned Ed Yourdon (*www.cutter.com/itjournal*). The *Microsoft Systems Journal* (*www.microsoft.com/msj*) is a good source of information about systems development. Programmers' professional organizations include the International Programmer's Guild, which you can find online at *www.ipgnet.com/ipghome.htm*.

2 Algorithms

To learn more about algorithms, start at the PC Webopaedia site (*www.pcwebopaedia.com*) and search for "algorithm." You'll find a clear definition of the term and links to sites with more in-depth information. Do you want to amaze your friends with your ability to predict the day of the week for any date? You can read about John Horton Conway's "Doomsday" algorithm at Rudy Limeback's Web site, *www.interlog.com/~r937/doomsday.html*. Computer algorithms are frequently employed for sorting and searching. Thomas Niemann provides an intuitive approach to these algorithms in his sorting and searching algorithm "cookbook" at *members.xoom.com/thomasn/s_man.htm*. A computer can also use an algorithm to solve Rubik's cube. Find out how at *www.sunyit.edu/~millerd1/RUBIK.HTM*. You might want to visit the Stony Brook Algorithm Repository at *www.cs.sunysb.edu/~algorith/index.html* where you will find a collection of algorithms for more than 70 fundamental problems. The classic text on algorithms is Donald Knuth's *Art of Computer Programming* (Addison-Wesley, 1998), now in its third edition (originally published in the 1970s). So far there are three volumes in this set, but Knuth is working on volumes four and five. For a progress update, you can connect to Knuth's home page at *www-cs-staff.stanford.edu/~knuth/taocp.html*.

3 Pseudocode & Flowcharts

You'll find a good definition of pseudocode by searching for "pseudocode" at online glossary sites, such as PC Webopaedia (*www.webopaedia.com*) or WhatIs? (*www.whatis.com*). You'll find out how to use pseudocode to express program control structures at *jeffconet.jeffco.k12.co.us/online_ed/cpp/nested.html*. To find some examples of pseudocode, use a search engine, such as *www.msn.com*, to search for "pseudocode."

In addition to using the search term "flowchart" at your favorite Web-based dictionary site or search engine, you can explore some flowcharting tools by connecting to PC Magazine Online at *www.zdnet.com/pcmag/features/flow/_open.htm*. You can download a trial version of SmartDraw from *www.smartdraw.com*, RFFlow from *www.rff.com*, or Micrografx FlowCharter from *www.micrografx.com/flowcharter*. The SmartDraw site also includes a variety of flowchart examples and a flowcharting tutorial.

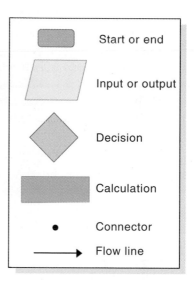

Start or end

Input or output

Decision

Calculation

Connector

Flow line

CHAPTER 15

4 Programming Careers

For practical advice on how to prepare for a programming career, check out to Eugene Eric Kim's article, "Making Your Move: Programming as a Career" in the Fall 1997 issue of *Dr. Dobb's Journal* (*www.ddj.com/articles/1997/9719/9719toc.htm*). The same issue includes the article "Programming in the Real World" by Allen Holub (*www.ddj.com/articles/1997/9719/9719n/9719n.htm*). The Bureau of Labor Statistics provides a detailed description of programmers' working conditions, employment outlook, salaries, and educational requirements at *stats.bls.gov/oco/ocos110.htm*. You can find up-to-date job listings for programmers at career Web sites, such as The Monster Board (*www.monster.com*), the Kaplan Career Services site (*www.kaplancareers.com*), or the Job Hunter link at the San Jose Mercury News (*www.sjmercury.com*). What does Bill Gates think is the key to becoming a successful programmer? You can find out in Susan Lammers' book, *Programmers at Work* (Microsoft Press, 1986), featuring Bill Gates and a cast of other luminaries from the early days of microcomputers. For a humorous look at programmers, read Ed Post's essay, "Real Programmers Don't Use Pascal," at *www.uio.no/~olews/real.men.html*.

5 GOTO

Dijkstra opened a can of worms when he submitted his famous letter, "Go To Statement Considered Harmful" to the Communications of the ACM in 1968. You can read the text of this letter on the Web at *www.acm.org/classics/oct95/*. Steve McConnell discusses the issue in his book, *Code Complete* (Microsoft Press, 1993). The Construx Web site (*www.construx.com/stevemcc/ccgoto.htm*) carries an excerpt from this book. You can learn more about the use of GOTO in an *IEEE Software* article called "Keep It Simple" at *www.construx.com/stevemcc/bp06.htm*.

6 Technical Writing

To learn more about prospects for technical writers, connect to the Bureau of Labor statistics page about writers and editors (*stats.bls.gov/oco/ocos089.htm*). You can get some great tips about starting a technical writing career from the Micro Search site article, "How to Break into Technical Writing" at *www.microsearchsf.com/breakin.htm*.

Several other Web sites provide good resources for technical writers, such as links to articles about improving your writing, technical writing tutorials, classes on technical writing, and job listings. Three of the best sites include Writer's Block (*www.niva.com/original/writblok/index.htm*), Internet Resources for Technical Communicators (*members.home.net/ksoltys/index.htm*), and the Mining Company (*techwriting.miningco.com/arts/techwriting*). You'll find an excellent bibliography of technical books at *library.afit.af.mil/bibs/repwrit.html*. The premiere professional organization for technical writers is the Society for Technical Communication (STC) at *stc.org*. David A. McMurrey has produced a truly wonderful technical writing text that you can read online by connecting to *www.io.com/~hcexres/tcm1603/acchtml/acctoc.html*.

7 OOP

Terry Montlick has written an excellent introduction to object-oriented technology called "What Is Object-Oriented Software?" at *www.soft-design.com/softinfo/objects.html*. For a quick overview of object-oriented terminology, connect to *www.justpbinfo.com/techdocs/ooterms.asp*. If you are looking for a more in-depth overview of object-oriented programming, connect to Bob Hathaway's Object-Orientation FAQ at *www.cyberdyne-object-sys.com/oofaq2*. If you're looking for a site with lots of links to OOP sites, you can connect to *iamwww.unibe.ch/~scg/OOinfo?infopage*. Grady Booch is a well-respected authority in object-oriented programming, and his book, *Object-Oriented Analysis and Design with Applications* (Addison Wesley, 1994), is already a classic. You can find out more about object-oriented development, including a tutorial, at a site maintained by Philipp Schneider (*www.hsr.ch/div/Booch/BoochReference*). Object-oriented programming is most successful when it is based on object-oriented analysis (OOA) and design (OOD). The Web article "Object-Oriented Methodologies" at *www.pencom.com/case/oo.html* compares the Booch, Coad-Yourdon, Rumbaugh, and Shlaer-Mellor methodologies. For in-depth information on this subject, browse through the online version of the book, *Object-Oriented System Development*, by Champeaux, Lea, and Faure (Addison Wesley, 1993) at *gee.cs.oswego.edu/dl/oosdw3*.

8 Visual Basic

Visual Basic is a Microsoft product, so the Web site at *msdn.microsoft.com/vbasic* is a good place to get technical information. According to many VB programmers, the most useful site is Carl & Gary's Visual Basic Home Page (*www.cgvb.com*). Carl & Gary's site includes links, articles, and downloads.. Another Web page specially targeted at beginning VB programmers is Gary Beene's Visual Basic Information Center at *www.vbinformation.com*.

You can learn to program by downloading a Visual Basic Self-Study Tutorial from TegoSoft, Inc., at *www.tego.com/Items/LearnVisualBasicFast/LearnVBFast.htm*. You'll find another tutorial at the Visual Basic Palace (*home.computer.net/~mheller/hints.html*). For news about the latest VB components and programming techniques, programmers like the DevX site (*www.vb-zone.com*) and the Visual Basic Online Magazine site (*www.vbonline.com/vb-mag*). The *Visual Basic Programmer's Journal* is the standard paper-based reference resource for Visual Basic programmers, and you can link to its subscription site at the DevX site.

9 C++

C++ was created in 1980 by Dr. Bjarne Stroustrup of Bell Laboratories. You can visit his C++ Web page for information and links at *www.research.att.com/~bs/C++.html*. C++ language vendors include Microsoft (*msdn.microsoft.com/visualc*) and Inprise (*www.inprise.com/borlandcpp/turbosuite*). For an excellent overview and examples of C++ programs, connect to the C++ for Beginners Web page at *www.wtvl.net/mike/webjr/begcpp.htm*. At this site, you'll also find a description of C++ command words, a bibliography of good reference books, and links to other C++ Web sites. The Visual C++ Developer's Journal (*www.vcdj.com*) is a good resource for C++ programming tips, code samples, and information on conferences. Are you thinking about pursuing C++ as your career option? If so, visit *www.cplusplusjobs.com/public/default.asp* for an up-to-date listing of C++ programming jobs.

🔟 Java, Etc.

Java was developed by Sun Microsystems and its "official" Java page at *java.sun.com* has links to FAQs, articles, tutorials, documentation, and programming tips. The place to begin learning about Java is Marshall Brain's "Introduction to Java" at *devcentral.iftech.com/learning/tutorials/java/javaintro*. You can find several online Java tutorials, including "Introducing Java—Your First Applet" at *www.freewarejava.com/tutorials/index.shtml*. You'll find a Java glossary, articles, and applets that you can download at the Java Boutique (*javaboutique.internet.com/how_to/glossary.html*. Despite all the hype about Java, some industry analysts remain skeptical about its usefulness. Can Java improve your life? Check out Mark Hurst's article at *www.creativegood.com/help/c011.html*. JavaScript differs from Java in several ways, but it is nevertheless, a useful Web development tool in its own right. HotSyte (*www.serve.com/hotsyte*), which bills itself as the JavaScript Resource, has a good set of links to articles, downloads, and sample scripts, including a link to the JavaScript Guide offered by JavaScript's creator, Netscape.

1️⃣1️⃣ Professional Ethics

You'll find the article by Dr. N. Ben Fairweather (mentioned in the *Issue* section) online at *www.ccsr.cms.dmu.ac.uk/resources/professionalism/codes/cei_command_com.html*. A comprehensive list of the Codes of Ethics Web sites is available through the Centre for Computing and Social Responsibility in the United Kingdom (*www.ccsr.cms.dmu.ac.uk/resources/professionalism/codes*). Its information includes links to the codes followed in Australia, Canada, Hong Kong, Germany, and the United States, including those developed by the ACM and IEEE.

IS IT Ethical?, a 1998 Survey of Professional Practice, describes ethical issues in the areas of data security, software development, using corporate computers, and electronic surveillance. You'll find the survey online at *www.ccsr.cms.dmu.ac.uk/resources/general/ethicol/Ecv9no1.html*. For some sample ethics cases at the corporate level, connect to the Center for Applied Ethics at *www.ethics.ubc.ca/resources/computer/pubs.html*.

QUICK CHECK ANSWERS

CHAPTER 1

QuickCheck A
1. Processing (process)
2. Data
3. Central
4. Memory (RAM, random access memory)
5. Storage

QuickCheck B
1. Microcomputer
2. Terminal
3. Mainframe
4. Keyboard, monitor
5. Compatible
6. Network

QuickCheck C
1. Prompt
2. Wizards
3. Enter
4. Syntax
5. Submenu
6. Windows
7. Cursor, insertion point
8. Control

Interactive Summary
1. Input
2. Stored
3. Memory (RAM, random access memory)
4. Central processing unit
5. Output
6. Hardware
7. Software (computer program)
8. Microcomputers
9. Platforms
10. Compatible

1. Network
2. Internet
3. Web
4. Browser
5. Interface
6. Graphical
7. Menu
8. Icons
9. Windows
10. Manual
11. Help

Interactive Quizzes
1. Input
2. Memory (RAM, Random access memory)
3. Software
4. Minicomputer (Mainframe computer)
5. Supercomputers (Supercomputer)

6. Mainframe
7. Platforms
8. Web (World Wide Web)
9. Hardware
10. Artificial intelligence

1. D
2. I
3. H
4. A
5. E
6. G
7. F
8. C
9. B

CHAPTER 2

QuickCheck A
1. False
2. False
3. Pirated
4. Program
5. Multiple user (multiuser)
6. Site
7. Shareware
8. System, application

QuickCheck B
1. Desktop
2. Micro
3. Multitasking
4. Linux
5. Utility
6. Device driver
7. Computer programming language

QuickCheck C
1. Suite
2. Desktop publishing
3. Wireframe
4. False
5. Connectivity (communications)
6. Vertical

QuickCheck D
1. True
2. Sound card
3. True
4. Desktop

Interactive Summary
1. Program
2. Copyright
3. Software
4. Shareware
5. Domain
6. Languages
7. Server
8. Desktop
9. Application

1. Multimedia
2. Sound
3. Scanner
4. Setup
5. Pirated

Interactive Quizzes
1. True
2. Internal
3. Desktop
4. Multitasking
5. Office
6. Formatting
7. Driver
8. Desktop
9. False

1. True
2. False
3. True
4. False

CHAPTER 3

QuickCheck A
1. Production
2. True
3. Word wrap
4. False
5. Document template, document wizard (wizard)
6. Electronic (desktop)
7. Concordance
8. HTML (Hypertext Markup Language)

QuickCheck B
1. Column, row
2. References (addresses)
3. Functions
4. False
5. True
6. True
7. What-if

QuickCheck C
1. Structured, freeform
2. True
3. Query by example (QBE)
4. Query language
5. True

Interactive Summary
1. Processing
2. Word wrap
3. Proofread
4. Worksheet
5. Reference
6. What-if
7. Charts (graphs)

1. Structured
2. Fields
3. Freeform
4. Access
5. Language
6. Index

Interactive Quizzes
1. Quality
2. Electronic
3. Worksheet, spreadsheet
4. Formulas
5. Relative
6. Access
7. URL

1. False
2. False
3. False
4. True
5. False

CHAPTER 4

QuickCheck A
1. Data, information
2. Wildcard
3. .exe (exe)
4. Open
5. Generic
6. False

QuickCheck B
1. False
2. Root
3. Subdirectories
4. .dat (dat)
5. True
6. Logical
7. False

QuickCheck C
1. False
2. Magnetizing
3. Optical
4. Tracks
5. FAT (file allocation table)
6. Fragmented

QuickCheck D
1. Bytes (gigabytes), milliseconds
2. Random, sequential
3. True
4. False
5. False
6. DVD (DVD-ROM)

Interactive Summary
1. Executable (program)
2. Data
3. Manager

4. Directory
5. Folders

1. Bits
2. Byte
3. Pits
4. Tracks
5. Clusters
6. Allocation
7. Kilobyte
8. Megabyte
9. Gigabyte
10. Terabyte
11. Access time
12. Transfer
13. DVD
14. Record (write, save)

Interactive Quizzes
1. Conventions
2. Extension
3. True
4. Root
5. False
6. False
7. Clusters
8. False
9. Fragmented
10. DVD

1. 69,000 (69 K, 69000)
2. 1
3. 12
4. .exe (exe)
5. 2
6. 3
7. C

CHAPTER 5

QuickCheck A
1. Integrated circuit
2. Digital, analog
3. ASCII
4. Binary
5. Data bus (bus)

QuickCheck B
1. Memory (RAM)
2. Volatile
3. Megabytes
4. Capacitors
5. Nanoseconds
6. Virtual
7. ROM (read-only memory)
8. CMOS

QuickCheck C
1. Microprocessor
2. ALU (arithmetic logic unit)
3. Control unit
4. Operand
5. Megahertz
6. System clock

QuickCheck D
1. Expansion bus
2. Expansion card

3. Slot, port
4. USB (universal serial bus)

Interactive Summary
1. Architecture
2. Binary
3. EBCDIC
4. Integrated
5. Data bus (bus)
6. Operating
7. DIMM
8. Volatile
9. BIOS
10. CMOS

1. Microprocessor (processor)
2. ALU (arithmetic logic unit)
3. Control
4. Parallel
5. Expansion
6. Slot
7. Port

Interactive Quizzes
1. Digital, analog
2. Character
3. Data, Address
4. Nanoseconds
5. False
6. Virtual
7. True
8. Registry
9. Safe

1. C
2. A
3. B
4. D
5. E
6. F

CHAPTER 6

QuickCheck A
1. Benchmark
2. False
3. False
4. False
5. Sound Blaster
6. Notebook
7. PCMCIA

QuickCheck B
1. Ink jet
2. Duty
3. Ink jet
4. Dot matrix
5. Multifunction

QuickCheck C
1. Vaporware
2. True
3. Competitive

4. Tiers (categories)
5. VAR (value added reseller)
6. False

QuickCheck D
1. True
2. Information systems
3. Northeastern
4. Experience
5. Organizations
6. Job fairs

Interactive Summary
1. Specifications (technical specifications)
2. AMD
3. Pentium
4. Ultra
5. LCD (active matrix, TFT)
6. Ink jet

1. Industry
2. Tiers
3. Cycle
4. Obsolete
5. Channels
6. Science
7. Engineering
8. Systems

Interactive Quizzes
1. True
2. Benchmark
3. AGP
4. Memory
5. Dot matrix
6. Version, revision
7. Upgrades
8. Specific

1. 466 MHz
2. Celeron
3. 6X
4. Creative Labs
5. AGP
6. 4 MB
7. 800 X 600
8. 13.9"
9. 64 MB
10. Windows (Windows 98)

CHAPTER 7

QuickCheck A
1. Server (file server)
2. Mapped
3. True
4. False
5. Default

QuickCheck B
1. NIC (network interface card)
2. File

3. Non-dedicated file server (non-dedicated server)
4. True
5. Host

QuickCheck C
1. False
2. False
3. Network (site, multiuser)
4. Groupware
5. Workflow

Interactive Summary
1. Network
2. LAN (local area network)
3. Node
4. Servers (server)
5. Mapped
6. Locked
7. Groupware

1. Interface
2. Hub (network hub)
3. File
4. Application (non-dedicated)
5. Host
6. Client
7. Workstation

Interactive Quizzes
1. Local, WAN (wide area network)
2. Mapping
3. RAM (memory, random access memory)
4. Locks
5. False
6. Workstation
7. False
8. Attachment

1. Thanks
2. Hotmail.com
3. Poster (Poster.bmp)
4. >

CHAPTER 8

QuickCheck A
1. Cyberspace
2. Internet
3. Terabytes
4. False
5. TCP/IP
6. URL

QuickCheck B
1. Home
2. Streaming
3. Plug-in (player, viewer)
4. Portal
5. True
6. True

QuickCheck C
1. Links
2. False
3. Body
4. Web authoring
5. True
6. Navigation (navigational)
7. True
8. E-commerce

Interactive Summary
1. Arpanet
2. Terabytes
3. TCP/IP
4. Host (Internet host)
5. IP
6. Domain
7. Browser
8. URL
9. Plug-in (player, viewer)
10. Self-extracting

1. HTML
2. Authoring
3. ISP (Internet service provider)
4. Modem
5. Connection

Interactive Quizzes
1. Backbone
2. TCP/IP
3. ISP (Internet service provider)
4. URL
5. FTP
6. HTML
7. False
8. Hosting
9. False
10. PPP (point-to-point)

1. B
2. A
3. D
4. C
5. E

C H A P T E R   9

QuickCheck A
1. Operator
2. False
3. UPS (uninterruptible power supply)
4. Surge
5. True
6. False
7. Backup

QuickCheck B
1. Virus
2. Macro
3. Trojan Horse
4. Worm
5. e-mail attachments

6. False
7. Signature (virus signature)

QuickCheck C
1. Risk management
2. Policy
3. True
4. User rights (rights)
5. Trapdoor
6. Cookie
7. Downtime
8. Redundancy

Interactive Summary
1. Spikes
2. Surge
3. RAM (memory, random access memory)
4. UPS (uninterruptible power supply)
5. Backup
6. Viruses
7. Trojan horse
8. Worm
9. Antivirus

1. Acceptable
2. Procedures
3. Biometric
4. Rights
5. Encrypted
6. Java
7. Certificate
8. Firewall
9. SSL (secure sockets layer)
10. Tape
11. Registry

Interactive Quizzes
1. False
2. File, Macro
3. True
4. Signature
5. False
6. Trapdoor
7. Public
8. Cookie

1. Incremental
2. Full
3. True
4. 1 (one)
5. Label

C H A P T E R   10

QuickCheck A
1. Information theory
2. Four (4)
3. Binary
4. ASCII
5. Unicode
6. Localization

QuickCheck B
1. Bitmap (bitmapped)
2. 8 (eight)
3. Dithering
4. Vector
5. False
6. False

QuickCheck C
1. Waveform, MIDI
2. Sampling
3. False
4. False
5. True

QuickCheck D
1. Compression
2. Volume
3. .zip (zip)
4. Adaptive pattern substitution
5. Lossy
6. True
7. Encoder

Interactive Summary
1. Theory
2. N
3. 16
4. Seven (7)
5. Eight (8)
6. Sixteen (16)
7. Bitmap (bitmapped)
8. Eight (8)
9. Twenty-four (24, 32, thirty-two)
10. Vector

1. Waveform
2. MIDI
3. Compressed
4. Volume
5. File

Interactive Quizzes
1. Eight (8)
2. Character
3. One (1)
4. True color
5. Bitmap (bitmapped)
6. MIDI
7. False
8. False
9. Lossy, lossless

1. E
2. D
3. C
4. A (B)
5. B (A)
6. F

C H A P T E R   11

QuickCheck A
1. Noise
2. Bandwidth
3. Star, bus
4. Protocols
5. Even
6. True

QuickCheck B
1. False
2. Coaxial (coax)
3. Electrical, light
4. Single-mode
5. True
6. Microwave

QuickCheck C
1. Circuit
2. Access
3. Software
4. True
5. False
6. Token
7. Communications protocols (protocols)
8. False

Interactive Summary
1. Source (sender, modem)
2. Channel
3. Analog
4. Digital
5. Bandwidth
6. Broadband
7. Narrowband
8. Noise
9. Protocols
10. Circuit
11. Voiceband

1. Cable
2. Downstream
3. Switching
4. Ethernet
5. TCP/IP
6. IPX/SPX
7. NetBIOS/NetBEUI

Interactive Quizzes
1. Frequency
2. True
3. Duplex (duplex communication)
4. Parity
5. True
6. Circuit, packet
7. Access
8. Open

1. D
2. B
3. C
4. E
5. A

C H A P T E R   1 2

QuickCheck A
1. Information system
2. Mission
3. Threats
4. Automation
5. Total quality management (TQM)
6. Rightsize

QuickCheck B
1. Executive management
2. Goods
3. Strategic
4. Tactical
5. Unstructured
6. Internal, external

QuickCheck C
1. Office automation
2. Transaction
3. Management information
4. Exception
5. Decision support
6. Expert
7. Expert system shell
8. Neural network

Interactive Summary
1. Information
2. Mission
3. Chart
4. Information
5. Service
6. Goods
7. Strategic
8. Automation
9. Processing

1. Management
2. Detail
3. Summary
4. Exception
5. Support
6. What-if
7. Expert
8. Knowledge
9. Inference
10. Fuzzy

Interactive Quizzes
1. False
2. Analysis
3. Transaction
4. False
5. Neural
6. Predicate
7. Chaos

1. Transaction
2. Detail
3. Exception
4. E-commerce
5. Service (information)

C H A P T E R   1 3

QuickCheck A
1. SDLC (system development life cycle)
2. Systems analysts
3. Problem statement
4. CASE
5. System requirements
6. Prototype

QuickCheck B
1. Design (system design)
2. Application development tool
3. RFP (request for proposal)
4. RFQ (request for quotation)
5. Application

QuickCheck C
1. Programming (software engineering)
2. Knowledge engineering
3. Unit
4. Integration
5. Test area
6. System

QuickCheck D
1. Procedure handbook
2. Conversion software
3. System conversion
4. Direct
5. Parallel
6. Phased
7. Pilot
8. Acceptance

QuickCheck E
1. Maintenance
2. Eighty (80)
3. Bugs (fixing bugs, support)
4. Cost-effective
5. SDLC (system development life cycle)

Interactive Summary
1. Analysis
2. Life
3. Analyze
4. Team
5. Problem
6. Success
7. Design
8. Application
9. Proposal
10. Quotation

1. Construction
2. Development
3. Unit
4. Integration
5. System
6. Implementation
7. Acceptance
8. Maintenance
9. System
10. Desk

Interactive Quizzes
1. Analysts
2. Performance
3. Structured
4. CASE
5. False
6. Direct
7. Maintenance

1. Data flow diagram (DFD)
2. Three (3)
3. Customer
4. Flows
5. Store

C H A P T E R   1 4

QuickCheck A
1. Variable-length, (memo)
2. Character
3. Numeric
4. Type, occurrence
5. Flat
6. True

QuickCheck B
1. Model
2. Cardinality
3. One
4. Hierarchical (hierarchical database)
5. False
6. Relational
7. True

QuickCheck C
1. Custom
2. Data independence
3. Object-oriented
4. Database management
5. Client/server
6. False

QuickCheck D
1. Field format
2. Range check
3. Redundancy
4. Case-sensitive
5. Query
6. Warehouse
7. Index

Interactive Summary
1. Field
2. Type
3. Record
4. Entity
5. Flat file
6. Database
7. Relationships (relationship)
8. Cardinality
9. Hierarchical
10. Network
11. Relational
12. Object-oriented
13. Methods

1. Custom
2. File
3. Database
4. Language (languages)
5. Redundancy
6. Range

Interactive Quizzes
1. Type, occurance
2. True
3. Relational
4. Independence
5. False
6. Character
7. Sort
8. Index
9. Boolean

1. Nine (9)
2. 96
3. 48,000
4. 1,500
5. No
6. Bonus points

C H A P T E R   1 5

QuickCheck A
1. Software engineer (computer programmer)
2. False
3. Problem statement
4. Algorithm (computer program)
5. Pseudocode
6. Flowchart

QuickCheck B
1. Coding
2. Sequence
3. Selection (decision, branch)
4. Repetiton (loop, iteration)

QuickCheck C

1. Testing (debugging)
2. Syntax
3. Run-time
4. Logic
5. Remarks
6. Program, reference (user)

QuickCheck D

1. Procedural
2. Declarative
3. Low-level (machine, assembly)
4. Source
5. Interpreter
6. Event-driven (object-oriented)
7. Components
8. Event (program event)

Interactive Summary

1. Engineering
2. Programming
3. Assumptions
4. Known
5. Algorithm
6. Coding
7. Sequence
8. Selection (decision, branch)
9. Repetition (loop, iteration)

1. Syntax
2. Run-time
3. Logic
4. Documentation (program documentation)

5. Declarative
6. Scripting

Interactive Quizzes

1. Flowchart
2. Subroutine
3. Loop
4. Remark
5. Syntax
6. Compiler
7. Event
8. Component
9. False

1. 170
2. 190
3. 100
4. 125
5. 150
6. 140
7. 130
8. 200

GLOSSARY

16-color graphic A digital image in which each pixel can have one of 16 colors. 453

24-bit color graphic Also called true-color graphic, a photographic-quality graphic that can display up to 16.7 million colors. It requires 24 bits for each pixel. 453

256-color graphic A digital image in which each pixel can have one of 256 colors. 453

3-D graphics software The software used to create three-dimensional wireframe objects, then render them into images. 68

4GL A programming language (fourth-generation language) that contains built-in commands for complex tasks such as sorting data or creating columnar reports. 582

Absolute reference In a worksheet formula, cell references (usually preceded by a $ symbol) that cannot change as a result of a move or copy operation. 125

Accelerated graphics card A type of graphics card that contains special circuitry to increase the speed at which graphics can be displayed. 264

Acceptable use policy A set of rules and regulations that specify how a computer system should be used and set the penalties for misuse. 407

Acceptance testing The final phase of testing for a new information system, in which the system's new owner determines whether the system performs as required. 593

Access time The estimated time for a storage device to locate data on a disk, usually measured in milliseconds. 180

Accounting The process of tracking the flow of money through an organization (see also Financial management). 537

Accumulator A part of the ALU that holds the results of processing operations until they can be sent to RAM. 221

Active matrix screen A type of LCD technology that produces a clear, sharp image because each pixel is controlled by its own transistor. 264

Active Server Page A method used to allow access to a Web-based database by creating Web pages that contain program code for data access. 635

ActiveX controls A set of commands and components that can be used by programmers to add interactive features to Web pages. 365

Adaptive pattern substitution A compression technique that replaces repetitive patterns of bytes with a shorter sequence of bytes, producing a sort of "short hand" that can later be reconstructed into the original data. 464

Address lines The circuitry on the data bus that carries a signal indicating the location or address of data. 214

ADSL service Asymmetric digital subscriber line. A telephone company service that offers digital communication over existing telephone lines. 505

AGP Short for accelerated graphics port, an AGP is a type of interface, or slot, that provides a high-speed pathway for advanced graphics. 231

Algorithm An abstract or general procedure for solving a problem, typically expressed as pseudocode, structured English, or a flowchart. 671

Alpha test One of the first phases of software testing, usually conducted by the software publisher's in-house testing team. 275

ALU (arithmetic logic unit) The part of the CPU that performs arithmetic and logical operations on the numbers stored in its registers. 221

Amplitude The distance from the baseline to the peak of a sound wave. Amplitude is a measure of a wave's strength, or volume. 489

Analog device A device that operates on continuously varying data, such as a dimmer switch or a watch with a sweep second hand. 211

Animated GIF A type of GIF image that displays a sequence of frames to create the appearance of continuous motion. 357

ANSI A character representation code devised by the American National Standards Institute (ANSI). The code is similar to ASCII, but uses eight, instead of seven, bits to represent each character. 450

Antivirus software A computer program used to scan a computer's memory and disks to identify, isolate, and eliminate viruses. 403

Applet A program created using Java or J++, that contains customized Web page controls. 697

Application development tool Software, such as 4GLs, expert system shells, and component objects that can be assembled into the applications software for an information system. 582

Application server A network server that runs a specific application program, usually a database application, and carries out processing tasks as directed by workstations. 321

Application software Computer programs that help you perform a specific task such as word processing. Also called application programs, applications, or programs. 66

Application specifications A detailed description of the way that the software for an information system should interface with the user, store data, process data, and format reports. 586

Application testing The process of testing newly developed application software by running unit tests, integration tests, and system tests. 589

Application-specific filename extension A filename extension that is associated with the files created using a specific software program, such as the .doc extension associated with Microsoft Word files. 166

Archiving The process of moving infrequently-used data off a primary storage device to a storage medium such as a CD-ROM. 189

ARPANET A network created in 1969 by the Advanced Research Projects Agency (ARPA), ARPANET was the first network to use the technology that is the basis for today's Internet. 346

Artificial intelligence (AI) A characteristic of computers that exhibit human-like intelligence or behaviors. A field of research that includes robotics, expert systems, and speech recognition. 33

ASCII American Standard Code for Information Interchange A code that represents characters as a series of 1s and 0s. Most computers use ASCII code to represent text, making it possible to transfer data between computers. 212

ASCII file A file that contains text data that is stored using the ASCII code. 449

Assumption In the context of programming, a condition that you accept to be true, which often places limits on the scope of the programming problem. 669

Asynchronous protocol A data transmission method in which the sender and receiver are not synchronized by a clock signal and must use start and stop bits to control the beginning and ending of transmissions. 494

Asynchronously A term referring to communication that does not take place in real time. One person posts a message, then other people respond whenever they log on. Contrast to "synchronously." 361

Attributes In the context of a relational database, the columns of data equivalent to fields. 627

Auditing In spreadsheet terminology, the process of testing a worksheet to make sure that it produces accurate results. 124

Automation The use of electrical or mechanical devices to accomplish a task; in a business, using computers to improve manufacturing or other processes. 538

Backup A backup is a duplicate copy of a file, disk, or tape. Also refers to a Windows utility that allows you to create and restore backups. 420

Backup software The software used to specify the folders and files that should be included when making a backup of hard disk data. 421

Bandwidth The data transmission capacity of a communications channel. The bandwidth of a digital signal is measured in bits per second; of an analog signal in Hertz. 491

Benchmark test A set of tests used to measure computer hardware or software performance. 256

Beta test A testing phase near the end of the software development process in which a software product is tested in real-world computer environments, often by end-users. 275

Binary codes Any code that represents data using only two states, such as 0 and 1. 448

Binary number system A method for representing numbers using only two digits, 0 and 1. Contrast this system to the decimal system, which uses ten digits: 0, 1, 2, 3, 4, 5, 6, 7,8, and 9. 212

Biometrics Biological measurements, such as fingerprinting, that are used in the context of computers to verify a person's identity. 410

Bit A bit is the smallest unit of information handled by a computer. A bit can hold one of two values, either a 0 or a 1. Eight bits comprise a byte which can represent a letter or number. 174

Bitmap display A monitor or other display device that uses an on-screen matrix of pixels to display text and graphics. 28

Bitmap image An image, such as a digital photo, that is stored as a grid work of colored dots. 68

Black hole An error on a DFD that depicts a process that has no output. 599

Block In data communications, a series of bits. Typically one or more bytes of data. 494

BNC connector The silver or gold connector on a coaxial cable. Looks similar to a cable television connector. 318

Boolean operators The operators AND, OR, and NOT. 645

Boolean string A sequence of key words, field names and logical operators that specify a query. 645

Boot process The sequence of events that occurs within a computer system between the time the user starts the computer and the time it is ready to process commands. 234

Boot sector virus A computer virus that infects the sectors on a disk that contain the data a computer uses during the boot process. The virus spreads every time the infected disk is in the computer when it boots. 398

Bootable floppy disk A disk that contains essential operating system files and that can be used to boot a computer. 237

Broadband A term used to refer to communications channels that have high bandwidth. 491

Bus topology A straight-line configuration of cables or other communications pathways that creates a shared pathway from one node to another. 492

Business An organization that seeks profit by providing goods and services. 536

Business process redesign (BPR) A technique for improving a business by making radical changes to existing business procedures or organizational structure. 539

Button An on-screen user interface element that simulates the action of a push button. By clicking the button, a user initiates a command or action. 23

Byte An eight-bit unit of information that represents a single character. 174

Cable modem A communications device that can be used to connect a computer to the cable TV infrastructure. 509

Cache Special high-speed memory that gives the CPU more rapid access to data (also called RAM cache or cache memory). 226

Capacitors Electronic circuit components that store an electrical charge; in binary code, a charged capacitor represents an "on" bit, and a discharged one represents an "off" bit. 215

Cardinality A description of the numeric relationship (one-to-one, one-to-many, or many-to-many) that exists between two record types. 623

Case sensitivity A condition in which uppercase letters are not equivalent to their lowercase counterparts. 639

CASE tool (Computer Aided Software Engineering) Software that is used to summarize requirements, diagram information systems, schedule development tasks, prepare documentation, and develop computer programs. 580

CD-R An acronym for compact disc-recordable. CD-R is a type of optical disk technology that allows the user to create CD-ROMs and audio CDs. 189

CD-ROM A storage device that uses laser technology to read data from a CD-ROM. 188

CD-ROM disk A high capacity read-only optical disk that can store up to 680 MB of data. An acronym for compact disc read-only memory. 12

CD-ROM drive A storage device that uses laser technology to read data from a CD-ROM. 12

CD-RW An acronym for compact disc-rewritable. CD-RW is a type of optical disk technology that allows the user to write data onto a CD, then change that data much like on a floppy or hard disk. 189

Cell In spreadsheet terminology, the intersection of a column and a row; in cellular communications, a limited geographical area surrounding a cellular phone tower. 121

Cell reference The column letter and row number that designates the location of a worksheet cell. For example, the cell reference C5 refers to a cell in column C, row 5. 121

Cellular modem A modem that can be used to connect a computer to a cellular phone for data transmission and Internet access. 507

Central processing unit (CPU) The main processing unit in a computer, consisting of circuitry that executes instructions to process data. 5

CGI (Common Gateway Interface) An interface that allows a user to access a Web-based database from a Web browser. 635

Chaos theory The theory of complex dynamic nonlinear systems, which encompasses the qualitative study of unstable behavior in complex systems. 560

Character data Letters, symbols, or numerals that will not be used in arithmetic operations (name, social security number, etc.). 212

Character data type A data type assigned to fields in a data file containing data that does not need to be mathematically manipulated (also called string data type). 617

Character representation The way in which non-numeric data, such as a letter of the alphabet, is represented by a series of bits. 449

Character representation code A series of bits that represents a letter, symbol, or numeral (also called simply "code"). These codes include ASCII, EBCDIC, ANSI, and Unicode. 449

Character-based display Method of display in which the monitor screen is divided into a grid of rectangles, each of which can display a single character from the standard character set. 28

Chat group A discussion in which a group of people communicate online simultaneously. 361

Check box An on-screen box that allows the user to select options clicking the box. 22

Checksum A value, calculated by combining all the bytes in a file, that is used by virus detection programs to identify whether any bytes have been altered. 403

Chief information officer (CIO) The highest-ranking executive responsible for information systems. 575

Child node In a hierarchical database, a record type connected to a record type higher up in the hierarchy. 625

Chip package The housing for an integrated circuit, a chip package can be a single DIP or PGA, or it can include a circuit board as in a DIMM or SEC. 209

Circuit switching The method used by the telephone network to temporarily connect one telephone with another for the duration of a call. 504

CISC A general-purpose microprocessor chip designed to handle a wider array of instructions than a RISC chip. CISC stands for complex instruction set computer. 227

Class In object-oriented programming, a group with specific characteristics to which an object belongs. 628

Client/server architecture A network architecture in which processing is split between workstations (clients) and the server. 321

Clip art Graphics designed to be inserted into documents, Web pages, and worksheets, usually available in CD-ROM or Web-based collections. 113

Cluster A group of sectors on a storage medium that, when accessed as a group, speed up data access. 177

CMOS memory A type of battery-powered integrated circuit that holds semi-permanent configuration data (acronym for complementary metal oxide semiconductor). 218

Coaxial cable A type of cable in which a center wire is surrounded by a grounded shield of braided wire. Used in connecting nodes on a network with silver BNC connectors on both ends (also called coax cable). 318

Codec Short for COmpressor/DECompressor, a hardware or software routine that compresses and decompresses digital graphics, sound, and video files. 462

Coding The process of using a computer language to express an algorithm. 677

Collision A disruption of communication that occurs when two packets are sent at the same time. 513

Color depth The number of bits that determines the range of possible colors that can be assigned to each pixel. For example, an 8-bit color depth can create 256 colors. 264

Command An instruction that the user inputs into the computer to tell it to carry out a task. 20

Command-line interface A type of user interface that requires the user to type in commands. 20

Commercial information services Companies that provide access to computer-based information, for a fee (for example, America Online, CompuServe, Microsoft Network, and Prodigy). 356

Commercial software Copyrighted computer applications sold to consumers for profit. 52

Communications channel Any pathway between the sender and receiver, channel may refer to a physical medium or a frequency. 490

Communications medium The material that carries one or more communications channels and provides a link between transmitting and receiving devices (for example, twisted-pair, coaxial, and fiber-optic cable). 490

Communications protocol A set of rules that ensures the orderly and accurate transmission and reception of data. 493

Communications software Computer programs that interact with a computer's modem to dial up, and establish a connection with, a remote computer. 73

Communications system A combination of hardware, software, and connecting links that transports data. 488

Compatible platforms Computer brands or models that operate in essentially the same way, use the same software, and accept the same peripheral devices. 13

Competitive upgrade A special price offered to consumers who switch from one company's software product to the new version of a competitor's product. 276

Compiled language A computer language that must be compiled to produce executable program code. 691

Compiler Software that translates a program written in a high-level language into low-level instructions before the program is executed. 691

Component object An application development tool in the form of a pre-programmed software module that a programmer can combine with basic program code to create software for an information system. 582

Component programming Using components to create a program. 695

Components In object-oriented programming, prewritten objects that programmers can customize and add to their own programs. See Component object. 695

Compressed volume A disk volume that contains files, which have been recoded by means of disk compression in order to use storage space more efficiently. 462

Compression ratio A measurement of the amount of shrinkage that occurs when data is compressed. 462

Computer A device that accepts input, processes data, stores data, and produces output. 5

Computer architecture The design and construction of a computer that is the basis for designating its platform. 208

Computer engineering A career that focuses on the design and development of computer hardware and peripheral devices. 284

Computer industry The corporations and individuals that supply goods and services to people and organizations that use computers. 273

Computer industry trade journals Publications about computing and computers that target computer professionals.

Computer magazines Publications that contain articles and advertisements about computing, computers, and other computer equipment.

Computer network A collection of computers and related devices, connected in a way that allows them to share data, hardware, and software. 15

Computer platform A hardware and software configuration shared by a group of computers that use the same software and peripheral devices. 13

Computer program A set of detailed, step-by-step instructions that tells a computer how to solve a problem or carry out a task. 46

Computer programmer A person who codes or writes computer programs. 677

Computer programming The process of writing instructions that direct a computer to carry out a specific task. 667

Computer programming language A standardized set of specific English-like phrases or predefined instructions used for writing computer programs. 65

Computer retail store A store that typically sells several brands of computers from a store-front location, such as a mall or shopping center. 278

Computer science A career field that focuses on developing fast and efficient computers, from their construction, to their programming and operating systems. 284

Computer virus A program designed to attach itself to a file, reproduce, and spread from one file to another, destroying data, displaying an irritating message, or otherwise disrupting computer operations. 397

Computerization The control, processing, and storage of information by means of an automated electronic device. 538

Computer-related jobs Jobs in the computer industry that are similar to jobs in other industries (computer sales, high-tech recruiting, etc.). 283

Computer-specific jobs Jobs that are unique to the computer industry (computer programmer, Webmaster, etc). 283

Computer-use jobs Jobs that require the use of computers to accomplish tasks in fields other than computing (laboratory technician, accountant, etc.). 283

Computing journals Computer publications that target academia, contain fairly technical information, and do not typically carry advertisements.

Concordance An alphabetized list of words in a document and the frequency with which each word appears. 116

Concurrent-use license Legal permission for an organization to use a certain number of copies of a software program at the same time. 53

Connection speed The maximum speed at which your modem communicates with your ISP's modem. This speed can be considerably less than your modem's top speed. 372

Connectivity software A category of application software that includes communications software, remote control software, e-mail software, and Web browsers. 73

Control structures Instructions that specify the sequence in which a program is to be executed: sequence, selection, and repetition controls. 678

Control unit The part of the ALU that directs and coordinates processing. 222

Controller A circuit board in a hard drive that positions the disk and read-write heads to locate data. 258

Conversion software Programs used to read data and convert it into a format that is usable by a different computer system. 591

Cookie A message sent from a Web server to a browser and stored on a user's hard disk, usually containing information about the user. 415

Copy disk A utility program that duplicates the contents of an entire floppy disk. 420

Copy utility A program that copies one or more files. 420

Copyright A form of legal protection that grants certain exclusive rights to the author of a program or the owner of the copyright. 50

Crackers People who break into a computer system with intent to damage files or steal data. 396

CRT (cathode ray tube) A display technology that uses a large vacuum tube, similar to that used in television sets. Although CRT technically refers to the vacuum tube, it is often used to refer to the entire monitor. 262

CSMA/CD Carrier sense multiple access with collision detection. A method used by Ethernet networks to deal with collisions. 513

Cursor A symbol, usually an underline, that marks the user's place on the screen and shows where typing will appear. 26

Custom software Software that has been written specifically to meet the needs of a particular user. 630

Cyberpunks People who break into computers, especially Internet computers, to steal data, modify files, or plant viruses. 396

Cyberspace A term coined in 1984 by science-fiction writer William Gibson to describe a computer-generated conceptual environment shared among computers. 345

Cylinder A vertical stack of tracks on a hard disk. 183

Data In the context of computing and data management, data refers to the symbols that a computer uses to represent facts and ideas. 5, 160

Data access software The interface used to search for information in a database. 134

Data bus An electronic pathway or circuit that connects the electronic components (mainly the processor and RAM) on a computer's motherboard. 214

Data communications The process of transmitting and receiving data in an orderly way. 488

Data compression The process of condensing data so that it requires fewer bytes of storage space. 462

Data dictionary A tool used by systems analysts to document detailed descriptions of the data that flows through an information system and the data that is stored by that system. 579

Data file A file containing words, numbers, and/or pictures that the user can view, edit, save, send, and/or print. 164

Data flow diagram (DFD) A diagram that illustrates how data moves through an information system. 578

Data flows On a DFD, a line with an arrow on the end, which indicates the direction in which data flows. 578

Data-grade cable Types of cable suitable for data transmission, such as Category 5 UTP or STP cable. 496

Data independence The separation of data from the programs that manipulate the data. 631

Data lines The wires in the data bus that carry the signals that represent data. 214

Data management The tasks associated with maintaining and accessing data stored in data files. 616

Data mining Analyzing data to discover patterns and relationships that are important to decision making. 640

Data model A description of the way that data is stored in a database, often depicted graphically with a data structure diagram. 623

Data redundancy Repetition of data within a database. 638

Data security Techniques that provide protection for data. 406

Data store A filing cabinet, disk or tape that holds data. On a DFD usually represented by an open-ended rectangle. 578

Data transfer rate The amount of data that a storage device can move from a storage medium to computer memory in one second. 180

Data type Used to specify the type of data that can be entered into a field in a data file; data types include character, numeric, date, logical, and memo. 617

Data warehousing Collecting vast amounts of data. 640

Database Popularly refers to any collection of information; technically, a collection of data in related files or record types treated as a single unit. 71, 132, 621

Database administrator A person who supervises database design, development, testing, and maintenance. 622

Database management system (DBMS) Application software that assists the user in manipulating, storing, and maintaining database files. 632

Database models A conceptual model of the structure for a database; models include hierarchical, network, relational, and object-oriented. 624

Database software The application software used to create and manage a database. 71

Date data type A data type that indicates that the data in a field represents a date. 617

Debugging The process of testing a section of code and correcting errors. 684

Decision model A numerical representation of a realistic situation, such as a cash flow model of a business. 552

Decision query A question or set of instructions that describes the data that needs to be gathered to make a decision. 552

Decision support system (DSS) A computer system that allows decision makers to manipulate data directly, to incorporate data from external sources, and to create data models or "what-if" scenarios. 522

Declarative language A computer language that lets a programmer write a program by specifying a set of statements and rules that define the conditions for solving a problem. 689

Decompressing The process of expanding compressed data files (also called uncompressing, extracting, and expanding). 462

Dedicated file server A file server devoted solely to the task of distributing programs and data files to workstations. 319

Dedicated line A permanent telecommunications connection between two locations (also called a leased line). 505

Default drive The drive that a computer attempts to read from or write to unless an alternate drive is specified. 237

Default printer The printer to which your PC sends documents unless an alternative printer is specified. 316

Defragmentation utility A software tool used to rearrange the files on a disk so that they are stored in continuous clusters. 179

Demodulation The process of changing a received signal back to its original state (for example when a modem changes an audio signal back to a digital pulse). 505

Desktop microcomputer A computer that is built around a single microprocessor chip and is small enough to fit on a desk. 8

Desktop publishing software Software used to create high-quality output suitable for commercial printing. DTP software provides precise control over layout. 67

Desktop video Videos stored in digital format on a PC's hard disk or CD. 83

Detail report An organized list generated by a management information system (for example, an inventory list). 551

Device driver The software that provides the computer with the means to control a peripheral device. 65

Device letter The unique character by which each of the computer's storage devices can be identified. For example, the floppy disk drive is usually assigned device letter A. 168

DHTML DHTML (dynamic HTML) is a variation of the HTML format that allows elements of Web pages to be changed while they are being viewed. 365

Dialog box An on-screen window that provides options associated with a command. 22

Dial-up connection A connection that uses a phone line to establish a temporary Internet connection. 349

Differential backup A copy of all the files that have changed since the last full backup of a disk. 423

Digital animation A series of frames, stored as digital images. When displayed in sequence, the series of frames creates the illusion of movement. 82

Digital certificate A security method that identifies the author of an ActiveX control. A computer programmer can "sign" a digital certificate after being approved. 414

Digital device A device that works with discrete (distinct or separate) numbers or digits. 211

Digital video Video footage that has been converted into digital format so it can be stored, modified, and displayed on a computer screen. 82

DIMM Short for dual in-line memory module, a DIMM is a small circuit board that holds RAM chips. A DIMM has a 64-bit path to the memory chips. 216

Direct conversion The simultaneous deactivation of an old computer system and activation of a new one. 592

Direct satellite service (DSS) A service that uses a geosynchronous or low-earth orbit satellite to send television, voice, or computer data directly to satellite dishes owned by individuals. 510

Directory A list of files contained on a computer storage device. 169

Discussion group Online communications in which multiple participants interact asynchronously to share views on a specific issue or topic (for example, a cat lovers' discussion group). 361

Disk cache Part of RAM used to temporarily hold information read from a disk, speeding up processing. 185

Disk compression A type of data compression that shrinks files and places them in a special volume on the hard disk. 462

Disk density The closeness of the particles on a disk surface. As density increases, the particles are packed more tightly together and are usually smaller. 181

Disk drive A computer storage device that records and retrieves data on disks. Drive types include floppy, Zip, and hard disk drives. 12

Disk volume A disk or an area of a disk that has a unique name and is treated as a separate disk. 462

Dithering A means of reducing the size of a graphics file by reducing the number of colors. Dithering uses patterns composed of two or more colors to produce the illusion of additional colors and shading. 454

DMA Short for direct memory access, DMA refers to specialized circuitry that transfers data between drives and RAM, bypassing the CPU. 258

Document production software Computer programs that assist the user in composing, editing, designing, and printing documents. 104

Document template A preformatted document into which the user types text. 110

Document wizards Tools that take the user step-by-step through the process of entering text in a wide variety of documents. 111

Documentation A permanent record that explains how a computer program works. 684

Domain name Short for ""fully qualified domain name;"" an identifying name by which host computers on the Internet are familiarly known (for example, ""cocacola.com""). 350

DOS DOS (disk operating system) was the operating system software shipped with the first IBM PCs, then used on millions of computers until the introduction of Microsoft Windows. 62

Dot matrix printer A printer that creates characters and graphics by striking an inked ribbon with small wires called ""pins,"" generating a fine pattern of dots. 271

Dot pitch The diagonal distance between colored dots on a display screen. Measured in millimeters, dot pitch helps to determine the quality of an image displayed on a monitor. 263

Double-density (DD) disk A type of floppy disk with a higher storage capacity than single-density disks due to increased disk density. 182

Double-sided (DS) disk A floppy disk that stores data on both the top and bottom sides of the disk. 181

Downloading The process of transferring a copy of a file from a remote computer to another computer's disk drive. 359

Downstream In direct satellite service terminology, the direction in which DirecPC satellites transmit, from the satellite to the user. 510

Downtime Time during which a computer system is not functioning. 416

Downwardly compatible The ability of an operating system to run application software designed for earlier versions of the operating system, but not those designed for later versions. 85

Dpi Dpi refers to the resolution of an image. Images with more dots per inch (dpi) appear more realistic than images with fewer dots per inch. 268

Drive mapping In network terminology, assigning a drive letter to a network server disk drive. 310

Drop-down list A list of options that is displayed when the user clicks an arrow button. 22

DSU (data service unit) A communications device that is used instead of a modem to connect a computer to a digital circuit, such as a T1 line. 505

Duty cycle The amount of output that can be expected from a printer, typically measured in pages per month. 268

DVD An optical storage medium similar in appearance and technology to a CD-ROM but with higher storage capacity. The acronym stands for "digital video disc" or "digital versatile disc." 12, 190

DVD disk An optical storage medium similar in appearance and technology to a CD-ROM but with higher storage capacity. The acronym stands for "digital video disc" or "digital versatile disc." 12

DVD drive (Digital Video Disc) An optical storage device that reads data from CD-ROM and DVD disks. 12

DVD+RW A DVD technology that allows users to record and change data on DVD disks. 190

DVD-RAM A blend of technologies that allow users to record data on a DVD disk. 190

DVD-ROM A DVD disk that contains data that has been permanently stamped on the disk surface. 190

EBCDIC (Extended Binary-Coded Decimal Interchange Code) A method by which digital computers represent character data. 213

Echoplex communication A communications technique in which communications are sent and then echoed back to the sender as a means of checking accuracy. 495

E-commerce Short for electronic commerce, it is the business of buying and selling products online. 369

E-commerce enabled Web site A Web site that is ready for e-commerce business as soon as you add product information and prices. These sites are typically provided for a monthly fee by Web hosting services. 370

E-commerce system A computer system that collects online orders, typically from a Web site, and processes credit card payments. 548

EIDE Short for enhanced integrated drive (or device) electronics, EIDE is a disk drive technology formally known as ATA. 258

Electronic publishing The manipulation, storage, and transmission of electronic documents by means of electronic media or telecommunications services. 114

E-mail Messages that are transmitted between computers over a communications network. Short for electronic mail. 327

E-mail address The network address for an individual's e-mailbox. Usually a user ID, an @ symbol, and the name of the e-mail server. 328

E-mail attachment A separate file that is transmitted along with an e-mail message. 331

E-mail client software Software that is installed on a client computer and has access to e-mail servers on a network. This software is used to compose, send, and read e-mail messages. 327

E-mail message A computer file containing a letter or memo that is transmitted electronically via a communications network. 327

E-mail server software The software that assists the e-mail server in organizing, sorting, and routing e-mail messages over a communications network. 327

E-mail software Software that manages one person's computer mailbox. 73

E-mail system The collection of computers and software that work together to provide e-mail services. 327

Employee empowerment Giving employees the authority to make business decisions. 539

Encryption The process of scrambling or hiding information so that it cannot be understood without the key necessary to change it back into its original form. 412

End-user procedures A set of formalized steps that a person must follow to perform a computing task. 407

Entity A person, place, thing, or event about which a user wants to store data. 618

Ethernet A type of network in which network nodes are connected by coaxial cable or twisted-pair wire; the most popular network architecture, it typically transmits data at 10 or 100 megabits per second. 317

Even parity In a parity bit error-checking protocol, the requirement that there be an even number of 1 bits in a data block. 493

Event-driven language A computer language that helps programmers create programs that continually check for, and respond to, program events. 694

Exabyte A quintillion bytes. 347

Exception report A report generated by a management information system, listing information that is outside normal or acceptable ranges, such as a reorder report showing low-stock inventory items. 551

Executable file A file, usually with an .exe extension, containing instructions that tell a computer how to perform a specific task. 163

Executive managers Managers responsible for making long-range plans and setting goals for an organization (also called senior managers). 543

Expanding The process of expanding compressed data files (also called uncompressing, extracting, and decompressing). 462

Expansion bus The segment of the data bus that transports data between RAM and peripheral devices. 229

Expansion card A circuit board that is plugged into a slot on a PC motherboard to add extra functions, devices, or ports. 230

Expansion port A socket into which the user plugs a cable from a peripheral device, allowing data to pass between the computer and the peripheral device. 232

Expansion slot A socket or "slot" on a PC motherboard designed to hold a circuit board called an expansion card. 230

Expert system A computer system incorporating knowledge from human experts, and designed to analyze data and produce a recommendation or decision (also called knowledge-based system). 553

Expert system shell A software tool used for developing expert system applications. 554

Export data The process by which a program transforms data into a format suitable for another program and then transmits it. 140

Expression A combination of symbols and characters that represents an operation or value to a computer. In database usage, an expression usually has a field name on the left and the information desired on the right. 648

External bay An opening in the computer case that allows the user to install a device, such as a floppy disk drive, that must be accessed from outside the case. 265

External entity A person, organization, or device that exists outside an information system, but provides it with input or receives output. On a DFD, usually represented by a square. 578

External information Information obtained by organizations from outside sources. 545

External services Services provided by the operating system that help users start programs, manage stored data, and maintain security. 57

Extracting The process of expanding compressed data files (also called uncompressing, expanding, and decompressing). 462

Feedhorn A component attached to a satellite dish, containing a microwave antenna in the form of a small metal probe. 502

Fiber-optic cable A bundle of thin tubes of glass used to transmit data as pulses of light. 498

Field The smallest meaningful unit of information contained in a data file. 617

Field format A specification for the way that data is displayed on the screen and printouts, usually using a series of Xs to indicate characters and 9s to indicate numbers. 636

Field name A name that identifies the contents of a field. 617

File A named collection of data (such as a computer program, document, or graphic) that exists on a storage medium such as a hard disk, floppy disk, or CD-ROM. 160

File allocation table (FAT) A special file that is used by the operating system to store the physical location of all the files on a storage medium, such as a hard disk or floppy disk. 177

File compression A type of data compression that shrinks one or more files into a single file that occupies less storage space than the files did separately. 463

File format The method of organization used to encode and store data in a computer. Text formats include DOC and TXT. Graphics formats include BMP, TIFF, GIF, and PCX. 444

File locking A process by which a network prevents two workstations from opening the same data file at the same time. 313

File management software Computer programs that help the user organize records, find records that match specific criteria, and print lists based on the information contained in records. 631

File manager utility software Software, such as Windows Explorer, that helps users locate, rename, move, copy, and delete files. 168

File naming conventions A set of rules, established by the operating system, that must be followed to create a valid filename. 161

File specification A combination of the drive letter, subdirectory, filename, and extension that identifies a file (for example, A:\word\filename.doc). Also called a "path." 170

File structure A description of the way in which data is stored in a file. 616

File virus A computer virus that infects executable files, that is programs with .exe filename extensions. 397

Filename A unique set of letters and numbers that identifies a file. 161

Filename extension A set of letters and/or numbers added to the end of a filename that helps to identify the file contents or file type. 161

Financial management The process of tracking the flow of money through an organization and making decisions about the best way to allocate available funds. 537

Firewall A method for preventing hostile programs, such as Java applets, from entering a network, usually by installing firewall software that filters out suspicious packets. 414

Fixed-length field A field in a data file that has a predetermined number of characters. 617

Flat file The electronic version of a box of index cards which stores information about one entity on each card. 71

Floppy disk A removable magnetic storage medium, typically 3.5" in size with a capacity of 1.44 MB. 12, 181

Floppy disk drive A storage device that writes data on, and reads data from, floppy disks. 12

Flowchart In software engineering, a graphical representation of the way a computer should progress from one instruction to the next when it performs a task. 674

Folders The subdirectories (a subdivision of a directory) that can contain files or other folders. 169

Font A typeface or style of lettering, such as Arial, Times New Roman, and Gothic. 112

Footer Text that appears in the bottom margin of each page of a document. 116

Formatting The process of dividing a disk into sectors so that it can be used to store information. 64

Formula In spreadsheet terminology, a combination of numbers and symbols that tells the computer how to use the contents of cells in calculations. 121

Fragmented When data in a file is stored in non-contiguous clusters. 179

Frame An outline or boundary, frequently defining a box. For document production software, a predefined area into which text or graphics may be placed. 113

Freeform database A loosely structured collection of information, usually stored as documents rather than as records. 133

Frequency The number of times per second the wave cycle of an electromagnetic wave repeats. 489

FTP client software Software that allows a user to upload and download files from a FTP server. Many browsers include download capability, but not upload capability. 359

FTP servers Computers that maintain a collection of data that can be transferred between two Internet computers using FTP (file transfer protocol). 352

Full backup A copy of all the files on a disk. 422

Full-duplex communication A system that allows messages to be sent and received simultaneously. 495

Function In worksheets, a built-in formula for making a calculation. In programming, a section of code that manipulates data, but is not included in the main sequential execution path of a program. 122, 680

Function key The keys numbered F1 through F12, located at the top of the computer keyboard, that activate program-specific commands. 26

Fuzzy logic A technique used by an expert system to deal with imprecise data by incorporating the probability that the input information is correct. 555

Gateway An electronic link that connects one computer system to another. 329

General accounting system A system that records the financial transactions of a business, keeping track of income, expenses, assets, and liabilities. 548

Generic filename extension A filename extension, such as .bmp or .txt, that indicates the type of data that a file contains, but does not indicate the specific program that was used to create the file. 165

Geosynchronous orbit (GEO) A type of orbit in which a satellite stays continuously above the same part of the earth by orbiting the earth at the same speed at which the earth rotates. 501

GIF Graphics Interchange Format. A bitmap graphics file format popularized by CompuServe for use on the Web. 467

Gigabyte (GB) Approximately one billion bytes; exactly 1,073,741,842 bytes. 180

Global updates The changing of data in more than one record at a time, by means of a computer. 641

Goods workers Employees who produce and manipulate physical objects. 541

Grammar checker A feature of word processing software that coaches the user on correct sentence structure and word usage. 109

Graphical object A small picture on the computer screen that the user can manipulate, using a mouse or other input device. 23

Graphical user interface (GUI) A type of user interface that features on-screen objects such as menus and icons, manipulated by a mouse. Abbreviated GUI (pronounced "gooey"). 24

Graphics card A circuit board inserted into a computer to handle the display of text, graphics, animation, and videos. Also called a "video card." 79, 230

Graphics software Computer programs for creating, editing, and manipulating images. 68

Grayscale graphics Digital images represented by shades of gray. 452

Ground station The earth-based equipment that sends signals to and receives signals from a communications satellite. 501

Groupware Software that provides ways for multiple users to collaborate on a project, usually through a pool of data that can be shared by members of the workgroup. 66

Hackers The term "hacker" once meant a computer hobbyist and has also been used to describe a computer novice. In most contexts today, it means a person who has gained illegal access into a computer system. 396

Half-duplex communication A communications technique that allows the user to alternately send and receive transmissions. 495

Hard disk One or more hard disk platters and their associated read-write heads (often used synonymously with hard disk drive). 183

Hard disk drive A computer storage device that contains a large-capacity "hard disk" sealed inside the drive case. A hard disk is NOT the same as a 3.5" removable disk that has a rigid plastic case. 12

Hard disk platter The component of the hard disk drive on which data is stored; a flat, rigid disk made of aluminum or glass and coated with a magnetic oxide. 183

Hardware Electronic and mechanical devices used for input, output, processing, and storing data. 7

Hardware redundancy Maintaining equipment that duplicates the functions of equipment critical to computing activities. 416

Head crash A collision between the read-write head and the surface of the hard disk platter, resulting in damage to some of the data on the disk. 185

Header Text that appears in the top margin of each page of a document, e.g., "Page 5". 116

Help desk Part of the IS department designated to assist users experiencing problems with their computers or applications. 595

Hierarchical database A database model in which record types are arranged as a hierarchy or tree of child nodes that can have only one parent node. 625

High-density (HD) disk A floppy disk that can store more data than a double-density disk. 181

High-level language A computer language that allows a programmer to write instructions using human-like language. 690

Home page (1) A document that is the starting, or entry, page at a Web site. (2) The Web page that a browser displays each time it is started. 351

Horizontal market software Any computer program that can be used by many different kinds of businesses (for example, an accounting program). 77

Host computer A central minicomputer or mainframe to which multiple terminals are attached. All processing takes place on the host computer. In Internet terminology, any computer connected to the Internet. 321

Hot swap Switching batteries or other plug-in devices while the computer is on. 267

HTML (Hypertext Markup Language) A standardized format used to display Web page documents. 115

HTML tag An instruction, such as <B>, inserted into an HTML document to provide formatting and display information to a Web browser. 364

Human resources management The management of matters relating to the personnel employed by an organization (for example, benefits and hiring). 537

Hypertext index A screen-based menu that allows the user to access information in specific categories by clicking a hypertext link. 135

Hypertext Transfer Protocol (HTTP) The communications system used to transmit Web pages. HTTP:// is an identifier that appears at the beginning of each Web page URL (for example, http://www.fooyong.com). 351

I/O (input/output) The circuitry that allows a computer to collect data (input) and the transportation of the results to display, print, or storage devices (output). 229

Icon A graphical representation of an object such as a disk, printer, or program. 23

Import data The process by which a program reads and translates data from another source. 140

Incremental backup A copy of the files that have changed since the last backup. 424

Index files Automatically created during the indexing process, an index file contains pointers that allow data to be accessed in an order other than the order of the original file. 642

Indexing Method of organizing records that maintains the records in their original order, but creates additional files called index files. 642

Inference engine Software that manipulates information in an expert system. 554

Information The words, numbers, and graphics used as the basis for human actions and decisions. 160

Information analysis tools Programs or utilities that help people to model problems (for example, spreadsheets and flow charts). 546

Information system Refers to a computer system that stores data and supplies information, usually within a business context. Also refers to the career field that focuses on developing such systems. 284, 535

Information systems department The part of a business or organization responsible for developing and maintaining the computers, data, and programs for an information system. 575

Information theory The study of the ways in which information can be represented or encoded. 444

Information workers Employees who produce and process information (for example, accountants, bookkeepers, and systems analysts). 541

Infrared transmissions A transmission technology that uses a frequency range just below the visible light spectrum to transport data. 500

Ink jet printer A non-impact printer that creates characters or graphics by spraying liquid ink onto paper or other media. 269

In-line spelling checker A spelling checker that checks for misspellings as you type. 108

In-place multimedia technology An Internet multimedia technology that plays a media element as part of a Web page. 357

Input As a noun, "input" means the information that is conveyed to a computer. As a verb, "input" means to enter data into a computer. 5

Input list A list of valid data items for a particular field, such as a list of state names, that allows the data entry person to select, rather than type, an entry. 639

Insertion point A flashing vertical bar that appears on the screen, indicating where the user can begin entering text. 26

Installation process In reference to software, the process by which programs and data are copied to the hard disk of a computer system. 85

Instruction Computer code that tells the computer to perform a specific arithmetic, logical, or control operation. 223

Instruction cycle The steps followed by a computer to process a single instruction; fetch, interpret, execute, then increment the instruction pointer. 224

Instruction pointer A sort of placeholder that the CPU's control unit uses to keep track of the location of the instructions that are scheduled for processing. 222

Instruction register A location in the CPU's control unit that holds a processing instruction retrieved from RAM. 222

Instruction set The collection of instructions that a CPU is designed to process. 223

Integer A whole number. 617

Integrated circuit (IC) A thin slice of silicon crystal containing microscopic circuit elements such as transistors, wires, capacitors, and resistors; also called chips and microchips. 209

Integration testing The testing of the completed modules of an application, to ensure that they operate together correctly. 589

Internal bay A location inside the system unit case where devices that do not need to be accessed from outside the case can be installed. 265

Internal information Information obtained by an organization from its own resources, such as the accounting or personnel departments. 545

Internal services Functions run by the operating system without user input, such as allocation of system resources and detection of equipment failure. 57

Internet The worldwide communication infrastructure that links computer networks using TCP/IP protocol. 16

Internet backbone The major communications links that form the core of the Internet. 348

Internet communications software Computer programs that allow a computer to transmit and receive data using the Internet TCP/IP communications protocol. 373

Internet host A computer that is permanently connected to the Internet and acts as a Web server, FTP server, e-mail server, or router. 347

Internet traffic The number of bytes transmitted from one Internet computer to another. 347

Interpreted language A computer language that uses an interpreter rather than a compiler to generate code that the computer can execute. 692

Interpreter A program that reads an instruction written in an interpreted language and converts it into a machine language instruction, which the computer executes. 692

Intraframe compression A technique in which each frame in a video file is shrunk through the use of a standard graphics compression format such as JPEG. 468

Intranet A LAN that uses TCP/IP communications protocols, typically for communications services within a business or organization. 511

IP address A unique identifying number assigned to each computer connected to the Internet. 350

IPX/SPX Internetwork packet exchange. The network communications protocol used by Novell NetWare. 515

IRC servers An Internet Relay Chat (IRC) computer that offers real-time chat over the Internet. 352

ISA (Industry Standard Architecture) A standard for moving data on the expansion bus. Can refer to a type of slot, a bus, or a peripheral device. An older technology, it is rapidly being replaced by PCI architecture. 231

ISAPI Internet Server Application Program Interface; a high-performance interface used to interact with Web-based databases. 635

ISDN service Integrated services digital network. A telephone company service that transports data digitally over dial-up or dedicated lines. 505

ISP (Internet service provider) A company that provides Internet access to businesses, organizations, and individuals. 349

Java A platform-independent, object-oriented, high-level programming language based on C++, typically used to produce interactive Web applications. 365

Java applet Small programs that add processing and interactive capabilities to Web pages. 414

JPEG Short for Joint Photographic Experts Group, a format that uses lossy compression to store bitmap images. JPEG files have a .jpg extension. 467

Justification The alignment of text against the right, left, or both margins. 112

Just-in-time inventory management The business practice of ordering inventory just before it is needed. Pioneered by Japanese firms, JIT as it is sometimes called, reduces the amount of money that a business ties up in inventory. 539

Key In the context of data encryption, a key is the method used to encrypt or decipher information as in which numbers in a code match each letter of the alphabet. 412

Keyboard An arrangement of letter, number, and special function keys that acts as the primary input device to a computer. 12

Keyboard shortcut A combination of keys, such as Ctrl+C, that allows the user to activate a program function without clicking a series of menu options. 26

Keyword search engine A means of accessing data about a particular subject, by searching for a significant word or keyword relevant to that subject. 136

Kilobyte (KB) Approximately one thousand bytes; exactly 1,024 bytes. 180

Knowledge base The collection of facts and rules obtained from experts that forms the information base of an expert system. 554

Knowledge engineering The process of designing, entering rules into, and testing rules in an expert system. 588

Known information In a problem statement, information supplied to the computer to help it solve a problem. 670

Laser printer A printer that uses laser-based technology, similar to that used by photocopiers, to produce text and graphics. 270

LCD (Liquid Crystal Display) A type of flat panel computer screen, typically found on notebook computers. 262

Level 1 cache (L1 cache) Cache memory built into a microprocessor chip. L1 cache can typically be read in one clock cycle. 256

Level 2 cache (L2 cache) Cache memory that is located in a chip separate from the microprocessor chip. 256

Line-of-sight communication Communication in which the transmitter must have an unobstructed path to the receiver for transmission to take place. 500

Links Underlined areas of text that allow users to jump between Web pages. 354

Linux A server operating system that is a derivative of Unix and available as freeware. 63

Local area network (LAN) An interconnected group of computers and peripherals located within a relatively limited area, such as building or a campus. 308

Local communications The process of sending electronic data over a short distance, such as from your computer to your printer. 488

Local resources The memory, storage, and peripheral devices attached to an individual user's workstation on a network. 308

Localization The modification of software for use in specific countries, often through the use of Unicode, which provides the ability to represent the alphabets of non-English languages. 450

Logic bomb A computer program that is triggered by the appearance or disappearance of specific data (for example, when the word "terminated" appears in an employee's record or when a password begins with the letters "DB"). 400

Logic error A run-time error in the logic or design of a computer program. 685

Logical data type A data type specifying that a field in a data file is used to store true/false or yes/no data. 617

Lossless compression A compression technique that provides the means to reconstitute all of the data in the original file, hence "lossless" means that this compression technique does not lose data. 467

Lossy compression Any data compression technique in which some of the data is sacrificed to obtain more compression. 467

Low-earth orbit (LEO) Type of orbit, used by many of the most recently launched communications satellites, about 1,000 miles above Earth. 501

Low-level language A computer language that requires a programmer to write instructions for specific hardware elements such as the computer processor, registers, and RAM locations. 690

MAC OS The operating system software designed for use on Apple Macintosh and iMac computers. 61

Machine language A low-level language written in binary code that the computer can execute directly. 690

Macintosh computer (Mac) A microcomputer platform manufactured primarily by Apple Computer Inc. and based on a proprietary architecture. 13

Macro A small set of instructions that automate a task. Typically, a macro is created by performing the task once and recording the steps. Whenever the macro is played back, the steps are repeated. 398

Macro virus A computer virus that infects the macros that are attached to documents and spreadsheets. (see macro) 398

Magnetic storage The recording of data onto disks or tape by magnetizing particles of an oxide-based surface coating. 175

Mail merge A feature of document production software that automates the process of producing customized documents such as letters and advertising flyers. 117

Mail-order supplier A merchant that takes orders by telephone or from an Internet site, then ships orders by mail or other courier service. 278

Mainframe A large, fast, and expensive computer generally used by businesses or the government to provide centralized storage processing and management for large amounts of data. 10

Management information system (MIS) A type of information system that manipulates the data collected by a transaction processing system to generate reports that managers can use to make business decisions. 550

| Exit | Home | Glossary | Jump Back | Jump To | ◀ Page | Page ▶ |

728   G L O S S A R Y

Managers People who make decisions about how an organization carries out its activities. 540

Manufacturer direct The selling of products by hardware manufacturers directly to consumers, by means of a sales force or mail order. 279

Many-to-many relationship A relationship in which one record in a particular record type can be related to more than one record in another record type, and vice versa. 624

Mathematical modeling software Software for visualizing and solving a wide range of math, science, and engineering problems. 70

Maximum resolution The maximum number of pixels a monitor can display, measured in number of horizontal pixels x number of vertical pixels. 263

Megabyte (MB) Approximately one million bytes; exactly 1,048,576 bytes. 180

Megahertz Megahertz (MHz) is a measure of frequency equivalent to one million cycles per second. 226

Members In a network database model, those record types related to another record type higher up in the network model. 626

Memo data type A data type that specifies that a field in a data file can contain variable-length text comments (also called memo field). 617

Memory The computer circuitry that holds data waiting to be processed. 5

Menu A list of commands or options. 21

Methods In an object-oriented database, the means by which objects are manipulated. 628

Microcomputer A category of computer that is built around a single microprocessor chip. The computers typically used in homes and small businesses (also called a personal computer). 8

Microprocessor An integrated circuit that contains the circuitry for processing data. It is a single chip version of the Central Processing Unit (CPU) found in all computers. 221

Microsoft Windows An operating system, developed by Microsoft Corporation, that provides a graphical interface. Versions include Windows 3.1, Windows 95, Windows 98, and Windows NT, and Windows 2000. 59

Microwave An electromagnetic wave with a frequency of at least 1 gigahertz. 501

Microwave transmission A technology in which a high-frequency radio signal is sent from a ground or satellite microwave-transmitting station to a microwave-receiving station. 501

Middle managers Managers responsible for designing ways to achieve the plans laid out by executive managers. 543

MIDI A standardized way in which sound and music are encoded and transmitted between MIDI devices. An acronym for musical instrument digital interface. 460

Millisecond (ms) A thousandth of a second. 180

Mils A measurement of the size of an integrated circuit, one mil is .001 inch. 220

Minicomputer A midrange computer, somewhat larger than a microcomputer, that can carry out processing tasks for many simultaneous users. 9

Miracle An error on a DFD, depicting a process that has no input. 599

Mission statement The written expression of an organization's goals and how those goals will be accomplished. 536

Modem A device that sends and receives data to and from computers over telephone lines. 230

Modulation The process of changing the characteristics of a signal (for example, when a modem changes a digital pulse into an analog signal). 505

Module A discrete sequence of instructions that performs activities or manipulates data but is not included in the main sequential execution path of a program. 680

Monitor A display device that forms an image by converting electrical signals from the computer into points of colored light on the screen. 12

Monochrome graphic A bitmap image that contains only the colors black and white. 451

Motherboard The circuit board in the computer that houses the chips that control the processing functions. 210

Motion compensation A video compression technique that stores only the data that changes between one video frame and the next. 468

Mouse An input device that allows the user to manipulate objects on the screen by moving the mouse on the surface of a desk. 12

MP3 MP3 is a type of audio compression that provides highly compressed audio files with very little loss of sound quality. 469

MP3 encoder Software that compresses a WAV file into an MP3 file. 469

MP3 player Software that plays MP3 music files. 469

MP3 ripper Software that converts the music on an audio CD to a WAV file. 469

MPEG A highly compressed file format for digital videos. MPEG is short for Moving Pictures Expert Group. Files in this format have a .mpg extension. 469

MTBF (mean time between failures) A measurement of reliability that is applied to computer components. MTBF is derived by dividing the number of failures in test equipment by the total time they were tested. 394

Multifunction printer An output device that combines printing capability with other functions, such as scanning, faxing, copying, and answering machine. 272

Multimedia An integrated collection of computer-based digital media, including text, graphics, sound, animation, photo images, and video. 78

Multimedia overlay technology An Internet multimedia technology that adds a separate window to the user's screen, in which multimedia elements appear. 358

Multi-mode cable A type of fiber-optic cable that has a 50-100 micron core. 499

Multi-player gaming Online gaming in which multiple players in various locations participate simultaneously. 362

Multiple-user license Legal permission for more than one person to use a particular software package. 52

Multisession support Allows a CD device to write data during more than one session or read data that has been written on a CD during more than one session. 189

Multitasking Running two or more programs at the same time. 59

Narrowband A term that refers to communications channels that have low bandwidth. 491

Natural language A language spoken by human beings, as opposed to an artificially constructed language such as machine language. 138

NetBIOS/NetBEUI A communications protocol developed by Microsoft. 515

Network access method A set of specifications that define how a network will physically transport data (for example, Ethernet and Token Ring). 513

Network access points (NAPs) Connections between network service providers on the Internet backbone. 348

Network administrator The person responsible for setting up user accounts and maintaining a network (also called network supervisor). 309

Network client software Programs that are installed on the local hard drive of each workstation to facilitate network interactions. Most desktop operating systems have built-in network client software. 323

Network communications protocol The communications protocol used on a particular network (see communications protocol.) 515

Network database A collection of physically linked records, in a one-to-many relationship, in which a member (child) can have more than one owner (parent). 626

Network hub A device that joins communications lines together. Typically used in computer networks as a point of connection for workstations, servers, and printers. 318

Network license Legal permission for the use of a software program by multiple users on a network. Similar to a multi-user or site license. 324

Network operating system (NOS) Programs designed to control the flow of data, maintain security, and keep track of accounts on a network. 323

Network patch cables A pre-made cable with connectors on each end, typically used to connect network devices to a hub. 517, 518

Network printer A printer on a network to which all network users can send output from their own workstations. 308

Network resources Processing capabilities, storage space, data, peripheral devices and application software available to users through a central server on a network. 308

Network server A computer connected to a network that "serves," or distributes, resources to the network users. 308

Network server software Programs installed on a file server that control file access from the server hard drive, manage the print queue, and track user data such as IDs and passwords. 323

Network service provider (NSP) A company that maintains a series of nationwide Internet links. 348

Neural network A type of expert system that uses computer circuitry to simulate the way in which the brain processes information, learns, and remembers. 555

NIC (network interface card) A small circuit board that sends data from a workstation out over a network, and collects incoming data for the workstation. 317

Node Each device on a network, including workstations, servers, and printers; in a hierarchical database, a segment or record type. 308, 625

Noise A disruption of data transmission, usually caused by electrical interference. 488

Non-dedicated file server A network computer that acts as both a server and a workstation. The use of non-dedicated servers is often called peer-to-peer capability. 320

Normalization The process of analyzing data to create the most efficient database structure. 638

Notebook computer A small lightweight portable computer that usually runs on battery power. Sometimes called a laptop. 8

Novell NetWare Operating system software designed specifically to run on microcomputer networks. 63

NSAPI Netscape Server Application Program Interface; a high-performance interface used to interact with Web-based databases. 635

Number A symbolic representation of a quantity, such as a value used in a calculation. 121

Numeric data Numbers that represent quantities and can be used in arithmetic operations. 212

Numeric data type A data type assigned to fields in a data file containing numbers that can be manipulated mathematically. 617

Numeric keypad A calculator-style input device for entering numbers and arithmetic symbols. Often part of a standard computer keyboard. 26

Object In an object-oriented database or programming language, a discrete piece of code describing a person, place, thing, event, or type of information. 628

Object code The low-level instructions that result from compiling source code. 691

Object ID number A unique identifier associated with a specific object in an object-oriented database. 639

Object-oriented database model A database model that organizes data into classes of objects that can be manipulated by programmer-defined methods. 628

Object-oriented DBMS Database management software used to construct an object-oriented database. 634

Object-oriented languages Programming languages that focus on the manipulation of objects rather than on the generation of procedure-based code. 693

Odd parity In a parity bit error-checking protocol, the requirement that there be an odd number of 1 bits in a data block. 493

Office automation system A system that automates or computerizes routine office tasks, such as producing documents, tracking schedules, making calculations, and facilitating interoffice communications. 547

Office suite A number of application programs that are packaged together and sold as a unit. 66

One-to-many relationship A relationship in which one record in a particular type may be related to more than one record of another record type. 624

One-to-one relationship An association between database entities in which one record type is related to one record of another type. 624

Online banking A means of using a computer and modem to conduct banking transactions, such as transferring funds among accounts and paying bills. 76

Online Help On-screen documentation that is available to a user while a software application is running. 29

Op code Short for operation code, an op code is a command word that designates an operation, such as add (ADD), compare (CMP), or jump (JMP). 223

Open reel tapes Large spools of computer tape that are sometimes used as a distribution medium for mainframe and minicomputer systems. 187

Operands An operand is the part of an instruction that specifies the data, or the address of the data, on which the operation is to be performed. 223

Operating system (OS) The software that controls the computer's use of its hardware resources, such as memory and disk storage space. 56

Operational planning The scheduling and monitoring of workers and processes. 543

Operations The primary activities of an organization, also called "production." 537

Operator error A mistake made by a computer user. 392

Optical fiber A single strand of glass tubing used in a fiber-optic cable. 498

Optical storage A means of recording data as light and dark spots on a CD, DVD, or other optical media. 176

Option button An on-screen control that allows a user to select one of two or more options in a dialog box. Also referred to as radio buttons. 22

Order-entry/invoice system A system that provides ways to input, view, modify, and delete customer orders. 548

Organization A group of people working together to accomplish a goal. 536

Outline feature A feature of document production software that helps the user develop a document as a hierarchy of headings and subheadings. 107

Output The results produced by a computer (for example, reports, graphs, and music). 5

Owner In a network database model, a record type that has relationships with other record types at lower levels of the network. 626

Packet switching A technology employed by data communications network, such as the Internet, whereby a message is divided into smaller units called "packets" for transmission. 511

Packets A small unit of data transmitted over a network or the Internet. 511

Paint software The software required to create and manipulate bitmap graphics. 69

Parallel computer A computer that has more than one processor and can process more than one instruction at a time. Also called non-von-Neumann machines. 228

Parallel conversion A type of system conversion in which the old computer system remains in service while some or all of the new system is activated. 592

Parallel processing A technique by which two or more processors in a computer perform processing tasks simultaneously. 228

Parallel transmission A method of communicating digital data in more than one bit of data is sent at the same time. 491

Parameter A delimiting variable used to modify a command, i.e., /ON modifies the DIR command so it displays files in order by name. 20

Parent node In a hierarchical database, a record type that has paths to other record types lower in the hierarchy. 625

Parity bit An bit added to the end of a data block to allow for error checking during data transmission (see Even parity and Odd parity). 493

Passive matrix screen A display found on older notebook computers that relies on timing to ensure that the liquid crystal cells are illuminated. 264

Password A special set of symbols used to restrict access to a user's computer or network. 15

Payload The disruptive instructions or message delivered by a computer virus. Payloads can range from just being annoying to destroying data and files on a computer system. 397

PC 1) A microcomputer that uses the Windows software and contains an Intel-compatible microprocessor. 2) A personal computer. 13

PCI (Peripheral Component Interconnect) A method for transporting data on the expansion bus. Can refer to type of data bus, expansion slot, or transport method used by a peripheral device. 231

PCMCIA card A small credit card-sized circuit board used to connect a modem, memory, network card, or storage device to a notebook computer. 265

PCMCIA slot A PCMCIA (Personal Computer Memory Card International Association) slot is an external expansion slot typically found on notebook computers. 265

PCX The PC Paintbrush file format that incorporates a compression algorithm. 467

Peer-to-peer The process by which one workstation/server shares resources with another workstation/server. Refers to the capability of a network computer to act as both a file server and as a workstation. 320

Peripheral devices Components and equipment that expand a computer's input, output, and storage capabilities, e.g., a printer or scanner. 7

Personal digital assistant (PDA) A computer that is smaller and more portable than a notebook computer (also called a palm-top computer). 8

Personal finance software Software geared toward individual finances that helps track bank account balances, credit card payments, investments, and bills. 76

Phase change technology A CD and DVD technology that uses disks with a modifiable crystal structure and allows users to add, modify, and delete data. 189

Phased conversion A type of information system conversion in which one module of a new information system is activated at a time. 592

Photo editing software The software used to edit, enhance, retouch, and manipulate digital photographs. 68

PIECES framework A concept developed by James Wetherbe, to help identify problems in an information system. Each letter of PIECES stands for a potential problem (Performance, Information, Economics, Control, Efficiency, and Service). 577

Pilot conversion A type of system conversion in which a new information system is first activated at one branch of a multi-branch company. 592

Pipelining A technology that allows a processor to begin executing an instruction before completing the previous instruction. 227

Pirated software Copyrighted software that is copied and used without authorization from the software developer. 50

Pixel Short for picture element, a pixel is the smallest unit in a graphic image. Computer display devices use a matrix of pixels to display text and graphics. 28

Player A device or software module designed to play or display files that have been stored in a particular format, such as MPEG, DVD, or MP3. 358

Plug and play The ability of a computer to automatically recognize and adjust the system configuration for a newly added device. 219

Plug-in A software module that adds a specific feature to a system. For example, in the context of the Web, a plug-in adds a feature to the user's browser, such as the ability to play RealVideo files. 358

Pointer A symbol on the computer screen, usually shaped like an arrow, whose movement corresponds to the movement of the mouse. 25

Point-of-sale (POS) system A computerized system that records items purchased at a cash register, and calculates the total amount due for each sale. 547

Port replicator A device that connects to a notebook computer, by means of a bus connector plug, and contains a duplicate of the notebook computer's ports for connecting devices such as an external monitor, mouse, or keyboard. 266

PostScript A printer language, developed by Adobe Systems, which uses a special set of commands to control page layout, fonts, and graphics. 270

POTS An acronym for "plain old telephone service." 505

Power failure A complete loss of power to the computer system. 393

Power spike A sudden increase of power that lasts less than a millionth of a second. 393

Power strip A device that provides multiple outlets, but no protection for power surges and spikes. 394

Power surge A sudden increase of power that can last several seconds. 393

Power-on self-test (POST) A diagnostic process that runs during startup to check components of the computer such as the graphics card, RAM, keyboard, and disk drives. 236

PPP (Point-to-Point Protocol) A version of PCP/IP software designed to handle Internet communications over dial-up connections. 373

Predicate logic A type of coding notation used in the Prolog programming language for constructing expert systems. 557

Presentation software Software that provides tools to combine text, graphics, graphs, animation, and sound into a series of electronic "slides" that can be output on a projector or as overhead transparencies, paper copies, or 35-millimeter slides. 69

Pretty Good Privacy (PGP) A popular public key encryption system. 413

Print job A file sent to the printer. 320

Print queue A special holding area on a network server, where files are stored until they are printed. 320

Print server A network computer that manages the activities of one or more printers. 320

Printer Control Language (PCL) The unofficial standard language used to send page formatting instructions from a PC to a laser or ink jet printer. 270

Problem statement In an organization, a one-sentence statement that identifies what needs to be improved or fixed; in software engineering, a definition of elements that must be manipulated in order to achieve a result or goal. 577

Procedural languages Computer languages used to create programs composed of a series of statements that tell the computer how to perform the processes of a specific task. 688

Procedure A section of code that performs activities but is not included in the main sequential execution path of a program. 680

Procedure handbook Step-by-step instructions for performing a specific job or task. 591

Process A systematic series of actions that a computer performs to manipulate data; typically represented on a DFD by a rounded rectangle. 5, 578

Process specification A written explanation of what happens to data within a process. 579

Production The primary activities of an organization engaged in manufacturing goods. 537

Productivity paradox The apparent lack of productivity increases in the U.S. economy, despite massive deployment of computers and other information technology. 144

Productivity software Computer programs that help the user work more effectively. 66

Program documentation Information about a computer program, including how it works, its algorithm, its features, and its user interface. 685

Program event An action, such as pressing a key or clicking a mouse, to which a program responds. 694

Program manual Documentation for programmers that contains information about a program. 687

Program specification A description of the elements to be included in a computer program. 677

Programming The process of creating applications or programs for an information system using a programming language or application development tool (also called software engineering). 588

Prompt A message displayed on the computer screen that asks for input from the user. 18

Prototype An experimental or trial version of a device or system. 581

Pseudocode A notational system for algorithms that combines English and a programming language. 674

Public domain software Software that can be freely used by anyone, either because it has not been copyrighted, or because the author has made it available for public use. 54

Public key encryption (PKE) An encryption method that uses a pair of keys, a public key (known to everyone) that encrypts the message, and a private key (known only to the recipient) that decrypts it. 413

Public relations The activities involved in promoting an organization. 537

Query A search specification that prompts the computer to look for particular records in a file. 640

Query by example (QBE) A type of database interface in which the user fills in a field with an example of the type of information that she is seeking. 137

Query language A set of command words that the user uses to direct the computer to create databases, locate information, sort records, and change the data in those records. 138

QuickTime A video and animation file format developed by Apple Computer that can also be run on PCs. QuickTime files have a .mov extension. 468

Radio waves A means of wireless transmission for mobile communications, such as cellular telephones. 500

RAID (Redundant Array of Independent Disks) Disks used by mainframes and microcomputers, in which many disk platters are used to provide data redundancy for faster data access and increased protection from media failure. 185

RAM (Random Access Memory) A type of computer memory circuit that holds data, program instructions, and the operating system while the computer is on. 215

RAM address Like the address on a house, a RAM address identifies a specific area in RAM that can hold data. 215

Random access The ability of a storage device (such as a disk drive) to go directly to a specific storage location without having to search sequentially from a beginning location. 180

Range check A method used in data management environments to specify what constitutes the range of valid entries in each field. 637

Read-only An indication that a computer can retrieve data from a storage medium such as a CD-ROM, but cannot write new data onto it. 188

Read-write head The mechanism in a disk drive that magnetizes particles on the storage disk surface to write data, or senses the bits that are present to read data. 175

Real number A number containing decimal units. 617

Receiver The destination of a message, such as a person, a computer, or another communications device. 500

Record In the context of database management, a record is the fields of data that pertain to a single entity in a database. 618

Record length The total bytes allocated for all of the fields in a record. 618

Record number In a database, a unique identifier associated with a specific record. 639

Record occurrence A record that has been filled with data for a particular entity. 619

Record type The structure of a record, including the names, length, and data types for each field. 619

Registers A sort of "scratch pad" area of the ALU and control unit where data or instructions are moved so that they can be processed. 221

Relational operators Symbols such as > < = and <> in an expression. 648

Relationship In the context of databases, an association between entities that can be used to link records in more than one file. 623

Relative reference In a worksheet, cell references that can change if cells change position as a result of a move or copy operation. 125

Remarks Explanatory comments inserted into lines of code in a computer program. 686

Remote control software Computer programs used to establish a connection, via modem, between two machines that are located at a distance from each other. 73

Removable hard disks Hard disk cartridges that contain platters and read-write heads, and that can be inserted into and removed from the hard drive. 185

Rendering In graphics software, the process of creating a 3-D solid image by covering a wire-frame drawing and applying computer-generated highlights and shadows. 68

Repetition control structure A component of a computer program that repeats one or more instructions until a certain condition is met (also called loop or iteration). 682

Report generator The component of a data management environment that provides a user with the ability to design reports. 643

Report template A predesigned pattern that provides the outline or general specifications for a report. 643

Request for proposal (RFP) A document sent by an organization to vendors to solicit proposals; it specifies the problem that needs to be solved and the requirements that must be met. 584

Request for quotation (RFQ) A document sent by an organization to vendors requesting a formal price quotation on a list of hardware and/or software. 585

Resolution The density of the grid used to display or print text and graphics. The greater the horizontal and vertical density, the higher the resolution. 28

Revision An updated form (indicated by .x) of a software program, incorporating minor enhancements and eliminating bugs found in the most recent version. 275

Rightsize To find the most effective configuration for computer resources. 539

Ring topology A configuration of cables or other communications pathways that form a closed loop. 492

RISC (Reduced Instruction Set Computer) A microprocessor chip designed for rapid and efficient processing of a small set of simple instructions. 227

Risk management The process of weighing threats to computer data against the expendability of that data and the cost of protecting it. 406

RJ-45 connector A small, square plastic connector that looks similar to a telephone connector. Used for the connection between network interface cards and hubs. 318

ROM Read-only memory; one or more integrated circuits that contain permanent instructions that the computer uses during the boot process. 218

ROM BIOS A small set of basic input/output system instructions stored in ROM, which cause the computer system to load critical operating files when the user turns on the computer. 218

Root directory The main directory of a disk. 169

Root node In a hierarchical database, the topmost node in the hierarchy. 625

Router A computer found at each intersection on the Internet backbone that examines incoming data's IP address and forwards the data towards its destination. 350

Run length encoding A graphics file compression technique that looks for patterns of bytes and replaces them with messages that describe the patterns. 466

Run-time error An error that occurs when a computer program is run. 685

Safe Mode A menu option that appears when Windows is unable to complete the boot sequence. By entering safe mode, a user can gracefully shut down the computer, then try to reboot it. 239

Sales and marketing The activities involved in selling and promoting an organization's goods and/or services. 537

Sampling rate The number of times per second a sound is measured during the recording process. 460

Sandbox A metaphor for the limited areas and equipment that a Java applet can access on a computer. 414

Satellite dish A parabolic device that captures transmissions from communications satellites. 502

Scripting language A computer language, such as HTML, in which a task is defined in the form of a script. 689

SCSI (Small Computer System Interface) An interface standard used for attaching peripheral devices such as disk drives. Pronounced "scuzzy." 258

SDRAM Short for synchronous dynamic RAM, it is a type of RAM that synchronizes itself with the CPU, thus enabling it to run at much higher clock speeds than conventional RAM. 257

Search and replace A feature of document production software that allows the user to automatically locate all instances of a particular word or phrase and substitute another word or phrase for it. 108

Search feature A feature of document production software that allows the user to automatically locate all the instances of a particular word or phrase. 108

Sectors Subdivisions of the tracks on a storage medium that provide a storage area for data. 177

Selection control structure A component of a computer program that tells a computer what to do, depending on whether a condition is true or false (also called decision structure or branch). 681

Self-extracting file A file that contains compressed data and the software necessary to decompress it. 360

Semi-structured problems Problems for which a general procedure has been established, but which require some degree of discretionary judgment to arrive at a solution. 544

Sequence In MIDI terminology, instructions that indicate which musical notes to play; these instructions include the pitch of a note, when it begins, which instrument plays it, the volume of the note, and its duration. 461

Sequence control structure A component of a program that changes the sequence, or order, in which instructions are executed by directing the computer to execute an instruction elsewhere in the program. 679

Sequential access A form of data storage, usually on computer tape, that requires a device to read or write data one record after another starting at the beginning of the medium. 180

Sequential execution The computer execution of program instructions performed in the sequence established by a programmer. 678

Serial transmission A method of communicating digital data in which each bit of data is sent one after the other. 491

Service workers Employees whose primary activity is providing services to customers (for example, sales associates and technicians). 541

Set In a network database model, a group of related record types. 626

Setup program A program module supplied with a software package for the purpose of installing the software on a PC. 86

Shareware Copyrighted software marketed under a license that allows users to use the software for a trial period and then send in a registration fee if they wish to continue to use it. 53

Sharing On a network, the use of the same program by multiple people at the same time. 312

Shrink-wrap license A legal agreement printed on computer software packaging, which goes into effect when the package is opened. 52

S-HTTP (Secure HTTP) A method of encrypting data transmitted between a computer and a Web server by encrypting individual packets of data as they are transmitted. 415

Simplex communication A communications technique that allows communication in only one direction. 495

Single-mode cable A type of fiber-optic cable that has a very narrow core, usually less than 10 microns in diameter. 499

Single-user license A legal usage agreement limiting the use of a software program to one user at any given time. 52

Site In Internet terminology, a computer with a domain name. 350

Site license Legal permission for software to be used on any and all computers at a specific location (for example, within a corporate building or on a university campus). 53

SLIP (Serial Line Internet Protocol) A version of TCP/IP software designed to handle Internet communications over dial-up connections. 373

Smalltalk An object-oriented programming language. 634

Software The instructions that set up a computer to do a task, indicate how to interact with a user, and specify how to process data. 7, 49

Software customization The process of modifying a commercially available software application to meet the needs of a specific user. 588

Software engineering The systematic approach to the development, operation, maintenance, and retirement of software. 588, 668

Software license A legal contract that defines the ways in which a user may use a computer program. 51

Software pirates Individuals who illegally copy, distribute, or modify software. 50

Software publisher A company that produces computer software. 275

Sort key A field used to arrange records in order. 641

Sorting Rearranging the sequence of records on a disk. 641

Sound card A circuit board that gives the computer the ability to accept audio input from a microphone, play sound files stored on disks and CD-ROMs, and produce audio output through speakers or headphones. 230

Source code Computer instructions written in a high-level language. 691

Spelling checker A feature of document production software that checks each word in a document against an electronic dictionary of correctly spelled words, then presents a list of alternatives for possible misspellings. 108

Spin box A control within a graphical user interface that lets the user increase or decrease a number by clicking arrow buttons. 22

Spreadsheet A numerical model or representation of a real situation, presented in the form of a table. 119

Spreadsheet modeling Setting up numbers in a worksheet format, to simulate a real-world situation. 130

Spreadsheet software Software for creating electronic worksheets that hold data in cells and perform calculations based on that data. 70

SQL (Structured Query Language) A popular query language used by mainframes and microcomputers. 640

SSL (Secure Sockets Layer) A security protocol that uses encryption to establish a secure connection between a computer and a Web server. 415

Stand-alone computer A computer that is not connected to a network. 308

Star topology A configuration of cables or other communications pathways that fan out from a central hub. 492

Start bit A signal sent by a transmitting computer, using an asynchronous protocol, to indicate that data is ready to be transmitted. 494

Statistical software Software for analyzing large sets of data to discover patterns and relationships within them. 70

Stop bit A signal sent by a transmitting computer, using an asynchronous protocol, to indicate the end of a block of data being transmitted. 494

Storage The area in a computer where data is retained on a permanent basis. 5

Storage capacity The maximum amount of data that can be recorded on a storage medium, usually measured in kilobytes, megabytes, gigabytes, or terabytes. 180

Storage device A mechanical apparatus that records data to and retrieves data from a storage medium. 174

Storage media The physical material used to store computer data, such as a floppy disk, a hard disk, or a CD-ROM. 12, 174

Storage medium The physical material used to store computer data, such as a floppy disk, a hard disk, or a CD-ROM. 12, 174

Storage technology A term used to describe a storage device and the media it uses. 174

Store-and-forward technology A technology used by communications networks in which an e-mail message is temporarily held in storage on a server until it is requested by a client computer. 327

Strategic planning The process of developing long-range goals and plans for an organization. 543

Streaming media An internet multimedia technology that sends a small segment of a media file to a user's computer and begins to play it while the next segment is being sent. 357

Street price The average discounted price of a product. 276

Structured database A collection of related information organized into records and fields. 133

Structured English Vocabulary and syntax used by systems analysts to concisely and unambiguously explain the logic of a process. It is limited to words defined in a data dictionary and to specific logical terms such as "if...then,". 579

Structured problems Problems for which there exists a well-established procedure for obtaining the best solution. 544

Submenu An additional menu of choices that appears when a menu option is selected. 21

Subroutine A section of code that performs activities or manipulates data but is not included in the main sequential execution path of a program. 680

Success factors System requirements that also serve as an evaluation checklist at the end of a development project. 581

Summary report A report generated by a management information system that combines or groups data and usually provides totals, such as a report of total annual sales for the past five years. 551

Supercomputer The fastest and most expensive type of computer, capable of processing more than one trillion instructions per second. 11

Supervisors People in an organization who are responsible for overseeing daily operations. 543

Surge strip A device that protects computer equipment from electrical spikes and surges (also called a surge suppressor or surge protector). 394

SVGA (Super Video Graphics Array) SVGA typically refers to 800 x 600 resolution. 264

Synchronous protocol A method of serial communication in which the transmission of data occurs at regular intervals synchronized by the computer's internal clock. 494

Synchronously A term used in the context of communications to mean simultaneously or in real time. A phone conversation or Internet chat are examples of synchronous communication. 361

Syntax Specifications or rules for the sequence and punctuation of command words and parameters. 20

Syntax error An error that results when an instruction does not follow the syntax rules, or grammar, of the programming language. 20, 685

System clock A device in the computer that emits pulses to establish the timing for all system operations. 226

System conversion The process of deactivating an old information system and activating a new one. 592

System development life cycle The series of phases that outlines the development process of an information system. 574

System development project team A group of people assigned to analyze and develop an information system. 576

System operator A person who operates a mainframe or minicomputer on a day-to-day basis. 594

System requirements 1) Specifications for the operating system and hardware configuration necessary for a software product to work correctly. 2) The criteria that must be met for a new computer system or software product to be a success. 84, 581

System resource Any part of a computer system, such as disk drive space, memory capacity, or processor time, that can be used by a computer program. 57

System software Computer programs that help the computer carry out essential operating tasks. 54

System testing The process of testing an information system to ensure that all the hardware and software components work together. 589

System unit The case or box that contains the computer's power supply, storage devices, the main circuit board, processor, and memory. 12

Systems analysis and design The process of planning and building an information system. 574

Systems analysts Computer professionals responsible for analyzing information requirements, designing new information systems, and supervising the implementation of new information systems. 575

Systems programmer The person responsible for installing new versions of the operating system and modifying system settings to maximize performance. 594

T1 service A high-bandwidth telephone line that can also transmit text and images. T-1 service is often used by organizations to connect to the Internet. 505

T3 service A type of ISDN service that uses fiber-optic cable to provide dedicated service with a capacity of 45 megabits per second. 505

Tables An arrangement of data in a grid of rows and columns; in a relational database, a collection of record types with their data. 627

Tactical planning Short- or near-term decisions and goals that deploy the human, financial, and natural resources necessary to meet strategic goals. 543

Tape backup A copy of data from a computer's hard disk, stored on magnetic tape and used to restore lost data. 186

Tape cartridge A removable magnetic tape module, similar to a cassette tape. 187

TCP/IP TCP/IP (Transmission Control Protocol/Internet Protocol) is a standard set of communication rules used by every computer that connects to the Internet. 348

Technical writer A person who specializes in writing explanations of technical concepts and procedures. 687

Telecommunications The process of sending electronic data over communications lines, or the transmission of data from a sender to a distant receiver. 488

Terabyte Approximately one trillion bytes. 180

Terminal A device with a keyboard and a monitor, used for input and output, but not for processing. 9

Terminal emulation software Programs that make it possible for a microcomputer to connect to a host computer and behave as if it were a terminal of the host computer. 322

Test area A location where software testing can occur without disrupting an organization's regular information system. 589

Text In spreadsheet terminology, words used for worksheet titles and for labels that identify columns and rows. 121

Text block In an online document, sections of text such as a group of words, sentences, or paragraphs. 107

Thesaurus A feature of documentation software that provides synonyms. 108

TIFF (Tag Image File Format) A file format (.tif extension) for bitmap images that automatically compresses the file data. 467

Time bomb A type of computer program that stays in a computer system undetected until it is triggered at a certain date or time. 400

Time-sharing system A configuration in which terminals share the host computer's processing time, in contrast to a network, in which processing is performed on workstations as well as on the server. 321

Toggle key A key such as the Caps Lock key that switches a device back and forth between two modes. 26

Token A unit of data that can carry a packet for delivery, as it travels continuously around a Token Ring network. 515

Token Ring A type of network in which the nodes are sequentially connected in the form of a ring; the second most popular network architecture. 317

Top-level domain The major categories into which groups of computers on the Internet are divided: com, edu, gov, int, mil, net, and org. 350

Topology The pattern or path of communications pathways, such as star, bus, and ring. 492

Touchpad A touch-sensitive input device that allows the user to control an on-screen pointer by moving the fingertips over the pad's surface. 260

TQM (total quality management) The process by which an organization analyzes and implements ways to improve the quality of its products and/or services. 539

Track point A small pencil-eraser-shaped device embedded among typing keys that controls an on-screen pointer when the user pushes the track point up, down, left, or right. 260

Trackball A pointing device consisting of a ball that is rotated in a frame to move a pointer around a computer screen. 260

Tracks A series of concentric or spiral storage areas created on a storage medium during the formatting process. 177

Transaction A business activity that involves the exchange of information, goods, or services. 547

Transaction processing system (TPS) A system that keeps track of transactions for an organization by providing ways to collect, display, modify, and cancel transactions. 547

Transfer rate The speed (measured in Kbps) at which data is transmitted between your computer and another device. Often used to specify the speed of data transfer over the Internet. 372

Transmitter A device that sends a signal at a particular frequency or group of frequencies. 500

Transponder A device on a telecommunications satellite that receives a signal on one frequency, amplifies the signal, and then retransmits the signal on a different frequency. 501

Trap door A way to bypass the normal security precautions and enter a computer system. A trap door is often created during computer installation and testing, but should be removed before the computer is placed into service. 411

Trojan horse A computer program that appears to perform one function while actually doing something else, such as inserting a virus into a computer system or stealing a password. 399

True-color graphic A color image with a color depth of 24 bits or 32 bits. Each pixel in a true color image can be displayed using any of 16.7 million different colors. 453

Tuple In a relational database, a row in a table, which is equivalent to a record. 627

Twisted-pair cable A type of cable in which two separate strands of wire are twisted together. Used in connecting nodes on a network with RJ-45 connectors on both ends. 318

Ultra ATA A disk drive technology that is an enhanced version of EIDE. Also referred to as Ultra DMA or Ultra IDE. 258

Uncompressing The process of expanding compressed data files (also called extracting, expanding, and decompressing). 462

Undelete utility An operating system subcomponent, that, in some cases, allows the user to retrieve all or part of a deleted file. 179

Unicode A 16-bit character-representation code that can represent more than 65,000 characters. 450

Unit testing The process of testing a completed application module, to make sure that it operates reliably and correctly. 589

UNIX A multi-user, multitasking server operating system developed by AT&T's Bell Laboratories in 1969. 63

Unstructured problems Problems for which there is no established procedure for arriving at a solution. 544

Unzipping In computer jargon, decompressing a file. 463

Uploading The process of sending a copy of a file from a user's computer to a remote computer. 359

UPS (uninterruptible power supply) A device that contains a battery to provide a continuous supply of power to a computer system in case of a power failure and contains circuitry to protect a computer from power spikes and surges. 393

Upstream The process of transmitting data from your home computer to the Internet. 510

URL (Uniform Resource Locator) The address of a Web page. 351

Usenet servers Computers that handle the exchange of comments among members of Internet discussion groups. 352

User account A means of providing a user with access to network resources and of accumulating information about the user, such as log-in and log-out times. 309

User ID A combination of letters and numbers that serves as a user's "call sign" or identification. Also referred to as a user name. 15

User interface The software and hardware that enable people to interact with computers. 17

User rights Rules that specify the directories and files that an individual user can access. 411

Utilities A subcategory of system software designed to augment the operating system by providing ways for a computer user to control the allocation and use of hardware resources. 64

Value-added reseller (VAR) A company that combines commercially available products with additional hardware, software, and/or services to create a system designed to meet the needs of specific customers or industries. 279

Vaporware Software that is announced but not produced. 273

Variable-length field A field in a data file that can accept any number of characters up to a maximum limit. 617

Vector graphics Images generated from descriptions that determine the position, length, and direction in which lines and shapes are drawn. 68

Version A new or totally redesigned product (for example, in the identifying number 6.1, the 6 is the version number). 275

Version upgrade price A special price for a new version of a software package, offered to owners of an earlier version. 276

Vertical market software Computer programs designed to meet the needs of a specific market segment or industry (for example, medical record-keeping software for use in hospitals). 77

Video for Windows A file format developed by the Microsoft Corporation for storing video information. Files in this format have an .avi extension. 468

Video memory Memory chips located on a graphics card that store images as they are processed. More video memory allows a computer to display images at higher resolutions and color depth. 264

Viewable image size (vis) A measurement of the maximum image size that can be displayed on a monitor screen. 262

Viewer A software module that allows you to view the contents of a specific type of file. For example, you can use a viewer to see the contents of a .dbf file even if you do not have the software that allows you to create and edit files of that type. 358

Virtual memory A computer's use of hard disk storage to simulate RAM. 217

Virus signature The unique computer code contained in a virus that helps in its identification. Antivirus software searches for known virus signatures to identify a virus. 403

Voiceband modem The type of modem that would typically be used to connect a computer to a telephone line (see modem). 505

Voice-grade cable Cable that is suitable for transmitting voice signals, but not data signals. 496

Waveform audio A digital representation of sound, in which a sound wave is represented by a series of samples taken of the wave height. 459

Waveforms The shape of an electromagnetic waves (also called wave patterns). 489

Wavelength The distance between waves. 489

Wavetable synthesis A MIDI standard that creates music by playing digitized sound samples of actual instruments. 261

Web Short for World Wide Web. An Internet service that links documents and information from computers distributed all over the world. Uses HTTP protocol. 16

Web authoring software Computer programs for designing and developing customized Web pages that can be published electronically on the Internet. 67

Web browser software Computer software, such as Netscape Navigator and Microsoft Internet Explorer, that allows users to view Web pages and follow links to jump from one document to the next. 31

Web hosting service An organization that provides space on its Internet servers for other organizations' and individuals' Web pages, in return for a monthly fee. 369

Web pages Documents on the World Wide Web that consist of a specially coded HTML file with associated text, audio, video, and graphics files. A Web page often contains links to other Web pages. 351

Web portal A Web site that provides a group of services, such as a search engine, news, weather, and chat groups. Designed to be used as a portal or entry into the Web. 356

Web search engine A feature of a Web site that allows users to search for information by entering key terms. 32

Web server A computer that uses special software to transmit Web pages over the Internet. 351

Web site A location on the World Wide Web that contains information relating to a specific topic. 350

Web-enabled databases Databases that can be accessed over the Internet by means of a standard Web browser. 635

What-if analysis The process of setting up a model in a spreadsheet and experimenting to see what happens when different values are entered. 130

Wide area network (WAN) An interconnected group of computers and peripherals that covers a large geographical area, such as multiple branches of a corporation. 308

Wildcard character A symbol, such as an asterisk, used to represent a group of characters in a filename (for example, *.exe means all files with an .exe extension). 162

Window A rectangular representation of a work area in a graphical user interface. 23

Windows Registry A crucial data file maintained by the operating system that contains the settings needed by a computer to correctly use any hardware and software that has been installed on the system. 238

Windows software Software that has been designed to run on computers with the Windows operating system. 13

Wireframe A representation of a 3-D object using separate lines, which resemble wire, to create a model. 68

Wireless networks Networks that use radio or infrared signals (instead of cables) to transmit data from one network device to another. 318

Wizard A sequence of dialog boxes that direct the user through multi-step software tasks, such as creating a graph. 19

Word processing software Computer programs that assist the user in producing documents such as reports, letters, papers, and manuscripts. 67

Word size The number of bits the CPU can manipulate at one time, which is dependent on the size of the registers in the CPU and on the number of data lines in the bus. 226

Word wrap A feature of document production software that automatically moves the cursor to the beginning of the next line of text when it reaches the end of the current line, allowing the user to type continuously. 106

Workbook A collection of individual worksheets that are stored together as one file. 128

Workers People who perform the tasks necessary to carry out an organization's mission. 540

Workflow software Programs that automate the process of electronically routing documents from one person to another, in a specified sequence and time frame. Also called document routing software. 326

Worksheet A computerized, or electronic, spreadsheet. 121

Worksheet template A worksheet form created by professionals and provided for your use by your spreadsheet software. 124

Workstation A computer connected to a local area network. 308

Workstation installation Installation of software on a network server to be accessed from workstations. The process copies some of the program files to a workstation's local hard drive and updates the workstation's Windows Registry and Start menu. 324

Worm A software program designed to enter a computer system, usually a network, through security "holes" and replicate itself. 401

Written documentation Written information in a form external to the program, designed to assist programmers and individuals who use a program. 686

XGA (Extended Graphics Array) XGA usually refers to 1024 x 768 resolution. 264

XML XML (extended markup language) is a document format similar to HTML, but one that allows the Web page developer to define customized tags, generally for the purpose of creating more interactivity. 365

Y2K bug A time bomb unintentionally created by programmers when they wrote programs that used a two-digit field for the year, with the result that computers will read the digits 00 as 1900 rather than as 2000. 400

Zip disk A high-capacity floppy disk manufactured by Iomega Corporation, frequently used for backups. 181

Zipping In computer jargon, compressing a file. 463

INDEX

CREDITS

Chapter 1: Chapter Opener: HAL photo credits: Photofest, Planet photo: Courtesy of NASA. Figure 1-1: Corbis-Bettmann. Figure 1-4: Courtesy of IBM Corporation. Figure 1-6: Courtesy of IBM Corporation. Figure 1-7: Courtesy of American Airlines. Figure 1-8: Image of the Cray T3E courtesy of Cray. Cray is a registered trademark of Cray Research, L.L.C., a wholly owned subsidiary of Silicon Graphics, Inc. "(c) 1999 Silicon Graphics, Inc. Used by permission." All rights reserved. Figure 1-9: Courtesy of Synchromic Studios, Inc. Figure 1-11A: Courtesy of ViewSonic Corporation. Figure 1-11B: Courtesy of 3M Visual Systems. Figure 1-11D: Courtesy of Hewlett-Packard Company. Figure 1-11H: Courtesy of PictureTel. Figure 1-11J: (c) 1999 Wacom Technology Corporation. IW1: Photofest. IW2: AP/Wide World Photos. IW3: Courtesy of Microsoft Corporation.

Chapter 2: Figure 2-0B: AP/Wide World Photos. Figure 2-5A/B: Durvin & Co. Figure 2-13A: Bonnie Kamin. Figure 2-14A: Courtesy of IBM Corporation. Figure 2-17: Courtesy of CompUSA, Inc. Figure 2-18: Shelly R. Harrison. Figure 2-21: Courtesy of Proxima Corporation. Figure 2-24: Courtesy of Microsoft Corporation. Figure 2-27: Courtesy of Virgin Interactive Entertainment. Figure 2-33: Photofest.

Chapter 3: Chapter Opener Video: IBM Archives. Chapter Opener A: Corel Corporation. Chapter Opener B: James Pozarik/Liaison Agency. Figure 3-1: North Wind Picture Archive and Corbis-Bettmann. Figure 3-3: Claudio Edinger/Liaison Agency. Figure 3-6: Courtesy of Vatican Library. Figure 3-12: National Archives and Records Administration. Figure 3-14: Jacques M. Chenet/Liaison Agency. Figure 3-26: Courtesy of Kinkos, Inc. Figure 3-28: Courtesy of Rodale Press and Jerry O'Brien. Figure 3-29: (c) Jeff Lowenthal/Chicago. Figure 3-34: Photofest. Figure 3-38: Courtesy of Proxima Corporation. IW1: North Wind Picture Archive. IW3: Jacques M. Chenet/Liaison Agency.

Chapter 4: Chapter Opener: Dilip Mehta/Contact Press Images. Figure 4-16: Courtesy of IBM Corporation, Research Division, Almaden Research Center. Figure 4-24: Courtesy of Western Digital Corporation. IW2: Courtesy of IBM Archives.

Chapter 5: Chapter Opener video: Courtesy of Western Digital Corporation. Chapter Opener video still: Courtesy of Intel Corporation. Chapter Opener art: James Kaczman. Figure 5-2: Courtesy of Motorola Semiconductor products Sector, (c)1999 SEMATECH, INC., Portions of Silicon Magic used with permission of Semicnductor Equipment and Materials International, (c) 1991. Figure 5-3A: Courtesy of Texas Instruments. Figure 5-3B/C/D: Courtesy of Intel Corporation. Figure 5-5: Courtesy of Western Digital Corporation. Figure 5-13: Smithsonian Institution. Figure 5-16: Courtesy of Motorola Semiconductor products Sector, (c)1999 SEMATECH, INC., Portions of Silicon Magic used with permission of Semicnductor Equipment and Materials International, (c) 1991.

Chapter 6: Chapter Opener video and still: Bonnie Kamin and Courtesy of CompUSA, Inc. Chapter Opener photo: Bonnie Kamin. Figure 6-5: Courtesy of Microsoft Corporation. Figure 6-6: (trackpoint) Courtesy of IBM Corporation; (trackball) Courtesy of Toshiba America Information Systems, Inc. (touchpad) Courtesy of Sharp Electronics Corporation. Figure 6-8: Courtesy of ViewSonic Corporation. Figure 6-11: Courtesy of Mobile Communications Division of U.S. Robotics. Figure 6-16: Courtesy of PriceScan.com, Inc. Figure 6-17: Courtesy of Micron Electronics. Figure 6-20: Courtesy of CompUSA, Inc. Figure 6-22: Bonnie Kamin. Figure 6-23: Computer Chronicles/Stewart Cheifet Productions. Figure 6-24: InfoWorld, May 31, 1999 issue. Figure 6-26: Courtesy of Motorola Semiconductor products Sector, (c)1999 SEMATECH, INC. Figure 6-27: Courtesy of MIT Media Lab; photo: (c) Sam Ogden.

Chapter 7: Preview video: Bruce Ayers/Tony Stone Images. Figure 7-5: Bruce Ayers/Tony Stone Images. Figure 7-17: Courtesy of Novell, Inc. Figure 7-20: Screen shot reprinted by permission from Microsoft Corporation. 7-KEY: Bruce Ayers/Tony Stone Images.

Chapter 8: Preview video: Courtesy of NCSA/UIUC Courtesy of NASA. Figure 8-1 video: Courtesy of NCSA/UIUC. Figure 8-2: Courtesy of MIDS, Austin, TX http://www.mids.org. Figure 8-3: Graphic courtesy of UUNET, an MCI WorldCom Company. Figure 8-7: Theodor Holm Nelson, Project Xanadu. Figure 8-11: Courtesy of JPL/NASA/Caltech. Figure 8-12: Courtesy of NASA. Figure 8-25 video: Internet Café/Stewart Cheifet Productions. Figure 8-P1: © 1993 The New Yorker Magazine.

Chapter 9: Figure 9-0a Preview video and still: Courtesy of Western Digital Corporation, Digital Imagery © Copyright 1999 PhotoDisc, Inc. (for both lightning and magnifying glass photos). Figure 9-0b: Stock Montage/SuperStock. Figure 9-2: Computer Chronicles/Stewart Cheifet Productions. Figure 9-11: AP/Wide World Photos. Figure 9-12: Courtesy of Fischer International Systems Corporation. Figure IW-1: AP/Wide World Photos.

Chapter 10: Part Opener: David Hanover/Tony Stone Images. Figure 10-0A: Digital Imagery © Copyright 1999 PhotoDisc, Inc. Figure 10-0B: Corbis/Bill Ross. Figure 10-26: Gilles Mingasson/Liason Agency Inc.

Chapter 11: Figure 11-0A: Digital Imagery © Copyright 1999 PhotoDisc Inc. Figure 11-0B: Carol Palmer Photography. Figure 11-12 (video): Courtesy of Corning Incorporated. Figure 11-13 (video): Computer Chronicles/Stewart Cheifet Productions. Figure 11-14 (animation): Image created by Robert Thurman and Patrick Worfolk using SaVi, the satellite visualization tool from The Geometry Center (http://www.umn.edu) at the University of Minnesota. Used with permission. Figure 11-16 (video): Property of AT&T Archives. Reprinted with permission of AT&T. Figure 11-21A: Courtesy of Com21, Inc. Figure 11-29: Bonnie Kamin Photography.

Chapter 12: Figure 12-0A: Digital Imagery © Copyright 1999 PhotoDisc Inc. Figure 12-0B: © Ted Nasmith, First printed in the J.R.R. Tolkien Calendar published by Harper Collins Publishers. Figure 12-6: Photos a – c, e, f are Courtesy of IBM Corporation; Photo d (man fixing computer): Shelly Harrison. Figure 12-15 (video): WGBH. Figure 12 IW1: Courtesy of IBM Corporation.

Chapter 13: Figure 13-0A: Courtesy of IBM Corporation. Figure 13-0B: Minden Pictures. Figure 13-3: Courtesy of IBM Corporation. Figure 13-14: Steven Peters/Tony Stone Images. Figure 13 Key: Courtesy of IBM Corporation. Figure 13 IW1: Courtesy of IBM Corporation.

Chapter 14: Figure 14-0A: Phil Jason/Tony Stone Images. Figure 14-0B: Photofest. Figure 14-16: Courtesy of Microsoft Corporation. Figure 14-25: Corbis/Bettmann. Figure 14 IW1: Photofest. Figure 14 IW3: Courtesy of Microsoft Corporation.

Chapter 15: Figure 15-0A: Dennis O'Clair/Tony Stone Images. Figure 15-0B: © 1991 Ken Reid/FPG International. Figure 15-14 (video): WGBH. Figure 15-22: Dennis O'Clair/Tony Stone Images. Figure 15 IW1: Stewart Cohen/Tony Stone Images.